NUMBERS
1–20

VOLUME 4A

THE ANCHOR BIBLE is a fresh approach to the world's greatest classic. Its object is to make the Bible accessible to the modern reader, its method is to arrive at the meaning of biblical literature through exact translation and extended exposition, and to reconstruct the ancient setting of the biblical story, as well as the circumstances of its transcription and the characteristics of its transcribers.

THE ANCHOR BIBLE is a project of international and interfaith scope. Protestant, Catholic, and Jewish scholars from many countries contribute individual volumes. The project is not sponsored by any ecclesiastical organization and is not intended to reflect any particular theological doctrine. Prepared under our joint supervision, THE ANCHOR BIBLE is an effort to make available all the significant historical and linguistic knowledge which bears on the interpretation of the biblical record.

THE ANCHOR BIBLE is aimed at the general reader with no special formal training in biblical studies; yet, it is written with the most exacting standards of scholarship, reflecting the highest technical accomplishment.

This project marks the beginning of a new era of cooperation among scholars in biblical research, thus forming a common body of knowledge to be shared by all.

William Foxwell Albright
David Noel Freedman
GENERAL EDITORS

THE ANCHOR BIBLE

NUMBERS
1–20

♦

A New Translation
with
Introduction and Commentary

BARUCH A. LEVINE

THE ANCHOR BIBLE

Doubleday

New York London Toronto Sydney Auckland

The Anchor Bible
PUBLISHED BY DOUBLEDAY
a division of Bantam Doubleday Dell Publishing Group, Inc.,
666 Fifth Avenue, New York, N.Y. 10103.

Library of Congress Cataloging-in-Publication Data

Bible. O.T. Numbers I–XX. English. Levine. 1993.
Numbers 1–20 : a new translation with introduction and commentary / Baruch A. Levine. — 1st ed.
p. cm. — (The Anchor Bible: 4)
Includes bibliographical references and index.
1. Bible. O.T. Numbers I–XX—Commentaries. I. Levine, Baruch A. II. Title. III. Series: Bible. English. Anchor Bible. 1964 : v. 4.
BS192.2.A1 1964.G3 vol.4
[BS1263]
220.7′7 s—dc20
[222′.14077] 92-12262
CIP

ISBN 0-385-15651-0

Printed in the United States of America
March 1993
First Edition

To my wife,
Corinne

He who finds a wife has found happiness,
And has won the favor of the Lord.

—Proverbs 18:22

Contents

♦

CONTENTS

CONTENTS

CONTENTS

Preface

♦

In retrospect, I acknowledge several forms of support and guidance that have enabled me to accomplish this translation and commentary, the first of two projected volumes on Numbers. I am grateful to my gifted student Anne Robertson for her indispensable assistance in preparing the original manuscript. The staff of the library of the École Biblique, Jerusalem, and my scholarly colleagues in attendance there, deserve my gratitude for their spirit of helpfulness. I am appreciative of the support given to me by the Dean of the Faculty of Arts and Sciences at New York University, C. Duncan Rice, and by my colleagues in the newly established Skirball Department of Hebrew and Judaic Studies. Their recognition of my commitment to research, and of my need for repeated periods of leave, has greatly abetted my scholarly progress.

David Noel Freedman, through the instrumentality of his incisive critiques and through the experience of genuinely friendly scholarly discourse, has instructed me significantly not only as regards knowledge of the biblical text, of which he is a master, but in all that pertains to exposition and presentation. Once again, I feel impelled to acknowledge the guidance of numerous scholarly colleagues in North America, Israel, and Europe, as well as the responses of my many students, whose interest and insight have contributed to this present effort.

Mr. Michael Iannazzi and his staff at Doubleday afforded valuable assistance. Ultimately, we are all in the debt of William F. Albright, who first envisioned the Anchor Bible and whose considerable contribution to my understanding of Numbers will emerge more clearly in the second volume of the commentary, on Numbers 21–36.

In dedicating this work to my wife, Corinne, I wish to acknowledge her appreciation of those scholarly efforts which continue to stimulate me and reward me with fulfillment. As one who seeks to interpret the words of the Torah, I profess the ancient blessing in gratitude:

"It is You who graciously imparts knowledge to humans, and teaches discernment to mortal beings."

ABBREVIATIONS

♦

AHw	W. von Soden, *Akkadisches Handwörterbuch.* 3 vols. Wiesbaden: Harrassowitz, 1965–1981
ANET	*Ancient Near Eastern Texts Relating to the Old Testament,* 3d ed. with suppl. Princeton: Princeton University Press, 1969
ARM	Archives royales de Mari
AP	A. E. Cowley, *Aramaic Papyri.* Oxford: The Clarendon Press, 1923
ASOR	American Schools of Oriental Research
BA	*Biblical Archaeologist*
BAR	*Biblical Archaeology Review*
BASOR	*Bulletin of the American Schools of Oriental Research*
BHS	*Biblia Hebraica Stuttgartensia*
BMAP	E. G. Kraeling, *The Brooklyn Museum Aramaic Papyri.* New Haven: Yale University Press, 1953
CAD	*The Assyrian Dictionary of the University of Chicago,* ed. L. Oppenheim et al. (cited as *CAD K, CAD S,* etc.)
CBQ	*Catholic Biblical Quarterly*
DISO	C.-F. Jean and J. Hoftijzer, *Dictionnaire des inscriptions sémitiques de l'ouest.* Leiden: E. J. Brill, 1965
EA	J. A. Knudtzon, *Die el-Amarna Tafeln.* 2 vols. (1915); reissue, Aaten: Otto Zeller, 1964
EAEHL	*Encyclopaedia of Archaeological Excavations in the Holy Land.* 4 vols. Jerusalem: Massada Press, 1975–1978
EB	*Encyclopaedia Biblica* (Hebrew). 8 vols. Jerusalem: Bailik Institute, 1950–1982
Gray—ICC	G. B. Gray, *Numbers.* International Critical Commentary. Edinburgh: T. & T. Clark, 1903
HALAT	W. Baumgartner et al., *Hebräisches und aramäisches Lexikon zum Alten Testament.* 4 vols. Leiden: E. J. Brill, 1967–1990

HUCA	*Hebrew Union College Annual*
IDBSup	*Interpreter's Dictionary of the Bible: Supplementary Volume*. Nashville: Abingdon Press, 1976
IEJ	*Israel Exploration Journal*
JAOS	*Journal of the American Oriental Society*
JBL	*Journal of Biblical Literature*
JJS	*Journal of Jewish Studies*
JNES	*Journal of Near Eastern Studies*
JSS	*Journal of Semitic Studies*
KTU	M. Dietrich, O. Loretz, and J. Sanmartin, *Die keilalphabetischen Texte aus Ugarit*. Alter Orient und altes Testament 24. Neukirchen-Vluyn: Neukirchener Verlag, 1976
Liddell-Scott	H. G. Liddell and R. Scott, A *Greek-English Lexicon*. A new edition. 2 vols. Oxford: Carendon Press, 1925
NEB	*New English Bible*
NJPS	*New Jewish Publication Society* (1955 translation)
PEQ	*Palestine Exploration Quarterly*
RA	*Revue d'assyriologie et d'archéologie orientale*
RB	*Revue biblique*
Sifre	*Sifre*, ed. M. Friedmann. Vienna: Selbstverlag der Verfassers, 1864.
ThWAT	*Theologisches Wörterbuch zum Alten Testament*, ed. G. J. Botterweck, H. Ringgren, and H. J. Fabry. 6 vols. Stuttgart: Kohlhammer, 1970–
Ugaritica V	*Mission de Ras Shamra*, vol. 16. Paris: Imprimerie Nationale, 1968
VT	*Vetus Testamentum*
VTSup	*Vetus Testamentum*, Supplements
Yalqûṭ Shimeoni	*Yalqûṭ Shimeoni, Bemidbar*, ed. D. Hyman and I. Shiloni. Jerusalem: Mossad Harav Kook, 1986

Translation of Numbers 1–20

♦

1 1 YHWH spoke to Moses, in the Wilderness of Sinai, at the Tent of Meeting, on the first day of the second month, in the second year after their
departure from Egypt, as follows:
2 Take a poll of the entire community of the Israelites by their clans and
their patriarchal "houses," according to the number of names, every male, by
their heads;
3 those above twenty years of age: all those eligible for military service
among the Israelites. You shall muster them by their divisions, you and Aaron.
4 With you there shall be one man from each tribe, a man who is head of his
own patriarchal house.
5 These are the names of the men who shall stand with you:
Representing Reuben—Elizur son of Shedeur.
6 Representing Simeon—Shelumiel son of Zurishaddai.
7 Representing Judah—Nahshon son of Amminadab.
8 Representing Issachar—Nethanel son of Zuar.
9 Representing Zebulun—Eliab son of Helon.
10 Representing the descendants of Joseph:
Representing Ephraim—Elishama son of Ammihud.
Representing Manasseh—Gamaliel son of Pedahzur.
11 Representing Benjamin—Abidan son of Gideoni.
12 Representing Dan—Ahiezer son of Ammishaddai.
13 Representing Asher—Pagiel son of Ochran.
14 Representing Gad—Eliasaph son of Deuel.
15 Representing Naphtali—Ahira son of Enan.
16 These are the elect of the community, the chieftains of their patriarchal
tribes; they are the heads of the sibs of Israel.
17 Moses and Aaron gathered these men, who had been specified by name.
18 They assembled the entire community on the first day of the second
month. They, [in turn,] registered their affiliations, by their clans and patriarchal houses, according to the number of names, of those twenty years of age
and above, by their heads.

19 Just as YHWH had commanded Moses, so did he muster them in the Wilderness of Sinai.
20 There were the descendants of Reuben, the firstborn of Israel; those born to them, by their clans and patriarchal houses, according to the number of names, by their heads, every male twenty years of age and above, all of those eligible for military service.
21 The musters of those affiliated with the tribe of Reuben: 46,500.
22 Of the descendants of Simeon, those born to them, by their clans and patriarchal houses; his musters, according to the number of names, by their heads, every male twenty years of age and above, all of those eligible for military service.
23 The musters of those affiliated with the tribe of Simeon: 59,300.
24 Of the descendants of Gad, those born to them, by their clans and patriarchal houses; according to the names of those twenty years of age and above, all of those eligible for military service.
25 The musters of those affiliated with the tribe of Gad: 45,650.
26 Of the descendants of Judah, those born to them, by their clans and patriarchal houses; according to the names of those twenty years of age and above, all of those eligible for military service.
27 The musters of those affiliated with the tribe of Judah: 74,600.
28 Of the descendants of Issachar, those born to them, by their clans and patriarchal houses; according to the names of those twenty years of age and above, all of those eligible for military service.
29 The musters of those affiliated with the tribe of Issachar: 54,400.
30 Of the descendants of Zebulun, those born to them, by their clans and patriarchal houses, according to the names of those twenty years of age and above, all of those eligible for military service.
31 The musters of those affiliated with the tribe of Zebulun: 57,400.
32 Of the descendants of Joseph—of the descendants of Ephraim, those born to them, by their clans and patriarchal houses; according to the names of those twenty years of age and above, all of those eligible for military service.
33 The musters of those affiliated with the tribe of Ephraim: 40,500.
34 Of the descendants of Manasseh, those born to them, by their clans and patriarchal houses; according to the names of those twenty years of age and above, all of those eligible for military service.
35 The musters of those affiliated with the tribe of Manasseh: 32,200.
36 Of the descendants of Benjamin, those born to them, by their clans and patriarchal houses; according to the names of those twenty years of age and above, all of those eligible for military service.
37 The musters of those affiliated with the tribe of Benjamin: 35,400.
38 Of the descendants of Dan, those born to them, by their clans and patriarchal houses; according to the names of those twenty years of age and above, all of those eligible for military service.

[39]The musters of those affiliated with the tribe of Dan: 62,700.
[40]Of the descendants of Asher, those born to them, by their clans and patriarchal houses; according to the names of those twenty years of age and above, all of those eligible for military service.
[41]The musters of those affiliated with the tribe of Asher: 41,500.
[42]Of the descendants of Naphtali, those born to them, by their clans and patriarchal houses; according to the names of those twenty years of age and above, all of those eligible for military service.
[43]The musters of those affiliated with the tribe of Naphtali: 53,400.
[44]These are the musters that Moses and Aaron arrayed, together with the chieftains of Israel; twelve men, one man each, affiliated with his patriarchal house.
[45]Total musters of the Israelite people, by their patriarchal houses; those twenty years of age and above, all of those eligible for military service in Israel:
[46]The total musters amounted to 603,550.
[47]But the Levites, affiliated with their patriarchal tribe, had not been included in their musters.
[48]YHWH spoke to Moses as follows:
[49]Moreover, as regards the tribe of Levi, you must be certain not to muster, or take a poll of them among the Israelite people.
[50]And as for you, appoint the Levites in charge of the Tabernacle of the Covenant, and in charge of all of its vessels, and everything pertaining to it. They shall transport the Tabernacle and all of its vessels, and they shall perform its service, encamping around the Tabernacle.
[51]Whenever the Tabernacle sets out on the march, the Levites shall dismantle it; and whenever the Tabernacle is encamped, the Levites shall set it up. Any alien who intrudes shall be put to death.
[52]The Israelite people shall encamp, each corps by itself and each *degel* by itself, according to their divisions.
[53]But the Levites shall encamp around the Tabernacle of the Covenant, so that rage will not be brought against the community of the Israelite people. The Levites shall be charged with maintaining the Tabernacle of the Covenant.
[54]The Israelites complied with all that YHWH had commanded Moses; they acted accordingly.

2 [1]YHWH spoke to Moses and to Aaron as follows:
[2]The Israelites shall encamp, each person with his *degel* alongside standards, according to their patriarchal houses. They shall encamp opposite one another, around the Tent of Meeting.
[3]Those encamped all the way to the east: the *degel* of the Judahite corps, by their divisions. Chieftain of the Judahites: Nahshon son of Amminadab.
[4]The musters of his division: 74,600.

5Those encamped alongside him: the tribe of Issachar. Chieftain of the Issacharites: Nathanel son of Zuar.
6The musters of his division: 54,400.
7The tribe of Zebulun: chieftain of the Zebulunites: Eliab son of Helon.
8The musters of his division: 57,400.
9Total musters of the Judahite corps: 186,400, by their divisions. They shall be at the head of the march.
10The *degel* of the Reubenite corps, to the south, by their divisions. Chieftain of the Reubenites: Elizur son of Shedeur.
11The musters of his division: 46,500.
12Those encamped alongside him: the tribe of Simeon. Chieftain of the Simeonites: Shelumiel son of Zurishaddai.
13The musters of his division: 59,300.
14The tribe of Gad. Chieftain of the Gadites: Eliasaph son of Reuel.
15The musters of his division: 45,650.
16Total musters of the Reubenite corps: 151,450, by their divisions. They shall march in second place.
17The Tent of Meeting shall then be set forth, with the levitical corps in the midst of the [other] corps. Just as they encamp, so shall they march; each group in its own place, by their *degels*.
18The *degel* of the Ephraimite corps, by their divisions, to the west. Chieftain of the Ephraimite corps: Elishama, son of Ammihud.
19The musters of his division: 40,500.
20Those alongside him: the tribe of Manasseh. Chieftain of the Manassites: Gamaliel son of Pedahzur.
21The musters of his division: 32,200.
22The tribe of Benjamin. Chieftain of the Benjamites: Abidan son of Gideoni.
23The musters of his division: 35,400.
24Total musters of the Ephraimite corps: 108,100, by their divisions. They shall march in third place.
25The *degel* of the Danite corps, to the north, by their divisions. Chieftain of the Danites: Ahiezer son of Ammishaddai.
26The musters of his division: 62,700.
27Those encamped alongside him: the tribe of Asher. Chieftain of the Asherites: Pagiel son of Ochran.
28The musters of his division: 41,500.
29The tribe of Naphtali. Chieftain of the Naphtalites: Ahira son of Enan.
30The musters of his division: 53,400.
31Total musters of the Danite corps: 157,600. They shall march at the rear, by their *degels*.
32These are the musters of the Israelite people, by their patriarchal houses. Total musters of the corps, by their divisions: 603,550.

33 The Levites had not been mustered as part of the Israelite people, as YHWH had commanded Moses.

34 The Israelites acted in accordance with all that YHWH had commanded Moses. Accordingly, they encamped by their *degels*, and accordingly, they marched; each [group] with its clans, and together with its patriarchal houses.

3 1 These are the persons who had been born to Aaron and Moses, at the time that YHWH spoke with Moses at Mount Sinai.

2 These are the names of the sons of Aaron: Nadab, the firstborn, and Abihu; Eleazar and Ithamar.

3 These are the names of Aaron's sons, who were the anointed priests, whom he had empowered to serve in the priesthood.

4 Nadab and Abihu died in the presence of YHWH, as they were about to bring an improper incense offering in the presence of YHWH, in the Wilderness of Sinai; they left no sons. Instead, Eleazar and Ithamar served as priests during the lifetime of Aaron, their father.

5 YHWH spoke to Moses as follows:

6 Bring the tribe of Levi and station them in the presence of Aaron the priest, so that they may serve him.

7 Let them serve under his charge, and under the charge of the entire community, in front of the Tent of Meeting, performing the tasks of maintaining the Tabernacle.

8 They are to maintain all of the appurtenances of the Tent of Meeting, discharging duties on behalf of the Israelite people by performing the tasks of maintaining the Tabernacle.

9 You shall subordinate the Levites to Aaron and his sons. They are completely dedicated to him, by act of the Israelite people.

10 You shall likewise commission Aaron and his sons to perform the duties of their priesthood. Any outsider who intrudes shall be put to death!

11 YHWH spoke to Moses as follows: I hereby select the Levites from among the Israelite people in place of every firstborn, the first issue of every womb from among the Israelite people; the Levites shall belong to me.

12 For every firstborn became mine at the time I slew every firstborn in the land of Egypt.

13 For I consecrated for myself every firstborn among the Israelites; both man and animal shall belong to me. I am YHWH.

14 YHWH spoke to Moses in the Wilderness of Sinai as follows:

15 Muster the descendants of Levi, by their patriarchal houses, according to their clans. Every male one month of age and older shall you muster them.

16 Moses mustered them, by order of YHWH, as he had been commanded.

17 These are the sons of Levi, listed by their names: Gershon, Kohath, and Merari.

18 These are the names of the sons of Gershon, by their clans: Libni and
Shimei.
19 The sons of Kohath were, by their clans: Amram and Yizhar, Hebron and
Uzziel.
20 The sons of Merari were, by their clans: Mahli and Mushi. Following are
the clans of the Levites listed according to their patriarchal houses.
21 Affiliated with Gershon: the Libnite clan, and the Shimeite clan; these are
the Gershonite clans.
22 Their musters according to the number of males one month of age and
older; their total counts: 7,500.
23 The Gershonite clans shall encamp behind the Tabernacle, on its western
side.
24 The chieftain of the patriarchal house representing the Gershonites is
Eliasaph son of Lael.
25 The charge of the Gershonites in the Tent of Meeting consists of the
Tabernacle compound and the Tent, including its cover and the screen at the
entrance of the Tent of Meeting,
26 as well as the hangings of the courtyard and the screen at the entrance of
the courtyard that surrounds the Tabernacle and the altar, including its lashings, in its complete construction.
27 Affiliated with Kohath: the Amramite clan, the Yizharite clan, the
Hebronite clan, and the Uzzielite clan. These are the Kohathite clans,
28 according to the number of all males, one month of age and older: 8,600
maintenance personnel for the shrine.
29 The Kohathite clans shall encamp along the southern side of the Tabernacle.
30 The chieftain of the patriarchal house representing the Kohathite clan is
Elizaphan son of Uzziel.
31 Their charge consists of the Ark and the table, the lampstand and altars,
and the vessels of the Sanctuary used in conjunction with them, as well as the
curtain and its complete construction.
32 The chief of the chieftains of the Levites is Eleazar son of Aaron the priest,
[over] the marshaled force of those assigned to the maintenance of the
Shrine.
33 Affiliated with Merari: the Mahlite clan and the Mushite clan; these are
the Merarite clans.
34 Their musters, according to the number of all males, one month of age and
older: 6,200.
35 The chieftain of the patriarchal house representing the Merarite clans is
Zuriel son of Abihail. These shall encamp along the northern side of the
Tabernacle.
36 The marshaled force bearing the Merarite assignment is charged with the

planks of the Tabernacle, and its bolts; its posts and its sockets, and all of its
appurtenances, and their complete construction,
37 also the posts of the courtyard, on every side; and their sockets, their tent
pegs, and their lashings.
38 Those who are to encamp in front of the Tabernacle to the east are Moses
and Aaron and his sons, charged with the duties of the sanctuary, in fulfillment of the duties of the Israelites. Any outsider who intrudes shall be put to
death!
39 The total musters of the Levites, which Moses and Aaron tallied by order
of YHWH, by their clans: all males one month of age and older amounted to
22,000.
40 YHWH spoke to Moses: Muster every firstborn male among the Israelite
people, one month of age and older, and take a count of the number of their
names.
41 You shall acquire the Levites for me, I am YHWH, in place of every firstling among the Israelite people; and the livestock of the Levites in place of
every firstling among the livestock of the Israelite people.
42 Moses accomplished the muster, as YHWH had commanded him, including every firstborn among the Israelite people.
43 All firstborn males by name, one month of age and older, totaled 22,273.
44 Then YHWH spoke to Moses as follows:
45 Recruit the Levites in place of every firstborn among the Israelites, and the
animals of the Levites in place of their animals. The Levites shall be mine, I
am YHWH.
46 As the redemption price of the 273 firstborn of the Israelites in excess of
the Levites,
47 you shall collect five shekels per head. You shall collect them by the sanctuary weight, at twenty grains a shekel.
48 You shall remit the silver to Aaron and to his sons, comprising the redemption prices of those outstanding among them.
49 So Moses collected the silver of redemption of those in excess of the
persons redeemed by the Levites.
50 He collected the silver from the firstborn of the Israelite people, in the
amount of 1,365 sanctuary shekels.
51 Moses remitted the silver of those who were redeemed to Aaron and
to his sons, by order of YHWH, just as YHWH had commanded
Moses.

4 1 YHWH spoke to Moses and to Aaron as follows:
2 Take a head count of the Kohathites, who are part of the Levites, by their
clans and patriarchal houses,
3 of those thirty years of age and older, until fifty years of age, all who are

eligible for performing assigned tasks in the work force, pertaining to the Tent of Meeting.

4This is the task of the Kohathites within the Tent of Meeting: the most sacred objects.

5Whenever the encampment sets out on the march, Aaron and his sons shall enter, and take down the *pārôket* screen, and wrap the Ark of the Covenant with it.

6They shall place over it a covering of dolphin skin, and spread a wrap of entirely blue cloth on top [of it], and insert its [carrying] poles.

7Over the table of the [bread] of display they shall spread a wrap of blue cloth, and set upon it the bowls, the ladles, the storage jars, and the libation jugs; and the regularly offered bread shall also be placed on it.

8They shall spread a crimson cloth over this, which they shall then wrap with a covering of dolphin skin, and insert its carrying poles.

9They shall take a cloth of blue, and wrap the lampstand [used] for lighting, together with its lamps, its tongs, and its pans, and all of the utensils for its oil, which are to be used in conjunction with them.

10They shall place it together with all of its vessels inside a covering of dolphin skin, and place it on a [carrying] frame.

11Over the altar of gold they shall spread a cloth of blue, and wrap it with a covering of dolphin skin, and insert its [carrying] poles.

12They shall take all of the vessels that are used in the Shrine and place them inside a cloth of blue, and wrap them with a covering of dolphin skin, and place [them] in a [carrying] frame.

13They shall remove the ashes from the altar [of burnt offerings] and spread a purple cloth over it.

14They shall place on it all of the vessels of the altar that are used in connection with it: the firepans, the forks, and the scrapers, and the basins all of the vessels of the altar and they shall spread over this a covering of dolphin skin and insert its [carrying] poles.

15Aaron and his sons shall complete the wrapping of what is in the Shrine, including all of the vessels of the Shrine, whenever the encampment sets out on the march. Afterward, the Kohathites shall arrive to do the transporting, but they may not have contact with the Shrine, lest they die. These are the transport duties of the Kohathites pertaining to the Tent of Meeting.

16The charge of Eleazar the son of Aaron the priest shall consist of the oil for lighting and the aromatic incense; the regular grain offering, and the oil of anointing the charge of the entire Tabernacle and everything in it pertaining to the Shrine and pertaining to its vessels.

17YHWH spoke to Moses and to Aaron as follows:

18Do not allow the tribal clans of the Kohathites to be cut off from the [rest of] the Levites.

19This is how you shall manage them, so that they may remain alive and not risk death whenever they approach the Holy of Holies: Aaron and his sons shall enter and assign them, each one, to his workload,

20 so that they do not have to come inside and view the Shrine for even a split second, and die as a result.

21 YHWH spoke to Moses as follows:

22 Take a head count of the Gershonites, as well, by their clans and patriarchal houses.

23 You shall muster all of them, thirty years of age and older to fifty years of age, all who are eligible to perform the tasks of the work force relevant to the Tent of Meeting.

24 This is the duty of the Gershonite clans: the task of transportation.

25 They shall transport the flaps of the Tabernacle and the Tent of Meeting—its wrapping, and the covering of dolphin skin that is over it, on top, and the curtain at the entrance of the Tent of Meeting,

26 as well as the hangings of the courtyard, and the curtains at the gate of the courtyard, which surrounds the Tabernacle and the altar of burnt offerings, and their lashings, and all of their functional accessories; they shall perform whatever is necessary for their maintenance.

27 The entire assignment of the Gershonites shall be conducted by order of Aaron and his sons, pertaining to all of their transportation tasks. You shall dutifully oversee all of their transportation work.

28 This is the task of the Gershonite clans pertaining to the Tent of Meeting, their charge being under the authority of Ithamar, son of Aaron the priest.

29 As for the Merarites, you shall muster them by their clans and patriarchal houses.

30 You shall record those of them thirty years of age and older to fifty years of age, all who are eligible for the work force, to perform assigned tasks relevant to the Tent of Meeting.

31 This is their transport assignment, comprising their complete task relevant to the Tent of Meeting: the planks of the Tabernacle, and its bolts, and its posts and its sockets,

32 and the posts of the courtyard on every side, and their sockets, and their tent pegs and their lashings, for the maintenance of all of their appurtenances. You shall list this transport assignment by the types of their assigned appurtenances.

33 This is the complete assigned task of the Merarite clan, relevant to the Tent of Meeting, under the authority of Ithamar, son of Aaron the priest.

34 So Moses and Aaron and the chieftains of the community mustered the Kohathites by their clans and patriarchal houses,

35 those thirty years of age and older to fifty years of age, all who were eligible for the work force, for assigned work relevant to the Tent of Meeting.

36 Their total musters by their clans came to 2,750.

37 These are the musters of the Merarite clans, of all who worked at the Tent

of Meeting, which Moses and Aaron listed, by order of YHWH, under the authority of Moses.

38 The musters of the Gershonites, by their clans and patriarchal houses,

39 of those thirty years of age and older to fifty years of age, all who were eligible to serve on the work force, at the Tent of Meeting.

40 Their musters, by their clans and patriarchal houses: 2,630.

41 These are the musters of Gershonite clans, all who performed tasks at the Tent of Meeting, whom Moses and Aaron registered by order of YHWH.

42 The musters of the Merarites, by their clans and patriarchal houses,

43 of those thirty years of age and older to fifty years of age, all who are eligible for service in the work force, at the Tent of Meeting.

44 Their musters, by their clans, came to 3,200.

45 These are the musters of the Merarite clans, which Moses and Aaron listed, by order of YHWH, under the authority of Moses.

46 The total musters of the Levites listed by Moses and Aaron and the Israelite chieftains, by their clans and patriarchal houses,

47 of those thirty years of age and older to fifty years of age, all who are eligible for assigned maintenance and transport tasks relevant to the Tent of Meeting.

48 Their musters came to 8,580.

49 They were listed by Moses, by order of YHWH, each unit for its assigned maintenance and transport task. Each was listed, just as YHWH commanded Moses.

5 1 YHWH spoke to Moses as follows:

2 Issue a command to the Israelite people to expel from the encampment any person suffering from *ṣāraʿat*, or experiencing a bodily discharge, as well as any person impure because of contact with a corpse.

3 You must expel both males and females, expelling them from the encampment, so that they will not defile their encampment, where I maintain a residence in their midst.

4 The Israelites did accordingly, and expelled them from the encampment. Just as YHWH had instructed Moses, so did the Israelites do.

5 YHWH spoke to Moses as follows:

6 Speak to the Israelite people: When a man or woman commits any of the offenses affecting persons, thereby also committing an act of betrayal against YHWH, and that person thereby incurs guilt—

7 he must confess his offense, which he committed, and he must make restitution for his liability equal to the amount of its principal, adding to it one-fifth of the amount. He shall pay [it] to the person who suffered a loss by the guilt he had incurred.

8 If that person had no [clan] redeemer to whom the liability could be repaid, the liability that is to be repaid belongs to YHWH, [credited] to the

priest. This is apart from the ram of the expiation rites, with which expiation rites shall be performed on his behalf.

9 Any levied donation for any of the sacred offerings that the Israelites deliver to the priest shall be for him.

10 For every person shall possess his own sacred offerings; each priest shall possess what is delivered to him.

11 YHWH spoke to Moses as follows:

12 Speak to the Israelite people and say to them: Should any man's wife become errant and commit an act of betrayal against him,

13 with the result that another man had carnal relations with her, and this was hidden from her husband's eyes, because she defiled herself in secret, there being no witness against her and she was not apprehended.

14 Now, if a fit of envious possessiveness overtakes him, so that he becomes envious of his wife in a case wherein she had in fact defiled herself, or a fit of envious possessiveness so that he becomes envious of his wife in a case wherein [as it turned out] she had not defiled herself—

15 the man must [in any case] bring his wife before the priest and present her offering on her behalf, of one-tenth of an ephah of barley flour. He shall not pour oil over it, nor place frankincense upon it, for it is a grain offering occasioned by jealous feelings; a grain offering of record, which calls attention to wrongdoing.

16 The priest shall bring her near, stationing her in the presence of YHWH.

17 The priest shall take holy water in a ceramic vessel, and the priest shall also take some earth from the floor of the Tabernacle and place it in the water.

18 The priest shall station the woman in the presence of YHWH and loosen the hair of the woman's head, and place on her palms the grain offering, the grain offering of record, the grain offering occasioned by envious feelings. The priest shall hold in his hands the bitter water of condemnation.

19 The priest shall administer the oath to her, saying to the woman, "If no man has had carnal relations with you, and if you have not been errant in an impure manner, while under your husband['s jurisdiction], may you be cleared of the charge by means of this bitter water of condemnation.

20 "But if you have been errant, while under your husband['s jurisdiction], and you have defiled yourself, in that a man other than your husband has inseminated you carnally—"

21 (the priest shall then administer to the woman the imprecation section of the oath). The priest shall say to the woman, "May YHWH make of you an accursed oath-violator among your kin, even as YHWH causes your thigh to sag and your belly to swell!

22 "May this water of condemnation enter into your intestines, to cause swelling of the belly and sagging of the thigh!" And the woman shall reply, "Amen! Amen!"

23 The priest shall inscribe the words of the imprecation on a document, and he shall then wash [them] away in the bitter water.

24 He is to give the woman the bitter water of condemnation to drink, and the water of condemnation will enter into her and turn bitter.

25 The priest shall take the grain offering of envious feelings from the woman's hand and present the grain offering before YHWH, and move her (= the woman) nearer to the altar.

26 The priest shall scoop up a fistful of the grain offering—its token portion—and turn it into smoke on the altar, after which he shall give the woman the water to drink.

27 He must give her the water to drink. It will happen that if she has defiled herself and has acted disloyally against her husband, the water of condemnation will turn bitter, with the result that her belly will swell and her thigh sag. The woman will become a curse in the midst of her kin.

28 But if the woman has not defiled herself, and she turned out to be pure, she shall be cleared of the charge, and retain seed.

29 This is the prescribed instruction regarding feelings of jealousy, in cases wherein a wife was errant while under [the jurisdiction of] her husband, and had defiled herself,

30 or in cases wherein a fit of envious possessiveness overtook a man, with the result that he became envious of his wife. The priest is to station the woman before YHWH and perform with respect to her this entire, prescribed instruction.

31 [In this way] the husband may be cleared of any wrongdoing, while the woman in question will bear punishment for her offense.

6 1 YHWH spoke to Moses as follows:

2 Speak to the Israelite people and say to them: When anyone, man or woman, sets [himself] apart by pronouncing a vow as a Nazirite, to place restrictions on himself for YHWH,

3 he must restrict [himself] from wine or any other intoxicant, not drinking the vinegar of wine, or the vinegar of any other intoxicant; nor may he imbibe any liquid in which grapes have been steeped. He may not eat either moist or dried grapes.

4 For the entire term of his restriction, he may not ingest any product of the grapevine, neither seeds nor skins.

5 For the entire term of his restriction, a razor may not pass over his head. Until the completion of the days during which he placed restrictions on himself for YHWH, he is to remain sacred, allowing the hair of his head to grow loose.

6 For the entire term during which he placed restrictions on himself for YHWH, he may not come near the body of a dead person.

7 Even on account of his father and his mother, or for his brother and sister

—even on account of them—he may not render himself impure at their death. For hair reserved for his God covers his head.

8For the entire term of his restriction, he remains sacred to YHWH.

9Should any person related to him pass away suddenly, so that he has defiled his dedicated hair, he must shave his head on the day of his purification. On the seventh day he must shave it.

10On the eighth day he must deliver to the priest two turtledoves or two young pigeons, at the entrance of the Tent of Meeting.

11The priest shall assign one as a sin offering and the other as a burnt offering, and perform expiation on his behalf for the guilt he has incurred concerning a corpse. He must reconsecrate his "head" on that day.

12He must recommit the days of his restriction for YHWH and deliver a yearling lamb as a guilt offering. The prior days fall away because his state of restriction has been impaired by an impurity.

13This is the prescribed instruction for the Nazirite: On the day that his term of dedication is complete, he is to be brought to the entrance of the Tent of Meeting.

14He is to present as his offering to YHWH a yearling lamb without blemish for a burnt offering, and one ewe a year old without blemish for a burnt offering, and one ewe a year old without blemish for a sin offering, and one ram without blemish for sacred gifts of greeting;

15a basket of unleavened bread made of semolina flour, prepared as loaves with oil mixed into them, and prepared as thin cakes of unleavened bread smeared with oil, along with their grain offerings and libations.

16The priest shall draw near to the presence of YHWH and perform his sin offering and his burnt offering.

17He shall sacrifice the ram as an offering of sacred gifts of greeting in the presence of YHWH, together with the basket of unleavened bread. The priest shall likewise perform his grain offering and his libation.

18The Nazirite shall then shave his restricted "head" at the entrance of the Tent of Meeting. He shall take the hair of his restricted "head" and place it on the fire that is under the sacred gifts of greeting.

19The priest shall take the boiled shoulder of the ram and one loaf of unleavened bread from the basket, along with one thin, unleavened cake, and place them on the palms of the Nazirite, after he has shaved off his restricted [hair].

20The priest shall raise them as a presentation in the presence of YHWH. This shall be a sacred offering for YHWH, in addition to the breast of the presentation offering and the shoulder of the levied donation. Only afterward may the Nazirite drink wine.

21This is the prescribed instruction for the Nazirite. But one who pledges his offering to YHWH in excess of his required restriction, in accordance with what his means allow, must fulfill the vow he has pledged in excess of the instruction prescribed for his restriction.

[22]YHWH spoke to Moses, saying:
[23]Instruct Aaron and his sons as follows: In this manner shall you bless the Israelite people. Say to them:
[24]"May YHWH bless you and watch over you.
[25]"May YHWH look kindly upon you and deal graciously with you.
[26]"May YHWH look with favor upon you and grant you well-being."
[27]Whenever they pronounce my name over the Israelite people, I will bless them!

7 [1]On the day Moses finished setting up the Tabernacle he anointed it, thereby consecrating it along with all of its vessels, the altar and all of its appurtenances. He anointed these, thereby consecrating them.

[2]The chieftains of Israel, heads of their patriarchal houses, made their presentations. They were the tribal chieftains, the ones in charge of the musters.

[3]They brought their offering in the presence of the YHWH, consisting of six transport wagons and twelve oxen; a wagon by every two chieftains, and one ox apiece. They presented these in front of the Tabernacle.

[4]YHWH then addressed Moses as follows:

[5]Accept [the offerings] from them, and they shall serve for maintaining the Tent of Meeting. Allot them to the Levites, to each [group] according to its maintenance tasks.

[6]Moses accepted the wagons and the oxen, and allotted them to the Levites.

[7]He allotted two of the wagons and four of the oxen to the Gershonites, in accordance with their maintenance tasks.

[8]He allotted four of the wagons and eight of the oxen to the Merarites, in accordance with their maintenance tasks, under the charge of Ithamar son of Aaron, the priest.

[9]He did not allot [wagons] to the Kohathites, for they were charged with maintaining the Shrine, and [customarily] carried their burdens on the shoulder.

[10]The chieftains presented their offering for the dedication of the altar on the day it was anointed. They presented their offering in front of the altar.

[11]YHWH then instructed Moses:
One chieftain a day, one chieftain a day, let them present their offering for the dedication of the altar.

[12]The one who presented his offering on the first day was Nahshon son of Amminadab, representing the tribe of Judah.

[13]His offering:
One silver bowl, its weight 130 shekels.
One silver basin, its weight 70 shekels, by the sanctuary weight.

Both of them were filled with semolina flour, mixed with oil, for grain offerings.
14 One gold ladle of 10 shekels, filled with incense.
15 One bull of the herd, one ram, and one yearling lamb, for burnt offerings.
16 One goat, for a sin offering.
17 For the sacred gifts of greeting:
oxen—2,
rams—5,
he-goats—5,
yearling lambs—5.
This was the offering of Nahshon son of Amminadab.
18 On the second day, Nethanel son of Zuar, chieftain of Issachar, presented his offering.
19 He presented as his offering:
One silver bowl, its weight 130 shekels.
One silver basin, its weight 70 shekels, by the sanctuary weight.
Both of them were filled with semolina flour, mixed with oil, for grain offerings.
20 One gold ladle of 10 shekels, filled with incense.
21 One bull of the herd, one ram, and one yearling lamb, for burnt offerings.
22 One goat, for a sin offering.
23 For the sacred gifts of greeting:
oxen—2,
rams—5,
he-goats—5,
yearling lambs—5.
This was the offering of Nethanel son of Zuar.
24 On the third day, chieftain of the Zebulunites, Eliab son of Helon.
25 His offering:
One silver bowl, its weight 130 shekels.
One silver basin, its weight 70 shekels, by the sanctuary weight.
Both of them were filled with semolina flour, mixed with oil, for grain offerings.
26 One gold ladle of 10 shekels, filled with incense.
27 One bull of the herd, one ram, and one yearling lamb, for burnt offerings.
28 One goat, for a sin offering.
29 For the sacred gifts of greeting:
oxen—2,
rams—5,
he-goats—5,
yearling lambs—5.
This was the offering of Eliab son of Helon.

30 On the fourth day, chieftain of the Reubenites, Elizur son of Shedeur.
31 His offering:
One silver bowl, its weight 130 shekels.
One silver basin, its weight 70 shekels, by the sanctuary weight.
Both of them were filled with semolina flour, mixed with oil, for grain offerings.
32 One gold ladle of 10 shekels, filled with incense.
33 One bull of the herd, one ram, and one yearling lamb, for burnt offerings.
34 One goat, for a sin offering.
35 For the sacred gifts of greeting:
oxen—2,
rams—5,
he-goats—5,
yearling lambs—5.
This was the offering of Elizur son of Shedeur.
36 On the fifth day, chieftain of the Simeonites, Shelumiel son of Zurishaddai.
37 His offering:
One silver bowl, its weight 130 shekels.
One silver basin, its weight 70 shekels, by the sanctuary weight.
Both of them were filled with semolina flour, mixed with oil, for grain offerings.
38 One gold ladle of 10 shekels, filled with incense.
39 One bull of the herd, one ram, and one yearling lamb, for burnt offerings.
40 One goat, for a sin offering.
41 For the sacred gifts of greeting:
oxen—2,
rams—5,
he-goats—5,
yearling lambs—5.
This was the offering of Shelumiel son of Zurishaddai.
42 On the sixth day, chieftain of the Gadites, Eliasaph son of Deuel.
43 His offering:
One silver bowl, its weight 130 shekels.
One silver basin, its weight 70 shekels, by the sanctuary weight.
Both of them were filled with semolina flour, mixed with oil, for grain offerings.
44 One gold ladle of 10 shekels, filled with incense.
45 One bull of the herd, one ram, and one yearling lamb, for burnt offerings.
46 One goat, for a sin offering.
47 For the sacred gifts of greeting:
oxen—2,
rams—5,

he-goats—5,
yearling lambs—5.
This was the offering of Eliasap hson of Deuel.
48On the seventh day, chieftain of the Ephraimites, Elishama son of Ammihud.
49His offering:
One silver bowl, its weight 130 shekels.
One silver basin, its weight 70 shekels, by the sanctuary weight.
Both of them were filled with semolina flour, mixed with oil, for grain offerings.
50One gold ladle of 10 shekels, filled with incense.
51One bull of the herd, one ram, and one yearling lamb, for burnt offerings.
52One goat, for a sin offering.
53For the sacred gifts of greeting:
oxen—2,
rams—5,
he-goats—5,
yearling lambs—5.
This was the offering of Elishama son of Ammihud.
54On the eighth day, chieftain of the Manassites, Gamaliel son of Pedahzur.
55His offering:
One silver bowl, its weight 130 shekels.
One silver basin, its weight 70 shekels, by the sanctuary weight.
Both of them were filled with semolina flour, mixed with oil, for grain offerings.
56One gold ladle of 10 shekels, filled with incense.
57One bull of the herd, one ram, and one yearling lamb, for burnt offerings.
58One goat, for a sin offering.
59For the sacred gifts of greeting:
oxen—2,
rams—5,
he-goats—5,
yearling lambs—5.
This was the offering of Gamaliel son of Pedahzur.
60On the ninth day, chieftain of the Benjaminites, Abidan son of Gideoni.
61His offering:
One silver bowl, its weight 130 shekels.
One silver basin, its weight 70 shekels, by the sanctuary weight.
Both of them were filled with semolina flour, mixed with oil, for grain offerings.
62One gold ladle of 10 shekels, filled with incense.
63One bull of the herd, one ram, and one yearling lamb, for burnt offerings.
64One goat, for a sin offering.

65 For the sacred gifts of greeting:
oxen—2,
rams—5,
he-goats—5,
yearling lambs—5.
This was the offering of Abidan son of Gideoni.
66 On the tenth day, chieftain of the Danites, Ahiezer son of Ammishaddai.
67 His offering:
One silver bowl, its weight 130 shekels.
One silver basin, its weight 70 shekels, by the sanctuary weight.
Both of them were filled with semolina flour, mixed with oil, for grain offerings.
68 One gold ladle of 10 shekels, filled with incense.
69 One bull of the herd, one ram, and one yearling lamb, for burnt offerings.
70 One goat, for a sin offering.
71 For the sacred gifts of greeting:
oxen—2,
rams—5,
he-goats—5,
yearling lambs—5.
This was the offering of Ahiezer son of Ammishaddai.
72 On the eleventh day, chieftain of the Asherites, Pagiel son of Ochran.
73 His offering:
One silver bowl, its weight 130 shekels.
One silver basin, its weight 70 shekels, by the sanctuary weight.
Both of them were filled with semolina flour, mixed with oil, for grain offerings.
74 One gold ladle of 10 shekels, filled with incense.
75 One bull of the herd, one ram, and one yearling lamb, for burnt offerings.
76 One goat, for a sin offering.
77 For the sacred gifts of greeting:
oxen—2,
rams—5,
he-goats—5,
yearling lambs—5.
This was the offering of Pagiel son of Ochran.
78 On the twelfth day, chieftain of the Naphtalites, Ahira son of Enan.
79 His offering:
One silver bowl, its weight 130 shekels.
One silver basin, its weight 70 shekels, by the sanctuary weight.
Both of them were filled with semolina flour, mixed with oil, for grain offerings.
80 One gold ladle of 10 shekels, filled with incense.

81 One bull of the herd, one ram, and one yearling lamb, for burnt offerings.
82 One goat, for a sin offering.
83 For the sacred gifts of greeting:
oxen—2,
rams—5,
he-goats—5,
yearling lambs—5.
This was the offering of Ahira son of Enan.
84 This comprised the dedication offering of the altar, at the time of its anointing, as presented by the Israelite chieftains:
Silver bowls—12,
Silver basins—12,
Gold ladles—12.
85 Each bowl weighed 130 shekels, and each basin, 70 shekels. Total silver for the vessels: 2,400 shekels, by the sanctuary weight.
86 Gold ladles—12; filled with incense, at 10 shekels per ladle, by the sanctuary weight. Total gold for the ladles: [120 shekels].
87 Total livestock for burnt offerings:
12 oxen;
rams—12,
yearling lambs—12, with their grain offerings,
goats—12, for sin offerings;
88 Total livestock for the sacred gifts of greeting:
24 bulls;
rams—60,
he-goats—60,
yearling lambs—60.
Such was the dedication offering of the altar, subsequent to its anointing.
89 Whenever Moses entered the Tent of Meeting to speak with him, he heard the voice continuously speaking to him, from [the space] above the expiation lid, which covered the Ark of the Covenant, from between the two cherubs. [In this way] he spoke to him.

8 1 YHWH spoke to Moses as follows:
2 Speak to Aaron and say to him: When you mount the lamps, let the seven lamps cast light toward the [area] in front of the lampstand.
3 Aaron did accordingly. He mounted its lamps toward the [area] in front of the lampstand.
4 Such was the manufacture of the lampstand: it was made of hammered gold; it was hammered from its base to its petal. In accordance with the depiction that YHWH had shown Moses, just so did he fashion the lampstand.
5 YHWH spoke to Moses as follows:

6 Separate the Levites from among the Israelite people, and purify them.

7 This is what you must do to them in order to purify them: sprinkle on them water of purification. They shall pass a razor over their entire body, launder their garments, and thereby become pure.

8 They must secure a bull of the herd, with its [accompanying] grain offering, to consist of semolina flour mixed with oil. You shall secure a second bull of the herd for a sin offering.

9 Bring the Levites near the front of the Tent of Meeting, and then assemble the entire community of Israelites.

10 Bring the Levites into the presence of YHWH. Then have the Israelites lay their hands on the Levites.

11 Aaron shall make a presentation offering of the Levites in the presence of YHWH on behalf of the Israelites, that they may serve by doing YHWH's work.

12 The Levites, in turn, shall lay their hands on the heads of the bulls, assigning one as a sin offering and the other as a burnt offering to serve as redemption for the Levites.

13 You shall station the Levites in front of Aaron and in front of his sons, and make of them a presentation offering to YHWH.

14 You shall separate the Levites from among the Israelites; the Levites shall belong to me!

15 Afterward, the Levites shall arrive, and perform the tasks of the Tent of Meeting; after you have purified them and made a presentation offering of them.

16 For they are to be completely dedicated to me, from among the Israelites, in place of the first issue of every womb; [in place] of every firstborn of the Israelites have I selected them for myself.

17 For every firstborn within the Israelite people belongs to me, both man and beast. At the time I slew every firstborn in the land of Egypt, I declared them dedicated to me.

18 I have appropriated the Levites in place of every firstborn within the Israelite people.

19 I have delegated the Levites to be assigned to Aaron and to his sons from among the Israelite people, to perform the tasks of the Tent of Meeting and to serve as redemption for the Israelite people, so that no plague may afflict the Israelite people as a result of Israelites' approaching the Sanctuary.

20 Moses and Aaron, with the entire community of the Israelites, carried out with respect to the Levites everything that YHWH had commanded Moses regarding the Levites; just so did the Israelites do to them.

21 The Levites purified themselves, laundering their garments. Moses then made of them a presentation offering in the presence of YHWH, with Aaron performing rites of expiation on their behalf so as to purify them.

22 Afterward the Levites arrived to perform their tasks at the Tent of Meeting,

under Aaron and under his sons. They did to them just as YHWH had commanded Moses regarding the Levites.

23 YHWH spoke to Moses as follows:

24 This is what applies to the Levites: everyone twenty-five years and older must serve in the work force, performing the tasks of the Tent of Meeting.

25 All those fifty years of age and older may retire from the work force, and need not serve any longer.

26 The Levites shall then assist their kinsmen at the Tent of Meeting, performing various duties, but no longer serving on the work force. That is how you shall assign the Levites with respect to their duties.

9 1 YHWH spoke to Moses in the Wilderness of Sinai in the second year after their exodus from Egypt, in the first month, as follows:

2 Let the Israelite people perform the paschal sacrifice at its set time.

3 On the fourteenth day of this month, at twilight, you shall perform it, at its set time. You must perform it in accordance with all of its statutes and its rules.

4 So Moses instructed the Israelite people to perform the paschal sacrifice.

5 They performed the paschal sacrifice in the first month, on the fourteenth day of the month, at twilight, in the Wilderness of Sinai, in accordance with all that YHWH had commanded Moses. So did the Israelites perform it.

6 It happened that some persons were impure because of contact with a dead human body, and could not perform the paschal sacrifice on that day. They approached Moses and Aaron on that day.

7 These persons stated to him, "We are impure because of contact with a dead body. Why should we be deprived of presenting the offering of YHWH at its set time, together with the Israelite people?"

8 Moses said to them, "Stay here, until I hear what YHWH commands concerning you."

9 YHWH spoke to Moses as follows:

10 Speak to the Israelite people as follows: Any person who becomes impure because of contact with a dead body, or is away on a distant journey, of you or your future generations, and desires to perform the paschal sacrifice—

11 they may perform it in the second month, on the fourteenth day, at twilight. Together with unleavened bread and bitter herbs let them partake of it.

12 They may not leave any part of it until morning, nor break any bone in it. They must perform it completely in accordance with the statute of the paschal sacrifice.

13 Any person who is pure, and was not away on a journey, and yet fails to perform the paschal sacrifice—that person shall be cut off from his kinsmen, for he failed to present the offering of YHWH at its set time. That person must bear the punishment for his offense.

14 Should an alien reside among you and wish to perform the paschal sacrifice to YHWH, he must perform it in accordance with the statute of the paschal sacrifice, and according to its rule. There shall be only one statute applying to the alien, just as it applies to the native-born citizen of the land.
15 On the day that the Tabernacle was set up, the cloud covered the Tabernacle of the Tent of the Covenant. At evening, it appeared over the Tabernacle as fire, until morning.
16 So it was regularly: the cloud covered it, appearing as fire at night.
17 As the cloud lifted off from atop the Tent, the Israelites would promptly set out on the march. Wherever the cloud came to rest, there the Israelites would make camp.
18 The Israelites marched by order of YHWH, and by order of YHWH they encamped. As long as the cloud rested over the Tabernacle, they remained encamped.
19 When the cloud remained over the Tabernacle for a long period of time, the Israelites obeyed YHWH's ordinance and did not march.
20 It would happen that the cloud would remain over the Tabernacle for only a few days. In that event, they encamped by order of YHWH, just as they marched by order of YHWH.
21 It happened that the cloud would remain only from evening until morning, and then lift off in the morning.
22 Whether for two days, for a month, or for a year—when the cloud rested over the Tabernacle for a long period of time—the Israelites would remain encamped, and would not march. When it lifted—they marched.
23 By order of YHWH they made camp, and by order of YHWH they marched. They obeyed YHWH's ordinance, by order of YHWH, through the authority of Moses.

10 1 YHWH spoke to Moses as follows:

2 Fashion two trumpets of silver; make them of a hammered piece. They shall serve you for assembling the community and for undertaking the march of the corps.

3 When both are sounded, the entire community shall assemble before you, at the entrance of the Tent of Meeting.

4 When only one is sounded, the chieftains, heads of the Israelite militias, shall assemble before you.

5 When you sound prolonged blasts, the corps encamped on the eastern side shall set out on the march.

6 At the second sounding of prolonged blasts, the corps encamped on the southern side shall set out on the march. Prolonged blasts shall be sounded for their marches,

7 but for assembling the congregation, you must sound short blasts, not prolonged blasts.

[8]The sons of Aaron, the priests, shall sound the trumpets. They shall serve you on a permanent basis, throughout your generations.

[9]When you wage war in your land, against any aggressor who attacks you, sound prolonged blasts on the trumpet, so that you will be brought to the attention of YHWH, your God, and be rescued from your enemies.

[10]And at the time of your rejoicing, on your annual festivals and your new moons, you must blast the trumpets over your burnt offerings and your sacred gifts of greeting. The [blasts] will serve as a reminder of you before your God. I am YHWH, your God!

[11]In the second year, on the twentieth day of the second month, the cloud lifted from the Tabernacle of the Covenant.

[12]The Israelites set out on their marches from the Wilderness of Sinai. The cloud settled in the Wilderness of Paran.

[13]They had commenced their march at the command of YHWH, transmitted by Moses.

[14]The *degel* consisting of the Judahite corps set out in the lead, by their divisions. In command of its (Judah's) division was Nahshon son of Amminadab.

[15]Commanding the division of the tribe of Issachar was Nethanel son of Zuar,

[16]and commanding the division of the tribe of Zebulun was Eliab son of Helon.

[17]The Tabernacle was then disassembled, and the Gershonites and Merarites, bearers of the Tabernacle, took to the march.

[18]The *degel* consisting of the Reubenite corps then set out on the march, by their divisions. In command of its (Reuben's) division was Elizur son of Shedeur.

[19]Commanding the division of the tribe of Simeon was Shelumiel son of Zurishaddai,

[20]and commanding the division of the tribe of Gad was Eliasaph, son of Deuel.

[21]Then the Kohathites, bearers of the inner sanctuary, set out on the march. By the time they arrived, others would have erected the Tabernacle.

[22]The *degel* consisting of the Ephraimite corps then set out on the march, by their divisions. In command of its (Ephraim's) division was Elishama son of Ammihud.

[23]Commanding the division of the tribe of Manasseh was Gamaliel son of Pedahzur,

[24]and commanding the division of the tribe of Benjamin was Abidan son of Gideoni.

[25]The *degel* consisting of the Danite corps, the rear guard of all the corps, then set out on the march, by their divisions. In command of its (Dan's) division was Ahiezer son of Ammishaddai.

26 Commanding the division of the tribe of Asher was Pagiel son of
Ochran,
27 and commanding the division of the tribe of Naphtali was Ahira son of
Enan.
28 These were the deployments of the Israelites, by their divisions, when
they set out on the march.
29 Moses addressed Hobab son of Reuel, the Midianite (the father-in-law of
Moses), "We are marching to the place of which YHWH has declared: 'That
very one will I grant to you!' Accompany us, and we will be generous to you,
for YHWH has assured Israel of good things."
30 He responded, "I will not come along; I prefer to return to the land of my
birth."
31 Moses went on, "Please do not part company with us; for truly, you know
where we should make camp in the wilderness, and you could serve as our
eyes.
32 "If you accompany us, we will share with you the good things YHWH is
about to confer on us."
33 They marched three days' distance from the mountain of YHWH, with
the Ark of YHWH's Covenant marching ahead of them < three days' distance > to scout out for them a place to encamp.
34 The cloud of YHWH remained above them during the day as they set
forth from the encampment.
35 Whenever the Ark set out on the march, Moses proclaimed,

"Attack, YHWH!
Your enemies disperse;
Your foes flee from your presence!"

36 When the Ark came to a halt, he would declare,

"Bring back, O YHWH,
The myriads of Israel's militias!"

11 1 The people continued to grieve bitterly, within earshot of YHWH, and
YHWH overheard, and his wrath flared. The flame of YHWH blazed at them,
consuming [those at] the edge of the encampment.
2 The people raised their grievance with Moses, and after Moses entreated
YHWH the flame subsided.
3 That site was named Taberah, for the flame of YHWH had blazed at
them.
4 The rabble in their midst had insatiable appetites. They complained again
and again, as did the Israelites, in the following words:
5 "Who will feed us meat? We recall the fish we dined on in Egypt without
cost; the cucumbers, melons, leeks, onions, and garlic.
6 "But now, our throats are dry; there is nothing to eat. All we can look
forward to is manna."

[7]Now, manna was similar to coriander seed, and its texture was like that of bdellium.

[8]The people would move about, gathering it up. They would grind it or pound it in a mortar, to be boiled in a pot or made into cakes. It tasted like creamy oil.

[9]At night, when dew fell over the encampment, manna would alight on top of it.

[10]Moses overheard the people as they complained, clan by clan, each person at the entrance of his tent. YHWH's wrath had flared, and Moses regarded the situation as dangerous.

[11]Moses addressed YHWH: "Why have you brought misfortune on your servant? What have I done to displease you, that you have imposed the burden of this entire people on me?

[12]"Did I conceive this entire people; did I give birth to it? Yet you command me: 'Carry him in your lap!'—as a male nurse carries an infant—to the land you promised to his ancestors.

[13]"Where can I find enough meat to feed this entire people? For they complain to me, saying, 'Give us meat to eat!'

[14]"I cannot bear responsibility for this entire people by myself. It is too burdensome for me!

[15]"If you insist on treating me this way put me to death, if I please you—but let me not witness my own misfortune."

[16]Thereupon, YHWH instructed Moses: Assemble in my presence seventy men from among the elders of Israel, whom you know to be truly the elders of the people and its senior officers. Bring them to the Tent of Meeting, and let them station themselves there, beside you.

[17]I will descend to communicate with you there. Then I will withdraw some of the spirit that rests upon you and confer it on them, so that they can share responsibility for all of the people with you, and you will not have to bear it alone.

[18]And to the people say: Make yourselves ritually fit for tomorrow, when you will eat meat. For you have been complaining within earshot of YHWH, saying, "Who will feed us meat? It was better for us in Egypt!" Indeed, YHWH will give you meat and you shall eat.

[19]You shall eat it not for one or two days, or for five or ten days, or even for twenty days;

[20]rather, up to a whole month of days, until it comes out of your nostrils and is loathsome to you. For you have rejected YHWH who is present in your midst, and have complained to him, saying, "Why, indeed, did we leave Egypt?"

[21]But Moses spoke up: "The people in whose midst I find myself include six hundred thousand foot soldiers, and yet you say, 'I will give them enough meat to eat for a whole month of days!'

[22]"Could flocks and herds be slaughtered for them in quantities sufficient for them? Were all the fish of the sea to be caught for them, would that meet their needs?"

[23]YHWH replied to Moses: Is anything beyond the reach of YHWH's arm? You will presently observe whether what I have spoken will happen to you.

[24]Moses came out of the Tent of Meeting and conveyed YHWH's message to the people. He then assembled seventy men from among the elders of the people and stationed them around the Tent.

[25]YHWH descended in the cloud and spoke to him. He withdrew some of the spirit that had rested on him, and bestowed it on the seventy elders. As the spirit settled on them, they began to prophesy ecstatically, but did not persist.

[26]Now, two men had remained in the encampment; one was named Eldad and the other was named Medad. The spirit had come to rest on them, for they were among those registered [as elders]. They had not gone out to the Tent, and [now] they continued to prophesy ecstatically inside the encampment.

[27]A youth ran over to Moses and reported to him as follows: "Eldad and Medad are prophesying inside the encampment."

[28]Joshua son of Nun, Moses' attendant since his youth, spoke up and said, "My lord, Moses, restrain them!"

[29]Moses replied to him, "Are you being zealous on my account? Would that the entire people of YHWH were prophets, if only YHWH would bestow his spirit on them."

[30]Moses reentered the encampment in the company of the elders of Israel.

[31]A wind gusted from YHWH, and swept up quail from the sea, dropping them over the encampment about the extent of one day's march in either direction around the encampment, and about two cubits over the surface of the ground.

[32]The people set about that entire day, the entire night and the entire day following to gather the quail—the one with the least gathered ten homers—and they spread them all around the encampment.

[33]While the meat was still between their teeth, even before it had been eaten, YHWH's wrath flared at the people. YHWH struck down the people in great numbers.

[34]That site was named Qibhroth Ha-Taavah, for those who had insatiable appetites were buried there.

[35]From Qibhroth Ha-Taavah, the people marched to Hazeroth, and they remained in Hazeroth.

12 [1]Miriam and Aaron spoke against Moses on the matter of the Cushite woman whom he had married: "He has taken a Cushite wife!"

[2]They went on to say, "Has YHWH spoken to Moses alone? Has he not also spoken to us?" YHWH took note of this.

[3]As for Moses, the man, he was exceedingly unassuming, more so than any person on the face of the earth.

[4]Suddenly, YHWH addressed Moses, Aaron, and Miriam: Go out all three of you to the Tent of Meeting! The three of them departed.

[5]Then YHWH descended in a pillar of cloud and stood at the entrance of the Tent. He called out: Aaron and Miriam! The two of them emerged.

[6]He said: Take heed of my words!
If there should be a prophet of yours,
[who is] of YHWH,
In a vision would I make myself known to him;
In a dream would I speak to him.
[7]Not so my servant, Moses!
Of all my household
He is most trusted.
[8]Mouth to mouth I speak to him;
In clear view, not in riddles.
He looks upon the likeness of YHWH.

How is it then, that you were not afraid to speak against my servant, against Moses?

[9]YHWH's wrath flared at them. Then he departed.

[10]The cloud moved away from the Tent, and Aaron turned to Miriam, and behold—she was covered with scales, as white as snow.

[11]Aaron besought Moses: "By my life, master! Pray do not impose on us punishment for the sin we have so foolishly committed.

[12]"May she not remain as a stillbirth, who issues from his mother's womb with half of his body eaten away!"

[13]Moses petitioned YHWH with these words: "*No more*, I beseech you! Heal her, I beseech you!"

[14]Then YHWH said to Moses: Suppose her father had spat directly in her face, would she not remain in disgrace for seven days? Let her be confined for seven days outside the encampment and only afterward be readmitted.

[15]So Miriam was confined outside the encampment for seven days. The people delayed their march until Miriam had been readmitted.

[16]Only thereafter did the people set out from Hazeroth, and they encamped in the Wilderness of Paran.

13 [1]The Lord spoke to Moses as follows:

[2]Dispatch important personages to scout the land of Canaan, which I am granting to the Israelite people. Send one such person to represent each of their patrilineal tribes, every one of them a chieftain.

[3]Moses dispatched them from the Wilderness of Paran, in accordance with
YHWH's command. All of them were important personages; they were the
heads of the Israelite people.
[4]Their names were as follows:
Representing the tribe of Reuben—Shammua son of Zaccur.
[5]Representing the tribe of Simeon—Shaphat son of Hori.
[6]Representing the tribe of Judah—Caleb son of Jephunneh.
[7]Representing the tribe of Issachar—Igal son of Joseph.
[8]Representing the tribe of Ehpraim—Hosea son of Nun.
[9]Representing the tribe of Benjamin—Palti son of Raphu.
[10]Representing the tribe of Zebulun—Gaddiel son of Sodi.
[11]Representing the tribe of Joseph, that is, the tribe of Manasseh—Gaddi
son of Susi.
[12]Representing the tribe of Dan—Ammiel son of Gemalli.
[13]Representing the tribe of Asher—Sethur son of Michael.
[14]Representing the tribe of Naphtali—Nahbi son of Vupsi.
[15]Representing the tribe of Gad—Geuel son of Machi.
[16]These are the names of the personages whom Moses dispatched to scout
the land. (Moses called Hosea son of Nun by the name of "Joshua.")
[17]Moses dispatched them to scout the land of Canaan. He charged them,
"Proceed northward through the Negeb, and make your ascent into the
mountains.
[18]"Observe the land: what is its condition? And the people inhabiting it: are
they strong or feeble, few or numerous?
[19]"And what of the land they inhabit: is it bountiful or lacking? And what
of the towns where they dwell: are they built as unwalled settlements or as
fortified towns?
[20]"And how is the land: is it rich in produce or lean? Is it wooded or not?
Make an effort to bring back some of the fruit of the land." (This was at the
season of first ripe grapes.)
[21]They proceeded northward, scouting the land all the way from the Wilderness of Zin to Rehob, at Lebo of Hamath.
[22]They proceeded northward through the Negeb, arriving at Hebron.
Ahiman, Sheshai, and Talmai, born of the Anakites, were there. (Hebron had
been built seven years before Tanis, in Egypt.)
[23]Arriving at Wadi Eshcol, they cut off a branch with a cluster of grapes,
which they carried on a pole, [borne] by two [men], along with some pomegranates and figs.
[24]That place was named Wadi Eshcol in token of the *cluster* that the Israelites had cut off while there.
[25]They returned from scouting the land forty days later,
[26]and went straight to Moses and the entire Israelite community, in the

Wilderness of Paran, at Kadesh. They brought to them and to the entire community a report, and showed them the fruit of the land.

27They reported to him as follows: "We entered the land to which you dispatched us. It is truly flowing with milk and sap, and here is a sample of its fruit.

28"In contrast, the people inhabiting the land are fierce and the cities are fortified and very large. We also noticed men born of the Anakites there.

29"Amalekites inhabit the Negeb region, with Hittites, Jebusites, and Amorites occupying the mountains; while Canaanites are settled near the sea and along the Jordan."

30Caleb silenced the people near Moses, exclaiming, "We should, by all means, invade and take possession of [the land], for we can certainly prevail over it."

31But the men who had accompanied him said, "We dare not mount an attack against that people, for it is more powerful than we are!"

32They presented the Israelite people with a discrediting report of the land they had scouted, as follows: "The land we traversed for the purpose of scouting it is a land that devours its inhabitants, and all of the people whom we observed in it are of enormous proportions.

33"There we saw Nephilim (Anakites are descended from Nephilim), and we felt like grasshoppers; and so we must have seemed to them!"

14 1The entire community raised [its voice] and gave forth with weeping on that night.

2All of the Israelite people protested to Moses and Aaron. The entire community said to them, "If only we had died in Egypt, or in this wilderness if only we had died!

3"Why is YHWH leading us to this land, only to fall by the sword, with our wives and small children taken as spoils? It would be preferable to return to Egypt!"

4They said to one another, "Let us head back and return to Egypt!"

5Moses and Aaron fell prostrate before the entire assembled Israelite community.

6Joshua son of Nun and Caleb son of Jephunneh, from among those who had scouted the land, tore their garments.

7They addressed the entire Israelite community as follows: "The land we traversed for the purpose of scouting it—that land is exceedingly bountiful!

8"Surely YHWH is well disposed toward us; he will enable us to enter this land, and will grant it to us—a land flowing with milk and sap.

9"As for you—do not rebel against YHWH! You must have no fear of the people of the land, for they are prey for us! Their Protector has abandoned them, and YHWH is on *our* side. Have no fear of them!"

10 The entire community was threatening to stone them, when the glorious presence of YHWH appeared at the Tent of Meeting, before the entire Israelite people.

11 YHWH said to Moses: How long will this people continue to reject me? How long will they refuse to place their trust in me, in all of the signs I have performed in their midst?

12 I will afflict them with pestilence, and dispossess them, and then make you into a nation greater and more numerous than they.

13 But Moses replied to YHWH, "The Egyptians will learn of this, for you brought this people out of their midst by your power.

14 "Now, they will learn of this, and relate it to the inhabitants of this land. They, in turn, have heard how you, O YHWH, appear to them in plain view, while your cloud remains above them; how you march in advance of them, within a pillar of cloud by day, and within a pillar of fire by night.

15 "If you should put this people to death, to the last person, the nations who have heard of your renown would then say,

16 " 'It was because YHWH lacked the capacity to bring this people to the land he had promised them that he slaughtered them in the wilderness!'

17 "Now, then, let my LORD's forbearance be great, as you, yourself, have declared, in the following words:

18 " 'YHWH is long-tempered, and shows great kindness. He forgives iniquity and disloyalty, but will not grant full exoneration. Rather, he reserves the punishment due the fathers for their children; for the third and for the fourth generations!'

19 "Pardon, I beseech you, the iniquity of this people, commensurate with your great kindness; just as you have pardoned this people from Egypt until now."

20 YHWH responded: I grant forgiveness, in accordance with your word.

21 But, as I live, and just as my glorious presence expands to fill the entire earth—

22 just so, none of these men who now see my glorious presence, and [who saw] my wondrous signs that I performed in Egypt and in the wilderness, and yet challenged me [at least] ten times, refusing to heed me,

23 will ever see the land I promised to their ancestors. All who would reject me shall never see it!

24 Except for my servant, Caleb, because he was possessed of a different spirit and remained committed to me. Him will I bring to the land he has already entered, and his descendants will conquer it.

25 Now, as the Amalekites and Canaanites inhabit the valley, redirect your march into the wilderness tomorrow, on the way to the Sea of Reeds.

26 YHWH spoke to Moses and Aaron as follows:

27 How long will this evil community persist in their agitation against me?

The protests of the Israelite people, which they continually inveigh against
me, I have heard.
28 Say to them: As I live, says YHWH, precisely what I have heard you wish
for, I will grant you!
29 Your corpses shall fall in this very wilderness, all of your numbered divisions, twenty years of age and above, who have agitated against me.
30 You will never enter the land where I swore I would settle you, except for
Caleb son of Jephunneh, and Joshua son of Nun.
31 But as for your small children, who, you predicted, would be taken as
spoils, these will I, indeed, allow to enter, and they will experience the land
that you have disparaged.
32 But your own corpses will fall in this wilderness!
33 And your [grown] children will roam about in this wilderness for forty
years, bearing the punishment for your faithlessness, until your own corpses
decompose in the wilderness.
34 In proportion to the number of days you scouted the land, for each day a
year, you shall bear the punishment for your iniquities; for forty years, so that
you may know what the denial of me entails!
35 I, YHWH, have spoken, and this I shall surely do to this evil community
who conspire against me. In this very wilderness they shall meet their end,
and here they shall die!
36 (And the men whom Moses had dispatched to scout the land, and who
returned to incite the entire community against him, presenting a discrediting
report of the land—
37 these men who presented a discrediting report of the land actually died in
a plague, in the presence of YHWH.
38 Only Joshua son of Nun and Caleb son of Jephunneh survived, of those
men who went to scout the land.)
39 When Moses communicated these words to the entire Israelite people,
the people mourned deeply.
40 They arose early on the morrow and climbed toward the summit of the
mountain range, proclaiming, "We are ready to invade the place designated
by YHWH. We have been remiss!"
41 But Moses warned, "Why are you countermanding YHWH's directive?
Such a course will not succeed!
42 "Do not invade, because YHWH is not present in your midst. Or else you
will be repulsed by your enemies!
43 "For the Amalekites will confront you there, and you will fall by the
sword! Because you have deserted YHWH, he will no longer be at your side."
44 Nevertheless, they surged ahead, attempting to climb to the summit of
the mountain range; but neither the Ark of YHWH's Covenant, nor Moses
himself, budged from within the encampment.

[45]The Amalekites and the Canaanites, who inhabited the mountains, swept down and pounded them to pieces all the way to Hormah.

15 [1]The LORD spoke to Moses as follows:

[2]Speak to the Israelite people, and say to them: When you arrive at the land of your settlement, which I am granting to you,

[3]and perform a sacrifice by fire to YHWH, consisting of a burnt offering or a sacred feast, for the purpose of setting aside a votive, or as a voluntary offering, or on the occasion of your festivals—producing a pleasing aroma for YHWH, from the herd or from the flocks—

[4]the one making his offering to YHWH shall present a grain offering consisting of a one-tenth measure of semolina flour, mixed with one-fourth of a *hin* of oil;

[5]also wine for the libation, in the amount of one-fourth of a *hin.* [These] you shall perform in addition to the burnt offering, or for the sacred feast, for each head of sheep.

[6]Or in the case of a ram, you shall perform a grain offering consisting of two one-tenth measures of semolina flour, mixed with one-third of a *hin* of oil;

[7]also wine for the libation in the amount of one-third of a *hin.* These you shall present, [producing] a pleasing aroma for YHWH.

[8]In the event you perform a burnt offering or a sacred feast, consisting of a head of large cattle, for the purpose of setting aside a votive, or as a sacred gift of greeting to YHWH,

[9]you must present, together with the head of large cattle, a grain offering, consisting of three one-tenth measures of semolina flour, mixed with one-half of a *hin* of oil;

[10]also wine for the libation, in the amount of one-half of a *hin,* to produce a pleasing aroma for YHWH.

[11]The same shall be performed for each ox and for each ram, or other head of small cattle, sheep, or goats.

[12]For as many as you perform, so shall you do for each one, corresponding to their number.

[13]Every native-born citizen of the land shall perform these [rites] in this way, when presenting an offering by fire, to produce a pleasant aroma for YHWH.

[14]When an alien who resides among you, or anyone else who may be among you at any time in the future, wishes to perform a sacrifice by fire, producing a pleasing aroma for YHWH, he shall perform [it] just as you perform [it].

[15]For the congregation [as a whole] there is only one statute, for you as well as for the resident alien; an everlasting statute throughout your generations. It shall [always] be the same for the alien as it is for you, in the presence of YHWH.

16There shall be only one prescription and rule applying both to you and to the alien who lives among you.

17YHWH spoke to Moses as follows:

18Speak to the Israelite people, and say to them: When you enter the land to which I am bringing you,

19and partake of the food of the land, you shall collect a donation for YHWH.

20The first product of your bread-baking utensils you shall collect as a donation, collecting it just as you do the donation from the threshing floor.

21You must prepare a donation to YHWH from the first product of your baking utensils, throughout your generations.

22In the event you inadvertently fail to perform all of these commandments, which YHWH communicated to Moses,

23including all that YHWH commanded you through Moses from the day that YHWH first issued commandments, and forward, throughout your generations:

24If an offense was inadvertently committed without the awareness of the community, the entire community must offer the sacrifice of one bull from the herd as a burnt offering, producing a pleasing aroma for YHWH, with its accompanying grain offering and libation, according to the rule; also one he-goat as a sin offering.

25The priest shall perform rites of expiation for the entire Israelite community, and they shall be pardoned. For it was, after all, an inadvertent offense, and they have duly presented their offering, a sacrifice by fire to YHWH, as well as their sin offering to YHWH consequent to their inadvertent offense.

26Pardon shall therefore be granted to the entire community of the Israelite people, as well as the alien residing among them, for the offense was committed by the entire people inadvertently.

27If an individual commits an offense inadvertently, that person must offer a yearling she-goat as a sin offering.

28The priest shall perform rites of expiation for that person who commits an inadvertent offense (because that person offended only inadvertently), in the presence of YHWH, securing expiation for him so that he may be pardoned.

29As regards both the permanent resident of the land from among the Israelites and the alien residing among them, there shall be one prescription for all of you, for one who acts inadvertently.

30But the person who acts defiantly, either permanent resident of the land or alien, is maligning YHWH. That person must be cut off from among his people.

31For he has shown disrespect for the word of YHWH and has transgressed his commandment. That person must surely be cut off and bear the punishment for his iniquity.

32While the Israelites were in the wilderness, they found a man gathering wood on the Sabbath.

33Those who discovered him gathering wood brought him before Moses and Aaron, and before the entire community.

34They placed him under guard, for it had not yet been specified what was to be done with him.

35YHWH said to Moses: That man must be put to death! The entire community must stone him to death outside the encampment.

36So the entire community took him outside the encampment and stoned him to death, just as YHWH had commanded Moses.

37YHWH addressed Moses as follows:

38Speak to the Israelite people and say to them that when they fashion fringes for themselves on the corners of their garments throughout their generations, they must join a cord of blue cloth to the fringe, at each corner.

39It (= the cord) shall serve you as a fringe, and when you see it, you will be reminded of all of YHWH's commandments and perform them. Then you will not be drawn after your heart and your eyes, which you follow so faithlessly!

40You must remember to perform all of my commandments and thereby be consecrated to your God.

41I am YHWH, your God, who brought you out of the land of Egypt, thereby becoming your God. I am YHWH, your God.

16 1Korah son of Izhar, son of Kohath, son of Levi, took counsel, along with Dathan and Abiram, and On son of Peleth, all Reubenites.

2They confronted Moses, accompanied by 250 personages from among the Israelites; chieftains of the community, those called in the assembly, men of renown.

3They rallied en masse against Moses and Aaron, and charged them, "You seek too much! The community in its entirety is sanctified, for YHWH is present in their midst. Why, then, do you exalt yourselves over YHWH's congregation?"

4When Moses heard this, he fell prostrate.

5He addressed Korah and his entire faction as follows: "In the morning YHWH will make known who is consecrated to him, and will declare [him] his intimate. He will declare as his intimate the one whom he chooses.

6"Do the following: Provide yourselves with firepans, Korah and his entire faction.

7"Place hot coals in them, and put incense over them when you stand in the presence of YHWH tomorrow. The person whom YHWH chooses—he is the sacred one! It is you who seek too much, you Levites!"

8Then Moses said to Korah, "Pay attention, you Levites!

9“Is it of so little importance to you that the God of Israel has distinguished you from the community of Israel by declaring you his intimates? He has assigned you to the maintenance of the Tabernacle of YHWH, to stand in attendance before the community to serve them.

10“He has declared you and all your Levite kinsmen his intimates. Do you seek priestly status as well?

11“In truth, it is against YHWH that you and your entire faction are conspiring! As for Aaron—what has *he* done that you incite grievances against him?”

12Moses sent word to summon Dathan and Abiram, sons of Eliab, but they replied, “We refuse to appear!

13“Haven't you done enough harm by leading us out of a land flowing with milk and sap, only to bring about our death in the wilderness, that you also persist in lording over us?

14“You have not even brought us to a land flowing with milk and sap, or granted us fields and vineyards as our estate. Do you intend to gouge out the eyes of those men? We refuse to appear!”

15Moses became exceedingly angered and addressed YHWH: “Do not accept their offering! I have never misappropriated the mule of a single one of them, nor have I ever harmed one of them!”

16Then Moses said to Korah, “You and your entire faction be present before YHWH; you and they, along with Aaron, tomorrow!

17“Let each person bring along his firepan and place incense over [the coals] and offer it in the presence of YHWH; each person with his own firepan, 250 firepans, in addition to you and Aaron, each with his firepan.”

18So each person took his firepan, they put coals in them, and they placed incense over them, and stood at the entrance to the Tent of Meeting, alongside Moses and Aaron.

19Korah then rallied his entire faction against them, at the entrance to the Tent of Meeting. The presence of YHWH appeared in view of the entire community.

20YHWH spoke to Moses as follows:

21Break away from this evil faction that I may annihilate them instantly!

22They fell prostrate, exclaiming, “Lord, God of the spirits of all flesh! When only one person has offended, will you become enraged at the entire community?”

23YHWH addressed Moses, saying:

24Speak to the community as follows: “Withdraw from the area around the residence of Korah, Dathan, and Abiram!”

25Moses then went over to Dathan and Abiram, and the elders of Israel followed him.

26He addressed the assemblage as follows:

"Move away from the tents of these wicked men and have no contact with anyone aligned with them, lest you, too, be terminated because of all their offenses!"

27 So they withdrew from the area around the residence of Korah, Dathan, and Abiram, as Dathan and Abiram were standing outside the entrances of their tents, along with their wives, their grown children, and their infants.

28 Then Moses spoke: "By this shall you know that it is YHWH who has sent me to carry out these actions; that they are not of my own devising.

29 "If these persons die in the manner usual for all human beings, if the fate of all mankind befalls them, then it is not YHWH who has sent me.

30 "But if YHWH creates a [special] creation and the earth opens its mouth and swallows them up, as well as all aligned with them; so that they descend live into Sheol—then you must acknowledge that these persons have rejected YHWH."

31 Just as he finished speaking these words, the earth beneath them split open.

32 The earth opened its mouth and swallowed them up, and their families, and all personnel who belonged to Korah, and their possessions.

33 They, and all associated with them, descended live into Sheol. The earth closed over them, so that they vanished from the midst of the congregation.

34 All Israelites who were in their proximity fled at the sound of their [cries], for they said, "The earth may swallow us, too!"

35 A fire issued forth from YHWH and consumed the 250 men, the offerers of the incense.

17 1 YHWH spoke to Moses as follows:

2 Order Eleazar son of Aaron the priest to remove the firepans from the remains of the fire and to scatter the incense away, for they have [both] become holy—

3 the firepans of those persons whose sinfulness cost them their lives. Let them be hammered into sheets as plating for the altar. Once having been offered in the presence of YHWH they had become holy. Let them serve as a sign to the Israelite people.

4 So Eleazar the priest took the copper firepans offered by those who perished in flame, and they were hammered into plating for the altar;

5 < as YHWH had commanded him through Moses. > This was a reminder to the Israelite people to ensure that no outsider, one not of the seed of Aaron, would ever approach, bearing incense, into the presence of YHWH, or behave in the manner of Korah and his faction.

6 On the morrow, the entire community of Israelites protested to Moses and Aaron, saying, "You have brought death upon the people of YHWH!"

7 As the community rallied en masse against Moses and Aaron, they turned

toward the Tent of Meeting, and behold! The cloud had enveloped it! The glorious presence of YHWH had appeared.

8 Then Moses approached the Tent of Meeting.

9 YHWH spoke to Moses as follows:

10 Withdraw from the midst of the community and I will annihilate them instantly! They fell prostrate.

11 Thereupon Moses instructed Aaron, "Take one firepan and put hot coals from the altar in it, and add incense. Quickly carry it over to the community and perform a rite of expiation over them. For the fuming rage has issued from the presence of YHWH; the plague has begun!"

12 Aaron took what Moses had instructed. He ran into the midst of the congregation, and behold! The plague had begun among the people. He prepared the incense and performed a rite of expiation over the people.

13 He stood between the dead and the living, and the plague was contained.

14 The number of those who died in the plague was 14,700, not counting those who perished in the Korah incident.

15 Aaron returned to Moses at the entrance of the Tent of Meeting. The plague had been contained.

16 YHWH spoke to Moses as follows:

17 Speak to the Israelite people. Collect from them one rod apiece from each patriarchal house, from all of the chieftains, for their patriarchal houses; twelve staffs. Write the name of each person on his rod.

18 And the name of Aaron you shall write on the rod of Levi, for there is also to be one rod for the head of their patriarchal house.

19 Place them inside the Tent of Meeting, in front of the Ark of the Covenant, where I customarily meet with you.

20 The man whom I select—his rod shall sprout, and I will then be relieved of the grievances of the Israelites that they incite against you!

21 Moses spoke to the Israelite people, and all of their chieftains delivered to him one rod for each chieftain, for their patriarchal houses, twelve rods. The rod of Aaron is [to be placed] among their rods.

22 Moses placed the rods in the presence of YHWH, inside the Tent of the Covenant.

23 It happened on the morrow that when Moses arrived at the Tent of the Covenant—lo and behold! The rod of Aaron, of the house of Levi, had sprouted. It gave forth sprouts, produced blossoms, and bore almonds.

24 Moses brought out all of the rods from the presence of YHWH before the entire Israelite people. Each person identified and retrieved his own rod.

25 YHWH then spoke to Moses: Replace Aaron's rod in front of the Ark of the Covenant for safe keeping, as a [warning] sign to rebellious persons; so that their protestations against me may cease, and they will not die.

26 Moses did as YHWH commanded him; so he did.

27 The Israelite people then addressed themselves to Moses as follows: "We are about to perish; we are all lost; we are all lost!

28 "Every person who ever approaches the Tabernacle of YHWH will die! Will we ever cease perishing?"

18 1 YHWH said to Aaron: You, your sons and your patriarchal house with you shall incur [punishment] for defilement of the Sanctuary, just as you and your sons with you shall incur [punishment] for the defilement of your [own] priestly group.

2 Dedicate as well your kinsmen with you, the tribe of Levi, your paternal tribe, that they may be associated with you and assist you and your sons with you in front of the Tent of the Covenant.

3 They shall be charged with caring for you, and with maintaining the overall Tent structure, but they may not have access to the vessels of the Shrine, or to the altar, lest both they and you meet with death!

4 They shall be associated with you in maintaining the Tent of Meeting, in all tasks pertaining to the Tent structure. No alien shall encroach upon you,

5 but you, yourselves, must undertake the maintenance of the Shrine and the altar, so that wrath may never again assail the Israelite people.

6 I hereby select your kinsmen, the Levites, from among the Israelite people to be given in service to you. [They are] dedicated to YHWH, to perform the tasks that pertain to the Tent of Meeting.

7 But you, and your sons with you, shall carefully fulfill the charge of your priesthood in all that pertains to the altar, and to what is located inside the *pārôket* screen. I will make of your priesthood a service of dedication, and any alien who intrudes shall be put to death.

8 YHWH spoke to Aaron: I hereby grant to you control over my levied donations, including all of the sacred offerings of the Israelite people. To you and to your sons I grant them as a share, as a permanent entitlement.

9 This is what you are to receive from the most sacred offerings, from the offerings by fire: all of their offerings, including all of their grain offerings and sin offerings, and guilt offerings that they must deliver to me as most sacred offerings—all this shall belong to you and your sons.

10 You must eat this in the most sacred precincts. Every male shall partake of it; it shall be consecrated as yours.

11 This, too, shall be yours: the levied donations that comprise their gifts, as well as all of the presentation offerings of the Israelite people, to you have I granted them and to your sons and your daughters with you, as a permanent statutory allocation. Every pure person in your household may partake of it.

12 All of the richest, new oil and all of the richest contents of wine and grain, their prime yield, which they [regularly] devote to YHWH—to you have I granted them.

13 The first yield of all that grows in their land, which they [regularly] convey

to YHWH, shall belong to you. Every pure person in your household may partake of it.

14Whatever has been proscribed on the part of Israelites shall be yours.

15The first issue of the womb of every living creature, which they [regularly] dedicate to YHWH, of human and beast, shall be yours. But you must provide for the redemption of the first issue of humans, and redeem as well the firstlings of impure animals.

16You shall collect their redemption payments, on behalf of all over one month of age, in the equivalent of five shekels of silver, according to the shekel of the Sanctuary, which contains twenty grains.

17You may not, however, permit the redemption of the firstlings of oxen, or the firstlings of lambs, or the firstlings of goats. These are preconsecrated; their blood you must dash on the altar, and their fatty portions you must burn as an offering by fire, producing a pleasant aroma for YHWH.

18Their flesh shall be yours, like the breast of the presentation offering; like the right thigh—they shall belong to you.

19All of the sacred levied donations that the Israelite people raise for YHWH have I granted to you and to your sons and your daughters with you, as a permanent statutory allocation. It is like the permanent rule [requiring use] of salt in the presence of YHWH, for you and your descendants with you.

20YHWH said to Aaron: You will not be granted an estate in their land, nor any territory among them. I represent your territory and the estate you are granted among the Israelite people.

21To the Levites I have awarded every tithe in Israel, in lieu of a land grant; as exchange for the tasks they will be performing by attending to the Tent of Meeting.

22This is so that Israelite persons will no longer encroach upon the Tent of Meeting, thereby incurring the penalty of dying.

23It is the Levites who shall perform the tasks pertaining to the Tent of Meeting, and they shall bear any punishment for their neglect. It (= the tithe) is a permanent statutory allocation throughout your generations. But they (= the Levites) will not receive a land grant among the Israelite people.

24For I have given to the Levites, in lieu of a granted estate, the tithes of the Israelite people, which they collect for YHWH as levied donations. Consequently, I have informed them that they will not receive a land grant among the Israelite people.

25YHWH spoke to Moses as follows:

26You shall address the Levites and say to them, "When you collect from the Israelite people the tithe that I have given to you in lieu of your land grant, you shall withhold from it as the levied donation for YHWH a tenth of the tithe.

27"Your levied donation will count for you the same as grain from the threshing floor and ripe fruit from the vat.

[28]“In this way you shall withhold the levied donations for YHWH from all of your tithes, which you collect from the Israelite people. Out of that you shall remit the levied donation for YHWH to Aaron, the priest.

[29]“From all gifts conveyed to you, you shall withhold the entire levied donation for YHWH; from all of its richest contents—the consecrated portion of it.”

[30]You shall say to them, “When you have withheld [an amount] from its richest contents, it shall count for the Levites the same as the yield from the threshing floor and the yield from the vat.

[31]“You may then partake of it (= the tithe) anywhere, you and your household. For it is compensation to you, in exchange for performance of your tasks relevant to the Tent of Meeting.

[32]“By withholding its richest contents from it, you will avoid bearing punishment over it, and will not cause the defilement of the sacred offerings of the Israelite people and thereby meet with death.”

19 [1]YHWH addressed Moses and Aaron as follows:

[2]This is the statute of the prescribed instruction that YHWH has ordained, as follows: Order the Israelite people to provide to you a red cow, physically perfect and without blemish, one that has never borne a yoke.

[3]Deliver it to Eleazar, the priest, and let it be taken outside the encampment and slaughtered in his presence.

[4]Eleazar, the priest, shall take some of its blood on his finger and sprinkle [it] seven times in the direction of the Tent of Meeting.

[5]The cow shall then be burned in his presence; its hide, meat, and blood shall be burned, together with its dung.

[6]The priest shall take cedar wood, hyssop, and crimson cloth, and cast them into the fire where the cow is being burned.

[7]The priest must then launder his clothing and bathe his body in water, after which he may reenter the encampment. He remains impure until evening.

[8]The person who burned [the cow] must likewise launder his clothing in water, and bathe his body in water. He remains impure until evening.

[9]A pure person shall gather up the ashes of the cow and deposit them in a pure place. This shall be conserved by the community of the Israelite people as water of lustration; it is a sin-offering.

[10]The person who gathers up the ashes of the cow shall launder his clothing. He remains impure until evening. This shall be a permanent statute for the Israelite people, as well as for the alien who resides among them.

[11]Whoever had contact with the corpse of any human being shall be deemed impure for seven days.

[12]He must purify himself with [the ashes] on the third day and on the

seventh day, and then shall become pure. Should he fail to purify himself on the third day and on the seventh day, he shall not be deemed pure.

[13]One who had contact with a corpse belonging to any human being who had died, but failed to purify himself, has defiled the Tabernacle of YHWH. That person shall be cut off from Israel, because water of lustration was not dashed on him. He remains impure; his impurity endures within him.

[14]This is the prescribed instruction: in the event that a person dies inside a tent, everyone who enters that tent and everyone found inside that tent becomes impure for seven days.

[15]Every open vessel that does not have a lid fastened around it becomes impure.

[16]Anyone having contact, in the open field, with a slain human body, or a corpse, or a human bone, or a grave, becomes impure for seven days.

[17]Some of the "dust" of the burned sin-offering shall be used for the impure person, and living water shall be poured over it, into a vessel.

[18]A pure person shall then take hyssop and dip it into the water, and sprinkle it on the tent, and on the persons who were there, and on the one who had contact with the bone, or the slain body, or the corpse, or the grave.

[19]The pure person shall perform the sprinkling over the impure person on the third day, and on the seventh day, finally removing the impurity on the seventh day. He must then launder his clothing and bathe in water, and at eventide he is restored to purity.

[20]But any person who becomes impure, but fails to purify himself—that person shall be cut off from the midst of the congregation, for it is the Sanctuary of YHWH that he has defiled. Water of lustration was not dashed on him: he remains impure.

[21]This shall be a permanent statute for you. The person who sprinkled the lustration water must launder his clothing: and anyone who had contact with the water of lustration remains impure until evening.

[22]Anything that the impure person touches is rendered impure, and a person who [in turn] touches [such objects] remains impure until evening.

20 [1]The Israelite people, the entire community, arrived at the Wilderness of Zin in the first month, and the people were residing at Kadesh. Miriam died there, and was buried there.

[2]There was no water for the community, and they assembled en masse against Moses and against Aaron.

[3]The people quarreled with Moses, expressing themselves as follows: "Had we only expired when our kinsmen expired in the presence of YHWH!

[4]"Why did you bring the congregation of YHWH to this wilderness to die here, we and our livestock?

[5]"And why did you take us up from Egypt to bring us to this awful place;

not a place of seed, or fig trees, or vines, or pomegranates, and with no water to drink?"

6 Moses and Aaron withdrew from the advance of the congregation to the entrance of the Tent of Meeting, and they fell on their faces. The glorious presence of YHWH appeared to them.

7 YHWH addressed Moses as follows:

8 Take the staff and assemble the community, you and Aaron, your brother. Both of you speak to the rock in sight of them, and it will produce its water. You shall extract water for them from the rock, and provide water for the community and their livestock.

9 Moses took the staff from the presence of YHWH as he had commanded him.

10 Moses and Aaron assembled the congregation in front of the rock. He said to them: "Take heed, then, O rebellious ones! Shall we from this rock actually extract water for you?"

11 Thereupon Moses raised his arm and hit the rock with his staff twice. Abundant water gushed forth, and the community and its livestock drank.

12 But YHWH said to Moses and to Aaron: Because you did not place your trust in me, which would have affirmed my sanctity in the sight of the Israelite people—for that reason you shall not bring this congregation to the land that I have granted to them.

13 Those are the Waters of Meribah, where the Israelite people quarreled with YHWH, and through which his sanctity was affirmed.

14 Moses dispatched messengers from Kadesh to the king of Edom. Thus says your brother, Israel: "You are surely aware of all of the distress that has overtaken us.

15 "Our ancestors descended to Egypt, and we resided in Egypt for many years, but the Egyptians dealt harshly with us and with our ancestors.

16 "We cried out to YHWH, who heard our voice. He sent an angel who brought us out of Egypt, and now we are in Kadesh, a town bordering on your territory.

17 "May we traverse your land? We will not pass through fields or vineyards, nor will we drink well water. We will travel on the King's Highway, without turning to the right or to the left, until we have traversed your territory."

18 But Edom said to him, "You shall not pass through me, lest I come out to meet you with the sword!"

19 The Israelite people said to him, "We will make our way up the highway, and should we drink of your waters, I or my livestock, I will remit their cost. Only make no issue of it; let me traverse on foot."

20 But he said, "You shall not pass through!" Then Edom came out to confront him with a large fighting force and with a powerful arm.

21 Edom refused to allow the Israelites to pass through his territory, and Israel turned away from him.

22They marched from Kadesh, and the Israelite people, the entire community, arrived at Hor Hahar.

23YHWH said to Moses and to Aaron at Hor Hahar, on the Edomite border, as follows:

24Let Aaron be taken away to his kin, for he shall not enter the land that I have granted to the Israelite people, because [the two of] you disobeyed my command at the Waters of Meribah.

25Take Aaron and Eleazar, his son, and bring them up to Hor Hahar.

26Divest Aaron of his garments, and clothe Eleazar, his son, with them, and let Aaron be taken away, and let him die there.

27Moses did as YHWH had commanded him. They ascended Hor Hahar in sight of the entire community.

28Moses divested Aaron of his garments and clothed his son, Eleazar, with them. Then Aaron died there, atop Hor Hahar. Moses and Eleazar came down from the mountain.

29The entire community saw that Aaron had expired, and they mourned Aaron for thirty days, the entire household of Israel.

Introduction to the Book of Numbers

♦

A. The Casting of the Wilderness Period

Go, proclaim to Jerusalem: YHWH has spoken as follows:
I account to your favor
The devotion of your youth,
Your love as a bride;
That you followed me through the wilderness,
Through a land unsown. (Jer 2:2)

YHWH has spoken as follows:
He found favor in the wilderness,
A people who escaped the sword;
Israel, en route to his secure place.
YHWH appeared to me from afar:
"I love you with an eternal love;
Therefore, I show you continuous devotion." (Jer 31:2–3)

The prophet Jeremiah, ever a fiery castigator of Israel's past sins, could nevertheless find an occasional good word for his flock. He reasoned that Israel must have been devoted to God at some time in the past so as to have been the recipient of his *ḥesed*. Before the conquest and settlement of Canaan Israel had, indeed, acted toward God with *ḥesed*, and God would reward Israel's devotion in kind, and in due time restore the exiles from Babylonia and from other lands.

Such positive resonances of Israel's wilderness experience contrast not only with Jeremiah's normally critical posture, but with a great part of biblical tradition. More often than not, Israel's conduct during its formative period as a nation served as a paradigm of religious infidelity, callous ingratitude, and blindness to the dramatic demonstrations of God's providence. In fact, the Exodus generation is held up as a *māšāl,* an object lesson to future Israelites:

Give ear, my people, to my teachings,
Bend your ear to my utterances.
I will expound a theme,
Hold forth on the lessons of the past;
Things we have heard and known,
That our fathers have told us.
We will not withhold them from our children,
Telling the coming generation
The praises of YHWH and his might,
And the wonders he performed.

He established covenant law in Jacob,
Implanted teachings in Israel;
Charging our fathers
To make them known to their children.
That a future generation might know
—children yet to be born—
And in turn tell their children;
That they might put their confidence in God,
And not forget God's great deeds,
But observe his commandments.
May they not be like their fathers,
A wayward and defiant generation;
A generation whose heart was inconstant,
Whose spirit was not true to God. (Ps 78:1b–8)

In a significant way, the literary function of Numbers as part of Torah literature is to assure that future generations realize how certain habitual shortcomings have complicated Israel's relationship with God, ever since that relationship was initiated after the Exodus from Egypt. From the start, the Israelites exhibited a lack of confidence in God's power to accomplish what he had promised—to establish his people, Israel, in the land of Canaan. The inconstancy of the Israelites expressed itself in various ways: in nostalgia for the dependency of Egypt, in an unwillingness to endure current hardships in pursuit of future security, in chronic rebellions against the divinely designated leadership of Moses, in fear of the Canaanites, and in a seemingly irrepressible attraction to paganism.

After the Exodus, such behavior had evoked wrathful reactions from God, whose patience was sustained only through Moses' appeals to his good name, to his covenant promises, and to his attribute of compassion. For his part,

God ultimately kept his promise, delaying the conquest of Canaan but not voiding his covenant with Israel. God continued to feed his people in the wilderness and to provide for their life-sustaining needs, pinning his hopes on the next generation of Israelites to accomplish the conquest and settlement of Canaan. That second generation, though not immune to sinfulness, emerged as a formidable fighting force, a nation so powerful it had no need for allies. Israel was now blessed by YHWH and favored by him.

The modern critical commentator would do well to take his cue from biblical literature itself. The main objective of the commentator is to identify and clarify the several agenda that inform the text of Numbers. This objective demands careful analysis, the pursuit of several lines of inquiry, both textual and contextual. A commentator must on the one hand probe the formulation, composition, and structure of Numbers; and, on the other, attempt to discover what this book says about the wilderness period. The pursuit of these objectives requires source-critical study in historical perspective of the several documents that comprise the book of Numbers. Only in this way can one hope to identify the various ancient Israelites for whom this composite book of the Torah speaks.

1. The Names of Numbers

The talmudic name of Numbers is *ḥômeš happequddîm* 'the "fifth" of the census totals,' namely, that one of the five Torah books which records the census of Numbers 1–4, and the later census of Numbers 26 (see Mishna, *Yômāʾ* 7:1; *Menāḥôt* 4:3; and Babylonian Talmud, *Sôṭāh* 36b). As a characterization, the Hebrew name *ḥômeš happequddîm* correlates with the Greek name *Arithmoi* and with Latin *Numeri*, from which we get "Numbers."

The mnemonic method of referring to a biblical book by a significant word in its opening verse has yielded less-known *Wayyedabbēr* 'He spoke' (see Rashi to Exod 38:26 and to Mishna, *Yômāʾ* 7:1) and better-known *Bemidbar* 'in the wilderness of—'. Curiously, the latter title also epitomizes the content of Numbers, which focuses on the wilderness period. In contrast, the talmudic, Greek, and Latin names capsulize the theme of Israel's deployment and organization in the wilderness, preparatory to conquering and settling Canaan.

2. The Content of Numbers

For purposes of publication it was decided to divide the Anchor Bible commentary on Numbers into two volumes: volume 1 will cover Numbers 1–20, and volume 2 will cover Numbers 21–36. It was not a simple matter to determine the best point at which to conclude volume 1 of the commentary, because of the complicated interaction of the documentary sources comprising Numbers. It seemed reasonable to program the break after Numbers 20, because at that point the Israelites had left Kadesh, or were about to do so, according to the chronology informing all of the literary sources. Numbers 21 begins the documentation of the Israelite advance through Transjordan that eventually brought them to the Plains of Moab, across the Jordan from Jericho.

In its textual makeup, Numbers is the most diverse of all Torah books. It includes historiographic narratives, collections of early Hebrew poetry, and extensive legal and ritual texts. In addition to its generic diversity, Numbers also exhibits a complex literary history. As a book of the Torah, it is held together in an intricate manner: a collection of relatively early Hebrew poetry and a limited body of collected historiography were greatly expanded by priestly writers, who radically recast the depictions of the wilderness period conveyed in them.

3. The Presentation of Content: Documentary Sources Interacting

The commentator must decide how best to present the content of Numbers. Instead of offering a detailed outline of the book, chapter by chapter, it would be more fruitful to discuss what the major contributors to Numbers, the historiographers of the source JE, and the writers of P (= the Priestly source) sought, in accordance with their respective agenda, to communicate to succeeding generations.

It is source analysis that holds the key to literary development. A word about the sources of Numbers is, therefore, required before we proceed farther. "JE" is the siglum given to a composite Torah document, primarily historiographic in substance and narrative in form. It is largely comprised of two earlier sources: J (= Jahwist), a Judean source, and E (= Elohist), a northern Israelite source. Both J and E go back to the ninth to eighth centuries B.C.E., perhaps even earlier (Gray 1971: xxiv–xxxix).

Recently it has been suggested that a third source, representing biblical creativity in Transjordan, is to be identified in Numbers, primarily in the poetic sections of Numbers 21 and 23–24. These poems, part of an El repertoire, relate to the experience of the Israelites in Transjordan and include the Balaam orations (Levine 1985b; 1991). I tentatively designate this Transjordanian archive T (= Transjordan) and regard it as a subsource of the E tradition.

The materials available from J and E (+ T) were combined, edited, and elaborated by the JE writers, probably during the seventh century B.C.E., in

Judah. JE presents a fairly sequential historiography, running through Genesis, Exodus, and Numbers, though sizable gaps are noticeable in Numbers. (Leviticus is entirely of priestly authorship, and Deuteronomy represents a separate school of biblical writers.)

At points, one can identify either J or E as the ultimate documentary source of a passage in Numbers, but we should normally be content to engage the composite source, JE, and to evaluate the materials it utilized. As regards the book of Numbers, the primary challenge is to explain how priestly writers recast the JE traditions and expanded upon them, thereby reconstructing the record of the wilderness period so as to focus on their central concerns.

The diachronic perspective basic to source criticism, namely, the proposition that in order to understand a Torah book we are required to disassemble and reassemble its sources in a chronological sequence, has been challenged in recent scholarship (Milgrom 1989: xii–xiii). It has been argued that source criticism, even if accurate (and certainly if not), tells us relatively little of importance about what Numbers, or any Torah book, truly means. It is argued that a synchronic, structural analysis of the finished product—as some call it, a "holistic" engagement of the complete book—would be more enlightening. Numbers should stimulate source-critical study by virtue of its complex composition, if for no other reason. Such analysis, if undertaken carefully, holds forth the promise of identifying significantly different perceptions of the wilderness experience, perceptions that might be lost to us were we to study only the final product of the biblical process at the expense of the phases reflected in its literary development.

A debate persists, even among the proponents of source criticism, regarding the *Sitz-im-Leben* of the priestly authors, their own historical situation as it is reflected in their characterization of the wilderness period. Some regard P as an essentially preexilic collection while others see it as a younger, later source, preceded historically by JE and D (= Deuteronomistic source). (Haran 1981; Levine 1989b: xxv–xxx.)

The textual limits of P are not the principal issue in this debate. Biblical scholars can quite reliably identify a particular text as either priestly or of another provenance on the basis of language, terminology, and other fairly precise criteria. Such determinations do not, however, answer questions pertaining to the literary history of P (Levine 1982c).

In the present commentary, the priestly content of Numbers (P) will be considered to be chronologically subsequent to the earlier, nonpriestly materials preserved in JE and the poetic selections of Numbers. This is not to imply that priestly writers did not utilize early materials in their writings, but only to emphasize the likelihood that, in their present form, priestly writings represent a later stage in the development of Torah literature than does the JE corpus. The reasoning for this critical judgment can hardly be taken for granted, and will be argued extensively in sections D.1 and E of the introduction. In anticipation of that discussion, the review of content will proceed here.

4. The Beginning of the Wilderness Period

As background to a source-critical discussion of Numbers, we should show how this method would work for Exod 15:22–40:38, those sections of Exodus which cover the earliest phase of the wilderness period. In Exodus we observe how a core of relatively early material, collected by the writers of JE, was elaborated by the priestly school. If all we possessed were the nonpriestly texts of Exodus, our perception of the beginning of the wilderness period could be summarized as follows.

The Israelites crossed the Reed Sea (wherever it was) and entered the Wilderness of Shur, proceeding thence to southern Sinai where they encamped at Rephidim. There the Israelites did battle with the Amalekites and were victorious, vowing eternal enmity against them. In the narratives, attention is given to the complaints of the people and their challenges to Moses' leadership. God provided water and manna to sustain the people (Exodus 16–17). Moses' Midianite father-in-law, named Jethro, advised him on proper governance of the people, and Moses accordingly appointed officers of various ranks to assist him (Exodus 18).

In the third month following the Exodus the Israelites experienced a dramatic theophany at Mount Sinai that was formative to their way of life (Exodus 19). The Decalogue was proclaimed by God, followed by a brief law on proper worship (Exodus 20). Exodus 21–23 comprise the Book of the Covenant, a collection of early laws governing family and society, that includes a brief calendar of festivals. In its composition, the Book of the Covenant generally resembles an ancient Near Eastern law code, with curses predicted for disobedience and rewards promised for the Israelites' compliance with its provisions (Levine 1987a: 9–34). The Book of the Covenant is, in turn, followed by the record of a cultic covenant, enacted at Mount Sinai (Exod 24:1–11).

The sequence of events projected in the early historiography of Exodus is not entirely clear. It is likely that we have two versions of the sinaitic covenant. The accounts preserved in Exodus 19–20 relate that Moses, after receiving the Tablets of the Covenant atop Mount Sinai, descended the mountain and conveyed them to the people. In contrast, the E tradition expressed in Exodus 32–34 resumes the cultic theme of Exod 24:1–11: Moses had, indeed, ascended the mountain to receive God's law, but had failed to return at the expected time, generating anxiety among the people.

This is the situation as Exodus 32 opens. Upon descending the mountain and seeing the Israelites engaged in pagan worship at the foot of the mountain, sacrificing to the golden bull-calf, Moses smashed the Tablets. This act required him to ascend a second time in order to secure their replacement. So it seems that the events of Exodus 19–20 are replayed in another version, consisting of Exod 24:1–11 and chaps. 32–34. In Exodus 32–34 we read of God's wrath and of Moses' intercession. God reaffirmed the selection of Moses as leader of the people of Israel and restated his intention to grant the Israelite people the land of Canaan. There is also reference to an oraculum, called *ʾôhel môʿēd* 'the Tent of Meeting', where God spoke with Moses. It was located outside the encampment.

How did the priestly writers of Exodus modulate these earlier traditions about the beginning of the wilderness period? We begin with Exodus 15–17, where priestly writers amplified complaints voiced by the people as they entered the Sinai peninsula. The priestly writers introduced the theme of the Sabbath into the manna narrative. We are informed that gathering manna on the Sabbath was prohibited and that a double portion of manna was provided on the previous day so as to avoid the violation of Sabbath law. As was their custom, the Israelites disobeyed the instructions given them regarding the Sabbath and were accordingly punished. Here and there the priestly writers also added captions that fixed the dates and places of important events.

Beginning in Exod 24:12 and continuing throughout the remainder of Exodus, with an interruption in Exodus 32–34, the priestly school introduced materials intended to link its agenda to the impressive existing records of the Sinai theophany. The oraculum narrative of Exod 33:7–11 is anticipated in the detailed prescriptions of the priestly Tabernacle, which housed the Ark, and where sacrifices were to be offered by the Aaronide priests (Exod 24:12–31:18, restated in chaps. 35–40). The priestly writers wanted the reader to know that when Moses ascended the mountain, he was shown the actual plan of the Tabernacle and was commanded to build the cult complex to its specifications (Exod 25:40, 26:30). It is as if the priestly writers had applied to their own creative efforts the well-known dictum of Rabbi Ishmael, cited in the Mekhilta on Exod 21:1: "*And these are the norms*—These add to the preceding. Just as the preceding were given from Sinai, so are the following given from Sinai" (Lauterbach 1976: 1). Not only did Moses receive the Decalogue and the Book of the Covenant, as well as further laws and commandments, at Sinai, he was also shown the specifications of the Tabernacle and all of its vessels, the design of an earthly residence for the God of Israel. In the priestly view, initiation of proper worship and the ordaining of complete Sabbath observance in the days of Moses, pursuant to instructions communicated to him directly by God, were subjects surely to be included in the Torah's record of that momentous time.

What the priestly writers did in treating the texts available to them in what was to become the book of Exodus is instructive for an understanding of what these same priestly writers and their successors accomplished in Numbers. But whereas in Exodus the input of the priestly school was joined to a more imposing structure of nonpriestly narratives and codes of law, the core of JE materials in Numbers was less dominant, and less definitive at the start. As a result, the work of the priestly school in Numbers had the effect of altering the character of the entire book.

5. The Contribution of JE to Numbers: An Earlier Historiography

We first encounter JE material in Num 10:29–12:16. The Israelites are in southern Sinai, near the mountain of God, where we left them in Exodus 34. The reference to Hazeroth in Num 11:35 makes this location fairly certain. Moses is conferring with his Midianite father-in-law, here named Hobab. After some persuasion, Hobab most probably decided to join company with the Israelites and, at least implicitly, was promised a share in the Promised Land as a reward for his friendship. This passage recalls Exodus 18, in that it further emphasizes an early friendly relationship with the Midianites. The Israelites begin their march, with the Ark preceding them in battle (Num 10:29–36).

Numbers 11 recounts the problems faced by Moses in his role as leader of the Israelites, a recurrent theme in Torah literature. In scenes reminiscent of Exodus 16–18, we read that God provided food in the wilderness, but the people complained that it was unsatisfying. Moses was instructed to appoint a council of seventy elders to assist him in the governance of a rebellious and unruly people. In Numbers 11–12 we also find further endorsement of Moses' unique status as a charismatic prophet. This theme is introduced in connection with the appointment of the seventy elders and against the background of a family dispute involving Miriam and Aaron, who had been critical of Moses. Miriam was punished for raising her voice against Moses, and her punishment dramatized the inviolability of Moses' person.

JE material next appears in Numbers 13–14. These two chapters present difficult redactional problems resulting from the interaction of JE and P in their formation. Such problems are pivotal for the overall historiographic interpretation of Numbers. For this reason it will be necessary to digress in order to clarify the interaction of JE and P in these two chapters. As best we can reconstruct the JE narratives within Numbers 13–14, they relate that Moses dispatched a group of tribal leaders to reconnoiter southern Canaan up to the Hebron area in the Judean hill country. The delegation included Caleb, who is affiliated with the tribe of Judah in certain biblical traditions. The statement in Num 13:21 that extends the scope of the mission to the northern border of Canaan is generally recognized as a priestly interpolation.

The spies, as they are usually called, brought back a discouraging report to Moses. They were unanimous in praising the productivity of Canaan but, with the exception of Caleb, they expressed fear of the Canaanite forces and anxiety over the impregnability of their fortified towns. They doubted the capacity of the Israelites to mount a successful invasion. Such negativism was interpreted as a lack of confidence in God's power, and it evoked his wrath. God vowed that none of those who currently doubted his power would see the Promised Land.

a. The Kadesh Traditions. The most significant problem posed by the interaction of JE and P in Numbers 13–14 pertains to the location of the Israelites at the time the spies were dispatched. According to P, whose writers rewrote the opening verses of Numbers 13, the Israelites had already marched to northern Sinai. In the vocabulary of P, northern Sinai is called the Wilderness of Paran, in contrast to the southern part of the peninsula, which the priestly writers refer to as the Wilderness of Sinai. This priestly nomenclature, which is problematic in itself, is verified by Num 10:12 and 12:16, where the actual march from the south to the north is recorded (see the NOTES on Num 10:12).

Accordingly, in the final version of Numbers 13 the spies were dispatched from the Wilderness of Paran, as we read in Num 13:3. We must remember, however, that in their original form the opening verses of Numbers 13 had undoubtedly registered a more precise location for the Israelite encampment from which the spies were dispatched, most likely Kadesh. We would conclude as much from Num 32:8, a JE passage, which states explicitly that the spies were dispatched from Kadesh.

And yet, the first explicit mention of Kadesh in the JE narrative comes only in Num 13:26 and, after that, not certainly until Num 20:14 (see the NOTES on Num 20:1). The importance of identifying the whereabouts of the Israelites at the time the spies were dispatched, an event that must have occurred near the beginning of the wilderness period, is far-reaching, as we shall observe presently.

Num 13:26 is a pivotal verse but one that has been rewritten by P, so that its textual analysis becomes difficult. In fact, Num 13:26 had to be rewritten if P's view of the wilderness period was to be sustained in Numbers as a whole. The precise question of concern is whether locative *Qādēšāh* 'at Kadesh' is original to Num 13:26. It is the site to which the spies returned, and therefore logically the place from which they had been dispatched. If the reference to Kadesh in Num 13:26 is textually secure, then we may assume that the JE tradition recorded the dispatch of the spies from Kadesh.

Kadesh (Barnea) is not in Sinai, as this peninsula is usually delimited geographically, but in the Wilderness of Zin, located in the southern Negeb. This is its explicit location in three separate priestly passages: (a) Num 20:1, recording the Israelite arrival at Kadesh; (b) Num 33:36, part of the wilderness itinerary according to P; and (c) Num 34:3–4, in the delineation of Canaan's borders, also according to P.

Inevitably, a degree of geographical "fudging" has occurred: in P's rewriting of Num 13:26, Kadesh has slipped southward into the Wilderness of Paran, or, alternatively, the Wilderness of Paran has expanded northward so that it overlaps the border of the Wilderness of Zin. This fudging allows Kadesh to be, simultaneously, both in Paran and in Zin. A perusal of recent biblical atlases reveals the instability of these toponyms, as historical geographers take their cues uncritically from differing textual traditions (Aharoni and Avi-Yonah 1979: 40–41, maps 48 and 51).

What we read in Num 13:26, as rewritten by P, with its geographical inaccuracy, resulted from an editorial process that may be plotted as follows:

> *wayyēlekû wayyābṓ'û 'el Moseh [we'el 'Aharôn we'el kol ʿadat benê Yisrā'ēl 'el midbar P'ārān] Q̱ādēšāh, wayyāšîbû 'ôtô < 'ôtām > dābār [we'et kol hāʿēdāh], wayyar'ûhû < wayyar'ûm > 'et perî hā'āreṣ.*
>
> They proceeded, coming to Moses [and to Aaron and to the entire community of the Israelites in the Wilderness of Paran] at Kadesh, and brought him < them > a report [and to the entire community] and showed him < them > the fruits of the land.

There are valid reasons for endorsing the originality of the reference to Kadesh in Num 13:26. We possess other fairly early attestations of Kadesh as the Israelite base near the beginning of the wilderness period. In addition to the testimony of Num 32:8 (JE), already mentioned, there is the record of D. It admittedly differs in some respects from that of JE, but it nevertheless reports that the spies were dispatched from Kadesh. By the reckoning of D, the Israelites arrived at Kadesh very soon after they left southern Sinai (Deut 1:19, 46; 2:14; and cf. Josh 14:6–12, Judg 11:16–17).

The spies were certainly dispatched close to the beginning of the schematic forty-year wilderness period. This chronology is more or less required by all of the historiographies represented in Torah literature, otherwise there would have been little meaning to the divine decree delaying Israel's entry into the land of Canaan as punishment for the spies' report and popular reaction to it. If the spies were, indeed, sent from Kadesh, one must conclude that the Israelites had arrived at Kadesh early on, most likely within a year or so after the Exodus.

The JE source is not explicit on (a) the duration of the Israelite encampment at Kadesh, that is to say, the time that elapsed from Numbers 13 to 20:21 and 21:4b, or (b) the time that elapsed in the JE record from Num 21:4b, which records the beginning of the skirting of Edom, to Num 21:11, which records the arrival of the Israelites at Nahal Zered in Transjordan.

The two questions are related, of course. In Num 20:14 we find the Israelites still at Kadesh and about to dispatch a delegation to the Edomites. The failure of this mission prompted their move toward southern Transjordan, via the Gulf of Elath. It is noteworthy that Kadesh is characterized in Num 20:16 as being near the boundary of the expanded Edomite territory, so that the skirting of Edom would have begun virtually as soon as the Israelites left Kadesh.

Actually, this move had been ordered in Num 14:25, a verse identifiable as part of the JE narrative (Num 14:11–25). There the Israelites were told to proceed to the Red Sea, namely, the Gulf of Elath. This order is rationalized by calling attention to the strength of the Canaanites and Amalekites in the Negeb, a situation that made a direct penetration into Canaan through the Negeb inadvisable at the time.

When the JE record resumes in Num 14:39–45, we read of a futile attempt by the Israelites to move into the Judean hill country that was repulsed at Hormah, near Arad (Num 14:40–45; cf. Deut 1:44). It should be mentioned that Num 21:1–3 also record an initial defeat at Hormah, but one that was reversed and turned into a victory. Of this discrepancy more will be said in due course.

It was the brief report of the Israelite defeat at Hormah in Num 14:40–45 that led to the decision to approach Canaan via Transjordan, a strategy that the Israelites begin to implement in Num 20:21 and 21:4b. That report is, therefore, of pivotal importance because of the consequential response it generated. As regards the projected schedule of the JE historiographers we note that for the presumed period of time between the narratives of Numbers 13–14 and the report of Num 20:14–21, JE records only the rebellion against Moses recounted in Numbers 16.

As was true of the opening verses of Numbers 13, so in the opening verses of Numbers 16 priestly writers have reworked the text to an extent that has obscured its original context. We read of a rebellion against the authority of Moses, led by a group of Reubenites that included Dathan and Abiram. Once again, Moses' leadership was endorsed by God, who unleashed his wrath in the form of an earthquake that swallowed up the insurgents and their households.

To return to the historiographic sequence in JE, I tentatively conclude that the Israelites passed relatively little time in Kadesh after the failure of their attempted penetration into southern Canaan. In turn, this deduction means that the Israelites remained in the Wilderness of Paran—or Kadesh, depending on which tradition one adopts—for only a brief period of time, and that for about thirty-eight of the forty years projected, they were elsewhere. Most probably the JE historiographers would agree with the statement in Deut 2:14: "And the time it took us to proceed from Kadesh Barnea until we crossed Nahal Zered came to thirty-eight years, until the extinction of the entire generation, the warriors, from the encampment, just as YHWH had sworn to them." If this reconstruction of the historiographic evidence is correct, about thirty-eight years of adventure were compressed by the JE historiographers between Num 21:4b and 21:12, a space of nine verses. Similarly, it took the Deuteronomist only sixteen verses, from Deut 2:1 through 2:16, to span the same thirty-eight years.

We can learn still more from D in reconstructing JE's version of the Israelite itinerary. The Deuteronomist uses the cliché *yāmîm rabbîm* 'many days' in Deut 1:46 to indicate the duration of the Israelite stay at Kadesh, and in Deut 2:1 to indicate how long it took to circumvent Seir. This cliché is ambiguous, of course, but in the present context it probably indicates a period of several months or a year. After all, if it took thirty-eight years to get from Kadesh to Nahal Zered, how long could the Israelites have spent in Kadesh? After leaving Kadesh they then set about circumventing Mount Seir for an additional period of *yāmîm rabbîm.* It is significant that Num 14:25 correlates with Deut 2:1a, in that both statements speak of an early advance of the Israelites toward the Red Sea.

The Deuteronomist does not mention Edom, and the JE historiographer fails to mention Seir. Some have proposed that the two names are sometimes interchangeable in biblical sources, which is probably so in Numbers 20 and Deuteronomy 2 (Bartlett 1989: 90–93). According to either tradition, the Israelites spent most of the thirty-eight years that elapsed between Kadesh and Nahal Zered somewhere else than in Sinai, as that peninsula is usually delimited. In the traditions of both JE and D, most of those years were spent in the wilderness east of Edom and south of Moab and the Dead Sea.

Both the JE and the Deuteronomistic historiographers probably agree that within a year's time, approximately in the fortieth year, the Israelites moved northward east of Moab and reached the Arnon River, avoiding conflict with the Ammonites and ultimately fighting victoriously against the Amorites of Gilead and Bashan. The events occurring along this route are recorded by JE, beginning in Num 21:13.

b. The Wilderness Period: The Differing Priestly Perspective. The critical student of the biblical text will want to know why the priestly writers went to such lengths to keep the Israelites in Sinai rather than elsewhere for most of the wilderness period, and why they reported the arrival of the Israelites at Kadesh only in the fortieth year (Num 20:1, 33:38).

To do so, they had to rewrite Num 13:3 so that the spies would be dispatched from Paran, not from Kadesh, and they also had to get the name of Paran into Num 13:26, the report of the spies' return. In Numbers 33, the priestly version of the Israelite itinerary from Egypt to the Plains of Moab, the same schedule is projected: in Num 33:1–17 the Israelites proceed from Egypt to southern Sinai, encamping at Hazeroth. Num 33:18–35 transport the Israelites from Hazeroth to Ezion-Geber to Elath, through no less than seventeen mostly unidentified toponyms, never touching Kadesh! What is more, Num 33:35 brings the Israelites from Ezion-Geber to Kadesh in what must have been the fortieth year. In other words, the command issued to the Israelites in Num 14:25, near the beginning of the wilderness period, to proceed to the Red Sea is fulfilled in P's vision only in the fortieth year, just as the mission to Edom recorded in Num 20:14–21 had been deferred to the end of the wilderness period. The priestly authors were compelled to produce an impractical itinerary, leading first to the Red Sea, then to Kadesh, and then back to the Red Sea and Edom by virtually the same route! Before the Israelites left the area of Kadesh, they buried Aaron in the fortieth year after the Exodus (Num 33:36–39; cf. Num 20:22–29). In the continuation of Numbers 33 (vv 40–49), we read of what may have been another tradition of the Israelite advance through Transjordan, but that route need not concern us here.

Perhaps the priestly writers sought to retain geographic proximity between the formative sinaitic theophany and the revelation of the elaborate laws and rituals they had retrojected into the wilderness period. If their enactments were to bear the same sanction as the Decalogue and the Book of the Covenant, they would have had to have been revealed in the same sinaitic setting, albeit in the north of the peninsula rather than in its southern region. Whereas the movements preparatory to the Transjordanian campaign required the Israelites to be within reach of the Gulf of Elath, it was not required that they exit the Sinai peninsula entirely.

We must also examine priestly attitudes and policy regarding the Israelite conquest and settlement of Transjordan. It appears that P had a special reason for telescoping the route of the Israelites from Kadesh to the Plains of Moab, as we shall have occasion to observe.

To summarize the discussion of the content of Numbers thus far: as a result of the interplay of the two sources, JE and P, we emerge from a reading of Numbers 1–20 with two primary wildernesses of reference. According to the priestly tradition of Numbers, the Israelites spent most of the forty years in Sinai, more precisely, in northern Sinai, making Sinai the primary wilderness of reference. This is the case no matter where we locate Kadesh, technically speaking. Even if one insists that Kadesh was in Sinai, by a particular territorial definition, the fact is that according to P the Israelites did not arrive there until the fortieth year and were somewhere in northern Sinai up to that time.

According to the JE tradition, however, the march toward Transjordan from Kadesh began within a year or so after the Exodus, and the wilderness of primary reference is east of Edom and Moab.

c. The Structure of Numbers: The Analysis of Sources. The foregoing discussion has implications for comprehending the overall structure of the book of Numbers, as well as for historiographic reconstruction. In placing recorded events in chronological sequence, the commentator attempts to establish a correlation between (a) the projected historical position and (b) the textual position of the events in question. One way of probing the structure of Numbers is, therefore, to trace the generational succession of the Israelites during the wilderness period. At what point did the new generation enter upon the scene, and how did respective schools of biblical historiographers mark that turning point?

We can assume that for the JE narrators, the Exodus generation had passed away before the Israelites arrived at Nahal Zered, early in the fortieth year (Num 21:12). The Deuteronomist explicitly states as much in Deut 2:14, and the same view should be attributed to the historiographers of JE in Numbers. There is hardly a logical alternative. After all, the message of the forty-year postponement of Israel's conquest and possession of Canaan is precisely that the Exodus generation was found wanting; that it was incapable of victory, having reacted so negatively to the prospect of conquering Canaan, even after witnessing many demonstrations of God's power. Could these Israelites overpower the Amorites and merit the praise of Balaam, who not only extols their impressive military might, but even eulogizes their favored relationship to YHWH? Unquestionably, it was the second generation who, in the fortieth year, accomplished the Transjordanian victories.

It is difficult, nevertheless, to understand why, if this analysis is correct, the succession of generations is so elusive in the historiography of JE, in contrast to its explicitness in the Deuteronomist's account (Deut 2:14). We find ourselves reading Num 21:4–20 without sensing that something is changing radically. In v 12 the Israelites arrive at Nahal Zered, and in v 13 they simply move on. Yet this is a critical juncture. The Israelites are now poised on the northern border of Moab facing the land of the Amorites. A few verses later, the stage will be set for the battles against Sihon, the Amorite king (Num 21:21).

We should not exclude the possibility that priestly writers condensed the record in order to produce Numbers 21 in its current form. Furthermore, when we read Numbers 20–21 critically we become aware of a time warp. In Numbers 20, P dramatized the approaching end of the wilderness generation by recording the deaths of Miriam and Aaron in and near Kadesh, at the border of the Edomite territory. (It is possible that Num 20:1b, recording the death and burial of Miriam in Kadesh, derives from JE.)

According to P, the Israelites had just arrived at Kadesh in the first month of the fortieth year; consequently, P's adjusted time frame for the JE record of the Edomite mission (Num 20:14–21), which P incorporates, is early in the fortieth year.

It follows that for P, the march from Hor Hahar around Edom (Num 21:4) also began in the fortieth year, so that it took only a brief time to get from Hor Hahar to Nahal Zered. But in the JE time frame, we are still near the beginning of the wilderness period as we read Num 20:14–21 and 21:4, with about thirty-eight years to go until the wilderness generation will have passed away. So it is that the critical student of the Hebrew Bible reads the same texts through the eyes of more than one school of biblical authors. Read through the eyes of JE, Num 20:14–21 and 21:4 report events that occurred, or commenced, near the beginning of the wilderness period; but read through the eyes of P, whose editors cited these texts and encased them in different rubrics, these passages report events of the fortieth year.

Some scholars have maintained that the generational progression in the book of Numbers is structured by the positioning of the two census records, in Numbers 1 and Numbers 26, respectively. On this basis, chaps. 1–25 are speaking of the Exodus generation, and chaps. 26–36 of the next generation (Milgrom 1989: xiii–xv). This view presupposes symmetry: just as the Exodus generation was introduced by a census record in Numbers 1, so the second generation is introduced in Numbers 26 by a later census list.

There is also the fact that at the conclusion of the second census, in Num 26:64–65, we actually find a statement to the effect that the Exodus generation had all passed on, except for Caleb and Joshua, as decreed in chaps. 13–14. One recalls the similar registering of the end of the wilderness generation in Deut 2:14.

In critical terms, all of this textual evidence in Numbers derives from P. The statement in Num 26:64–65 would appear to indicate that P's view of the succession of generations differed from the earlier JE view. The wilderness generation would have ended in the Plains of Moab, and the priestly writers would actually have attributed the Israelite victories over the Amorites of Transjordan to the Exodus generation.

How does such a projection of the succession of generations square with the divine decree of Numbers 13–14 condemning the wilderness generation? I refer to Numbers 13–14 in their full version, including the priestly amplifications. The JE sections of Numbers 13–14 emphasize, in their formulation of the divine decree, the exclusion of the wilderness generation from entry into the Promised Land. Those who had doubted God's power would never see the Land (Num 14:21–24). Ironically, it is precisely in priestly sections of Numbers 13–14 such as Num 14:26–39 that the emphasis is on the death of the wilderness generation *bammidbār hazzeh* 'in this wilderness' (Num 14:29, 32–33, 35). For the priestly writers, "this wilderness" can only refer to Sinai. Could the priestly historiographers have intended the first generation to survive all the way to the Plains of Moab? Literally speaking, it would have been possible for the JE historiographers to interpret their own version of the decree of Numbers 13–14 to allow for this interpretation, but it was hardly possible for the priestly writers themselves.

It is more likely that for P the first generation, the generation of the Exodus, actually came to a close before the Israelites left the region of

Kadesh. With a degree of geographical "fudging," the decree that the entire generation of Israelites, save Joshua and Caleb, would die "in this wilderness" would have been carried out. Even Miriam and Aaron die and are buried in Kadesh and Hor Hahar, respectively, and for the priestly authors Kadesh lies in the Wilderness of Paran, outside Canaan proper.

The decree of Numbers 13–14 had never included Moses. The denial of his entry into Canaan was not on JE's agenda and had to be rationalized by P, whose writers echoed the Deuteronomist's tragic reference to that divine decree (cf. Deut 3:23–29; Num 20:12–13).

The statement at the end of the second census (Num 26:64–65) marking the extinction of the first generation need not compel the conclusion that P meant that generation actually to survive until the Israelites arrived at the Plains of Moab and to accomplish the Transjordanian victories over the Amorites. There is, after all, another agenda to be considered, and it has to do with marking the beginning and end of the wilderness period itself. This is a geographical as well as a temporal determination. The statement in Num 26:64–65 merely recapitulates the succession of generations at a point in time when the Israelites were about to cross over the Jordan into Canaan, thus ending the period of migration.

Perhaps it is possible to probe the viewpoint of P even further: P seems exceptionally uninterested in the Transjordanian victories. Between Num 21:4 and 25:6, where P begins to amplify the JE account of the Baal Peor incident recorded in Num 25:1–5, the only priestly input is to be found in Num 22:4 and 7. There P introduced Midianites as allies of the Moabites and set the stage for the priestly version of the Midianite war, subsequently to be recounted in chap. 31.

As far as military ventures are concerned, P was interested almost exclusively in the conquest of Canaan proper and, of course, in the destruction of Israel's enemies in Canaan. For P, Transjordan is not part of Canaan, the land promised to the Israelites, as is made explicit in the boundaries of the Promised Land delineated in Numbers 34, a predominantly priestly document. In Numbers 32, the effect of priestly amplifications is to add admonitions to, and express increased criticism of, the Transjordanian settlement by the two and one-half tribes. In Joshua 22, a text under evident priestly as well as Deuteronomic influence, the two and one-half Transjordanian tribes are told in no uncertain terms that the God of Israel may not be worshiped on an altar that stands east of the Jordan.

This priestly policy might also explain why a report of the battle with the Canaanites of Arad at Hormah suddenly appears at the beginning of Numbers 21 (vv 1–3). This seemingly misplaced report converts the defeat of Num 14:45 (cf. Deut 1:44) into a victory. Logically, the priestly writers must have been the ones who interpolated this item, which they cited from a separate archive. We would gather as much from the fact that it is positioned in the priestly itinerary precisely at this point in the sequence of events (Num 33:40).

Once the priestly writers, for their own reasons, had deferred the arrival at Kadesh to the fortieth year, they were more or less compelled to fix the end of the first generation at a point in time before the Israelites left the Kadesh area to begin their circumvention of Edom, a move recorded in Num 21:4a. Originally, Num 21:4 had probably followed Num 20:21 and had not contained any reference to Hor Hahar:

> Num 20:21: But Edom refused to allow Israel to traverse his territory, and Israel turned away from him.
>
> Num 21:4: So they marched <from Hor Hahar> by way of the Red Sea in order to circumvent the land of Edom, and the people became impatient along the way.

This sequence posed no difficulty for the historiographers of JE, for whom the departure from Kadesh was an event occurring early in the wilderness period. But for the priestly historiographers, it was problematic. They consequently added Num 20:22–29, effectively ending the first generation in Num 20:29, and slightly delaying the Israelite departure from the region of Kadesh. They then interpolated Num 21:1–3. For the priestly writers this account of a successful battle with the Canaanites heralds the entrance of the second generation.

A subtle message would be conveyed by the priestly interpolation of a victory over Negeb Canaanites in the fortieth year by the new generation of warriors. This victory did not change anything, because the historiographers of JE had committed the Israelites to the Transjordanian campaigns, which proceeded as planned. Yet the interpolation may have been an effort to upstage the Transjordanian victories. The priestly message is that achieving victory over Canaanites in Canaan was the critical challenge, not defeating the Amorites of Transjordan.

Nothing that has been said about the redactional status of Num 21:1–3 is to be taken as undermining the historicity of the account itself. In fact, some scholars, most notably R. de Vaux (1978: 1.419–425, 2.523–549), regard the account in Num 21:1–3 as historical and conclude that it preserves an alternative tradition of early Israelite incursions into Canaan. The present reference would substantiate other biblical records of Calebite and Judahite conquests in the region of Judah, such as those preserved in Judges 1 (cf. Judg 3:8–11; Josh 14:6–15).

The Israelites were victorious over the Negeb Canaanites after they demonstrated added faith in God's power by pronouncing a vow of *ḥērem* devotion, which ensured that all of the spoils of the conquered Canaanite cities would be dedicated cultically. Reference to the *ḥērem* suggests a Deuteronomic derivation for Num 21:1–3.

What was for JE a decisive defeat that led to the Transjordanian adventure and necessitated thirty-eight years of harsh migrations became for P a victory that heralded the advent of a new generation of Israelites. If this analysis is correct, it would indicate how remarkably keen the priestly writers were. They found an alternative version of the Hormah battle, one that reversed the defeat of Num 14:45 by attributing religious devotion to the Israelites, and they placed it in Num 21:1–3.

d. The Israelites in Transjordan. In the historiography of JE we read that the march from Ezion-Geber, east of Edom, to Nahal Zered near the southern border of Moab was extremely harsh. The people were troublesome along the way, repeatedly arousing God's anger. The episode of the bronze serpent, fashioned as a cure for the plague of snake bites unleashed by God, is set in this context (Num 21:4–12).

Numbers 21:13–20 record that the Israelites proceeded northward east of Moab, encamping in the desert across the Arnon River, which marked the border between Moab and the lands of the Amorites. Several poetic selections are cited here; they will be discussed, along with all of the poetry concentrated in Numbers 21–24, in section B.1.a of this introduction.

A delegation was then sent to Sihon, king of the Amorites, whose capital was at Heshbon, but he refused passage to the Israelites. This time the Israelites had no alternative to war if they hoped to reach the Jordan. The second generation of Israelites consequently engaged the Amorites in a series of battles, and they triumphed. The battle between Sihon and the Israelites at Yahsah, north of Qedemoth, produced an important Israelite victory. The Israelites settled Gilead and Bashan after conquering Jazer, a town on the Ammonite border then said to be inhabited by Amorites, not Ammonites. There was no need to engage the Ammonites at that point, especially because their border was strongly fortified (Num 21:21–35).

The ballad preserved in Num 21:27–30, and introduced by the caption in 21:26, was conceivably intended to compensate for the lack of a recorded negotiation with the Moabites, which, if we possessed it, would have explained why the Israelites were compelled to proceed east of Moab instead of through Moabite territory. As it stands, this ballad establishes Israel's right to Gilead, which was once ruled by Moab, but which had been lost by them to the Amorites before the Israelites arrived on the scene.

After the Israelites reached the Plains of Moab, having eliminated all impediments to their advance (Num 22:1), we read the Balaam pericope of chaps. 22–24. This section of Numbers exploits the hostility between Israel and Moab as a setting for poetic orations extolling God's providence over Israel.

Earlier in this introduction, in discussing the source-critical makeup of Numbers, I suggested that the poetry cited in the Balaam pericope (Numbers 22–24) derives from an El repertoire, preserving the creativity of the Israelites in Gilead. This attribution would also apply to the poetic selections preserved in Numbers 21, which also speak to events in Transjordan and reveal regional literary distinctiveness.

Numbers 22–24 tell us that the Moabites (allied with the Midianites in the priestly tradition) were extremely fearful of the powerful Israelites poised at their northeastern border (Num 22:5). Balak, the Moabite king, engaged the services of Balaam, a foremost foreign diviner who was supposed to employ ritual and magical techniques as well as spells to weaken the Israelites. Subsequent to a narrative that conveys the message that Balaam was powerless to act without the authorization of the God of Israel, who clearly stood with his people and fought at their side, we encounter the poetic orations themselves. These poems extol Israelite power and portray Israel as extremely blessed. Several "oracles against the nations" were appended to the original orations and serve to characterize Balaam as an international personality.

The JE version of the Baal Peor incident recorded in Num 25:1–5 takes place at Shittim, in the Plains of Moab, where the Israelites had encamped (see Num 22:1). Positioned as it is subsequent to the accounts of brilliant Israelite victories over the Amorites reported in chap. 21, and subsequent to the Balaam pericope (chaps. 22–24), which dramatizes God's providence over Israel, the lapse into paganism epitomized in the Baal Peor incident brings home a sobering message: Even the second, heroic generation of Israelites was susceptible to the lure of paganism. Such backsliding was to become a chronic pattern in biblical historiography. Israel often forgot its debt and promise to God and lapsed into the very kinds of behavior that had brought defeat and suffering upon the people in the past.

Subsequent to Num 25:1–5, the JE narrative recurs solely in chap. 32, a highly composite and carefully reworked text. The JE sections of chap. 32, which are actually quite difficult to isolate, address the legitimization of the permanent settlement of Gilead (and Bashan) by the tribes of Reuben and Gad and by the Machirite clan, affiliated with Manasseh (de Vaux 1978: 2.551–592). These two tribes pledged to take part in the conquest of Canaan west of the Jordan alongside their Israelite brothers. The underlying political reality reflected in the historiography of JE is that of a tribal confederation galvanized into a unified militia during times of war. As far as can be ascertained, the JE material in Numbers 32 is mostly concentrated in vv 6–9, 16–19, and possibly in vv 34–42.

e. The Themes of JE. There are several themes prominent in the non-priestly, primarily JE materials of Numbers. Basic to the agenda of JE is the status of Moses as leader of the Israelites. We therefore encounter in Numbers more of the same kinds of challenges to Moses' leadership that we first observed in Exodus. In every instance, we find the unique status of Moses being endorsed by God, often in dramatic ways. JE narratives vary, nonetheless, in the degree of importance they attach to Moses' clout as an intercessor and in the degree of sinfulness they attach to Israel's disaffection. There are also reports of modifications in governance, intended to alleviate the burdens borne by Moses and to address the pressing needs of the people.

Still another theme of note in the JE materials is the notion that God had prepared the Israelites for their future life in the Promised Land; that they brought their way of life with them. This theme is, of course, common to all Torah traditions.

The JE tradition explains the forty-year delay in arriving at the Promised Land as God's punishment for Israel's lack of trust in him. The Israelites doubted his power and reliability, which is a traditional way of interpreting more realistic factors that would actually have caused the postponement of the conquest, or that might explain the refusal of the Israelite leadership to endorse a policy of conquest.

6. The Priestly Contribution to Numbers: A Loaded Agenda

How did the priestly school transform existing perceptions of the wilderness period? We initially observe that all of Num 1:1–10:28 is the work of P. As the book of Numbers begins, the Israelites are in the south of the Sinai peninsula, near Mount Sinai. A priestly caption records a communication between God and Moses on the first day of the second month of the second year after the Exodus (Num 1:1). The next dated caption in the priestly source comes in 9:1, where we read that sometime before the twentieth day of the same month and year, God communicated to Moses certain revisions in the laws governing the paschal sacrifice. Soon thereafter, in 10:11–12, we read that on the twentieth day of the same month and year the Israelites began their march northward to the Wilderness of Paran, which is P's designation for the northern part of the Sinai peninsula.

In the light of JE's record, which reports on further movement in southern Sinai in Num 11:35, the statement of P in 10:11–12 appears anticipatory. To correct the discrepancy between the JE and P schedules, P added a postscript in 12:16 stating that only after all that happened in 10:29–12:15 did the Israelites actually depart for the Wilderness of Paran. According to P's chronology, all that is contained in 1:1–10:28 transpired during a period of less than one month, namely, in the second month of the second year following the Exodus.

The priestly school has contributed the following content in Num 1:1–10:28. In Numbers 1–4, we are provided a record of the plan and organization of the Israelite encampment. According to priestly tradition, this system went into operation near the beginning of the forty-year wilderness period. After a census of all males twenty years old and older who were eligible for military service, administered by the tribal chieftains *(neśîʾîm)*, we find a statement anticipatory of Numbers 3–4 to the effect that the Levites were to be registered separately.

Numbers 2 outlines the plan of the encampment, repeating some of the census figures. The priestly plan projected an encampment, with the Tabernacle complex at its core and the various tribes grouped around it. The priests were positioned on the favored eastern side of the Tabernacle, and the clans of Levites on its other three sides. Moving outward from the center of the encampment, we encounter four groups of three tribes each, with the Judahite corps given the preferential location on the eastern side.

Provisions were made for transporting the portable shrine, earlier described in the latter chapters of Exodus, by the appropriate levitical clans. These instructions anticipate the levitical assignments detailed in Numbers 3–4, which outline the organization of the Aaronide priesthood and its Levite assistants, clan by clan. Clearly, the most significant announcement by the priestly school in Numbers 1–4 is the stratification of the priesthood into (a) priests, as strictly defined, and (b) the rest of the tribe of Levi. These Levites would not serve as officiants or celebrants, but as servitors bearing assigned tasks relevant to the transport, maintenance, and handling of cultic materiel. Prior to the first four chapters of Numbers, priestly sources in Exodus and Leviticus had given no explicit indication of any such stratification within the tribe of Levi as had been described between priests and Levites. This system is introduced and highlighted in Numbers.

The contents of Numbers 5–6 are only loosely linked to chaps. 1–4, on the one hand, and to the contents of 7:1–10:28, on the other. Whatever linkage is evident pertains to purification of the Israelite Tabernacle and of the encampment as a whole. To be specific: Num 5:1–4 ordain the expulsion of certain impure persons, pursuant to the provisions of Leviticus 13–15. Num 5:5–10 summarize, with notable revisions, the expiatory sacrificial practices first prescribed in Leviticus 4–7. In a related vein, Num 5:11–31 prescribe a judicial ordeal for a wife suspected of adultery, again with the objective of sustaining sexual purity. Num 6:1–21 are devoted to an aspect of the votive system, naziritism, in which the impurity caused by contact with a corpse figures prominently.

A frank evaluation of Numbers 5–6 leads to the conclusion that various matters bearing on the purity of the Israelite encampment and its Tabernacle were stated (or restated) in anticipation of the actual dedication of the Tabernacle, an event recorded in chap. 7. In 6:22–27 the priestly benediction appears, cited from an independent source. Since late antiquity it has been recognized that its logical place in the Torah is directly after Lev 9:22–23, where we read that Aaron pronounced a blessing over the people after his consecration and the consecration of his sons as Tabernacle priests. Numbers 7 preserves an archival record of the dedication of the Tabernacle and its altar, listing contributions by all twelve tribal chieftains over a twelve-day period.

The dominant subject of Num 8:1–10:28 is the dedication of the Levites. First, 8:5–26 present a description of that event modeled after the consecration of the Aaronide priests recorded in Leviticus 8–9, but with marked differences reflecting the lower status of the Levites. Preceding the dedication of the Levites, we have an ordinance on the Tabernacle Menorah (8:1–4). Following the levitical dedication, there are provisions for a deferred paschal sacrifice in the second month for those impure at the required time in the first month, or too distant to undertake the required pilgrimage (9:1–14). This festival code should be interpreted against the background of Exodus 12–13, where the primary Pesaḥ regimen is presented. Num 9:15–23 preserve a narrative associated with the "cloud *(cānān)*," a manifestation of God's presence. This theme is also significant in the JE traditions of Exodus 33–34 and Numbers 11. In the P tradition, the cloud's movement specifically signaled either a divinely ordered march or an order to make camp at the end of the march. Num 9:15–23 are linked to the date on which the Tabernacle was erected and put into operation. Thus we see that priestly literature itself preserves more than one record of the erection and dedication of the Tabernacle.

In Numbers 10–12 there is very little interaction between JE and P. In chap. 10, vv 1–28 are consistently priestly, while 10:29–12:15 are nonpriestly, with only a postscript in 12:16 having been provided by a priestly editor. Taken as a whole, chaps. 1–12 comprise a discernible division of the book in its final form, covering the Israelite experience in southern Sinai. Chapters 13–20 cover the Israelite experience in Kadesh, according to the JE tradition; and in Paran, or northern Sinai, according to the priestly tradition.

a. Priestly Content in Numbers 13–20. The priestly contribution to chaps. 13–20 is of a varied character. In historiographic terms, chaps. 13–14 are critical, as has already been explained at length in the review of the JE materials (section A.5.a, above).

The remaining contribution of P to Numbers 13–14 is merely expansive. The delegation sent to reconnoiter the land of Canaan is instructed in Num 13:21, a verse inserted by P, to proceed all the way to Lebo of Hamath, on the northern border of Canaan. This target point corresponds to the limits of Canaan in some priestly traditions, as for instance in Numbers 34, where the borders of Canaan are delineated. In the priestly passages of chaps. 13–14, the delegation is neatly structured, in typical priestly fashion. It is made to consist of one tribal chieftain from each of the twelve tribes, and it includes Joshua, who is absent from the JE narrative. The negative report of the spies is more reprehensible in P, denigrating the productive capacity of the country and cynically referring to Egypt, not Canaan, as a land flowing with milk and honey. In P, Joshua joins Caleb in dissenting from the *dibbāh* 'malignment' of the other spies.

In a similar way, the priestly version of the decree postponing possession of Canaan by the Israelites is spelled out more specifically than is the JE account. We read of retribution—forty years for forty days—and we encounter terms such as *zenût* 'harlotry' and *nāśāʾ ʿawôn* 'bear the punishment of sin', so typical of P's vocabulary. P also records the immediate death of the spies themselves, as divine punishment strikes swiftly. All of these thematic expansions lend to chaps. 13–14, in their final form, the impression of meticulous divine management of Israel's fortunes in the wilderness.

Leaving the cultic laws of Numbers 15 aside for the moment, we move directly to chaps. 16–17, noting that the JE content is limited to chap. 16. JE's original view of the rebellion against Moses, stated in the opening verses of chap. 16, has been obscured by the priestly writers. The textual situation resembles the one that obtained in the opening verses of chap. 13. In effect, the priestly school transformed whatever had been the issue at stake in the rebellion into an internecine rivalry among the clans of the tribe of Levi. Moses and Aaron were of the Amramite clan, which held the right to the priesthood. A leading member of the Kohathites, named Korah, sought a priestly role for his clan and fomented an insurrection in pursuit of that objective. The situation is resolved in two incompatible ways: in JE, an earthquake swallows up the insurgents, and in P a fire consumes them. The priestly writers effectively delegitimized the Kohathites, who were, after the Amramites, the privileged levitical clan. In so doing, they established Aaron's clan as the sole legitimate priests. There are further characteristically priestly elements in chaps. 16–17, such as the utilization of consecrated materials in refurbishing the altar, expressions of the *ʿānān* tradition, and references to the Tent of Meeting.

We can now backtrack and consider the ritual material in Numbers 15, continuing then with a summary of chaps. 18–19, which contain important codes of priestly law. Why all of these law codes were positioned precisely where they were is unclear. Chapter 15 is of several parts: vv 1–16 prescribe the appropriate grain offerings *(minḥāh)* and libations *(nesek)* that were to accompany the major sacrifices, the *ʿôlāh* and the *zebaḥ*. Verses 17–21 introduce a new levy *(terûmāh)* from the dough of baking vessels. Verses 22–31 capsulize the more detailed and expansive codes of Leviticus 4–5 and parts of Leviticus 6–7 on the subject of the expiation of inadvertent offenses. We find a strong statement objecting to ritual expiation of flagrant offenses. Verses

32–36 relate an actual incident of Sabbath violation, which serves to introduce additional Sabbath laws. Finally, vv 37–41 ordain the fashioning of fringes to be worn on the garments of Israelite males, as a visual reminder of the duty of Israelites to fulfill God's commandants.

Numbers 18 sets forth the perquisites of the clergy, both the Aaronide priests and the Levites, outlining what amounted to their support system. It speaks of tithes and levies, as well as of sections of actual sacrifices allotted to the priests, as well as of firstlings. In effect, this elaborate chapter of Numbers may be characterized as a summary codex. All of its provisions capsulize stated Torah laws. Chapter 19, in contrast, is an unprecedented priestly statement on corpse contamination, prescribing the complex purification required to restore an Israelite so defiled to a proper ritual state. The ultimate objective of these rites was to assure the continuing purity of the Tabernacle complex and its clergy, as well as the entire Israelite encampment. These prescriptions are best understood as responses to the cult of the dead, and they recall the restrictions on priestly participation in funerary activity prescribed in Leviticus 21.

Num 20:1 records the arrival of the Israelites at Kadesh, in the fortieth year, the year in which Miriam and Aaron died. This caption virtually reorders the schedule of the Israelite wilderness experience, making it clear that the wilderness of the wanderings was Sinai. As has been explained earlier, the JE tradition scheduled the arrival of the Israelites in Kadesh near the beginning of the forty-year wilderness period.

To introduce the first maneuver aimed at approaching Canaan from Transjordan, the priestly school, in Num 20:2–13, reports yet another episode of Israelite recalcitrance, in the course of which both Moses and Aaron showed a lack of trust in God. This lapse ultimately justified God's decree denying Moses entry into the Promised Land. As an etiological narrative, the story of Moses' lapse was probably triggered by the Deuteronomist's treatment of the tragic theme of Moses' death in Transjordan (Deut 3:23–29). Farther on, in Num 20:22–29, after the JE narrator spoke of the delegation to Edom (20:14–21), P recounts the journey from Kadesh to Hor Hahar, an unidentified site near the border of Edom. There Aaron, the high priest, died. The priesthood is then transferred to Aaron's son, Eleazar, thus assuring inclusion of a record of the priestly succession during the wilderness period, while Moses was still Israel's leader.

Volume 1 of the Anchor Bible commentary on Numbers concludes at this point. In chaps. 21–36, to be covered in volume 2, the priestly school completed its historiographic record, as well as seeing to it that its institutional agenda was fully represented in Torah literature.

b. Further Priestly Content in Numbers 25–36. The next encounter with priestly material comes in Num 25:6–15, an addendum to the JE record of the incident of Israelite paganism at Baal Peor. In a spirit blatantly priestly, the text records that Phineas, Eleazar's son, rose to the occasion and killed the two leading offenders. One was a chieftain of Simeon and the other, the daughter of a Midianite chieftain. Together they had made a public spectacle of pagan behavior. Again, in the spirit of the priestly tradition, God punished the Israelites with a plague, finally stemmed only by Phineas's intervention.

These priestly narratives attribute religious zeal to the successors of Aaron. They also set the stage for the priestly tradition of a Midianite war, first mentioned in the ensuing passage, Num 25:16–18, and later recounted in chap. 31. The role of the Midianite war in the historiography of Numbers will be discussed in section D.6, below.

Numbers 26–31 are entirely of priestly authorship, and we do not encounter further JE material until chap. 32, in the narrative account of the Transjordan settlement. As was true with respect to the positioning of priestly texts in earlier sections of Numbers, so too, in the latter part of the book, we cannot fully explain their sequence. Chapter 26 presents the second census, registering the new generation. This census is formulated differently from the earlier record preserved in chap. 1, and it makes occasional references to intervening events. The census record concludes in 26:64–65 with a significant statement to the effect that no one, save Caleb and Joshua, remained alive of the Exodus generation, in fulfillment of God's decree.

Numbers 27 attends to two essentially unrelated, yet important, subjects in the priestly agenda: inheritance law and the succession of Joshua to Moses' role as leader of the Israelites. The complaint of Zelophehad's daughters at being potentially disinherited occasions a brief code of estate law, incorporating significant revisions of customary practice. When a man left no sons, his daughters would henceforth inherit his estate. This provision was subsequently qualified in chap. 36, almost as an afterthought: an heiress under the provisions of chap. 27 would qualify only if she married a man from her own tribe, as the daughters of Zelophehad eventually did. This restriction was clearly intended to prevent loss of landed estates by any of the Israelite tribes, or clans, which would happen were the daughter of one tribe to marry a man from another, who would ultimately hand the estate down to his own son.

The second part of chap. 27 (vv 12–23) records the transfer of leadership from Moses to Joshua by divine decree. The ritual empowering Joshua included both the laying on of hands and a public charge by Moses. We are also informed, somewhat indirectly, of Eleazar's appointment to oracular functions involving the Urim and Tummim. Moses is afforded a distant view of the Promised Land before his death.

Numbers 28–29 preserve an important liturgical calendar, covering the entire year and listing the prescribed sacrifices to be presented in the public cult. Its provisions are to be viewed against the background of Leviticus 23, an earlier calendar of festivals, to which a Sabbath law had been added. The code of Numbers 28–29 is more complete and detailed than Leviticus 23, in prescribing all of the sacrificial components of public worship on a daily, weekly, monthly, and seasonal schedule. It undoubtedly represents a subsequent stage in the formulation of temple activity, if not a later stage in actual praxis.

The remaining chapters of Numbers (30–36) exhibit a mixed agenda. As already noted, the only JE material is to be found in chap. 32. Chapter 30 presents a priestly law governing vows. It was applicable to Israelite daughters at various stages of their personal lives, while resident in their fathers' houses and after marriage. The point of law operative throughout chap. 30 is that an adult Israelite male, either father or husband, must deal responsibly with obligations incurred by the women of his family. Women did not enjoy legal autonomy.

Numbers 31 may be regarded as a priestly response to the laws of war stated in Deut 20:1–21:14 and to the laws of the king in Deut 17:13–20, which also deal with the conduct of war. Logically, the priestly writers turned their attention to a vested interest, the perquisites of the clergy. In effect, chap. 31 legislates temple income from the spoils of war, a reflection of known royal policies. Kings customarily dedicated spoils of war to temples under their sponsorship. The immediate historiographic trigger for the priestly laws of chap. 31 is the enmity against Midian expressed in the Balaam pericope, where priestly writers allied Midian with Moab against Israel (Num 22:4, 7), and in the Baal Peor incident, which had involved only Moabites in the JE version, but which now involved Midianites introduced by P (Num 25:6–9). The hostility against Midian is epitomized by the telling statement in Num 31:9 that the Israelites made certain to kill not only the kings of Midian, but Balaam son of Beor as well.

In Numbers 32, P expands the JE material relevant to the Israelite settlements of Transjordan and, in part, reworks it. The agreement that is struck with the tribes of Reuben and Gad, and with the Machirite clan affiliated with Manasseh, is spelled out legalistically, providing for all contingencies by formulating the agreement in the terms of a vow. The priestly writers, who liked to think in neat units, registered the Machirite clan as representing half of the tribe of Manasseh. There are other giveaways of priestly tendencies in chap. 32, but also valuable geographical information about Transjordan provided by priestly writers.

After Numbers 32 we find only priestly materials, although priestly writers may have availed themselves of independent sources in composing the remainder of Numbers in its final form. Thus, chap. 33 provides a detailed itinerary of the Israelite journeys from Egypt to the Plains of Moab. This itinerary, which lists many unidentified locations alongside known toponyms, correlates in significant respects with what we know from other priestly sources and is helpful in elaborating the projection of the wilderness period underlying the priestly historiography. Nevertheless, the route listed from

Num 33:40–49 apparently went through Edom and Moab, thereby contradicting all that is said in Numbers and Deuteronomy about the refusal of the Transjordanian peoples to allow the Israelites passage through their territories. Num 33:40–59 may preserve an alternative tradition on the Transjordanian route taken by the Israelites.

Numbers 34 thereupon outlines the geographic limits of the Promised Land, Canaan, and prescribes how it was to be allotted to the twelve tribes, under priestly authority. The governing principle was to be the respective population of each tribe, which would determine its territorial needs. Once again, we have in chap. 34 a priestly text of relatively late origin that, nonetheless, preserves valuable geographical information, albeit reflecting later periods of history. Canaan, as the land to be granted to the Israelites, is delimited as extending in the south from Wadi-el-Arish *(Naḥal Miṣrayîm)* to the southern edge of the Dead Sea; in the north, from the Mediterranean, via Lebo of Hamath (cf. Num 13:21), to a point near the Golan, perhaps Baneas; on the east, all the way down along the Sea of Galilee and the Jordan River to the Dead Sea. It has long been recognized that these borders are remarkably similar to those negotiated in the Egyptian-Hittite treaty enacted following the battle of Kedesh on the Orontes, ca. 1280 B.C.E. (Aharoni 1979: 39, map 45; 41, map 51).

Numbers 35 designates forty-eight localities as levitical towns. We find legal references to such entities in Lev 25:33–34. Because these towns included the so-called "cities of asylum" legislated in Deuteronomy (Deut 4:41–43, 19:1–13), the stage was set for an important code of law on the subject of homicide. It is here that we have an explicit differentiation between what we would term manslaughter and intentional murder. Further, chap. 35 spells out the system of asylum and provides for an amnesty at the death of the incumbent high priest, a provision that reveals the priestly provenance of the chapter. Those who had sought refuge in cities of asylum are to be released with immunity at the death of the high priest, and blood redeemers would thereafter be forbidden to pursue them in retaliation.

As explained above, Numbers 36 is an addendum to 27:1–11, imposing restrictions on the right of daughters to inherit their fathers' estates and insisting on tribal endogamy.

c. Numbers in Final Form. The book of Numbers, as restructured by the priestly writers, focuses our attention on the cultic and religious policies of the priestly school in ancient Israel. In its historiography, P establishes the sole legitimacy of the Aaronide priesthood within the tribe of Levi and legislates the functions of the Levites as a separate corps of temple servitors relegated to nonsacral functions. P also lays the foundation for the leadership role of Joshua son of Nun who, in the JE tradition, is merely regarded as Moses' assistant or attendant. In P's historiography, Joshua emerges as a tribal chieftain and as the heir apparent, ultimately ordained by Moses to carry on after his death as leader of the Israelites. He will lead the Israelite conquest of Canaan. In presenting Joshua as a leader, the priestly writers may have taken their cue from the Deuteronomist (Deut 1:38, 3:21, 28).

B. The Literary Character of Numbers

The source-critical orientation that has governed the discussion of content will also inform the forthcoming analysis of the diverse genres represented in the book of Numbers. Some genres are common to the two main contributors to Numbers, JE and P. Nonetheless, significant features of style and formulation distinguish the two textual sources from each other, and these differences often affect our understanding of a particular genre when it is present in both sources. Thus, the priestly narratives of Numbers hardly resemble the narratives of the JE source. The source-critical method is, therefore, instructive even for literary analysis. The generic diversity of Numbers, when considered together with its varied sources, compounds the problem of establishing its coherence and makes of Numbers the most loosely organized of all the Torah books.

1. The Nonpriestly Materials

The nonpriestly sections of Numbers consist of two genres: poetry and narrative historiography. The poetry is concentrated in chaps. 21–24, but two verses appear elsewhere in 10:35–36. They are called the Song of the Ark: an invocation recited or sung when the Ark set out on the march and when it came to rest. Some would consider the characterization of Moses as a prophet, in 12:6–8, to be a form of poetry (see the Notes on those verses). The literary provenance of the Song of the Ark is the biblical epic tradition, as is suggested by the paraphrase of the first verse of the song in Ps 68:2. The priestly benediction cited in Num 6:22–27 is also to be regarded as poetic, and will be discussed as an aspect of priestly literature. The fairly extensive poetic passages in Numbers 21–24 are cited from various sources, as their captions indicate. They are eloquent examples of early biblical poetry.

All the rest of the textual material in Numbers that is attributable to JE may be classified as historiographic, in that it relates events and describes situations in the manner of the narrative and the chronicle.

a. Biblical Poetry. The poetic selections of Numbers cannot be appreciated apart from the narratives within which they are presented. Basic to understanding the literary function of the poetic selections preserved in the book is the technique of the historiographers who incorporated them in their narratives. It is quite clear that the poetic selections in chaps. 21–24 are of separate authorship. In diachronic perspective, it is further likely that the several poems in chap. 21, and the four principal orations of Balaam in chaps. 23–24, existed before the historiographic narratives that now encompass them. In contrast, the three brief orations in 24:20–24 were probably appended to the four major poems. They logically originated in separate collections, which may in themselves have been quite ancient.

In Numbers 21, the independent derivations of the poetic selections are indicated by the captions used in citing them. Thus, in 21:14, a fragment of a poem is attributed to *sēper milḥamôt YHWH* 'The Record of the Wars of YHWH', and 21:17 refers to a known poem entitled *ʿalî beʾēr* 'Rise up, o spring'. Farther on, in 21:27, we read of the *môšelîm* 'bards' who contributed a ballad that celebrates an Amorite victory over the Moabites. These poetic selections were introduced by the JE narrator as evidence for the reliability of the historiographic record. Their function is conveyed by the explanatory phrase *ʿal kēn* 'On this matter' (21:14, 27). This method of citation refers the reader directly to an epic source, cited as proof of what has been related in the narrative (Levine 1989a: 202).

The Balaam pericope, encompassing Numbers 22–24, contains four major poems and several additional brief orations, likewise attributed to Balaam. All four of the Balaam orations probably derive from the same archive, which would account for the distinctive poetic diction that informs all of them. Not only are these poems relatively old, by biblical standards, but it has been suggested here that they are of Transjordanian authorship. This subsource of E has been labeled T. There is, therefore, a synchronic regional factor to be taken into account in their interpretation, not merely the acknowledged diachronic factor, which is highlighted by early Hebrew usage and syntax.

That the literary creativity of the Israelites in Gilead should have found its way into the Hebrew Bible is only to be expected. Archaeologists have discovered epic texts at Deir ʿAlla, in the Jordan Valley, in what was known in the early biblical period as the Valley of Sukkoth, near the Jabbok-Zerqa River. These texts, relating the exploits of one Balaam son of Beor, are changing our perceptions regarding the level of contemporary culture in Transjordan. The Deir ʿAlla texts, which date from about the middle of the eighth century B.C.E., are written in a regional dialect of Canaanite that exhibits certain Aramaic features. They are literary creations of impressive quality. Assuming that the Balaam texts at Deir ʿAlla represent Transjordanian creativity and were not imported from Syria, as some had thought to be the case, it is plausible that the Balaam orations were composed in Transjordan. The prominence of the Syro-Canaanite deity El in the Deir ʿAlla texts points scholars in the direction of additional biblical texts that might also have been part of the El repertoire (Levine 1981; 1985b; 1991).

The brief orations about neighboring peoples appended to the four major poems (Num 24:20–24) serve to raise Balaam to the status of an international prophet. The same method is apparent in the major prophetic books, where similar types of "oracles against the nations" were inserted and attributed to Isaiah and Jeremiah, for instance. As would be expected, these shorter orations are unrelated in content to the prose narratives of Numbers 22–24.

The Balaam orations, as well as the appended poems, all of which occur in Numbers 23–24, attest an unusual number of hapax legomena, words and forms that are unique in the Hebrew Bible. These poems are composed in a laconic, staccato style, producing verses that say a lot in a few words, and in which finite verbs are expressed in the simple tenses. In fact, in all four orations there is not a single instance of *waw*-conversive, which is the primary feature of the so-called narrative tenses. There is also a high incidence of nominal verses. These syntactic patterns are the earmarks of early Hebrew poetry (Levine 1978: 155–160).

b. Narrative Historiography. We may now turn to an analysis of the JE narratives in Numbers, whose textual limits have been delineated earlier (section A.5, above). The discussion presented here is largely restricted to literary analysis and to such considerations as theme, style, and diction.

Beginning in Num 10:29–36, we observe that the JE narrators employ the familiar converted tenses in succession, avoiding monotony by interspersing circumstantial clauses and other syntactic variations in the ongoing narrative. Most interesting in this connection is the role of dialogue, more precisely, the manner in which speech is introduced within historical narratives. One notes in dialogue a much greater reliance on simple tenses and participles, rather than on the converted tenses so characteristic of historiographic narrative. We also encounter asides, or explanatory digressions, in which syntax is markedly altered.

Several examples will make the point. In Num 11:4b–9 we read how the people felt about the manna. This unpleasant report is followed by a parenthetical digression describing the manna and telling how it was harvested. There is not a single converted verbal form in this entire passage. Further on, in Num 11:11–15, we encounter a complaint that Moses addressed to God, yet another instance of speech in which no converted tenses occur subsequent to the initial narrative form, *wayy'ômer* 'He said'. Another noteworthy passage, in terms of style, is Aaron's plea to Moses in Num 12:11–12, and Moses' response to it in v 13. The negative-imperative *'al nāʾ* 'Pray, do not!' is thrice repeated, thereby indicating the capacity of biblical historiographers to express speech artistically and revealing their penchant for liturgical forms.

Notwithstanding the complex braiding of narratives from JE and P that is evident in Numbers 13–14, it is possible to observe once again how speech adds interest to what otherwise would be a rather dull narrative. Moses' charge to the spies (13:17b–20) is punctuated by successive rhetorical questions, each introduced by *mah* 'What?' and followed by a conditional formula: interrogative *heh* + X, . . . *'im* Y: 'Is it X or is it Y?'—for example, *haṭôbāh hîʾ ʾim rāʿāh* 'Is it beautiful or unpleasant?' We encounter a series of no less than five rhetorical inquiries of this type, referring variously to the land, the people, and the towns of Canaan:

> He charged them, "Proceed northward through the Negeb, and make your ascent into the mountains. Observe the land: what is its condition? And the people inhabiting it: are they strong or feeble, few or numerous? And what of the land they inhabit: is it bountiful or lacking? And what of the towns where they dwell: are they built as unwalled settlements or as fortified towns? And how is the land: is it rich in produce or lean? Is it wooded or not?"

Perhaps the most dramatic passage in the JE narratives is preserved in Num 12:6–8, where we have a speech by YHWH that may qualify as poetry, or as what some have called "heightened prose." The passage reads as follows:

> If there should be a prophet of yours,
> [who is] of YHWH,
> In a vision would I make myself known to him;
> In a dream would I speak to him.
> Not so my servant, Moses!
> Of all my household
> He is most trusted.
> Mouth to mouth I speak to him;
> In clear view, not in riddles.
> He looks upon the likeness of YHWH.

I have already spoken of the poetic selections in Numbers 21. Actually, this chapter contains a remarkable assemblage of literary components. At the same time, the narrator has set out to record a most important phase in the Israelite settlement of Transjordan. Topically, chap. 21 covers the Israelites' advance all the way from the Red Sea to the Jordan River, preparatory to their entry into Canaan. It is replete with precise geographical indicators and offers historical explanations for one situation or another. As a result, this chapter carries an exceptionally heavy historiographic load within the JE narratives of Numbers, and may have been condensed by priestly writers.

Despite all of the historiographic detail presented, there was still space in Numbers 21 to relate an episode that dramatized God's providence over Israel, even in moments of wrath. Although God punished the people with pernicious snakebites in an angry reaction to their grumblings, he nevertheless provided Moses an effective method for their cure.

Moving ahead of the text, we note that the Baal Peor incident (Num 25:1–5, in the JE version) provides an anticlimax to the glory of the Israelite victories celebrated in Numbers 21. The report in 25:1–5 is exceedingly terse and expresses the theme of *haron* 'wrath'. Usage of the verb *hôqaʿ* 'to impale', describing the punishment of the offenders, links this account to an incident recounted in 2 Samuel 21. There we read of the impalement of seven descendants of Saul, whose execution was in retribution for Saul's earlier crime in violating the treaty with the Gibeonites by putting some of them to death.

One of the questions that has occupied scholars with respect to the Balaam pericope is the relation of the overall narrative to the story of Balaam's jenny (Num 22:22b–35a; cf. Rofé 1979: 40–45). This tale presupposes a different sequence of events from the one projected in the rest of the pericope, and it is generally recognized that it derives from a separate source. The episode of the jenny was included in order to epitomize God's authority over Balaam. In the words of the tale, it was an angel of YHWH who communicated with Balaam, not YHWH himself. The role of the angel associates this tale with a series of similar stories in Judges, Samuel, and Kings, all of which portray angelic manifestations to "men of God" and to other charismatic leaders.

For the rest, the JE narrators of the Balaam pericope verbalize, in a somewhat more doctrinaire manner, the underlying phenomenology of Balaam's acts and the source of his powers. Ultimately, the E source is represented most prominently in these narratives, as we would expect, for Gilead and other areas of Transjordan were ruled by the northern kingdom of Israel over a long period.

2. The Priestly Materials

Numbers preserves a wide variety of priestly texts, ranging from narratives to several descriptions of ritual celebrations associated with important events in the religious history of Israel. Most of all, the priestly sections of Numbers preserve an abundance of ritual prescriptions and priestly legislation. There is probably one instance of liturgical poetry, namely, the priestly benediction preserved in Num 6:24–26. The preceding types of texts contrast with a significant group of priestly documents, which may be classified as administrative. These texts include census records, lists of tribal leaders, and detailed accountings of donations to the Tabernacle.

The proper reading of priestly texts, even of historiographic narratives, involves decoding technical terms and ritual formulas. In fact, we refer to the style of priestly law and ritual as "formulaic."

a. Priests as Poets. Interpretation of the priestly benediction (Num 6:24–26) has been advanced by the recent discovery, in 1986, of a version of the same blessing inscribed on silver amulets. These items of jewelry had been buried in caves together with the dead in the environs of Jerusalem, at a site now known as Keteph Hinnom (Barkai 1989: 37–76; Haran 1989: 77–89).

The priestly benediction is characterized by ascending verse length and by the repetition of primary themes, amplified by secondary themes. The absence of parallelism has led some scholars, such as M. Haran, to regard the benediction as liturgical, but not poetic. Others, most notably D. N. Freedman, espouse a definition of poetry broad enough to permit the inclusion of the priestly benediction, and this view has much to recommend it (Freedman 1975: 35–47).

b. Priests as Historiographers. The historiography of the priestly writers has been discussed earlier in this introduction, in reviewing how priestly writers amplified and modulated the JE narratives they had before them. Attention has also been paid to the function of priestly narratives as a means of introducing new themes of importance in the priestly agenda. Here, the intent is to clarify the literary character of the priestly narratives in Numbers, showing how they differ in style, vocabulary, and composition from their counterparts in the JE corpus. It would be well to examine several substantial sections of priestly narrative, noting their distinctive features.

We return to Numbers 13–14, which earlier served as an example of JE narrative. In 14:26–38 a continuous priestly narrative is preserved. It utilizes many of the familiar terms and formulas characteristic of priestly law, ritual, and administrative recording. Thus the Israelites comprise an *ʿēdāh* 'community' and are arrayed by *pequddîm* 'musters', manned by male Israelites *mibben ʿeśrîm šānāh wāmaʿalāh* 'twenty years of age and above' (Num 14:29).

In Numbers 16, vv 16–24 record a cultic ordeal whose orchestration is described by such technical terms as *lipnê YHWH* 'in the presence of YHWH' and *kebôd YHWH* 'the glorious presence of YHWH', and by verbs such as *hiqrîb* 'to offer, present'. In effect, we are reading the story of a cultic event told by priests.

One need only compare the priestly narratives in Numbers 13–14 and in chaps. 16–17 with the detailed prescriptions of chaps. 3–4 or with the census of chap. 1 to realize to what extent priestly narrative style is punctuated by the same terms and formulas that inform administrative and ritual texts. This affinity is somewhat less apparent in the priestly narratives of Genesis and Exodus than it is in Numbers.

An unusual etiological narrative is presented in Num 20:1–13 and 22–29. In 20:5 a Deuteronomic cliché that also appears in Deut 8:7–9, characterizing Canaan as bountiful and productive, as a land yielding specific grains and fruits, was paraphrased by the priestly writers. Here, the characterization is expressed with irony and is applied to the desolate Wilderness of Zin by the disgruntled Israelites. They protest that this arid area lacked seed, fig trees, grapevines, and pomegranates, the very crops and fruits attributed to Canaan!

That Moses worked wonders in the wilderness is hardly a notion monopolized by any single documentary source. One need only compare Num 21:8–10, part of a JE passage, where we read that Moses deals with serpent bites and fashions a bronze serpent, to the priestly narrative in Num 20:7–11, where he brings out water from a rock.

Num 20:22–29 present a brief narrative recording the death of Aaron. Once again, we encounter the theme of obedience to divine command so basic to the priestly ideology, and expressed by the formula *ka'ăšer ṣiwwāh YHWH 'et Môšeh* 'as YHWH commanded Moses' (Num 20:27). To this is added an atmosphere of piety: the people mourned Aaron for thirty days.

Num 25:6–19 depict a crisis, a lapse into pagan worship initially reported by JE in the preceding verses (1–5). In elaborating the Baal Peor incident, the priestly writers introduce two relevant subjects from their agenda: after introducing the Midianites as enemies to be attacked and destroyed, P proceeds to endorse the Aaronide succession, from Aaron to his son Eleazar. Phineas son of Eleazar is made the hero of the Baal Peor episode, which now involves Midianites along with Moabites. With religious zeal, Phineas rises up in the congregation to punish a leading Israelite and a leading Midianite who had offended against God, and thereby demonstrates the worthiness of Aaron's line to succeed to the office of the high priesthood. In this way, P confirms the line of succession within the high priesthood of Aaron, which has now reached the third generation. At the same time, this passage sets the stage for the Midianite war, to be recounted in Numbers 31.

In terms of diction, Num 25:6–19 exhibit a plethora of priestly locutions and formulas. The theme of *berît* 'covenant' predominates in such combinations as *berît kehunnat 'ôlām* 'the covenant promise of an everlasting priesthood' or *berît šālôm* 'a covenant of alliance'. There is also reference to *bêt 'āb* 'patriarchal "house" ' and the verb *kipper* 'to expiate', so typical of priestly ritual, is used in a rather unusual context. All of these terms occur in a narrative.

c. Law and Narrative: Mutual Reinforcement. A basic pattern in the priestly sections of Numbers is the introduction of a novel law through the medium of a story. In the story, a specific situation is presented as prompting the necessity, or as lending the justification, for the presented legislation. There were two salient instances of this pattern in Leviticus: in chap. 10, a law forbidding priests to imbibe intoxicants prior to officiating in the cult is introduced by a horrendous story telling of improper conduct by two of Aaron's sons. In a similar manner, a new law governing blasphemy is introduced in Lev 24:10–23 by a report of an actual case of blasphemy (Levine 1989b: 58–63, 166–168).

In Numbers, this pattern seems to be even more evident. Num 9:1–14 pursue an interesting sequence: vv 1–5 relate that in the second year after the Exodus, the Israelites were commanded to observe the Pesaḥ sacrifice at the appointed time. The Israelites obediently complied, and performed the commemorative sacrifice. Thereupon, vv 6–8 report the complaint of some Israelites who were in a state of ritual impurity at the scheduled time of the sacrifice, and who resented being denied the right to participate. Verses 9–14 then present a novel law, providing for a deferred Pesaḥ in the second month. The deferral was specifically intended for those who were impure during the first month, or who were too distant from the Sanctuary to participate at the appointed time.

Chapters 15, 27, 31, 32, and 36 of Numbers provide even more examples of the pattern under discussion. In Num 15:32–36 there is a brief tale about an Israelite discovered gathering wood on the Sabbath (vv 32–34), which is immediately followed by a law condemning such violators to death (vv 35–36). Chapter 27 opens with a scene set in Moses' presence. The daughters of an Israelite named Zelophehad protested their exclusion from their father's estate. Zelophehad had died leaving no male heirs, and we are to presume that daughters, prior to the registering of this novel legislation, had not been acceptable as legal heirs. We are therefore informed to the contrary in the ensuing statement of law. Furthermore, chap. 36, apparently a brief addendum to the book, records a complaint by some tribal leaders who feared that allowing daughters to inherit their fathers' estates might result in major shifts of land from tribe to tribe. This was a consequence surely to be avoided, and we consequently read a statement of law requiring endogamous marriages by inheriting daughters, like those of the deceased Zelophehad.

Numbers 32, which contains both JE and P materials, also exhibits the process by which narratives serve to introduce legislation. In the probable JE portions of the chapter, of which vv 16–19 are surely a part, the Reubenites and Gadites offer to fight along with the other Israelite tribes in the conquest of Canaan, west of the Jordan, without being specifically ordered to do so. They insist only on the right to settle thereafter in Gilead and Transjordan. In the priestly version, which occupies most of the rest of chap. 32, the same commitment had to be exacted by Moses, pursuant to divine command. The granting of land in Transjordan for settlement was accompanied by binding conditions, spelled out in legalistic formulas. It seems to be particularly important in the priestly view of things that behavior be determined by divine commands and that events be understood to occur as they do and when they do because God had specifically commanded them.

Numbers 31 has been left for last. Although it narrates a battle, it does so in a mixed literary medium, bordering on legal formulation. It exemplifies the pattern under discussion very clearly: a battle narrative occasions a statement of law governing the spoils of war.

Before leaving the subject of the priestly narratives in Numbers, I must call attention to several stylistic features of considerable interest. In Num 16:22 we find the divine epithet *'el 'elôhê hārûḥôt lekol bāśār* 'Lord, God of the spirits of all flesh', elsewhere attested only in Num 27:16, where the Tetragrammaton, *YHWH*, is employed instead of *'el*. In both instances the immediate context is one of prayer, and in both, the danger of death was imminent.

In Num 17:23 we find a proverbial cliché, something unusual in priestly narrative:

wayyôṣēʾ peraḥ
wayyāṣēṣ ṣîṣ
wayyigmôl šeqēdîm

It gave forth sprouts,
Produced blossoms,
Bore almonds.

Partial elements of this rare cliché are expressed in Isa 18:5; 40:6–8; Ps 103:15; and Job 14:9. The textual distribution of the components of the cliché reveals the links existing between priestly writings and the proverbial repertoire of biblical prophecy and wisdom.

d. Chiasm and Its Limits. There has been considerable interest of late in the subject of chiasm, when it can be identified in prose or in legal formulations. The presence of chiasm in nonpoetic texts is hardly limited to priestly literature, but it is perhaps most evident in it. A good example is Num 14:2, a priestly passage:

"If only we had died—in the land of Egypt;
In this wilderness—if only we had died!"

An example of chiasm occurring in a legal text occurs in Num 30:15, a statement on the subject of vows:

If her husband is silent to her from one day to the next—he has confirmed all of the vows and obligations she had assumed.

He has confirmed them—because he remained silent to her on the day he had heard.

These examples have been cited by Milgrom (1989: xxii–xxix), and similar examples of chiasm, in such notable priestly compositions as Genesis 1, have been analyzed by David Howlett (1993). The literary implications of the use of chiasm in prose narratives and in legal formulations are far reaching, though some of the recent identifications of chiasm by biblical scholars exaggerate its applicability. Chiasm is a feature best restricted to small textual units. It enhances style and focuses the attention of the reader through the reinforcement that comes with repetition, and by shifting the order of the discrete components that comprise a complete statement. To characterize the sequential relationship of large textual units, of complete chapters or whole narratives, as chiasm is a questionable application of this feature.

e. Formulaic Texts: Ritual and Administration. There remain several other types of priestly texts in Numbers that warrant special attention. These include descriptive ritual texts, census lists, temple records, and actual prescriptions of ritual and law.

There is a significant distinction to be drawn between "descriptive" and "prescriptive" ritual texts. It is reasonable to posit, based on comparative evidence from the ancient Near East, that ritual prescriptions were adapted from descriptions, originally composed in the form of temple records. Temple records became progressively more narrative in form, and at a later stage, modal forms of the key verbs began to appear in them, thereby transforming a description of a cultic event into an obligatory set of procedures.

We turn first to Num 8:5–22, a record of the dedication of the Levites to the service of the Tabernacle. The major part of this record is formulated as a prescription, conveying divine commands. Only vv 20–22 are formulated descriptively, using narrative verbal forms that express compliance with those commands. It is instructive to show how this passage, as a record, differs from the record of the consecration of the Aaronide priests in Leviticus 8, on which it is undoubtedly modeled. In Leviticus 8, the major part of the record is formulated descriptively, as we read how Moses performed a complex series of religious rites on that occasion. Actually, Numbers 8 more closely resembles Exod 29:1–33, a parallel record of the investiture of the Aaronide priests probably based on Leviticus 8.

We observe, therefore, how a primary description of the initiation of the Aaronide priesthood (Leviticus 8) generated a secondary prescriptive account of the same occasion (Exod 29:1–33) and, in addition, provided the model for a mirror record of the dedication of the Levites, largely prescriptive in its formulation (Num 8:5–22; cf. Levine 1965a: 307–318).

In Num 8:5–22 we also note the consistent downgrading of the terms of status applicable to the Levites, as compared with Leviticus 8 in its definition of the priestly status. Such differentiation was intended to punctuate the subordinate status of the Levites: they are not consecrated, but only dedicated; they do not officiate, they only serve.

Numbers 7 is of paramount importance for the proper analysis of all administrative records in the Hebrew Bible. It is a remarkable adaptation of an originally tabular temple record. This type of ancient Near Eastern document is illustrated in the commentary.

In substance, Numbers 7 records the donations of the twelve tribal chieftains to the Tabernacle on the occasion of its dedication. Verses 1–3 are formulated descriptively, a feature quite unusual in priestly records, which usually open with a prescriptive introduction and then proceed to describe what is happening. It appears that Num 7:4–9 were interpolated so as to convey an added requirement deriving from the levitical assignments of chaps. 3–4. The remainder of Numbers 7 (vv 10–88) is based on a temple record and is perhaps the most archival of all biblical texts of this type. It is almost completely devoid of narrative elements, which vanish entirely after the first few entries. Because it was preserved in a form so close to its original composition, Numbers 7 brings us into touch with the accounting methods in use during the biblical period.

Closest in form to Numbers 7 are the census lists of chaps. 1 and 26, which, nevertheless, differ from each other in certain respects. In chap. 1, prominence is given to the tribal chieftains *(neśîʾîm)*, who are, in contrast, conspicuously absent from chap. 26. Instead, chap. 26 lists the "clans" *(mišpāḥôt)*, the subdivisions of each tribe, by name. The levitical assignments of chaps. 3–4 carry these classifications even farther, to the patriarchal "houses" (the Hebrew term is *bêt ʾāb)* that constituted each clan.

The liturgical calendar presented in Numbers 28–29 warrants special attention because of its considerable religious significance. It was undoubtedly composed subsequent to Leviticus 23, also a liturgical calendar. Numbers 28–29 specify all of the components of the composite rituals to be performed in the public cult, providing for daily worship as well as for the New Moons and Sabbaths, and for the annual festivals, including even the offerings for each day of the Sukkoth festival. Leviticus 23 lacks much of this detail, most probably because it represents an earlier stage in the development of Israelite religion (Levine 1989b: 153–164, 261–268).

In interpreting the liturgical calendar of Numbers 28–29 we are once again warranted in projecting an editorial process whereby temple records that described public rituals were adapted and reformulated as prescriptions. This was done so as to express a major principle of the priestly ideology: all of the details of the cult were directly communicated by God to Moses in the wilderness period, during the formative stage of Israel's history. The transformation of temple records into ritual codes of law illustrates how form responds to ideology, and how customary practices assume the authority of law and commandment.

f. The Formulation of Ritual Law. In priestly law the casuistic formulation, which expresses a condition or circumstance, is clearly favored, and this tendency is especially evident in the content of Numbers. We encounter legal statements that begin with *'îš kî* 'a person if—' (or *nepeš kî, 'ādām kî*), all with essentially the same meaning. Thus Num 27:8b: *'îš kî yāmût ûbēn 'ên lô*, literally, "A man if he dies, having no son—." In addition to its conditional formulation, this statement also exemplifies a syntactic pattern wherein the subject precedes the conditional particle. In legal statements that emanate from non-priestly sources, the syntax is usually different: conditional + verb + subject. Compare Deut 22:13: *kî yiqqaḥ 'îs 'iššāh* 'If a man took a wife'.

There are many other observable differences in formulation between priestly and nonpriestly laws, and they will be duly noted in the NOTES. Similarly distinctive is the priestly legal vocabulary, which freely utilizes the known legal terminology of the other Torah sources, but registers its own mark by terminology distinctive to the priestly school.

Some of these features have already been mentioned in earlier discussion, where the prominence of legal diction in priestly narratives was noted. Here, we may add a term of considerable institutional importance, *'aḥuzzāh* 'acquired land', which is distinctive to the priestly school and to writers under its influence. The Deuteronomist favored the term *yeřûšāh* 'estate, homestead' for classifying land under Israelite ownership, whereas earlier sources, both within and outside Torah literature, favored *naḥalāh* 'land grant, patrimony' (Levine 1983: 69–82).

What we observe in the formulation of priestly legislation in Numbers is the tendency of priestly writers to use distinct terms of reference as though they were synonymous. Thus they often place such terms in attribution to each other, instead of allowing them to express their separate histories and different meanings. Priestly writers also appropriate earlier, nonpriestly terms in their effort to lend an aura of antiquity to their legislation. A classic example comes from the law of inheritance. In Num 27:7 we read, *nātôn tittēn lāhem 'aḥuzzat naḥalāh* 'You shall surely grant them an estate as acquired land'. Usage of the term *'aḥuzzāh* definitely assigns this statement to the priestly source, whereas usage of the older term *naḥalāh* does not contradict this source-critical assignment. One reading this statement would assume that *'aḥuzzāh* modifies *naḥalāh*, whereas a knowledge of the origins of each of these terms makes one aware of how different their respective meanings are.

The point to be made about priestly ritual texts is that their terms of reference are encoded. It would be instructive to analyze a sample passage in order to illustrate how much must be known about each of the technical terms used in it before it can be understood in depth. I have chosen Num 15:3 for this purpose:

> *wa'ăśîtem 'iššeh leYHWH 'ôlāh 'ô zebaḥ lepallē' neder 'ô binedābāh 'ô bemô'adêkem la'aśôt rēaḥ niḥôaḥ leYHWH min habbāqār 'ô min haṣṣô'n*

> and [you] perform a sacrifice by fire to YHWH, consisting of a burnt offering or a sacred feast, for the purpose of setting aside a votive, or as a voluntary offering, or on the occasion of your festivals—producing a pleasing aroma for YHWH, from the herd or from the flocks.

The following issues should be addressed in commenting on this single verse:

(1) It must be explained that the verb *ʿāśāh* takes on a specialized nuance in the context of ritual, where it means "to perform a rite, to celebrate."

(2) The following terminology must be defined, both etymologically and functionally: (a) the term *ʾiššeh* as it relates to *ʾēš* 'fire'; (b) the referent of the term *ʿôlāh* must be identified: is it the fire that "ascends" heavenward, or is it the sacrifice "put atop" the altar, or is it the officiant who "ascends" in the course of offering it? (c) the Hebrew term *zebaḥ* is cognate with Akkadian *zību* 'a meal, offering of food': how does this affect our understanding of the related Hebrew and West Semitic verbal forms? and (d) the terms *neder* and *nedābāh* both pertain to the practice of individual religion in ancient Israel and require a study of the biblical votive system.

(3) The precise sense of infinitival *lepallēʾ* requires analysis. It seems to mean "to separate, set apart," and is sometimes spelled *lepallēh*, with final *heh*.

(4) The term *môʿēd* is basic to biblical religion. What is its underlying concept?

(5) What does *rēaḥ niḥôaḥ* 'pleasing aroma' tell us about the phenomenology of burnt offerings in biblical religion?

C. Texts, Versions, Translations, and Commentaries

Both the translation and the commentary presented here are based on the Masoretic Hebrew text of Numbers. Specifically, this author used Leningrad Codex B 19A, completed in 1009 C.E. and copied from a text written by Aaron ben Moses ben Asher. Allowance has been made for occasional emendations. Such suggested textual changes are based either on the testimony of ancient Hebrew versions and early translations, or on the acumen of modern critical scholars.

This method is preferable to generating an eclectic Hebrew text, one that has never existed in reality. It is more constructive initially to endorse the Masoretic text, and then deal in the commentary with the specific problems it presents.

The five books of the Torah held greater authority in the ancient Synagogue than did the other two sections of the tripartite canon. The theological postulations that informed ancient Jewry brought it about that manuscripts of the books of the Torah were more carefully curated in late antiquity, and during the early Middle Ages, than were other biblical books, prophetic and hagiographic. Within the Torah books themselves the most significant textual problems emerge in the poetic selections and, next to them, in narrative. This is not meant as a statistical assessment, but as an interpretation of the relative significance of the attested variants. The texts of laws and rituals were most closely monitored, for obvious reasons.

1. The Character of Masoretic Texts

The term "Masoretic" is hardly precise, nor can it be adequately defined (Orlinsky 1966). It customarily designates a collated corpus of ancient copies of the Hebrew Bible. The consonantal, or orthographic, content of existing copies—that is to say, the wording of the texts and the spelling of the words—was meticulously checked. As part of the same process, the pointing, or vocalization, of the texts was collated. It must be remembered that in Semitic languages written alphabetically, as is true of Hebrew, vocalization often determines meaning.

Ancient and medieval Masoretes made progressive textual determinations in the process of establishing a uniform text that would be regarded as authoritative by all Jewish communities. With respect to the Torah, in particular, they sought to standardize the wording of the text, as well as to decide what, precisely, was represented vocalically and morphologically by the accepted consonantal readings. In absolute terms, this process has never been completed.

My specific concern here is to arrive at an educated approximation of what might have been the earliest canonical Hebrew text of Numbers. This effort has been abetted by the newly obtained Numbers scroll, and related fragments, from Qumran cave 4, part of the trove of biblical texts preserved at Qumran. A sectarian Jewish commune flourished at this Dead Sea site from about 135 B.C.E. to about 70 C.E., when the Romans destroyed the second Jewish Temple of Jerusalem. The caves of Qumran and the repositories of nearby sites have yielded many biblical texts, some of which remain to be published.

2. Textual Evidence from Qumran

Nathan Jastram (1989) has now edited the Numbers scroll from Qumran cave 4 (4 QNumb) as his 1989 Harvard University doctoral dissertation. Pursuant to paleographic studies by Frank M. Cross, Jr., cited by Jastram, the script of the fragments from Qumran cave 4 may be dated to the beginning of the period between 30 B.C.E. and 20 C.E. In other words, paleographic considerations suggest a late Hasmonean or early Herodian date for this manuscript. The Numbers scroll from Qumran is, therefore, at least two thousand years old.

Jastram not only provides a careful and precise analysis of the Qumran texts themselves, but also offers comparisons with the Septuagint translations (most significantly with what is known as the Old Greek text), with the Samaritan Hebrew version of the Pentateuch, and, of course, with the Masoretic text itself. Significant variants evidenced by the manuscript of Numbers found in Qumran cave 4 will be mentioned in the NOTES.

The sections of the Numbers scroll preserved at Qumran cave 4 begin with Num 11:31 and continue with interruptions through all of the remaining columns of the manuscript, which initially contained forty-eight columns. From column 17 (Num 11:3–13:5) to column 48 (Num 36:2a–36:13), only five (19, 20, 21, 23, and 26) are completely lost.

Taken as a whole, the variants exhibited by the Qumran scroll cannot be said to undermine the Masoretic text of Numbers, and they seldom indicate that the Qumran scribes had before them, to start with, texts different from those underlying the Masoretic version. This is, after all, the primary question confronting the text critic: does a particular reading give evidence of textual fluidity in antiquity, of different ancient versions; or do the evident variants merely reflect early efforts to render the same primary text more comprehensible?

Jastram analyzes every textual variant evidenced by the Qumran manuscript and concludes that, in most instances, they are secondary. This is to say that most of the 4QNumb variants represent conscious adaptations of one primary text instead of reflecting dependence on different base texts, although instances of this process can also be detected. Jastram found it instructive to compare the Qumran fragments with the Samaritan version, in particular, because many of the more distinctive variations of content correlate with the Samaritan version, thus suggesting a relationship between these two text traditions.

Whereas orthographic and morphological variants are of considerable interest to the linguist, lexical variants hold the greatest fascination for the commentator. When the actual wording of the text differs, in any of several significant ways—through addition, omission, juxtaposition, or even through changes in syntax—the commentator senses that the meaning of the text may be substantially affected.

On occasion, the lexical variants evidenced in the Numbers scroll from Qumran also have hermeneutic import in that they are aimed at resolving inconsistencies, as between Numbers and Deuteronomy, for example. Some of the evident differences in the record pertain to such subjects as relations with neighboring nations, like the Edomites, and justification of the wars fought by the Israelites. The Qumran Numbers scroll utilizes interpolation and juxtaposition in much the same way as does the Samaritan version. These techniques are also characteristic of the Temple Scroll, a sectarian document published and interpreted by Yigael Yadin (1977) of which a copy was extant at Qumran (Levine 1979a). All of these processes indicate a fluid attitude regarding the received text of the Torah in the last pre-Christian centuries, one that permitted considerable editorial license.

3. Ancient Texts and Translations

Ancient translations differ in character from actual texts of the Torah. Any number of projects are currently in the works, providing the scholar with better texts of ancient translations. We are now able to benefit from the contribution of John Wevers (1982), who produced the Septuagint on Numbers in the Göttingen critical edition, and from the valuable insights of Emmanual Tov (1981) into the nature of the Septuagint corpus.

We also possess critical editions of the Aramaic Targums to the Torah, including the edition of the Babylonian Targum, known as Onkelos by A. Sperber (1944), and the Samaritan Targum, recently edited by A. Tal (1981). The Syriac Peshitta is now in the course of appearing in a critical edition by the Peshitta Institute of Leiden, *Vetus testamentum Syriace.* Jerome's Latin translation is also being studied anew, and Numbers has appeared in *Biblia Sacra iuxta vulgatam versionem adiuvantibus,* in 1969.

Essentially, ancient (and other) translations inform us of how their authors understood the text of the Torah and how they dealt with the problems presented by it. For this reason, translations have the rather obvious value of assisting the modern commentator with lexicographic and philological problems. Occasionally, there is reason to suppose that one or another ancient translator was reading from a differently worded Torah text, and this possibility may inform us about the formation of the text of the Torah.

4. Modern Interpretation of Numbers

The relatively few textual emendations proposed in the present commentary occur predominantly in poetic texts, and with few exceptions are the product of modern critical investigation, instead of deriving from ancient versions and translations.

The bibliography lists a selection of traditional and modern commentaries, as well as scholarly studies on Numbers. I have found it helpful to adopt one modern commentary as a primary guide to an interpretation of Numbers. It is the commentary by George Buchanan Gray, first published as part of the International Critical Commentary (1903), and abbreviated henceforward as "Gray—ICC." Gray's commentary has been of the greatest assistance because he possessed a fine philological sense and was a student of biblical poetry (Gray 1913). Intellectually, Gray was fully liberated from theological restraints. His independent studies of the biblical cult made him a penetrating interpreter of biblical religion, a subject basic to a proper understanding of Numbers (Gray 1971). Notwithstanding the extensive lapse of time since Gray's commentary appeared, I know of no other modern critical commentary on Numbers that has been as instructive as his.

The English translation presented here is original. It was, however, greatly influenced by the new Jewish translation of the Torah published by the Jewish Publication Society (*NJPS*). My intention was to avoid leveling the syntax and style of the Hebrew original, a penchant unfortunately evident in *NJPS*. This effort was particularly important in translating the formulaic style of the ritual and legal texts that are so prominent in Numbers.

The reader should be informed that in the present translation, the name of the God of Israel is represented as "YHWH," a consonantal transcription of the Tetragrammaton that avoids the form "Yahweh," which I regard as uncertain.

D. Numbers in Context

So far the introduction has addressed the content, formulation, and composition of the text of Numbers, as well as summarizing the text-critical information now available on the formation of the text. The foregoing discussion has dealt with the preserved text of Numbers, read as presented. The objective has been to understand what the text is saying and how it expresses its statements. Except for a methodical differentiation between the two major contributors to Numbers, JE and P, there has been no attempt to discuss the context of Numbers, the *Sitz-im-Leben* of its respective authors, or the literary history of the documentary sources themselves.

The study of context introduces realism into the analysis of biblical literature. It necessarily involves an attempt to identify ancient realities—events and institutions, movements and ideas—and to place them in historical perspective. What is the book of Numbers speaking about, in realistic terms? As stated, Numbers records the Israelite experience during the wilderness period, a schematic time-frame beginning with the Exodus from Egypt and concluding as the Israelites stood in the Plains of Moab just east of the Jordan, preparing to cross over into Canaan. Historically, the wilderness period, assuming that period to be in itself historical, would belong to the late thirteenth or early twelfth century B.C.E.

The modern critical scholar of the Hebrew Bible is aware, however, that the received text of Numbers, as compiled from various literary or documentary sources, reflects the literary creativity, as well as the policies, ideologies, and attitudes, of later periods of Israelite history.

Before engaging the context of Numbers, it should be clarified that the present discussion will address only Numbers 1–20, the textual content covered by Volume 1 of the Anchor Bible commentary on Numbers. The context of Numbers 21–36 will be discussed in the introduction to Volume 2 of this commentary. So, whereas the preceding discussion of *content* embraced the entire book of Numbers, the discussion of the *context* of Numbers will be presented in two parts.

1. JE in Context

We begin with a contextual consideration of the JE content of Numbers 1–20, which will be followed by a treatment of P's contribution to Numbers 1–20, in context.

Based on the investigation of JE, as this source traverses Exodus and Numbers, and based on its comparison with the more systematic presentation of the presettlement period in Deuteronomy 1–4, we may formulate a working hypothesis regarding context: the JE narratives retroject certain events and realities of the settlement period and of the period of the monarchy into a prior age, about which we know relatively little historically. By so doing, the JE authors laid a foundation for later realistic relations between Israelites and some of their enemies—such as Amalekites, Midianites, Ammonites, Moabites, Edomites—as well as between the Israelites and some of their friends. The task of the student of biblical historiography is to identify those later realities, thereby making it possible to identify the *Sitz-im-Leben* of the historiographers themselves; to know when they lived and wrote, and what were their central concerns. Pursuant to this effort, we should attempt to explain why all that was, indeed, projected into the wilderness period held special importance for the narrators of JE, and was consequently preserved.

2. Archaeological Considerations

The archaeological record of the time frame we have been calling "the wilderness period" is severely limited for the relevant regions. What is more, events and situations that JE projects into the Late Bronze or Early Iron Age are not always corroborated by the archaeological record, when such a record exists, and are occasionally blatantly contradicted by it. In some instances, where archaeological evidence is available for a certain locale at a later period, this evidence suggests that the JE narrators have shifted its historical import and have altered the dynamics of later circumstances through a process known as "refraction." By this process, actual evidence bearing on a later set of realities was recast in a way that produced an attributed record of the earlier presettlement period. How this historiographic process works may be illustrated by any number of examples. What Numbers in the JE version has to say, for instance, about Kadesh as the Israelite base near the beginning of the wilderness period must be understood in this light. The considerable evidence now available about Kadesh Barnea comes from the period of the United Monarchy in the tenth century B.C.E. and thereafter, and suggests a different function for the fortifications uncovered there.

Recent excavations at Kadesh Barnea (ʾAin Qudeirat), headed by Rudolph Cohen, afford a reconstruction of the history of that site (R. Cohen 1983; and see the NOTES and the COMMENTARY to Numbers 13–14). The archaeological record indicates that in two main periods of Israelite history, Kadesh Barnea served as the hub of a network of fortifications in the southern Negeb: during the United Monarchy, under Solomon, and during the reign of Josiah, toward the end of the seventh century B.C.E. Archaeological evidence also indicates construction activity at unspecified intermediate periods. There is however, no evidence of construction at the site before the tenth century B.C.E. This fact alone would prompt us to identify a later historical reality as the one underlying the JE narratives, which are set as I have said in the Late Bronze or Early Iron Age (in the thirteenth and twelfth centuries), the traditional wilderness period.

The actual purpose of this Negeb network was to control the southern border of Judah and the territories south of it. Most probably the JE narrators refracted what was known to them about one or more of the identified historical settings and made of Kadesh the principal Israelite base at the beginning of the wilderness period, when the Israelites had sought to penetrate southern Canaan through the Negeb.

3. The Kadesh Traditions: Their *Sitz-im-Leben*

If we accept the hypothesis that JE refracts later realities, we should search for the *Sitz-im-Leben* of the JE narrators who wrote about Kadesh, either in the days of Solomon or during the reign of Josiah, or at some time between. Because J and E, as independent sources, were most probably composed before the seventh century, when JE was compiled, it is more likely that the JE narrators utilized J materials originally generated by an early Judean author. That author would have known of the importance of Kadesh either from his own contemporary situation in the tenth century, if he wrote at that time, or from preserved records of the United Monarchy, if he wrote during the ninth century or thereafter. A network built to keep out invaders and to control the area south of the Negeb became, for the biblical historiographer of Numbers, a base of operations and a jumping-off point for the advancing Israelites, in their effort to penetrate Canaan from the south.

The same method can be applied to the Caleb traditions of Numbers 13–14, which are reflected in Deut 1:36 and Joshua 14–15 and 21. These sources from the Hexateuch should be studied in tandem with the reports concerning the activities of Caleb and of the tribe of Judah in Judges 1 (cf. 1 Sam 30:14).

A hero of the conquest-settlement period, named Caleb, was active in the territory of Judah, as reported in Judges 1, as was his younger brother, Othniel son of Qenaz (cf. Judg 3:8–11). The same hero was portrayed by the JE narrators of Numbers and by the Deuteronomist as having been the sole loyal leader of the earlier wilderness period, a person whose faith in the conquest enterprise had never faltered. Caleb was given a Judahite affiliation, as we might have expected, and was made to serve as a living link between the Exodus and the conquest, spanning the wilderness period (de Vaux 1978: 2.523–526).

4. The Mission to Edom

A telling instance of historiographic refraction is to be found in Num 20:14–21, JE's record of the mission to Edom. In Num 20:16b, Moses informs the Edomite king that he is near his border: "Now we are in Kadesh, a town bordering on your territory *(ʿîr qeṣēh gebûlekā)*." For the student of historiography, the question is obvious: At what period had the Edomite kingdom expanded far enough west of Elath that it bordered on southern Judah, and one could say that Kadesh was near Edom? This question has been discussed most recently by J. R. Bartlett (1989: 85, 90–93, 128–143). He observes that Edomite expansion began in the eighth century B.C.E., after Edom rebelled against Judah, following the death of Jotham, king of Judah (2 Kgs 16:5–6). The oracle preserved in Amos 1:11–12 is probably a reaction to this situation. Amos accuses Edom of pursuing his brother with a sword *(baḥḥereb)*, and Num 20:18 has the king of Edom threaten to confront Israel with a sword *(baḥḥereb)*. An ostracon from Arad found in stratum VIII at the site, and which speaks of hostile Edomites, may also be dated to this general period (Aharoni 1981: 70–74, inscription 40). Edomite expansion continued and became extensive in the mid to late seventh century, as we now know from the Qiṭmit excavations (Beit Arieh 1989: 135–146). But under Assyrian domination, beginning in the late eighth century, the Edomites had little power to threaten Judah. So we are required to decide whether Num 20:16b reflects the realities preceding the Assyrian campaigns or the reality of a period about a century later, when it again became possible for Edom to expand and represent a threat to Judah. Some have even related Num 20:14–21 to the time of the Babylonian campaigns of the early sixth century. The period of the eighth century recommends itself on literary grounds, because of the diction shared by Num 20:8 and Amos 1:11. In the Late Bronze Age and Early Iron Age, on which Numbers 20 is reporting historiographically, the border of Edom did not extend west of Aqaba (Bartlett 1989: 67–82).

It should be noted that Edom is mentioned in the fourth oration of Balaam (Num 24:18):

> Edom shall be dispossessed,
> Seir dispossessed by its enemies;
> But Israel is triumphant!

In context, this brief reference to the subjugation of Edom probably reflects the realities of the reign of David (Levine 1989a).

5. Disguised Kenites

A problem of a different sort is represented by the account of Moses and Hobab the Midianite in Num 10:29–32. In an atmosphere reminiscent of Exodus 18 (cf. Exod 2:16–3:1), the brief episode in Numbers 10 depicts an intimate and friendly people, who are related by marriage to Moses himself.

Here it is not historiographic refraction that may help to clarify the anomaly of friendly Midianites, elsewhere unheard of in the historical books of the Bible, where we read only of hostile Midianites. It is rather the juxtaposition of ethnographic nomenclature, a known technique of biblical historiographers. There are reasons to conclude that the early friendly relationship between Israelites and Midianites, as portrayed in Exodus and Numbers, had Kenites in mind rather than actual Midianites.

Our information about the land of Midian is scant, and we know much less about the Midianites than we do about others of Israel's early neighbors, the Ammonites, Edomites, and Moabites, for example. There is little contemporary information about the Midianites to supplement the evidence available from classical sources of a later age. The land of the Midianites would appear to have been in the northwestern region of the Arabian peninsula. The most precise biblical information we have about its location comes from a chance reference. In 1 Kgs 11:17–18 we read that Hadad, an Edomite prince, once fled from Midian through Paran to Egypt. His route would have traversed northern Sinai, south of Kadesh Barnea, to the border of Egypt. This route points to northwestern Arabia as the land of Midian, the starting point of the fleeing prince (de Vaux 1978: 1.330–338).

What we read in Judges about the Midianite wars led by Gideon, a Benjaminite, took place, however, in northern Israel and involved northern tribes, predominantly Manasseh, Zebulun, and Naphtali (Judges 6–8). Thus it is that in terms of historical geography, as we know it from later classical sources, the presence of Midianites in Sinai would pose no problem. But in terms of what we read about Israelite wars with the Midianites in the historical books of the Bible, placing them so far south requires explanation.

As is explained in the commentary, these inconsistencies, though not irreconcilable, suggest that we would be closer to reality if we were to use the familial relationship of Moses to a leading Midianite, elsewhere characterized as the same relationship to a Kenite, to explain the ethnography underlying the record of friendship preserved in Exodus 18 and Numbers 10. The friendship between Moses and Hobab/Jethro is explained by reference to the narratives of Judges, which, however, speak of the Kenites, not the Midianites, as the clan of Moses' father-in-law (Judg 4:2, 17, 21; 5:24). These narratives correlate with information provided in Judg 1:15 and 4:11, as well as in 1 Sam 15:6, where we read of Kenites living among Amalekites and Canaanites in Canaan. Some Kenites enacted treaties with the Canaanites, as Judg 4:11 informs us; but, like Jael, wife of Heber the Kenite, they may have remained loyal to the Israelites in times of crisis.

There is reason to assume from the narrative of Num 10:29–32 that Hobab and his tribe responded positively to Moses' persuasion and decided to join the Israelites in their journey to the Promised Land. This background would have laid the foundation for actual relations between the two groups during the settlement period and the early monarchy, when Kenites would have been helpful to the Israelites and at the same time protected by them, and exempted from the decreed fate of the other Canaanite peoples.

By accepting this juxtaposition, we can explain the intimacy between Moses and the so-called Midianites of Exodus 18 and Numbers 10 as a retrojection of a later reality, namely, the friendly relations that existed between the Israelites and an exceptional group of Canaanites, the Kenites. In ethnographic terms, this retrojection makes a significant statement: not all Canaanites were enemies!

That ethnographic designations are occasionally inconsistent in biblical literature is brought home by further comparisons between Numbers and the historical books of the Bible. In the words of the ballad cited by JE in Numbers 21, the Israelite settlement of Transjordan is defended against the claims of the Moabites, whereas in Judges 11 the same argument is used against the Ammonites. The Ammonites were, after all, Jephtah's current enemies, and this fact explains the "recycling" of an ancient ballad. As a corollary, we note that in Num 21:29 (cf. Isa 48:13, 46; 1 Kgs 11:7, 33) Kemosh is the god of the Moabites, whereas in Judges 11 he is god of the Ammonites.

Once we agree, then, that a degree of juxtaposition occurred in biblical historiography, we can propose that the so-called Midianites of Exodus and Numbers were disguised Kenites. Having raised the question of the identity of the Midianites of Num 10:29–36, it might be informative to pursue the subject of Midianite relations a bit further.

6. Hostile Midianites

The fact is that retrojection of hostile Midianites is noticeably missing in JE, and we have reason to think that the priestly writers were sensitive to this omission. In view of P's primary interest in the conquest of Canaan, one would have expected the priestly school to lay a foundation for the later conflicts with the Midianites, conflicts pivotal in the conquest itself. In fact, the priestly writers introduced the Midianites into their narrative as a hostile force in Num 22:4 and 7, at the beginning of the Balaam pericope, where the Midianites join the Moabites in an effort to overcome the Israelites through other than direct military means. It is entirely possible that the words *ziqnê Midyān* 'the elders of Midian' were interpolated by the priestly writers in Num 22:4a and 7 for this purpose. The elders of Midian never reappear thereafter in the Balaam pericope, as a matter of fact.

In a similar way, priestly writers added Midianite involvement to the record of the Baal Peor incident of Num 25:1–9, of which only vv 1–5 are attributable to JE. There is, however, no mention of Midianites in vv 1–5, only of Moabites. JE disposes of the entire incident in Num 25:5 by putting the sinful Israelite leaders to death. Num 25:6–9 tell a different story, one in which the Midianites are actually featured. The remainder of chap. 25, which is also of priestly authorship, goes so far as to command a war against the Midianites. Finally, Numbers 31, which, at least in its final form, is of priestly authorship, generates a full-blown war against the Midianites, to which it adds a code of law governing the disposition of spoils.

Every group whom the JE and priestly narrators considered relevant was accounted for in some way. The first battle was with the Amalekites. The Ammonites were avoided; the Moabites were neutralized without war, it seems, and the Israelites skirted the Edomites. The priestly writers saw to it that Midianite hostility was also projected into the wilderness period. Let us trace the agenda of JE further in Numbers.

7. The Inhabitants of Canaan

Numbers provides several lists of the inhabitants of Canaan. We begin with Num 13:29, a list of these inhabitants at the beginning of the wilderness period. It mentions the Amorites and the Hittites and speaks of the antiquity of Hebron. As has been argued persuasively by J. van Seters (1976), most biblical references to Amorites and Hittites, especially those in the proverbial lists of the inhabitants of Canaan, cannot be taken as evidence bearing on the historical Amorites and Hittites of the second millennium B.C.E. Based on an examination of how Egyptian and Assyrian writers of the first millennium used such nomenclature, van Seters concluded that these designations actually refer to the first-millennium inhabitants of Canaan and the regions west of the Euphrates. These ethnographic designations are transparent, in the sense that they betray the first-millennium *Sitz-im-Leben* of the biblical narrators of the JE school who employed them, and of the later priestly writers who subsequently adopted them as well.

In Num 13:22 we find an unusual record of the history of Hebron, in which the early founding of Tanis is also mentioned by comparison. As explained most recently by S. Ahituv (1971), Tanis was actually founded long after the Ramesside period, so that the author of Num 13:22, who refers to its chronology, must have known of Tanis from its existence during the later Saitic period, which is when he wrote about it. Surely the same could be said of the biblical writer of the first millennium B.C.E. who refers to Hebron as an Amorite city of the Late Bronze Age (see the COMMENTS on Numbers 13–14).

8. Amalekites

Numbers 13:29 also mentions the Amalekites, who are subsequently characterized in an oracle (Num 24:20) as being the "first" (or "foremost") of the various Canaanite peoples, who would, nevertheless, ultimately meet with destruction. In Num 14:25 and 43–45 we find references to Amalekites who inhabited the Negeb alongside Canaanites. When we apply the hypothesis of historiographic retrojection to the Amalekites, we arrive at the following conclusions: The historical books make some commonplace references to Amalekites fighting in the company of Midianites, Moabites, and *benê qedem* 'eastern peoples', whoever they were (Judg 5:14; 12:15). For the most part, however, the historical books speak about the Amalekites as a people inhabiting the Negeb and southern Judah, with their settlements extending through northern Sinai to the Wilderness of Shur at the approaches of Egypt (1 Sam 15:7; 27:8). One of the principal Israelite battles against the Amalekites is reported in 1 Samuel 15, where we read that Saul defeated them. There we find reference to *ʿîr ʿAmālʾēq* 'the town of Amalek', which was located somewhere near a Negeb wadi (1 Sam 15:5).

It is reasonable to conclude that by attributing the first battle of the Israelites after the Exodus to an enemy named Amalek, the JE historiographers of Exodus 15 (and of Deuteronomy 25 as well) were laying the foundation for the later real enmity between the conquering Israelites and the Canaanite Amalekites. Not only Saul, but David as well, had a major encounter with the Amalekites (1 Samuel 30; 2 Sam 1:1). Etiological intent is further implied by an editorial interpolation in 1 Sam 15:1–3, which rationalizes Saul's great victory as retribution for Amalek's attack upon Israel soon after the Exodus. What better primal enemy to be the first to confront the Israelites departing from Egypt than the Amalekites, whose hegemony extended all the way westward to the approaches of Egypt?

When we examine the references to Amalekites in Numbers, we also find them in the Negeb. This is most clearly stated in Num 13:29: *ʿAmālēq yôšēb beʾereṣ hannegeb* 'The Amalekites inhabit the Negeb region'. This is also their reported locale in Num 14:25 and 43–45, notwithstanding some geographical ambiguity evident in those passages. What is more, these references correlate well with the area said to be inhabited by the Amalekites according to Gen 14:7.

Genesis 14 is a remarkable document in many respects. It records an international war in which Abram became involved, and refers somewhat cryptically to battles waged in Transjordan and near the Gulf of Elath, encompassing the southern Negeb in the process. In Gen 14:7 we read the following report: "They headed back (from the Gulf of Elath), arriving at ʾEin Mishpat, now called Kadesh, and they ravaged the entire Amalekite mountain range, as well as the Amorites who inhabited Haseson Tamar (=ʿAin Gedi, 2 Chr 20:2)." One is left with the clear impression that the Amalekites constituted a major component of the Canaanite ethnography during the settlement period and the early monarchy, and that the words of the oracle in Num 24:20 are to be understood realistically: Amalek was a foremost nation, and its eventual subjugation was a matter of considerable importance. Genesis 14, like those JE sources of Numbers which speak of Amalekites, may well reflect realities during the reigns of Saul and David. One senses that the Amalekites served to represent the Canaanites of the conquest period, and that the hatred expressed regarding them capsulizes the hostility of the Israelite tradition against Canaanites generally.

9. JE in Numbers: A Doctrine

What has been said so far about the context of JE in Numbers 1–20 may be summarized as follows: the governing doctrine of the JE narrators is that Israel's conflicts and relations with other peoples during the conquest period and the early monarchy were primal; they did not commence during the settlement and monarchic periods, after the Israelites had possessed Canaan. These hostilities are not to be regarded as the consequence of ascendant Israelite power, or of its conquest of Canaan. They are, rather, attributable to some ancient hatred on the part of Moabites, Amalekites, Edomites, Midianites, and, at least implicitly, Ammonites. Israel had sought peaceful relations with these peoples, who had refused their friendship and who confronted Israel with hostility when the Israelites were on their way to the Promised Land and in desperate straits. Ultimately the Israelites were to become exceedingly powerful, but not before they suffered during long treks through inhospitable deserts, all because those hostile peoples would not allow them passage through their territories or because, like the Amalekites, they attacked them without cause.

In effect, what the JE narrators of Exodus and Numbers relate about these peoples seeks to sanction or to justify later Israelite policies toward them. What they are saying is that these peoples had either to be defeated and their lands seized, or to be subjugated and rendered tributary if Israelite sovereignty over Canaan were to be held securely. This is the hidden agenda of the JE historiographers.

In literary-historical terms, we should look to E (and T) as the ultimate source of retrojections from the historical realities of the northern Israelite kingdom, and to J for similar traditions regarding Judah and the Negeb. This subject will reemerge in the introduction to Volume 2 of this commentary, because the relevant JE narratives occur, for the most part, in Numbers 21–36, where the record of the Israelite experience in Transjordan unfolds.

In a broader perspective, the JE narrators were addressing the question of Israelite self-definition. Ethnography served to classify the Israelites as other than Canaanites or Amorites, and as not being related to the Transjordanian peoples either. Just as these indigenous and neighboring peoples were the "other," so was Israel distinct from the nations whose lands it eventually seized, settled, and possessed, or rendered tributary. It is interesting, therefore, to take note of those groups which are not mentioned in the JE narratives of Numbers.

I have already made mention of the failure of the JE historiographers of Numbers to project hostile Midianites into the wilderness period, and of how priestly writers, sensitive to this omission, created an etiology for them.

10. Israelites and Other Non-Canaanites: Ethnography

There is much more to the ethnographic picture, however. There is no reference to the Philistines in the historiography of Numbers. A passing reference to Philistines in the historiography of Exodus occurs in Exod 13:17, a verse derived from E. There we read that the departing Israelites avoided the coastal road, known as Via Maris, for fear of the Philistines. Similarly, in Exod 23:31, part of an idealized covenant promise, we read that God will establish the borders of Israel all the way from the Gulf of Elath to the "sea of the Philistines," which, of course, refers to the southern Mediterranean seacoast. Contrast such quiescence on the part of historiographers with the verses of the Song of the Sea (Exodus 15), where we find a more realistic ethnography of Canaan, one that correlates with what we know of the settlement period and the early monarchy. We read of Philistia, of Moabites and Edomites, all of whom are said to have feared the Israelites.

Stories about Philistines during the patriarchal age, such as those in Gen 26:1–33 (J), may also be seen as retrojections. They do not pertain to the wilderness period, and do not contradict the insight that the JE narrators of Numbers fail to come up with an etiology to explain the battles Israelites later fought against Philistines.

The historical confrontation between the Israelites and the Philistines surely fits the time frame of similar encounters with Amalekites, Midianites, and other Canaanites, even the so-called Amorites. Why, then, if the proposed hypothesis be accepted, is there no groundwork in the JE historiography of Numbers for the sustained military confrontations that were to dominate the reigns of Saul and David?

It is entirely conceivable, though hardly demonstrable, that no need was felt to justify the elimination or subjugation of the Philistines because they were not indigenous to Canaan proper or to Transjordan. Like the Israelites, so, too, the Philistines were foreign invaders. Like the Israelites themselves, Philistines were not Canaanites, and it was not their land that the Israelites were in the process of possessing by means of conquest and settlement.

Without entering into a full-blown discussion of the patriarchal narratives, it is obvious that the agenda of J and E, and of the composite source JE, change as we move through the Torah books, and as various earlier periods are recast historiographically. The Patriarchs were legal residents in Canaan, and not conquerors. They were able to resolve most of their differences with all whom they encountered without recourse to war. The adventure of the wilderness period is treated in a radically different spirit, however. The enterprise of the conquest and settlement of Canaan, as portrayed in Exodus and Numbers, was fraught with protracted military engagements, said to have occurred before Israel reached the Jordan. In such terms it was felt, perhaps, that the Israelite-Philistine wars required no historiographic groundwork, no justification or precedent.

What about the Egyptians? Almost without exception, the only Egyptians known to the Torah books, as a whole, are living in Egypt, not in Canaan, notwithstanding the considerable biblical and archaeological evidence available on the Egyptian presence in Canaan. Were it not for the cryptic reference in Gen 50:11 to the burial of Egyptians in Canaan, one would hardly guess, based solely on Torah literature, that they had ever been there! There are, of course, a few hints in the Table of Nations (Genesis 10) to genealogical connections between Egyptians and Canaanites and even Philistines, but such references are more puzzling than illuminating.

Similarly, were it not for a verse in the first oration of Balaam (Num 23:6) we would not imagine that Arameans had ever appeared on the Canaanite and Transjordanian scenes. Even that verse portrays Aram as a distant land (cf. Deut 23:5). Again we notice a difference between the patriarchal traditions and the historiography of the wilderness period. The Patriarchs were, in a sense, Arameans who had migrated to Canaan. As regards the wilderness period and its etiologies, as preserved in Exodus and Numbers, there is no retrojection of any of the major wars later fought between Israelites and Arameans, nor of any other connections with Arameans.

Do these blatant omissions have literary-historical implications? Are we to assume, for instance, that the JE narrators of Numbers used sources composed prior to the extensive campaign of Pharaoh Shishak (Shoshenq) in the Land of Israel, in the late tenth century, or considerably after that campaign had ceased to be relevant (1 Kgs 14:25–31)? Is the absence of Arameans from the ethnographic equation to be interpreted to mean that the sources used by the JE narrators of Numbers were composed before the Arameans appeared on the scene? A good argument could be advanced that some of the J and E traditions go back to the period before the late ninth century, when the Aramean expansion threatened Transjordan and the northern Israelite kingdom. And yet the Edomite factor is included in the JE record (Num 20:14–21; 21:4), in a manner that recalls the eighth century.

Literary-historical considerations do not override certain issues of policy that may more convincingly account for the significant omissions we have noted here. Like Philistines, the Egyptians and Arameans were foreign elements in Canaan, and there need have been no sensitivity about doing battle with them or about seizing land from them.

11. The Ethnography of the Deuteronomist

Before leaving the subject of ethnography and its putative value in establishing the context of the JE narrators of Numbers, a word should be said about the policies reflected in the Deuteronomistic historiography, especially in Deuteronomy 1–4, that focus on the wilderness period. Such a query may shed light on the reason for some of the significant omissions from the ethnography of Numbers.

The Deuteronomist voices a different policy with respect to Israelite relationships with the Canaanite and Transjordanian peoples. There are two major differences between the JE narratives and Deuteronomy in this regard. In the first place, the Deuteronomist adopts a different attitude regarding those lands and peoples bordering on Canaan. The Amorites of Canaan are, of course, enemies, but not the peoples of Esau/Lot who inhabit Seir (Deut 2:2–8). These peoples were granted their land by God himself, and the Israelites were consequently commanded to skirt Seir on their way to Transjordan. Similarly, when Israel was traversing the desert east of Moab they were told, in Deut 2:9–16, not to attack Moab because that land had been granted to the Moabites by Israel's God. Finally, in Deut 2:17–24, the same ideology is applied to the Ammonites. The Deuteronomist does not refer in this connection to Edom, as had the JE historiographers of Numbers, but Seir and Edom may have been synonymous in the Deuteronomistic nomenclature.

What is more, the Deuteronomist becomes involved in the internal history of these neighboring lands. We read that the peoples of Lot/Esau had seized Moab from an earlier indigenous people, variously named Eimim or Anakites, of the stock of the Rephaim, whom they had dispossessed (Deut 2:11–12). In a similar spirit, the Ammonites, so we read, had dispossessed other Rephaim (Deut 2:20–23). Pretty much as an afterthought, we are informed that Seir as well had at one time belonged to an indigenous people who were eventually displaced (Deut 2:22).

Deut 2:23 is especially significant because it introduces an element of reality: the same kind of ethnographic replacements that were recorded for Ammon, Moab, and Seir are also reported for the southern seacoast and coastal plain, from Hatserim (Raphiah) to Gaza. We are informed that the indigenous people of that region, called Awwim, had been dispossessed by Caphtorites, which is to say, Philistines (Amos 8:7).

The Deuteronomist was unquestionably also guided by an ideological agenda in his treatment of ethnography, in which justification for the Israelite conquest and settlement of Canaan was paramount. When dealing with peoples perceived to be genealogically related to the Israelites, such as those of Lot/Esau, the Deuteronomist projects a positive background: Israel, for its part, had respected the territorial integrity of the neighboring peoples, giving them no cause for complaint.

Perhaps the reference to Caphtorites in Deut 2:23 affords the greatest support for the hypothesis that has been elaborated in the foregoing discussion. What Israel did in Canaan was no different, as a matter of fact, from what Philistines had done or from what those nations generally considered to be the legitimate contemporary possessors of their own territories had done. They had all displaced indigenous peoples in the past.

In their distinctive ways both the Deuteronomist and the JE narrators of Exodus and Numbers set the stage for the conquest-settlement agenda of the historical books, primarily Judges and Samuel and, for all its problems, Joshua as well. To focus on Numbers specifically, I conclude that JE retrojects into the preconquest or wilderness period an ideological justification for the conquest and settlement, one rooted in a particular reconstruction of that earlier age. More will be said on this subject in the introduction to the second volume of this commentary, as I explore the Transjordanian experience central to Numbers 21–36.

There are few if any additional contextual indicators in the JE sections of Numbers 1–20. If there is a clue to historical context in Num 11:1–12:15, the narratives about Moses that epitomize his unique status as a prophet, it is to be found in 12:6–8. There Moses is referred to as God's *ʿebed* 'servant', and as a member of his *bayît* 'household'. Such language is elsewhere reserved for David (see the NOTES and COMMENTS to 10:29–12:16). Once again, our attention is directed to the period of the United Monarchy. The image of Moses is made to anticipate David. In the image given him by the JE narrators of Numbers, Moses is both prophet and king.

E. THE CONTEXT OF THE PRIESTLY SOURCE

The context of the priestly materials in Numbers 1–20 is best discussed within the larger framework of P as a documentary source continuing through the Tetrateuch (Genesis through Numbers), with a few addenda in Deuteronomy. The texts assigned to P, on the basis of source analysis, are of two principal types: (1) historiography and (2) law and ritual. The relationship of these two types of literature is dynamic. In the beginning, there is the cult, with all of its rituals and celebrations. The institution of the cult and the formulation of its codes of practice generated a priestly historiography intended to lend sanction to the cult, historically and politically (Levine 1983).

The message of this historiographic tradition is clear: what later Israelites were being called upon to perform and to fulfill in their practice of religion by the dicta of the Torah was anticipated by their dutiful ancestors in the time of

Moses. It was then that God had revealed to those earliest Israelites all of the detailed practices required in religious life. In fact, the priestly historiography reaches back to the patriarchal period recorded in Genesis, and even to the primeval history of Genesis 1–11. This entire body of literature was written so as to confirm the great antiquity and original significance of the cult in God's plan for the people of Israel.

There is, of course, movement in the other direction as well. Major events and episodes of Israelite history, such as the Egyptian sojourn and the Exodus, generated cultic responses and commemorations. Most notable are the Pesaḥ celebrations, variously legislated in Exodus, Leviticus, Numbers, and Deuteronomy.

This process is hardly limited to P; it is equally characteristic of JE and D, except that in the book of Numbers specifically, there is no strictly legal or ritual content directly attributable to JE or D. All of the legal material in Numbers, including the laws concerning homicide in chap. 35 and the estate laws expounded in chap. 27 (and further in chap. 36) have been adapted and modulated by the priestly school, as their legal vocabulary and formulation indicate. So it is that the dynamic interaction of law and historiography is effectively confined to the priestly materials in Numbers.

At one point in the forgoing discussion of the content of Numbers it was stated that P, in its diverse materials, legal and historiographic, should be regarded as generally subsequent to JE and D. It is now time to discuss this diachronic alignment of the Torah sources, in an attempt to validate the alleged lateness of P. What is required is nothing short of a relative literary-historical chronology of Pentateuchal literature.

The crux of the literary-historical issue regarding the diachronic position of P rests in the Deuteronomic question; specifically, the extent to which P reflects or is dependent on the Deuteronomic school. The most distinctive Deuteronomic legislation is expounded in Deuteronomy 12–16 and pertains to the restriction of all cultic activity to one central Temple that would be erected in an unnamed place selected by God.

H. L. Ginsberg (1982) has contributed seminal studies on the development of the Israelite festivals and concerning the origin and transmission of core Deuteronomy from northern Israel to Judah. He shows how the priestly writers responded to Deuteronomic legislation governing the scheduling of the festivals and the limitation of sacred space to one altar and one sanctuary. The seven-week deferral of the spring harvest festival, renamed *Šābûʿôt* 'Weeks' in Deuteronomy 16, is accepted in the priestly liturgical calender of Leviticus 23. Undoubtedly, this deferral was prompted by practical considerations. If one lines up the Torah sources pertaining to the annual festivals, as Ginsberg did, in three phases—pre-Deuteronomic, Deuteronomic, and post-Deuteronomic—it is possible to reconstruct what occurred in the development of those festivals designated *ḥag* 'pilgrimage'. In the pre-Deuteronomic

Book of the Covenant (Exodus 21–23), the spring harvest festival, called *qāṣîr*, occurred directly after the Pesaḥ sacrifice, as soon as a sheaf of new grain became available for presentation. But such a schedule made sense only when Israelites could fulfill their religious obligations by undertaking a short pilgrimage to a nearby cult site and then returning home quickly to harvest their grain. As a result of the Deuteronomic legislation, it would henceforth be required that Israelites undertake a prolonged pilgrimage to the central Temple. Agricultural pursuits would be interrupted considerably, at the worst season of the year for a farmer to be absent from home, and rescheduling thus became necessary. It is clear from a close reading of Leviticus 23 that the priestly school not only accepted the postponement of seven weeks but in fact generated additional celebrations during the seven-week period between the Pesaḥ and the Pentecost. Furthermore, Ginsberg's tracing of the Deuteronomic core, those parts of the book which we consider primary, to northern Israel of the mid eighth century instead of to Judah of the seventh century changes the absolute chronology of the Pentateuchal sources. The primary Deuteronomic legislation emerges as more ancient than we thought it was, so that one who maintains that P antedates D must now assume a provenance for P in the early eighth century, not in the early seventh.

There are additional considerations that recommend endorsement of the traditional alignment of the Torah sources in the order J, E, D, P, making the priestly source the latest in the literary chronology. By accepting this alignment one need not, however, accept the original basis for it. We need not endorse the same reconstruction of Israelite religion as had been proposed in the nineteenth century by Julius Wellhausen and others, who formulated the most widely accepted source-critical hypotheses. At the present time, the traditional order, which has been challenged most poignantly by Yehezkel Kaufmann and his followers, seems persuasive for other reasons, most notably because of internal evidence, augmented by comparative considerations (Kaufmann 1960: 451–801).

1. Contextual Indicators

There are contextual indicators within the priestly source itself that point to an early postexilic provenance for at least some of the essential content of P. These indicators suggest renewed priestly creativity, beginning in the period of the Return, during the late sixth century B.C.E., and continuing long afterward, well into the period of the Second Temple. One would surely expect such creativity at a time that the newly constituted Jewish community in Jerusalem and Judea, with its restored temple, was preoccupied with the reordering of religious life under new conditions of collective existence.

In particular, Leviticus 25 and 27 suggest a postexilic provenance. In its provisions for land tenure and indenture Leviticus 25 presents legislation that figures to be subsequent to the provisions of Deuteronomy 15, on some of the same legal issues. Notions of *ge'ullāh* 'restoration' and *derôr* 'release' likewise represent further developments of legal practices that first emerged in the Israelite context during the near-exilic period, though they have a long history in other ancient Near Eastern societies (Levine 1989a: xxxi–xxxix, 270–274).

It was Wellhausen's seminal insight that the provisions of Leviticus 17, requiring that all sacrificial offerings be brought to the opening of the Tent of Meeting, inevitably reflect Deuteronomic doctrine on cult centralization, albeit in a wilderness environment. The priestly requirement is hardly explicable unless we assume that P is reacting to Deuteronomic policy on restructuring the Israelite cult. Wellhausen's insight is particularly apt as a point of departure for discussing the literary history of the priestly materials in Numbers (Wellhausen 1965: 376–385).

The priestly content of Numbers shares the overall context of P within Torah literature. P is a source that most probably took shape over a protracted period of time, beginning in the late preexilic period; it preserved some quite early material and continued to develop during the postexilic period. As regards the priestly content of Numbers, especially what is preserved in Numbers 1–20, we encounter fairly clear expressions of postexilic institutions. The emergence of the Levites as a distinct class of cultic servitors is a case in point. This subject has been discussed in depth in various sections of this commentary, most extensively in the COMMENTS to chaps. 3–4, 8, and 16–17.

2. Levites and Priests

It has been proposed that the stratification of the priestly tribe into two groups, consecrated priests and subordinate, unconsecrated Levites, can be traced to a policy first advocated in Ezek 44:9–14. There we are told that the Levites who had been part of the apostasy associated with Israel's earlier sins, a veiled reference to the sin of the *bāmôt* 'high places', would henceforth be forbidden to officiate in the temple cult. These Levites would serve the priests and slaughter the sacrifices, whereas cultic officiation would be reserved for the Zadokite priests.

Without entering into the source analysis of Ezekiel 44, or addressing the originality of Ezekiel 40–48 as a whole, it is obvious that the content of Ezek 44:9–14 is exilic, at the earliest. We note further that even Ezek 44:9–14 do not yet speak of the Aaronide priesthood, but rather of the priesthood of Zadok, indicating that the notion of an Aaronide priesthood, so basic to the priestly traditions of Exodus, Leviticus, and Numbers and yet so conspicuously absent from any preexilic biblical source outside of Torah literature, might represent an even later, postexilic development. To be more specific: the separation of the Levites is central to Numbers 3–4, where the several levitical clans are mustered separately, and where the Aaronide priests of the Kohathite clan are featured as the exclusive bearers of the priestly office. As part of this stratification process, the important task of transporting the Ark of the Covenant, traditionally a priestly assignment in preexilic sources, becomes the assignment of a levitical clan, the Kohathites. The same Kohathites figure again in Numbers 16–17, where an earlier record of a rebellion against Moses' authority has been transformed by the priestly writers into an internecine rivalry between the clan of Kohath, represented by Korah, and the Aaronides. The outcome of an ordeal (or more than one ordeal) establishes the exclusive right of the Aaronides to the priesthood. Finally, Numbers 8, which mirrors Leviticus 8, itself a record of the installation and consecration of the Aaronide priesthood, tells of the dedication of the Levites to the service of the Tabernacle, under the authority of the Aaronide priesthood.

It is further evident that the composition of the priestly materials in Numbers is late not only with respect to JE and D, neither of which know of the stratification of the tribe of Levi into priests and subordinate Levites, but relatively late even with respect to the priestly traditions of Exodus and Leviticus, which also know nothing about this arrangement. Although Exodus 6 preserves genealogies that more or less correlate with the data provided in Numbers 3–4, there is no reference in Exodus to the subordination of the Levites. For its part, whatever little Leviticus mentions about the Levites pertains to urban property owned by Levites, and to the acknowledged tithe remittable to them, according to chaps. 25 and 27. It is not even certain that Leviticus is employing the term "Levite" any differently than does Deuteronomy, which regards all priests as Levites.

3. Laws of Purity

The laws and rituals prescribed in Numbers 19 relevant to corpse contamination and the resultant purifications seem to be predicated on yet another late passage, Ezek 43:7–9. There we read, for the first time outside of Torah literature, the doctrine that corpses and bones of the dead and their flesh are potent contaminators, and that the defilement that they generate is permanent and irreversible. Ezek 43:7–9 protest the burial of kings in the Temple complex, stating that such a practice defiles the Temple. This statement is to be viewed against the background of 2 Kgs 23:14, 16, 20, where it is reported that Josiah used the bones of the dead to delegitimate the altar near the necropolis of Bethel, as well as altars in the environs of Jerusalem where cults of the dead were operative. The provisions of Numbers 19 effectively institutionalize the concepts first expressed in Ezek 43:7–9, itself an exilic, or even postexilic, text (Levine 1990).

It has already been suggested that the Tabernacle traditions are to be considered post-Deuteronomic, because they are predicated on the effective restriction of all sacrifice to the opening of the Tent of Meeting, as ordained in Leviticus 17. But there is more: in Exodus 24:12–31:18 and chaps. 35–40, all priestly sections, the architecture of the portable Tabernacle complex is provided. In Numbers 1–4, and again in 10:1–28, we find that this sanctuary complex has been integrated within an encampment planned around it, with assigned locations for the Aaronide priests, the several levitical clans, and the Tribes of Israel. We are warranted in concluding, therefore, that in Numbers the priestly writers built upon the priestly traditions of Exodus and Leviticus, which, in turn, had taken their cue from the older E tradition of an oraculum located outside the encampment (Exod 33:7–11; and cf. Num 11:16; 12:4). Thus we are instructed not only by the subsequence of priestly writings to other, datable texts of exilic and postexilic provenance, but by internal developments within priestly literature itself. These developments indicate that the priestly content of Numbers is often of a later provenance than that of Exodus and Leviticus.

4. Internal Sequences

Some fairly precise internal sequences can be traced in the area of law and ritual. Purifications from various sorts of defilement are, of course, basic to the legislation of Leviticus. In particular, the funerary restrictions imposed on the priesthood according to Leviticus 21 have a direct bearing on the provisions of Numbers 19.

The nexus of these two codes of law is, precisely, opposition to the cult of the dead, a notion basic to the biblical outlook. This subject is addressed in the COMMENTS to chap. 19. Preventing priestly involvement in funerary rites was one way of distancing such rites from the purview of the Temple and the priesthood. In this instance, one assumes that both Leviticus 21 and Numbers 19 reflect fairly late developments in Israelite religion and were part of the same movement to combat cults of the dead.

The same spirit animates Numbers 6, the Nazirite law. A Nazirite may not defile himself by contact with the dead, even to attend to the burial of a consanguineal relative. This was also the law affecting the high priest, according to Leviticus 21.

We note several additional examples of subsequence in the priestly materials of Numbers 1–20. Num 5:5–10 are based on Lev 5:14–16 and 20–26, the primary laws of *maʿal* 'cultic misappropriation'. Numbers adds the requirement of a confessional by the officiating priest and mandates an estate provision not specified in Leviticus. Further, Num 5:9–10 echo Lev 7:9 and 14 on the rights of individual priests to what they had collected and offered in the Sanctuary. Num 9:1–14 presuppose normal rules for the scheduling of the Passover festival and its attendant paschal sacrifice as stated in Exodus 12–13, Leviticus 23, and Numbers 29, all priestly codes of religious law. In itself, the provision for a deferred Pesaḥ in the second month is reminiscent of Hezekiah's Pesaḥ, according to 2 Chronicles 30. Numbers 15, which calls for accompanying offerings, the *minḥāh* 'grain offering' and the *nesek* 'libation', is ancillary to the major codes prescribing burnt offerings and sacred gifts of greeting. In form, it resembles a type of ancient Near Eastern temple rituals in which accompanying offerings of wine and grain are collected separately (Levine 1983b). Numbers 18 is a comprehensive summary of all of the priestly and levitical emoluments and, except for an innovation or two, is entirely based on previously stated legislation.

It would be accurate to state in summary that the priestly materials in Numbers 1–20 (as in Numbers as a whole) represent, by and large, the further development of priestly law and historiography well into the postexilic period. Such development was not merely a matter of redactional activity, but also involved new writings by the postexilic priesthood of Jerusalem and their associates. It is worth mentioning, in this context, that some of the postexilic Psalms may have been composed by priests and Levites.

5. The Evidence of Language

One of the criteria employed by modern scholars in dating biblical texts, most notably the content of P, is the evidence of language. It is possible to determine, at least in relative terms, whether certain biblical Hebrew locutions are early or late. Disagreement persists on this score, but there is a growing body of evidence to suggest that the priestly vocabulary contains many late components. The methodological principle governing the chronology of language is that late texts often preserve early language. Wherever we encounter evidently late locutions, however, we are warranted in concluding that the texts in which these locutions occur were composed, or at least reworked, at a late date.

A good example of late language in the priestly materials is the term *degel*, otherwise known from Aramaic documents of the Persian period as the designation for a military unit arrayed around a fort or command post. Its occurrences are restricted to Numbers 2 and 10, in their references to the plan of the Israelite encampment and the order of march. Usage of this term by a biblical writer strongly suggests a date for his creativity during the Persian period, beginning in the late sixth century and continuing throughout most of the fifth. It was then that such contemporary vocabulary would have been introduced into the priestly source. In this instance, we should not conclude that the texts of Numbers 2 and 10, in which this distinctive term occurs, were initially composed during the Achaemenid period, only that they were redacted or adapted at that time.

In other instances, the likelihood that a particular text from the P source was initially composed in the Persian period is much greater. A case in point is Numbers 30, which repeatedly employs the legal term *ʾissār* 'ban' (variously *ʾesār)* in the context of legislation governing the vows pronounced by Israelites. This term is basic to the entire votive system embodied in that chapter, and in no way can it be regarded as editorial. What is more, this very term has now turned up in the Samaria Papyri from Wadi Daliye, dated to the third quarter of the fourth century (Cross 1985). The logical conclusion to be derived from the existence of such comparative evidence is that Numbers 30 was also composed during the fifth or fourth century, when this previously unattested term was in use. It occurs nowhere else in the Hebrew Bible but, significantly, it does occur in the Aramaic sections of Daniel—repeatedly in Daniel 6, in its final form a product of the second century.

The use of language in dating biblical texts emerges as only one among several significant criteria relevant to this process. The language of P incorporates both early and late usage and diction but, in the last analysis, does more to suggest a relatively late date for the completion of P.

6. Realistic Interpretation

A contextual or historical treatment of the priestly materials in Numbers (for now, in Numbers 1–20) must also counter the argument that the laws and rituals of the priestly source of the Torah may be essentially programmatic, and therefore unrealistic in character. To put it another way: priests may never have offered sacrifices in the manner prescribed in Leviticus and Numbers during the biblical period. The community projected in the priestly source may not have existed in reality. In the present scholarly climate, there is a tendency to regard ancient law codes and records as canonical, a label that tends to distance them from reality and to brand them as artificial, or ossified, as once removed from living religion.

The discussion of context is, therefore, more than an effort to date biblical texts or to establish the *Sitz-im-Leben* of their authors. It has to do with assessing their value as windows on ancient reality. Are the priestly texts informative about the meaning and perceptions of religiosity in biblical Israel in specific periods?

The view endorsed in this commentary is that, in many ways, records of religious praxis reveal dimensions of religious life more realistic than prophetic pronouncements on what ought to be the proper practice of religion. In ancient Near Eastern studies generally, the value of administrative records, temple documents, and other types of descriptive evidence is now recognized as every bit as valuable as the messages of myth and narrative.

Reference Bibliography

Abou-Assaf, A. 1982 *La Statue de Tell Fekherye* (with P. Bordreuil and A. R. Millard). Paris: Éditions Recherche sur les civilisations.

Abusch, I. Tzvi 1987 *Babylonian Witchcraft Literature.* Atlanta: Scholars Press.

Aharoni, Y. 1967 Forerunners of the Limes: Iron Age Fortresses in the Negev. *IEJ* 17: 1–17.

1974 Excavations at Tell Masos (Khirbet el-Meshash). *Tel Aviv* 1: 64–74 (with A. Kempinsky, V. Fritz, et al.).

1976 Arad. *IDBSup.* Nashville: Abingdon Press, 38–39.

1977 Excavations at Tell Masos. *Tel Aviv* 4: 13–158 (with A. Kempinsky et al.).

1979 *The Land of the Bible: A Historical Geography,* rev. by A. F. Rainey. Philadelphia: Westminster Press.

1981 *Arad Inscriptions,* trans. A. F. Rainey. Jerusalem: Israel Exploration Society.

——— and M. Avi-Yonah 1979 *The Modern Bible Atlas.* 2d ed. prepared by Carta, Ltd. Boston: Allen & Unwin.

Ahituv, S. 1971 *Ṣôʿan. EB* 6.744–747.

1976 *Reʿuʾēl. EB* 7.387.

Ahituv, Y. 1982 *Sélâw. EB* 8.306–307.

Albright, W. F. 1942 A Votive Stele Erected by Ben-Hadad I of Damascus to the God Melcarth. *BASOR* 87: 23–29.

1968 *Archaeology and the Religion of Israel.* 5th ed. Garden City, N.Y.: Doubleday, 210.

Amiran, R. 1964 Arad: A Biblical City in Southern Palestine. *Archaeology* 17: 43–53 (with Y. Yadin).

1980 The Early Canaanite City of Arad. *Qadmônîot* 13: 2–19 (with C. Arnon, D. Alon, R. Goethert, and P. Louppen).

Astour, M. C. 1965 The Origins of the Terms "Canaan," "Phoenician," and "Purple." *JNES* 24: 346–350.

Barkai, G. 1989 The Priestly Benediction on Silver from Keteph Hinnom in Jerusalem (Hebrew). *Cathedra* 52: 37–76.

Bartlett, J. R. 1989 *Edom and the Edomites*. Sheffield: JSOT Press.

Beit Arieh, I. 1989 An Edomite Shrine at Horvat Qitmit (Hebrew). *Eretz-Israel* 20 (Y. Yadin Volume): 135–146.

Ben Sira 1973 *The Book of Ben Sira: Text, Concordance and an Analysis of the Vocabulary*. Jerusalem: Academy of the Hebrew Language.

Brichto, H. C. 1975 The Case of the Sota and a Reconsideration of Biblical "Law." *HUCA* 46: 55–70.

Burshtin, M. 1988 *Hattĕkelet* (Hebrew). Tel Aviv: A. Gitler.

Caquot, A. 1977 *Debaš*. *ThWAT* 2.135–139.

Cohen, C. 1993 The Priestly Benediction (Num. 6:24–26) in the Light of Akkadian Parallels. *Tel Aviv*. Forthcoming.

Cohen, R. 1983 Excavations at Kadesh Barnea, 1976, 1982 (Hebrew). *Qadmoniot* 16: 2–14.

Cross, F. M. 1953 The Council of Yahweh in Second Isaiah. *JNES* 30: 274–277.

1985 Samaria Papyrus I: An Aramaic Slave Conveyance of 335 B.C.E. Found in the Wadi ed-Daliyeh. *Eretz-Israel* 18 (N. Avigad Volume): non-Hebrew section, 7–17.

——— and D. N. Freedman 1948 The Blessing of Moses. *JBL* 67: 191–210.

Cunchillos, J.-L. 1989 Correspondance. In *Textes ougaritiques*. Vol. 2 pt. 2. Paris: Cerf.

Dossin, G. 1978 *Correspondance feminine*. ARM 10. Paris: Librairie Orientaliste Paul Geuthner.

Driver, G. R. 1954 *Aramaic Documents of the Fifth Century B.C.* Rev. and abr. Oxford: Clarendon Press.

1956 Three Technical Terms in the Pentateuch. *JSS* 1: 97–105.

——— and J. C. Miles 1955 *The Babylonian Laws*. Vol. 2. Oxford: Clarendon, 282–285.

Dupont-Sommer, A. 1970 Une Inscription phénicienne archaique, récemment trouvée à Kition (Chypre). *Académie des Inscriptions et Belles Lettres, Mémoires* 44: 2–28.

Ehrlich, A. 1969 *Mikra Ki-Pheshuto* (Hebrew). Vol. 1. New York: Ktav.

Eilat, M. 1982 *Tekēlet we'argaman, EB* 8:543–546.

Einige, C. A. and R. R. Durfee 1966 Pelvic Prolapse: Four Thousand Years of Treatment. *Clinical Obstetrics and Gynecology*, December: 997–1032.

Eissfeldt, O. 1956 El and Yahweh. *JSS* 1: 25–37.

Fensham, F. C. 1962 Salt as Curse in the Old Testament and the Ancient Near East. *BA* 25: 48–50.

Finkelstein, I. 1988 *The Archaeology of the Israelite Settlement.* Jerusalem: Israel Exploration Society.

Fishbane, M. 1974 Accusations of Adultery: A Study of Law and Scribal Practice in Numbers 5:11–31. *HUCA* 45:25–45.

Fitzmyer, J. A. 1959 The Aramaic Qorban Inscriptions. *JBL* 78: 60–65.

Freedman, D. N. 1975 The Aaronic Benediction. In *No Famine in the Land,* ed. J. W. Flanagan and A. Weisbrod Robinson. Claremont, Calif.: Claremont Graduate School, 35–47.

1986 Verbal communication to the author.

Friedrich, J. 1970 *Phönizisch-Punische Grammatik.* Rome: Pontificium Institutum Biblicum.

Frymer-Kensky, T. 1983 Pollution, Purification, and Purgation in Biblical Israel. In *The Word of the Lord Shall Go Forth,* ed. C. L. Meyers and M. O'Connor. Winona Lake: Eisenbrauns, 399–414.

1984 The Strange Case of the Suspected *Sôṭāh* (Numbers V 11–31). *VT* 34: 11–26.

Garfinkel, Y. 1987 The Meaning of the Word MPQD in the Tel 'Ira Ostracon. *PEQ* 119: 19–23.

Gaster, T. H. 1969 *Myth Legend and Custom in the Old Testament.* New York: Harper and Row.

Gesenius 1960 *Gesenius' Hebrew Grammar,* ed. E. Kautzch, trans. A. E. Cowley. 2d English ed. Oxford: Clarendon.

Gibson, J. C. 1971 *Textbook of Syrian Semitic Inscriptions,* vol. 1: *Hebrew and Moabite Inscriptions.* Oxford: Clarendon.

1975 *Textbook of Syrian Semitic Inscriptions,* vol. 2: *Aramaic Inscriptions.* Oxford: Clarendon.

1978 *Canaanite Myths and Legends.* 2d ed. Edinburgh: T & T Clark.

1982 *Textbook of Syrian Semitic Inscriptions,* vol. 3: *Phoenician Inscriptions.* Oxford: Clarendon.

Ginsberg, H. L. 1945 Psalms and Inscriptions of Petition and Acknowledgement. In *Louis Ginzberg Jubilee Volume,* ed. A. Marx et al. New York: American Academy of Jewish Research, 159–171.

1982 *The Israelian Heritage of Israel.* New York: Jewish Theological Seminary of America.

1988 Verbal communication to the author.

Good, R. 1983 *The Sheep of His Pasture: A Study of the Hebrew Noun*

'*Am(m) and Its Semitic Cognates*. Chico, Calif.: Scholars Press.

Gray, G. B. 1913 The Forms of Hebrew Poetry. *Expositor* 1913: A.421–441, 552–568; B.45–60, 117–140, 221–244, 306–328, 529–553.

1971 *Sacrifice in the Old Testament*, with a prolegomenon by B. A. Levine. New York: Ktav.

See also Gray—ICC *in the Abbreviations.*

Greenberg, M. 1983 *Biblical Prose Prayer as a Window to the Popular Religion of Ancient Israel*. Berkeley and Los Angeles: University of California Press.

Hackett, J. A. 1980 *The Balaam Text from Deir 'Alla*. Harvard Semitic Monographs 31. Chico, Calif.: Scholars Press.

1987 Religious Traditions in Israelite Transjordan. In *Ancient Israelite Religion*, ed. P. D. Miller et al. Philadelphia: Fortress Press, 125–136.

Hallo, W. W. 1991a Royal Ancestor Worship in the Biblical World, "*Sha'arei Talmon.*" In *Studies in the Bible, Qumran, and the Ancient Near East, Presented to Shemaryahu Talmon*, ed. M. Fishbane et al. Winona Lake: Eisenbrauns, 381–402.

1991b The Death of Kings: Traditional Historiography in Contextual Perspective. *Ah, Assyria, Studies in Assyrian History and Ancient Neareastern Historiography* Presented to Hayim Tadmor, ed. M. Cogan, et al., *Scripta Hierosolymitana* 33, 148–165.

Haran, M. 1960 The Uses of Incense in the Ancient Israelite Ritual. *HUCA* 36: 217–223.

1962 *Mattenôt Kehunnāh* (Priestly Emoluments). *EB* 4.39–45.

1981 Behind the Scenes of History: Determining the Date of the Priestly Source. *JBL* 100: 321–333.

1989 The Priestly Benediction from Keteph Hinnom—The Biblical Significance of the Discovery. *Cathedra* 52: 77–89.

Haupt, P. 1918 Assyrian *dagālu*- "to look" in the Old Testament. *JBL* 37: 229–232.

Herodotus 1971 *Herodotus*, ed. and trans. A. D. Godley. Loeb Classical Library. Cambridge, Mass.: Harvard University Press, book 4.

Hinke, W. J. 1911 *Selected Babylonian Kudurru Inscriptions*. Leiden: E. J. Brill.

Hoftijzer, J. 1967 Das Sogenannte Feueropfer. VTSup 16, 114–134.

——— and G. van der Kooij 1976 *Aramaic Texts from Deir ʿAlla*. Leiden: E. J. Brill.

Howlett, D. 1992 *British Books in Biblical Style*. Forthcoming.

Jackson, K. P. 1983 Ammonite Personal Names in the Context of the West Semitic Onomasticon. In *The Word of the Lord Shall Go Forth*, ed. C. Meyers and M. O'Connor. Winona Lake: Eisenbrauns, 507–521.

Japhet, S. 1983 People and Land in the Restoration Period. In *Das Land Israel*. Göttingen: Vandenhoeck & Ruprecht, 103–125.

Jastram, N. 1989 "4Q Num-b from Qumran." Ph.D. diss., Harvard University.

Kaufmann, Y. 1960 *The Religion of Israel*, trans. and abridged by M. Greenberg. Chicago: University of Chicago Press.

1967 *The History of Israelite Religion* (Hebrew). 2d ed., 4 vols. Jerusalem: Bialik Institute.

Kelso, J. A. 1948 *The Ceramic Vocabulary of the Old Testament*. *BASOR* suppl. 5–6.

Kempinsky, A. 1982 *Talmaî*. *EB* 8.575–576.

——— and N. Neeman 1973 The Idrimi Inscription Reconsidered. In *Excavations and Studies (S. Yeivin)* (Hebrew). Tel Aviv: Institute of Archaeology, 211–220.

Kinnier-Wilson, J. V. 1966 Leprosy in Ancient Mesopotamia. *RA* 60: 47–58.

Knudtzon, J. A. 1964 *Die Amarna Tafeln*. Aalen: Otto Zeller, vols. 1 and 2.

Kochavi, M. 1970 The First Season of Excavations at Tell Malhata. *Qadmoniot* 3: 22–24.

1973 Khirbet Rabud—Ancient Debir (Hebrew). *Publications of the Institute of Archaeology at Tel Aviv University* 1: 111–118.

1977 Malḥata, Tell. *EAEHL* 3.771–772, 774–775.

1980 Rescue in the Biblical Negev. *BAR* 6: 24–27.

Kraemer, J. R. 1966 *Šeqʿarûrôt:* A Proposed Solution for an Unexplained Hapax. *JNES* 25: 125–129.

Lambert, W. 1960 *Babylonian Wisdom Literature*. Oxford: Clarendon Press.

Lauterbach, J. Z. 1976 *Mekhilta de Rabbi Ishmael*. Philadelphia: Jewish Publication Society, vol. 3.

Levine, B. A. 1963 The *Netînîm*. *JBL* 82: 207–212.

1965a The Descriptive Tabernacle Texts of the Pentateuch. *JAOS* 85: 307–318.
1965b Comments on Some Technical Terms of the Cult (Hebrew). *Leshonenu* 30: 3–11.
1968a On the Presence of the Lord in Biblical Religion. In *Religions in Antiquity*, ed. J. Neusner. Leiden: E. J. Brill, 1.17–27.
1968b *Nergal. EB* 5.924–926.
1974 *In the Presence of the Lord.* Leiden: E. J. Brill.
1975 On the Origins of the Aramaic Formulary at Elephantine. In *Christianity, Judaism and Other Greco-Roman Cults*, ed. J. Neusner. Leiden: E. J. Brill, 3.37–54.
1976 More on the Inverted Nuns of Num. 10:35–36. *JBL* 95: 122–124.
1978 Chapters in the History of Spoken Hebrew (Hebrew). *Eretz-Israel* 16: 155–160.
1979a The Temple Scroll: Aspects of Its Historical Provenance and Literary Character. *BASOR* 232: 4–26.
1979b On the Arad Inscriptions (Hebrew). *Shenaton—Annual of Bible and Semitic Studies*, ed. M. Weinfeld, 3: 283–294.
1981 The Deir ʿAlla Plaster Inscriptions. *JAOS* 101: 195–205.
1982a From the Aramaic Enoch Fragments: The Semantics of Cosmography. *JJS* 33 *(Yadin Volume)*: 311–326.
1982b Assyriology and Hebrew Philology: A Methodological Re-examination. In *Mesopotamien und seine Nachbarn*, ed. J. Renger et al. XXVe Rencontre Assyriologique. Berlin: 1.521–550.
1982c Research in the Priestly Source: The Linguistic Factor (Hebrew). *Eretz-Israel* 16 *(Orlinsky Volume)*: 124–131.
1983 Late Language in the Priestly Source: Some Literary and Historical Observations. In *Proceedings of the Eighth World Congress of Jewish Studies, Panel Sessions: Bible Studies and Hebrew Language.* Jerusalem: World Union of Jewish Studies: 69–82.
1985a The Pronoun *Še* in Biblical Hebrew in the Light of Ancient Epigraphy (Hebrew). *Eretz-Israel* 18 *(Avigad Volume)*: 147–152.
1985b The Balaam Text from Deir ʿAlla: Historical Aspects. In *Biblical Archaeology Today.* Jerusalem: Israel Exploration Society, 326–339.

1987a The Epilogue to the Holiness Code: A Priestly Statement on the Destiny of Israel. In *Judaic Perspectives on Ancient Israel,* ed. J. Neusner et al. Philadelphia: Fortress Press, 9–34.

1987b The Language of Holiness: Perceptions of the Sacred in the Hebrew Bible. In *Backgrounds for the Bible,* ed. M. O'Connor and D. N. Freedman. Winona Lake: Eisenbrauns, 241–255.

1989a The Triumphs of the Lord. *Eretz-Israel* 20: 202–214.

1989b *Leviticus.* The JPS Torah Commentary. Philadelphia: Jewish Publication Society.

1990 The Impure Dead and the Cult of the Dead: Polarization and Opposition in Israelite Religion (Hebrew). *Bitzaron* 10: 80–89.

1991 The Plaster Inscriptions from Deir ʿAlla: General Interpretation. In *The Balaam Text from Deir ʿAlla Re-evaluated,* ed. J. Hoftijzer and G. van der Kooij. Leiden: E. J. Brill, 58–72.

——— and J.-M. de Tarragon 1984 Dead Kings and Rephaim: The Patrons of the Ugaritic Dynasty. *JAOS* 104: 649–659.

Levy, J. 1963 *Wörterbuch über die Talmudim und Midraschim.* 4 vols. Darmstadt: Wissenschaftliche Buchgesellschaft (reprint of Berlin-Wier ed., 1924).

Licht, J. 1965 *The Rule Scroll* (Hebrew). Jerusalem: Bialik Institute, 277–286.

1985 *A Commentary on the Book of Numbers (I–X)* (Hebrew). Jerusalem: Magnes Press.

1991 *A Commentary on the Book of Numbers (XI–XXI)* (Hebrew). Jerusalem: Magnes Press.

Lieberman, S. 1950 Critical Marks *(semeia kritika)* in the Hebrew Bible. In *Hellenism in Jewish Palestine.* New York: Jewish Theological Seminary.

1967a *The Tosefta,* part 6: *Order of Nashim.* New York: Jewish Theological Seminary.

1967b *Tosefta Ki-fshutah: A Comparative Commentary on the Tosefta,* part 6: *Order of Nashim.* New York: Jewish Theological Seminary.

Liver, J. 1968a *Chapters in the History of the Priests and Levites* (Hebrew). Jerusalem: Magnes Press.

1968b *Mešîḥāh. EB* 5.526–531.

Loew, I. 1881 *Aramäische Pflanzennamen.* Vol. 1. Leipzig: Engelman.

Loewenstamm, S. 1976 *Qehāt. EB* 7.84–87.

Malamat, A. 1970 The Danite Migration and the Pan-Israelite Exodus-Conquest (Hebrew). *Eretz-Israel* 10: 173–179.

Mazar, B. 1950 'Ôn. *EB* 1.148.

1962 *Lebô' Ḥamāt. EB* 4.416–418.

1965 The Sanctuary of Arad and the Family of Hobab the Kenite. *JNES* 24: 297–308.

1969 *The Excavations in the Old City of Jerusalem.* Jerusalem: Israel Exploration Society.

McCarter, P. K. 1980 *I Samuel.* Anchor Bible 8. Garden City, N.Y.: Doubleday, 1980.

1984 *II Samuel.* Anchor Bible 9. Garden City, N.Y.: Doubleday, 1984.

McKane, W. 1980 Poison, Trial by Ordeal and the Cup of Wrath. *VT* 30: 474–492.

Meier, S. 1989 House Fungus: Mesopotamia and Israel. *RB* 96: 35–53.

Mendenhall, G. E. 1957 The Census Lists of Numbers 1 and 26. *JBL* 76: 52–66.

Meshel, Z. 1978 *Kuntillet ʿAjrud: A Religious Center from the Time of the Judean Monarchy on the Border of Sinai.* Israel Museum Catalogue 175. Jerusalem: Israel Museum.

Meyers, C. 1976 *The Tabernacle Menorah.* ASOR Dissertation Series 2. Missoula, Mont.: Scholars Press.

Midrash Hagadol 1932 *Midrash Hagadol, Leviticus,* ed. E. N. Rabinowitz. New York: Jewish Theological Seminary.

Milgrom, J. 1970 *Studies in Levitical Terminology.* Near Eastern Studies 14. Berkeley and Los Angeles: University of California Press.

1972 The Alleged Wave Offering in Israel and the Ancient Near East. *IEJ* 22: 33–38.

1976 *Cult and Conscience.* Leiden: E. J. Brill.

1989 *Numbers.* The JPS Torah Commentary. Philadelphia and New York: Jewish Publication Society.

Miller, P. and J. J. M. Roberts 1977 *The Hand of the Lord: A Reassessment of the Ark Narratives of I Samuel.* Baltimore: The Johns Hopkins University Press.

Moran, W. 1969 New Evidence from Mari on the History of Prophecy. *Biblica* 50: 17–56.

Muffs, Y. 1978 Reflections on Prophetic Prayer in the Bible (Hebrew). *Eretz-Israel* 14: 48–54.

Musil, A. 1928 *The Manners and Customs of the Rwala Bedouins,* New York: American Geographical Society.

Naveh, J. 1981 Inscriptions of the Biblical Period (Hebrew). In *Thirty*

Years of Archaeology in Eretz-Israel, 1948–1978. Jerusalem: Israel Exploration Society, 75–85.

Neusner, J. 1973 *The Idea of Purity in Ancient Judaism.* Leiden: E. J. Brill.

Noth, M. 1962 *Exodus, a Commentary,* trans. J. S. Bowden. The Old Testament Library. Philadelphia: Westminster Press.

Ofer, A. 1989 Excavations at Biblical Hebron. *Qadmoniot* 22: 88–93.

Orlinsky, H. M. 1966 The Massoretic Text: A Critical Evaluation. In *Introduction to the Massoretico-Critical Edition of the Hebrew Bible,* by C. D. Ginsburg. New York: Ktav, i–xlv.

Palmoni, Y. 1954 *Debôrāh* (Hebrew). *EB* 2.584–587.

Pardee, D. 1982 *Handbook of Hebrew Letters.* Chico, Calif.: Scholars Press.

Pettinato, G. 1979 *Culto officiale ad Ebla durante il regno di Ibbi-Šipiš.* Orientis antiqui collectio 16. Rome: Centro per le Antichità e la Storia dell'Arte de Vicino Oriente.

1982 *Testi lexicali bilingui della Biblioteca L 2769.* Naples: Isituto Universitario Orientale.

Pope, M. 1977 *Song of Songs.* Anchor Bible 24a. Garden City, N.Y.: Doubleday.

Porten, B. 1968 *Archives from Elephantine.* Berkeley and Los Angeles: University of California Press.

Rainey, A. F. 1968 The Scribe at Ugarit, His Position and Influence. *Israel Academy of Arts and Sciences* 111.4: 1–22.

1970 The Order of Sacrifices in Old Testament Rituals. *Biblica* 51: 485–498.

1973 Gleanings from Ugarit. *Israel Oriental Studies* 3: 34–62.

Roesel, H. 1986 Zur Formelierung des aaronitischen Segens auf den Amuletten von Ketef Hinnom. *Biblische Notizen* 35: 30–36.

Rofé, A. 1979 *The Book of Balaam (Numbers 22:2–24:25)* (Hebrew). Jerusalem: Sinor.

1988 *Introduction to Deuteronomy* (Hebrew). Jerusalem: Akademon.

Scott, R. B. Y. 1959 "Weights and Measures of the Bible," *BA* 22, 1959, 22–40.

Schuler, E. von 1957 *Hethitische Dienstanweisungen, für höhere Hof- und Stadtsbeamte.* (*Archiv für Orientforschung, Beiheftio*) *Im Selbstverlage des Herausgebers,* 1957.

Segal, J. B. 1983 *Aramaic Texts from North Saqqara.* London: Egypt Exploration Society.

Segal, M. Z. 1971 *The Books of Samuel* (Hebrew). Jerusalem: Qiryat Sepher.

Seters, J. van 1976 The Terms "Amorite" and "Hittite" in the Old Testament. *VT* 22: 64–81.

Smith, W. R. 1969 *Lectures on the Religion of the Semites.* 3d ed. with intro. and notes by S. A. Cook, prolegomenon by J. Muilenberg. The Library of Biblical Studies, ed. H. M. Orlinsky. New York: Ktav.

Speiser, E. A. 1963a Background and Function of the Biblical Nasi'. *CBQ* 25: 111–117.

1963b Unrecognized Dedication. *CBQ* 25: 111–117.

Sperber, A. 1944 *The Bible in Aramaic,* vol. 1: *The Pentateuch according to Targum Onkelos.* Leiden: E. J. Brill.

Spiegel, S. 1953 Verbal communication to the author.

Stern, E. 1962 *Mišqālôt. EB* 4.846–878.

Stern, P. 1991 *The Biblical Ḥerem: A Window on the Religious Experience of Biblical Israel.* Atlanta: Scholars Press.

Tadmor, H. 1968 "The People and the Kingship in Ancient Israel: The Role of Political Institutions," *Cahiers d'Histoire Mondïale* 11, 1968, 46–68.

1982 *Taḥaš. EB* 8.520.

Tal, A. 1981 *The Samaritan Targum of the Pentateuch,* part 2: *Numeri.* Tel Aviv: Tel Aviv University.

Tigay, J. 1970 Psalm 7:5 and Ancient Near Eastern Treaties. *JBL* 89: 178–186.

Tov, E. 1981 *The Text-Critical Use of the Septuagint in Biblical Research.* Jerusalem: Sinor.

Vaux, R. de 1968 Le Pays de Canaan. *JAOS* 88: 23–30.

1970 The Settlement of the Israelites in Southern Palestine and the Origins of the Tribe of Judah. In *Translating and Understanding the Old Testament: Essays in Honor of Gordon May,* ed. H. T. Frank et al. Nashville: Abingdon Press.

1978 *The Early History of Israel,* trans. J. Smith. 2 vols. London: Dartman, Longman & Todd, and Philadelphia: Westminster Press.

Weinberg, J. P. 1973 Das Beit 'abot in 6.–4 Jh. v.v. Z. *VT* 23: 400–414.

Wellhausen, J. 1965 *Prolegomena to the History of Ancient Israel,* trans. Black and Menzies. Cleveland: Meridian Books.

Wevers, J. W. 1982 *Septuaginta Vetus Testamentum Graecum: Numeri.* Göttingen: Vandenhoeck & Ruprecht.

Whitaker, R. 1972 A *Concordance of the Ugaritic Literature.* Cambridge, Mass.: Harvard University Press.

Wilson, J. A. 1969 The Protestation of Guiltlessness. In *ANET*, 34–36.

Wright, D. 1986 The Gesture of Hand Placement in the Hebrew Bible and in Hittite Literature. *JAOS* 106: 433–446.

Yadin, Y. 1962 *The Scroll of the War of the Sons of Light Against the Sons of Darkness,* trans. B. Rabin and C. Rabin. Oxford: Oxford University Press.

1978 *The Temple Scroll* (Hebrew). 3 vols. Jerusalem: Israel Exploration Society.

Yardeni, A. 1991 Remarks on the Priestly Blessing on Two Ancient Amulets from Jerusalem. *VT* 41: 176–185.

PART I.

NUMBERS 1–4: GETTING ORGANIZED

NUMBERS 1: THE WILDERNESS CENSUS

The book of Numbers begins by recording a census of the Israelites, undertaken at God's command by Moses and the chieftains of the twelve tribes of Israel. Numbers 1 actually introduces the reader to a larger unit, comprising Numbers 1–4, in which the Israelites of the Sinai period are portrayed as a military force, a camp on the march consisting of adult fighting men. No mention is made in these chapters of the Israelite families. The Levites, who were dedicated to Tabernacle service, were exempt from military service and were accordingly left out of the census. This exemption is stated in Num 1:48–54, in anticipation of the provisions of Numbers 3–4, where the alternative functions of the Levites are spelled out in detail.

Numbers 2 sets forth the arrangement of the Israelite encampment *(maḥaneh)* and prescribes the order in which the tribes were to set out on the march. Chapters 3 and 4 focus on the Tabernacle complex located at the core of the encampment, and they detail the internal organization of the tribe of Levi. The various levitical clans were assigned specific duties in transporting and servicing the portable Tabernacle and its furnishings.

As for the tribe of Levi, as a part of the Israelite people, we are told that this tribe consisted of two parts: the Levites are separate from the Aaronide priests, who were also of the same tribe. The internal division of the tribe of Levi is introduced by the priestly traditions of Numbers and represents one of the highlights of the book of Numbers as a whole. In Deuteronomy, for instance, all Levites are priests, whereas Exodus and Leviticus speak for the most part only of the Aaronide priests.

Priestly historiography proceeds from Exodus, through Leviticus, and continues in Numbers. In this way, the events recorded in Numbers 1–4 are dated just subsequent to the erection of the Tabernacle, an event recorded in Exod 40:17. All of the intervening material preserved in Leviticus is "dateless," it being presumed that the regulations for the priestly conduct of the cult were communicated by God to Moses (and occasionally to Aaron) during a period of about one month, between the first and second months of the second year after the Exodus from Egypt.

As we would expect, Numbers 1 resembles Numbers 26 in significant respects, for Numbers 26 is the record of a second census taken at the conclusion of the forty-year period of the wilderness migrations.

Numbers 1 may be divided into three parts. (1) Verses 1–19 record the divine command to take a census and proceed to list the chieftains of the twelve tribes, beginning with Reuben, who were to assist Moses in accomplishing it. The two sons of Joseph, Ephraim and Manasseh, take up the slack resulting from the exclusion of the tribe of Levi from the list of twelve. This adjustment is epitomized in Gen 48:5b, in the words of Jacob's blessing: "Ephraim and Manasseh shall be for me as Reuben and Simeon!" (2) Verses

20–47 list the total musters of each tribe in turn and conclude with the anticipatory statement that the Levites were to be counted separately. (3) Finally, vv 48–54 expound the policy of the book of Numbers regarding the distinct status of the Levites as cultic servitors, thus anticipating Numbers 3–4, as well as the consecration of the Levites recorded in Numbers 8.

Numbers 1, all of Numbers 1–4, and Numbers 10, which records the march from south to north in Sinai, serve to tighten the historiographic link between the Exodus and the wilderness experience. The key term in this link is *ṣābāʾ* and its plural form *ṣebāʾôt*, variously translated "force(s), division(s)." Thus we read in Exod 6:26; 12:41, 51 that God brought the Israelite "forces" out of Egypt, or that these "forces" marched out of Egypt (cf. Num 33:1). In Numbers 1, 2, and 10 we are told that the same "forces" or "divisions" were mustered and deployed in the wilderness.

In terms of its form, Numbers 1 may originally have been written as a tabular record in several columns. The clearest example of this format is Numbers 7, and in the COMMENT to that chapter this method of recording is explained with reference to comparative sources from the ancient Near East.

TRANSLATION

1 [1]YHWH spoke to Moses, in the Wilderness of Sinai, at the Tent of Meeting, on the first day of the second month, in the second year after their departure from Egypt, as follows:

[2]Take a poll of the entire community of the Israelites by their clans and their patriarchal "houses," according to the number of names, every male, by their heads;

[3]those above twenty years of age: all those eligible for military service among the Israelites. You shall muster them by their divisions, you and Aaron.

[4]With you there shall be one man from each tribe, a man who is head of his own patriarchal house.

[5]These are the names of the men who shall stand with you:
Representing Reuben—Elizur son of Shedeur.
[6]Representing Simeon—Shelumiel son of Zurishaddai.
[7]Representing Judah—Nahshon son of Amminadab.
[8]Representing Issachar—Nethanel son of Zuar.
[9]Representing Zebulun—Eliab son of Helon.
[10]Representing the descendants of Joseph:
Representing Ephraim—Elishama son of Ammihud.
Representing Manasseh—Gamaliel son of Pedahzur.
[11]Representing Benjamin—Abidan son of Gideoni.
[12]Representing Dan—Ahiezer son of Ammishaddai.
[13]Representing Asher—Pagiel son of Ochran.

14 Representing Gad—Eliasaph son of Deuel.
15 Representing Naphtali—Ahira son of Enan.
16 These are the elect of the community, the chieftains of their patriarchal tribes; they are the heads of the sibs of Israel.
17 Moses and Aaron gathered these men, who had been specified by name.
18 They assembled the entire community on the first day of the second month. They, [in turn,] registered their affiliations, by their clans and patriarchal houses, according to the number of names, of those twenty years of age and above, by their heads.
19 Just as YHWH had commanded Moses, so did he muster them in the Wilderness of Sinai.
20 There were the descendants of Reuben, the firstborn of Israel; those born to them, by their clans and patriarchal houses, according to the number of names, by their heads, every male twenty years of age and above, all of those eligible for military service.
21 The musters of those affiliated with the tribe of Reuben: 46,500.
22 Of the descendants of Simeon, those born to them, by their clans and patriarchal houses; his musters, according to the number of names, by their heads, every male twenty years of age and above, all of those eligible for military service.
23 The musters of those affiliated with the tribe of Simeon: 59,300.
24 Of the descendants of Gad, those born to them, by their clans and patriarchal houses; according to the names of those twenty years of age and above, all of those eligible for military service.
25 The musters of those affiliated with the tribe of Gad: 45,650.
26 Of the descendants of Judah, those born to them, by their clans and patriarchal houses; according to the names of those twenty years of age and above, all of those eligible for military service.
27 The musters of those affiliated with the tribe of Judah: 74,600.
28 Of the descendants of Issachar, those born to them, by their clans and patriarchal houses; according to the names of those twenty years of age and above, all of those eligible for military service.
29 The musters of those affiliated with the tribe of Issachar: 54,400.
30 Of the descendants of Zebulun, those born to them, by their clans and patriarchal houses, according to the names of those twenty years of age and above, all of those eligible for military service.
31 The musters of those affiliated with the tribe of Zebulun: 57,400.
32 Of the descendants of Joseph—of the descendants of Ephraim, those born to them, by their clans and patriarchal houses; according to the names of those twenty years of age and above, all of those eligible for military service.
33 The musters of those affiliated with the tribe of Ephraim: 40,500.
34 Of the descendants of Manasseh, those born to them, by their clans and

patriarchal houses; according to the names of those twenty years of age and
above, all of those eligible for military service.
35 The musters of those affiliated with the tribe of Manasseh: 32,200.
36 Of the descendants of Benjamin, those born to them, by their clans and
patriarchal houses; according to the names of those twenty years of age and
above, all of those eligible for military service.
37 The musters of those affiliated with the tribe of Benjamin: 35,400.
38 Of the descendants of Dan, those born to them, by their clans and patriarchal houses; according to the names of those twenty years of age and above,
all of those eligible for military service.
39 The musters of those affiliated with the tribe of Dan: 62,700.
40 Of the descendants of Asher, those born to them, by their clans and patriarchal houses; according to the names of those twenty years of age and above,
all of those eligible for military service.
41 The musters of those affiliated with the tribe of Asher: 41,500.
42 Of the descendants of Naphtali, those born to them, by their clans and
patriarchal houses; according to the names of those twenty years of age and
above, all of those eligible for military service.
43 The musters of those affiliated with the tribe of Naphtali: 53,400.
44 These are the musters that Moses and Aaron arrayed, together with the
chieftains of Israel; twelve men, one man each, affiliated with his patriarchal
house.
45 Total musters of the Israelite people, by their patriarchal houses; those
twenty years of age and above, all of those eligible for military service in Israel:
46 The total musters amounted to 603,550.
47 But the Levites, affiliated with their patriarchal tribe, had not been included in their musters.
48 YHWH spoke to Moses as follows:
49 Moreover, as regards the tribe of Levi, you must be certain not to muster,
or take a poll of them among the Israelite people.
50 And as for you, appoint the Levites in charge of the Tabernacle of the
Covenant, and in charge of all of its vessels, and everything pertaining to it.
They shall transport the Tabernacle and all of its vessels, and they shall perform its service, encamping around the Tabernacle.
51 Whenever the Tabernacle sets out on the march, the Levites shall dismantle it; and whenever the Tabernacle is encamped, the Levites shall set it up.
Any alien who intrudes shall be put to death.
52 The Israelite people shall encamp, each corps by itself and each *degel* by
itself, according to their divisions.
53 But the Levites shall encamp around the Tabernacle of the Covenant, so
that rage will not be brought against the community of the Israelite people.
The Levites shall be charged with maintaining the Tabernacle of the Covenant.

[54]The Israelites complied with all that YHWH had commanded Moses; they acted accordingly.

NOTES

1 1. Priestly historiographers often provide precise dates for the events they are recording, as if formulating an official chronicle. This practice was undoubtedly intended to enhance credibility. Compare Num 9:1; 10:11; 20:1; 33:3 for similar chronological formulations. In Gen 8:5, 13 we even find a chronology of the primeval flood.

The fact that the order to take the census came so shortly after the completion of the Tabernacle reveals the priestly agenda, as explained in the introduction to Numbers 1–4. The census had a military function, to be sure, but it also prepared the way for a delineation of the levitical assignments and for the provisions for maintaining the Tabernacle, both when stationary within the Israelite encampment and when on the march.

the Wilderness of Sinai. Hebrew *midbar Sinaî* is used here as the name of the southern part of the peninsula, where all of the events recorded between Exod 19:1 and Num 10:12 occurred. At that point, the Israelites began their march northward to the part of the Sinai peninsula called *midbar pāʾrān* 'the Wilderness of Paran'. Hebrew *midbār,* which more precisely means "steppe, desert," is nevertheless translated "wilderness," especially when it is used in priestly nomenclature, because of the atmosphere of harsh desolation projected in these texts. The problem of identifying toponyms in JE and P was discussed in the introduction to this volume, sections A.5.a–b.

Tent of Meeting. The Hebrew term *ʾôhel môʿēd* is one of the ways of referring to the tent structure where the Ark was housed, and which was the focal point of sacrifice. In some sources, the term *miškān* 'tent, Tabernacle' is used and functionally, the two designations refer to the same institution. As described in Exodus 25–27 and 35–40, this sanctuary complex was surrounded by an enclosed courtyard, open to the sky. The sacrificial altar stood in the courtyard and was oriented toward the entrance of the Tent, in line with the outside entrance to the courtyard itself. Sacrificial activity was thus directed toward the Tent, which was conceived as God's residence, where he was present during sacrifice and celebration.

The Tent itself was divided into two parts, separated by the *pārôket,* a screen embroidered with cherubs. Beyond the screen was the innermost section of the Tent, the Holy of Holies, where the Ark was kept, with its sculpted lid, the *kappôret.* In front of the screen, in the section encountered when entering the Tent, stood the Menorah, a standing candelabrum; the altar of incense overlaid with gold; and a presentation table.

The name *ʾôhel môʿēd* reflects the verb *y-ʿ-d* 'to come together, meet, assemble'. There were, however, differing traditions regarding the functions of this cult complex. In the priestly traditions, the "assembling" conveyed by the name is the assembly of the people for purposes of worship, and for other meetings on matters of common concern. In this conception, the Tent complex stood at the center of the Israelite encampment.

There is, however, another conception of the *'ôhel mô'ēd* as an oraculum, a site where God communicated his word to Moses. According to this conception, stated most clearly in Exod 33:6–11, which is not a priestly text, Moses would enter the Tent on occasion to receive a communication from God or to seek an audience with him. Whenever such a "meeting" took place, a cloud pillar appeared at the Tent's entrance, to separate this sacred area from the people and the surrounding environment. In this description, there is no reference to sacrificial activity at all, and the Tent in question stood outside the encampment.

It is, therefore, logical to assume that the name *'ôhel mô'ēd* expresses at least two conceptions that ought not to be synthesized, but rather seen as they are—two functions that were blended in the course of time. As regards Numbers 1–4 and priestly literature in general, it is cultic activity that is of major concern. And yet, we find in Num 7:89 a passing reference to the oracular function in a priestly text (see the NOTES on Num 7:89).

2. *Take a poll.* The idiom *nāśā' rō's*, literally, "to lift the head," means to take a head count or poll. Compare Exod 30:12, where the same idiom is used in yet another census associated with the Tabernacle project. There we read that to help finance the construction and furnishings of the Tabernacle, each adult male was taxed one-half shekel *laggulgôlet* 'by the head', the same language used in the present verse. (Cf. further in Num 26:2 and in Exod 16:16; 38:26.)

Israelites. There is a particular significance to the terms of reference that characterize the Israelites as a group. Because such terms will be employed throughout much of Numbers, it would be useful to explain them here, at the outset. Hebrew *'adat benê Yiśrā'ēl* combines two discrete terms, *'ēdāh* and *benê Yiśrā'ēl.* Hebrew *'ēdāh* is the characteristic term for the Israelites in the priestly literature of the Torah, whereas *benê Yiśrā'ēl* (which was traditionally rendered "children of Israel") is a more widely used ethnographic designation, in which *bēn* 'son' functions to express group affiliation. Thus, *benê 'Ammôn* designates "the Ammonite people" (Num 21:24), whereas *benê hannebî'îm* is best understood as "members of the prophetic guild," in which *bēn* signifies professional affiliation rather than kinship (1 Kgs 20:35).

Hebrew *'ēdāh,* in contrast, expresses an association based on social organization and is best rendered "community." Like *mô'ēd* 'assembly; appointed time', Hebrew *'ēdāh* derives from the root *y-'-d* 'to come together'. In Judg 14:8 we read of "a nest of bees (*'adat debôrîm*)," a usage that reveals the basic sense of *'ēdāh.* In Ugaritic epic we read of *'dt ilm* 'the assembly of the gods'

(Gibson 1978: 91; text 15, col. 2, lines 7, 11), just as we have *ʿadat ʾēl* 'the council of El' in Ps 82:1. Ugaritic poetry also attests the cosmic reference *ʿdt thmtm* 'the confluence of the two deeps', in parallelism with *mbk nhrm* 'the confluence of the two rivers' (Gibson 1978: 138; *Ugaritica* V, 564; text 7, line 3). The term *ʿēdāh* is also known in the Aramaic papyri from Egypt of the fifth century B.C.E. The Jewish mercenary colony of Elephantine was itself known as the *ʿēdāh,* and one who had a grievance would rise in the *ʿēdāh* to press his suit (*AP*, text 15, line 26; *BMAP* text 2, line 7; text 7, line 21; Levine 1989b: 22, to Lev 4:13; 202, n. 16 to Leviticus 4).

Priestly writers had a penchant for combining discrete terms of reference to produce composite terminology, and in so doing they implied synonymous meanings. This was undoubtedly part of their effort to embrace all of the acceptable traditions on Israelite origins and to blend them with one another. On this basis terminology like *ʿadat benê Yiśrāʾēl* was formulated.

clans . . . patriarchal "houses." Verse 2 uses two additional social terms, *mišpāḥāh* and *bêt ʾāb,* both of which require considerable explanation. I will translate *mišpāḥāh* as "clan," for want of a better term, and *bêt ʾāb* as "patriarchal 'house.' "

Mišpāḥāh designates what we would today call an extended family, one that included cousins, probably even those once or more removed. In the story of Ruth, Boaz was of the *mišpāḥāh* of Elimelek, Naomi's deceased husband (Ruth 2:13). In Numbers 27, where laws of inheritance are set forth, we gain further information on the parameters of the Israelite *mišpāḥāh.* Similarly, Lev 25:48–49 provide information about who one's *mišpāḥāh* relations are, for they are the ones exhorted to redeem an Israelite who had become indentured to a gentile. Leviticus 18, whose provisions are restated in Leviticus 20, defines the *mišpāḥāh* in terms of the prohibition of incest, prohibiting marriage with certain close clan relatives, while leaving open the option of marriage with others.

A measure of flexibility is to be assumed in the usage of most of the social terms of reference. At times, *mišpāḥāh* for example is synonymous with *šēbeṭ* 'tribe' (Judg 18:19), and even the entire Israelite people may be called one large *mišpāḥāh* (Jer 8:3; Amos 3:1; Mic 2:3). Such extended usage serves to emphasize the common bonds uniting all Israelites. The root *š-p-ḥ* is attested in Ugaritic, where the noun *špḥ* is parallel with *yrṭ* 'heir' (Hebrew *yôreš*; Gibson 1978: 82, on Keret, col. 1, line 24; 86, Keret, col. 3, lines 144, 152). In one Ugaritic passage we find the designation *špḥ bkrk,* which is best translated "your firstborn son," resembling *bēn bekôr* in biblical Hebrew (2 Kgs 3:27; Gibson 1978: 86, col. iii, line 144). How precisely Hebrew *šipḥāh* fits into the etymology of *mišpāḥāh* remains somewhat uncertain. Hebrew *šipḥāh* is often synonymous with "slave" (Gen 32:6; Isa 24:2). Conceivably, a *šipḥāh* was a female child born into the *mišpāḥāh* that owned her parents, or one of her parents. This status would be similar to that of *yelîd bayît,* literally, "one born into the household" (Gen 17:12f.), or *ben bayît* 'member of the household' (Gen 15:3), a reference to Eliezer, Abraham's slave, who served as his steward.

More difficult to define, notwithstanding its obvious etymology, is the term *bêt 'āb* as a unit within the Israelite social structure. The *bêt 'āb* has a long history in Israelite society, and cognate social terms were known in other West Semitic cultures. The mid-second-millennium Syrian leader Idrimi speaks of a person with É *a-bi-šú* "his patriarchal house" as being fortunate, whereas one without this status is a virtual slave (Kempinsky-Neeman: 1973, on Idrimi line 10). In the Bible's patriarchal narratives, *bêt 'āb* is at least once synonymous with *mišpāḥāh* (Gen 24:38). One has the same impression regarding the parameters of the *bêt 'āb* of Gideon (Judg 6:27), and of Abimelek (Judg 9:18). In fact, in Judg 6:15, which also comments on Gideon's social status, *bêt 'āb* is synonymous with *'elep,* a social term to be discussed in the NOTES on v 4, below. It was certainly a unit larger than the immediate family.

Particularly relevant to a consideration of the Aaronide priesthood and of the Levites are the statements in 1 Sam 2:27–36 in which Eli, the chief priest of Shiloh, is told that his *bêt 'āb,* which had been granted the exclusive right to the priesthood while yet in Egypt, had betrayed its trust. The implication is clear that the *bêt 'āb* was a social unit similar to the *mišpāḥāh.* The translation "patriarchal house" is intended to convey the patrilineal descent basic to this social structure as well as the transactions on the notion of *bayît* 'house, household' expressed by the term itself.

The connotation of the term *bêt 'āb* in the priestly sources of the Torah, especially in Numbers, most likely reflects a considerably later social reality, of the late sixth to fourth centuries B.C.E. (Weinberg 1973). The most proximate sources of information within the priestly source are Numbers 3–4, which outline the internal organization of the tribe of Levi in the course of enumerating the specific assignments of the various levitical clans. As a result of P's specific agenda in Numbers, we possess detailed information about the tribe of Levi but not about other tribes. We may, however, generalize from what we read in Numbers 3–4, on the assumption that in the priestly view all of the tribes were structured in the same way as the tribe of Levi. As we shall observe in the NOTES to v 15, below, this method will shed light on other social terminology as well. The priestly school revived ancient terms of reference, like *nāśî'* 'chieftain' and *'elep* 'sib, militia', as well as *bêt 'āb,* in the effort to lend to their later projections an atmosphere of presettlement or premonarchic Israel.

The pattern evident in Numbers 3–4 may be charted as follows:

Generation 1: Tribe *(maṭṭeh),* listed by epigone (example: Levi, son of Jacob)

Generation 2: Patriarchal house *(bêt ʾāb)*, listed by son of tribal epigone (example: the *bêt ʾāb* of Gerson, son of Levi)

Generation 3: Clan *(mišpāḥāh)*, listed by son of the head of the *bêt ʾāb* (example: the *mišpāḥāh* of Libni, son of Gerson)

In the synchronic perspective, we can state that a tribe of Israel consisted of several primary patriarchal houses *(bêt ʾāb)*, each of which was divided into clans *(mišpāḥāh)*. Diachronically, we perceive a generational factor at work, whereby over a period of three generations the tribes of Israel, including the tribe of Levi, progressively split up into smaller units. This process stops with the third generation, and for a fairly obvious reason: the intent of the priestly writers in Numbers 1–4 was to summarize the formative stages of presettlement tribal development within the time frame extending from the initial designation of the tribes to the wilderness period. In Gen 15:16 it is predicted that the fourth generation would return to Canaan, namely, the generation born during the Sinai-Transjordanian period. The tribal structure, according to priestly tradition, was fixed before the Israelites entered Canaan.

Gray—ICC (p. 5) saw things differently and concluded that the *bêt ʾāb* was a smaller unit than the *mišpāḥāh*. He cites as evidence the progression stated in Josh 7:14. In seeking to apprehend an offender, lots are cast, and the procedure moves in on the offender in the following order: (1) *šēbeṭ* 'tribe', (2) *mišpāḥāh* 'clan', and (3) *bātîm* 'houses, households'.

There is, however, a difference between the simple term *bayit* as a way of referring to a family or household, and the discrete term *bêt ʾāb*. In certain contexts, Hebrew *bayît* designates the immediate family, as in Ruth 1:9 and more systematically in Lev 18:9, where the term *bayît* designates a family headed by a husband and wife, sharing the same domicile. Hebrew *bêt ʾāb* is a different matter, however.

according to the number of names. Hebrew *bemispar šēmôt* recalls Isa 40:26, where God is portrayed as commanding the heavenly hosts: "He leads forth their hosts *(ṣebāʾām)* by number *(bemispār)*, calling them all out by name *(bešēm)*." Closer to home, we find a similar formulation in Num 3:40: *weśāʾ ʾet mispar šemôtām* 'take a count of the number of their names'.

3. There are various systems evident in Torah literature for classifying adults. In Numbers 1 no retirement age is mentioned, but only the minimum age for being counted in the census, namely, twenty years of age. This is also the case in Exod 30:14, in another poll taken for purposes of taxation. According to Numbers 4, however, the Levites were to begin their service only at age thirty, and complete it at age fifty (cf. Ezra 3:8). Because the term *ṣābāʾ* 'military, work force' is used both in the general census of chap. 1 and in the separate levitical census of chap. 4, indicating the affinity of the two texts, some explanation should be sought for this apparent discrepancy. The situa-

tion is further complicated by the provisions of Num 8:24–27, which require Levites twenty-five years old to report for Tabernacle service, and those fifty years old and over to retire from active service (see the NOTES on 8:24–27). Num 8:24–27 serve as an appendix to the record of the dedication of the Levites, and may represent a divergent tradition. A minimum age of twenty-five years has no currency elsewhere in biblical records. Perhaps some years of training were required for levitical duties, so that only at a later age would the Levites actually commence their Tabernacle service. The minimum age of twenty years merely marked eligibility. According to Lev 27:1–8, the valuations stipulated for purposes of votary donations imply a retirement age of sixty years.

military service. The formula *yôṣēʾ ṣābāʾ* connotes military service, and it is important to establish this precise sense because *ṣābāʾ* itself exhibits a wide range of meanings. Hebrew *ṣābāʾ* is cognate with Akkadian *ṣābu,* whose basic meaning is "manpower, work force, personnel," also "fighting force" (CAD Ṣ, 46–54, under *ṣābu).* The same semantic range is evident, though less elaborately, in biblical Hebrew usage. Thus, women called *haṣṣôbeʾôt* in Exod 38:8 and 1 Sam 2:22 were the female personnel who worked in the sanctuaries. In Num 4:23 and 8:24, the formula *liṣbôʾ ṣābāʾ* means "to perform service." In Num 4:3, Hebrew *liṣbôʾ ṣābāʾ* is synonymous with *laʿabôd ʿabodah* 'to do service'—namely, to work at the sanctuary.

In contrast, the verb *yāṣāʾ* 'to go out', when used with *ṣābāʾ*, refers consistently to "marching forth"—to war. We find the same usage in Deut 20:1 and in Num 31:27–28, where warriors are called *hayyôṣeʾîm laṣṣābāʾ* 'those who *go out* to the army', and in Deut 24:5 we read of exemption from military service, stated as *lôʾ yēṣēʾ baṣṣābāʾ* 'He shall *not go out* as one of the military force'.

you must muster them. That Numbers 1–4 are describing a military force, one that alternately encamps and sets forth on the march, is also indicated by the verb *pāqad,* which appears first in the present verse, and which subsequently becomes basic to the content of this unit of the book of Numbers in the form of the nominal derivative, *pequddîm* 'musters'.

The verb *pāqad* is ambiguous, and connotes both "counting" and "mustering, arraying, assigning." Judging from the meanings known for the Akkadian cognate, *paqādu,* which is a verb of widespread usage, it seems that the basic sense is "to hand over, deliver, assign," hence: "to turn one's thoughts, or attention to—" (1 Kgs 20:15; 1 Sam 14:17; 18:1; Zech 10:3). In a curious way, this is its sense in Gen 21:1, where we read that God turned his attention to Sarah. The sense of "counting" is therefore derivative and not primary, as some have maintained, just as the basic sense of Hebrew *sāpar* is "to list, record," and only in a derivative sense "to number, count." The sense of "counting" derives from contexts projected for the verb *pāqad,* because so often mustering an army or force of conscripts involves counting off the number of those arrayed or deployed. A similar system is reflected in an early Phoenician inscription (Garfinkel 1987).

The present verse is to be translated "You shall *muster* them by their divisions." The important consequence of the proposed interpretation, which sees more than counting or numbering as being involved in the process, is that the noun *pequddim* is not to be translated "totals, tallies" in most instances. This caveat applies throughout Numbers 1–4 (see the NOTES on Num 3:22). The adult males were to be counted, of course, but they were also to be arrayed and assigned to military units, *leṣib'ôtām* 'by their divisions'. Hebrew *ṣebā'ôt* is actually the plural of masculine *ṣābā'*, the designation of a military unit, whose exact strength is not specified. In Numbers 2, we shall observe that the overall Israelite military force consisted of twelve *ṣebā'ôt*, so that we could define a *ṣābā'*, in the present context, as a tribal militia. The translation "division" is merely functional, for there were three *ṣebā'ôt* in each *mahaneh* 'corps' according to the provisions of Numbers 2 (Levine 1982a).

you and Aaron. The final two words of v 3, *'attāh we'aharôn,* are probably an explanatory gloss.

4. *tribe.* Hebrew *maṭṭeh,* like *šēbeṭ,* the other term for "tribe," literally means "staff." Whereas *šēbeṭ* is of more general usage, *maṭṭeh* is most often used by the priestly writers, and seldom by others. Idiomatic *'îš 'îš* 'each person' is common in priestly formulations (cf. Lev 16:17; 17:3, 8, 10, 13; 20:2, 9; 22:4; and Num 4:19, 49; 5:12).

head of his own patriarchal house. The point of v 4 is that each of the twelve tribal representatives was, in his own right, head of a *bêt 'āb* (cf. Josh 22:14, and see the NOTES on Num 10:4; 13:2). This position indicated high status. In v 16, below, the terminology has changed somewhat, and we find the composite term *neśî'ê maṭṭôt 'abôtām* 'the chieftains of their patriarchal tribes'. In Exod 6:14 we find the titulary *rā'šê bêt 'abôtām* 'the heads of their patriarchal groups', as in the present verse. In Num 25:15, we read that the Midianites were similarly organized.

Now, when we combine the preceding variations in the titles given to leaders with the evidence of Num 7:2, where the tribal leaders are designated *neśî'ê Yiśrā'ēl, rā'šê bêt 'abôtām* 'the chieftains of Israel, the heads of their patriarchal houses', we produce an equation: *nāśî'* = *rō's bêt 'āb.* On this basis, Eleazar, Aaron's son, is entitled *neśî' neśî'ê hallēwî* 'chief of the chieftains of Levi' in Num 3:32, indicating that there were any number of *neśî'îm* within the tribe of Levi. Incidentally, this evidence reinforces the conclusion, adopted in v 2 above, that the *bêt 'āb* was a unit larger than the *mišpāḥāh* 'clan' but smaller than the tribe.

5. *Representing. . . .* Prepositional *lamed,* as in *lammaṭṭeh,* functionally connotes representation and is a reflex of the possessive sense: "of each tribe; belonging to each tribe." This is the function of prepositional *lamed* through-

out the list of tribal leaders. Thus *lirʾûbēn* means "representing Reuben," and so forth. This is also the force of prepositional *lamed* in other lists in Numbers 7, 13, 26, and 34. In Num 7:24, we find, for example, *nāśîʾ libnê Zebulûn* 'the chieftain representing the Zebulunites'.

Gray notes that except for the names *Naḥšôn* and *ʿAmmînādāb* (Ruth 4:20), all the rest of the twenty-four names listed here are known only from the similar lists in Numbers 2, 7, and 10 and have no currency elsewhere in biblical literature.

5–15. It is now proper to discuss the names of the tribal chieftains. Most of them are shared with the lists of Numbers 2, 7, and 10, notwithstanding some differences in the order of the tribes, and are replaced in Numbers 13 and 34.

(1) *ʾElîṣûr ben Šedêʾûr* of Reuben (v 5). These names are limited to Numbers 1, 2, and 7, and both represent the El and Shaddai names so prevalent in the lists of Numbers. *Šĕdêʾûr* probably means "Shaddai is/gives light," just as *ʾUrîyāh* means "Yah is my light." *ʾElîṣûr* means "The 'Rock' is my god."

(2) *Šelûmîʾēl ben Ṣûrîšaddaî* of Simeon (v 6). These names are limited to Numbers 1, 2, 7, and 10. *Šelûmîʾēl* probably means "El is my friend, ally," on the basis that forms of the verb *šālam* may connote treaty alliance (Tigay 1970).

(3) *Naḥšôn ben ʿAmmînādāb* of Judah (v 7). This person is known elsewhere. His name appears in the geneaology of Ruth (4:20; and cf. 1 Chr 2:10–11). According to Exod 6:23, Aaron married the sister of one Nahshon, namely, Elisheva daughter of Amminadab. The name *Naḥšôn* means "snake-like" (*nāḥāš + ôn*, a characterizing affix). In the first instance, this is a heroic name, associated with the power of the snake. In Gen 49:16–17 Jacob speaks of the tribe of Dan as a snake that foils the chariotry, or cavalry, of the enemy! As a personal name, *Naḥāš* is associated with the kings of the Ammonites in the historical books of the Bible (1 Sam 11:1; 2 Sam 10:2). *ʿAmmînādāb* means "my [divine] kinsman has been generous."

(4) *Netanʾēl ben Ṣûʿar* of Issachar (v 8). This name is unknown outside Numbers 1, 2, 7, and 10, and this *nāśîʾ* was replaced in Num 13:8 and 34:26 by two different persons. *Ṣûʿar* is probably a form of *Ṣāʿîr* 'young, small', and may be compared with Akkadian *Ṣeḫer-ilī* "the youth of the god" (*HALAT* 949).

(5) *ʾElîʾāb ben Ḥēlôn* of Zebulun (v 9). Whereas *Ḥēlôn*, which may mean "powerful one" (*ḥayîl + ôn*), is limited to Numbers 2, 7, and 10, the name *ʾElîāb* enjoyed wider usage. This personage may or may not be identical with the father of Dathan and Abiram (Num 16:1–17; Deut 11:6). *HALAT* 53, under *ʾElîʾāb*, lists several cognates, and Ugaritic attests a deity named *ilib*, which probably means "Il is father" (*KTU* 1.47, line 2; 1.91, line 5).

(6) *ʾElišāmāʿ ben ʿAmmîhûd* of Ephraim (v 10). Cognates of *ʾElîšāmāʿ* are

attested outside biblical literature (*HALAT* 55), and its meaning is clear: "my god has heard." *ʿAmmîhûd* means "my kinsman is the Majestic One," referring to an unnamed deity. Within biblical literature, it is a fairly well-attested name (2 Sam 5:16; Jer 36:12).

(7) *Gamlî'ēl ben Pedāhṣûr* of Manasseh (v 10). Both names are limited to the early chapters of Numbers, but their meanings are clear—and somewhat synonymous with each other, as a matter of fact. Thus *Gamlî'ēl* means "El has been gracious to me," and *Pedāhṣûr* means "the Rock has redeemed me." Cf. *Pedah'el* in Num 34:28, a *nāśî'* of Naphtali.

(8) *'Abîdān ben Gidʿônî* of Benjamin in (v 11). *'Abîdān* is limited to some of the Numbers traditions, whereas *Gidʿônî,* specifically, is limited to Numbers 1, 2, 7, and 10 and relates to the better-known name *Gidʿôn,* the Israelite leader (Judg 6:13). Based on the root *gādaʿ* 'to cut down, cut off, break' + *ôn,* the characterizing affix, *Gidʿôn* means, literally, "the destroyer, shatterer." *'Abîdān* probably means "my Father is strong," which is more likely than "My Father judges/vindicates."

(9) *'Aḥîʿezer ben 'Ammîšāddaî* of Dan (v 12). Here we have yet another Shaddai name, "Shaddai is my kinsman," and another kinship name, "my brother/kinsman is a help." The name *'Aḥîʿezer* occurs in 1 Chr 12:3.

(10) *Pagʿî'ēl ben ʿOchrān* of Asher (v 13). Both names are limited to Numbers 1, 2, 7, and 10. *Pagʿî'ēl* should mean something like "my entreaty of El," namely, the child I asked of El (cf. Jer 7:16; Ruth 1:16 for the relevant meaning of the verb *p-g-ʿ*). *ʿOkrān,* assuming a positive rather than negative connotation, should mean, literally, "the defeater, subduer." In all biblical occurrences of the verb *ʿākar,* the orientation projects negative acts of disgracing or destruction, but, as is typical of horrendous words, they may be understood positively or heroically as well.

(11) *'Elyāsāp ben Deʿû'ēl* of Gad (v 14). The correct spelling is undoubtedly *Reʿû'ēl* 'the companion of El', as this name appears in Num 2:14. One bearing the name *Rēʿû 'êl* appears in the patriarchal narratives as an Edomite (Gen 36:4, 10). S. Ahituv (1976) mentions the Aramaic name *rʿbʿl,* in the Latin transliteration *Reibelus,* and Phoenician *rʿmlk.* Another *'Elyāsāp* appears in the levitical lists of Num 3:24 as a chieftain of the Gershonites. The meaning of *'Elyāsāp* is "El has added."

Before continuing to list the twelfth and final name in the list of tribal *neśî'îm,* it should be mentioned that in the ordinal numeral, *ʿaštê ʿāśār* 'eleventh', *ʿaštê* is cognate to Akkadian *ištēn* 'one, first' (*CAD I/J,* 275). Compare similar usage in other biblical records, primarily in 2 Kgs 25:2; Jer 1:3; Deut 1:3.

(12) *'Aḥîraʿ ben ʿÊnān* of Naphtali (v 15). Both names are limited to Numbers 1, 2, 7, and 10. *'Aḥîraʿ* means "my brother/kinsman is a friend," and *ʿÊnān* probably derives from the root *ʿ-y-n* 'to see' + *ān,* literally, "the one who

sees/knows." In 1 Sam 18:9, *ʿôyēn (qere)* means, literally, "to look upon with hostility," but in Ugaritic the verb *ʿyn* is used more simply to mean "to look, see," and it is denominative of *ʿyn* 'eye'.

A general overview of the list of tribal chieftains shows that the names registered are largely limited to the traditions of the first ten chapters of Numbers. Here and there we find names elsewhere attested, but except for Nahshon and Eliab, none have any role at all in biblical historiography. The same is true of the lists in chaps. 13 and 34, which break with the traditions of chaps. 1–10. In the list of chap. 13 two historical names are introduced, Caleb and Joshua, but only one, Caleb, survives into the list of chap. 34, because Joshua has since become leader of the entire people.

We find an abundance of El and Shaddai names in the list of tribal leaders, a fact that may be significant (Hackett 1987). Several of the names are attested in the Ammonite onomasticon of the seventh century B.C.E. (Jackson 1983), including *ʿmndb (= ʿAmmînādāb), [n]tnʾl (=Netanʾēl),* and *ʾlsmʾ (= ʾElîsāmāʿ).* There are also variations on the biblical names in the Ammomnite onomasticon. It would be reasonable to conclude that the list is more traditional than historical as regards biblical Israel, that it reflects a particular cultural and religious setting.

The order of this list is Reubenite, as is also the case in chaps. 13 and 26, whereas in chaps. 2, 7, 10, and 34 the lists begin with Judah.

16. *the elect of the community.* Some of the terms occurring here are anticipated in v 4, where they were discussed. It remains, however, to explain the reference to *qerîʾê hāʿēdāh* (following the *ketîb, qryʾy),* literally, "those called, invited." In Ezek 23:22 the term *qeruʾim* occurs in a list of official titles that also includes two terms for "governors," *paḥôt* and *seganîm,* as well as the term *šālîš,* a military title. The *neśîʾîm* 'chieftains' are the *qerûʾîm,* and they are also the heads of the *ʾalāpîm* 'militias' (cf. Num 10:4). In cultic contexts, the term *qerûʾîm* designates those invited to participate in a sacral meal (1 Sam 9:13, 22) or in an important ceremony, such as Adonijah's coronation (1 Kgs 1:41). Metaphorical usage of *qerûʾîm* is evident in Zeph 1:7 and Prov 9:18.

heads. Speiser has explained the title *nāśîʾ* as one "raised, elevated" to leadership, with the form *nāśîʾ* representing a passive form on the Aramaic model (Speiser 1963a). In a sense, *neśîʾîm* and *qerûʾîm* are redundant terms, both designating leaders who were chosen.

The term *nāśîʾ* occurs in at least one early biblical source, Exod 22:27: "You shall not curse God, nor damn a chieftain of your own kin." For the most part, however, attestations of this title come in relatively late sources, such as Ezek 34:24; 37:25; and Ezekiel 40–48, as well as, of course, in priestly literature.

sibs. In the comments on vv 2 and 4 above, the term *ʾelep* was mentioned in passing. This term occurs in certain relatively early sources (Judg 6:15; 1 Sam 18:13; Num 10:36). It would be more reasonable to derive it from *ʾelep*

(Akkadian *alpu)* 'a head of large cattle; bull' rather than from *'elep* 'one thousand'. Most likely, some confusion entered into biblical usage, but originally the two derivations were distinct. The head of an *'elep* was called *śar hā'elep* 'the chief of the *'elep*' (1 Sam 18:13), or *'allûp*. According to Genesis 36, the major social units by which such peoples as the Edomites, Seirites, and Horites were grouped were headed by a leader entitled *'allûp*. Although these units are not referred to as *'elep* in Genesis 36, they are referred to as *mišpāḥāh* in Gen 36:40. By metonymy, we could call the social group *'allûp* as well as *'elep*. The NJPS translates Exod 15:15 accordingly: "Now are the *clans* of Edom *('allûpê 'Edôm)* dismayed, the tribes of Moab *('êlê Mô'āb)*—trembling rips them." Now, the parallelism of *'allûp* and *'ayîl*, literally, "bull" and "ram," is suggestive: the social connotations are metaphors for the lead animals of the flock and herd! Once again, it must be understood that later priestly writers reintroduced social terms like *'elep* as part of their effort to link their projected social structure to early, presettlement and premonarchic institutions.

17. *had been specified.* The basic sense of the verb *nāqab* is "to pierce, incise," hence "to specify." This is forensic language, and the verb *nāqab* often takes "name" *(šēm)* as its direct object (cf. Isa 6:22; Ezra 8:20; 1 Chr 12:31). One may also "fix" wages by this verb (Gen 30:28). The punctuation as a *niph'al* form, *niqqebû*, may mask the internal *qal* passive, in the perfect tense:* *nuqbû*, for the active form is usually expressed in the *qal* stem (Gen 30:28; Lev 24:16). In Amos 6:1 we find the passive *qal* participle *nequbê rē'šît haggôyîm* 'notables of the leading nation'.

18. *They assembled . . . They registered. Hiph'il hiqhîlû* is common in social and political contexts (Lev 8:3; Num 8:9; 10:7; 20:8). The form *wayyityaldû* is, however, unique to this passage, and connotes something like registering one's own geneaology. This verbal form is not pointed as a *hithpa'el*, but rather in a manner similar to the classical Aramaic *hithpe'el.* A later expression for the same process is *wayyityaḥasû* 'they registered their geneaologies' (Ezra 2:62).

20–43. The historical significance of the numerical totals listed here has often been exaggerated. We are dealing with a tradition that attributes great numbers to the wilderness Israelites. A sexigesimal system, employing multiples of sixty, is made to yield an overall total of approximately 600,000. In Exod 12:37 and Num 11:21, JE speaks of the 600,000 *raglî* 'foot soldiers' who marched out of Egypt, just as other fairly early sources mention armies consisting of thousands of foot soldiers (Judg 20:2; 1 Sam 4:10; 15:4). The word *'elep* in the census list must surely mean "one thousand," because it alternates with *mē'ôt* 'hundreds' and with other numbers. There is no basis for interpreting *'elep* here as the designation of a social unit so as to render the totals more realistic, as Mendenhall attempted to do (Mendenhall 1957). The text of Numbers is using military formulas in the census record, in contradistinction to its earlier use of *ʾelep* as a social term, as in v 4, above. With a few minor discrepancies, the totals here are the same as those given in Numbers 2.

Here, I will merely point out some features of administrative formulation. At the beginning of the census list we note a narrative tendency, which quickly gives way to the predominantly formulaic structure of the record. In the first entry we find a trace of narrative style: *wayyihyû benê Reʾûbēn* 'There were the descendants of Reuben'. From that point on, the nonverbal administrative formulation is consistent, except for minor variations. Hebrew *tôlādāh* is characteristic of the priestly genealogies, and literally connotes the result of begetting, an act conveyed by the *hiphʿil hôlîd;* hence, one who has been begotten or born into a family is its *tôlādāh.* Compare Akkadian *tālittu* (from *tālidtu)* 'born to the herd or flock' *(AHw,* 1310).

44–47. These verses merely recapitulate what has transpired. It is preferable to translate *pequddîm* as "musters, arrays" in v 45, but as "totals" in v 46 (see above, in the NOTES on v 3), because vv 45 and 46 run into each other syntactically.

In mathematical contexts, the verb *hāyāh* has the sense of comprising or amounting to a total. Hence, *wayyiheyû kol happequddîm* is best translated "The total musters amounted to—." Compare Gen 6:3: *wehāyû yamâw meʾāh weʿeśrîm šānāh* 'And his days shall amount to one hundred twenty years'.

Verse 47 explains that the totals just provided exclude the Levites. The form *hotpoqdû* is unusual, and might mask a *hithpaʿel* form, originally vocalized *hitpaqqedû* 'they registered themselves'. See above, in the NOTES on v 18.

48–49. The concluding section of chap. 1 (vv 48–54) states the policy of excluding the Levites from the collective of the twelve tribes, thereby anticipating the contents of chaps. 3–4 and 8.

50. *appoint . . . in charge.* The *hiphʿil hipqîd* means "to place in charge" —over an array or an assignment—and this verb is often complemented by the preposition *ʿal,* as is true here (cf. Isa 62:6; Jer 1:10; Josh 10:18; Gen 41:34). There is an obvious play on usage: one appoints Levites (the form *hipqîd)* in charge of certain cultic tasks just as we are told that the leadership of the twelve tribes did not "muster" them (the form *pāqad)* in the normal manner!

Tabernacle of the Covenant. The term *miškan hāʿēdût* may be analyzed as an abbreviation of *miškan lûḥôt hāʿēdût* 'the Tabernacle of the *Tablets* of the Covenant'. Compare the similar abbreviation, *ʾarôn hāʿēdût* 'the Ark of the [Tablets of the] Covenant', and simply *hāʿēdût* in Lev 16:13 (see Num 10:11 and Exod 31:18; 38:21). Hebrew *ʿēdût* is an abstract form of the root *ʿ-w-d* 'to give testimony' and refers to the oath of covenant enactment.

perform its service. In the priestly traditions of Numbers, the verb *šērēt* 'to serve' often characterizes the service of the Levites (Num 3:6; 8:26; 16:9; 18:2). It is of uncertain etymology and is explained in the NOTES on Num 18:2, where its application to the Levites is most clearly expressed.

The Levites were encamped around the Tabernacle. More particulars on their deployment will be provided in the NOTES on Numbers 2–4, where the Israelite encampment *(maḥaneh)* as well as the levitical assignments are outlined.

51. *shall dismantle . . . shall set up.* The two verbs *yôrîdū* and *yāqîmû* 'they will pull down, disassemble' and 'they will set up', respectively, recall 1 Sam 6:15, where we read that the Levites handled the Ark after the Philistines had returned it to the Israelite camp. For similar usage with respect to tents and other structures, see Jer 10:20; Amos 9:11; and cf. priestly usage in Num 7:1; 9:15.

Any alien who intrudes shall be put to death. The relative clause *wehazzār haqqārēb yummat* has been discussed at great length by J. Milgrom (1970: 5–59). He has clarified the fact that this formula mandates capital punishment for the violation of sacred space. The noun *zār* 'alien', literally, 'one hated' (cf. Akkadian *zêru* 'to hate') has connotations that depend on context. In Lev 20:10–12 and Num 17:5, it designates nonpriests, whereas here it more likely refers to both unconsecrated Israelites and non-Israelites (cf. Num 3:10, 38; 18:7).

52. The sense of this verse is that the Israelite tribes—in contradistinction to the Levites, who were encamped immediately around the Tabernacle—would encamp along the four sides of the encampment area. As will be clarified in the NOTES to chap. 2, the term *degel* is functionally equivalent to *maḥaneh,* though it has a different history in extrabiblical literature.

53. *maintaining.* The precise import of this verse has been the subject of considerable scholarly debate, especially as regards the formula *šamar mišmeret.* J. Milgrom, in the course of his discussion on the tasks of the Levites, interprets *mišmeret* as guard duty, the actual guarding of the Tabernacle and its immediate area by the Levites (Milgrom 1970: 8–16). Actually, the term *mišmeret* enjoys several connotations in Numbers. The Hebrew verb *šāmar,* and nominal *mišmeret,* are subject to subtle shifts in meaning that can significantly affect our understanding of the text, as well as of the duties of the Levites. Several connotations may be identified: there is first the sense "to guard, watch over," hence "to care for, maintain." Compare *šāmar-mišmeret* in 2 Kgs 11:5–7: "He commanded them as follows: 'This is what you are to do: a third of you will *serve* a weekly tour of *guard duty (šomerê mišmeret)* in the royal palace' "; and compare similar usage in Exod 12:6 and 16:23–34. In Num 18:8, however, a different sense is conveyed by *mišmeret:* "control, jurisdiction." In that verse *mišmeret terûmôtaî* means "control over my levied donations." This connotation is an extension of the sense of "keeping." All of the preceding nuances seem not to apply in the present context.

Another connotation is "to fulfill (= keep) a charge, perform a duty"—whatever it may consist of. This is the sense in Num 18:3: the Levites are to perform the "charge" of the priests and the "charge" of the Tent, just as the priests themselves are to keep the charge of their priestly office (Num 18:7). Similarly, in Lev 8:35, the priests are ordered to remain within the Sanctuary for seven days. This order itself constituted their *mišmeret.* Compare usage in Zech 3:7 and in Gen 26:5, where *mišmeret* is synonymous with *miṣwāh* 'command' and *tôrāh* 'instruction'. (Also see Ezek 44:16; 48:11.) This sense of "charge, duty," of a task that does not necessarily involve watching or guarding, seems to apply in the present verse, as it does in Num 3:28, 32, and 38. In Num 8:26 we read that after reaching the age of fifty years, Levites would no longer perform tasks *('abôdāh)* in the Tabernacle, but only be of assistance to their fellow Levites "by performing various duties *(lišmôr mišmeret).*"

Although Levites were actually stationed as guards, it is more likely that in the preceding passages reference is to the general duties of the Levites, and not specifically to their role as guards. To read these provisions as limited to guard duty would be to miss their meaning.

It is more likely, despite the admitted ambiguity of this verse and those surrounding it, that here the functional sense of *mišmeret* is not specifically the prevention of human intrusion but rather the proper maintenance of the Tabernacle and its furnishings. Milgrom (1970: 21) may also have erred in his understanding of *qeṣep* 'rage'. He thought that it referred to danger from intruding humans, when it more likely refers to the danger of divine wrath, the anticipated reaction to such intrusion and to the neglect of the Tabernacle generally.

54. The chapter concludes with the almost proverbial compliance formula (Levine 1965a).

NUMBERS 2: THE ISRAELITE ENCAMPMENT —A MIGRATORY COMMUNITY ON THE MARCH

Following upon the census of Israelite musters recorded in Numbers 1, Numbers 2 presents the plan of the Israelite encampment. It is depicted as a quadrilateral zone, with the rectangular Tent of Meeting occupying its central area. On all four sides, facing the sanctuary complex, four groups of consecrated personnel were correspondingly encamped: the Aaronide priests and the three levitical patriarchal houses. Moving outward, we encounter four military units, one occupying each side of the encampment, and each comprising the combined forces of three tribes (figure 1).

An analysis of this simple plan reveals that it nevertheless reflects concepts basic to the priestly traditions of Numbers. The east, which lies to the right of one facing north, was reserved for two groups deemed most important—the Aaronide priests in the cultic dimension, and the Judahite corps in the military dimension. These groups were aligned with the entrance to the Tent of

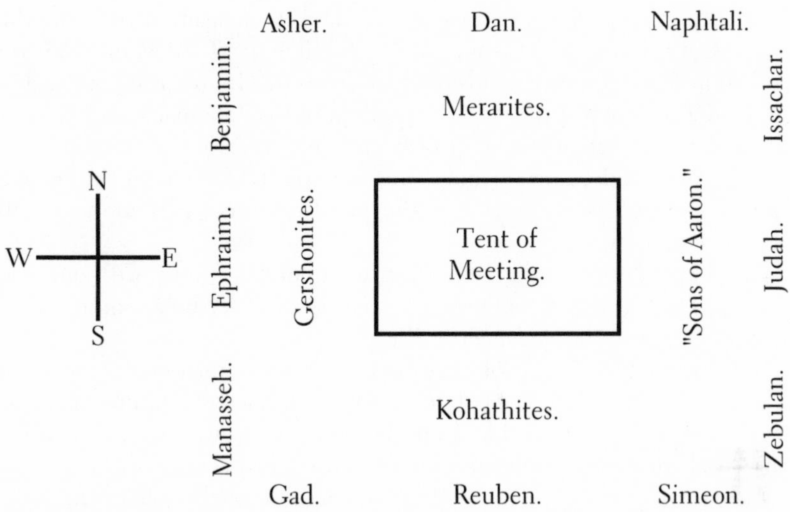

Figure 1. The Israelite Encampment according to Numbers 2. Adapted from G. B. Gray, *Numbers, The International Critical Commentary,* Edinburgh: T & T Clark Ltd., 1903 (latest impression 1976) 17.

Meeting. In contrast to chap. 1, which begins its tribal lists with Reuben, the plan underlying chap. 2 recognizes Judah as the leading tribe, thus parting company with those traditions which assigned preeminence to the firstborn son, Reuben.

One finds almost no social or familial terminology in Numbers 2, within the projected organization of the Israelite forces. The only exception is an initial passing reference in v 2 to the *nāśî'* 'chieftain', which serves to link the two chapters. This is curious because the military role of the *nāśî'* was, in fact, basic to his status in certain biblical traditions. In place of *mišpāḥāh* 'clan' and *bêt 'āb* 'patriarchal house' we have in Numbers 2 such regularly occurring terms as *ṣābā'* 'division' (cf. plural *ṣebā'ôt* in v 3), *maḥaneh* 'corps', and *degel,* a term designating a unit, whose precise meaning will be explained presently (cf. Num 1:52).

If the east was the favored side of the encampment, the south must have been next in line of importance, as Gray—ICC (16–18) correctly noted. In the cultic dimension, the Kohathites represented the levitical house from which the Aaronide priests had sprung. In the tribal, military dimension Reuben, like Issachar and Zebulun (and Simeon as well), were all sons of Leah, Judah's mother (Gen 46:15). Furthermore, the southern units followed directly after the eastern units in the order of march, and the Kohathites had the most important levitical assignment of transporting the sacral vessels of the Tabernacle, including the Ark of the Covenant (Num 4:1–16; 10:6).

The depiction presented in Numbers 2 is taken up again in 10:1–28, which functions in a traditional manner as the fulfillment of the command: what God had instructed in the words of chap. 2 was dutifully carried out in 10:1–28. Only v 17 of chap. 2 refers to the position of the Tabernacle and its vessels in the order of march, whereas 10:1–28 primarily concern the march itself. By then, the time had come to move on from southern Sinai to the northern sector of the peninsula, known in the priestly sources of Numbers as the Wilderness of Paran.

The plan of Numbers 2 groups the tribes in units of three, with one of the three tribes regarded as preeminent, so that its *nāśî'* served as commander of the entire "corps," the *maḥaneh* or *degel.*

The resulting structure of tribal organization is meaningful on several levels. That Reuben, Israel's firstborn, would be a lead tribe of one of the four groupings is fairly obvious. From another point of view, one less traditional than genealogical, Judah's leadership is self-evident because of the historical role of that tribe or, to put it another way, because of the role of the Judean kingdom. The same would be true of Ephraim, the leading tribe of the northern kingdom of Israel. The three eponyms associated with the northern kingdom—Ephraim, Manasseh, and Benjamin—would be expected to be linked together (Gen 46:19–22). Of course, there is a point beyond which it is pedantic to seek significance in the tribal arrangement, but one could say that a pro-Judean tendency is clearly evident.

The plan detailed in Numbers 2 presents the Israelite marches and the military encampment in a cultic frame of reference. The army carried the shrine forth into battle and protected it while the Israelites were encamped. This concern for the cult complex as well as its utilization on the march and in battle reflect very ancient traditions, here recast by the priestly writers (see the NOTES on Num 10:29–36 and the COMMENTS to Num 10:29–12:16).

TRANSLATION

2 [1]YHWH spoke to Moses and to Aaron as follows:

[2]The Israelites shall encamp, each person with his *degel* alongside standards, according to their patriarchal houses. They shall encamp opposite one another, around the Tent of Meeting.

[3]Those encamped all the way to the east: the *degel* of the Judahite corps, by their divisions. Chieftain of the Judahites: Nahshon son of Amminadab.

[4]The musters of his division: 74,600.

[5]Those encamped alongside him: the tribe of Issachar. Chieftain of the Issacharites: Nathanel son of Zuar.

[6]The musters of his division: 54,400.

[7]The tribe of Zebulun: chieftain of the Zebulunites: Eliab son of Helon.

8 The musters of his division: 57,400.

9 Total musters of the Judahite corps: 186,400, by their divisions. They shall be at the head of the march.

10 The *degel* of the Reubenite corps, to the south, by their divisions. Chieftain of the Reubenites: Elizur son of Shedeur.

11 The musters of his division: 46,500.

12 Those encamped alongside him: the tribe of Simeon. Chieftain of the Simeonites: Shelumiel son of Zurishaddai.

13 The musters of his division: 59,300.

14 The tribe of Gad. Chieftain of the Gadites: Eliasaph son of Reuel.

15 The musters of his division: 45,650.

16 Total musters of the Reubenite corps: 151,450, by their divisions. They shall march in second place.

17 The Tent of Meeting shall then be set forth, with the levitical corps in the midst of the [other] corps. Just as they encamp, so shall they march; each group in its own place, by their *degel*s.

18 The *degel* of the Ephraimite corps, by their divisions, to the west. Chieftain of the Ephraimite corps: Elishama, son of Ammihud.

19 The musters of his division: 40,500.

20 Those alongside him: the tribe of Manasseh. Chieftain of the Manassites: Gamaliel son of Pedahzur.

21 The musters of his division: 32,200.

22 The tribe of Benjamin. Chieftain of the Benjamites: Abidan son of Gideoni.

23 The musters of his division: 35,400.

24 Total musters of the Ephraimite corps: 108,100, by their divisions. They shall march in third place.

25 The *degel* of the Danite corps, to the north, by their divisions. Chieftain of the Danites: Ahiezer son of Ammishaddai.

26 The musters of his division: 62,700.

27 Those encamped alongside him: the tribe of Asher. Chieftain of the Asherites: Pagiel son of Ochran.

28 The musters of his division: 41,500.

29 The tribe of Naphtali. Chieftain of the Naphtalites: Ahira son of Enan.

30 The musters of his division: 53,400.

31 Total musters of the Danite corps: 157,600. They shall march at the rear, by their *degel*s.

32 These are the musters of the Israelite people, by their patriarchal houses. Total musters of the corps, by their divisions: 603,550.

33 The Levites had not been mustered as part of the Israelite people, as YHWH had commanded Moses.

34 The Israelites acted in accordance with all that YHWH had commanded Moses. Accordingly, they encamped by their *degel*s, and accordingly,

they marched; each [group] with its clans, and together with its patriarchal houses.

NOTES

2 2. The term *bêt ʾāb* has been explained in the NOTES on Num 1:2. Two new terms are introduced in chap. 2 that require explanation. In fact, they may be considered reflexes of each other: *ʾôtôt* 'standards' and *degel,* which I leave untranslated, but which can now be explained on the basis of comparative evidence. The verb *ḥānah* 'to encamp' also appears in this verse, and its nominal derivative *maḥaneh* 'corps' first occurs in v 3 and is used repeatedly throughout chap. 2.

The key to a proper understanding of the plan and military organization underlying Numbers 2 is the term *degel,* which has not been correctly understood in the past. Functionally, it is synonymous with *maḥaneh* 'corps', in that it designates a unit comprising three tribes. One need only compare v 3 with v 9: In v 3, the formulation is redundant: *degel maḥaneh Yehûdāh* 'the *degel* of the Judahite corps', whereas in v 9 we have simply *maḥaneh Yehûdāh.* The Hebrew term *maḥaneh* has two principal meanings: (1) an area of encampment or settlement (Exod 33:7, 11; Lev 14:18; Deut 23:15; Judg 7:19), and (2) a fighting force, a large body of men (Deut 23:10; Gen 33:8; 50:9; 1 Sam 13:17; 2 Kgs 7:5–6; Ps 27:3). It is the latter connotation that is expressed in Numbers 2.

Characteristically, priestly writers use terms synonymously that are, in reality, discrete terms of reference, each with its own history. This tendency has already been noted in the NOTES on Num 1:2 concerning designations for the Israelite people as a whole. Thus *qehal ʿadat Yiśrāʾēl* 'the congregation of the community of Israel' represents the same kind of redundancy as we now observe with respect to *degel maḥaneh Yehûdāh.*

Can we be certain that *degel* initially designated a *unit* of fighting men and does not simply mean "banner, insignia," as many have explained it? After all, it is common for units to be called by their insignia; witness *maṭṭeh* and *šēbeṭ,* which both mean "staff, scepter," but are used to signify a tribe.

In the immediate context, it is the Hebrew term *ʾôtôt* 'signs' that refers specifically to the insignia of the tribes. The tribes encamp "alongside standards" *(beʾôtôt)* but are not themselves the *ʾôtôt.* The tribes are grouped according to *degel* units. As a matter of fact, these definitions also apply in the War Scroll from Qumran, whose descriptions closely mirror the plan of encampment and the order of battle as set forth in the priestly traditions of Numbers. Y. Yadin (1962: 168–181) has demonstrated this correlation, independently of the evidence for the meaning of *degel* to be presented here.

The verb *dāgal* 'to see' is relatively rare in biblical Hebrew, but its cognate *dagālu* 'to see, look upon' is common in Akkadian (*CAD D*, 21–25, under *dagālu*). The usual reflex of this Semitic verbal root in biblical Hebrew is the noun *migdāl* 'watchtower'. Hebrew *migdāl* does not derive from a verb meaning "to be big, high," as is often assumed, but rather reflects the metathesis of **madgal*, a term known in various forms in Akkadian and Ugaritic. The derivation from *dāgal* was long ago proposed by Haupt (1918). In Cant 6:6 we read that the beloved woman is described as *'ayummāh kannidgālôt* 'awesome as the watch towers' (preformative *mem* of original *midgālôt* has shifted to *nun*). This meaning is reinforced by Cant 8:10, where the beloved woman says of herself, "I am a wall and my breasts are like watchtowers *(kammigdālôt)*."

In biblical Hebrew there is no evidence to suggest that *degel* means "standard," literally, "something looked upon, visible." The meaning "standard" would express a passive function for the Segollate form, *degel*. Cant 2:4 has been cited in support of the meaning "standard, banner": *wediglô 'ālây 'ahabāh* 'His banner over me is love'. This interpretation is unsubstantiated, however, and the verse in question is better translated "*His gaze upon me* is amorous" or "His *inclination toward me* is love," as proposed by M. Pope (1977: 377, to Cant 2:4). Such connotations are actually attested for Akkadian *diglu*. The passive sense in Hebrew is conveyed by the passive participle, as in Cant 5:10: *dāgûl mērebābāh* 'favored of ten thousand' (literally, "seen, singled out"). Even Ps 2:6 does not really refer to "banners," as traditional exegesis suggests. There we read *ûbešēm 'elôhênû nidgôl* 'We shall *look forward* in the name of our God!' (not "We shall carry banners in the name of our God!"). Although ancient Mesopotamian lexical series list the form *diglu* in the sense of "mirror, sight" ("something looked upon"), there seems to be no evidence for such a meaning in actual documents (*CAD D*, 136, under *diglu* A).

As against this scant evidence for a passive sense, which would allow for translating *degel* as "banner, standard," we have abundant information on the term *degel* as designating a sociomilitary unit within the Persian army. We know this from Aramaic papyri found at Elephantine, in upper Egypt, where mercenary units, some consisting of Jews, guarded the borders of the Persian Empire during most of the fifth century B.C.E. We read of units named *diglā'* (plural *diglîn*). Each of these units was commanded by the *rēš diglā'* 'head of a *degel* unit'. Various individuals mentioned in such documents are identified by the following formula: *x le-degel Y* 'So-and-So of the *degel* headed by So-and-So' or *min degel Y* 'from the *degel* of So-and-So' (Porten 1968: 28–29). The term *dgl* has been discovered on ostraca from Saqqara, in northern Egypt, recently published by J. B. Segal (1983: 32, no. 15, line 2; 85, no. 63, line 3; 113, no. 113, line 2). This term has also turned up on an Aramaic ostracon from the Persian period at Arad, published by J. Naveh (Aharoni 1981: 158, no. 12, line 2). The Arad source demonstrates that the term *degel*, Aramaic *dgl*, for the Persian sociomilitary unit was known in the land of Israel during the Achaemenid period (ca. 546–330 B.C.E.). Some scholars had assumed that only the Jewish units in Egypt were called *diglîn,* and that this term of reference was of Israelite Jewish origin. This cannot be so, however, because Egyptian units were also identified in the same way, and invariably the commanders of the *degel* units had non-Jewish names. One such head of a *diglāʾ*, named in the Arad ostracon, was *ʿbd nny* 'Servant of Nannai', the name of a Persian deity, and at Saqqara we also find Persians heading the *dgl* units.

The *degel* was, then, a unit of the Persian military, especially appropriate for settled military outposts, where soldiers lived with their families. The compiler (or author) of Numbers 2 and 10 (and of 1:52) most probably knew of this term precisely because he lived and wrote in the fifth century B.C.E., when such units were operative in the Near East. In projecting his plan for the Israelite encampment of the wilderness, preconquest period he would have used the term *degel,* as a synonym of conventional *maḥaneh.* He would have done so in an effort to be contemporary, to convey to his readers a realistic sense of what the more ancient Israelite experience had been initially. This is, after all, the primary literary function of anachronism.

If the preceding analysis is correct, we have telling evidence of the *Sitz-im-Leben* underlying the final version of the wilderness traditions generated by the priestly school. The priestly writers would have lived in the period beginning with the first return in the latter part of the sixth century B.C.E. and continuing to nearly the end of the fifth (Levine 1982c). This hypothesis has serious implications for the dating of the priestly writings of the Torah, a subject that has been discussed in the introduction, section E.

In terms of earlier background, it is interesting to note that Hittite sources of the second millennium B.C.E. refer to a military personage known as *bēl madgalti* 'commander of the watchtower'. That officer commanded the military units stationed in the watchtowers of towns, who sallied forth into the countryside to protect the region. E. von Schuler (1957) has published a collection of Hittite instructions addressed to such commanders, and these documents employ the title *bēl madgalti* as an akkadogram, an Akkadian term adopted by Hittite scribes. At the present time, we only know this title from Hittite, but it must of necessity hark back to an Amorite title or to some other early Semitic title that has not been preserved. Of interest in interpreting Numbers is the fact that *bēl madgalti* (and infrequent occurrences of such forms as *madgallu* and *madgaltu* in other Syro-Mesopotamian sources) derive from the same root, *d-g-l,* as do Hebrew *degel* and Aramaic *dgl.*

3. Here begins the description of the encampment. The "corps" *(maḥaneh, degel)* consisted of three tribes. The translation "corps" is merely for convenience, designating a unit larger than *ṣābāʾ* 'division', because three divisions constituted a *maḥaneh* or *degel.* On the derivation of the term *ṣābāʾ* see the NOTES on Num 1:3. The strength of a *ṣābāʾ* clearly corresponds to the quota of the tribal unit, according to the plan of Numbers 2, although the

term itself bears no relation to the tribal system, as has been explained. The description begins with Judah and his affiliated tribes, Issachar and Zebulun (vv 3–9).

all the way to the east. Adverbial *qēdmāh mizrāḥāh* has incremental force; compare Gen 13:14; 28:14 for adverbial *qēdmāh,* as one of the four "winds" of the earth. For the redundant formula occurring here, see Exod 27:13; 38:13; Josh 19:12–43. What we have is the combination of two or more directional systems, one that expresses a solar perception *(mizrāḥ* 'where the sun shines') and another, a positional orientation, literally, "facing toward the east," with the east at the *front* of the viewer. The same system operates in v 10, where "to the south" is signified by *têmānāh,* literally, "to the right." In v 18 the system is geographic, hence *yāmāh* 'toward the sea', just as in v 25 we have *ṣāpônāh* 'to the north', a common directional indicator.

4. *The musters of his division.* The formulation *ûṣebā'ô ûpequddêhem,* literally, "and his division and their muster" (normally *ûpequddâw* 'and its musters') requires clarification, though its meaning is clear. The sequence *w A . . . w B* has circumstantial force, as if to say, "And his division, consisting of its musters; the musters of his division being—."

5. *Those encamped alongside him.* Formulaic *wehaḥônîm ʿālâw* means "those encamped near him" or, with relational force, "—in association with him." The lead tribe is designated *(degel) maḥaneh Yehûdāh,* but the other two tribes in the Judahite corps are termed *maṭṭeh* 'tribe'.

9. *Total musters.* Hebrew *kol happequddîm* reflects administrative formulation, as is typical of accounts and lists. Compare Num 7:85: *kol kesep hakkēlîm* 'total silver for the vessels' and similar formulas in Num 7:86–88 (see the NOTES to Num 7:85 and following). Similar accounting techniques are apparent in Josh 21:26, 39 and Ezra 2:64. For the same formulation in a family record, see Gen 46:15b: *kol nepeš bānâw ûbenôtâw* 'Total persons, of his sons and daughters'.

The Judahite corps took up the march "at the head" *(ri'šônāh).* Compare Gen 33:2, where we read that Jacob placed the concubines *ri'šônāh* 'at the head' when he marched toward an encounter with Esau (also cf., in a cultic context, Lev 5:8). In the present chapter, in vv 16, 24, and 31, we find sequential indicators with adverbial force: "second, third," and so forth.

With v 9, the record concludes a delineation of the first of four major units. Subsequent units are enumerated in vv 10–16, 18–24, and 25–31. With only minor variations, the same formulation is repeated in each case. The paucity of copulatives, and of narrative, syntactic structures in chap. 2, more pronounced than in chap. 1, is significant. It suggests that in its original form, chap. 2 was a tabular list, registered in horizontal columns rather than sequentially, as we have it. This format was observed in chap. 1, and in the COMMENT on chap. 7 it is explained.

16. *in second place.* Adverbial *šeniyyîm* 'in second place', and *šelîšîm* 'in third place' (v 24), recall the decks of Noah's ark as described in Gen 6:16.

17. The portable sanctuary, carried by the Levites, was to be positioned between the second and third units, a measure aimed, no doubt, at its protection. In v 17b *ʿal yādô* has the unusual sense of "in its *own* place," literally, "next to itself."

32–33. Generally, vv 32–34 provide the sum total of all of the musters, identical with the totals listed in Num 1:46. Again, *kôl* means "total" (see NOTE to v 9, above). Verse 33 paraphrases Num 1:47 and anticipates the detailed assignments of the various levitical clans in chaps. 3–4, which immediately follow.

34. Once again, a priestly record concludes with a compliance formula. The polarity of the two verbs—*ḥānû* 'they encamped' and *nāsāʿû* 'they marched'—suggests that, indeed, the verb *nāsaʿ* in these records means "to march" rather than merely "to journey." The context is decidedly military (Levine 1982a).

NUMBERS 3–4: THE CULTIC ESTABLISHMENT —GENEALOGY, RANK, AND FUNCTIONS

The first two chapters of Numbers recorded a census of the Israelite fighting forces and provided a plan of the Israelite encampment as it was organized, according to the priestly tradition, at the beginning of the wilderness period. Numbers 3–4 focus on the internal organization of the tribe of Levi, which was comprised of three principal patriarchal houses, Gershon, Kohath, and Merari.

In a larger sense, these two chapters inform us of priestly traditions regarding the overall tribal organization of the Israelites in the presettlement period, not just about the tribe of Levi specifically (see the NOTES on Num 1:2). As portrayed here, the tribe of Levi represented a work force structured in much the same fashion as were the fighting forces manned by the other twelve tribes of Israel.

Of the three patriarchal houses, the most prominent was Kohath, as already explained in the introduction to Numbers 2. Aaron and Moses were affiliated with one of the Kohathite clans, the clan of Amram. Thus the Aaronide priesthood was in effect a part of the house of Kohath. Appropriately, the Kohathite Levites were assigned the most intimate tasks associated with the Tabernacle, those requiring proximity to sacred space and the handling of the vessels and appurtenances of the inner Shrine, including the Ark itself.

Numbers 3 and 4 seem to have been compiled from various records, loosely joined to each other so as to fill out the priestly description of the

Israelite people, as the Israelites were marshaled during the wilderness period. In part, they anticipate the contents of Numbers 8, the record of the dedication of the Levites to Tabernacle service.

The agenda of Numbers 3 includes several topics: (1) a brief statement on the family history of Aaron, the chief priest, covering his lifetime and mentioning the death of his two sons, Nadab and Abihu (vv 1–4); (2) the commissioning of the Levites and the command to dedicate them collectively to Tabernacle service. The dedication of male Levites was to serve as repayment of God's claim on the firstborn of Israel, whom he had spared in Egypt (vv 5–13); (3) a census of male Levites, one month of age and older, that refers in passing to the assignments of the several houses (vv 14–39); and (4) an adjustment of the differential between the total number of Israelite firstborn males and the total number of male Levites available for service. The sanctuary was compensated at the rate of five shekels for each of 273 firstborn Israelite males in excess of available Levites (vv 40–51). In summary, Numbers 3 deals quite literally with "numbers!"

Numbers 4 details the specific assignments of the three levitical houses. Accordingly, the genealogical sequence characteristic of chap. 3 gives way in chap. 4 to a functional arrangement of the data. Thus the record begins with the Kohathites, whose functions were considered most vital (vv 1–20). The rest of chap. 4 is divided as follows: vv 21–28 outline the duties of the Gershonites, and vv 29–33, the duties of the Merarites; finally, vv 34–49 report the fulfillment of what had been commanded previously, namely, the registering of adult male Levites available for service in the Tabernacle.

The records of Numbers 3–4 specify what had to be done each time the Tabernacle was to be transported, reviewing how each work force went about performing its assigned tasks. The census records begin with Kohath and continue with Gershon and Merari. The span of cultic service extended from thirty to fifty years of age, not from twenty years of age. The problems created by differences in the prescribed age of service were discussed in the comments on Num 1:3.

Numbers 4 highlights the Kohathites because of their position of eminence among the levitical houses. Indicative of this emphasis are the statements in Num 4:17–20 that express particular concern for the Kohathites, because they handled the most sacred furnishings of the Tabernacle and were consequently in greater danger from God's wrath.

TRANSLATION OF NUMBERS 3

3 1These are the persons who had been born to Aaron and Moses, at the time that YHWH spoke with Moses at Mount Sinai.

2These are the names of the sons of Aaron: Nadab, the firstborn, and Abihu; Eleazar and Ithamar.

3 These are the names of Aaron's sons, who were the anointed priests, whom he had empowered to serve in the priesthood.

4 Nadab and Abihu died in the presence of YHWH, as they were about to bring an improper incense offering in the presence of YHWH, in the Wilderness of Sinai; they left no sons. Instead, Eleazar and Ithamar served as priests during the lifetime of Aaron, their father.

5 YHWH spoke to Moses as follows:

6 Bring the tribe of Levi and station them in the presence of Aaron the priest, so that they may serve him.

7 Let them serve under his charge, and under the charge of the entire community, in front of the Tent of Meeting, performing the tasks of maintaining the Tabernacle.

8 They are to maintain all of the appurtenances of the Tent of Meeting, discharging duties on behalf of the Israelite people by performing the tasks of maintaining the Tabernacle.

9 You shall subordinate the Levites to Aaron and his sons. They are completely dedicated to him, by act of the Israelite people.

10 You shall likewise commission Aaron and his sons to perform the duties of their priesthood. Any outsider who intrudes shall be put to death!

11 YHWH spoke to Moses as follows: I hereby select the Levites from among the Israelite people in place of every firstborn, the first issue of every womb from among the Israelite people; the Levites shall belong to me.

12 For every firstborn became mine at the time I slew every firstborn in the land of Egypt.

13 For I consecrated for myself every firstborn among the Israelites; both man and animal shall belong to me. I am YHWH.

14 YHWH spoke to Moses in the Wilderness of Sinai as follows:

15 Muster the descendants of Levi, by their patriarchal houses, according to their clans. Every male one month of age and older shall you muster them.

16 Moses mustered them, by order of YHWH, as he had been commanded.

17 These are the sons of Levi, listed by their names: Gershon, Kohath, and Merari.

18 These are the names of the sons of Gershon, by their clans: Libni and Shimei.

19 The sons of Kohath were, by their clans: Amram and Yizhar, Hebron and Uzziel.

20 The sons of Merari were, by their clans: Mahli and Mushi. Following are the clans of the Levites listed according to their patriarchal houses.

21 Affiliated with Gershon: the Libnite clan, and the Shimeite clan; these are the Gershonite clans.

22 Their musters according to the number of males one month of age and older; their total counts: 7,500.

23 The Gershonite clans shall encamp behind the Tabernacle, on its western side.

24 The chieftain of the patriarchal house representing the Gershonites is Eliasaph son of Lael.

25 The charge of the Gershonites in the Tent of Meeting consists of the Tabernacle compound and the Tent, including its cover and the screen at the entrance of the Tent of Meeting,

26 as well as the hangings of the courtyard and the screen at the entrance of the courtyard that surrounds the Tabernacle and the altar, including its lashings, in its complete construction.

27 Affiliated with Kohath: the Amramite clan, the Yizharite clan, the Hebronite clan, and the Uzzielite clan. These are the Kohathite clans,

28 according to the number of all males, one month of age and older: 8,600 maintenance personnel for the shrine.

29 The Kohathite clans shall encamp along the southern side of the Tabernacle.

30 The chieftain of the patriarchal house representing the Kohathite clan is Elizaphan son of Uzziel.

31 Their charge consists of the Ark and the table, the lampstand and altars, and the vessels of the Sanctuary used in conjunction with them, as well as the curtain and its complete construction.

32 The chief of the chieftains of the Levites is Eleazar son of Aaron the priest, [over] the marshaled force of those assigned to the maintenance of the Shrine.

33 Affiliated with Merari: the Mahlite clan and the Mushite clan; these are the Merarite clans.

34 Their musters, according to the number of all males, one month of age and older: 6,200.

35 The chieftain of the patriarchal house representing the Merarite clans is Zuriel son of Abihail. These shall encamp along the northern side of the Tabernacle.

36 The marshaled force bearing the Merarite assignment is charged with the planks of the Tabernacle, and its bolts; its posts and its sockets, and all of its appurtenances, and their complete construction,

37 also the posts of the courtyard, on every side; and their sockets, their tent pegs, and their lashings.

38 Those who are to encamp in front of the Tabernacle to the east are Moses and Aaron and his sons, charged with the duties of the sanctuary, in fulfillment of the duties of the Israelites. Any outsider who intrudes shall be put to death!

39 The total musters of the Levites, which Moses and Aaron tallied by order of YHWH, by their clans: all males one month of age and older amounted to 22,000.

[40]YHWH spoke to Moses: Muster every firstborn male among the Israelite people, one month of age and older, and take a count of the number of their names.
[41]You shall acquire the Levites for me, I am YHWH, in place of every firstling among the Israelite people; and the livestock of the Levites in place of every firstling among the livestock of the Israelite people.
[42]Moses accomplished the muster, as YHWH had commanded him, including every firstborn among the Israelite people.
[43]All firstborn males by name, one month of age and older, totaled 22,273.
[44]Then YHWH spoke to Moses as follows:
[45]Recruit the Levites in place of every firstborn among the Israelites, and the animals of the Levites in place of their animals. The Levites shall be mine, I am YHWH.
[46]As the redemption price of the 273 firstborn of the Israelites in excess of the Levites,
[47]you shall collect five shekels per head. You shall collect them by the sanctuary weight, at twenty grains a shekel.
[48]You shall remit the silver to Aaron and to his sons, comprising the redemption prices of those outstanding among them.
[49]So Moses collected the silver of redemption of those in excess of the persons redeemed by the Levites.
[50]He collected the silver from the firstborn of the Israelite people, in the amount of 1,365 sanctuary shekels.
[51]Moses remitted the silver of those who were redeemed to Aaron and to his sons, by order of YHWH, just as YHWH had commanded Moses.

NOTES TO NUMBERS 3

3 Verses 1–4 review the status of Aaron's immediate family, his *toladot*, the record of those born to Aaron (see the NOTE on Num 1:20).

1. *at the time that [YHWH] spoke.* The formula *beyôm dibber* has its analogue in Exod 6:28, at the conclusion of another priestly genealogy. The syntax is not uncommon: *beyôm* + a finite verb in the perfect tense; compare 2 Sam 22:1 || Ps 18:1: *beyôm hiṣṣîl* 'at the time he rescued'. The verb *dibbēr* may also take an indirect object, introduced by prepositional *'et* 'with' (cf. Exod 31:18; 34:34–35; Num 7:89). The point is that what we have in this caption is typical of the formulation of priestly records. Aaron had four sons, of course, but he lost two of them, Nadab and Abihu, as is reported in Lev 10:1–7.

2. One finds alternative genealogical formulations in various biblical records. Here we have *habbekôr* + *PN* 'the firstborn—*PN*' (cf. 1 Sam 8:2; 1 Chr 3:1, 15). But note as well the formula *PN* + *habbekôr* '*PN*—the firstborn' (1 Sam 17:13; 1 Chr 26:2).

The names of Aaron's sons warrant comment. The name *Nādāb* is a shortened form, in which the name of the deity is missing but understood. *Nādāb* resembles *ʿAmmînādāb* (see the NOTES on Num 1:7). It means "the deity has been generous"—in granting a son. *Elʿāzār* has a clear meaning: "God (or El) has helped me." The name of the other dead son, *ʾAbîhû*, means "he is my (divine) father." The name *ʾÎtāmār* is of uncertain derivation. Some have suggested that it expresses the root *ʾ-m-r* (cf. Akkadian *amāru*) 'to see', and means "I have been shown wonders."

3. *anointed priests.* Reference to "the anointed priests *(hakkôhanîm hammešuḥîm)*" is significant. In the priestly literature of the Torah, we find two discrete traditions or viewpoints regarding the status of the high priest. According to Leviticus 8, the record of the investiture of the Aaronide priesthood, only Aaron himself was anointed with pure oil, not his sons; they were purified in another manner. Furthermore, in Leviticus 8 Aaron, the high priest, is instructed to don distinctive vestments not worn by his sons. This view is also expressed in Lev 21:10–15, where the high priest is distinguished from other priests by virtue of his unique unction. Lev 4:3 speaks of "the anointed priest *(hakkôhen hammāšîaḥ)*" as the effective leader of the Israelite community (also cf. Exod 29:7). The Yom Kippur ritual of Leviticus 16 ordains a distinct role for Aaron, the chief priest, who alone enters the Holy of Holies to seek expiation for the community, and whose efforts in this regard are indispensable. In contrast, we find references to the unction of Aaron's sons in Exod 30:22–23; 40:1–38; and Lev 7:34–38, just as we do here. This represents the alternative view of the Israelite priesthood.

whom he had empowered. The formula *millēʾ yād* has a technical sense: "to appoint, empower." It also occurs in the record of priestly investiture in Leviticus 8, which has just been discussed. This is its only occurrence in the book of Numbers, where, for the most part, concern centers on the Levites rather than the priests themselves. In biblical literature, *millēʾ yād* is used only with respect to the appointment of priests. Literally, *millēʾ yād* means "to fill the hand," referring to a symbolic act that transfers authority from one person to another. In Lev 8:27–29 we read that parts of the sacrifice of investiture were actually placed on the palms of Aaron and his sons.

The Akkadian expression *mullû ana (ina) qatê* has often been cited as a parallel of Hebrew *millēʾ yād.* It means "to hand over, assign," as one "fills" something "into" another's hand. This is not a precise parallel, but it is close enough to be instructive *(CAD M* 1.187, under *mullu,* 9c).

4. The death of two of Aaron's sons, Nadab and Abihu, is recounted in Lev 10:1–5 and recalled in Lev 16:1–2. They presented "an alien fire *(ʾēš zārāh)*" inside the Tabernacle and met instant death at God's hands by means of a fire that issued from within the Sanctuary. The precise import of *ʾēš zārāh* has been debated since late antiquity, because the text of Leviticus 10 does not specify the offense committed by Aaron's two sons. From Exod 30:9 we learn

that only the daily incense offering could be placed on the golden incense altar. Any other offering would be regarded as *qetoret zarah* 'alien incense'. Because *'ēš zārāh* probably has the same meaning as *qeṭôret zārāh,* we may conclude that Aaron's two sons violated ritual practice by offering incense that was not expressly ordained by priestly law (Levine 1989b: 58–59, to Lev 10:1).

These two priests met their death before begetting sons. They may have been quite young at the time of their death, suggesting that priests entered into cultic service at a relatively young age. This left only Eleazar and Ithamar to serve as priests during Aaron's lifetime. The book of Numbers records the priestly succession prior to the time of Aaron's death in 20:22–29.

served as priests. The denominative verb *kihhēn* is common in biblical parlance (Hos 4:6; Isa 61:10) and is especially favored by priestly writers (Ezek 44:13; Exod 29:1, 44; 30:30; Lev 7:35; 16:32).

during the lifetime. Idiomatic *ʿal penê* occasionally has temporal force, as is true here. Compare Gen 11:28: "And Haran died during the lifetime of Terah (*ʿal penê Teraḥ*), his father."

5–13. These verses comprise a discrete section of Numbers 3. Certain locutions occurring here link this section closely to the diction of Num 8:5–26, the record of the dedication of the Levites. In fact, the sequence *hiqrîb . . . heʿemîd* 'to bring . . . to station', occurring here in v 5, is paralleled in Num 8:13. More links of diction will be noted as we pursue the analysis of the text. Quite clearly, vv 5–13 were included at this point as a preamble to the census of the tribe of Levi that takes up most of Numbers 3 (precisely, 3:14–39).

6. *the tribe of Levi.* We have already encountered the designation *maṭṭeh Lēwî* in Num 1:49, and it recurs in Num 18:2.

they may serve. The verb *šēret* 'to serve' is explained in the NOTES on Num 8:26, where it figures prominently. This verb has particular significance in Torah sources pertaining to the tribe of Levi, where it appropriately characterizes the type of service performed by the Levites.

7. The cognate clause *šāmar mišmeret* is explained in the NOTES on Num 1:53, where it is shown that, when it refers to the Levites, it has nothing to do necessarily with standing guard and simply means "to fulfill assigned duties." In the present context, the clause *ʿābad ʿabôdāh* 'to perform a task' similarly refers to the maintenance functions of the Levites. In the NOTES on Num 8:26 it is explained that in certain cases the formula *ʿābad ʿabôdāh,* when it refers to what the Levites were *not* allowed to do, means "to officiate in the cult," an office restricted to the priests.

9–10. In its formulation, v 9 closely parallels what is stated in Num 8:16 and 19 regarding the status of the Levites vis à vis the Aaronide priests. The Hebrew term *kehunnāh* 'priesthood' here connotes the priestly fraternity, the group of priests. This is also its sense in Num 18:1 and 1 Sam 2:36, where an outcast priest begs to be admitted "into one of the priestly orders *(ʾel ʾaḥat hakkehunnôt).*" Most often, however, this term refers to the priestly office. The sense of the present statement is that the Aaronide priests bear collective responsibility for the duties assigned to their group, whereas the Levites are merely subordinate to the priesthood. Although Num 8:10 states theoretically that the Levites were dedicated "to me," namely, to God, the statement here is administrative in its force: the Levites were assigned to the priests and placed under their charge. This status is reflected in a specialized connotation of the verb *nātan,* namely, "to reduce, subordinate," explained in the NOTES on Num 8:16.

you shall likewise commission. It is worthy of mention that in v 10 the verb *pāqad* clearly suggests "mustering," rather than simply "counting," a point emphasized in the NOTES on Num 1:3. The sense is that the priests had been commissioned to their tasks just as the Levites were about to be assigned to theirs.

Any outsider who intrudes shall be put to death! The ban on entry into the sacred areas of the Tabernacle was explained in the NOTES on Num 1:51.

11–13. These verses explain the basis for the dedication of the Levites. In their content they closely parallel Num 8:16–19, where some of the relevant terms of reference are explained in greater detail.

11. *the first issue of every womb.* The Hebrew verb *pāṭar* is rare in biblical Hebrew. It means "to loose, dismiss, send forth" (1 Sam 19:10; Prov 17:14) and is cognate to Akkadian *paṭāru (AHw* 849–851, *paṭāru).* In 1 Kgs 6:18 *peṭûrê ṣîṣîm* seems to mean "floral reliefs," conveying the sense of "protrusion" basic to the sense of the verb *pāṭar.* On this basis, *peṭer reḥem* (Num 18:15) and feminine *piṭrat reḥem* (Num 8:16) would mean "offspring of the womb."

14. Here begins the census of the three levitical houses, which concludes in v 39. The explicit venue of the divine communication to Moses, the Wilderness of Sinai, links the census of the Levites to the prior general census of the Israelites, ordained in Num 1:18. There we likewise read that the Israelites were in Sinai at the time.

15. The Levites were to be registered somewhat differently from the other tribes. All males one month of age or older were to be listed. According to Numbers 1, the fighting forces included only adult males, twenty years of age or older. The logic of the distinction is fairly apparent: the Levites were a hereditary group, and a male became a member of the group as soon as he was deemed viable, at the age of thirty days, according to the definition of viability in the priestly votive system of biblical Israel (Lev 27:6; Num 18:16). After all, the Levites were devoted persons, in the cultic sense. In Num 8:24 we read that the Levites began their actual service in the Tabernacle only at the age of twenty-five, whereas Num 4:3 has them begin their service at the age of thirty.

Presumably Levites underwent a protracted period of training prior to assuming their active duties.

16. *by order of YHWH.* Idiomatic *ʿal pî YHWH* is common in priestly texts (cf. Exod 17:1; Lev 24:12). This is its first occurrence in the book of Numbers, where it will be used repeatedly. Like other references to divine authority, it serves to reinforce the notion that all of the particulars of priestly practice were directly ordained by God and were not merely matters of custom and convention.

had been commanded. The idiom *ʿal pî YHWH* is reinforced by the statement that Moses "had been commanded *(ṣuwwāh)*" to conduct the census and to marshal the levitical houses. The *puʿal* form of this verb is actually quite common (cf. Gen 45:19; Exod 34:34; Lev 8:35; 10:13; Ezek 12:7; 24:18; 37:7).

17. *by their names.* Adverbial *bišmôtām* is typical of the formulation of genealogies (Gen 25:13; 36:40).

17–39. Verses 17–20 list the three levitical houses and their respective clans. Following upon the introductory list, they use a fixed sequence for registering each of the houses—Gershon, Kohath, and Merari—listed in vv 21–39: (1) the house and its affiliated clans; (2) the total number of the census of all males one month and older; (3) the name of the chieftain *(nāśîʾ)* of the relevant house; and (4) the assignment *(mišmeret)* of the relevant house.

The names of the levitical houses are interesting in their own right. *Geršôn* (variant: *Geršôm)* may incorporate the verb *gērēš* 'to expel, drive out', With the affix *-on*, the name would mean "the expeller, conqueror." We have a folk etymology incorporating the term *gēr* 'alien, foreign resident' (Exod 2:22), but such a derivation of the name is merely interpretive. The Hebrew name *Qehāt* receives confirmation from the Ugaritic personal name Aqhat, the hero of Ugaritic epic. Also compare Akkadian *A-qá-tum* and the Canaanite name occurring in Egyptian inscriptions as *A-amqehataʾ* (Loewenstamm 1976). The name *Merārî*, solely attested as a son of Levi, probably means "the strong one," deriving from the verbal root *m-r-r* 'to be bitter, fierce, strong'.

The names of the respective clans of each house also require explanation. The name *Libnî* recalls *Lābān* (Gen 24:29) and connotes "whiteness," a motif present in toponyms such as *Lebānôn* and *Lebônāh*, a site on the way to Shechem (Judg 21:19). *Šimʿî* is a shortened form of a name such as *Šemaʾyāh*, expressing the notion that God "heard" the prayer of a parent. This theme is quite common in biblical nomenclature. The Kohathite name *Ḥebrôn* is of obvious geographic and political provenance. For the rest, the Kohathite names are restricted to the levitical traditions and to Ezra 10. The names *Maḥlî* and *Mûšî* remain somewhat enigmatic and are, in any event, restricted to the pertinent levitical clans.

22. *their total counts.* In this verse, the second occurrence of *pequddêhem* may be translated "their counts," in view of the fact that the same term has been repeated in a single census entry. As explained in the NOTES on Num 1:3, the term *pequddîm* means "muster, array," and although mustering troops usually involves counting, this term conveys more than merely totaling a series of numbers. In the present verse, and in vv 34 and 39 below, this fact is brought out by the formula *ûpequddêhem bemispar kol zākār* 'Their musters, according to the number of all males'. In one instance, v 28, the notion of "totals" is conveyed merely by the Hebrew *bemispar* 'according to the number of—'. The rule is that *pequddîm* means "musters," essentially, but it may designate the totals arrived at in a census when it occurs a second time in the same entry. Alternatively, the notion of "total" may be conveyed by a term such as the Hebrew *mispār* (Levine 1982a).

23–24. The Gershonites encamped to the west of the Tabernacle, behind it. Adverbial *'aḥare* has a spatial connotation here. The chieftain *(nāśî')* of the Gershonites was named *'Elyāsāp,* which means "El has increased" (see the NOTES on Num 1:14). The name *Lā'ēl* connotes devotion: "one who belongs to El." It is unique to this chapter.

25–26. The various sections and parts of the Tabernacle structures and the appurtenances listed here, in vv 25–39, carry us back to Exodus 25–27, 30, and 38, where the details of the Tabernacle are described.

25. *the Tent of Meeting.* The formulation in v 25 is specific: *'ôhel mô'ēd* is here used as the designation for the entire complex, including the fenced-in courtyard. The overall complex included "the Tent *(hā'ôhel),*" which is the Shrine with its interior chambers, and the *miškan* 'Tabernacle compound', namely, the area bounded by the courtyard.

This analysis of terminology emerges from the wording of vv 25–26. Thus, "its cover *(miksēhû)*" refers to the covering, in two layers, of the Shrine, made of tanned ram skins, over which an additional covering of dolphin skins was placed (Exod 26:14).

The "screen" *(māsāk,* fron the root *s-k-k* 'to cover over') refers to the screen at the entrance to the tent itself, as is clear from Exod 26:36–37, where it is referred to more precisely as *māsāk lepetaḥ hā'ôhel* 'a screen for the entrance of the Tent'. This screen is distinct from the one covering the entrance to the courtyard, which is mentioned in the next verse. The ambiguity arises from the fact that v 25 is inconsistent in its terminology. In the first instance it uses the term *'ôhel mô'ēd* to designate the entire complex, and in the second part of the verse it uses the same term for the Tent specifically. The screen at the entrance to the Tent was quite elaborate, made of blue, purple, and crimson yarns, and embroidered. It was held erect by five posts that were overlaid with gold.

26. In Exod 27:9 we read of the hangings *(qelā'îm)* made of linen, which

were tied with "thongs *(mêtarîm)*" to posts, and which surrounded the entire courtyard (cf. Exod. 35:18; 39:40). The entrance to the courtyard also had a screen (Exod 27:16), held up by four posts. The force of prepositional *ʿal* in v 26 is "around, near." It is the courtyard *(ḥāṣēr)* that surrounds the Tabernacle compound, and the altar of burnt offerings that stood inside it (Exod 27:1). The ambiguous term *ʿabôdāh* means "construction, fashioning," as it does in Exod 27:19 and below, in vv 31 and 36. Once again, idiomatic *šāmar mišmeret* refers to maintenance tasks (see the NOTES on Num 1:53; 18:2).

29. *the southern side.* The Kohathites were encamped "to the right" of the eastern entrance of the Tabernacle complex, namely, to the south of it, as described in Numbers 2. The Hebrew *yārēk* 'thigh' is one of those terms for a part of the human body used to designate architectural features (Exod 40:24). Cf. *yerek hammizbēaḥ* 'the "thigh" of the altar', namely, its side (2 Kgs 10:14; Lev 1:11). A similar appropriation of bodily terms is reflected in usage of *ṣēlāʿ* 'rib' to mean "buttress, ledge," as an architectural term (1 Kgs 6:2; Ezek 41:5, 11; Exod 26:26).

30. The Hebrew name *ʾElîṣāpān* most probably means "my God has protected." Compare the name *Ṣepanyāh* YH (= YHWH) has protected'. See Pss 27:5 and 31:21 for expressions of the concept of divine protection conveyed by the verb *ṣāpan. ʾElîṣāpān*'s father is named *ʿUzzîʾēl* 'El (God) is my strength'. In the episode of the death of two of Aaron's sons, recounted in Leviticus 10, we find the same person, whose name is given as *ʾĒlṣāpān* son of *ʾUzzîʾēl* , identified as Aaron's cousin (Lev 10:4). A review of Hebrew sentence names constructed on the model *ʾel* + verb in the perfect tense shows a number of cases of variation with *ʾēlî* + verb in the perfect tense: compare *ʾElîšāmāʾ* 'my God has heard' (Num 1:10) and *ʾElîšāpaṭ* 'my God has judged' (2 Chr 23:1). This evidence allows us to conclude that the person named here is the same as the one named in Leviticus 10.

31. The Ark, presentation table, and candelabrum are described in Exod 25:10–40, whereas the two altars are detailed elsewhere. The altar of burnt offerings was located in the open courtyard. Reference to *kelê haqqôdes* 'the vessels of the Sanctuary' recalls Exod 38:3 but also takes us forward to Num 4:14, where the various vessels are enumerated as the text specifies the tasks of the Kohathites. In the present verse, the term *māsāk* 'screen' is used for designating the *pārôket* (curtain), described in Exod 26:31–37, that separated the innermost chamber of the Tent from its outer chamber.

32. The chief of the chieftains of the three levitical houses was Eleazar, son of Aaron, who was actually a scion of the Kohathite clan, and for that reason is named here. Aaron was ultimately in charge of all of the levitical groups of workers, as well as of the priests. The Hebrew term *pequddâh* has several connotations in biblical usage. Here it means "marshaled force," referring to the group itself, not to the tasks the group was assigned or to the manner in which it was mustered. In 2 Chr 26:11 we read *bemispar pequd-*

dātām 'according to the number of their marshaled force'. The plural, *pequddôt*, also has this meaning, as in 2 Kgs 11:18; Ezek 9:1).

33. Here begins the section on the Merarite clans, which continues through v 38.

35. The *nāśîʾ* of the Merarites was *Ṣûrîʾēl* 'El is my rock, protector', son of *ʾAbîḥayîl* 'my Father is powerful'. The Merarites were encamped on the northern side of the Tabernacle complex.

36–37. The Hebrew formula *pequddat mišmeret* is somewhat redundant: "The marshaled force bearing the assignment." The Merarites were in charge of the structural sections of the Tent and courtyard—the planks and posts, bolts and lashings. The flaps and actual materials of the Tent and its coverings and trappings, as well as those of the courtyard enclosure, were assigned to the Gershonites. These structural parts are described in Exod 26:1–31.

38. After outlining the units encamped to the west, south, and north of the Tabernacle compound, the record proceeds to inform us that the Aaronide priests occupied the most honored position, to the east, facing the entrance to the Tabernacle. There Moses and Aaron and his sons, the priests, resided. They bore overall responsibility for the tasks relevant to the Shrine. The sense of *lemišmeret benê Yiśrāʾēl* is "in fulfillment of the duties of the Israelite people." The formula that concludes v 38, *wehazzār haqqārēb yummāt* 'Any outsider who intrudes shall be put to death', was explained in the NOTES on Num 1:51.

The term used in this verse to designate the entire Tabernacle complex is *miqdāš* 'sanctuary, temple' rather than *ʾôhel môʿēd* or *miškān*. The Hebrew term *miqdāš* more properly connotes a stationary building, but in priestly sources of the Torah it may also refer to the wilderness Tabernacle (Exod 25:8; Lev 12:4; 21:12; Num 10:21; 18:1).

39. This verse records the total number of male Levites as 22,000. It sets the stage for computing the differential between the number of firstborn male Israelites and the number of Levites potentially available for Tabernacle service, which is the subject of vv 40–43. It is curious that the cumulative total of the three levitical houses, as given successively in Num 3:22, 28, and 34 is actually 22,300. Conceivably an error occurred somewhere along the line, perhaps in Num 3:28, where *šēš meʾōt* 'six hundred' (consonantal *šš*) may be an error for *šelôš meʾôt* (consonantal *šlš*) '300'.

40. Moses was to register the names of all firstborn Israelite males one month of age and older. This count corresponds to the calculation of the number of male Levites, also based on the age of one month.

41. The subject of the second part of v 41, a reference to the firstlings of the livestock of the Levites as redemption for those belonging to Israelites, is not picked up in v 42 and may, therefore, represent an interpolation. Taken as it stands, this part of the verse states that the livestock possessed by the tribe of Levi was to be devoted to the Tabernacle at the time the Levites them-

selves were initially dedicated. This requirement was undoubtedly meant to be permanent, as was the case with respect to the firstborn of male Israelites, who were to be redeemed on a continuing basis (see the Introduction to Numbers 18, and cf. below, in v 45).

You shall acquire. The force of the verb *lāqaḥ* 'to acquire' requires comment. The formulation *lāqaḥ* + direct object + possessive *lamed,* which occurs here, is quite common; compare Gen 24:4: *welāqaḥtā 'iššâh libnî le-Yiṣḥāq* 'You shall acquire a wife for my son, for Isaac'. Also note Exod 6:7: *welāqaḥtî 'etkem lî le'ām* 'I shall acquire you for me, as a people'.

42. The syntax of v 42 is parenthetical, and should be rendered literally: "Moses mustered, as YHWH had commanded him, every firstborn among the Israelites."

43. *totaled.* Again, as in Num 1:46, we note technical usage of the verb *hāyāh* to connote a mathematical total, with the sense of "amounting to, totaling." The outcome of the census was that there were 273 more firstborn Israelites to be redeemed than there were Levites to stand in for them.

44–51. The remaining verses detail the adjustment of the differential of 273 persons, just recorded. The key verb is *pādāh* 'to redeem, buy back'. The primary context seems to be that of bondage, wherein the owner or master of one in service is compensated for the claim held on the person bound over to him. The Israelites had been in bondage to the Egyptians, and God bought them their freedom, a thought reiterated in Mic 6:4 and Deut 21:8.

46. *redemptive price.* The passive plural form *pedûyîm,* used repeatedly in this passage, represents either an abstract plural or a collective *(pluralis tantum).* See the NOTES on Num 18:15.

The language of this verse and of vv 48–49 below, recalls usage in Lev 25:25–28, the text of a law dealing with redemption of land that an owner had been compelled to sell. One was to compute "the balance *(hā'ôdēp),*" literally, the amount due in excess of what had been repaid previously, and to remit the same to the purchaser. The verb *'ādap* may also refer to size, connoting whatever overreached the edge of an object or extended beyond it (Exod 26:12), or to quantity, to what was left of the manna, for instance (Exod 16:23).

47. *by the sanctuary weight.* In ancient Israel, two standards were in use. There was the royal standard, known as *'eben hammelek,* literally, "the royal stone" (2 Sam 14:26), and *šeqel haqqôdeš* 'the sanctuary weight', the term occurring here, which was used in all transactions with the Temple. In Ezek 45:2 we find a summary statement of the precise content of the sanctuary standard.

48. *those outstanding among them.* Here the sense is that 273 male Israelites constituted a balance of firstborn sons, remaining to be redeemed; *hā'ôdepîm bāhem,* literally, "those in excess among them."

49. The form *pidyôm* (consonantal *pdywm)* may be erroneous for *peduyyîm* (written *pdym),* as is suggested by the occurrence of the latter form in v 51 below. The usual form is *pidyôn* 'redemption price' (Exod 21:30; Ps 49:9).

TRANSLATION OF NUMBERS 4

4 1 YHWH spoke to Moses and to Aaron as follows:

2 Take a head count of the Kohathites, who are part of the Levites, by their clans and patriarchal houses,

3 of those thirty years of age and older, until fifty years of age, all who are eligible for performing assigned tasks in the work force, pertaining to the Tent of Meeting.

4 This is the task of the Kohathites within the Tent of Meeting: the most sacred objects.

5 Whenever the encampment sets out on the march, Aaron and his sons shall enter, and take down the *pārôket* screen, and wrap the Ark of the Covenant with it.

6 They shall place over it a covering of dolphin skin, and spread a wrap of entirely blue cloth on top [of it], and insert its [carrying] poles.

7 Over the table of the [bread] of display they shall spread a wrap of blue cloth, and set upon it the bowls, the ladles, the storage jars, and the libation jugs; and the regularly offered bread shall also be placed on it.

8 They shall spread a crimson cloth over this, which they shall then wrap with a covering of dolphin skin, and insert its carrying poles.

9 They shall take a cloth of blue, and wrap the lampstand [used] for lighting, together with its lamps, its tongs, and its pans, and all of the utensils for its oil, which are to be used in conjunction with them.

10 They shall place it together with all of its vessels inside a covering of dolphin skin, and place it on a [carrying] frame.

11 Over the altar of gold they shall spread a cloth of blue, and wrap it with a covering of dolphin skin, and insert its [carrying] poles.

12 They shall take all of the vessels that are used in the Shrine and place them inside a cloth of blue, and wrap them with a covering of dolphin skin, and place [them] in a [carrying] frame.

13 They shall remove the ashes from the altar [of burnt offerings] and spread a purple cloth over it.

14 They shall place on it all of the vessels of the altar that are used in connection with it: the firepans, the forks, and the scrapers, and the basins "all of the vessels of the altar" and they shall spread over this a covering of dolphin skin and insert its [carrying] poles.

15 Aaron and his sons shall complete the wrapping of what is in the Shrine, including all of the vessels of the Shrine, whenever the encampment sets out

on the march. Afterward, the Kohathites shall arrive to do the transporting,
but they may not have contact with the Shrine, lest they die. These are the
transport duties of the Kohathites pertaining to the Tent of Meeting.
[16]The charge of Eleazar the son of Aaron the priest shall consist of the oil for
lighting and the aromatic incense; the regular grain offering, and the oil of
anointing the charge of the entire Tabernacle and everything in it pertaining
to the Shrine and pertaining to its vessels.
[17]YHWH spoke to Moses and to Aaron as follows:
[18]Do not allow the tribal clans of the Kohathites to be cut off from the [rest
of] the Levites.
[19]This is how you shall manage them, so that they may remain alive and not
risk death whenever they approach the Holy of Holies: Aaron and his sons
shall enter and assign them, each one, to his workload,
[20]so that they do not have to come inside and view the Shrine for even a split
second, and die as a result.
[21]YHWH spoke to Moses as follows:
[22]Take a head count of the Gershonites, as well, by their clans and patriarchal houses.
[23]You shall muster all of them, thirty years of age and older to fifty years of
age, all who are eligible to perform the tasks of the work force relevant to the
Tent of Meeting.
[24]This is the duty of the Gershonite clans: the task of transportation.
[25]They shall transport the flaps of the Tabernacle and the Tent of Meeting—
its wrapping, and the covering of dolphin skin that is over it, on top, and the
curtain at the entrance of the Tent of Meeting,
[26]as well as the hangings of the courtyard, and the curtains at the gate of the
courtyard, which surrounds the Tabernacle and the altar of burnt offerings,
and their lashings, and all of their functional accessories; they shall perform
whatever is necessary for their maintenance.
[27]The entire assignment of the Gershonites shall be conducted by order of
Aaron and his sons, pertaining to all of their transportation tasks. You shall
dutifully oversee all of their transportation work.
[28]This is the task of the Gershonite clans pertaining to the Tent of Meeting,
their charge being under the authority of Ithamar, son of Aaron the priest.
[29]As for the Merarites, you shall muster them by their clans and patriarchal
houses.
[30]You shall record those of them thirty years of age and older to fifty years of
age, all who are eligible for the work force, to perform assigned tasks relevant
to the Tent of Meeting.
[31]This is their transport assignment, comprising their complete task relevant
to the Tent of Meeting: the planks of the Tabernacle, and its bolts, and its
posts and its sockets,
[32]and the posts of the courtyard on every side, and their sockets, and their

tent pegs and their lashings, for the maintenance of all of their appurtenances. You shall list this transport assignment by the types of their assigned appurtenances.

33 This is the complete assigned task of the Merarite clan, relevant to the Tent of Meeting, under the authority of Ithamar, son of Aaron the priest.

34 So Moses and Aaron and the chieftains of the community mustered the Kohathites by their clans and patriarchal houses,

35 those thirty years of age and older to fifty years of age, all who were eligible for the work force, for assigned work relevant to the Tent of Meeting.

36 Their total musters by their clans came to 2,750.

37 These are the musters of the Merarite clans, of all who worked at the Tent of Meeting, which Moses and Aaron listed by order of YHWH, under the authority of Moses.

38 The musters of the Gershonites, by their clans and patriarchal houses,

39 of those thirty years of age and older to fifty years of age, all who were eligible to serve on the work force, at the Tent of Meeting.

40 Their musters, by their clans and patriarchal houses: 2,630.

41 These are the musters of Gershonite clans, all who performed tasks at the Tent of Meeting, whom Moses and Aaron registered by order of YHWH.

42 The musters of the Merarites, by their clans and patriarchal houses,

43 of those thirty years of age and older to fifty years of age, all who are eligible for service in the work force, at the Tent of Meeting.

44 Their musters, by their clans, came to 3,200.

45 These are the musters of the Merarite clans, which Moses and Aaron listed, by order of YHWH, under the authority of Moses.

46 The total musters of the Levites listed by Moses and Aaron and the Israelite chieftains, by their clans and patriarchal houses,

47 of those thirty years of age and above to fifty years of age, all who are eligible for assigned maintenance and transport tasks relevant to the Tent of Meeting.

48 Their musters came to 8,580.

49 They were listed by Moses, by order of YHWH, each unit for its assigned maintenance and transport task. Each was listed, just as YHWH commanded Moses.

NOTES TO NUMBERS 4

4 The terminology of Numbers 4 has been explained, for the most part, in the course of commenting on Numbers 1–3. This is true of terms governing the levitical assignments, as well as those identifying vessels, furnishings, and sections of the Tabernacle structure. Comments will be limited, therefore, to matters not previously discussed.

Verse 2 implies that the Kohathites enjoyed a certain preeminence among the three levitical houses, that they were distinguished. The Kohathites were to be counted "from among the sons of Levi *(mittôk benê Lēwî)*." In the subsequent statements introducing the assignments of the Gershonites (v 21) and the Merarites (v 29), we do not detect a similar nuance.

3. *thirty years of age and older.* It has already been noted that in the book of Numbers we find three traditions regarding the minimum age of service for Levites: twenty, twenty-five, and thirty years of age. The minimum age of thirty years is restricted to chap. 4, just as the minimum age of twenty-five years is restricted to chap. 8, which records the dedication of the Levites. In contrast, twenty years is a more general minimum age, common to a number of sources. It is likely, therefore, that the provisions of Numbers 4 and 8 are of separate textual origins.

4. *the most sacred objects.* This sense of *qôdeš haqqodāšîm* may be found elsewhere; compare *qôdeš qodāšîm* in Exod 30:29, where most of the same objects listed below, in v 7 of this chapter, are classified in the same manner. See also the Notes on Num 18:10 for more information on terms for sacred places and objects. Elsewhere, *qôdeš haqqodāšîm* often means "the most sacred precinct, the Shrine," as in 1 Kgs 8:6; Ezek 41:4; Exod 26:34.

5–14. In these verses we find a delineation of the specific tasks to be performed by the Kohathites whenever the Israelites prepared to set forth on the march. Briefly summarized, the procedure was as follows: the Aaronide priests were the only persons who actually touched the interior furnishings and vessels, and then only in order to cover them. The priests covered the Ark and other furnishings with various wraps and inserted the poles used to carry them, or placed the objects on frames. The Kohathites would take over only after the sacred objects had been carefully wrapped. The limited purification of the Levites, described in Numbers 8, and their lesser cultic status prevented their touching sacred objects.

First, the priests would disassemble the *pārôket* screen (*pārôket hammāsāk*; cf. Exod 35:12; 39:34; 40:21; and see the Notes on 3:25–26). This curtain served as the first wrap placed over the Ark.

6. *covering.* The word *kesuî* is rare and occurs only here and in v 14 below. The more normal term is *mikseh,* as in v 10 below, and repeatedly in this chapter. One covering was hardly sufficient for the Ark, and, in fact, all of the most sacred objects had at least two coverings. Over the *pārôket* curtain was placed a covering of dolphin skins *(taḥaš)*, and over that a third covering of perfectly blue cloth *(kelîl tekēlet)*, so that the Ark, which was the most sacred object of all, would be well protected.

dolphin skin. Not all scholars agree that Hebrew *taḥaš* means "dolphin." Some think that it refers to the pigment or color of a cloth fabric. Thus Tadmor (1982) has argued that Hebrew *taḥaš* is cognate with Akkadian *taḫ-si-a,* originally a Hurrian word, which designates leather colored with the yellow or red pigment of the *dūšū* stone. And yet we know that dolphin skins were used quite extensively in ancient Near Eastern cults.

blue [cloth]. We can now be precise about the composition of *tekēlet,* a pigment extracted from the *Murex* snail (see the NOTES on 15:38; and cf. Exod 28:31; 39:22).

entirely. Hebrew *kālîl* may have adverbial force: "entirely, perfectly" (cf. Deut 13:17; Isa 2:18; Judg 20:40).

[carrying] poles. Once the Ark was properly covered, the poles *(baddîm)* were inserted into four rings, located on both sides of the Ark. (The Ark's design is prescribed in Exod 25:10–15.) Once the poles were in place, the Ark could be carried by the Kohathites without danger of arousing God's wrath by having them touch it directly. In 2 Sam 6:68 we read that a man named Uzzah was struck dead upon accidentally touching the Ark.

7. *table of the [bread] of display.* Here the table is called *šulḥan happānîm,* a probable abbreviation of *šulḥan leḥem happānîm* 'the table for the bread of display', which is described in Exod 25:23–30. Along with the candelabrum and the golden incense altar, the presentation table stood in the larger section of the tent shrine. The priests would spread a blue cloth wrap over the table. On this tablecloth they would place the utensils used in the Tabernacle cult, along with the bread of display itself. Here these loaves of bread are called *leḥem hattāmîd* 'the regularly offered bread'.

The basic regulations governing the bread of display are presented in Lev 24:5–9. The practice of displaying loaves of bread in the presence of the Lord was very ancient in biblical Israel. It is mentioned in biblical accounts of David's early career, when he was fleeing from Saul. David's hungry men were given such bread to eat by the priest of Nob, just after it had been removed from the presentation table (2 Sam 31:75).

To return to the procedures for transporting the sacred vessels and appurtenances, we are informed that the entire package would be wrapped with two coverings, the first of crimson cloth, and the second of dolphin skin, and then the poles would be inserted.

the bowls, the ladles, the storage jars. The various utensils listed here are known from other biblical sources. The *qeʿārôt* were recessed bowls, often filled with flour (Num 7:13–15). The *kappôt* were "ladles," fashioned in the form of a palm (Hebrew *kap),* such as were used for incense (Num 7:14). The *menaqqîyôt* are best defined as storage jars for liquids, for elsewhere they are said to be used for libations (Exod 25:29; and cf. Jer 52:19; Exod 37:16). Some have suggested relating the Hebrew *menaqqîyôt* to the Akkadian verb *naqû* "to offer a libation" *(CAD* N 1.336–342, under *naqû).* An alternative is to see in this term the connotation of "removal, clearing away" associated with the verbal root *n-q-h* in Hebrew.

the libation jugs. The Hebrew term *qaswāh* (plural construct *qesôt)* is also spelled with a *samekh* and designates a "libation jug," used in pouring out the offering. The Septuagint renders *qesôt* as *spondeîa*, singular *spondeîon*, a vessel used for the *spondê* 'libation'. For information on the kinds of libations offered in the priestly cult, see the provisions of Numbers 15.

9. *the lampstand [used] for lighting.* The next object to be wrapped was the Menorah, first described in Exod 25:1–39. Here the candelabrum is called *menôrat hammāʾôr* (cf. Exod 35:14), just as the oil used in the lamps of the Menorah is called *šemen hammāʾôr* 'the oil for lighting' (cf. Exod 35:14). In her discussion of the Tabernacle Menorah, Meyers (1976) describes the seven *nerot* 'lamps' and the other parts of the Menorah in artistic terms, explaining how they were fashioned.

its tongs, and its pans. Hebrew *melqāḥayîm*, from the verbal root *l-q-ḥ* 'to take, carry off', designates the tongs, probably used to hold the wicks as they were inserted in the lamps. The *maḥtôt* 'pans', best known as containers for incense or hot coals (Lev 10:1; Num 16:17), here refer to the pans from which oil was poured into the lamps. Hebrew *maḥtāh* derives from the verb *ḥātāh* 'to remove, burn' (Ps 52:7; Prov 25:22).

10. The Menorah and its related untensils were wrapped in stages. First the candelabrum itself was covered with *tekēlet* cloth, and then the utensils were wrapped, together with the Menorah, in dolphin skins. This package was carried on a "frame *(môṭ)*," a term explained in the NOTES on Num 13:23.

11. Next came the golden incense altar, first described in Exod 30:27. *Tekēlet* cloth was spread over the incense altar, followed by a covering of dolphin skins. This altar was carried with poles.

12. All of the remaining vessels and utensils used in cultic service within the Shrine were also to be wrapped in two coverings and placed on a frame for transport.

13. Now came the altar of burnt offerings, which stood in the courtyard outside the Tent. It was first described in Exod 27:1–8. The denominative verb *diššēn* means "to remove the ashes" *(dešen* in Hebrew). In effect, this altar was cleaned and then wrapped with a purple cloth.

14. *the firepans, the forks, and the scrapers, and the basins.* The utensils of the altar included *maḥtôt* 'firepans', a term already explained in v 9, above, and here intended for carrying hot coals. The remaining three utensils are known from biblical usage. The Hebrew *mazlēg* 'fork' is mentioned in 1 Sam 2:13–14 as an implement used to remove cooked sections of offerings from the pots in which they were customarily boiled (cf. also Exod 27:3; 38:3). Hebrew *mizrāq*, from the verb *zāraq* 'to cast, sprinkle', means "basin," and is explained in the NOTES on Num 7:13 (cf. Zech 9:15; 14:20). In Amos 6:6 the *mizrāq* is said to contain wine, and it must have been a fairly large vessel, because the prophet mocks those who drink wine from "basins" in excessive quantities. Hebrew *yāʿeh* 'scraper' is first mentioned in Exod 27:3 (cf. Exod 38:3), and it designates a utensil used to remove ashes (1 Kgs 7:40, 45; Jer 52:18).

15. Only when the Aaronide priests had completed wrapping the Shrine's vessels and furnishings could the Kohathite Levites carry them, as the Israelites set out on the march. The Kohathites had to be protected from the danger of divine wrath by avoiding direct contact with the most sacred Tabernacle objects, while they were still exposed. This theme is made more explicit below, in vv 17–20.

16. We are now told that handling some of the special ingredients used in the Tabernacle cult was the assignment of Aaron's son Eleazar. These materials had to be transported whenever the Israelites set out on the march, but they were too sacred for others to handle. The relevant materials are (1) the oil for lighting the Menorah's lamps, already referred to in v 9, above (see Exod 35:14); (2) the special "spiced incense," Hebrew *qeṭôret hassammîm,* used on the golden incense altar (Exod 30:7; 31:11); (3) the ingredients of the daily *minḥāh* "grain offering," ordained as a priestly sacrifice in Lev 6:12–16, to be performed by the high priest; and (4) the oil of anointing *(šemen hammišḥāh),* whose main function is prescribed in Exod 25:6 and described in Exod 30:25–31. It was used to anoint Aaron and, according to certain sources, all of the priests as well (see the NOTES on Num 3:3). On occasion, this oil was used in other rites of consecration.

grain offering. As this is the first occurrence of the term *minḥāh* in Numbers, it would be best to discuss its origin and meaning here. The essential *minḥāh* is prescribed in Leviticus 2. It was made of semolina flour. Oil was mixed with the dough, or smeared over it, and frankincense was added. (There were several exceptions to this recipe, of course.) Once the dough was mixed, a fistful of it was burned on the altar, and the rest of the dough of the *minḥāh* was formed into cakes or thin wafers, and prepared in various ways.

The term *minḥāh* itself says nothing about the contents or preparation of the offering; rather, it relates to the manner of its presentation or disposition. The basic sense of the term *minḥāh* is "gift, tribute," and, like many terms for sacrificial offerings, it was adopted by priestly writers from the administrative vocabulary (cf. 2 Sam 8:26; 1 Kgs 5:1; 10:25; 2 Kgs 17:4). Basically, the term *minḥāh* could be used for any kind of sacrifice. The differing offerings of Cain and Abel are both termed *minḥāh* in Gen 4:3–5.

What made the term *minḥāh* so appropriate was its expressiveness of subservience or submission. How the term *minḥāh* came to designate offerings of grain specifically is not entirely clear. Hebrew *minḥāh* derives from the verb *nāḥāh* 'to lead, conduct', so that it connotes what was brought before the Deity or presented to him. In its earliest form, the grain offering was presented to the Deity; it was set before him instead of being burned to any extent on the altar. Thus the bread of display *(leḥem happānîm)* was presented in this way (Lev 24:5–6). According to Lev 7:12–14, the grain offering of thanksgiving included two loaves of leavened bread that were not burned on the altar at all. Deut 26:1–4 speak of firstfruits *(bikkûrîm)* that were to be "placed" before God. So perhaps the term *minḥāh* was used to describe grain offerings because they were largely "presented," and it is this act that relates to the root meaning of *minḥāh*.

the charge. The Hebrew term *pequddāh* is here translated "charge," referring to the duties incumbent on priests and other servitors of the Tabernacle. In the NOTES on Num 3:32 it was explained that this term may also designate the work force, those "charged" with certain duties. The point of v 16 is that Eleazar was in charge of specific consecrated materials, just as Ithamar was in charge of others (see below, in the NOTES on vv 28, 33).

17–20. The next four verses merely restate the special concern shown the Kohathites, whose duties have just been delineated (see the NOTES on v 15, above).

18. The sense of the *hiph'il* negative imperative *'al takrîtû* is "Do not allow . . . to be cut off," namely, do not allow the Kohathites to be so endangered that they will meet death at the hands of God (Levine 1989b: 241–242).

19. *each one*. The Aaronide priests were permitted entry into the Shrine, at least into the outer section of it; but the Levites were entirely barred from the interior of the Shrine. So the priests had to exercise care in assigning individual Kohathites to the appropriate tasks required for transporting the sacred objects. Idiomatic *'îš 'îš* usually means "any person," but here it seems to mean "every person, each person," as in v 49, below.

20. *for a split second*. The Levites were forbidden to gaze upon the interior of the Shrine. Adverbial *kebala'* literally connotes the time it takes to swallow one's spittle (Job 7:19).

21–49. Verses 21–33 detail the tasks of the Gershonites and Merarites in transporting the Tabernacle and its parts. Afterward, vv 34–49 report the results of the official census of all three levitical houses. Just as chap. 4 began with an introductory statement (vv 1–3) commanding the mustering of the Kohathites and then proceeded to enumerate their assigned tasks, so here vv 21–23 perform the same introductory function with respect to the Gershonites. Further on, v 29 similarly introduces the assignments of the Merarites, once again by referring to their musters.

24. *the task of transportation*. Hebrew *la'abôd ûlemassa'* represents hendiadys: "for the task of transporting" (rather than "for performing a task and for transporting").

25–26. These verses repeat the tasks listed as the *mišmeret* 'duties' of the Gershonites in Num 3:25–26 in the same general formulation, but in greater detail. It is, therefore, unnecessary to explain the pertinent technical terms again. In general, the Gershonites attended to the wrappings and flaps of the Tent structure and of the courtyard enclosure. Verse 26 ends with a summary statement: *we'et kol 'ašer yē'āśeh lāhem we'ābādû*, literally, "Whatever needs to be done with respect to them, let them perform!"

27. Once again, careful supervision by the priests was required to ensure

that all tasks were carried out properly. As in v 24 above, we have here another instance of hendiadys. Hence, *lekol maśśāʾām ulekol ʿabôdātām* means "pertaining to all of their transportation tasks." The conclusion of v 27 is characterized by a plethora of technical formulation involving the verb *paqad,* and the nouns *mišmeret* and *maśśāʾ*. The formula *ûpeqadtem ʿalêhem bemišmeret* means "You shall carry out your charge over them dutifully." The construction *bemišmeret* thus has adverbial force.

28. This verse concludes the section on the assignments of the Gershonites, noting that their tasks were under the supervision of Ithamar (see below, in v 33).

29–33. The next five verses detail the assignments of the third levitical house, the Merarites.

31–33. These verses repeat the duties listed as the assignment of the Merarites in Num 3:36–37 with a degree of elaboration. The pertinent technical terms have already been explained.

34–39. These verses record the fulfillment of what had been ordained throughout, namely, a complete muster of all of the Levites (Num 3:14; 4:1–29). The order here is functional, reflecting the maintenance and transport of the Tabernacle complex. It begins with the Kohathites and continues with the Gershonites and Merarites. Both the content and the formulation of vv 34–39 are repetitive. For this reason, further comments will be limited to what has not been explained so far.

41. Formulaic *kol hāʿôbēd* means "all who performed tasks *ʿabôdāh,*" with denominative connotation.

49. The point emphasized here is that everything Moses and Aaron did had been specifically ordained by God and was in fulfillment of precise divine commands. This theme is reinforced by reference to the chieftains of Israel, mentioned in v 46 above. In this way, all were included who had initially been instructed to conduct the census and to supervise the organization of the encampment, with the Tabernacle at its center.

We have come to the conclusion of the first major unit of the book of Numbers, consisting of chaps. 1–4. The encampment and its Tabernacle are now in place and have been made operational.

COMMENT: INTRODUCING THE LEVITES

Taken together, Numbers 3–4 provide a table of organization for the Levites as the group charged with maintaining the Tabernacle complex. The Levites were to dismantle it, transport it, and set it up again whenever the Israelites moved their encampment. Chapter 3 outlines the assignments of each of the three levitical clans, whereas chap. 4 describes how these assignments were to be carried out. Implicit in all of these procedures is the responsibility of the Levites for maintaining the Tabernacle and its furnishings in good repair, for cleaning the Tabernacle and performing related tasks. These assigned duties are laconically conveyed by the allusive term *mišmeret*, used repeatedly in Numbers.

Incorporated in the provisions of chap. 3 are the results of the separate census of all male Levites one month of age and older, a reflection of the genealogical orientation of this chapter. In contrast, chap. 4, exhibiting an administrative orientation, reports on the mature male Levites, those trained and available for service; namely, those of thirty to fifty years of age. It turns out that the number of adult male Levites, so defined, amounts to approximately 26 percent of all male Levites (see Num 1:48–54). Therefore, about three-quarters of the Levites were either too young, too old, or as yet untrained to serve in the sanctuary. It is curious that a twenty-year-old Israelite was fit to serve in the military, according to chap. 1, whereas a Levite was not ready for active Tabernacle service until age thirty. This discrepancy may mean that extensive training and initiation were required for functioning Levites, or it may indicate that the needs of the Tabernacle did not require as much manpower as was available at any particular time. It would be difficult to pinpoint any historical period in which such regulations would have made the most sense.

Chapter 3 expresses a theory of cultic service according to which male Levites were considered substitutes for the firstborn male Israelites spared by God when he smote the firstborn of Egypt (Num 3:11–13, 40–51). This subject is not resumed in chap. 4 but reemerges in Num 8:16–20 in the record of the Levites' dedication.

In attempting to position the provisions of chaps. 3–4 in literary-historical perspective, it must be borne in mind that the historicity of the Tabernacle traditions is highly questionable to start with. It is true that 2 Sam 6:17 and 7:2 report that the Ark had been located inside a tent prior to its installation in the Solomonic temple. But these passages may well be secondary in 2 Samuel (McCarter 1980: 131, to 1 Sam 6:19). Even if original, however, such simple statements are a far cry from the elaborate depictions of the Tabernacle found in the later chapters of Exodus, in Leviticus, and in Numbers. Even more, it is the portable character of the Tabernacle that clashes with the real forms of cult sites in the biblical period. Cult installations, however they may have been constructed, were stationary. The entire concept of a portable cult complex, wrapped up and carted away whenever the encampment set forth on the march, has no substantiation in the historical books of the Bible, except in certain passages clearly attributable to the priestly tradition, such as Josh 18:1.

The Ark, conversely, has an authentic history as a portable cult object. Early biblical sources relating to its functions exhibit a high degree of reality. The same could be said about certain of the Tabernacle furnishings, as regards their functions if not their precise forms. It is realistic to suppose that a presentation table *(šulḥān)* was in use, as well as some sort of Menorah, though not necessarily the one described in Exod 25:31–40. There is also a body of comparative evidence, some of it iconographic, which adds to the realism of such cult objects.

Thus it is that the specific assignment of the Levites of the Kohathite clan, to attend to the Ark and to the most sacred furnishings of the Tabernacle, can be discussed somewhat historically. It would be problematic, however, to attempt a historical treatment of the assignments of the Gershonites and Merarites, as outlined in chaps. 3–4, because the assignments of these clans all pertain to the portable tent shrine.

Methodological considerations recommend, therefore, that we begin our literary-historical quest with a discussion of the Ark itself. In Num 10:33–36 we read that the Ark was carried ahead of the Israelite forces when they set out on the march. That passage preserves two verses from an ancient epic poem (see the COMMENTS on Num 10:29–12:16). The utilization of the Ark in military campaigns is, of course, highlighted in the so-called "Ark narratives" of 1 Samuel 4–7 (Miller and Roberts 1977). The various biblical traditions of the Ark do not project a consistent conception of its functions, however. The Deuteronomic school emphasizes the conception of the Ark as a repository for the Tablets of the Covenant, a function not uniformly reflected in other biblical sources.

What is of particular interest regarding the assignments of the levitical clans is that in early biblical sources the priests were the ones who attended to the Ark. They customarily carried it about, when that task was required during the period preceding the installation of the Ark in the Shrine *(debîr)* of the Jerusalem Temple. This assignment is only to be expected in relatively early biblical sources, for the Levites, as a group separate from the priesthood, did not emerge before the exilic period, according to my calculations. This subject is elaborated in the COMMENTS to chaps. 8 and 16–17.

Biblical historiography preserves at least two recastings of the pre-Temple history of Israelite worship, one that has priests attending to the Ark, and another that has Levites performing this task in the same projected historical period. Numbers 3–4 belong with the latter set of traditions, of course, and accordingly have the preeminent Levites, namely, the clan of Kohath, transport the Ark. There is, however, one proviso: only the Aaronide priests were actually permitted to touch the Ark, as would be required in wrapping it, for instance (Num 4:5). No amount of recasting by the priestly writers of the Torah, or even by the Chronicler, dared challenge this cultic restriction.

The foregoing reconstruction emerges from a careful examination of certain biblical sources bearing on the handling of the Ark. In 1 Sam 6:15 we read that the Levites lowered the Ark from the wagon on which it had been returned to the Israelite camp by the Philistines. This account would seem to contradict what was said above and indicate a role for the Levites in a relatively early biblical source. But the reading *hallewiyyîm* in 1 Sam 6:15 has correctly been questioned. It is likely either that the text originally contained the Deuteronomic designation *hakkôhanîm hallewiyyîm* 'the levitical priests' (M. Z. Segal 1971: 32, to 1 Sam 6:15) or that 1 Sam 6:15, in its entirety, represents a priestly interpolation. I find the latter explanation more persuasive on exegetical grounds. The next verse, 1 Sam 6:16, follows logically upon v 14, whereas v 15 merely rephrases v 14 and is redundant. Most likely, a priestly editor inserted 1 Sam 6:15 with the express purpose of making the text conform to the priestly view of the Levites, as projected in the book of Numbers. In point of fact, no early biblical tradition would have explicitly accorded the Levites the right to touch the Ark, as was noted above.

Except for such interpolations, the preexilic historical books tell us consistently that priests attended to the Ark. In 1 Sam 7:1 we are told that when the Ark was brought to Gibeah, some time after the Philistine episode, a certain Amminadab, who had accepted the Ark and housed it on his property, consecrated *(qiddēš)* his son Eleazar to care for it. Usage of the verb *qiddēš* implies that he appointed his son as a priest. 1 Sam 14:17–20 (especially v 19) also indicate that priests cared for the Ark and transported it.

Most instructive is a comparison of the earlier biblical accounts of bringing the Ark to Jerusalem, in 2 Samuel 6 and 1 Kings 8, with the later reworkings of the same accounts, in 1 Chronicles 15–16 and 2 Chronicles 5. Second Samuel 6 relates that David had the Ark brought to Jerusalem, and there we once again find reference to the Amminadab of 1 Samuel 7. One of his sons, Uzza, who was in charge of caring for the Ark together with his brother Ahyo, was struck dead when he accidentally took hold of it while it was being transported on a wagon. Like Eleazar of 1 Samuel 7, these two sons of Amminadab had undoubtedly been consecrated as priests and assigned to care for the Ark. The account of 2 Samuel 6 makes no further mention of priests (or of Levites, for that matter), but instead expands on the perils of handling the Ark.

A careful analysis of the account in 1 Kings 8, the record of the dedication of the Solomonic Temple, makes us aware of the composite character of that source, which was edited by priestly writers. It clearly states in 1 Kgs 8:3 that the priests *(hakkôhanîm)* carried the Ark, and this assignment is restated in v 6 (cf. 1 Kgs 6:19). Furthermore, vv 10–11 imply the same priestly function by relating that the priests were enveloped in the cloud of God's glorious presence *(kābôd)*, which occurred, significantly, as they were leaving the Shrine after depositing the Ark inside it.

Only 1 Kgs 8:4–5 reveal the hand of a priestly writer. In the first instance, we read of *hakkôhanîm wehallewiyyîm* 'the priests and the Levites', and then we find reference to *'ôhel môʿēd* 'the Tent of Meeting'. Finally, v 5 mentions *kol ʿadat Yiśrāʾēl* 'the entire community of Israel'. These are all priestly locutions. Now, either the priestly editor split the Deuteronomic designation *hak-*

kôhanîm hallewiyyîm 'the levitical priests' by inserting conjunctive *waw;* or, as is more likely, he simply added *wehallewiyyîm* 'and the Levites' at the end of v 4 so as to make this account accord with the priestly laws of the Torah.

First Chronicles 15–16 represent a reworking of 2 Samuel 6. Most significant for the present discussion is the preeminence afforded the families of the Kohathite clan in these accounts. All of the levitical clans are represented, of course, and even the Aaronide priests are mentioned (1 Chr 15:4, 11). But a careful examination shows that the Kohathite families, Hebron and Uzziel, are the ones featured. Undoubtedly, the Elisaphan who is mentioned in 1 Chr 15:8 is identical with Elsaphan, who in Lev 10:4 is the son of Uzziel, Aaron's uncle (see the Notes on Num 3:30). A disproportionate role is given, therefore, to the Kohathite clan in the Chronicler's projection of the deposition of the Ark in Jerusalem during David's reign. Among the officers summoned to supervise the transportation of the Ark is none other than one named Amminadab, who in the levitical genealogy of 2 Chr 6:7–9 is a Kohathite (cf. 1 Sam 7:1; 2 Sam 6:3–4).

More telling, perhaps, is the absence of anyone from the Yizhar family, to which Korah belonged. Quite obviously, the condemnation of Korah, recounted in Numbers 16–17, was endorsed by the Chronicler. In 1 Chr 6:7 Korah is registered as a scion of the clan of Kohath in the record of the clan's formation, but by the time we reach the Chronicler's recounting of David's reign, Korah had long since been condemned; annihilated, in fact, so that descendants of his family would hardly be acceptable within the levitical hierarchy.

The analysis of 2 Chronicles 5, a later reworking of 1 Kings 8, is equally informative. In 2 Chr 5:4 it is stated explicitly that the Levites were the ones who carried the Ark. As the account unfolds, however, we encounter the same inconsistencies as were experienced in 1 Kings 8. In 2 Chr 5:5 we read that, working together, the priests and Levites brought all of the vessels of the Tent of Meeting, as well as the tent parts, to the Temple. But in v 7 only priests are mentioned as those who installed the Ark in the Shrine. This restriction is reinforced in v 11, which echoes the provisions of 1 Kgs 8:10–11. For the rest, Levites are only listed as musicians *(mešôrerîm)*. In other words, the shifting of responsibility for transporting the Ark from priests to Levites is clearly evident in 2 Chronicles 5, notwithstanding its close paraphrasing of 1 Kings 8, a textual situation that might confuse the reader.

According to Num 4:4–12 both priests and Levites were involved in attending to the Ark, but the division of labor is consistent: the Aaronide priests prepared the Ark for transport, because only they were permitted to handle it before it was wrapped and its poles had been inserted. Actually, only priests were permitted to enter the Shrine in order to remove the Ark (Num 4:17–20). But it is the nonpriestly Kohathites who transport the Ark, not the priests.

Numbers 3–4 differ from the Chronicler's accounts in that the Chronicles focus on the period of David and thereafter and pay relatively little attention to the presettlement period. In 1 Chr 6:17 the term *'ôhel mô'ēd* occurs in a reference to the erstwhile role of the Levites before the Temple of Jerusalem was built. In 1 Chr 23:32 we find a similar reference, in a passage closely paraphrasing Num 3:7–8 (cf. also 2 Chr 1:3; 5:5).

Because the Chronicles credit David with accomplishing practically everything except the actual construction of the Temple, we should not expect to find in Chronicles records of the detailed assignments of the levitical clans operative during the wilderness period. In the same accounts, the roles that Numbers assigns to the Gershonites and Merarites are dealt with abruptly, as a matter of fact.

For the most part, the Chronicles report on functions more realistic during the period of the Second Temple—the role of levitical musicians and other trained personnel. As we pursue the agenda of the Chronicler, we find Levites progressively assuming other roles as well, roles that were previously associated with the priesthood, including those of an administrative, educational, and judicial character (see 2 Chronicles 17, 24).

The traditions of Numbers stand somewhere between the historical books of Samuel and Kings, on the one hand, and the work of the Chronicler, on the other. The provisions of Numbers 3–4 were surely known to the Chronicler, but because of the difference in the period of primary reference, little is said in Chronicles of the levitical functions highlighted in Numbers 3–4. The salient exception is the transportation of the Ark. Conversely, Numbers says nothing of certain realistic levitical roles, for instance, their role as musicians, which is highlighted in Chronicles and reflected in the captions to the Psalms.

The omission of any reference to the musical role of the Levites can be explained in terms of the overall policy of the priestly writers of the Torah. Yehezkel Kaufmann characterized the sanctuary projected in the priestly Torah source as *miqdaš haddemāmāh* 'the sanctuary of silence' (Kaufmann 1967: 1.403–408, 551). This is an apt observation on the spirit of the priestly source, which never affords any role to music and hardly ever to ritual recitations. This is not to say that the *cultus* of the First Temple or of the Second Temple was performed without music. It merely signifies that the priestly writers of the Torah did not project music into their recasting of the beginnings of Israelite worship in the wilderness period. As a result, Levites were not assigned to musical functions in the priestly legislation of Numbers.

The role of gatekeepers (*šô'arîm*) is not explicit in Numbers (see the NOTES on Num 1:53). Nevertheless, the elaborate maintenance tasks projected in Numbers certainly included guarding the Tabernacle.

It is worth mentioning that the role of the Levites projected in Ezra and Nehemiah probably represents institutional developments even subsequent to the period of the Chronicler. It is likely that Chronicles antedates Ezra and

Nehemiah, which takes up where Chronicles leaves off, namely, with the edict of Cyrus. This literary-historical sequence, suggested by Ginsberg (1988), does not mean that Chronicles reports historically on the period of the First Temple, or that Ezra 1–7 report reliably on the period of the Return. It means only that, in terms of relative literary chronology, Chronicles antedates Ezra and Nehemiah, and that what Ezra and Nehemiah say about Levites, as an example, may refer to their role in a period subsequent to that of the Chronicler. Furthermore, S. Japhet has shown convincingly that what Ezra and Nehemiah say about the early postexilic period is less historical than had previously been thought (Japhet 1983).

The theme of substitution is prominent in the traditions about the Levites. Pursuant to anticipatory statements in Num 1:48–54, this theme is elaborated in Num 3:11–13 and 40–51, and it reemerges in Numbers 8. The key concept in these sources is conveyed by forms of the verb *pādāh* 'to redeem, restore'. In Num 3:43 we read that there were 273 more Israelite firstborn males than there were male Levites, and we are promptly informed that five shekels a head were to be paid as redemption for the surplus Israelite males, so that all Israelite firstborn males would be free of claims.

The theme of the consecration of the firstborn of Israel is more appropriately a subject for commentaries on Exodus (chapter 13) and Deuteronomy (15:19–23). The present concern focuses on the dynamics of substitution: what does it mean to have Levites serve most of their productive life in the Tabernacle in repayment of God's claim on the firstborn of Israel? From an institutional perspective, we could say that priestly tradition rationalizes the service of the Levites after the fact, by basing their compulsory service on an unsatisfied divine claim. The present claim recalls the votive, or Nazirite, consecration of children to cultic service, as is reflected in the narrative of Hannah, Samuel's mother (1 Samuel 1–2). In a more legalistic formulation, we find in Leviticus 27 a scale of valuations for the redemption of votive consecrations to the Temple that at least theoretically involved devoted persons.

Once a votive pledge was pronounced, the vower incurred a debt to God, which in practical terms meant a debt payable to the Temple and its priesthood. Based on the provisions of Leviticus 27, we would assume that, in most cases, priestly legislation intended such votive indebtedness to be repaid in silver or other objects of value, not by actually having the person pledged report for duty at the Temple! And yet the Samuel narrative informs us that priestly orders, attached to regional temples, augmented their numbers through just such forms of recruitment. Acceptance into priesthoods and other cultic orders stimulated economic mobility by offering opportunities to families in need. Dedicated children would be trained in certain specialized skills and be assured of support and sustenance, for themselves and for their families.

According to both the Deuteronomic and the priestly theories, the Levites were trading off this form of support and sponsorship for the more normal economies of the Israelite tribes who possessed productive lands. Inevitably, levitical service had its liabilities and was not likely perceived as an unqualified distinction. Whereas some priestly families in postexilic Jerusalem, and elsewhere in the land, are known to have possessed estates, less is known of any amassed wealth on the part of the postexilic Levites.

PART II.

NUMBERS 5: ASPECTS OF PURITY

INTRODUCTION: ENCAMPMENT AND COMMUNITY

As is true of certain other sections of Numbers, chapter 5 is not a coherent unit but rather a collection of diverse laws and rituals. There are, to be sure, suggestive thematic links pertaining to such subjects as impurity and betrayal, but as a whole Numbers 5 is best seen as a repository of priestly legislation appropriate to the needs of the Israelites after their "encampment" *(maḥaneh)* had become operational.

Verses 1–4 deal with impure persons of several sorts: those suffering from ailments called *ṣāraʿat,* those experiencing abnormal bodily discharges from the genitals, and those who became impure as a result of contact with a corpse. Such persons were to be expelled from the *maḥaneh,* lest their presence threaten its overall purity and the purity of the Tabernacle located within it. The provisions of vv 1–4 take us back to Leviticus 13–15, the basic legislation governing *ṣāraʿat,* and lead us forward to Numbers 19, which deals with the impurity of the dead.

Verses 5–10 present a brief code of law on the subject of sacrilegious misappropriation, a crime known as *māʿal* in biblical Hebrew. The essential legislation is found in Lev 5:14–16 and 20–26. The present law addresses a complication that might result from that legislation: if the original victim died without leaving an heir before restitution could be made and required penalties paid, all such payments were to go to the priesthood.

Verses 11–31, which comprise the main body of Numbers 5, prescribe an unusual ordeal to be imposed on a married woman whose husband suspects her of infidelity. The ordeal was prescribed in cases wherein no evidence of adultery was available. If witnesses testified to adultery on the part of the woman in question, and their testimony was substantiated, the penalty was death (Lev 20:10).

In the case projected here, the husband in question had cause to suspect his wife, most likely because she had become pregnant. The husband had reason to conclude that the pregnancy was not attributable to him. In such circumstances adultery was suspected and might actually have occurred. This possibility, in itself, was sufficient to threaten the purity of the Israelite community, if the matter were not actively pursued until the guilty party—if, indeed, guilt existed—was punished. Sexual misconduct was considered a form of impurity.

The ordeal of the errant wife was administered by the priest in front of the Tabernacle. A grain offering was prepared, but it was devoid of the usual oil and aromatics and was made of barley, not of wheat, the superior grain. In the course of the procedure the priest made use of holy water, mixed with earth taken from the floor of the Tent of Meeting. The inked words of an execration were washed into the liquid mixture, which was contained in a ceramic vessel. The priest read the charge to the woman and she drank the liquid, after accepting the terms of the execration.

If the woman was truthful in denying the charge, she would retain her conception and carry to term. If, however, she was lying, the liquid mixture would produce deleterious somatic effects, causing the woman's belly to distend and her thighs to sag. This is probably a way of describing a miscarriage. The theatrics of the ordeal, which included a meager grain offering, the loosing of the woman's hair, intoning the grim execration, and the ingestion of the bitter water of condemnation all served to dramatize the apprehension surrounding sexual misbehavior within the Israelite community. More will be said about the phenomenology of the ordeal of the errant wife in the COMMENTS to this chapter.

TRANSLATION

5 [1]YHWH spoke to Moses as follows:

[2]Issue a command to the Israelite people to expel from the encampment any person suffering from *ṣāraʿat*, or experiencing a bodily discharge, as well as any person impure because of contact with a corpse.

[3]You must expel both males and females, expelling them from the encampment, so that they will not defile their encampment, where I maintain a residence in their midst.

[4]The Israelites did accordingly, and expelled them from the encampment. Just as YHWH had instructed Moses, so did the Israelites do.

[5]YHWH spoke to Moses as follows:

[6]Speak to the Israelite people: When a man or woman commits any of the offenses affecting persons, thereby also committing an act of betrayal against YHWH, and that person thereby incurs guilt—

[7]he must confess his offense, which he committed, and he must make restitution for his liability equal to the amount of its principal, adding to it one-fifth of the amount. He shall pay [it] to the person who suffered a loss by the guilt he had incurred.

[8]If that person had no [clan] redeemer to whom the liability could be repaid, the liability that is to be repaid belongs to YHWH, [credited] to the priest. This is apart from the ram of the expiation rites, with which expiation rites shall be performed on his behalf.

[9]Any levied donation for any of the sacred offerings that the Israelites deliver to the priest shall be for him.

[10]For every person shall possess his own sacred offerings; each priest shall possess what is delivered to him.

[11]YHWH spoke to Moses as follows:

12Speak to the Israelite people and say to them: Should any man's wife
become errant and commit an act of betrayal against him,
13with the result that another man had carnal relations with her, and this was
hidden from her husband's eyes, because she defiled herself in secret, there
being no witness against her and she was not apprehended.
14Now, if a fit of jealous possessiveness overtakes him, so that he becomes
envious of his wife in a case wherein she had in fact defiled herself, or a fit of
envious possessiveness so that he becomes envious of his wife in a case
wherein [as it turned out] she had not defiled herself—
15the man must [in any case] bring his wife before the priest and present her
offering on her behalf, of one-tenth of an ephah of barley flour. He shall not
pour oil over it, nor place frankincense upon it, for it is a grain offering
occasioned by jealous feelings; a grain offering of record, which calls attention
to wrongdoing.
16The priest shall bring her near, stationing her in the presence of YHWH.
17The priest shall take holy water in a ceramic vessel, and the priest shall also
take some earth from the floor of the Tabernacle and place it in the water.
18The priest shall station the woman in the presence of YHWH and loosen
the hair of the woman's head, and place on her palms the grain offering, the
grain offering of record, the grain offering occasioned by envious feelings. The
priest shall hold in his hands the bitter water of condemnation.
19The priest shall administer the oath to her, saying to the woman, "If no
man has had carnal relations with you, and if you have not been errant in an
impure manner, while under your husband['s jurisdiction], may you be
cleared of the charge by means of this bitter water of condemnation.
20"But if you have been errant, while under your husband['s jurisdiction],
and you have defiled yourself, in that a man other than your husband has
inseminated you carnally—"
21(the priest shall then administer to the woman the imprecation section of
the oath). The priest shall say to the woman, "May YHWH make of you an
accursed oath-violator among your kin, even as YHWH causes your thigh to
sag and your belly to swell!
22"May this water of condemnation enter into your intestines, to cause swelling of the belly and sagging of the thigh!" And the woman shall reply, "Amen!
Amen!"
23The priest shall inscribe the words of the imprecation on a document, and
he shall then wash [them] away in the bitter water.
24He is to give the woman the bitter water of condemnation to drink, and
the water of condemnation will enter into her and turn bitter.
25The priest shall take the grain offering of envious feelings from the
woman's hand and present the grain offering before YHWH, and move her
(= the woman) nearer to the altar.
26The priest shall scoop up a fistful of the grain offering—its token portion—

and turn it into smoke on the altar, after which he shall give the woman the water to drink.

[27]He must give her the water to drink. It will happen that if she has defiled herself and has acted disloyally against her husband, the water of condemnation will turn bitter, with the result that her belly will swell and her thigh sag. The woman will become a curse in the midst of her kin.

[28]But if the woman has not defiled herself, and she turned out to be pure, she shall be cleared of the charge, and retain seed.

[29]This is the prescribed instruction regarding feelings of jealousy, in cases wherein a wife was errant while under [the jurisdiction of] her husband, and had defiled herself,

[30]or in cases wherein a fit of envious possessiveness overtook a man, with the result that he became envious of his wife. The priest is to station the woman before YHWH and perform with respect to her this entire, prescribed instruction.

[31][In this way] the husband may be cleared of any wrongdoing, while the woman in question will bear punishment for her offense.

NOTES TO 5:1–4: AILMENTS AND IMPURE EMISSIONS

5 2. *suffering from ṣāraʿat.* The first type of impure person dealt with is the one designated *ṣārûʿa* (*qal,* passive participle), namely, a person potentially infected or diseased with *ṣāraʿat.* The *piʿel* passive participle, *meṣôraʿ*, also occurs, most frequently outside the priestly laws of the Torah (2 Sam 3:29; 2 Kgs 5:1). The form occurring here, *ṣārûʿa,* is the one employed in Lev 13:44; 14:2; and 22:4, the very texts that provide the background to the present law.

The disease known as *ṣāraʿat* is definitely not to be identified as Hansen's Disease, commonly known as leprosy. The symptoms of Hansen's Disease are not those listed in Leviticus 13–14, which more closely resemble skin ailments such as vitiligo, psoriasis, and acute acne. The verb *ṣāraʿ* may be a variant of *sāraʿ* 'to spread over, extend, overflow'. It is used to describe limbs that are abnormally elongated (Lev 21:18; 22:28; and cf. literary usage in Isa 28:20). It should be noted that Greek *lepros* does not signify "leprosy" in the sense of Hansen's Disease, either. It means "scabby, scaly," or "enlarged," and some have associated it with elephantiasis. In ancient Mesopotamia, a skin ailment known as *saḫaršuppû* has been identified as similar to *ṣāraʿat,* as this ailment is described in Leviticus 13–14 (Kinnier-Wilson 1966; Meier 1989).

Characteristically, quarantine and isolation are prescribed for those who suffer from *ṣāraʿat.* We read in 2 Kgs 15:5 that Azariah/Uzziah, who was a *meṣôraʿ*, was confined to isolated quarters all his life. Lev 13:46 ordains that one diagnosed as having acute *ṣāraʿat* was to be permanently banished from the area of settlement. 2 Kings 7 tells a tale about four *meṣôrā'îm* who stood outside the city gate when speaking to the townspeople, suggesting that they were not allowed to enter the city.

And yet the present law more likely pertains to persons showing symptoms of *ṣāraʿat*, such as discoloration of the hair and recessed lesions on the skin. Such persons were quarantined outside the encampment for one or more seven-day periods, for purposes of observation (Lev 13:14; 14:8). This procedure parallels the disposition of one experiencing impure bodily discharges (Hebrew *zāb*), as well as of one impure because of contact with a corpse, the two other kinds of impure persons discussed in Num 5:1–4 (cf. Lev 15:13–14, 24; Num 19:12, 19). One recalls that Miriam was once confined for seven days outside the encampment when she was afflicted with *ṣāraʿat* (Num 12:14–15).

experiencing a bodily discharge. The second type of impurity pertains to a person classified as *zāb*, literally, "one flowing," that is to say, experiencing abnormal discharges from the genitals. This is the subject of Leviticus 15. The two classes of impurities, that of the *ṣārûʿa* and that of the *zāb*, are customarily paired, as in 2 Sam 3:29. In the case of a male, reference is to pus, or to some similar discharge emitting from the penis. In the case of females, reference is to some uterine disorder that produces chronic vaginal discharges outside the normal menstrual period. The verbal root *z-w-b* merely means "to flow, run" (Isa 48:21; Pss 78:20; 105:41) and has nothing to do per se with impurity. It occurs in the beautiful characterization of Canaan as a land "flowing *(zābat)* with milk and sap" (Num 14:8; 16:13).

In Leviticus 15, where the laws affecting the *zāb* are presented, removal from the encampment is not explicitly mandated. There, it is only required that such persons be barred from the area near the Tent of Meeting (Lev 15:13–14, 28–29), and then only while awaiting final purification over a period of seven full days. The present law thus imposes an added stringency.

any person impure because of contact with a corpse. The third category of impure persons is represented by those contaminated through contact with a corpse. The term *ṭāmēʾ lannepeš* 'impure because of a corpse' also occurs in Num 9:10 (the plural occurs in v 6, below). The purification of such persons is legislated in detail in Numbers 19. Precisely, the term *ṭāmēʾ lannepeš* recalls the formulation of the law in Num 19:13: "One who had contact *with a corpse belonging to any human being (bemēt benepeš hāʾādām)* who had died." In certain contexts, Hebrew *nepeš* may refer to dead persons as well as to the living, as in Num 6:6, thus adding a particular nuance to the usage of Hebrew *nepeš* in the present law.

Although the requirement that one impure as a result of contact with a corpse remain outside the encampment is nowhere stated explicitly in Numbers 19, the principal source governing the impurity of the dead, such exclusion was undoubtedly intended. This requirement may be inferred from other provisions stipulated in Numbers 19. Thus the materials instrumental for purification were prepared outside the encampment and were to be stored there. The apprehension expressed in Numbers 19 over the mere presence of contaminated persons inside the encampment also supports the conclusion that during the period of purification such persons were to be held outside the encampment. As stipulated in Num 19:13 and 20, a person who failed, in the proper period of time, to attend to the required purifications would be "cut off" from the Israelite community, a penalty that undoubtedly involved actual banishment.

expel. The *piʿel šillaḥ* is intensive and connotes "driving" or "dispatching." It is said of animals, as well as of humans (Exod 22:4; Lev 16:10).

3. *both males and females.* Both males and females come under the law, and this requirement is expressed by the merism *mizzākār ʿad neqēbāh,* literally, "from male to female."

defile. Were impure persons, such as those listed in v 2, to remain within the encampment, the effect would be to "defile" (the *piʿel* verb *ṭimmēʾ*) the encampment. The form *maḥanēhem* is singular, of course.

I maintain a residence. I have translated the verb *šōkēn* as a denominative, regarding it as a reflex of the noun *miškān* 'residence, tabernacle'. The point of this statement seems to be that the purity of the encampment must be sustained at all costs, precisely because the God of Israel had located his earthly residence within it. This verse recalls the language of other statements on the immanence of God, such as Exod 25:7; 29:45; Lev 16:16; Num 19:13, 20; 35:34, where the verb *šākan* also occurs. One could, of course, translate more simply: "where I reside in their midst."

In 1 Kgs 6:13, the same thought is expressed by the verb *šākan* in referring to the Solomonic Temple, and to its function as a divine residence. In Deut 23:15 we find the general statement "Your encampment must be holy *(qādôš)!*"

4. This verse expresses compliance. In the priestly idiom, compliance is normally expressed by reference to an antecedent divine command, conveyed by the verb *ṣiwwāh* 'to command' (see frequently in Leviticus 8–9, and in Num 1:54; 3:51; 4:49). The verb *dibbēr* 'to speak' often has the nuance "to command" in statements of compliance (Gen 12:4; Exod 24:3; 40:32), which serve to emphasize that the early Israelites were consistently obedient to their God, that they "performed" (the verb *ʿāśāh)* what God had commanded. It was also important to make the point that all of the details of law and ritual prescribed in the Torah came directly from God, through Moses.

NOTES TO 5:5–10: SACRILEGIOUS MISAPPROPRIATION

The crime of *maʿal* is essentially one of sacrilege, and so it is presented in Lev 5:14–16, the primary Torah source on this subject (Milgrom 1976: 16–35; Levine 1989b: 30–34). *Maʿal* is the misappropriation of sacred property. Intentional *maʿal* was undoubtedly punishable by death, as we learn from the fate of Achan, who misappropriated some of the spoils of Jericho, thereby violating the ban *(ḥerēm)* against personal aggrandizement from the spoils of war (Joshua 7; 22:20). But where doubt existed, and the offender could claim that his act had been inadvertent, the sentence was commuted. The offender was allowed the option making full restitution, plus paying a penalty of 20 percent of the loss incurred by the Sanctuary. Ritual expiation by means of an *ʾāšām* sacrifice was also required because of the sacrilegious nature of the crime. The term *ʾāšām* expresses the dominant theme of the law, and this term has a wide range of meanings, including "guilt" as a resultant legal state, and "penalty" as a liability incurred.

Farther on in Lev 5:20–26, the provisions of cultic law were extended to include the criminal misappropriation of another's property through fraud, embezzlement, and misuse of belongings entrusted to one's keeping. In the punishment of such crimes it was often required that the accused party swear to his own innocence, as actual evidence of wrongdoing was not available.

If the accused had lied under oath, there would be no way for the one who had suffered the loss of property to recover what he had lost. In order to provide an incentive, a certain immunity was allowed in the laws of Lev 5:20–26. One could come forth and admit the original crime and make full restitution, with the penalty of 20 percent imposed. An expiatory sacrifice would also be required, because the prior false oath had invoked God's name in vain.

As long as the original victim was alive, or if deceased had left heirs who could claim the requisite payments, there would be no problem in implementing the law. But if a man had passed away leaving no heirs, how would the system work? In such an event, the requisite payments would be credited to the priesthood; more precisely, to the priest of choice, the one who had been assigned to administering the original expiation. This provision resembles many laws, known the world over, which declare the state or a religious institution to be *de jure* heir to unclaimed estate benefits.

6. *a man or woman.* The formulation *ʾîš ʾô ʾiššāh* is actually quite rare in biblical law (cf. Deut 17:2).

offenses affecting persons. The characterization *ḥaṭṭʾôt hāʾādām* is unique to this verse. Its precise meaning is elusive, but in context it refers to offenses against persons, in contrast to religious sins, which we would regard as primarily offensive to God. Thus, NJPS translates "any wrongs toward a fellow man." It is possible, of course, that *ḥaṭṭ'ôt hā'ādām* simply means "offenses committed by persons," but this reading is less likely.

committing an act of betrayal against YHWH. The cognate formulation *lim'ôl ma'al b-YHWH* is to be understood as somewhat loose, rather than as precisely legal or technical. The same generalized meaning is evident in v 12 below, where marital infidelity is characterized as *ma'al* (cf. also Lev 25:40; Ezek 14:13; and in even later sources, Ezra 9:2–4; 10:6; Dan 9:7). What began as a legal category, defining the misappropriation of property, intentional or inadvertent, became idiomatic for describing other sorts of betrayal and disloyalty.

The noun *ma'al* generated the cognate verbal form, *ma'al* 'to misappropriate, betray'. The etymology of the noun *ma'al* remains uncertain. Possibly it derives from the verbal root *'-l-l* 'to perpetrate, to do', which often refers, in context, to horrendous or destructive deeds (Lam 1:12, 22; 2:20; Num 22:29). The morphology of *ma'al* would be analogous to that of *māgēn* 'shield', from the geminate root *g-n-n* 'to protect'. In the case of the noun form *ma'al*, the radical consonant, *ayin*, produced vowel harmony, so that we have *ma'al* rather than *mā'ēl*.

that person [thereby] incurs guilt. The statement *we'āšemāh hannepeš hahî* requires special comment because the verb *'āšam* enjoys such a wide semantic range that a degree of ambiguity surrounds it. In simple terms, this statement means that the person in question actually did something wrong; that he was *guilty* of wrongdoing. The guilt conveyed by the verb *'āšam* is the effect of a cause: the person is guilty because he did something wrong. He is not *'āšēm* merely because he admitted wrongdoing, or because he was aware that what he had done was wrong.

The verb *'āšam* and related forms enjoyed widespread usage in the West Semitic languages, especially in the Phoenician dialects and in Arabic (Levine 1974: 91–100). In biblical Hebrew its connotations are consistently negative, at least by implication. The root *'āšam* is part of the vocabulary of the tabu system operative in many ancient religions. It is part of a semantic grouping that, in the Semitic languages, included verbs (and their cognates) such as *ḥāram* 'to set apart as sacred, proscribe, condemn' and even *qādaš* 'to be holy, sanctified'. All of these verbs exhibit both positive and negative aspects, if not in Hebrew, then in the cognate languages.

In the present context, reference is to the guilt incurred by committing an offense, by the violation of the law. The stative *'āšam* (also *'āšēm*, a participial form) is common in priestly legislation governing all sorts of offenses requiring ritual expiation. This legislation is prescribed principally in Leviticus 4–5, where we find, in the protases of casuistic legal formulations, repeated references to incurring guilt conveyed by the stative verb *'āšam* (Lev 4:14, 23, 28; 5:3–4). In such statements it is clear that reference is to a *state* of guilt, not to awareness of, knowledge of, or admission of guilt. Such consequences are expressed by other verbs. Thus awareness or knowledge is conveyed by forms of the verb *yāda*ʿ 'to know, perceive'. This fact is expressed, for instance, in the transition from Lev 4:13 to 4:14: "And if the entire congregation of Israel should err, the matter being concealed from the eyes of the assembly, and should transgress by *doing* any of the things forbidden by YHWH's commandments, and *thereby incur guilt (weʾāšēmû)*—." The point is that guilt, as a legal state, may precede any knowledge or awareness of wrongdoing. Lev 4:13–14 are speaking about the fact of guilt in anticipation of its discovery or acknowledgment. It should also be emphasized that God is perceived as omniscient, and is aware of all human guilt even in cases when the human perpetrator is unaware of it or chooses to ignore it.

NJPS translates the statement *weʾāšemāh hannepeš hahîʾ* 'and that person realizes his guilt'. Such an interpretation is possible, of course, but it would relate the statement we are discussing to a point later on in the process, to the projected, hypothetical decision of the offender to come forth and assume responsibility. In the view argued here, *weʾāšemāh hannepeš hahîʾ* states the legal situation emerging from the crime itself, preliminary to the projected disposition of the case.

7. *he must confess.* If, subsequent to earlier denials stated under oath, the offender comes forth and confesses his crime, there is a way he can be reinstated, with God and with men. *Hithpaʿel wehitwaddû* 'they must confess' derives from the verbal root *y-d-h* (or *w-d-h)*, whose essential meaning is "to expose, reveal," thus expressing the reverse of concealment. This meaning underlies the *hiphʿil hôdāh* 'to acknowledge, admit' (Ps 32:5; Prov 28:13). The requirement of confession is not explicit in Lev 5:14–16 and 20–26, where we find the primary laws of *maʿal.* It is, however, conveyed by the verb *hitwaddāh* earlier in the same chapter, in Lev 5:5, within the law governing sins of omission. In circumstances of failure to do what the law required, detection was also improbable, as it was in cases of misappropriation involving a false oath. Whenever testimony was not available, expiation and restitution would not likely eventuate unless the guilty party came forth on his own initiative and confessed his omissions or misdeeds. In Lev 16:21 we read that the chief priest "confessed" the sins of all Israel as part of the process of expiation on the Day of Atonement. That confession was also an initiative of sorts, aimed at securing forgiveness.

To summarize the provisions of the law up to this point: a guilty party must, first of all, come forth and acknowledge his guilt both for the initial misappropriation of another's property, and for his subsequent false oath. Once he had done so, the process could continue. The wording of v 7 is technical: *wehēšîb ʾet ʾašāmô berōʾšô,* literally, "He must make restitution for his liability equal to the amount of its principal." Virtually every word in this clause requires clarification: *hiphʿil hēšîb* (and the *hophʿal* participle *muššāb* 'restored') have the specialized sense of "repaying, remitting." Compare Lev 5:23: "He must *repay* the robbery *(wehēšîb 'et haggezēlāh).*" In a more general context, compare 2 Kgs 3:4: "And he *remitted (wehēšîb)* to the king of Israel one hundred thousand fatling sheep"—as tribute.

The term *'āšām*, as it is used here, does not refer to the sacrificial offering by that name, but instead to the substance of a payment or penalty, and has therefore been translated "liability." In this sense, Hebrew *'āšām* conveys the notion of culpability, or penalization resulting from guilt.

principal. Hebrew *rô'š* 'head' reflects the semantics of finance, evident in many languages. The principal or, literally, "capital" is expressed by forms of a word meaning "head," in contrast to interest and penalties, for which other terms are used. Hence I translate *rô'š* 'principal'. The construction *berô'šô* employs *beth prettii*, "the beth of price," which connotes equivalence, hence: "equal to its principal."

The wording of this law appears to compress the statements of Lev 5:20–26. Thus Lev 5:24, the counterpart of Num 5:7, uses the verb *šillēm* 'to repay' instead of *hēšîb*, but *hēšîb* itself is used in Lev 5:23, in a related statement. The principal and the penalty of 20 percent are to be remitted: *la'ašer 'āšam lô* 'to the one with respect to whom he had incurred guilt, whom he had disadvantaged', namely, to the victim of the misappropriation who had sustained the loss.

8. In the biblical system of inheritance, one's heirs were his clan relatives, the members of his *mišpāḥāh*. These were also the persons who bore the duty to redeem him (the verb *gā'al*) in certain unfortunate circumstances. According to Lev 25:48–49, one's clan relatives were duty bound to redeem an Israelite indentured to a gentile if the person himself lacked the means to buy his freedom. These "redeemers" were listed, and they included one's uncles, first cousins, and "flesh" relatives (Hebrew *še'ēr*), those we would call consanguineous relatives. These *še'ēr* relatives are, in turn, listed in Lev 21:2. They include one's mother, father, son, daughter, and brother. The females in this list would not normally inherit property, but they would when male heirs were lacking. Num 27:8–11 state that if a man died leaving no son, but only one or more daughters, his daughters became his heirs. If no daughters survived him, the next closest clan relatives would inherit his estate—his brothers, his father's brothers, and in turn their *še'ēr* relatives. The present verse, in projecting a situation in which a man had no *gô'ēl* '[clan] redeemer' means to say that he had no relatives, no heirs at all! In such a situation, both the principal and penalties remitted by an earlier offender would accrue to the priesthood.

The way this verse formulates the practical result of this procedure is of interest. It states *ha'āšām hammuššāb le-YHWH lakkôhēn* 'the liability that is to be repaid belongs to YHWH, [credited] to the priest." Prefixed *heh* in the *hoph'al* participle *hammuššāb* functions as a relative, whereas the *hoph'al* form itself reflects *hiph'il wehēšîb* in v 7. This statement means that the payments first became God's property, and then God was perceived as assigning them to the priesthood. Compare the same formulation, *le-YHWH lakkôhēn*, in Lev 23:20. This is usually the practical result implied in priestly law. Whatever went to God, with the exception of sacrifices entirely consumed on the altar, actually went into the temple treasury, or was otherwise used in support of the priesthood. This system is summarized in Numbers 18.

The confessed offender was also required to expiate his wrongdoing by an *ʿāšām* sacrifice, consisting of a ram. Here that ram is called *ʾêl hakkippûrîm* 'the ram of the expiation rites', a unique combination of terms. Compare *ḥaṭṭāʾt hakkippûrîm* 'the sin offering of the expiation rites' in Num 29:11, in a reference to part of the rites of the Day of Atonement. The formulation here is redundant: *beʾêl hakkippûrîm ʾašer yekappēr ʿālâw*, literally, "by means of the ram of the expiation rites, with which he is to perform rites of expiation on his behalf." The same sacrifice, simply called *ʾāšām* in Leviticus 5, would be performed according to the provisions of Lev 7:1–10. Most of the edible meat was to be consumed by the priests, whereas the fatty inwards were burned on the altar.

9–10. *levied donation.* This section closes with a statement to the effect that whatever "levied donation" (Hebrew *terûmāh*) is collected by priesthood belongs to the particular priest who collected it, or to whom it was "presented" (the verb *hiqrîb*). The donor could choose the priest, and once that priest collected the levied donations, he could claim them as his own. The *ʾîš* at the beginning of v 10 may be the very same priest, hypothetically, as is referred to in the latter part of the verse. Further provisions for the support of the clergy are found in Num 18:8–20. Hebrew *terûmāh* is a generic term that literally means "what is lifted, taken," referring to a tax, or assessment, or even to a payment made on a voluntary basis. The term has nothing to do with "heaving" or "lifting," but rather with the act of collection. Most substances identified as *terûmāh* have to do with temple and cult, or with the emoluments of the clergy (Lev 7:14; Num 18:8, 29–30; Deut 12:6–11, 17).

The legislation of Num 5:5–10 raises crucial questions. The general rule, stated in Num 15:30–31, was that ritual expiation was possible only in cases of inadvertent violations of law, but not for flagrantly intentional violations. In such cases, the offender would be punished by established human agencies, by court and community, or be "cut off" from membership in the community, with no allowance for ritual expiation whatsoever. Here, although full restitution is demanded and additional penalties imposed, an expiatory sacrifice functions to reinstate the offender with God and community.

NOTES TO 5:11–31: SUSPICIONS OF MARITAL INFIDELITY

The basic outline of the ordeal has been presented in the introduction to chapter 5. Here the details of procedure will be explained, leaving the implications of the ordeal for discussion in the COMMENT that follows.

12. *Should any man.* The formulation *ʾîš ʾîš* 'any man, person' recalls the formulations in Leviticus 17, where a series of laws is introduced in this way. This is part of a casuistic formula, employing the conditional particle *kî* 'if, when, should'.

become errant. The key verb is *ś-ṭ-h,* whose meaning is quite graphic. In Prov 21:15, the proverbial son is warned to avoid the path of the wicked: "Turn away *(śeṭēh)* from it; pass it by!" In Prov 7:25, the same young man is further warned against indecent women: "Let your thoughts not wander *(ʾal yēśṭ)* along her ways; do not go astray in her paths!" A context of impropriety always seems to be associated with the verb *ś-t-h,* a straying from the true path.

commit an act of betrayal. Here the sense is that a married woman has acted improperly, has, literally, "erred" in so doing. She has betrayed her husband, a notion expressed by *limʿôl maʿal* (see the NOTES on v 6, above). As in the matter of false oaths, so in the matter of marital infidelity, there is a sacred dimension to be considered, and it is this aspect that makes it appropriate to speak of *maʿal.*

13. The betrayal consisted of an extramarital liaison. A man other than her husband had lain with this woman. Hebrew *šikbat zeraʿ* means "a layer of semen" (see below, in v 20, and cf. Lev 18:20). This idiom represents a play on the verb *šākab* 'to lie', which is the standard euphemism for sexual intercourse in biblical Hebrew.

because she defiled herself in secret. The act of infidelity had been concealed from the woman's husband. The verb *neʾelam* (the *niphʿal* stem) often conveys the sense of being unseen, escaping notice, as in Lev 4:13 and 5:2. The notion of concealment is reinforced by the verb *wenisterāh* 'she was hidden, she hid herself'. The intent of the law is clarified by translating *wenisterāh wehîʾ niṭmāʾāh* as hendiadys: "because she defiled herself in secret." Defilement is here conceived as the effect of an improper act and is not technically the same as ritual defilement resulting from contact with an impure substance or object. In a similar way, the *piʿel ṭimmēʾ* 'to defile' is used in connection with the rape of Dinah (Gen 34:5).

there being no witness against her. In formulaic *weʿēd ʾên bāh* prepositional *beth* means "against." The verb *hēʿîd* 'to bear witness, testify' often takes the indirect object (Amos 3:13; Exod 21:29; 2 Kgs 17:13).

and she was not apprehended. The proviso *wehîʾ lôʾ nitpāśāh,* literally, "but she was not held," is ambiguous. Two principal interpretations have been proposed: NJPS translates "without being forced." The verb *tāpaś* 'to hold, apprehend' connotes rape in the law of Deut 22:28. This interpretation is, therefore, decidedly possible here, but to accept it would be to introduce an additional variable into the legal equation, namely, consent. The entire ordeal would be applicable only in cases wherein the wife in question had consented to the liaison. One questions, however, whether such a qualification would have been stated, for a rape victim was never held accountable for her consequent defilement.

It is more logical to regard the final clause in the verse as relating to the conditions of concealment. It states that the woman had not been "caught" in the act, further emphasizing that no testimony against her was available. The verb *tāpaś* regularly connotes the apprehension of criminals, enemies, and fugitives (cf. Deut 21:9; Ezek 21:16; 1 Sam 23:26), and a degree of repetitiveness for purposes of emphasis should not appear to us as strange.

14. Before taking up the precise diction of this verse and the ones to follow, it would be useful to state the background of the projected ordeal. It is probably to be assumed that the husband became suspicious because his wife was pregnant. It is unlikely, as Gray and others have suggested, that the husband's suspicions need not have had any real basis. Such an interpretation would contradict the dynamics of the ordeal itself, for the ordeal focuses on pregnancy by its own binary alternatives: either the wife in question will retain her seed or she will not (see below, in the NOTES on v 28).

envious possessiveness. Hebrew *qin'ah* and the verb *qinnēʾ* attest subtle connotations, so their precise meanings must be established from immediate context. Here the notion of possessive jealousy is obviously appropriate. Milgrom (1989: 38, to Num 5:14) calls attention to Prov 6:32–35, where we read that an adulterer foolishly brings ruin and permanent disgrace upon himself: "For possessive envy *(qin'āh)* enrages a man, so that he will show no mercy on the day of revenge. He will not allow any ransom, or be agreeable even if you offer a large bribe." These are the emotions being addressed by the present priestly legislation.

The formulation of v 14 is somewhat redundant: whether the woman had not, in fact, defiled herself, or whether she had done so, the husband had become jealous.

15. If the husband sought to act on his suspicions so as to strengthen his case for divorcing his wife, he had to submit her to an ordeal, administered by a priest. The priestly view of divorce followed the Deuteronomic interpretation that the only basis for divorce was adultery or serious sexual misconduct (Deut. 24:1). Lacking evidentiary testimony of actual adultery on his wife's part, the suspicious husband would rely on the ordeal to determine innocence or guilt. One assumes that the woman in question would submit to the ordeal

only if she claimed her innocence and wanted to save her marriage and retain her rights.

The role of the required grain offering must be clarified. In any approach to the Deity, whether directly, for purposes of worship, or for other forms of access, one could not come empty-handed (Exod 23:15; 34:20; Deut 16:16). Here the objective was to seek God's judgment, to learn the truth in the absence of evidence. God, the divine judge, knows the hidden facts, and through the outcome of the ordeal will bring them to light.

The woman was to be given the potion to drink just before the priest presented the grain offering on her behalf (see the NOTES on vv 24–25, below). This sequence suggests that the ordeal would not be efficacious were the required offering not presented on the woman's behalf. This is the force of prepositional *ʿālêhā* 'on her behalf' in this verse. Here, of course, the statement is anticipatory: the grain offering is merely being prepared at this point, to be offered later in the proceedings. Hebrew *qorbān* is a generic term for various sorts of offerings, merely designating what is "brought near, presented."

The amount of flour to be used was standard for the *minḥāh* in many instances, namely, one-tenth of an ephah (cf. Num 15:4; 28:13; Exod 29:40). But its recipe was highly unusual. The offering was to be made of barley instead of semolina wheat *(sôlet)*, which was routinely prescribed. Furthermore, oil and frankincense were not to be applied to the dough, as was customary. The recipes used in preparing the *minḥāh* are set forth in detail in Leviticus 2. The verbs *yāṣaq* 'to pour over' and *nātan* 'to place upon' are also used in that legislation, as they are here. The closest we come to what is prescribed in the ordeal of the errant wife is to be found in Lev 5:11, where a *minḥāh* made of semolina, but devoid of oil and frankincense, may be offered as a sin offering by one unable to afford more expensive animal sacrifices.

grain offering occasioned by envious feelings. The language of the present verse (and of v 26, below) reproduces the formulary used in the basic statements on the preparation of grain offerings found in Leviticus 2. The term *minḥāh* itself is explained in the NOTES to Num 15:4, where the development of this term is traced. Here we must explain the peculiar term *minḥat qenāʾôt* (see below, in the NOTES on v 25). It is a normative term, one that says something about the emotions or attitudes prompting the offering, namely, that they are heated and hostile! Furthermore, the offering calls attention to wrongdoing. In v 18 below we find this term alongside another, *minḥat zikkārôn* 'the grain offering of record', expressing the same thought. Perhaps we should also compare the term *minḥat šāwʾ* 'a grain offering of falsehood' in Isa 1:13, which is parallel with *qetoret tôʿēbāh* 'incense offering of abomination'.

calls attention to. Together, the combination *minhat qenāʾôt mazkeret ʿawôn* produces yet another parallelism: 'a grain offering occasioned by envious feelings, a *memento* of wrongdoing'. It is preferable to take participial *mazkeret* as a syntactic substantive instead of translating it as a relative (= "that signifies wrongdoing"). In any event, the verb *zākar*, which appears in v 18 in the form *zikkārôn*, means more than "remembering," as a mental function. Akkadian *zikru* means "effigy, double," something that recalls another person or object by its appearance or substance. In v 26 below we encounter the term *ʾazkārāh*, which is translated "token portion." It consists of a fistful of the dough of the *minḥāh*. Here the sense is that this *minḥāh*, by its unusual concoction, would be associated with sinfulness by all who observed it and knew of its meager contents.

16. The verb *hiqrîb* 'to bring near, present' and *heʿemîd* 'to station' are used to depict the staging of the ordeal (cf. the sequential usage of the same two verbs in Num 8:9–10, 13; and in v 18, below). The ordeal was to take place in front of the Tent of Meeting, probably in the area encountered before one reached the altar of burnt offerings in the Tabernacle courtyard (cf. Exod 28:29–30, 35; 29:11). Hebrew *lipnê YHWH* 'in the presence of YHWH' is functionally equivalent with *lipnê ʾôhel môʿēd* 'in front of the Tent of Meeting' (Num 3:7, 38) and with *lipnê hammiškān* 'in front of the Tabernacle' (Num 7:3). See the NOTES on the relevant verses.

17. *holy water.* It is difficult to know for certain what is conveyed by *mayîm qedôšîm*, a unique combination of terms. Most likely, it simply means "pure water" *(mayîm ṭehôrîm)*, as in Ezek 36:25, or even *mayîm ḥayîm* 'living, running water' in Num 19:17, as suggested by Gray—ICC.

ceramic vessel. Utilization of a ceramic vessel *(kelî ḥereś)* is archaeologically interesting. Most vessels mentioned in the Bible whose manufacture is not specified as being of silver or gold were, in fact, ceramic vessels (cf. *kelî hayyôṣēr* 'the potter's vessel' in 2 Sam 17:28; Jer. 19:11; Kelso 1948). Ceramic vessels were used in other ritual procedures, though those vessels specified for use in the sanctuary cult were of silver and gold, as we gather most immediately from Numbers 7. Perhaps it is symbolic that simplicity dominates the ordeal of the errant wife. In Lev 14:5, 50 we read that ceramic vessels were used in the purification rites of persons stricken with some form of *ṣāraʿat*, and in the purification of plastered building stones that showed signs of discoloration and blight identified as *ṣāraʿat*. In those rituals, the priest took blood from a slaughtered bird and poured it into a ceramic vessel containing "living water," producing a mixture that he subsequently sprinkled on the person, or on the plastered surface. The *kelî* of Num 19:17, utilized in the purification of one contaminated by contact with a corpse, was also undoubtedly ceramic (see the NOTES on Num 19:17).

Here the priest concocted a mixture of pure water and earth taken from the floor of the Tabernacle. The Tabernacle had no wooden flooring, in contrast to the Solomonic temple, whose wooden floors were overlaid with gold (1 Kgs 6:15–16).

The significance of utilizing earth from the Tabernacle floor will be explored further in the COMMENT to Numbers 5. Quite clearly, this procedure served to link the ordeal to the Tabernacle by introducing into its procedures a substance taken from its sacred space. Earth would make the liquid ingested by the suspected woman taste unpleasant, a condition that would be enhanced because the prescribed liquid would ultimately contain ink as well. Earth would also associate the ordeal with death and punishment, because dust was so prominent in rites of mourning (Josh 7:6; Ezek 27:30) and is elsewhere associated with cursing (2 Sam 16:13).

18. The suspected wife, holding her unadorned offering in her palms, stood before the Deity in a shameful condition, with her hair loosened, seeking divine judgment. One may compare these rites to those ordained for the Nazirite in Num 6:19.

the bitter water of condemnation. The unusual designation *mayîm hamme'ārerîm hammārîm* reflects alliteration and internal assonance. Though unrelated etymologically, *mārîm* and *me'ārerîm* sound very much alike, and both evoke unfavorable associations. The verb *'ārar* means "to curse," and one "accursed" is *'ārûr,* as in the execration of Deuteronomy 27. It is also the key verb for conveying the impact of execration in Deut 28:10–19, and *'ārûr* is the antonym of *bārûk* 'blessed' in Deut 28:3–6. The *pi'el* of the verb, which we have here, is rare but attested, nonetheless. Thus, although God had "condemned" *('ērar)* the earth, Noah would bring consolation (Gen 5:29). The sense of the *pi'el* is intensive, so that *hamme'ārerîm* is best rendered "that condemn." Bitter water is a known phenomenon in magical practice, and Hebrew *mar* may be a way of saying poisonous, infectious, or simply undrinkable! This phenomenology accounts for the place-name Marah, where "bitter" water was miraculously sweetened (Exod 15:23).

19. *hiph'il hišbî'a* means to administer an oath, or to compel one to swear. The oath itself is termed *šebû'āh* (Gen 50:5; 1 Sam 14:2; 1 Kgs 22:16; Cant 2:7; 3:5).

Oath formulas abound in biblical literature, as they do in ancient Near Eastern documents generally. Here it suffices to analyze the particular formulation of the oath administered by the priest to a wife suspected of infidelity, leaving further discussion for the COMMENT. As is normal, this oath projects a binary response, with contrasting alternatives. This was an oath of purgation, as it has been called by modern scholars, whose purpose it was to clear the accused of a charge. Thus it is that the negative alternative signified innocence, because it indicated that the accused did *not* do wrong, whereas the positive alternative projected a charge of criminality, which if substantiated meant that the accused had, indeed, done wrong. Each of the alternative formulations is composed of a protasis and an apodosis, expressing the condition and its projected effects.

(A) The negative alternative: protasis. *'im lō'* . . . *we'im lō'* 'If not . . . and if not'. Each conditional introductory is then followed by a finite verb.

The present formulation differs from the rhetorical interrogative, which implies a positive conclusion, something like "Is it not?" (Gen 24:38; 34:17; 42:37). In the clause *'im lō' śātît ṭum'āh*, the noun *ṭum'āh* functions adverbially: "If you did not err in an impure manner." It is as though the word *ṭum'āh* was prefixed *beṭum'āh* 'with impurity'.

under your husband['s jurisdiction]. Hebrew *taḥat* 'under' is idiomatic for expressing the situation of a married woman who is under her husband's jurisdiction (Ezek 23:5). It may represent an abbreviation of *taḥat yad* 'under the authority of' (Gen 16:9; Lev 22:27; 1 Sam 21:4, 9).

Apodosis. The *niph'al* imperative *hinnāqî* is modal: "may you be cleared." Hebrew *nāqî* 'clean, clear' and cognate verbal forms regularly connote clearance of a charge or release from an obligation (Gen 24:41; Prov 19:5, 9; Jer 25:29). The sense is that the bitter water of condemnation will serve as a litmus test, we might say.

20. (B) The positive alternative: protasis. *we'att kî* + finite verb . . . *wekî* + finite verb 'But if, indeed you did . . . and, indeed, you did'. Compare assertive *kî* in Gen 3:14: *kî 'āśîtā zō't* 'Because, indeed, you have done this'; also the promise expressed in Gen 13:17, *kî lekā 'etnennāh* 'For I shall, indeed, grant it to you' (cf. Gen 21:17; 21:18). The protasis continues with a further specification of the alleged crime, by mentioning carnal relations with someone other than the woman's own husband (see the NOTES on v 13, above).

21–22. Apodasis. After a parenthetical statement, the imprecation is stated. The legal term *šebû'at hā'ālāh* means "the imprecatory section of the oath." Hebrew *šebû'āh* is an uncomplicated term, whereas *'ālāh* requires comment. It attests cognates in the West Semitic languages, where it occurs in royal inscriptions as part of the vocabulary of oaths and penalties stipulated in treaties (*HALAT* 50; *DISO* 14, under *'lh* II). Treaties regularly contain curse sections that give warning of the consequences of violating the obligations assumed under oath. This function is most clearly evident when *'ālāh* is used in conjunction with *berît* 'covenant' (Deut 29:11, 20). The *'ālāh* is that part of the treaty or oath that specifies the penalties for, or dire effects of, violation. The term *'ālāh* is of uncertain etymology.

It is at this point in the procedures that the priest specifies what will happen if the woman lies under oath. Wishes expressed by the verb *yittēn* 'may he make' abound in biblical statements of promise, in oaths, and in curses. Compare Deut 28:7: "May YHWH make *(yittēn YHWH)* your enemies . . . battered before you"; or Ruth 4:11: "May YHWH make *(yittēn YHWH)* this woman . . . as Rachel." The verb *nātan* seems to have a particular idiomatic function in precative statements.

an accused oath-violator. The combination *le'ālāh welišbû'āh* is best understood as hendiadys, and has been translated accordingly. The sense seems to be that if the woman is guilty, she will be physically affected; and these physical results, including the loss of her embryo, will signify to her kinsmen that she has sworn falsely, as well as having committed adultery. So Hebrew *ʾālāh* connotes both the words of the execration and their effects, the crime and its punishment.

The adjective *ṣābāh* and the verbal forms, *qal ṣābetāh* and *hiphʿil laṣbôt,* are unique to this chapter and recur below in vv 22 and 27. The accepted meaning of **ṣ-w-b* is conveyed by Targum Onkelos (Sperber 1944: to Num 5:21), where *bitnēk ṣābāh* is rendered by the Aramaic *mēʿaîkî nepîḥîn* '[may] your intestines be swollen'.

It is not certain what the combined effects of a swollen belly and sagging thighs mean, in medical terms. It is logical to interpret them as indicating a miscarriage, as may be concluded from the contrast between the stated outcome when the woman is guilty and the outcome when she is innocent, as expressed in v 28, below. If innocent, the woman would "retain her seed," and her pregnancy would continue. The reverse of that outcome would be the termination of pregnancy by what amounted to an induced miscarriage or abortion.

The apodosis continues into v 22. The bitter water will "enter into" the woman's bowels and cause swelling and sagging of the thighs. In biblical usage, *mēʿayîm* 'intestines' can refer to the womb (Gen 25:23). For the effects of a curse that enters the body as a liquid, compare Ps 109:18: "He donned curse as his garment; it entered inside him *(wattābôʾ beqirbô)* like water, and like oil, in his bones."

"Amen! Amen!" The repeated response, *ʾāmēn ʾāmēn,* is unusual. In Deut 27:15 and passim, the people respond *ʾāmēn* each time they accept as binding one of the many terms of the execration. Here the repetition probably reflects the binary formulation of the execration. The woman answers "Amen" to both the negative and the positive alternatives. The Sifre comes close to this interpretation: "*ʾāmēn,* that I did not defile myself; and if I did, in fact, defile myself, may the water enter me!" (*Sifre,* 5b, *Nāśôʾ*, par. 15).

23. The priest writes the words of the imprecation on a document *(sēper),* undoubtedly with ink (thus the Sifre), and washes the words off of the parchment or leather, so that they are erased. God's name occurs in the words of the imprecations, so it would also be erased in the process.

The condemnation water becomes "as bitter," *lemārîm;* that is to say, it turns bitter. The implication is that if the woman is guilty, the water will become bitter, in the sense of being injurious. There is also the variant construct formation *mê hammārîm hameʾārerîm,* literally, "the 'bitter ones of condemnation' waters" (v 24), with no significant difference in meaning intended.

25. At this point the priest attends to the grain offering in the usual manner. Before "scooping up" (the verb *qāmaṣ)* a fistful of dough as a "token portion *(ʾazkārāh),*" he "presents *(wehēnîp)*" the offering for God to view and

then places the token portion on the altar to be burned. The procedure known as *tenûpāh* 'presentation' is explained in the NOTES on Num 8:11.

26. *token portion.* Hebrew *'azkārāh* reflects Aramaic morphology, where the causative stem is expressed by preformative *aleph* instead of preformative *heh,* producing *'aphel* instead of *hiphʿil.* On this basis *'azkārāh* would literally mean "that which represents, signifies, resembles." Some have analyzed the form *'azkārāh* as reflecting prothetic *aleph,* in which case it would express the meaning of the simple stem, namely, "double, effigy, token," for which we note cognate Akkadian *zikru* 'effigy' (Driver 1956). This verse recalls the wording of Lev 2:2.

turn into smoke. The *hiphʿil* verb *hiqṭîr* means literally "to burn into smoke." Compare the intensive verb *qutturu* in Akkadian, which has the same meaning (*CAD Q,* 166–168). The Hebrew noun *qeṭôret* 'incense, incense offering' derives from the verb *qāṭar.* In Hebrew, the *piʿel* form *qiṭṭēr* came to be associated particularly with grain offerings (Amos 4:5).

After placing the token portion of the grain offering on the altar, the priest gave the liquid mixture to the woman to drink.

27–28. The alternatives projected in the ordeal are restated here. A significant point is added in v 28b, in the words *weniqqetāh wenizreʿāh zaraʿ* 'she shall be cleared and she shall retain seed'. This phrase is a reflex of the imperative *hinnāqî* 'May you be cleared', occurring in v 19, above, in the words of the charge addressed to the woman.

29–31. The final verses recapitulate the provisions of vv 11–28. The preceding is the *tôrāh* 'prescribed instruction' for dealing with feelings of suspicion and envy on the part of a husband (see above, in vv 15, 18). On the term *tôrāh* see the NOTES on Num 19:2, 14. The syntax in the second part of v 29 is unusual: *'ašer tiśṭeh 'ištô 'in cases wherein* a wife was errant'. Similar syntax is evident in Lev 14:32, also a priestly law.

30. The priest shall perform *(weʿāśāh)* with respect to the woman all of the required rites. On specialized meanings of the verb *ʿāśāh* see the NOTES on Num 8:2.

31. A problem ignored up to this point in the interpretation of the ordeal is the possibility that the husband may have libeled his wife and unjustly hurt her by his suspicions. We have no way of knowing whether ordeals of this sort could have been manipulated. Clearly, if the ordeal confirmed the woman's guilt, the husband would be cleared of any wrongdoing, whereas the condemned woman would bear the punishment of her wrongdoing. She would undoubtedly be divorced, and would henceforth be ostracized and considered undesirable as the wife of any other Israelite man.

COMMENT: THE ORDEAL OF THE ERRANT WIFE—STRUCTURE AND PHENOMENOLOGY

The contents of the first two sections of Numbers 5 have been adequately treated in the NOTES. Their relation to religious legislation earlier encountered in Leviticus has been emphasized. The appearance in the book of Numbers of summary legislation on the subject of certain prevalent illnesses, and regarding the *'āšām* sacrifice, is evidence of editorial activity within the P source itself. This phenomenon relates to one of the evident functions of the book of Numbers, which is to serve as a repository of previously unrecorded priestly texts. In this way, the content of Numbers helps to complete the priestly agenda.

The subject that invites discussion is the ordeal of the suspected wife (Num 5:11–31). Its phenomenology is truly distinctive among biblical rituals, combining as it does ingredients of a magical, cultic, and legal character. Determining how these factors interact is the key to a proper understanding of this complex text.

We are fortunate in having an abundance of ancient interpretations regarding the ordeal of the *sôṭāh* 'errant wife' preserved in the Mishna and Tosefta, and in the Gemaras of the talmudic tractate *Sôṭāh*. The ancient midrashic collection on the book of Numbers, the Sifre *(Sifre*, 3b–7a, *Nāśô'*, pars. 7–21) likewise comments on the meaning of the ordeal and its attendant circumstances. These sources will be cited as they are relevant. The ordeal of the errant wife also held considerable interest for Philo of Alexandria and for Josephus Flavius, the noted ancient historian (Gray—ICC, 43–48).

In modern times, as was true throughout the centuries since late antiquity, the ordeal of Num 5:11–31 has continued to fascinate biblical scholars. As comparative evidence has accumulated in modern times, so have attempts to place this ordeal in ancient Near Eastern perspective. At the same time, source-critical scholarship has struggled with the composition of the text and with its distinctive terms of reference and legal formulas.

Three principal aspects of the ordeal require clarification before its overall character can be properly assessed. The first is the projected alternative consequences of the ordeal. The unfavorable projection is formulated as a symptomatology whose diagnosis in precise medical terms is difficult to determine. It is unclear whether the text is speaking of a permanent disability, or only of a temporary or immediate disfunction. For its part, the favorable projection, the blessed outcome of the ordeal, is also expressed somewhat ambiguously. The second area requiring clarification consists of the preconditions or underlying circumstances that initially prompted the husband to subject his wife to the ordeal. These circumstances are expressed in emotional terms as suspicion, jealousy, and hostility, but one is left wondering whether there were not more realistic indications of infidelity resulting from the behavior of the wife in question or evident in her physical condition. The final aspect is the phenomenology of the ordeal, as it was to be administered by the priest. This subject has received most of recent scholarly attention. In particular, scholars have sought to clarify the relationship of the oath administered to the woman, on the one hand, and the cultic and magical aspects of the ordeal, on the other (Milgrom 1989: 37–43, 350–354; Fishbane 1974; Brichto 1975; Frymer-Kensky 1984; Licht 1985: 166–169).

The Projected Alternatives of the Ordeal

If the suspected wife was found out by the ordeal and determined to have committed adultery, she was permanently disgraced and declassed, to be sure. The physical or somatic consequences of a guilty verdict are described as the swelling of the womb (or belly) and the sagging or falling of the "thigh," probable euphemisms for the uterus and vagina, respectively. For the most part, ancient interpreters diagnosed these symptoms as dropsy, a hydrophilic condition. More recently it has been suggested that these symptoms refer to a condition known as pelvic prolapse, one wherein the uterus protrudes from the enlarged vagina, indicating a collapse of the pelvic structure that holds the uterus in its proper position, especially during pregnancy. It turns out that this condition was known to the ancient Egyptians, and after them to the Greeks, who had even devised mechanical methods of containing it. It was diagnosed as the result of excess sexual activity too soon after childbirth, or as the result of extreme exertion and fatigue, all of which adversely affect the physical condition of women (Einige and Durfee 1966). Some modern scholars have understood the symptoms as descriptive of an abortion or a miscarriage, leaving open the question of whether the threatened damage was viewed as permanent.

The unfavorable projection can only be understood, of course, in tandem with the blessed prediction, which would be fulfilled in cases wherein innocence was established by the ordeal. This outcome is stated in v 28: *weniqqetāh wenizreʿāh zāraʿ* 'she shall be cleared of the charge, and retain seed'. In the NOTES on v 28 it was explained that this formula must, if taken literally, assume conception, the result of successful insemination. It may of course be taken less literally to mean "she shall be granted offspring." After all, Hebrew *zeraʿ* often means "offspring, descendant." This sense is predicated by the view attributed to Rabbi Akiba in the Sifre, *Nāśôʾ*, par. 19: *šeʾim hāyetāh ʿaqqārāh-nipqedet* 'If she had been a barren woman, she would henceforth be the object of divine attention', in other words, she would conceive. (The Sifre is alluding to the language of Gen 21:1, which states that God was mindful of Sarah, the Matriarch.)

It seems that the modern commentator is caught between two emphases that are not necessarily exclusive of each other, but each of which leads to a different interpretation. The formulations of the ordeal may be projecting a more or less permanent condition, alternatively of fertility or of its denial by a disabling physical condition, such as pelvic prolapse. Or these formulations may be projecting a more immediate and limited result, simply the termination of a current pregnancy. How we understand the symptomatology depends, however, on how we understand the preconditions stated in the text.

The Preconditions or Underlying Circumstances

What was it that prompted the husband in question to accuse his wife of adultery? Based on what is said in the Mishna and Tosefta of the talmudic tractate *Sôṭāh*, one gathers that the rabbinic view was that the wife's behavior was the primary factor in bringing about the ordeal. A man had observed his wife in associations with men other than himself, which had aroused his suspicion. We are advised by the Sages that men should not ignore such behavior on the part of their wives. We do not find in these sources any clear suggestion that the wife's physical condition might have aroused her husband's suspicions; that she had, as an example, become pregnant and her husband questioned whether her pregnancy was attributable to him. This condition might have reinforced earlier doubts entertained by the husband, based on the observable behavior of his wife.

One is reminded of the Bathsheba episode, as recounted in 2 Sam 11:2–15. When Bathsheba, the wife of Uriah, becomes aware that she is pregnant she sends word secretly to David, who promptly sets about covering up his liaison with her. No doubt Bathsheba would have been in terrible trouble once those around her learned of her pregnancy, as her husband had been far away from home for some time. The only way out for David and Bathsheba was to bring Uriah home so that he could have relations with his wife, and the pregnancy be attributed to him. Had Uriah become aware of his wife's pregnancy, he might have subjected her to the ordeal of the *Sôṭāh*.

In the NOTES it was explained that biblical law recognized as proper grounds for divorce only adultery or incest, and that any sexual liaison by a married woman, even with an unmarried man, would be considered adulterous. But the evidentiary requirements for a conviction were exceedingly strict. A husband who sought to divorce his wife, but who lacked testimonial evidence of sexual misconduct on her part, could, nevertheless, secure a divorce if his wife were found guilty by the ordeal.

Although postbiblical Jewish sources do not explicitly refer to pregnancy as the usual prior circumstance for the ordeal of the errant wife, there are subtle indications that the Sages were thinking along these lines. Thus the Tosefta (*Sôṭāh* 5:3) states the following: "A woman pregnant by the husband himself, or one nursing his child, must either 'drink' (the potion of the ordeal) or forfeit her *ketubbāh* (the contract of her marriage settlement)." At the outset, this legal statement brings out a practical function of the ordeal: it served as a trigger for divorce. Faced with the prospect of a degrading and potentially injurious ordeal, a guilty woman might well be persuaded to accept an unremunerated divorce rather than fight her husband's charge to the finish.

The Tosefta's statement goes much farther, however. Admittedly, it refers to pregnancy as an exceptional circumstance, not as the usual situation that would call the ordeal into play. And yet it raises the issue of abortion, because it would authorize administering the ordeal even if it might terminate a pregnancy and cause the loss of a fetus.

According to biblical law, the unborn have value, as is evidenced by Exod 21:22–24, a law requiring compensation to be paid to a married man by one who accidentally caused his wife to lose her fetus. And yet the Tosefta and the Babylonian Talmud (*Sôṭāh* 26a) mandate the ordeal for a pregnant woman notwithstanding the potential loss of the value-bearing fetus. On the question of whether the ordeal could be deferred, there is disagreement among the medieval commentators of the Talmud. Rashi and Maimonides insisted that deferral of the ordeal was not allowed, whereas the Tosafists advocated deferral so as to protect the husband from loss.

In his commentary on the Tosefta, Saul Lieberman (1967b: 655, to Tosefta, *Sôṭāh* 5:3) cites the Midrash, *Sifre Zuṭah* in the name of Rabban Gamaliel: *weniqqetāh wenizreʿāh zāraʿ-perāṭ lizrûʿāh* ' "She shall be exonerated and will retain seed"—this excludes a woman already inseminated.' The hidden agenda of the disagreement over the import of the Tosefta's dictum in *Sôṭāh* 5:3, providing for administration of the ordeal during pregnancy, is the abortion issue. Whether the ordeal of the errant wife could be deferred in cases in which the woman was pregnant depended on whether the religious authorities supported or opposed abortion.

Abortion is not merely a postbiblical issue, however. It most probably informed the priestly legislation of the Torah as well. However we interpret the symptomatology or the preconditions of the ordeal, it is reasonable to conclude that at times, if not quite often, pregnancy was material to the implementation of the ordeal. If this conclusion is correct, a pregnant woman who was "found out" by the ordeal would in fact lose her fetus; the ordeal would terminate her pregnancy. If we take the symptomatology to indicate a permanent disability, she would, in addition, be effectively prevented from ever bearing children in the future.

The fact that these potential outcomes were even allowable according to the priestly law of the Torah means that what we today call "the right to life" was not regarded by that body of law as absolute. After all, a convicted adulteress was to be condemned to death according to the priestly law of Lev

20:10, and the concurrent loss of her fetus would inevitably result in cases in which the adulteress was pregnant.

It is another thing, however, to bring about the loss of a fetus in cases in which a woman could not be condemned by testimonial evidence. The readiness to do so was predicated on a mentality that regards certain sins and impurities as overriding the usual norms of law. To allow a child to be born who would then be denied proper membership in the religious community and be ineligible for its supportive care was unacceptable to the Israelite priesthood, based on its fundamental commitment to certain principles of family purity. That ancient Sages and medieval authorities sought to mitigate biblical law reveals their own sensibilities on the subject of abortion and on the meaning of community, but it hardly alters the implications of the original biblical ordeal. The execution of the ordeal of the *sôṭāh* was finally abolished by the Palestinian Amora, Rabbi Yohanan, of the third century C.E. (Mishna, *Sôṭāh* 9:9).

Modern scholars have cited comparative evidence from the *Code of Hammurabi* (henceforth *CH*) as germane to the interpretation of the biblical ordeal. They have correctly observed that the Babylonian evidence provides only a partial parallel, but more needs to be said about the relevance of these Old Babylonian laws to the priestly legislation of the Torah.

CH mandates the river ordeal in cases of suspected adultery, just as the same ordeal was employed in other legal situations wherein evidentiary testimony was unavailable. In the river ordeal, the suspect plunged into a torrential river. If the waters overtook him, it was concluded that he was guilty; in fact, he probably drowned. The river god, signifying the divine power manifested in the river, had judged that person and had found him to be guilty. If, however, the suspect survived the torrents, it was evidence of vindication, for the powers acting through the river had spared him.

Sexual behavior is, by its very character, a private matter seldom witnessed by others. This fact creates a situation ripe for other than the usual juridical procedures. Of course, the ordeal also bore a mythic character, because it invoked the sentence of a divine judge, whose verdict, whether innocent or guilty, was transmitted through the binary results of the ordeal.

The laws most directly relevant to the biblical ordeal are *CH* 131 and 132:

> 131. If the husband of a married woman has accused her but she is not caught lying with another man, she shall take an oath by the life of the god and return to her home.
>
> 132. If a finger has been pointed at the married woman with regard to another man and she is not caught lying with the other man, she shall leap into the divine river (or river god) for her husband. (Driver and Miles 1955: 53, 282–285)

The most significant difference between these two related laws pertains to the identity of the accuser in cases of suspected adultery on the part of a married woman. If the husband is the accuser, the woman may clear herself by an oath, but if the accusation comes from someone other than the husband, the perilous ordeal is required. The accusation of a husband carries, therefore, less legal force than one coming from an independent person whose objectivity was undoubtedly presumed to be greater, and who would not have had a personal motive such as divorce for maligning the woman in question.

It is significant that the two laws separate the two factors—the oath and the ordeal—both of which were appropriate in circumstances of uncertainty involving marital fidelity. The Babylonian river ordeal would most likely have caused the death of a guilty suspect, whereas the biblical ordeal, in similar circumstances, would have only disabled the suspected woman or terminated her current pregnancy. Biblical law would have consigned her to a permanently disgraced reputation, however.

The Phenomenology of the Ordeal

What has been said about the projected binary alternatives of the ordeal and about its underlying circumstances and their implications leads us directly to a consideration of its complex phenomenology. This phenomenology attests three interrelated features: the cult offering presented by the priest on behalf of the "impure" woman, ingestion of the bitter potion by the suspected woman and the proper concoction of the potion, and the oath of purgation taken by the suspected woman. Once the function of each of these three factors is clarified, it might also be possible to arrive at a conclusion about the degree of overall textual coherence exhibited by Num 5:11–31, in structural terms.

When all is said and done it can be stated reliably that what we have is primarily a magical ordeal, in which the cultic offering and the oath each play a corollary role. Such interaction is not uncommon in magical rites known throughout the ancient Near East, especially as evidenced in neo-Assyrian magic. Such an interpretation would seem preferable to saying that the magical component and the sacrificial offering were secondary, with the oath constituting the basic procedure.

The integrity of the ordeal will emerge as we analyze each of its three components in turn. The source-critical question of whether Num 5:11–31 is of one cloth is not nearly so important an issue as is its phenomenological integrity, in comparative perspective.

The cultic offering. As is true of the *nāzîr* of Numbers 6 (especially according to Num 6:19), so in the case of the suspected wife a person standing before the Deity and requesting to be judged by him should bear a gift in his or her palms (Num 5:18). It should be noted that all who appeared before

God in sacred precincts, for whatever purpose and even with no implication of guilt, were expected to bear gifts and were not to appear empty-handed (Exod 23:15; 34:20; Deut 16:10).

The prayerful gesture with palms raised was also made by the initiate Aaronide priests as they presented themselves before God for acceptance (Lev 8:27; Exod 29:24). The palms were held face up, perhaps raised in a gesture of devotion and presentation (Ps 141:2; and cf. Exod 9:29–33; 1 Kgs 8:22; Pss 63:5; 88:10; Ezra 9:5).

Uncovering the hair and loosening it were forms of shaming, and these procedures made of the woman so treated someone to be shunned. The person diagnosed as suffering from acute *ṣāraʿat* had to wear his hair in this fashion as a signal to all that he was impure and was to be avoided (see Lev 13:45; and cf. Lam 4:15). Baring one's head and loosening the hair were also gestures of mourning (Lev 10:6; 21:10).

In the present case, the sacrificial offering was also an instrument of purification, functioning much like a *ḥaṭṭāʾt* 'sin offering'. The woman in question was asking God to pronounce her pure. According to the phenomenology of sacrifice, God's acceptance of the wife's sacrifice would signal his readiness, at the very least, to judge her and, at the most, to declare her innocent and pure. Because of the horrendous nature of the accusation and the dire penalties potentially ensuing, barley instead of semolina was used for the grain offering *(minḥāh)*, and no aromatics were applied to it. It should be remembered that the *minḥāh* was the least costly offering to start with. It represented the option of last resort in the graduated scale of offerings listed in Lev 5:1–13, for one required to make offering because of some sin of omission on his part.

The actual presentation of the *minḥāh* occurred just before the woman ingested the bitter potion and just after she had taken the oath declaring her innocence. The *minḥāh* was first raised as a *tenûpāh* 'presentation offering', to be viewed by the Deity and then disposed of in the normal manner, as prescribed in Leviticus 2.

The sequence of the ordeal has its own logic: the suspected wife had protested her innocence and had submitted her request for judgment, accompanied by the proper offering. Now she would submit to the actual ordeal by allowing the potion to do its work! More will be said about the theme of "bitterness" farther on.

The entire procedure was to be carried out in the Sanctuary area, mainly because of the judicial appeal to God's verdict that was basic to its efficacy. Oaths would be taken in the Sanctuary complex, where the courts were normally located. The closeness of courts to temples and sacred space is virtually universal and is reflected in the planning of the acropolis complex in many parts of the ancient world.

The same architecture underlies the original import of the law stated in Exod 22:7–8: a homeowner accused of misappropriating property entrusted to him shall approach God and take an oath in his presence, namely, in the Temple. Whomsoever God finds guilty pursuant to such procedures will bear the appropriate penalty. The appeal to God's justice is a common theme in Psalms, and the formula that expresses the appeal is *šopṭēnî YHWH* 'Judge me innocent, O Lord!' (Pss 7:9; 26:1; 35:24; 43:1).

The orchestration of the ordeal in the presence of YHWH has additional significance. The sacred venue means, in effect, that the various impurities expressed by forms of the verb *ṭāmēʾ* 'to be impure' are not always of the same character. When it is associated with sexual violations, such impurity may not possess the same potency as ritual impurity, which inevitably collides with sacred space and distances the impurity from the sanctuary. In the present ordeal, the suspected woman is addressed in the language of impurity within the very precincts of the Sanctuary complex (Num 5:13–14, 27–28). This unusual circumstance requires further explanation.

It is the view of at least one version of priestly law that a person guilty of sexual offenses is defiled, or impure. This view is stated most emphatically in Lev 18:24–30, at the conclusion of a code of family law governing incest, adultery, and other sexual offenses. One who violates the law in such respects defiles himself, as well as bringing impurity upon the Israelite community and upon the land. In fact, it was as a result of widespread sins of this sort that the earlier peoples of Canaan had lost their right to possess the land, so we are told. The same essential view is shared by Deut 24:4, which also classifies the adulteress as impure. There were, of course, other terms for characterizing the effects of similar sexual offenses, such as *tôʿēbāh* 'abomination' and nominal forms of the verb *ḥāṭāʾ* 'to offend, sin'. Most such formulations also refer to defilement, however.

It is clear, nevertheless, that the defilement associated with sexual misconduct must be understood on its own terms. One could say that the impurity imputed to adultery would, by extension, have the same effect on God's temperament as would severe ritual impurity; that it would arouse his wrath in the same way. This notion is clearly expressed in Ps 106:39: "They became impure *(wayyiṭmeʾû)* through their acts, and committed harlotry through their deeds. YHWH then became enraged at his people, and he regarded as abominable his estate!"

The concept of "pure" and "impure" deeds was a favorite theme of the prophet Ezekiel. He predicted that God would restore his people to the land he had formerly granted to them. Once restored, Israel would recall the acts through which they had previously defiled themselves, thereby losing their land (Ezek 20:43). Elsewhere, Ezekiel refers explicitly to adultery as an act that defiles (Ezek 18:11, 15; 22:11; 33:26).

What we observe is the modulation of primarily ritual categories by applying them to interpersonal behavior, to morally offensive acts. Such modulation is expressed in Isaiah's dramatic call to his people to redress their social ills: "Wash yourselves, purify yourselves, remove your evil deeds from my sight. Cease to do evil; learn to do good!" (Isa 1:16–17). In the exilic period and thereafter, such modulated ritual concepts seem to have attracted a wide audience.

The themes of purity and impurity are expressed in yet another way in the ordeal of the suspected wife. Although their realization more precisely pertains to the magical and legal aspects of the ordeal and to the definition of its projected alternatives, it might be well to discuss these themes here. The verbal root *n-q-h,* which in biblical Hebrew is attested almost exclusively in the *pi'el* and *niph'al* stems (and in the adjectival form *nāqî* 'innocent, cleared'), figures quite prominently in Num 5:11–31. In v 19 we read that the priest assures the woman that if, indeed, she is innocent she will be "cleared, exonerated" by drinking the bitter potion. In v 28 the blessed outcome is likewise stated in terms of the woman's exoneration by the *niph'al* form of the same verb: *weniqqetāh* 'she shall be cleared'.

Ironically, forms of the root *n-q-h* in biblical Hebrew virtually never refer to purely ritual purification. The only possible exception is the rare term *menaqqiyyāh* 'cleaning utensil' (Num 4:7). Even when a worshiper states that he has washed his hands in cleanliness, we are to understand his declaration metaphorically as referring to avoidance of evildoing (Pss 26:6; 73:13). In other words, the semantic progression of the base meaning "to be clean, pure" has gone all the way into another context, that of legal purgation and clearance from liability or obligation. A similar semantic development is observable in the Akkadian verb *ebēbu* 'to be pure, clear', which most often relates to legal circumstances, not to actual cleansing or ritual purification *(CAD E,* 5–7, under *ebēbu,* D-stem *ubbubu).* So Hebrew *nāqî* means "innocent, exonerated," just as in Job 4:17 the verb *ṭāhar* 'to be pure' appropriates the connotation of being just or righteous: "Can a mortal be more righteous *(yisḍāq)* than God? Can a person be more just *(yiṭhār)* than his maker?"

The semantic fields of ritual and moral terms of reference often overlap; they move toward each other in biblical Hebrew usage. Their interaction is one of the most subtle and enlightening features of biblical diction.

What makes all of this significant for an understanding of the ordeal of the *sôṭāh* is that purification is integral to the magical dimension of judicial ordeals, just as it is in countering the effects of witchcraft and in the performance of therapeutic magic. In his recent study of the Assyrian magical series known as *Maqlû,* Abusch (1987: x–xviii) has outlined what a person seeking to avert the effects of witchcraft must do. It emerges that the acts prescribed for such a person in the *Maqlû* series are not very different from those undertaken by the suspected woman in the effort to counter the accusation against her during the course of the biblical ordeal. The Mesopotamian person appeals to a god, or to a group of gods; he emphatically and elaborately declares his purity and insists on his innocence. In so doing, he sends the accusation back to the accuser, with the effect of a boomerang, calling on the gods to bring the evil upon his accuser not on himself.

More will be said about the magical aspect of the present ordeal farther on. At this point it is important to understand that as a ritual process purification is at the core of the procedures whereby the accused sexual offender is reinstated. The unfaithful wife is said to be impure, defiled in a modulated sense. If declared innocent, the woman in question will be purified or exonerated in a similarly modulated sense!

The bitter waters: the magic of the ordeal. Utilization of a liquid substance more or less classifies the procedures of Num 5:11–31 as a "potion ordeal," a type of magical rite best known in Africa. J. Licht (1985: 166–169) has provided a valuable excursus on the ordeal of the suspected wife, including references to available studies of practices among the Ashanti and other African tribes.

It is important in such ordeals that the liquid be bitter, or distasteful, though it is definitely not to be assumed that such potions were concocted of toxic ingredients. After all, it is the sense of taste that immediately brings home the dire potential of the ordeal, by signifying peril. What operates to entrap the guilty, who are "found out" by the ordeal, is the inevitable psychological or psychosomatic association of bitterness and distaste with harm and injury and, consequently, with the fear of being poisoned.

What we have in the repetitive formulations of the "curse" (Hebrew *ʾālāh*) is a play, or more than one play, on the theme of bitterness, conveyed by the adjective *mar* 'bitter', which is assonant with the plural participle, *meʾārerîm* 'condemning'. The clearest formulation of the curse occurs in vv 22 and 24: *hammayîm hammeʾārerîm,* literally, "the waters that convey the execration; that condemn" (see the NOTES on Num 5:22–24). The waters have this power because the actual words of the *ʾālāh* have been dissolved into them, as we read in v 23. Then, too, we have a variant description of the waters as *mê hammārîm* 'the waters of bitterness; waters having bitter ingredients' in v 23, as part of the overall formulation.

When we contrast v 19b with v 24b we learn how the play on words worked: in formulating the favorable alternative the priest states, "Be exonerated from the effects of the waters of bitterness that convey the execration." But in projecting the unfavorable outcome he states, "May the waters conveying the execration enter into her, and become *as poisonous.*" The same eventuality is restated casuistically in v 27. So whereas the water is bitter from the start, it has a harmful effect—it becomes consequentially "bitter"—only in the event the water ultimately encounters guilt in the woman's inwards!

The ingredients of the potion are, of course, highly significant. The water is pure, which is what "holy" means in this context. W. R. Smith may have been correct in suggesting that the water was drawn from a sacred spring (Smith 1969: 181). This is not to suggest that the waters were perceived as having curative powers. It simply indicates that an ordeal being executed in the sanctuary must use pure ingredients, in this case the kind of water otherwise acceptable for ritual utilization.

The dust or earth taken from the floor of the sanctuary serves to bind the suspected woman to the sanctuary, and thereby to its resident God, who is judging her. Licht (1985: 169) cites J. Sasson, who called his attention to a text from Mari, ARM X:9, that tells how dust mixed with water figured in an oath procedure (Dossin 1978). Sasson suggested to him its possible relevance to the ordeal of the errant wife in Numbers 5, so Licht reports. Actually, this text had been studied by W. Moran (1969: 50–52), who clarified its meaning without discussing possible connections with biblical ritual.

The reverse side of the tablet is broken in many places, but there is clear reference to an oath *(ni-iš DINGIR-lim)* to be taken "where there is water *(a-šar m[u-ú i-ba-aš-su-ú])*." Someone, perhaps a prophet, reports that a deity named Asumum, along with Asumezumum and probably other deities of the Ea circle, were about to take an oath to another group of gods, presumably a larger group or one superior to them. Ea himself administered the oath.

The relevant speech, presumably spoken by Ea, reads as follows:

> *[la-ma ni-iš DINGIR-lim] ni-za-ak-ka-ru ru-[ša-am] ù sí-ip-pa-am ša ba-ab [Ma-ri-ki (x)]-x li-il-qú-nim-ma ni-is DINGIR-lim [i-ni-iz-ku-ur] ru-ša-am ù ši-ip-pa-am ša ba-[ab] Ma-ri-ki il-qú-ni-im-ma i-na me-e im-ḫu-[ḫu]-ma DINGIR.MEŠ ù i-la-tum iš-te-e*

> "Before we pronounce the oath, let them take the dirt and jamb of the gate of Mari . . . , and then let us pronounce the oath." The dirt and the jamb of the gate of Mari they took and dissolved in water, and then the gods and goddesses drank.

The continuation of the text is more clearly preserved and need be presented only in translation:

> Thus spoke Ea: "Swear to the gods that you will not harm the brickwork of Mari or a commissioner *(rābiṣu)* of Mari." The gods and goddesses swore, saying: "We shall not harm the brickwork of Mari or the commissioner of Mari."

Moran explains the procedure as follows: "The point of putting the jamb of the gate and dissolving some of its dirt in water (of a river?) is perhaps to put the 'essence' of the brickwork of Mari in a form that can be imbibed by the gods, who by their swearing about it interiorize, so to speak, the oath itself and put its power within themselves" (Moran 1969: 52).

Moran suggests that river water would have been appropriate in a rite involving Ea and his entourage. In any event, and notwithstanding certain mysteries left unresolved, it is clear that the Mari rite represents the same phenomenology as is evident in the ordeal of the errant wife. The oath, which involves a duty to the city of Mari, to its walls and its commissioner, becomes binding by means of a physical link to its gate, the symbol of the city. Something of the city gate has entered the bodies of the gods, so that their subsequent failure to preserve Mari would harm them.

Similarly, the woman suspected of adultery renders herself vulnerable by ingesting dust from the Tabernacle, because her duty to be pure is a duty to the God of Israel, resident in the sanctuary. If the gods in the Mari oath failed in their sworn duty, Mari would be impaired. If the woman of Numbers 5 had failed in her duty, the Tabernacle would be endangered.

To return to the biblical ordeal, we note that the woman who drinks the potion is surely aware that the words of the curse, in the form of dissolved ink, are also in the water, and that she has, therefore, no chance of escaping the *ʾālāh.* The liquid will penetrate her inwards and ascertain whether another man has planted his semen in her (Num 5:13, 20). The symmetry of sin and magic is blatant in the procedures of the ordeal.

Perhaps the adjective *mar* may yield yet another nuance, that of potency. There is, after all, a semantic overlap between notions of bitterness and those of strength, or ferocity. In biblical Hebrew this overlap is best expressed by the adjective *ʿaz,* which means both "strong" and "bitter," as reflected in Samson's well-known riddle (Judg 14:14–18). The same semantics are evident in English usage, as a matter of fact, because we often refer to a bitter substance as "strong." The potion is, therefore, potent.

The ʾālāh 'curse'. The Sages of the Sifre have been followed by most modern scholars in their interpretation of the repeated Amens: *ʾāmēn šellōʾ niṭmēʾtî—weʾim niṭmēʾtî—ûbāʾû lāh* " 'Amen'—that I have not been defiled; but if I have been defiled—'may they (the waters) enter into her.' " This interpretation echoes the wording of Num 5:24 and 27, as if to say, "May the words of the curse do what they must!" The specification of the binary alternatives, and the wife's acceptance of the rules of the game, are characteristic of biblical oaths, treaties, and versions of covenants enacted with the God of Israel.

Most immediately relevant to the function of the *ʾālāh,* a phenomenon whose manifold ramifications cannot possibly be discussed here, is the reference to the effects of an *ʾālāh* in Zech 5:1–4:

> I looked up again and I saw a flying scroll. "What do you see?" he asked, and I replied: "A flying scroll, twenty cubits long and ten cubits wide." "That," he explained to me, "is the curse which goes out over the whole land. For everyone who has stolen, as is forbidden on one side [of the scroll] has gone unpunished: and everyone who has sworn

> [falsely] as is forbidden on the other side of it, has gone unpunished. [But] I have sent it forth—declares YHWH of Hosts—and [the curse] shall enter the house *(uba'ah 'el-)* of the thief, and the house of the one who swears falsely by my name, and it shall lodge inside their houses and shall consume them to the last timber and stone!"

This is what happens when the words of the *'ālāh* "enter in." Its words are potent and, in the case of the ordeal of Num 5:11–31, they include the divine name. When the *'ālāh* lodges inside the woman's belly, the truth of the situation will be found out. One is reminded quite graphically of modern medical methods for examining the gastrointestinal system of the human body by introducing liquids that make it possible to see inside a person and to identify blood clots, ulcers, and cancerous growths.

Summary

One must object to some modern scholars who play down the magical character of the ordeal of Num 5:11–31 (Brichto 1975). There is widespread misunderstanding about the role of the gods in magical praxis, as there is about the integral relationship of prayer, magic, and the judicial ordeal. In substance, Num 5:11–31 presents an integrated phenomenology, and in structural terms there is likewise little basis for identifying diverse sources. One could predicate that the author of Num 5:11–31 utilized formulations known to him and blended them into his overall description of the proceedings without concern for their distinct original provenances, legal, cultic, or magical. The introduction and conclusion follow fairly well-attested methods of inclusion and resumption characteristic of the priestly source (Milgrom 1989: 350).

In functional terms, the legislation of this ordeal served to fill a gap in the law, so that mechanisms for divorce could operate in a religious community restrained by very limited grounds for divorce, on the one hand, and by strict insistence on evidentiary testimony, on the other. Applied concepts of impurity stigmatized the suspected wife who, if she protested her innocence when actually guilty instead of settling for an unremunerated divorce, might risk an abortion or worse—a permanently disabling condition, not to speak of disenfranchisement from her rights as an Israelite. Implicit in the workings of the ordeal are judgments about which sorts of children the community was prepared to accept and to care for. At least as a hidden agenda, a policy of "pro-choice," operated in priestly law and was exercised by the established religious authority, the Israelite priesthood.

PART III.

NUMBERS 6: THE VOW OF THE NAZIRITE, WITH A BENEDICTION ADDED

INTRODUCTION

Numbers 6 deals with a fascinating, albeit elusive, aspect of Israelite religion, the phenomenon of naziritism, a very ancient institution and one that persisted long after the biblical period (Milgrom 1989: 43–44, 355–358). As defined in Numbers 6, a *nāzîr* was a person who had pledged under terms of a vow *(neder)* to restrict his behavior in several areas so as to attain a greater measure of holiness in his life. It is often the case that no explanation is provided in the biblical sources for specific phenomena. Their motivations and purposes must be deduced or inferred from the ritual and legal provisions attendant upon them. This is true of naziritism, whose larger implications will be explored in COMMENT 1 on this chapter.

In effect, the Nazirite pledged to restrict himself in three areas: to abstain from any product of the vine, to avoid contact with the dead even with regard to his closest relatives, and to allow the hair of his head to grow loose (Num 6:1–8). We should assume that a person would normally commit himself to these restrictions for a specified period of time.

After defining the basic obligations of the Nazirite vow, Numbers 6 provides for emergencies that might interrupt the process. Should a close family relative die suddenly during the term of the vow, so that the *nāzîr* was unavoidably defiled by contact with a corpse, or as a result of being under the same roof with a corpse, he would have to begin all over again! Although the breach had been unavoidable, it had, nevertheless, made actual fulfillment of the vow impossible. The *nāzîr* was required to expiate the interruption of his vow during a seven-day period of purification, followed by sacrificial offerings on the eighth day (Num 6:9–12).

Num 6:13–21 prescribe the normal course of events, in cases in which the *nāzîr* was able to complete the term of his restriction without incident. An elaborate sacrificial regimen was performed on the day of completion, including a burnt offering, a sin offering, and the *šelāmîm* 'sacred gifts of greetings', all accompanied by libations and grain offerings.

Subsequent to these rites, the *nāzîr* was to shave his head and place the hair on the fire, under the last of the major sacrifices, the *šelāmîm.* Those parts of the sacrifices which accrued to the priests were first held up to God's view, and promptly assigned to the priests. Then the *nāzîr* could again drink wine.

Without a doubt, the most distinctive feature of the rites of the *nāzîr* is the disposition of the *nāzîr*'s hair, reflecting the widespread significance of hair in the phenomenology of religion, a subject to be explored in COMMENT 1, below. The emphasis on hair recalls the career of Samson, recounted in Judges 13–16. Samson had been devoted as a lifelong *nāzîr.*

Numbers 6 concludes, in vv 22–27, with the text of the priestly benediction, which survived in postbiblical Judaism and is part of Christian liturgy as well. This is the benediction referred to in Lev 9:22b: "Aaron lifted his arms toward the people and blessed them." He blessed them with the words preserved in this chapter! The first pronouncement of the priestly benediction occurred after Aaron and his sons had been consecrated as priests of YHWH and when, for the first time, they officiated at the Tabernacle cult (Lev 9:23–24). Thereafter, it was undoubtedly pronounced regularly, perhaps even every day.

In 1986, two thin silver amulets were discovered in the area of the Valley of Hinnom in the environs of Jerusalem, in an area now called Keteph Hinnom. These amulets have incised on them almost verbatim versions of the priestly benediction. They were found in a burial cave, among a trove of valuable items buried with the dead. The implications of this remarkable discovery, which has been dated as early as the late seventh century B.C.E. and as late as the early sixth century B.C.E., will be explored in COMMENT 2, below. There the relevance of other examples of ancient epigraphy to the priestly benediction will also be discussed.

TRANSLATION

6 [1]YHWH spoke to Moses as follows:

[2]Speak to the Israelite people and say to them: When anyone, man or woman, sets [himself] apart by pronouncing a vow as a Nazirite, to place restrictions on himself for YHWH,

[3]he must restrict [himself] from wine or any other intoxicant, not drinking the vinegar of wine, or the vinegar of any other intoxicant; nor may he imbibe any liquid in which grapes have been steeped. He may not eat either moist or dried grapes.

[4]For the entire term of his restriction, he may not ingest any product of the grapevine, neither seeds nor skins.

[5]For the entire term of his restriction, a razor may not pass over his head. Until the completion of the days during which he placed restrictions on himself for YHWH, he is to remain sacred, allowing the hair of his head to grow loose.

[6]For the entire term during which he placed restrictions on himself for YHWH, he may not come near the body of a dead person.

[7]Even on account of his father and his mother, or for his brother and sister —even on account of them—he may not render himself impure at their death. For hair reserved for his God covers his head.

[8]For the entire term of his restriction, he remains sacred to YHWH.

[9]Should any person related to him pass away suddenly, so that he has defiled his dedicated hair, he must shave his head on the day of his purification. On the seventh day he must shave it.

[10]On the eighth day he must deliver to the priest two turtledoves or two young pigeons, at the entrance of the Tent of Meeting.
[11]The priest shall assign one as a sin offering and the other as a burnt offering, and perform expiation on his behalf for the guilt he has incurred concerning a corpse. He must reconsecrate his "head" on that day.
[12]He must recommit the days of his restriction for YHWH and deliver a yearling lamb as a guilt offering. The prior days fall away because his state of restriction has been impaired by an impurity.
[13]This is the prescribed instruction for the Nazirite: On the day that his term of dedication is complete, he is to be brought to the entrance of the Tent of Meeting.
[14]He is to present as his offering to YHWH a yearling lamb without blemish for a burnt offering, and one ewe a year old without blemish for a burnt offering, and one ewe a year old without blemish for a sin offering, and one ram without blemish for sacred gifts of greeting;
[15]a basket of unleavened bread made of semolina flour, prepared as loaves with oil mixed into them, and prepared as thin cakes of unleavened bread smeared with oil, along with their grain offerings and libations.
[16]The priest shall draw near to the presence of YHWH and perform his sin offering and his burnt offering.
[17]He shall sacrifice the ram as an offering of sacred gifts of greeting in the presence of YHWH, together with the basket of unleavened bread. The priest shall likewise perform his grain offering and his libation.
[18]The Nazirite shall then shave his restricted "head" at the entrance of the Tent of Meeting. He shall take the hair of his restricted "head" and place it on the fire that is under the sacred gifts of greeting.
[19]The priest shall take the boiled shoulder of the ram and one loaf of unleavened bread from the basket, along with one thin, unleavened cake, and place them on the palms of the Nazirite, after he has shaved off his restricted [hair].
[20]The priest shall raise them as a presentation in the presence of YHWH. This shall be a sacred offering for YHWH, in addition to the breast of the presentation offering and the shoulder of the levied donation. Only afterward may the Nazirite drink wine.
[21]This is the prescribed instruction for the Nazirite. But one who pledges his offering to YHWH in excess of his required restriction, in accordance with what his means allow, must fulfill the vow he has pledged in excess of the instruction prescribed for his restriction.
[22]YHWH spoke to Moses, saying:
[23]Instruct Aaron and his sons as follows: In this manner shall you bless the Israelite people. Say to them:
[24]"May YHWH bless you and watch over you.
[25]"May YHWH look kindly upon you and deal graciously with you.
[26]"May YHWH look with favor upon you and grant you well-being."

[27]Whenever they pronounce my name over the Israelite people, I will bless them!

NOTES TO 6:1–21: THE RULES OF NAZIRITISM

6. 2. *man or woman.* The formula *ʾîš ʾô ʾiššāh* occurred in Num 5:5, where it was discussed. The conditional, somewhat hesitant tone of this opening statement has prompted religious authorities throughout the centuries to advise against vows, noting that nowhere are the Israelites commanded to pronounce vows. These authorities further base themselves on the wisdom of Koheleth (5:4), who states that it is preferable not to undertake vows in the first place, if one has any thought of not fulfilling them (cf. Deut 23:22).

sets [himself] apart. Generally, the language employed in laws pertaining to oaths and vows is subtle and redundant. The verb *pālāʾ*, here appearing in the *hiphʿil* stem, *yaplîʾ*, is difficult to define precisely. Then, too, the two verbs *nādar* and *nāzar*, forms of which recur in this chapter, are sufficiently close in meaning and in sound to suggest that they are related etymologically.

As for the verb *pālāʾ*, it is best understood as a phonetic variant of *pālāh*, with final *heh*, which means "to separate, differentiate, set aside." The verb, when spelled with final *heh*, occurs in the *niphʿal* (Exod 33:16; Ps 139:14) as well as in the *hiphʿil* (Exod 9:4; 11:7; Pss 4:4; 27:7), and its connotation is well established. There are several factors recommending the identification of the two vocables, aside from the fact that *aleph* and *heh* are often interchanged.

In Ps 17:7 we read *haplēh ḥasādêkā* 'make your acts of kindness *singular*', whereas Ps 31:22 has *kî hiplîʾ ḥasdô lî* 'for he [God] has made his acts of kindness *singular* on my behalf'. The two statements paraphrase each other, suggesting that the two verbal forms are merely variations of each other. The form with final *aleph* most often occurs in the *piʿel* stem (Lev 22:21; Num 15:3–5), but the *hiphʿil* also occurs in Lev 27:2: *ʾîš kî yaplîʾ neder* 'when a person *sets aside* a vow'. Actually, the present statement is a variation of Lev 27:2, expressed in a more verbose manner.

The point is that *yaplîʾ*, in the present verse, does not express how the vow is pronounced; it does not mean "to be explicit, profuse," or the like, as it was understood in NJPS. Rather, *yaplîʾ* refers to the purpose of the vow. In effect, the present statement is redundant, with *yaplîʾ* and the infinitive, *lehazzîr* 'to restrict', both conveying the purpose of the vow, which is to dedicate something or someone to God.

Whereas the meaning of the verb *nādar* is evident, the sense of *nāzar* is less obvious. Both roots, *n-d-r*, which is attested in Ugaritic and Phoenician, and *n-z-r*, are probably phonetic variants of the same verbal root, which is posited as **n-ḏ-r*, on the basis of the Arabic cognate *naḏara*. This identification has been argued by Albright (1942) and by Ginsberg (1945).

An analagous pattern of phonetic variation is evident in the case of *n-d-h* and *n-z-h*, both of which connote "casting off, hurling, sprinkling." In the NOTES on Num 19:9 it is argued that both forms derive from a common root, but were subsequently differentiated.

In the present law, the verb *nāzar*, in its various forms, has taken on a negative nuance. It connotes "restriction, abstinence, self-denial." The form *nādar*, in contrast, signifies "devotion, commitment, pledge," expressing the positive aspects inherent in the phenomenon of naziritism. In summary, the present legislation utilizes two differentiated phonetic variants of the same verbal root side by side, just as, in Numbers 19, *n-d-h* and *n-z-h* also occur side by side.

Returning to the present verse, we note that two active-transitive verbs, *yaplî'* and *lehazzîr*, both lack direct objects. (In v 12, below, *hizzîr* attests a direct object.) We should supply the direct object "himself" when an explicit direct object is lacking.

The term *neder*, it must be remembered, has dual aspects; it connotes the initial pronouncement of a vow, and it designates the substance or payment of the vow as pledged (Lev 7:16). Literally, the term *nāzîr* means "one restricted, set apart" and represents a *qal* passive participle, on the Aramaic model, analogous to *nāśî'* 'one elevated; a chief'. Here the noun *nāzîr*, without prepositional *lamed*, functions adverbially, as if written *lenazzîr* 'as a Nazirite'.

In summary, the present legislation, up to this point, has projected a situation in which a person intends to restrict himself by pronouncing a vow as a Nazirite. Verse 2 represents an extended protasis, with the apodosis beginning in v 3.

It should be explained that the translation adopted here is aimed at bringing out the fullest sense of technical terms employed in the formulation of the law. Admittedly, this method of translation may result in a more stilted rendering, but the alternative of smoothing out the language of law and ritual runs the risk of obscuring important nuances. Legal and ritual texts were not composed in a fluid style.

3. Here again we are required to supply a direct object for the verb *yazzîr*, namely, "he must restrict *himself*."

wine or any other intoxicant. Translating Hebrew *šēkār* as "beer" (the meaning of Akkadian *šikāru*) would be problematic, because we have no explicit evidence in biblical sources of libations made from grain, and yet Num 28:7 specifies *šēkār* as the substance of a libation. According to Numbers 15, all libations were to be made of wine, and as is routinely specified in priestly ritual prescriptions. In 2 Sam 23:16 we read that David once offered a libation of water; and later Jewish sources speak of libations of water offered in the

Second Temple of Jerusalem (Mishna, *Sukkôt* 4:1; Babylonian Talmud, *Sukkôt* 34a; *Šebîʿît* 63a; Jerusalem Talmud, *Sukkôt*, 54b).

It is doubtful, moreover, that fermented grain would have been allowed on the sacrificial altar according to priestly law, in light of the widespread aversion to the use of leavened dough *(ḥāmēṣ)* in grain offerings of which a part ascended the altar (Lev 2:11). Beer is brewed from fermented grain of one sort or another. Therefore, when Num 28:7 refers to *šēkār* as the substance of libations, we are prompted to identify it as a liquid made from grapes.

There is the added observation that in biblical Hebrew the verb *šākar* 'to be intoxicated' is often used with reference to the effects of wine (Isa 29:9; 51:21; Gen 9:21). Most likely, Hebrew usage was generalized, so that the denominative verb *šākar* came to describe intoxication from wine primarily, and the noun *šēkār* itself was used for wine that had an intoxicating effect, not for beer. The word *yayîn* 'wine' is of limited distribution and exhibits cognates in Ugaritic and some other West Semitic languages.

After all, it is unlikely that the *nāzîr* was required to refrain from any drink *not* made of grapes, in view of the extent to which the present law focuses on the fruit of the vine. On this basis, I translate *yayîn wešēkār* 'wine or *any other intoxicant*', reference being to a grape product of a quality different from wine. Hebrew *ḥômeṣ* 'wine vinegar' (Ps 69:22; Ruth 2:14) connotes fermentation, like *ḥāmēṣ* 'leaven', which is said of dough (Hos 7:4, Exod 12:34). We have no information about what type of intoxicant, made from grapes, would be designated by *šēkār*. Perhaps *šēkār* is new wine, known to be unusually heady.

in which grapes have been steeped. The Hebrew combination *mišrat ʿanābîm* is unique to this verse. The verb *šārah* 'to steep' is rare in biblical Hebrew (Job 37:3), but common in Aramaic and Late Hebrew, where *šerê/šārāh* means "to soak, dilute, steep," with cognates in Syriac *(teraʾ)* and Arabic *(tarāya)* (*HALAT* 1523, under *š-r-h* II; and cf. Mishna *Yādayîm* 1:3).

dried grapes. Raisins *(ṣimmûqîm)*, forbidden to the Nazirite, are a mainstay of the Middle Eastern diet (cf. 1 Sam 25:18; 30:12; 2 Sam 16:1). Some have speculated that enigmatic *ʾašîšê ʿanābîm* of Hos 3:1 also means "raisins" (cf 2 Sam 6:19; Cant 2:5).

4. *For the entire term of his restriction.* The formula *kol yemê nizrô,* and variations of the same, recur as a refrain in our chapter (vv 5, 6, 8) and clearly refer to the term of the restrictive vow, it being customary to specify a precise number of days. According to the Mishna (*Nāzîr,* 1:3; 6:3) one who failed to specify the duration of his vow would be bound to it for thirty days.

The Segollate noun *nēzer* 'Naziriteship, restriction' is probably unrelated to *nēzer* 'crown diadem' (Exod 29:6; Lev 8:9), even though one is tempted to relate the two vocables (see v 18, below). Actually, *nēzer* simply means "restriction," just as *neder* means "vow."

All products of the grapevine are forbidden to the Nazirite in any form.

The combination *gepen hayyayîn*, literally, "the wine vine," also occurs in Judg 13:14, in one of the Samson stories, and Samson was, after all, a kind of Nazirite.

neither seeds nor skins. The meanings of *ḥarṣānîm* and *zāg* are both uncertain. *Ḥarṣānîm* 'seeds' is better attested in Aramaic and Late Hebrew, and an Aramaic cognate *ḥiṣrin* has been adduced (*HALAT*, 342). What we have is a merism, meaning that no part of the grape, from inside out, was permitted to the Nazirite. On this basis, *zāg (zôg)* should yield the sense "skin, shell."

5. *razor.* Hebrew *taʿar* is usually derived from the root *ʿ-r-h* 'to uncover', so that *taʿar* would be an instrument for exposing one's head by shaving off the hair. In Ezra 5:1 we read of *taʿar haggallābîm* 'the barbers' razor'. The same vocable, *taʿar* connotes "sheath" (Ezek 21:8–9). Razors "pass over" (the verb *ʿābar*) one's head (Num 8:7). Throughout the present legislation, "head" is a way of referring to "hair."

sacred. The Nazirite is *qādôš* for the duration of his vow, a thought repeated in v 7, below. The implications of this definition of the Nazirite's status will be explored in the first COMMENT to this chapter.

allowing the hair of his head to grow loose. In the clause *gaddēl peraʿ śeʿar rôʾsô*, the verb *gaddel* represents an infinitive absolute, which takes a direct object. Hebrew *peraʿ* means "growing hair; long loose hair" (Ezek 44:20). In Num 5:18 we read that the priest loosened (the verb *pāraʿ*) the hair of a woman suspected of infidelity. All usages of this verb somehow connote dishevelment or disarray, but the phenomenology of the *nāzîr* differs from that pertaining to mourning or shaming (see the NOTES on Num 5:8).

6. The second restriction imposed on the Nazirite was avoidance of contact with a corpse. The basic regulations regarding the impurity of the dead may be found in Numbers 19. The degree of restriction is more severe in the case of the Nazirite than it is even with respect to ordinary priests, who were permitted to participate in the burial of close consanguineous relatives (Lev 21:1–4). The restrictions imposed on the Nazirite were effectively as severe as those applicable to the high priest (Lev 21:11). This severity allows us to infer that a high degree of purity was basic to the phenomenon of naziritism, so that death became a significant constraint affecting its realization.

he placed restrictions on himself. The Hebrew form *hazzîrô* is an infinitive construct, with the object suffix.

the body of a dead person. The construction *nepeš mēt* means, literally, "the corpse of a dead person"; it recalls the language of Num 19:11, 13, within the primary legislation governing the impurity of the dead, as well as Num 9:7, 10, in the law of the deferred Pesaḥ of the second month, where *nepeš* likewise refers to a corpse, in the immediate context.

7. *He may not render himself impure.* The verbal form *yiṭṭammāʾ* represents the *hithpaʿel* stem, consonantal *yṭṭmʾ*, assimilated.

The four family members listed here—one's father, mother, brother, and sister—recall Lev 21:1–4 and 11, as noted above. There, however, additional consanguineous relatives are listed, namely, one's son and daughter. We may also compare the lists of relatives in Lev 25:49 and Num 27:8–10 (see the NOTES on Num 5:8).

reserved for God. The term *nēzer 'elôhâw* 'the restriction of his God' requires comment, because it is a "pregnant" combination of terms. The sense is that one whose grown hair was dedicated or restricted to God ought not to be defiled by contact with the dead; that one's hair, allowed to grow loose in the fulfillment of a vow made to God, should not be so defiled. It is tempting to relate *nēzer,* as it is used here, to *nēzer* 'crown, diadem' (see above, in the NOTES on v 4), but this connection is unlikely.

8. This verse restates v 5, in referring to the status of the Nazirite as a sacred person.

9–12. The next four verses provide for an emergency: a close relative of a *nāzîr* died suddenly, perhaps in the same dwelling shared by the *nāzîr.* In such an event, the Nazirite had to begin his term all over again, after a seven-day period of purification. Subsequently, he would be required to sacrifice offerings on the eighth day.

suddenly. Idiomatic *kepetaʿ pitʾôm* means, literally, "unexpectedly, all of a sudden" (cf. Num 35:22; Isa 29:5; 30:13).

he had defiled. The *piʿel* intensive verb *weṭimmēʾ* would normally convey intent, but here it merely expresses a result. In effect, the *nāzîr* had defiled his devoted hair, though not intending to do so.

his dedicated [hair]. The construction *rôʾš nizrô* means "the dedicated [hair] of his head," not, of course, "the head of his dedicated [hair]." Construct formations may often be juxtaposed.

he must shave it. The verb *gillaḥ* means "to shave" near the skin, whereas cropping the hair is conveyed by the verb *kasam* (Ezek 44:20; and cf. Lev 14:8; Deut 21:12). In the situation projected here, the *nāzîr* was forced to end his term prematurely. Formulaic *beyôm ṭoharātô* (cf. Lev 14:2; Ezek 44:26) refers to the day on which the *nāzîr* is restored to purity. The shaving takes place on the seventh day after the defilement. Seven-day periods awaiting purification are normal for serious types of impurity, especially the sort contracted by contact with a corpse (Num 19:12).

10. Seven full days were to elapse because the sacrifices requisite for restoration to purity took place only on the eighth day (cf. the rites of purification prescribed for the ailment of *ṣāraʿat* in Lev 14:10; 15:29).

young pigeons. This meaning of Hebrew *benê yônāh* is suggested by Gen 15:9, where *tor* 'turtledove' is paired with *gôzāl* 'chick, young bird'. The two kinds of birds, turtledoves *(tôr)* and young pigeons, were regularly employed in sacrificial rites. Lev 1:14 provides that these birds may be offered as burnt offerings. According to Lev 5:7–8, these kinds of birds could also be offered to expiate certain sins of omission by one unable to afford animal sacrifices (also cf. the provisions of Lev 12:8).

11. *shall assign.* The priest shall "perform" (the verb *ʿāśāh)* one of the birds as a sin offering and the other as a burnt offering, in that order. The order is highly significant, because it was necessary first to reinstate the Nazirite and to expiate his abrogation of the term of restriction. Once this was done, an *ʿôlāh* 'burnt offering' served to test God's response. God's acceptance of the *ʿôlāh* indicated acceptance of the Nazirite's expiation. The same sequence obtains in Num 8:12, in the purification of the Levites as part of their dedication.

on his behalf. The construction *wekipper ʿālâw* is ambiguous, as employed here. The indirect object construction means "on behalf of"—as is its meaning in Num 5:8.

for the guilt he has incurred concerning a corpse. In the clause *mēʾašer ḥāṭāʾ ʿal hannepeš,* the function of adverbial *mēʾašer* is to express cause: because the Nazirite had been in contact with a corpse *(nepeš)* he was defiled. Compare Isa 43:4: *mēʾašer yāqarta beʿênâi* 'because you are dear in my sight'.

The Nazirite was to consecrate (the verb *qiddēš)* his hair on the eighth day. He would do so by placing it on the altar fire, just as is provided in the normal rites at the completion of the Nazirite's term, as stipulated in v 18, below. It is logical to conclude, notwithstanding some ambiguity in the formulation of the law, that whatever a Nazirite does in emergency circumstances would approximate what he would do at the successful completion of his period of restriction.

12. *He must recommit.* Here the verb *wehizzîr* takes a direct object, namely, the *days* of his restriction.

The obligation of the Nazirite who was unexpectedly defiled to offer an *ʾāšām* 'guilt offering' requires comment. Strictly speaking, the *ʾāšām* was required only where *maʿal* had occurred, namely, where there had been actual misappropriation of property (Lev 5:14–16, 20–26; Num 5:5–10). What loss of property had occurred in the case of the Nazirite? Most likely, the Nazirite was regarded as a form of sacred property, for he was, after all, sacred to God. His defilement, and the breach of his term of restriction, constituted a loss to God, just as if sacred property had been taken from the Sanctuary. No restitution of property would be required, but only a sacrifice in the form of a yearling lamb and, of course, the recommencing of the period of the vow. This process satisfied God's claim.

fall away. The prior days would "fall" *(yippelû)* from the count of the full term. Usage here approximates Josh 21:43; 23:14, where we read of fulfillment "falling short" (the verb *nāpal)* of obligation or of promise (also cf. usage in 1 Kgs 8:56; Esth 6:10).

has been impaired. Some read, instead of stative *ṭāmēʾ*, intensive *kî timmēʾ*

nizrô 'because he had defiled his restricted [hair]', to conform to v 9, above, but this emendation is unnecessary.

13–21. These verses prescribe the rites to be performed at the normal conclusion of the term of restriction.

This is the prescribed instruction for the Nazirite. The caption *zō't tôrat hannāzîr* recalls similar captions in Lev 14:2 and 15:32, where the referent of the construct formation is a person. The third-person form, *yābî'*, has stative/passive force: "he must be brought." This is often the sense of third-person verbal forms, when no subject is specified. Like most rites of purification, those of the Nazirite took place in front of the Tabernacle.

14. Three sacrifices are listed, this time in the administrative order in which they would be offered (Rainey 1970). The sin offering would be offered first, followed by the burnt offering (v 16, below). Finally, the *šelāmîm* 'sacred gifts of greeting' would be presented.

He is to present. The verb *wehiqrîb* conveys the presentation, preliminary to performance of the actual rites. Included is a female animal from the flock *(kabśāh* or *kibśāh).* There is no clear basis for explaining why female animals were requisite for certain sacrifices and not for others. Most animal sacrifices were of males, for the obvious reason that only relatively few males were needed for the reproduction of herds and flocks. A female of the flocks is also mandated for the rites of purification undergone by one showing symptoms of *ṣāraʿat* (Lev 14:10), a rite also scheduled on the eighth day, after a seven-day period of waiting. Lev 5:6 allows a female of the flock to be offered for the expiation of sins of omission.

without blemish. Sacrificial offerings had to be free of blemishes, of course, a state expressed by the Hebrew adjective *tāmîm.*

sacred gifts of greeting. This translation for the term *šelāmîm* requires special comment because it differs from the accepted understanding of this sacrifice. The basic procedures for the *šelāmîm* are presented in Leviticus 3, and again in Lev 7:11–34.

The many different renderings of the term *šelāmîm* reflect, of course, the wide range of meanings attendant upon the common Semitic root *š-l-m.* Virtually all suggested renderings of *šelāmîm* reflect one or another of these meanings, and the problem becomes one of determining which attested connotation applies. Thus, the common translation "peace offering" reflects the rendering of the Vulgate, *pacificus,* associated with Hebrew *šālôm.* Stative adjectival *šālēm* 'whole, complete' has generated such translations as "shared offering" *(NEB). NJPS* renders "offering of well-being." The rendering "sacred gifts of greeting" reflects the impact of comparative evidence, especially evidence from Ugaritic and Akkadian.

In the Ugaritic epic of *Keret,* we read that a besieged king offered *šlmm (šalāmūma)* 'tribute, gifts' to his attacker in order to induce him to withdraw the siege (Gibson 1978: 89, to *Keret,* col. VI, line 274). Quite a number of terms for sacrifices convey the notion of "gift," for the obvious reason that sacrifices are, in a very real sense, gifts proffered to God (or to the gods). A related Akkadian term, *šulmānu*, connotes "a gift of greeting," more precisely, the gift one presents when greeting another by saying *šulmu* 'Peace!' in Akkadian, or *šālôm* in Hebrew (Levine 1974: 3–52).

Applying these considerations to the biblical sacrifice known as *šelāmîm* or *zebaḥ šelāmîm*, one could say that it was offered to God by way of greeting, when God would arrive in response to the invocation of his worshipers. That is why the *šelāmîm* was offered after the *ʿôlāh*. First God had to be invoked, and then a sacred meal could be held in God's presence. The *šelāmîm* offering is classified as a *zebaḥ*, a kind of offering partially burned on the altar and partially prepared in pots (1 Sam 2:13–16).

15. *unleavened bread.* The use of a basket of unleavened baked goods *(maṣṣôt)* in these rites finds an analogue in the consecration of the Aaronide priesthood (Exod 29:3; Lev 8:2). Two types of *maṣṣôt* were conventional in the biblical cult: *ḥallôt maṣṣôt* 'unleavened cakes' and *reqîqêʾ maṣṣôt* 'unleavened wafers'. Hebrew *ḥallāh* designates "a thick, round cake" (Ibn Ezra). The etymology is uncertain, reflecting either a root *ḥ-w-l* 'to be round, circular' or a root *ḥ-l-l* 'to pierce', because *ḥallāh* bread is often pierced before baking. Hebrew *rāqîq* means "a thin, small cake." The root *r-q-q* means "to be thin, small, meager," as in Gen 41:19–20, where adjectival *raqqôt* describes lean cows. The Akkadian cognate *raqqu* shares this meaning, and this root accounts for the adverb *raq* 'only, but for' and the noun *raqqāh* 'temple' (Judg 4:21–22; 5:26; Cant 4:3; Levine 1965b).

The derivation of Hebrew *maṣṣāh* remains uncertain. It is the opposite of *ḥāmēṣ* 'leavened dough'. Some have suggested a connection with Greek *madza* 'barley cake', from the verb *massô* 'to knead dough' (Liddell-Scott, 1072, under *madza*; 1082, under *massô*). This identification is, however, uncertain, even though no Semitic etymology has been found for Hebrew *maṣṣāh*.

along with their grain offerings and libations. The last part of this verse, *uminḥātām weniskêhem*, probably refers to the three major sacrifices listed in vv 14–15, and not only to the *maṣṣôt* of v 15, which would not have been accompanied by yet more grain offerings! The basic procedures governing grain offerings are presented in Leviticus 2 and 6:7–11. The procedures regarding libations are presented in Numbers 15.

16. *shall draw near.* Now begins the prescribed procedure, once the necessary materials had been secured. The verb *wehiqrîb* lacks a direct object and has stative force, but of an intensive or elative character, hence: "to draw very near." Thus, Exod 14:10: *ûparʿôh hiqrîb* 'Pharaoh drew very near' (cf. Gen 12:11).

The sin offering was offered first, then the burnt offering (see the Notes on v 14, above). Once God had indicated that the expiation of the Nazirite was proper by his acceptance of the burnt offering, it was time to offer sacred gifts of greeting, which were realized as a sacred meal.

17. The *šelāmîm* were offered "together with" (*ʿal*) the basket of *maṣṣôt*. Then the priest performed the grain offerings and libations first mentioned in v 15, above.

18. The Nazirite would then shave his hair, which had been allowed to grow loose. He does so in front of the Tent of Meeting. He places his shaved hair on the altar fire, under the last of the sacrifices to have been placed there. This is the sense of *ʾašer taḥat* 'which was under,' namely, into the fire burning under the *šelāmîm* offering.

19. *boiled shoulder.* The priest takes the "cooked shoulder" (*hazzerôʿa bešēlāh*). This terminology reflects the fact that sacrifices of the *zebaḥ* type were boiled in pots, as is described in 1 Sam 2:13–16. It is assumed that the reader knows this fact of procedure. Absence of the definite article in the adjective of attribution (so that we have *bešēlāh* instead of *habbešēlāh*) is characteristic of Late Hebrew syntax, perhaps under the influence of Phoenician (Friedrich 1970: 296–297, 299).

Some of the sacrificial materials were placed on the palms of the Nazirite. This procedure resembles the one prescribed for a wife suspected of infidelity, according to Num 5:18. Such an offering could literally be termed *maśʾat kappayîm* 'the gifts of the palms' (Ps 141:2).

20. *the priest shall raise . . . as a presentation.* The cognate clause *wehēnîp . . . tenûpāh* occurs quite frequently in descriptions of religious rites (cf. Lev 8:29; 14:12, 24; 23:20). A shorter formulation, which merely employs the verb *hēnîp*, is explained in the NOTES on Num 5:25. In this case, the priest received more than he normally would. According to Lev 7:30–32, priests received the breast (*ḥāzeh*) and the thigh (*šôq*) from the *šelāmîm* sacrifice. Here the priest receives the shoulder, plus one-half of the *maṣṣôt* in the basket. Prepositional *ʿal* means "together with, in addition to."

When the rites were over, the Nazirite was permitted to drink wine again.

21. Here *zôʾt tôrat hannāzîr* serves as a postscript (cf. above, in v 13).

The syntax of v 21 is cumbersome, but the point seems to be clear: the Nazirite who has the means to offer more than what is required according to standard procedure is expected to do so. The key is provided by the preposition *ʿal*, which here means "in addition to, in excess of." Thus *ʿal nizrô* means "*in excess of* his restriction," and *ʿal tôrat nizrô* means "*in excess of* the instruction prescribed for his restriction." Though initially optional, the additional offerings became obligatory once pledged.

NOTES TO 6:22–27: THE PRIESTLY BENEDICTION

22–27. The concluding verses of chap. 6 present the priestly benediction. It was the duty and the privilege of the Aaronide priests to pronounce blessings over the people of Israel, and this act was referred to in Lev 9:22b, as noted in the introduction to Numbers 6.

23. *Say to them.* One assumes that priests blessed the people on any number of occasions. The infinitive absolute *'āmôr* 'Speak!' is here used as an imperative. This is often the function of the infinitive absolute in biblical Hebrew, as well as in ancient Hebrew epigraphy (Levine 1979b).

In this manner shall you bless. Idiomatic *kôh tebārekû* indicates that the words immediately to follow were the actual words of blessing. Very often, *kôh* introduces a direct quotation.

24. The priest expresses the wish or request that God grant blessings to a second-person addressee, "you," which is a way of identifying the Israelite people, collectively.

bless. No satisfactory etymology for the verb *bērēk* has been proposed. It is possible that the verb and the participial forms (most frequently *bārûk* 'blessed', the passive *qal* participle) are all denominative of *berākāh* 'gift, blessing'. In other words, "to bless" is to grant *berākāh,* or to request that it be granted. In any case, the point to be made about the verb *bērēk* and nominal *berākāh* 'gift, blessing' is that they are not to be understood as abstractions, nor do they refer primarily to a state of mind or express some spiritual condition. God's blessings would come in the form of substantial gifts and material benefits, of progeny and prosperity, of well-being and peace in the land. In Gen 24:1 we read that God "blessed" Abraham with everything *(bakkôl),* except with a son and heir. This passage implies what it is that blessings consist of (see Gen 17:16; 27:10; Exod 23:25; Deut 7:13; 14:24; 16:15; Job 1:10; 42:12).

watch over. The verb *šāmar* 'to guard', when used in statements of blessing, often conveys the request for safety and security. Frequently the word *derek* 'way, path' is connected with the verb *šāmar,* because journeys were perceived as particularly dangerous, as were assigned missions (Exod 23:20; Josh 24:17). The verb *šāmar* may also pertain to being protected from defeat by one's enemies (1 Sam 30:23).

The subtle import of the first statement is that the priest is invoking God's blessings over his people, hoping that God would safeguard them and, in so doing, grant them blessing.

25. The second statement expresses the request of God that he look upon his people favorably and be kind and generous to them. The concept of light,

more precisely, the light of the countenance, is clarified by several biblical statements. In Eccl 8:1 we read, "A man's skill *lights up (tāʾîr)* his face, so that the severity of his face is changed for the better." In other words, when one's face "lights up" he is well disposed, which is the antithesis of a fierce countenance (the adjective *ʿaz*), which conveys an unkind disposition. In anticipation of further references to God's countenance, let it be said that the countenance of God was believed to be a potent force. When God is well disposed, his face brings blessings and power, but when he is ill disposed, his face shows it, and danger follows.

deal graciously. The verb *ḥānan* 'to be gracious, kind' is often linked to words of blessing. As in the case of the verb *bērēk* itself, Hebrew *ḥānan* most often implies the granting of material well-being. Thus Gen 33:11: "For YHWH has been generous to me *(ḥannanî)*, with the result that I possess everything!" One is generous *(ḥônēn)* to the indigent (Prov 14:31). The Canaanite peoples were *not* to be treated generously or be considered as allies (Deut 7:2).

26. *look with favor upon you.* The third statement of the priestly benediction expresses the request of God that he pay attention to his people, that he look upon them favorably and grant them well-being. Idiomatic *nāśāʾ pānîm ʾel*, literally, "to lift up the face toward" means to treat favorably, even to show favoritism! Thus Deut 28:50: "He will not treat the elderly favorably," namely, the cruel enemy will show no special consideration, even for the elderly. In the simplest terms, this idiom means "to look someone in the face, to encounter a person" (2 Sam 2:22).

grant you well-being. The idiom *śîm šālôm* 'to provide well-being' is rare, but the sense is eminently clear nonetheless. The closest we come to it in biblical Hebrew is in Ps 147:14: "He who enstates *(haśśām)* well-being in your border."

27. It was the function of the Aaronide priests to pronounce God's name over the Israelite people. Once this is done, God will grant them blessings.

my name. The theme of God's "name" is relevant, but not central, to the priestly benediction. The point is that by pronouncing the divine name in the statements of the benediction, the priests opened the door to the granting of blessings by God. God must be invoked by name; the request of God must call upon him by name. The same effect is achieved by the invocation accompanying a sacrifice: "At every cult site where *I allow my name to be pronounced (ʾašer ʾazkîr ʾet šemî)*, I will arrive where you are, and grant you blessings *(ûbēraktîkā)*" (Exod 20:24).

COMMENT 1: A FORM OF ISRAELITE DEVOTION—THE *NĀZÎR*

The laws of the Nazirite (Hebrew *nāzîr)*, as we have them in chapter 6 of Numbers, represent a late, priestly codification of religious practices known in various forms from earlier biblical sources. In this diachronic perspective, the position of Numbers 6 parallels that of Numbers 30, which preserves a relatively late code of law on the subject of vows. The legislation of Numbers 30 is presented in the context of family law as affecting married women, but it harks back to earlier votive practices. The comparison of Numbers 6 and 30 is more than positional, however, for most kinds of naziritism involved vows of some sort. One normally assumed the status of a *nāzîr* pursuant to the terms of a vow, either voluntary or imposed, either time-constrained or lifelong.

The phenomenon of naziritism received considerable attention from William Robertson Smith (1969: 181–182, 481–485), and G. B. Gray (Gray—ICC 56–61) has provided for us an enlightening discussion of this institution in his commentary on Numbers 6. The search for contemporary comparative evidence has been rewarding, whereas biblical information is painfully sparse, and cryptic at that.

As Gray and others have emphasized, attention should be paid to the difference between (a) naziritism as a lifelong status, divinely designated, as was the devotion of Samson, and (b) the specific provisions of the present chapter, which speak of a time-constrained status, undertaken by an individual on his own initiative. And yet these differences are not absolute, and they do not point to entirely separate phenomena. As a result, the respective features of both manifestations can be brought to bear on each other in a methodical discussion.

Three behavioral restrictions are stipulated in the Nazirite legislation of Numbers 6: (1) the prohibition against shaving the hair of one's head; (2) abstinence from wine and products of the grapevine; and (3) avoidance of contact with the dead. The most consistent of the three, in biblical sources on the subject of naziritism, seems to have been the restriction regarding hair. Gray put the matter clearly in discussing the two aspects of this restriction, the ban on shaving the hair of the head and the requirement (or custom) of offering some part of one's hair to the Deity: "A common belief, that the hair is part of the man's vital being, seems to account for both treatments. If the one main object is to keep the man's power of vitality at the full, the hair is never shaven; if the object is to present the deity with part of the man's life, the hair is a suitable means of achieving this. Hence its frequency in offerings" (Gray—ICC, 69).

This survey of the biblical evidence bearing on the *nāzîr* will begin with the cycle of stories about Samson preserved in Judges 13–17. Samson is explicitly designated a *nāzîr* in the theophanic annunciation to his unnamed mother (Judg 13:5–7). The prohibition against shaving the hair of the son to be born is imposed at the outset, and it subsequently figures poignantly in the adventures of Samson. It is stated that the expected child will be a *nāzîr min habbeṭen* 'from the womb', words reminiscent of what was said to Jeremiah (1:5), whose assignment to the prophetic mission was likewise prenatal—*babbeṭen* 'in the womb' (Gray—ICC). A degree of rhetorical hyperbole was probably intended in the Jeremiah passage, whereas in the case of Samson there is the sense of legal assignment. Samson would remain a *nāzîr ʿad yôm môtô* 'until the time of his death'.

Peculiarly, abstinence from wine (and from impure foodstuffs) is a condition imposed on Samson's expectant mother, not on Samson himself. It seems inescapable, nevertheless, that abstinence from wine was perceived by the story's author as material to the status of a *nāzîr*. Quite possibly, existing narratives about a hero named Samson were modulated by the specific classification of Samson as a *nāzîr*, a status not original to the story. All that the hero Samson knew was that his strength was in his hair. As Samson is depicted as a carousing adventurer, reveling in wine, women, and song, it would have strained the credibility of the stories about him to have defined him as an ascetic, or holy warrior, abstaining from wine! So the independent author of the annunciation narrative displaced the ban on drinking wine from the hero himself and imposed it on his expectant mother, along with a ritual admonition against eating anything impure.

One questions Gray's assumption that Amos 2:11–12, a statement castigating the Israelite people, does not refer to abstinence from wine as a Nazirite rule. The prophet says,

And I raised up prophets from among your sons,
And Nazirites from among your men. . . .
But you made the Nazirites drink wine,
And ordered the prophets not to prophesy.

Gray compares these statements to Isa 28:7, a late passage, where the Israelite prophets and priests are accused of being muddled in their vision and judgment by excessive intoxication. He understands Amos 2:11–12 as a similar denunciation of a more general character, rather than as an indication that in the eighth century B.C.E., abstinence from wine was a restriction imposed on Nazirites. More likely, the sequential statements in Amos 2:11–12 are symmetrical: gagging the prophets eliminates their ability to function, because their job is to speak out. Similarly, forcing Nazirites to drink wine disqualifies them from doing whatever it was they were supposed to do. Would that we knew what it was!

Perhaps it would be best to explore the theme of hair first, and then attempt to deal with abstinence from wine. The starting point is Deut 33:16b. However we interpret this passage, it inevitably suggests the phenomenon of naziritism:

> May these [namely, blessings] rest on the head of Joseph,
> On the pate of the elect of his brothers *(nezîr ᵓeḥâw)*.

As explained in the NOTES on Num 6:2, the verbal root *n-z-r* connotes separation. If such separation is positively perceived and considered distinctive, the *nāzîr* stands apart as one selected for a holy or otherwise worthwhile purpose. Joseph might have been characterized as *nezîr ᵓeḥâw* because he had received his father Jacob's extraordinary blessing. References to "head" *(rôᵓš)* and "pate" *(qodqôd)* are highly suggestive when used in association with the verb *n-z-r*. A more literal rendering of Deut 33:16b would be

> May all of these rest on the head of Joseph,
> On the pate of *one whose hair is dedicated* from among his brothers.

One might even translate "On the pate of one whose hair was untrimmed."

To understand the preceding verse properly, we must digress for a moment and speak of grapes and wine, rather than hair, because the root *n-z-r* also occurs in that context. Gray observes that the figurative characterization *ʿinbê nezîrekā* in Lev 25:5, which may be rendered "your Nazirite grapes" for convenience, or "your untrimmed grapes" literally, is also significant in establishing the character of the Nazirite restrictions in force during the biblical period. Extended usage often serves as oblique evidence, if properly understood, because of its predications. Thus *ʿinbê nezîrekā* of Lev 25:5, which occurs in the context of the prohibitions obtaining during the seventh year, nevertheless suggests the prohibition against drinking wine imposed on the *nāzîr*. One could hardly characterize grapes in this way unless the Nazirite prohibition were widely known and virtually proverbial.

To return to the subject of hair, we note that an early reference to naziritism and its rule against shaving one's hair may possibly be expressed in the opening verse of the Song of Deborah (Judg 5:2), though this reading is not entirely certain. The *NJPS* translation seems to be near the mark:

> *biprôᵃʿa perāʿôt beyiśrāᵓēl*
> *behitnaddēb ʿam- bārekû* YHWH

> When locks go untrimmed in Israel,
> When fighting men dedicate themselves—bless YHWH!

The verb *pāraʿ* and its nominal reflexes may refer to the loosening of hair, to letting it grow untrimmed, as explained in the NOTES on Num 6:5. The connotation of unruly behavior or civil disturbance expressed by this verb is surely derivative (Exod 32:25; Prov 29:18).

Deut 32:42 is of interest in this connection, and may support the interpretation proposed here:

mērôʾš parʿôt ʾôyēb

From the long-haired heads of the enemy;
From the blood of the slain and the captives.

In the words of the Song of Deborah, allowing the hair to grow long, if this is what *biprōʿa perāʿôt* means, is associated with dedication, a theme conveyed by the verb *hitnaddēb*, there used in the heroic rather than the cultic sense. On the same basis, Hebrew *ʿam* is best translated "fighting men" in the opening verse, as is its sense farther on in the Song of Deborah (Judg 5:9, 11, 13), where *ʿam* clearly refers to the force of Israelite warriors. Those fighting in *milḥamôt YHWH* 'the wars of YHWH' would dedicate themselves; and this dedication, in votive form, would require them not to shave the hair on their heads.

Two other early biblical narratives add more to the heroic dimension of naziritism, even though they do not make explicit reference to this phenomenon or speak of hair as a motif of significance. They do, however, refer to abstinence of another sort—avoidance of sexual relations with women. We have, first of all, the insistence by Uriah the Hittite that it would be improper for him to sleep with his wife while his fellow Israelite soldiers were doing battle in Transjordan: "The Ark and Israel and Judah are located at Sukkoth, and my master Joab and Your Majesty's fighting men are camped in the open field, and I should enter my house to eat and drink and lie with my wife? As you live, and by your very life, I will not do this thing" (2 Sam 11:11). When we compare this incident with the episode at Nob (1 Sam 21:5–6), when David sought sustenance from the priest in charge of the sanctuary for his hungry fighting men, we learn more about the military aspect of dedication. David reassured the priest of Nob that his men had not had recent sexual relations with women, and only then were they permitted to eat of the bread of display just removed from the sanctuary.

Although the terms of the story are not entirely clear, it is reasonable to assume that sexual relations by the fighting men would have constituted a violation of the terms of their enlistment. The only basis for allowing the fighting men to eat sacred food, otherwise reserved for priests, would have been that they were engaged in a holy war. Although this was not the case in the present instance, David makes a point of informing the priest of Nob that his fighting men, though on an ordinary mission, were observing the restrictions of a holy war.

The connection between restrictions and abstentions, on the one hand, and the cultic and purificatory aspects of naziritism, on the other, is most evident in the story of Samuel (1 Samuel 1). Hannah's vow in the sanctuary of Shiloh also involved a ban on shaving the hair of her son's head. Although the term *nāzîr* nowhere occurs in that story, reference to the theme of hair and to lifelong dedication, in a cultic rather than heroic context, links Samuel, the cult-prophet, to the institution of naziritism.

We now possess a Phoenician inscription from Kition, in Cyprus, dated sometime before 800 B.C.E. and published by A. Dupont-Sommer (1970). It speaks about hair that was shaved and dedicated to a goddess in payment of a petitionary vow. The inscription appears on a bowl found in a temple, and although the text is not fully preserved, certain of its key formulas can be read without difficulty, or can at least be restored quite reliably. The following two excerpts are most relevant:

(1) . . . *śʿr z glb wypg[ʿ brbt ʿš]trt wʿ[štrt šmʿt qly]*
. . . the hair, which he shaved. And he petitioned Rabbat ʿAshtart, and ʿAshtart heard his voice."

(2) *wytqr[b . . . . . ś wk]bś*
And it was sacrificed . . . . . a head of sheep and a young lamb.

Some comment on this interesting Phoenician text is clearly required: the verb *gālab* 'to shave' appears only once in the Hebrew Bible, though it is common in Aramaic and Late Hebrew (Levy 1963: 1.328, under *gelab*). Significantly, the single biblical reference, in Ezek 5:1–4, is highly suggestive:

> "And you, O mortal, take a sharp knife: use it as a barber's razor *(taʿar haggallābîm)*, and pass it over your head and beard. Then take scales and divide the hair. When the days of siege are completed, destroy a third part in the city, take a third and strike it with the sword all around, and scatter a third to the wind and a sword I will unsheath after them. Take also a few [hairs] from there and tie them up in your skirts. And take some more of them and cast them into the fire. From this a fire shall go out upon the whole House of Israel."

One could interpret this Ezekiel passage as a literary dramatization of the *nāzîr*'s sacrifice. Just as the *nāzîr* casts his shorn hair into the altar fire, so is the prophet commanded to burn his shorn hair in a fire. The symbolic acts referred to in the prophetic communication signify destruction. Some of the inhabitants of Jerusalem will perish in fire, after a period of siege and deprivation is over.

The nexus of shorn hair and votive activity is established in the Phoenician inscription by the verb *wypgʿ* 'and he petitioned', known in biblical Hebrew as expressing petitionary prayer (Jer 7:16; 27:18; 36:25; Ruth 1:16; Isa 59:16). The verb *wytqrb* 'and it was offered' clearly indicates the act of sacrifice, though it is not entirely clear whether the antecedent of *wytqrb* is *śʿr* 'hair', or what follows the verb, namely, *ś wkbś* 'a sheep and a young lamb'. In any case, farther on in the inscription, in line 4, we find further indication of the role of hair in votive activity: *śʿ[r . . . . 7 bnd[r tms* 'hair . . . . seven, by the vow of Tomassos.' If the restorations are correct, the inscription explicitly refers to a vow *(ndr)* and associates hair with it. Putting all of the disparate sections of the inscription together, we come up with the following admittedly conjectural interpretation of its contents: a devotee of Astarte offered some of his hair, shaved off, as a dedicatory offering to the goddess whom he had petitioned, and who had heard his entreaty.

The provenance of the Phoenician inscription, which was found in a Cypriot Phoenician temple of the late ninth century B.C.E., suggests that the comparable Israelite phenomena as evidenced in the Hebrew Bible were parts of a larger regional system of votive dedication.

Turning to the prohibition against drinking wine, we encounter indications of nomadic symbolism, and of opposition to the urban way of life. The Hebrew Bible records that the Rechabites of Jeremiah's time remained loyal to the traditional avoidance of wine and continued to dwell in tents. They had moved to Jerusalem only from fear of the advancing Babylonians (Jer 35:65). The Nabataeans, according to Diodorus, were also forbidden to build homes or plant vines. Gray has the following to say about the meaning of such restrictions: "The original reason of the latter rule has been sought in the attempt of certain classes to maintain a more primitive way of life: the cultivation of the vine . . . is one of the marked differences between the nomadic life . . . and the settled agricultural life" (Gray—ICC, 62). Tending grapevines requires continuous habitation of the same area and full-time care of the vines. In Ezekiel's prophecy of restoration (Ezek 28:6), it is predicted that the returning Israelites "will again build houses and plant vineyards" in their homeland. We may compare the similar pairing of homes and grapevines in Deut 28:30–39 and Isa 65:21. The typology of "vines < > settlement" is also expressed in the prophecy of Jer 31:4–5:

> Again you shall plant vineyards
> On the hills of Samaria;
> Men shall plant and live to enjoy them.
> For the day is coming,
> When watchmen shall proclaim

On the hills of Ephraim:
Come, let us go up to Zion,
To the Lord our God!

In defining holiness in terms of abstinence from products of the vine, the biblical traditions were endorsing a traditional, perhaps nostalgic respect for the nomadic past of the Israelite people in the presettlement period. As Jeremiah said it elsewhere (2:2–3):

I accounted to your favor
The devotion of your youth,
Your love as a bride;
How you followed me in the wilderness
In a land *not sown (lôʾ zerûʿāh)*.

The most we can say is that the codified definition of naziritism presented in Numbers 6 reflects the coalescence or combination of various traditional practices associated with votive dedication. These practices were operative in various contexts—in heroic battle and in cultic sanctification. Both fighting men and priests and prophets could be part of this phenomenology, and the comparison of *nāzîr* and *nābîʾ* 'prophet' in Amos 2:11–12 suggests a high status for the *nāzîr*. We can further state that, on some level, naziritism as a votive status realizes itself in connection with a petition, pledge, or oath. These acts are either undertaken by the person himself, or they are predetermined for that person by a parent or by the Deity. The involvement of the votive system in naziritism requires that the two phenomena be studied in tandem.

One of the most interesting areas for further study is the search for groups of Nazirites, for religious and/or military orders operative in biblical Israel. For its part, votive activity is consistently individual or at least represents the act of an individual on behalf of his immediate family. It is noteworthy that Numbers 6 makes explicit mention of women as participants in naziritic, votive activity. Whether groups of votaries developed, and what form these groups would have assumed and what role they would have played, are questions that remain to be explored.

Avoidance of contact with the dead, one of the restrictions imposed on the Nazirite, links naziritism to the provisions of Numbers 19, the primary priestly statement within Torah literature on the impurity of the dead. This aspect of naziritism will, therefore, be addressed in the COMMENT to Numbers 19.

COMMENT 2: THE BIRTH OF A BENEDICTION

In the NOTES, the suggestive words and formulas of the priestly benediction were discussed in an effort to define the concepts that the blessing was intended to express. Two dimensions of interpretation have yet to be addressed. (1) Comparative evidence on the diction of the priestly benediction: the themes that inform its statements, themes such as the "shining" of the divine countenance and the "lifting" of the divine countenance toward someone, the notion of divine protection, and the concept of blessing, are hardly particular to biblical Hebrew and, in fact, were part of an extensive ancient Near Eastern rhetorical repertoire. (2) The Israelite, biblical background of the symmetrical priestly benediction and the process of its composition: recent archaeological discoveries have shed new light on this process.

(1) Comparative Diction

C. Cohen (1993) has studied the themes of the shining divine countenance and of the lifting of the divine countenance, as expressed in the biblical benediction, with special reference to Mesopotamian literary sources. The precise semantic equivalent in Akkadian of the Hebrew idiom *hē'îr pānîm* 'to cause the face to shine' is *panī nummuru* 'to cause the face to shine, be bright'. Cohen cites a statement from a twelfth-century boundary stone *(kudurru)* telling that the god Enlil looked favorably upon the Babylonian king, Nebuchadrezzar I: *ina nummur panīšu damqūti, ina bunnīšu namrūti* 'with his(Enlil's) beautiful, radiant face, with his shining countenance' (Hinke 1911: 144, Pines 22–24). Cohen also calls attention to a Ugaritic letter, written by a prince to his mother, the queen of Ugarit, in which he tells of his favorable reception by the Hittite king, referred to as "the Sun": *'umy td'ky 'rbt lpn špš, wpn špš nr by mid* 'My mother, know that I entered into the presence (= face) of "the Sun," and the face of "the Sun" shone strongly upon me' (*KTU* 2.16:7–10). There are other Akkadian idioms that closely approximate Hebrew *nāśā' pānîm 'el* 'to lift the face toward'. These include *panī nadānu* 'to direct the face toward', *rēša šuqqû* 'to lift the head (toward)', *panī suḫḫuru* 'to turn the face around toward', and *rēša našû* 'to lift the head toward'. Pairs of these idioms often occur together in parallelism, indicating their common meanings. Cohen cites a version of the Babylonian composition *Ludlul Bēl Nēmeqi*, which reads,

ila alšīma ul iddima panīšu
usalli ištarrī ul ušaqqâ rēšiša

I invoked the god, but he did not direct his face;
I beseeched my goddess, but she did not raise her head (Lambert 1960: 38:4–5).

All of these idioms express concern and attention on the part of one for another. We observe, therefore, an equivalence of diction as well as a comparison of context between the Akkadian and Ugaritic diction, on the one hand, and Hebrew diction, on the other. Body language is prominent in expressing the attitudes of gods and kings regarding their subjects.

When we examine the theme of protection conveyed by the verb *šāmar*, and that of well-being *(šālôm)*, we once again discover that the diction of the priestly benediction reflects a broad ancient Near Eastern rhetorical pattern, one that cuts across several types of textual and literary materials. A. Rainey (1968) has shown that Ugaritic epistolary salutations represent translations of standard Akkadian salutations. A comparison will demonstrate this relationship: the standard Ugaritic salutation *ilm tǵrk tšlmk* 'May the gods watch over you and bring you wellbeing' corresponds to the standard Akkadian salutation *ilānī ana šulmānī liṣṣurūka* 'May the gods protect you for well-being.'

Although idiomatic *śîm šālôm* 'grant well-being' is virtually unknown in biblical diction (possibly cf. Ps 147:14), we do find a similar idiom, once again in epistolary greetings. This time we are directed to one of the Achaemenid Aramaic letters of the fifth century B.C.E. This parallel was noted by J. Licht (1985: 97). The context of the Aramaic letter is highly significant: after thanking one who favored him with things he sorely needed, the author of the letter states, *wmnm [t]tm[tḥ] ṣlw kzy ʾlhyʾ šlm yśymw lk* 'And on our part, prayer will be offered, that the gods (or "god") grant you well-being' (Driver 1954: 35, letter XIII). Aramaic *šlm yśymw lk* parallels Hebrew *weyāśēm lekā šālôm.*

(2) The Biblical Background

It is probable that expressions of blessing drawn from social and official contexts, originally having no bearing on the cult, provided the discrete components of the fixed liturgical benedictions. These benedictions were most likely pronounced by priests and similar functionaries, both on an individual basis and within the public cult of the Jerusalem Temple during the late preexilic period. The tracing of the priestly benediction necessarily involves us, therefore, in an important determination regarding the development of liturgy in biblical Israel, one discussed at great length by M. Greenberg (1983), in a recent study of biblical prayer. Greenberg observes a progression from the less fixed formulas to the more fixed ones and, in the same vein, a progression from more general usage to more defined liturgical functions. It would be logical, therefore, to take note of the nonliturgical, often quotidian expressions of the very components of the priestly benediction.

In Ruth 2:4 we find an exceptional combination of greeting and response. Boaz greets the reapers, *YHWH ʿimmākem* 'YHWH be with you'. The reapers respond, *yebārekekā YHWH* 'May YHWH bless you!' (cf. Judg 6:12; 1 Sam 17:37; 20:13). We note, in a similar context, that when Joseph, disguised as he was, first beheld his younger brother, Benjamin, he greeted him with the words *ʾelôhîm yoḥnekā, benî* 'May God be kind to you, my son!' (Gen 43:29; cf. 2 Sam 12:22).

It is reasonable, therefore, to associate greetings and good wishes with the dicta of official liturgy in the realization that worshipers addressed God in ways similar to the way they addressed one another, and similar to the way they addressed kings and persons in authority, both orally and in writing. The name of God was on the lips of ordinary persons, and in the mouths of the highborn and powerful, as they went about their daily lives.

The formulaic and literary processes we are discussing were not, however, unidirectional. Normal forms of communication were surely influenced and stimulated by the formulas of liturgy. It would be inaccurate and misleading, however, to conclude that the language of blessings originated in the liturgy of the temple cult, and only then found its way into everyday conversation or into official writings and correspondence.

Our ability to reconstruct the actual text of the priestly benediction has been greatly enhanced by recent archaeological activity in the environs of Jerusalem, in an area now called Keteph Hinnom, near the Valley of Hinnom and adjacent to the Scottish Church of Saint Andrew. In the early spring of 1980, an expedition directed by G. Barkai discovered two small inscribed silver plaques, fashioned in the form of women's jewelry (Barkai 1989). They were found amid the large cache that filled a cavity within the burial caves at the site. These finds were dated by Barkai, on the basis of their archaeological context, to the late seventh century B.C.E., though others insist on a later date, in the early sixth century B.C.E. (Yardeni 1991). Inscribed on both of these plaques is a benediction, a text largely identical with the biblical, priestly benediction of Num 6:24–26. The inscriptions lack some of what appears in the biblical version, but what they actually preserve is almost verbatim.

When we add the evidence of these plaques to other epigraphic finds from such sites as Kuntillat ʿAjrud, on the southern route to Elath, dated to about 800 B.C.E., and to evidence from Khirbet el-Qom in southwestern Judah, and from Ain Gedi on the Dead Sea, we emerge with a considerable inventory of blessing formulas, utilized on an individual basis during the period of the First Temple and thereafter. This inventory is carefully cited and analyzed by J. Naveh (1981). Long before the discovery of the inscribed plaques from Keteph Hinnom, such scholars as G. B. Gray had dated the biblical benediction to the time of Josiah, near the end of the seventh century B.C.E., and had associated it with Josiah's efforts to reorganize the Judean priesthood.

The inscription on the smaller of the two plaques from Keteph Hinnom can be restored reliably to read as follows:

ybrk YHWH wyšmrk
y'r YHWH pnyw 'lyk
wyśm lk slwm

May YHWH bless and protect you;
May YHWH look favorably upon you,
And grant you well being

When compared with the version preserved in Numbers 6, we note the following differences, indicated by the bracketed words:

yebarekekā YHWH weyišmerekā
yā'ēr YHWH pānâw 'ēlêkā [wiyḥunnekā
yiśśā' YHWH pānâw 'ēlêkā]
weyāśēm lekā šālôm.

May YHWH bless [you] and protect you;
May YHWH look favorably upon you [and be kind to you;
May YHWH lift up his countenance toward you]
And may he grant you well-being.

The first question confronting the student of Torah literature is obvious: does the fuller scriptural version, with all of its acknowledged symmetry, represent the prototype underlying the inscription found at Keteph Hinnom, or is the scriptural version an expansion of shorter formulations, such as the one found at Keteph Hinnom?

In the Keteph Hinnom version, we note that the opening verb, *ybrk* (= *yebārēk*), lacks the object suffix, which produced *yebārekekā* 'May he bless *you*" in the biblical version. The simplest explanation is to assume haplography, the omission of the second *kaph* by scribal error; and indeed some have restored the Keteph Hinnom plaque to read *ybrk[k]*. After all, most biblical examples have the object suffix, and read *yebārekekā YHWH* (Ruth 2:4; Gen 27:10; Deut 14:24, 29; 15:10; Jer 31:23; Ps 128:5). And yet, one wonders if there was not a different syntax in use: *yqtl. . . . wyqtlk*, as we find at Kuntillat 'Ajrud: *[YHWH] ybrk wyšmrk wyhyh 'm 'd[n]y* 'May [YHWH] bless and protect you, and be "with" my lord!' (Meshel 1978).

Perhaps this syntax was utilized initially when the nominal or pronominal subject preceded the sequence of verbs, with the result that one verb followed immediately on the other. An anticipatory syntax operated, so that one object suffix did double duty, qualifying both verbs. We find such double duty elsewhere in biblical Hebrew. Thus, in Hos 6:1 we read *kî hûʾ ṭārap weyirpāʾēnû, yak weyaḥbešēnû* 'For he has torn apart, and will make *us* whole; he smote and will bind *us* up' (cf. Exod 13:13; 34:20 for similar phenomena).

Once this syntax became current, it may also have been utilized when the subject followed the first verb, thereby intervening between the first and second verbs. This possibility recommends against emending both the Keteph Hinnom and Kuntillat ʿAjrud versions just so as to have them agree with biblical syntax!

More significant, of course, are the apparent "omissions" in the Keteph Hinnom version of the benediction, as M. Haran (1989) would classify them. If we assume, as does Haran, that the inscriber of the Keteph Hinnom plaques had before him the version preserved in Numbers, we might postulate that the eye of the inscriber slipped from the first *ʾēlêkā* down past the second *ʾēlêkā* (from line 2 past line 3) and immediately proceeded to copy the line beginning with *weyāśēm*, omitting all that is bracketed in the citation presented above. It is Haran's view, however, that economy of space led the inscriber consciously to delete the bracketed words in preparing the talisman to be worn as jewelry. This explanation is, however, questionable.

It is distinctly possible, as recently proposed by H. Roesel (1986), that textually, the biblical version of the priestly benediction represents an expansion of the Keteph Hinnom version. Thematically, there is reason to assume such a development. The biblical benediction contains two primary verbs of reference: *bērēk* 'to bless' and *šāmar* 'to protect'. Each has its amplifications: the theme of *bērēk* is amplified first by *hēʾîr pānîm ʾel* 'to look with favor upon, be well disposed toward', and in the second instance by the verb *ḥānan* 'to be gracious, to be kind'. After all, these verbs uniformly connote the granting of material blessings and of blessings less material, perceived in various modes. As for the primary theme of *šāmar*, it is amplified, in the first instance, by *nāśāʾ pānîm ʾel* 'to show concern for', and, in the second instance, in the scriptural version, by *śîm šālôm l-* 'grant well being to'. These expansions are aspects of protection and safekeeping, expressed more positively than *šāmar*. In other words, each of the primary themes, only once amplified in the shorter version [(a) *bērēk* < > *hēʾîr pānîm ʾel*; (b) *šāmar* < > *śîm šālôm l-*] was amplified a second time in the expanded version, adding *ḥānan* to (a) and *nāśāʾ pānîm ʾel-* to (b). The result was a benediction that began and ended with the same words but had been expanded internally—"fattened," if you will. The two respective versions may be plotted as follows:

Keteph Hinnom

(1) a + b

(2) a^1

(3) b^1

Numbers

(1) a + b
(2) a^1 + [a^2
(3) b^2]
(4) b^1

Whereas no one questions the elegant symmetry of the biblical version or doubts its careful formulation, features that Haran and others have emphasized, the final form does not argue against the development and expansion outlined here. This type of expansion is precisely what may have occurred in the ongoing development of liturgy.

It is at this point that we ought to consider whether the priestly benediction is poetic in form or not. Haran disputes the views of G. B. Gray (Gray—ICC 71–72) and D. N. Freedman (1975), among others, who regard the priestly benediction as poetry. Haran fully accepts the hymnodic affinities of the benediction, whose diction inevitably draws us to the Psalter for comparison. He insists, nonetheless, that poetic parallelism is absent from the benediction, and he therefore objects to its classification as poetry, notwithstanding the ascending number of words in each successive line (3–5–7) and the ascending number of letters (15–20–25), yielding a total of 60 letters; and, according to Freedman, a similarly ascending syllable count.

Surely poetry can be composed in such ascending patterns. Semantically, the degree of synonymity or restatement that characterizes the benediction is almost tantamount to parallelism, as one would conclude from the brief charting of the shorter and longer versions of the benediction provided above.

So much for literary analysis. In terms of function, it becomes important to discuss the archaeological context of the Keteph Hinnom discoveries. In so doing, we may factor in the blessing formulas in evidence at Kuntillat ʿAjrud, Khirbet el-Qom, and ʿAin Gedi, as well as at other sites, analyzed by Naveh (1981). Two basic orientations are attested in such individualized utilizations of blessing formulas by local priests and functionaries: (a) formulas wherein the Deity is the syntactic object, such as brk X. *l-YHWH* 'So-and-so is recommended *(bārûk)* to YHWH for blessing' or *brkty ʾtkm lʾYHWH* (= *bēraktî ʾetkem-)* 'I have addressed a request for blessing to YHWH on your behalf'; (b) formulas wherein the Deity is the syntactic subject, such as the formula at Kuntillat ʿAjrud already cited: *[YHWH?] ybrk wyšmrk wyhyh ʿm ʾd[n]y* 'May [YHWH?] bless and protect you, and be "with" my lord'. This form is closest to the Keteph Hinnom orientation, and ultimately to the scriptural benediction as well.

We are warranted in assuming that at Kuntillat ʿAjrud and similar sites, as well as in the Jerusalem Temple, individuals could acquire such amulets as were found in Keteph Hinnom, or benedictions inscribed as graffiti, in return for donating votives. Who exactly manufactured such items of jewelry as the silver plaques of Keteph Hinnom is uncertain, but we would be close to the mark in saying that the priests had a hand in such commerce. Perhaps such items were sold exclusively to those who fulfilled particular religious duties, such as a pilgrimage that involved the donation of a votive. Was every participant blessed individually for his particular vows, as the medieval commentator Moses Ibn Ezra implied?

The discoveries at Keteph Hinnom raise questions that are even more complex. Assuming, as we must, that the priestly benediction, in one or another of its versions, served as a magical talisman, how did such items find their way into burial troves? It was a widespread ancient custom to bury valuable or useful possessions with the dead, on the notion that the deceased would require them or enjoy them in the afterlife, as biblical concepts would have it, in Sheol. The precise text of the benediction inscribed on the amulets, if we may call the plaques by that name, might indicate further that the benediction was interpreted as being particularly relevant to the dead, as expressing the wish that the dead be protected in death and on their way to Sheol. There was also the wish that the Deity would deal benevolently with the dead in the netherworld.

Two ingredients of the benediction point in this direction: there is, first of all, the term *šālôm,* and further, usage of the verb *šāmar* in suggestive contexts. Let us examine the verb *šāmar* first. The nexus of *šāmar* and *derek* 'way, voyage' is fairly obvious, because we normally worry more about being safe while journeying, or in unknown places (cf. Exod 23:20; Josh 24:17; Pss 91:11; 121:7–8; Job 33:11; Prov 2:8). God's protection on the way is guaranteed to his devoted ones *(ḥasîdîm).* Particularly relevant are statements in which protection is sought for the *nepeš* 'life, person, soul', because *nepeš* was also taken to refer to the deceased or to the afterlife of the soul (Pss 25:20; 34:21; 86:2; 97:11). Most interesting in this connection is 1 Sam 2:9:

> *raglê haṣîdâw yišmôr*
> *ûrešāʿîm baḥôšek yiddammû*

> He guards the footsteps of his devoted ones,
> But the wicked perish in darkness.

As for the theme of *šālôm,* it quite clearly expressed the situation hoped for in the afterlife. The blessed would "repose *(šākab)*" peacefully, in a state of "well-being *(bešālôm)*" after their death (1 Kgs 2:6; 2 Kgs 22:20; Jer 34:5).

We know that the later Jewish tradition explicitly associated the priestly benediction with the dead. Such interpretations are preserved in the Sifre, a tannaitic Midrash on Numbers and Deuteronomy. These interpretations once again focus on the theme of *šālôm* and on the notion of protection conveyed by the verb *šāmar.*

In the Sifre *(Sifre, Nāśō'*, par. 42) we read, "*Šālôm* is of great importance, for even the dead require *šālôm.*" In the same section of the Sifre *(Nāśō'*, par. 40), we find the following comments on the word *weyišmerekā* 'May he protect you': (a) "May he protect your *nepeš* at the time of death"; and (b) "May he protect your footsteps from Gehinnom." A medieval midrashic source, the *Yalqûṭ Shimeoni (Nāśō'*, par. 6, p. 125, line 14), offers the following comment: *weyišmerekā—lā'ôlām habbā'* 'May he protect you—for the world to come'. All of these are later, postbiblical comments, to be sure, but we should not dismiss the possibility, even the likelihood, that in biblical times the priestly benediction was also interpreted, at least on the popular level, as a talisman appropriate for the dead in burial, and that its dicta were understood accordingly.

The priestly benediction persisted in later Judaism, and is recited to this very day. Sir 50:20 records the daily pronouncement of the priestly benediction by the high priest in the Second Temple of Jerusalem in the following words: "Then he descended and raised his arms toward the entire assembly of Israel. And the benediction of the LORD *(birkat 'adônâi)* was on his lips; he pronounced words of praise in the name of the LORD." Not much later in the course of postexilic Jewish history, the legislators of Qumran (Licht 1965: 67; 1QS I, 2) required their priests to bless the entire community in the words of an interpretive version of the priestly benediction:

Yebārekekā—May he bless you—with every good thing.

Weyišmorkā—May he protect you—from every evil thing.

Weyā'îr libbekāh—May he enlighten your thoughts—with intelligence for living *(beśēkel ḥayîm)*.

Weyahonekāh—May he favor you—with everlasting knowledge.

Weyiśśā' penê ḥasādâw lekāh lišlôm 'ôlāmîm—May he show concern for you through his acts of kindness, for everlasting well-being.

The Mishna *(Tāmîd* 7:2) records that the priests who officiated daily in the Second Temple of Jerusalem pronounced the priestly benediction on the steps of the portico after having prostrated themselves inside the Temple hall. This passage of the Mishna also indicates that priests pronounced the benediction in synagogues, away from the Temple itself, thus documenting its early inclusion in synagogue liturgy.

The priestly legislation of the Torah, whenever it was originally authored, went into uninterrupted practice during the Persian period (538–ca. 330 B.C.E.) in the restored temple of Jerusalem. In priestly legislation it was Aaron, the first high priest, who pronounced the benediction at the consecration of the wilderness Tabernacle, as we learn from a statement in Lev 9:22. Since late antiquity, some have suggested that the benediction was originally recorded in the Torah immediately following Lev 9:22, but that it was subsequently shifted to the conclusion of Numbers 6; why, exactly, is not clear. Conceivably it was intended to serve as an introduction to the dedication of the Tabernacle altar, recorded in Numbers 7. In other words, the benediction was shifted from the conclusion of the Leviticus account of that dedication ceremony to a position immediately preceding the Numbers version of the same event!

For some, the alleged preexilic provenance of the inscriptions from Keteph Hinnom endorses the preexilic dating of the priestly source (P). Those who make this claim do not dispute that the benediction is quoted by the priestly author or compiler of Numbers 6, that it was a text known to him, not one initially composed by him. As such, its date, even if preexilic, cannot attest to the date of the document in which it is cited.

In conclusion, we are warranted in regarding the priestly benediction as multifunctional, surely in the exilic and postexilic periods. In its extraliturgical utilization, it may well have connoted the wish for well-being in the afterlife, as it did in later periods of Jewish religious experience.

PART IV.

NUMBERS 7: THE CONSECRATION OF THE TABERNACLE

INTRODUCTION: TRIBAL SPONSORSHIP OF THE TABERNACLE

Chapter 7 is primarily an administrative record, even though its subject matter is cultic. It lists the gifts tendered by the chieftains of the twelve tribes of Israel at the consecration of the Tabernacle. This event, recorded in Num 7:10–88, is termed *ḥanukkāh* 'dedication'. It signals the initiation of religious worship in biblical Israel, according to one priestly tradition.

The main body of Numbers 7 (vv 10–88) is composed in the form of an ancient Near Eastern temple account. The account is preceded by a brief introduction (vv 1–9) and is followed by a postscript, telling how God communicated with Moses in the Tabernacle (v 89).

Although Numbers 7 appears artificial and is highly repetitive, it can be reconstructed as a two-dimensional or tabular list, containing several columns. Listing uniform quantities and standard items was, in reality, a characteristic of ancient temple accounts, as it is of record-keeping generally. These features are discussed in the COMMENT, below, where the contents of Num 7:10–88 are charted in the format of an ancient temple record.

Numbers 7 dramatizes the participation of all twelve tribes of Israel in the dedication of the Tabernacle. No tribe could presume a greater role than any other, and every tribe had a role. In spirit, Numbers 7 recalls the statement characterizing the census taken at the initiation of the Tabernacle project: "The rich shall not pay more, and the poor shall not pay less" (Exod 30:15).

Numbers 7 is part of a larger group of priestly texts that record the Tabernacle project and the initiation of institutionalized worship in ancient Israel during the time of Moses. This chapter carries forward the chronology of Exodus 40 and of Numbers 1. It dates the events it records in the second year after the Exodus, though it is not entirely clear in which month of that year. The account is also linked to Leviticus 8, where the consecration of the Tabernacle and its vessels, as well as the consecration of the priesthood, are described as an integrated event. Together, Exodus 40 and Leviticus 8 provide background for the opening statements of the present chapter, which refer to the unction and consecration of the Tabernacle. Numbers 7 also presupposes the levitical assignments outlined in Numbers 3–4.

Gifts were first presented, some collectively and others individually, by the chieftains of the tribes, continuing over a period of twelve days. The gifts were presumably delivered to the Tabernacle in the wagons donated by the chieftains. These wagons, drawn by oxen, would subsequently be utilized for transporting the portable Tabernacle and its appurtenances. The tribal gifts consisted of silver bowls, basins filled with semolina flour *(sôlet)*, and gold ladles filled with incense. The chieftains also contributed large and small cattle for the regimen of altar sacrifices celebrating the dedication of the Tabernacle, a celebration that was, by all indications, quite elaborate. The order of the tribes begins with Judah, not with Reuben, and of course excludes Levi as a tribe. After all of the gifts are listed, they are totaled in the manner of an administrative account (Num 7:84–88).

Numbers 7 concludes with v 89, a cryptic statement telling how God and Moses communicated with each other in the Holy of Holies, within the Tent of Meeting.

TRANSLATION

7 [1]On the day Moses finished setting up the Tabernacle he anointed it, thereby consecrating it along with all of its vessels, the altar and all of its appurtenances. He anointed these, thereby consecrating them.

[2]The chieftains of Israel, heads of their patriarchal houses, made their presentations. They were the tribal chieftains, the ones in charge of the musters.

[3]They brought their offering in the presence of the YHWH, consisting of six transport wagons and twelve oxen; a wagon by every two chieftains, and one ox apiece. They presented these in front of the Tabernacle.

[4]YHWH then addressed Moses as follows:

[5]Accept [the offerings] from them, and they shall serve for maintaining the Tent of Meeting. Allot them to the Levites, to each [group] according to its maintenance tasks.

[6]Moses accepted the wagons and the oxen, and allotted them to the Levites.

[7]He allotted two of the wagons and four of the oxen to the Gershonites, in accordance with their maintenance tasks.

[8]He allotted four of the wagons and eight of the oxen to the Merarites, in accordance with their maintenance tasks, under the charge of Ithamar son of Aaron, the priest.

[9]He did not allot [wagons] to the Kohathites, for they were charged with maintaining the Shrine, and [customarily] carried their burdens on the shoulder.

[10]The chieftains presented their offering for the dedication of the altar on the day it was anointed. They presented their offering in front of the altar.

[11]YHWH then instructed Moses:

One chieftain a day, one chieftain a day, let them present their offering for the dedication of the altar.

[12]The one who presented his offering on the first day was Nahshon son of Amminadab, representing the tribe of Judah.

[13]His offering:

One silver bowl, its weight 130 shekels.

One silver basin, its weight 70 shekels, by the sanctuary weight.

Both of them were filled with semolina flour, mixed with oil, for grain offerings.

14 One gold ladle of 10 shekels, filled with incense.

15 One bull of the herd, one ram, and one yearling lamb, for burnt offerings.

16 One goat, for a sin offering.

17 For the sacred gifts of greeting:

oxen—2,
rams—5,
he-goats—5,
yearling lambs—5.

This was the offering of Nahshon son of Amminadab.

18 On the second day, Nethanel son of Zuar, chieftain of Issachar, presented his offering.

19 He presented as his offering:

One silver bowl, its weight 130 shekels.

One silver basin, its weight 70 shekels, by the sanctuary weight.

Both of them were filled with semolina flour, mixed with oil, for grain offerings.

20 One gold ladle of 10 shekels, filled with incense.

21 One bull of the herd, one ram, and one yearling lamb, for burnt offerings.

22 One goat, for a sin offering.

23 For the sacred gifts of greeting:

oxen—2,
rams—5,
he-goats—5,
yearling lambs—5.

This was the offering of Nethanel son of Zuar.

24 On the third day, chieftain of the Zebulunites, Eliab son of Helon.

25 His offering:

One silver bowl, its weight 130 shekels.

One silver basin, its weight 70 shekels, by the sanctuary weight.

Both of them were filled with semolina flour, mixed with oil, for grain offerings.

26 One gold ladle of 10 shekels, filled with incense.

27 One bull of the herd, one ram, and one yearling lamb, for burnt offerings.

28 One goat, for a sin offering.

29 For the sacred gifts of greeting:

oxen—2,
rams—5,
he-goats—5,
yearling lambs—5.

This was the offering of Eliab son of Helon.

30 On the fourth day, chieftain of the Reubenites, Elizur son of Shedeur.

31 His offering:
One silver bowl, its weight 130 shekels.
One silver basin, its weight 70 shekels, by the sanctuary weight.
Both of them were filled with semolina flour, mixed with oil, for grain offerings.
32 One gold ladle of 10 shekels, filled with incense.
33 One bull of the herd, one ram, and one yearling lamb, for burnt offerings.
34 One goat, for a sin offering.
35 For the sacred gifts of greeting:
oxen—2,
rams—5,
he-goats—5,
yearling lambs—5.
This was the offering of Elizur son of Shedeur.
36 On the fifth day, chieftain of the Simeonites, Shelumiel son of Zurishaddai.
37 His offering:
One silver bowl, its weight 130 shekels.
One silver basin, its weight 70 shekels, by the sanctuary weight.
Both of them were filled with semolina flour, mixed with oil, for grain offerings.
38 One gold ladle of 10 shekels, filled with incense.
39 One bull of the herd, one ram, and one yearling lamb, for burnt offerings.
40 One goat, for a sin offering.
41 For the sacred gifts of greeting:
oxen—2,
rams—5,
he-goats—5,
yearling lambs—5.
This was the offering of Shelumiel son of Zurishaddai.
42 On the sixth day, chieftain of the Gadites, Eliasaph son of Deuel.
43 His offering:
One silver bowl, its weight 130 shekels.
One silver basin, its weight 70 shekels, by the sanctuary weight.
Both of them were filled with semolina flour, mixed with oil, for grain offerings.
44 One gold ladle of 10 shekels, filled with incense.
45 One bull of the herd, one ram, and one yearling lamb, for burnt offerings.
46 One goat, for a sin offering.
47 For the sacred gifts of greeting:
oxen—2,
rams—5,
he-goats—5,

yearling lambs—5.
This was the offering of Eliasaph son of Deuel.
48On the seventh day, chieftain of the Ephraimites, Elishama son of Ammihud.
49His offering:
One silver bowl, its weight 130 shekels.
One silver basin, its weight 70 shekels, by the sanctuary weight.
Both of them were filled with semolina flour, mixed with oil, for grain offerings.
50One gold ladle of 10 shekels, filled with incense.
51One bull of the herd, one ram, and one yearling lamb, for burnt offerings.
52One goat, for a sin offering.
53For the sacred gifts of greeting:
oxen—2,
rams—5,
he-goats—5,
yearling lambs—5.
This was the offering of Elishama son of Ammihud.
54On the eighth day, chieftain of the Manassites, Gamaliel son of Pedahzur.
55His offering:
One silver bowl, its weight 130 shekels.
One silver basin, its weight 70 shekels, by the sanctuary weight.
Both of them were filled with semolina flour, mixed with oil, for grain offerings.
56One gold ladle of 10 shekels, filled with incense.
57One bull of the herd, one ram, and one yearling lamb, for burnt offerings.
58One goat, for a sin offering.
59For the sacred gifts of greeting:
oxen—2,
rams—5,
he-goats—5,
yearling lambs—5.
This was the offering of Gamaliel son of Pedahzur.
60On the ninth day, chieftain of the Benjaminites, Abidan son of Gideoni.
61His offering:
One silver bowl, its weight 130 shekels.
One silver basin, its weight 70 shekels, by the sanctuary weight.
Both of them were filled with semolina flour, mixed with oil, for grain offerings.
62One gold ladle of 10 shekels, filled with incense.
63One bull of the herd, one ram, and one yearling lamb, for burnt offerings.
64One goat, for a sin offering.
65For the sacred gifts of greeting:

oxen—2,
rams—5,
he-goats—5,
yearling lambs—5.
This was the offering of Abidan son of Gideoni.
66 On the tenth day, chieftain of the Danites, Ahiezer son of Ammishaddai.
67 His offering:
One silver bowl, its weight 130 shekels.
One silver basin, its weight 70 shekels, by the sanctuary weight.
Both of them were filled with semolina flour, mixed with oil, for grain offerings.
68 One gold ladle of 10 shekels, filled with incense.
69 One bull of the herd, one ram, and one yearling lamb, for burnt offerings.
70 One goat, for a sin offering.
71 For the sacred gifts of greeting:
oxen—2,
rams—5,
he-goats—5,
yearling lambs—5.
This was the offering of Ahiezer son of Ammishaddai.
72 On the eleventh day, chieftain of the Asherites, Pagiel son of Ochran.
73 His offering:
One silver bowl, its weight 130 shekels.
One silver basin, its weight 70 shekels, by the sanctuary weight.
Both of them were filled with semolina flour, mixed with oil, for grain offerings.
74 One gold ladle of 10 shekels, filled with incense.
75 One bull of the herd, one ram, and one yearling lamb, for burnt offerings.
76 One goat, for a sin offering.
77 For the sacred gifts of greeting:
oxen—2,
rams—5,
he-goats—5,
yearling lambs—5.
This was the offering of Pagiel son of Ochran.
78 On the twelfth day, chieftain of the Naphtalites, Ahira son of Enan.
79 His offering:
One silver bowl, its weight 130 shekels.
One silver basin, its weight 70 shekels, by the sanctuary weight.
Both of them were filled with semolina flour, mixed with oil, for grain offerings.
80 One gold ladle of 10 shekels, filled with incense.
81 One bull of the herd, one ram, and one yearling lamb, for burnt offerings.

82 One goat, for a sin offering.
83 For the sacred gifts of greeting:
oxen—2,
rams—5,
he-goats—5,
yearling lambs—5.
This was the offering of Ahira son of Enan.
84 This comprised the dedication offering of the altar, at the time of its anointing, as presented by the Israelite chieftains:
Silver bowls—12,
Silver basins—12,
Gold ladles—12.
85 Each bowl weighed 130 shekels, and each basin, 70 shekels. Total silver for the vessels: 2,400 shekels, by the sanctuary weight.
86 Gold ladles—12; filled with incense, at 10 shekels per ladle, by the sanctuary weight. Total gold for the ladles: [120 shekels].
87 Total livestock for burnt offerings:
12 oxen;
rams—12,
yearling lambs—12, with their grain offerings,
goats—12, for sin offerings;
88 Total livestock for the sacred gifts of greeting:
24 bulls;
rams—60,
he-goats—60,
yearling lambs—60.
Such was the dedication offering of the altar, subsequent to its anointing.
89 Whenever Moses entered the Tent of Meeting to speak with him, he heard the voice continuously speaking to him, from [the space] above the expiation lid, which covered the Ark of the Covenant, from between the two cherubs. [In this way] he spoke to him.

NOTES

7. 1. The opening verse recalls Exod 40:9–11 and Lev 8:10, both of which speak of the anointing of the Tabernacle. Textually, this recollection represents considerable distance, but chronologically, all of the activities described and prescribed in the Torah between Exodus 40 and Numbers 7 occurred within only a few weeks. Although no dates are given in the book of Leviticus for any events, the entire context of Leviticus belongs, as well, to the beginning of the wilderness period, according to the priestly chronology (see the NOTES on Num 9:1).

Sanctification by unction was a widespread practice in biblical Israel, as elsewhere in the ancient Near East. Unction served to confer status and was performed on kings, priests, and prophets. When oil was poured on objects, such as altars and stelae, it served to consecrate them as well (Liver 1968b). The verb *māšaḥ* is denominative of *mešaḥ* 'oil', a word best known in Aramaic (Ezra 6:9; 7:22).

2. *the ones in charge of the musters.* The pertinent social and political terms of reference employed in Numbers 7 have been explained in the NOTES on Num 1:2–5 and 16. The language of 7:2 recalls chap. 1 in other ways: characterizing the twelve chieftains as "the ones in charge of the musters," literally, "who stand over *(hāʿômedîm ʿal)* the musters," recalls Num 1:5, *ʾăšer yaʿamdû ʾitkem,* literally, "who shall stand with you." The Hebrew term *pequddîm,* translated "musters, arrays," is central to the entire system projected in the priestly descriptions of Numbers and has been explained in the NOTES on Num 1:3.

3. *transport wagons.* Whereas Hebrew *ʿagālāh* is a common word for "wagon" (1 Sam 6:7), Hebrew *ṣāb* is highly unusual, occurring elsewhere only in Isa 66:20, in the plural form, *ṣabbîm.* An Aramaic cognate occurs in the Targum to Isa 49:22, where enigmatic Hebrew *beḥôṣĕn* is rendered by Aramaic *beṣîbîn* 'in wagons', and in the Targum to Nah 2:8, where the incomprehensible Hebrew of the first part of the verse is rendered *wemalketāʾ yātebat ṣîbāʾ* 'and the queen is sitting on a wagon'. The Hebrew noun is also cognate with Akkadian *ṣumbu* 'wheel, wagon' (a form that itself developed from an earlier form, *ṣabbu*), a term for ceremonial wagons *(CADṢ,* 244, under *ṣumbu).* The combination *ʿeglôt ṣāb* is redundant and is best translated "transport wagons." The six wagons that were dedicated would henceforth be used to transport the portable Tabernacle and some of its appurtenances.

by every two chieftains. With a total of six wagons, each wagon would represent the shared gift of two chieftains. This is the sense of *ʿal šenê hannesîʾîm.* The various connotations of the Hebrew verb *hiqrîb* 'to present, donate, offer' are discussed in the NOTES on Num 8:9, where it is explained that this verb is not restricted in its usage to the presentation of sacrificial offerings.

5. Moses is instructed to "accept" (the imperative, *qaḥ* 'take') the gifts and then hand them over to the appropriate levitical groups for utilization in the performance of their tasks. The unusual construction *wehāyû laʿabôd* means "they shall serve for maintaining," reflecting the meaning of *ʿabôdāh* as "maintenance."

7. Moses allotted two wagons and four oxen to the Gershonites who, according to Num 3:25–26 and 4:21–28, were charged with transporting the tenting—its covers, drapes, and hangings.

8. Moses allotted four wagons and eight oxen to the Merarites, whose task was to transport the heavy equipment—poles, posts, and planks, according to

Num 3:36; 4:29–33. Ithamar, one of Aaron's sons, was in charge of two groups, the Gershonites and Merarites, according to Num 4:28 and 33.

9. We read in Num 3:31 and 4:1–15 that the Kohathites were charged with transporting the sacred appurtenances—the Ark, table, Menorah, altars, and sacred vessels. They received none of the donated wagons, because they carried the assigned objects on poles, held on the shoulder *(bakkātēp)*.

10–11. Logically, v 10 begins a new section of the chapter. Up to this point, the text has been speaking of wagons in which the donated offerings would be delivered to the Tabernacle initially, and which would normally be used thereafter to transport the Tabernacle. But there is an ambiguity in the wording of v 10, noted by Gray and others: the *qorbān* 'offering' of the *nesî'îm* included the wagons and oxen, to be sure, but these could hardly be characterized as "the dedication offering" *(ḥanukkāh)* of the Tabernacle! So v 10 is a textual link, doing double duty: it recapitulates what has preceded and anticipates what is to follow.

offering for the dedication. Hebrew *ḥanukkāh* (see below in vv 84, 88) more properly designates the offering of dedication, or the celebration of which the offerings were a part; it is not an abstract noun. The etymology of the verb *ḥānak* is uncertain. It is probably unrelated to the professional title *ḥānîk* 'trained soldier(?)' of Gen 14:14. It is that very noun, however, which produced the denominative verb *ḥānak* 'to train, educate', as in Prov 22:6: *ḥānôk lanna'ar* 'train the youth', also Late Hebrew *ḥinnēk* 'to educate' and nominal *ḥinnûk* 'education' (see CAD Ḫ 36, *under ḫanāku;* Albright 1942: 24, n. 87).

The present term, *ḥanukkāh,* connotes a variety of dedicatory acts, including pronouncing words of formal dedication, words that are lost to us. The verb *ḥānak* elsewhere occurs in 1 Kgs 8:63, characterizing the abundant sacrifices offered in dedication of the Solomonic temple (cf. 1 Chr 7:5–9; Neh 12:27). Psalm 20 bears the caption "a song for the dedication of the Temple *(mizmôr šîr ḥanukkat habbayît),*" but the psalm itself tells us little about the nature of dedication. In the laws of war in Deuteronomy 20, we read that one who had built a house but was unable to "dedicate" it (the verb *ḥānak*) before reporting to military duty should be allowed to return home, lest someone else consummate the project. This statement parallels the desacralizing of a vineyard and the consummation of a marriage, in the same series of Deuteronomic laws. The context suggests that *ḥanukkāh* is the term for a prerequisite celebration or ritual, performed before one could rightfully have use of what he had built or taken as his own.

In Num 7:3, 4, and 10 the place in which gifts were presented is variously listed as *lipnê YHWH* 'in the presence of YHWH', *lipnê hammiškān* 'in front of the Tabernacle', and *lipnê hammizbēaḥ* 'in front of the altar', namely, the altar of burnt offerings located in the courtyard facing the entrance of the Tent. There is probably no significance to these various designations of locale.

There is a further ambiguity, between vv 10 and 11, regarding the schedule of offerings, but this, too, is hardly significant. According to v 10, the chieftains presented their gifts on the day the Tabernacle was anointed, but in v 11 we read that each day thereafter, one of the *neśîʾîm* was to present his gift. Once again, we are mindful that v 10 both summarizes and anticipates, with the term *qorbān* 'offering' doing double duty. Adverbial *layyôm* means "each day" (Exod 29:38; Jer 37:21; Ezek 4:10), and its repetition conveys plurality.

their offering for the dedication of the altar. More significant, perhaps, is the fact that the celebration is termed *ḥanukkat hammizbēaḥ* 'the dedication offering of the altar'. This is probably an instance of *pars pro toto,* for the entire Tabernacle complex was being dedicated. Specifically, however, the gifts proffered by the chieftains over the twelve-day period were all intended for use in offering altar sacrifices—silver and gold vessels, animals for sacrifice, semolina flour mixed with oil and incense.

12. Verses 12–17 will be commented upon in considerable detail, and these NOTES will suffice for the eleven remaining sections. All twelve sections are virtually identical, except for the chieftain's name and tribal affiliation, of course, and except for minor differences in formulation. The names of the tribal chieftains have been explained in the NOTES on Num 1:5–15, where it is suggested, among other things, that Deuel, here appearing in v 47, should be read "Reuel."

The one who presented . . . was. Verse 12 begins in narrative fashion: *wayyehî hamaqrîb. . . .* Prefixed *heh* has relative force. In the entry for the second *nāśîʾ*, the formulation includes a verbal form: *bayyôm haššēnî hiqrîb* 'on the second day he offered'. From the third *nāśîʾ* onward, there are no verbal forms and no traces of narrative syntax, but simply an administrative record.

13. The first order of gifts, listed in v 13, consisted of a silver bowl *(qaʿarat kesep)* and a silver basin *(mizrāq ʾeḥād kesep)*, both filled with semolina flour. The singular form, *minḥāh,* has collective force.

silver bowl. The terms for the two types of bowls are difficult to identify precisely with archaeological finds, which are mostly ceramic, not metallic. Hebrew *qeʿārāh* should describe a vessel with a recession that was hollowed out (Num 4:7; Exod 25:29 ‖ 37:16). The verbal root *q-ʿ-r,* with a cognate in Arabic, means "to be deep." The anomalous form *šeqaʿarûrôt* 'sunken' in Lev 14:37 describes skin lesions, which may represent a Shafael formation of the same root (Kraemer 1966).

silver basin. Hebrew *mizrāq* designates a vessel for receiving blood or into which blood is dashed (1 Kgs 7:40, 45; Zech 9:15; 14:20). The Samaritan vocalization *mizrēq* would indicate that the vessel so named was used to dash blood on the altar, because that action is conveyed so frequently by the Hebrew verb *zāraq* (cf. Lev 1:4). The prophet Amos chides the rich northern Israelites of his time, who drink wine from *mizrāqîm* (Amos 6:6). Here these vessels do not contain liquids, and, in fact, there is no reference to libations in the list of dedication offerings.

The relative weights of these vessels are some indication of their function. In the next verse we read of a golden ladle *(kap)*, used as a censer, that weighed ten shekels. By the sanctuary weight, a shekel contained twenty grains, and it is calculated that a shekel weighed anywhere from 11.4 to 12.2 grams. This estimate is based on the known weight of *beqaʿ* as a half-shekel (Exod 38:26). Samples of the *beqaʿ* have been found by archaeologists, and they weigh 6.1 grams. In any event, the gold ladle weighed 114–122 grams. On this basis, the bowl of 130 shekels would have weighed about 1.5 kilograms, and the basin of 70 shekels more than .75 kilogram. These weights accommodate fairly large quantities (Scott 1959; E. Stern 1962).

14. *ladle.* Hebrew *kap* 'palm, hand' may signify a censer fashioned in that form. Many examples of ceramic censers have been found on biblical soil. 1 Kgs 17:12 refers to "a ladle full of flour *(melōʾ kap qemaḥ).*"

semolina flour. Hebrew *sôlet* means "semolina flour," which according to Lev 2:1 was required for grain offerings.

15. *ram.* Although Leviticus 1 does not specify the ram *(ʾayîl)* as a small animal suitable for the burnt offering, it is surprising just how often rams were used for this purpose. First of all, Balaam included rams in his burnt offerings (Num 23:2), and they were offered as burnt offerings in the Israelite cult on other occasions. According to Num 28:19, rams were offered on the first day of the Pesaḥ festival, and the same is true of some other festivals. Ezek 46:4–6 provides for burnt offerings consisting of rams on Sabbaths and New Moons, to be offered by the *nāśîʾ* of vision. There seems to be a function for rams in purificatory rites (Exod 29:15–18; Lev 9:2; 16:3–5; Num 6:14). What better testimony to the use of rams in burnt offerings than Isaiah's vehement statement, "I am sated with burnt offerings of rams *(ʿôlôt ʾêlîm)*" (Isa 1:11; see also Ezek 27:21; 39:18; 45:23; Ps 66:15; Job 42:8)?

16. *goat.* Goats were customarily used for the type of sin offering *(ḥaṭṭāʾt)* prescribed here (cf. Lev 4:23; 9:3). One may speculate about why goats were appropriate for sin offerings. On the basis of the rite of the scapegoat (Leviticus 16) and the reference in Lev 17:7 to the former practice of the Israelites in offering sacrifices to wilderness goats, it would appear that the wild goat was the symbol of the wilderness (Isa 13:21). The wilderness, in turn, was the domain of impurity, intimately associated with sinfulness. That is why the scapegoat was driven into the desert, never to return (Levine 1989b: 250–253).

17. The postscript reads *zeh qorban* X 'this was the offering of X', recapitulating what had been listed. More often, demonstrative *zeh* introduces what is to follow and appears in superscriptions. Thus Gen 5:1: *zeh sēper* 'This is the record of' (cf. Num 8:4; 28:3).

sacred gifts of greeting. The *šelāmîm* offering is explained in the Notes on

Num 6:7 (see also the NOTES on Num 15:8). It was appropriate for the dedication of the Tabernacle and was also offered at the dedication of the Solomonic Temple, as we are informed in 1 Kgs 8:63 (Levine 1974: 27–35, 45–46).

The system of numeration utilized in this entry (vv 12–17), and in each of the twelve entries to follow, is unusual and at the same time enlightening. This system may be analyzed as *item* + *numeral,* for instance, "oxen—2, rams —5," and so on. It is a feature of certain ancient records and accounts for which comparative evidence exists. This subject is addressed in the COMMENT on Numbers 7.

he-goats. Most of the designations of animals require no explanation. Hebrew *ʿattûdîm* designates mature goats and attests the Akkadian cognate *atūdu (CAD* A 2.521, under *atūdu).*

84–88. These verses provide the totals of all commodities donated by the *neśîʾîm.* In the COMMENT, below, these figures will be shown in graphic display, in the manner of an ancient record. The particle *kol* is here used technically, and means "total"; compare Josh 21:26, 39; Ezra 2:64 for similar usages of Hebrew *kol.* It parallels Akkadian *napḫāru,* Sumerian SU-NIGIN; PAB 'total'. Verse 87 mentions that the burnt offerings were accompanied by grain offerings, implying that the semolina mixed with oil was used in this way.

89. Chapter 7 concludes with a cryptic verse, intended to acknowledge the function of the Tabernacle as an oraculum. In Exod 25:22 we read that God would "meet" Moses in the inner chamber of the Tent and speak to him from the space above the *kappôret* 'the expiation lid'. We should also refer to Exod 33:6–11, a passage attributable to the Elohist, which emphasizes the function of the Tent of Meeting as an oraculum and makes no mention of its cultic function. How to deal with the differing traditions on the Tent, the Ark, and the cherubs is a problem discussed in the NOTES on Num 1:1. Suffice it to say that the priestly tradition, while laying great stress on cult and sacrifice, nevertheless endorses the oracular role of the Tent.

continuously speaking. The Hebrew form *middabbēr* represents the assimilated *hithpaʿel: mitdabbēr* < > *middabbēr* 'He continuously spoke'; compare the same form in 2 Sam 14:13; Ezek 1:2; 43:6. The Jewish tradition, represented by Rashi, explains this form as a tendentious repointing of the normal *piʿel* form, *medabbēr,* occasioned by the awesome fact that the speaker is God. But this is probably not the original intent. Targum Onkelos has *mitmallal,* an Aramaic *ithpaʿal* participle, having iterative force: "He spoke continually."

The Hebrew term *kappôret* refers to the function of the sculpted lid that covered the Ark (Exod 25:17–21). The Septuagint rendering *hilastērion* 'forgiveness seat' is accurate, and it is incorrect to translate *kappôret* as "lid" on the assumption that the verb *kippēr* means "to cover" (Levine 1982b).

cherubs. The God of Israel is pictured as "sitting astride the cherubs *(yôšēb hakkerûbîm)*" in any number of biblical depictions (1 Sam 4:4; 6:2; 1 Kgs 19:15; Isa 37:16; Ezek 9:3; 10:4). Hebrew *kerûb* designates both what we would call a mythological being and an iconographic object. The term *kerûb* is usually regarded as a cognate of Akkadian *karābu* 'to beseech, pray' *(CAD K,* 192–198). Akkadian also attests related forms, especially *kāribu,* feminine *karībtu,* terms designating a person or deity making a gesture of adoration or performing some religious act *(CAD K,* 216–217). The Hebrew form *kerûb* probably represents the active participial form *qāṭôl,* hence *kārôb* 'worshiper, adorer'. It indicates the function of the cherubs as worshipers of the Deity. The biblical *kerûbîm* have outstretched arms and, in some depictions, faces (Exod 25:20; 1 Kgs 6:25).

Ark of the Covenant. On the designation *ʾarôn hāʿēdût* see the NOTES on Num 1:50; 4:5.

The import of Num 7:89 is phenomenological. Moses would customarily hear God speaking to him from above the cherubs. The last words of the verse recapitulate what has been said: *wayyedabbēr ʾêlâw,* literally, "he (= God) spoke to him (= Moses)." This reading seems to accord with other priestly depictions of the process (Exod 25:22), though it is surely tempting to translate "he (= Moses) would [then] speak to him (= God)."

COMMENT: HOW TEMPLES KEPT RECORDS

Numbers 7 is a highly instructive source of information about the accounting methods employed by the priests of biblical temples and by representatives of other agencies operating within biblical society over an extended period of time. If actual records from biblical temples or from the royal archives of Judah and northern Israel had survived in meaningful quantities, as they have from Syro-Mesopotamian and Egyptian temples, we would know much more about the institutional provenance of the priestly writings of the Torah. But, possessing very little epigraphic evidence, we are compelled to rely on analytic methods in our effort to retrieve the original format of biblical texts such as Num 7:10–88 and to trace their progressive adaptation and reformulation to conform to the overall literary character of the Hebrew Bible. As a matter of fact, it emerges that Numbers 7 may be one of the *least* adapted records in the entire Bible!

If we were to plot the information presented in Num 7:12–88 as an actual record, we might end up with a tabular, or two-dimensional format, intended to be read both horizontally and vertically. It might have appeared as on page 260. This hypothetical reconstruction allows us to analyze several features of Num 7:12–88 in a clear manner and to compare them with fairly contemporary ancient Near Eastern records, preserved in several languages.

(yom) "day"	*(hammaqrib)* the offering prince	silver bowls 130šq@	silver basins 70šq@	golden ladles 10šq@	(herd animals) for burnt offerings			goats for sin-offerings	herd animals for the sacrifice of well-being				*(zeh qrôban)* "This is the offering of —"
		filled with fine flour		filled with incense	bull	ram	yearling lambs		bulls	rams	he-goats	yearing lambs	
I	Nahshon son of Amminadab of Judah	1	1	1	1	1	1	1	2	5	5	5	Nahshon son of Amminadab of Judah
II	Nethanel son of Zuar of Issachar	1	1	1	1	1	1	1	2	5	5	5	Nethanel son of Zuar of Issachar
III	Eliab son of Helon of Zebulun	1	1	1	1	1	1	1	2	5	5	5	Eliab son of Helon of Zebulun
IV	Elizur son of Shedeur of Reuben	1	1	1	1	1	1	1	2	5	5	5	Elizur son of Shedeur of Reuben
V	Shelumiel son of Zurishaddai of Simeon	1	1	1	1	1	1	1	2	5	5	5	Shelumiel son of Zurishaddai of Simeon
VI	Eliasaph son of Deuel of Gad	1	1	1	1	1	1	1	2	5	5	5	Eliasaph son of Deuel of Gad
VII	Elishama son of Ammihud of Ephraim	1	1	1	1	1	1	1	2	5	5	5	Elishama son of Ammihud of Ephraim
VIII	Gamaliel son of Pedahzur of Manasseh	1	1	1	1	1	1	1	2	5	5	5	Gamaliel son of Pedahzur of Manasseh
IX	Abidan son of Gideoni of Benjamin	1	1	1	1	1	1	1	2	5	5	5	Abidan son of Gideoni of Benjamin
X	Ahiezer son of Ammishaddai of Dan	1	1	1	1	1	1	1	2	5	5	5	Ahiezer son of Ammishaddai of Dan
XI	Pagiel son of Ochran of Asher	1	1	1	1	1	1	1	2	5	5	5	Pagiel son of Ochran of Asher
XII	Ahira son of Enan of Naphtali	1	1	1	1	1	1	1	2	5	5	5	Ahira son of Enan of Naphtali
	"total" *(kôl)*	12	12	12	12	12	12	12	24	60	60	60	"This was the dedication of the altar after it had been anointed."
		total silver: 2400 ŝq		total gold: 120 ŝq									

Figure 2.

In cuneiform tablets we often find lines for columns actually incised on the clay, with headings that provide various kinds of information: names of disbursing and receiving agencies and of individuals, commodities, dates, and quantities. In the same way, the consistent order in which items are listed for each of the twelve tribal chieftains in Numbers 7 suggests a similar format for the original. Two-dimensional records often show subtotals and totals for the columns tabulated.

The formulation of Num 7:12–88, in particular, shows very little narrative adaptation. Once we go beyond the introduction, we observe a progressive reduction in the utilization of clauses and encounter almost exclusive reliance on formulas. Thus, v 12 reads, *wayyehî hammaqrîb* 'The one who presented an offering . . . was', and in v 18 we find a rather abrupt verbal clause: *bayyôm haššēnî hiqrîb* 'On the second day . . . he offered'. From that point on, the entries are consistently formulaic: thus from vv 24–25 on we read, "On the third day: So-and-So, chieftain of the Such-and-Such tribe: X son of Y: His offering *(qorbānô)*." This formulation is extremely close, I surmise, to the archival headings that would originally have been found in the administrative record.

The system of numeration employed in Num 7:12–88 is perhaps the most revealing feature of all, because it directly links biblical records to known methods of ancient Near Eastern accounting. In Num 7:12–88 the sequence of numeration is (a) item, (b) numeral (quantity); for example: *bāqār—šenayîm* 'oxen—2'. There is hardly an exception to this sequence in this main section of chap. 7. In biblical texts quantities are usually registered differently, as follows: (a) numeral (quantity) (b) item; for example: *šibʿāh kebāśîm* 'seven lambs' (or the construct formation *šibʿat kebāśîm* 'seven of lambs'). See examples in Num 28:19; Lev 23:18.

It must be understood, of course, that we find two types of numerals in ancient records, and in records generally: ideographic numerals, namely, characters to be read as numerals (such as the roman characters I, X, or arabic 10, 30); and nonideographic numerals, namely, words (such as English "seven," "one thousand").

In ancient Near Eastern documents one observes two principal systems of numeration: in cuneiform records in Akkadian and Sumerian, ideographic numerals, when they are used, normally *precede* the items they quantify. By contrast, in Ugaritic, Aramaic, Phoenician, and epigraphic Hebrew lists and records, ideographic numerals, when they are employed, normally *follow* the items they quantify.

An informative example in Empire Aramaic, from Elephantine of the fifth century B.C.E., is the following citation from a papyrus, *AP* 22, which begins

> *b3 lmpḥtp šnt 5 znh šmht ḥylʾ yhwdyʾ zy yhb ksp lyhw ʾilhʾ lgbr l[g]br ksp š 2*

On the *3rd* of Phamenhotep, year 5. This is [a list] of the names of the Jewish military garrison, [everyone] who donated silver to Yahow, the God, man by man: silver, shekels, 2.

In this papyrus, the ideographic numerals are written as slanted or vertical markings (\////= 5; \//= 3, and so forth). As the list proceeds, name by name, we find entries such as the following: *mlkyh br ytwm br hddnr [kl]š 2 lh* 'Malkiyah, son of Yatom, son of Hadadnur. [Total]: shekels 2, of his'. This system applies only when ideographic numerals are used, not, of course, when numerals are written as words, as is normal in literary documents.

In the Arad inscriptions of the late seventh and early sixth centuries B.C.E. from that Negeb Judean garrison, we also find lists of commodities employing the sequence of numeration under discussion: (a) item (b) ideographic numeral, as is clearly the case with ostracon no. 11, in the collection published by Y. Aharoni (1981):

1. *ʾl ʾlyšb*
2. *wʿt ntn lktm*
3. *[ ] b 2 yyr*
4. *w[*
5. *m[n]ḥmyhw*

1. To Eliashib:
2. Now, then: Deliver to the Kittim
3. [ ] *bat* 2, of wine.
4. And[
5. From Nehemyahu.

On this ostracon hieratic ideographic numerals are used, but the sequence is the same. It is worth mentioning that the same western system is evident in the Linear B records from Mycenae, where we quite regularly find the sequence (a) item (b) ideographic numeral. It is not entirely clear why this is so in the proto-Greek documents, and what the implications of this correlation might be (Levine 1965a).

Now, there are no ideographic numerals evident in the Hebrew Bible; all numerals are written out in words. And yet, certain biblical records are formulated in such a way as to suggest that originally ideographic numerals had been subsequently replaced by words. This is most likely the case, as it turns out, in biblical lists, records, and even cultic prescriptions that employ the West Semitic system of numeration, as is true of Numbers 7.

In Josh 12:9–14 there is a list of city-states conquered during the Israelite settlement of Canaan. In all, thirty-one kings are listed, according to the following consistent formula: "King of X-city—one *(ʾeḥād)*; King of Y-city—one"; and so forth. The kings are unnamed, and the list concludes as follows: *kol melākîm šelôšîm weʾehād* 'Total kings: thirty-one'. Similarly, in Gen 46:15, after a list of the sons of Leah, we find a total expressed as follows: *kol nepeš bānâw ûbenôtâw—šelôšîm wešālôš* 'Total persons, his sons and his daughters: thirty-three'. Note also the total of the list of towns in the territory of Judah, in Josh 15:32: *kol ʿārîm ʿeśrîm wātēšaʿweḥaṣrêhem* 'Total towns: twenty-nine, and their ajacent plots' (cf. further Josh 18:28; 19:6–7, 15; 21:1, 6–7).

In Ezra and Chronicles, this system of numeration is particularly evident. Let us examine Ezra 1:9–11a as an example:

> Following is their quantity:
>
> Golden sashes—thirty;
>
> Silver sashes—one thousand;
>
> Suits of clothes—nine and twenty;
>
> Golden bowls—thirty;
>
> Silver bowls—four hundred ten;
>
> Other vessels of gold and silver: five thousand four hundred.

Similar calculations occur in Ezra 8:35 and in 1 Chr 6:46–48; 7:40.

When we encounter this system of numeration in cultic texts, as in Numbers 7 and in Num 28:11 and 29:13, 17 within the calendar of the public cult, it is reasonable to assume that priestly scribes employed an accounting method essentially identical to that used in other administrative agencies of biblical Israel, and that in all such instances the originals upon which the biblical texts were based had ideographic numerals, such as we have seen in West Semitic epigraphy.

It was A. F. Rainey (1970) who first explained that the administrative order of donations and disbursements, as set forth in records such as Numbers 7, did not normally correspond to the *operative* order followed in the actual performance of the cult. In the celebration of the cult, the *ḥaṭṭāʾt* 'sin offering' normally preceded the offering of other sacrifices in composite rites. The *ḥaṭṭāʾt* was, in a sense, a preparatory offering that had the effect of reinstating the worshiper in the eyes of God, in cases wherein the sacrifices had been occasioned by particular offenses. Usually the *ḥaṭṭāʾt* was also necessary for the preliminary purification of the Sanctuary, to assure that the Sanctuary had been tended properly, and was fit for sacrificial activity. The ḥaṭṭāʾt would most often be followed by the *ʿôlāh* 'burnt offering, holocaust', which functioned as an invocation, testing the readiness of the Deity to respond to the petitions of his worshipers. Only then would the *šelāmîm* 'sacred gifts of greeting' be offered. This sacrifice was shared by priests and worshipers and constituted a sacral meal, in the presence of God.

The order in which the donations are listed in Numbers 7 is administrative; it is the order suitable for keeping temple records. The list of donations, in each case, begins with the most costly items—bowls and vessels of gold and silver, filled with precious incense and finely ground semolina flour. The list then proceeds to record animals, first large and then small cattle, which had been donated for sacrifices, with the *ḥaṭṭā't* intervening between the *'ôlāh* and the *šelāmîm.* The organizing principle in administrative records would reflect the commodities listed—their size, generic character, and cost—and not the actual order of cultic performance.

It might be instructive to produce an example of a two-dimensional or tabular cuneiform record, so as to demonstrate just how closely Num 7:12–88 follows the Syro-Mesopotamian accounting system. For this purpose, a neo-Babylonian temple record from the reign of Nabonidus, the last king of Babylon, has been selected. It will be plotted only partially, but this sample will suffice for purposes of illustration (see fig. 3).

The final verse (v 89) of chap. 7 warrants special comment for its bearing on the several traditions regarding the functions of the Tabernacle, or Tent of Meeting *('ôhel mô'ēd).* Brief mention was made of these differing conceptions of the Tent in the NOTES. According to Exod 33:6–11, a nonpriestly source attributed to the Elohist, the Tent was to be pitched outside the encampment and was not to have any cultic function as the locus of sacrifice. It was to serve as an oraculum, where Moses would receive verbal communications from God: where he would "meet" with God. This is the etymology of *mô'ēd,* from the verbal root *y-'-d,* implied in the account of Exod 33:6–11.

Priestly writers occasionally recall this conception of the Tent. In Exod 25:22, in the midst of the detailed prescriptions for the construction of the Tabernacle, there is a statement on its oracular function quite similar to Num 7:89 (cf. also Exod 29:42–43; 30:6–36). The book of Leviticus opens with the statement that God called to Moses from the Tent of Meeting and communicated to him precise instructions on the proper manner of sacrificing. According to Leviticus 16, however, the high priest was to enter the Holy of Holies on the Day of Atonement for the sole purpose of seeking expiation for the Israelites. Although these rites included a confessional, pronounced by the high priest, there is no reference, in that context, to verbal communication from the Deity or to oracular inquiry.

Priestly writers often caption cultic prescriptions and descriptions with a statement to the effect that God directly communicated their contents to Moses, to Moses and Aaron, or to the Israelites generally. In such instances, the emphasis does not seem to be on the locus of these divine communications, but on the specificity of their content. When, as in v 89, reference is made to the oracular role of the Tent, we observe an effort to reconcile the

Bulls	Full-grown cows	3-year-old oxen	3-year-old cows	2-year-old oxen	2-year-old cows	Young steers	Young cows	Total oxen	Inventory *(amirtum)* of temple gods of Ištar and Nanâ
10, of which 5 pure	37	13, of which 6 pure	10	12, of which 6 pure	10	8, of which 4 pure	10	Total 110	Innina-šarru-uṣur son of Nergal-ušallim
[1]6, of which x pure	270	17, of which 15 pure	43	48, of which 40 pure	62	70, of which 56 pure	81	Total 607	of Nanâ-êreš, son of Marduk-erîba, on behalf of Iqîša, his son; 9 bulls, 3 3-year-old oxen for the tax *(ṣibtu)*
. . .]	85	5, of which 3 pure	12	7, of which 5 pure	18	13, of which 7 pure	25	165	Manna-ki-Dada, son of Nabû-zabada
. . .	. . .]	3	14	9, of which 6 pure	12	24, of which 18 pure	26	183	Nabû-mušêtiq-urri, son of Balâṭsu
. . .	. . .	. . .]	12	9, of which 6 pure	19	30, of which 23 pure	20 [+x]	194	Innina-zêru-ušabšu, son of Bal'āṭsu, on behalf of Rêmût and his brother
. . .	. . .	. . .	. . .]	3, of which 1 pure	5	9, of which 3 pure	5	60	Ibnî-Ištar, son of Šumu-ukîn

13th day of Kislîmu, 9th year of Nabû-na'îd, King of Babylon

Figure 3. A Neo-Babylonian Two-Dimensional Temple Record. *Yale Babylonian Texts* VI, 130, dated: 547/6 B.C.E. Translated and adapted from M. San Nicolò, "Materialen zur Viehwirtschaft in den neübabylonischen Tempeln, II," *Orientalia* 18, 1949, 304–305.

two traditions regarding the function of the Tent of Meeting, the oracular and the cultic.

The noticeable shift in emphasis from the oracular to the cultic in characterizing the function of the Tent of Meeting may reflect the growing importance of the Israelite priesthood. Priests replaced prophets in the postexilic period. Divine verbal communication had been a feature of prophecy, not forgotten in priestly projections of the Mosaic period, but hardly functional in the later priesthood. The priesthood utilized oracular methods of a different sort, some of great antiquity. For the most part, the divine will and disposition were communicated through the act of sacrifice and through rites of purification. The divine response was silent, but assuredly effective.

PART V.

NUMBERS 8: THE DEDICATION OF THE LEVITES

♦

INTRODUCTION

Numbers 8 is best understood against the background of the first four chapters of Numbers. In chaps. 1–4 the plan of the Israelite encampment was presented, and the assignment of the several levitical clans to maintenance tasks associated with the Tabernacle was set forth in detail. Once the Tabernacle and its altar were dedicated, an event recorded in chap. 7, it was logical to provide a record of the devotion of the Levites to sanctuary service. Chapter 8 opens, however, with brief instructions addressed to Aaron on the mounting of the lamps *(nerot)* atop the branches of the Tabernacle Menorah. Once the Tabernacle became functional, the Menorah also went into use (Num 8:1–4).

Just as the Aaronide priesthood had been consecrated, as reported in Leviticus 8–9, so were the Levites to be initiated as cultic servitors. Numbers 8 conveys the special role of the Levites in the priestly traditions of Numbers, where the distinction between Aaronide Levites, who are priests, and the rest of the tribe of Levi, who are *not* priests, is most clearly drawn (Num 8:5–23). The chapter concludes with a statement defining the period of levitical service as from twenty-five to fifty years of age (Num 8:24–26).

TRANSLATION

8 1 YHWH spoke to Moses as follows:

2 Speak to Aaron and say to him: When you mount the lamps, let the seven lamps cast light toward the [area] in front of the lampstand.

3 Aaron did accordingly. He mounted its lamps toward the [area] in front of the lampstand, as YHWH commanded Moses.

4 Such was the manufacture of the lampstand: it was made of hammered gold; it was hammered from its base to its petal. In accordance with the depiction that YHWH had shown Moses, just so did he fashion the lampstand.

5 YHWH spoke to Moses as follows:

6 Separate the Levites from among the Israelite people, and purify them.

7 This is what you must do to them in order to purify them: sprinkle on them water of purification. They shall pass a razor over their entire body, launder their garments, and thereby become pure.

8 They must secure a bull of the herd, with its [accompanying] grain offering, to consist of semolina flour mixed with oil. You shall secure a second bull of the herd for a sin offering.

9 Bring the Levites near the front of the Tent of Meeting, and then assemble the entire community of Israelites.

10 Bring the Levites into the presence of YHWH. Then have the Israelites lay their hands on the Levites.

11 Aaron shall make a presentation offering of the Levites in the presence of

YHWH on behalf of the Israelites, that they may serve by doing YHWH's work.

12The Levites, in turn, shall lay their hands on the heads of the bulls, assigning one as a sin offering and the other as a burnt offering to serve as redemption for the Levites.

13You shall station the Levites in front of Aaron and in front of his sons, and make of them a presentation offering to YHWH.

14You shall separate the Levites from among the Israelites; the Levites shall belong to me!

15Afterward, the Levites shall arrive, and perform the tasks of the Tent meeting; after you have purified them and made a presentation offering of them.

16For they are to be completely dedicated to me, from among the Israelites, in place of the first issue of every womb; [in place] of every firstborn of the Israelites have I selected them for myself.

17For every firstborn within the Israelite people belongs to me, both man and beast. At the time I slew every firstborn in the land of Egypt, I declared them dedicated to me.

18I have appropriated the Levites in place of every firstborn within the Israelite people.

19I have delegated the Levites to be assigned to Aaron and to his sons from among the Israelite people, to perform the tasks of the Tent of Meeting and to serve as redemption for the Israelite people, so that no plague may afflict the Israelite people as a result of Israelites' approaching the Sanctuary.

20Moses and Aaron, with the entire community of the Israelites, carried out with respect to the Levites everything that YHWH had commanded Moses regarding the Levites; just so did the Israelites do to them.

21The Levites purified themselves, laundering their garments. Moses then made of them a presentation offering in the presence of YHWH, with Aaron performing rites of expiation on their behalf so as to purify them.

22Afterward the Levites arrived to perform their tasks at the Tent of Meeting, under Aaron and under his sons. They did to them just as YHWH had commanded Moses regarding the Levites.

23YHWH spoke to Moses as follows:

24This is what applies to the Levites: everyone twenty-five years and older must serve in the work force, performing the tasks of the Tent of Meeting.

25All those fifty years of age and older may retire from the work force, and need not serve any longer.

26The Levites shall then assist their kinsmen at the Tent of Meeting, performing various duties, but no longer serving on the work force. That is how you shall assign the Levites with respect to their duties.

NOTES TO 8:1–4: THE TABERNACLE MENORAH

8 2. The basic features of the Tabernacle Menorah are set forth in Exod 25:31–40, and repeated, with minor variations, in Exod 37:17–24. The present statement concerning the lamps more closely parallels that of Exod 25:37. The specific object of the instructions was to ascertain that the seven Menorah lamps would cast their light in a certain direction, over a particular area.

The instructions are addressed to Aaron, the priest, as he is the one charged with mounting the Menorah lamps. Hebrew *behaʿalôtekā* means "When you *mount, set up*" and not "When you *kindle,*" as Rashi concluded. Admittedly, *hiphʿil heʿelāh* is ambiguous; in Exod 27:20 and Lev 24:2, for example, the sense is "to kindle," whereas in Exod 25:37 and 40:25, as well as in this verse, the sense is to place the lamps *(nerot)* atop the branches of the Menorah.

The Tabernacle Menorah consisted of a central upright shaft, termed *qāneh* 'stem', a botanical term. The central shaft rested on a base called *yārēk* 'thigh', an anatomical term! Fanning out on either side of the central *qāneh* were three branches, also called *qānîm,* the plural of *qāneh.*

toward the area in front of the lampstand. The Hebrew term *menôrāh* is itself ambiguous. It is difficult to ascertain, in certain statements, whether it refers only to the base and central shaft of the lampstand, or to the entire artifact with its six additional branches. This ambiguity comes to the fore in the phrase *ʾel mûl penê hammenôrāh,* which has been translated "toward the [area] in front of the lampstand." In the parallel passage (Exod 25:37), the wording is *ʾel ʿēber pānêhā* 'across the [area] facing its front'. If we assume that the two statements are synonymous, then the intent was that the seven lamps would light the area in front of the Menorah.

Those who have concluded that the seven lamps were to face the central shaft (perhaps because they understood the term *menôrāh* in Num 8:2 to designate only the base and central shaft of the lampstand) were on the wrong track, it seems, because, graphically, how could all seven *nerot* shine toward the center? Only six of them could do so!

The precise meaning of idiomatic *ʾel mûl penê-* is established by its usage elsewhere. Thus, we read that two gold cords were affixed to the priestly garment, the *ʾēpôd,* "on its front side *(ʾel mûl pānâw),*" in contrast to the two gold rings attached to the breastplate of the high priest "facing the *ʾēpôd* inward *(ʾel ʿēber hāʾēpôd hāytāh),*" according to Exod 28:25–26 and Exod 39:18–20 (cf. also usage in Exod 28:37; 39:31). In Ezek 1:9–12, we read that the beasts of Ezekiel's vision moved each *ʾel ʿēber pānâw* 'in the direction of its front', without turning as they moved. This text establishes the sense of v 2: the lamps were intended to shed light in front of the Menorah.

According to Exod 26:35 and 40:24 the Menorah stood at the southern side of the first chamber of the Tent, across from the table for the bread of display, which stood at the northern side of the chamber. To the east was the *pārôket* curtain, covering the entrance to the Holy of Holies. According to certain depictions, the golden incense altar stood in the center of this chamber (Exod 30:1–10; 39:38).

Aaron was to insert each of the seven *nerot* into the *gābîʿa* 'bowl' at the top of the stems. A wick and some oil would be put into each lamp and kindled. Many such lamps have been uncovered in archaeological excavations.

The Hebrew term *menôrāh* from the root *n-w-r* 'to shine, blaze' attests a cognate, *mnhrt* in Minaean, South Arabic (Meyers 1976: 46, n. 16).

3. The formula *kaʾašer ṣiwwāh YHWH ʾet Môšeh* 'as YHWH commanded Moses' confirms compliance and is characteristic of the formulation of priestly law and ritual (see the NOTES on Num 1:19). It stresses two related ideas basic to the priestly ideology: not only were all of the details of law and ritual directly communicated by God to Moses, but they were promptly carried out by Moses and the Israelites of his time.

4. The Menorah was made of hammered gold sheet, as was also true of the trumpets whose manufacture is prescribed in Num 10:2. Meyers has studied the graphics of the Tabernacle Menorah in depth. She concludes that a wooden model was utilized and that gold sheet, which was thicker than gold leaf, was formed over the model in the desired shape. This process contrasted with the use of a mold in sculpture. By that process, a mold was fashioned, and melted gold was poured into it.

Gold is a highly malleable metal, suitable for hammering and rubbing. The term *miqšāh* remains somewhat elusive, but inevitably involves use of a hard instrument, such as a hammer. This verse emphasizes that the entire *menôrāh* (whether by this is meant the entire artifact with its branches, or only the central lampstand) was hammered from a single sheet of gold, stated here as "from the base *(yārek)* to the petal *(peraḥ)*," which was a floral component of the *gābîʿa* 'bowl'.

The "depiction, view" (Hebrew *marʾeh)* of the Menorah had been shown to Moses, just as in Exod 25:39 we read that the "model *(tabnît)*" of the entire Tabernacle had been shown to him. Whereas Hebrew *marʾeh* connotes a picture or drawing, *tabnît*, from the verbal root *b-n-h*, may well connote a model, something actually constructed. This meaning is further suggested by the abundant artifactual evidence, from tombs and temples, of votive models or miniatures of edifices and objects of cultic function.

NOTES TO 8:5–26: THE LEVITES AS TABERNACLE SERVITORS

A comparison of the present description of the dedication of the Levites with the consecration of the Aaronide priests, recounted in Leviticus 8–9, may serve to pinpoint significant differences between the two groups. The Levites were to serve under the priests, performing maintenance and support functions, but they were not consecrated as officiants in the sacrificial cult. The levitical assignments are outlined in Numbers 3–4. In Numbers 18 we find information on the income to which the Levites were entitled and on their obligations to the priests. The Aaronide priests were consecrated, a concept conveyed by the verb *qiddēš*, and they donned sacral vestments and distinctive insignia. A mixture of sacrificial blood and oil was dashed on them, and Aaron himself was anointed with pure oil. The priests bathed their entire bodies. In Leviticus 8, such consecration is referred to as *millûʾîm* 'appointment' to a prestigious office. The Levites, by contrast, were "purified," a process conveyed by the verb *ṭihhēr*, and "dedicated," an act expressed by the verb *nātan*. They are presented as an offering to God, and both the verb *nātan* and the characterization of the Levites as *tenûpāh* 'presentation offering' imply submission. The Levites were handed over to the Deity in substitution for the firstborn of the Israelites, spared by God when he smote the firstborn of Egypt.

In full view of the Israelite community, the Levites were presented to the God of Israel. Representatives of the community laid their hands upon them, and in turn the Levites placed their hands on the sacrifices that they had donated in celebration of their dedication as Tabernacle servants. The sequence of sacrifices, beginning with a sin offering *(ḥaṭṭāʾt)* and continuing with a burnt offering *(ʿôlāh)*, is significant. The *ḥaṭṭāʾt* served to remove impurity and made the Levites ready for their presentation to God. Then the *ʿôlāh* served as the first act of worship by the purified Levites, a test of God's acceptance of them in their new role. The same sequence is observable in the ceremonies of the priestly investiture, as recorded in Lev 8:14–21, as well as in the purification of the Sanctuary, as prescribed in Lev 16:3.

In contrast to the Aaronide priests, the Levites donned no special vestments. Special water was sprinkled on them, but not sacrificial blood or oil. The Levites had to meet certain purificatory requirements, however. They were to launder their clothing and shave off their body hair. In these respects, their purification resembles what would be undertaken by a person undergoing purification from disease, according to the provisions of Leviticus 13–14. We may also draw a comparison with the duty of the Nazirite to shave his head at the conclusion of the period of his vow (see the NOTES on Num 6:9, 18).

6. *Separate . . . from among.* This meaning of the Hebrew idiom *qaḥ . . . mittôk* is suggested by the parallel statement in v 14, below: *wehibdaltā . . . mittôk* 'You shall separate . . . from among'.

purify. The verb *ṭihhēr* 'to purify', used to characterize procedures that were part of the levitical dedication, is highly significant. One normally purifies someone or something that was impure to start with. Thus the Sanctuary required purification because it would be defiled by the impurities of the Israelites (Lev 16:19, 30). A diseased person also required purification, a fact that further links this chapter to the rites prescribed for the treatment of disease in Leviticus 13–14.

At no point is the verb *ṭihhēr* employed in describing the investiture of the Aaronide priests, in Leviticus 8–9; though, to be sure, purification was essential for the soon-to-be priests. But such procedures are not conveyed by the verb *ṭihhēr.* The implications of this distinction will be explored in the COMMENT that follows. For now, it suffices to point out that it is the conception of the Levites as an offering presented to God that holds the key to their purification.

7. *water of purification.* Three acts were involved in purifying the Levites: laundering their clothing, shaving their body hair, and sprinkling special water on their persons. Laundering and shaving are hardly exceptional procedures in purificatory rites (cf. Lev 14:8–9; Numbers 19). It remains, however, to explain the precise function of water in the present process, a function expressed in the unique term *mê ḥaṭṭāʾt,* translated "water of purification." It is unlikely that the term *ḥaṭṭāʾt* refers here to a sin offering, in the usual sense, because no water is directly associated with such sacrifices. Some commentators, medieval and modern (thus Gray—ICC, for instance) have identified *mê ḥaṭṭāʾt* with *mê niddāh* 'water of lustration, of sprinkling', which occurs in Num 19:9, 13, 20 and 31:23. This identification is improbable, as is explained in the NOTES on Num 19:9.

The verbal form *wehiṭṭehhārû* represents the *hithpaʿel* stem, in a pausal position. The unassimilated form *hitṭahhārû* became *hiṭṭahhārû* by assimilation of the first *tau* to *ṭet*. In turn, the pausal position produced *hiṭṭehhārû.* The *hithpaʿel* of *ṭ-h-r* is employed quite frequently in ritual contexts (cf. Gen 35:2; Lev 14:19, 28; Isa 66:17; Neh 13:22).

Although *mê ḥaṭṭāʾt* is probably not to be identified with *mê niddāh* of Numbers 19, it is in Num 19:9 that we find a usage of *ḥaṭṭāʾt* that approaches its sense here. Thus *ḥaṭṭāʾt hîʾ* 'It is a [virtual] sin offering' of Num 19:9 means that the water of lustration, mixed with the ash of the red cow used there to purify those contaminated by contact with a corpse, *resembles* a sin offering because it, too, serves to purify! Literally, the sense of *mê ḥaṭṭāʾt* is "Water for the removal of impurity, sinfulness." Perhaps we should vocalize consonantal *ḥ-ṭ-ʾ-t* as *ḥaṭṭôʾt*, an infinitival form: "purifying, expiating," hence "water for purifying." The form *hazzēh* represents the *hiphʿil* imperative of *n-z-h* 'to spatter', hence "to sprinkle." The rare *qal* form of this verb occurs in Lev 6:20.

8. Two bulls were provided, one for the sin offering and the other for the burnt offering. The sin offering *(ḥaṭṭāʾt)* was accompanied by a grain offering *(minḥāh)*. The character of the burnt offering in biblical ritual was clarified in the NOTES on Num 6:14 and that of the grain offering in the NOTES on Num 4:16. Because this is the first occurrence of the term *ḥaṭṭāʾt* 'sin offering' in Numbers, it would be best to discuss its meaning and functions here. The force of the *piʿel ḥiṭṭēʾ* is to undo or remove the effects of the action conveyed by the simple stem *ḥāṭāʾ* 'to commit an offense, to sin'. Literally, the term *ḥaṭṭāʾt* designates an offering or ritual aimed at redressing an offense against God, and this process usually involved purification and expiation.

In Leviticus 4–5, two principal types of sin offerings are prescribed. There is, first of all, the *ḥaṭṭāʾt* offered on behalf of the entire community or on behalf of its leader, the high priest. An example would be the *ḥaṭṭāʾt* included in the rites of Yom Kippur (Leviticus 16). This type of sin offering involved special blood rites and shared certain features with riddance rituals, such as those prescribed in Numbers 19. The entire victim was destroyed (Lev 4:1–21). The second type of sin offering served various functions. In addition to securing expiation, it also compensated the priesthood for its services on behalf of transgressing Israelites. This secondary function is intimated in Hosea's condemnation of the priests of his own day: "They feed on my people's sin offerings, and so they desire its iniquity." In other words, the priests secretly wished that the people would sin excessively, so as to increase their own revenue (Lev 4:22–5:13)!

It was often the case that a grain offering accompanied other more substantial sacrifices. Compare the provisions of Num 28:1–7 for its use in the public cult.

9. *Bring . . . near.* The verb *hiqrîb* is ambiguous, because its basic sense of "bringing near" can describe various acts involved in consecration and worship. In Lev 1:13, for instance, *wehiqrîb* means "he brought near," namely, he presented the Aaronide priests before God on the occasion of their consecration. In fact, Num 8:9–10 prescribe two sequential stages of a process: first the Levites were brought to an area near the entrance of the Tent of Meeting; then, once the Israelite community had been assembled, the Levites were brought even closer, into the presence of YHWH. In spatial terms, they came even closer than they had been to the entrance of the Tent of Meeting. At that point, representatives of the people placed their hands on the Levites.

10. *lay their hands on.* The symbolic act of "laying on of hands," conveyed by the verb *sāmak* 'to lean on, place upon', is a pervasive feature of cultic and juridical activity. Essentially it served to assign a particular sacrifice for use in a specific rite. Thus the donor of a burnt offering assigned his sacrifice in this

way, according to Lev 1:4. Below, in v 12, we read that the Levites themselves placed their hands upon the sacrifices to be offered in celebration of their own devotion.

In a juridical context, we read that Moses designated Joshua as his successor by placing his hands upon him (Num 27:18–23; Deut 34:9). In still another passage, we read that members of the Israelite community laid their hands upon a person convicted of blasphemy, thereby consigning him to execution (Lev 23:10–16). Hittite rituals evidence widespread utilization of the symbolic laying on of hands (Wright 1986).

Because the Levites constituted a veritable offering to God, it was appropriate to assign them to Tabernacle service by means of the laying on of hands. We must assume, of course, that representatives of the Israelite community performed this symbolic act, because it would have been practically impossible for the entire people to do so. In the same way, the statement in Exod 12:6 that the entire Israelite community slaughtered the paschal sacrifice must be understood to mean that representatives of the community did so, as was recognized by the Sages of the *Mekhilta'* (Lauterbach 1976: 40, to *Bô'*, par. 5). Presumably representation would involve the chieftains, who were often heads of the patriarchal houses.

11. *presentation offering*. This verse, and the several that follow, define the dedication of the Levites as an act similar in its effect to the *tenûpāh* 'presentation offering'. The verb *hēnîp* means "to raise," and this mode of presentation is described in the Mishna *(Menāḥôt* 5:6). The offering was not "waved," as many have explained it, but was rather carried to and fro, while being held high, in order to display the offering before the Deity (see the NOTES on Num 5:25; and cf. Num 18:11, 18; Milgrom 1972). Usage here is more figurative than literal. Referring to the Levites as a *tenûpāh* merely meant that they were being presented to God as an offering, *mē'ēt benê Yiśrā'ēl* 'on behalf of the Israelite people'.

that they may serve by doing YHWH's work. The syntax of the final clause of v 11, *wehayu la'abôd 'et 'abôdat YHWH*, is unusual. The precise sense of *'abôdāh* 'work', and of the cognate construction *la'abôd 'abôdāh* 'to perform work', as used here, is explained in the NOTES on Num 4:23. The term *'abôdāh* characteristically designates the functions of the Levites, as set forth in Numbers. It must be emphasized that the Levites did not officiate, a function often attendant on the verb *'ābad*, but merely "served" in other capacities.

12. *assigning*. The Levites assigned the two primary sacrifices celebrating their dedication. The key verb here is *'āśāh* 'to make of', which in the context of sacrificial rites often has the functional meaning "to assign, designate." Compare its usage in Lev 16:9: *we'āśāhû ḥaṭṭā't 'he assigned it* as a sin offering'. It was necessary to stipulate that the victim was reserved for a specific offering.

to serve as redemption for the Levites. The clause *lekappēr 'al hallewiyyîm* requires special comment, because the verb *kippēr* most often describes expiatory rites involving the use of sacrificial blood (see the NOTES on Num 6:11). We might attribute usage of the verb *kippēr* in this verse to the overall looseness of terminology characteristic of chap. 8 (see below, in the NOTES on v 21). Quite possibly *kippēr* merely connotes some manner of purification in this instance. And yet another idea may be operative here: In certain contexts *lekappēr ʿal* represents the more complete formula *lekappēr ʿal nepeš* 'to serve as ransom for a life' (Exod 30:15; Lev 17:11). In such cases the *piʿel* form, *kippēr*, does not mean "to expiate" directly, but is denominative of *kôper* 'ransom' and means, literally, "to serve as *kôper*, ransom." This is the sense of *lekappēr ʿālâw* in Lev 1:4: "to serve as *redemption* for him," namely, for the person who has donated a burnt offering, having placed his hand upon it.

Here, too, it is best to understand the statement in question as conveying the notion that proper assignment of the burnt offering by the Levites served to "redeem" them, or to protect them, if you will, from God's wrath. Anyone standing in close proximity to the Deity was in danger of incurring God's wrath, regardless of whether he had committed an actual offense. God's acceptance of the burnt offering signaled his acceptance of the Levites' devotion. This interpretation is virtually explicit in v 19, below, which speaks of the role of the Levites themselves. Their dedication to cultic service would serve to avert the plague of God's wrath. This was also the rationale given for the payment of half a shekel to finance the building of the Tabernacle by each male Israelite on the occasion of a census, according to Exod 30:12–16.

In summary, the *ʿôlāh*, as part of the rites of Numbers 8, tested God's disposition. If God accepted it, he was pleased by the dedication of the Levites; they were protected from divine wrath. This attitude contrasts sharply with God's displeasure at the Qorahites on another occasion. Not only was their offering rejected, but they were struck down by God's wrath, as we read in Numbers 16–17.

14. *The Levites shall belong to me!* The second part of this verse is emphatic: *wehāyû lî hallewiyyîm*. This meaning of idiomatic *hāyāh l-* expresses possession; compare Gen 32:6: *wayyehî lô šor waḥamôr* 'he *possessed* oxen and mules' (cf. also the usage in Num 3:12, 45).

15. The second part of this verse was quite possibly interpolated, because the sequence of the rites up to this point logically concludes with the statement that the Levites were to begin their tasks at the Tent of Meeting (v 15a). Verse 15b has been translated as a recapitulation: "after you have purified them and made a presentation offering of them."

16. *completely dedicated.* The Levites are "dedicated, given over." This is the sense of *netûnîm netûnîm* Repetition conveys emphasis (cf. *ʿāmôq ʿāmôq* 'exceedingly deep' in Eccl 7:24). As has been emphasized in previous NOTES, the verb *nātan* is of primary importance in defining the status of the Levites. Its usage in the present chapter may serve to clarify its significance even

further. Hebrew *nātan* may, in certain contexts, specifically connote compulsory assignment to cultic service, when the recipient is a deity or a religious establishment. Thus Joshua "consigned" the Gibeonites (Hebrew *wayyittenēm* 'he consigned them') to cultic service (Josh 9:27). Cultic servitors are known as *netînîm* 'devoted cultic servitors' in Ezra 2:43. In Akkadian, the verb *šarāku* 'to donate, hand over, devote' is used in the same way, and neo-Babylonian documents actually speak of temple servants called *širkūtu* 'devotees' (Levine 1963).

Use of the passive participle *netûnîm* is a particular way of characterizing the status of the Levites (cf. Num 3:9; 18:6; 1 Chr 6:33; and below, v 19). It inevitably conveys subservience, even though the context is religious dedication. This diction emphasizes the subordination of the Levites vis à vis the Aaronide priests.

first issue of every womb. The Levites were "claimed" by God, an act conveyed by the verb *lāqaḥ,* in place of the first issue of the womb of every Israelite. The feminine *piṭrat reḥem* 'first issue of the womb' is unique to this verse. Elsewhere, the masculine form *peṭer reḥem* is emphasized (see the Notes on Num 3:11). This, then, is the basic theory sanctioning the assignment of the Levites to cultic service, and the concomitant denial of their claim to a territorial state (see the Notes on Num 18:21–24). It is the book of Numbers that establishes this theory, against the background of the requirement to surrender the firstborn, which is stated in Exod 13:2; 34:19–20; and Deut 15:19–23.

18–19. These verses amplify the preceding statements. The Levites were "dedicated" *(netûnîm)* both to God and to Aaron and his sons. Their dedication was realized on two levels, which do not contradict each other: God exercised his claim on the Levites, and he assigned them to the jurisdiction of the priests. Verse 19 is best understood against the background of the earlier discussion of the formula *lekappēr ʿal* 'to serve as redemption for' in v 12, above. The performance of the Levites would also serve to avert God's predictable wrath at having ordinary Israelites encroach upon the space of the Sanctuary (cf. Num 18:2–5, 22).

21. *purified themselves.* The rare *hithpaʿel wayyitḥaṭṭeʾû* occurs elsewhere in Numbers (19:12; 31:19–20), in the context of purification after contact with a corpse. Here it simply refers to the purificatory measures undertaken by the Levites, including the laundering of their garments.

with Aaron performing rites of expiation. In this instance the formula *wayyekappēr ʿalêhem* means "he (= Aaron) performed *rites of expiation over* the Levites." This is a loose way of referring to the purification of the Levites, though it is an extension of the more common technical connotation of the verb *kippēr.* Normally, such rites involved the utilization of sacrificial blood, but not in the dedication of the Levites (see above, in the Notes on v 12).

24. The period of service for Levites was to extend from twenty-five to

fifty years of age. This duration is unusual and probably indicates that Num 8:23–26 derive from a different code of practice. See the NOTES on Num 4:2 for a discussion of the different minimum ages of service.

must serve in the work force. The cognate formula *liṣbōʾ ṣābāʾ* requires special comment. It is the book of Numbers that uses the term *ṣābāʾ* in its most basic sense of "work force," the sense most common for the Akkadian cognate *ṣabu (CAD* Ṣ, 40–45, under *ṣābu)*. Elsewhere in biblical literature, Hebrew *ṣābāʾ* most often refers to the heavenly "hosts" (Isa 40:26), and quite frequently to military "forces" (1 Chr 9:11).

25. At the age of fifty, a Levite could retire from active service in the Tabernacle.

26. The meaning of this verse is ambiguous. Does it mean to say that after the age of fifty Levites would no longer perform maintenance functions, but only "assist" (the verb *šērēt)* in other ways, performing less demanding duties? To put the question another way: does v 26 link up directly with the preceding statements in vv 24–25, or does it recapitulate the overall characterization of the status of the Levites, as "serving" but not officiating? (See the NOTES on vv 15 and 19, above, and cf. Num 18:2–5.) The former alternative is preferable, because vv 23–26 appear to be a separate statement.

duties. The plural *mišmārôt* means "duties." It represents the plural of the feminine singular form *mišmeret* used so frequently in chap. 8, and in other texts dealing with levitical assignments. In late biblical and postbiblical Hebrew the homophone *mišmārôt* represents the plural of masculine singular *mišmār*, and means "tour of duty" (Neh 7:3; 13:30; 1 Chr 26:12; 2 Chr 35:2; and in the Mishna, *Taʿanît* 4:2).

COMMENT: THE OBSCURE HISTORY OF THE LEVITES IN BIBLICAL ISRAEL

The composition of priestly literature seems to follow a teleological sequence. First the scene is set, and all is made ready; then the actors enter on stage! This sequence was characteristic of Leviticus: the book opened with seven chapters of prescriptions pertaining to the various sacrifices performed in the Tabernacle cult. Thereupon, chaps. 8–10 proceeded to record the investiture of the Aaronide priesthood, who served as the cast of the Tabernacle cult, initiating the formal worship of the God of Israel.

So, too, in the composition of the book of Numbers: chaps. 1–4 and 7 set the stage for the dedication of the Levites. (The contents of chaps. 5 and 6 represent a digression of sorts.) Anticipated by statements in 1:48–53, chaps. 3 and 4 outline the detailed assignments of the several levitical clans and position them within the Israelite encampment. These chapters state the policy that the Levites were not to be included in the census of the Israelite people, but were to be registered separately. The levitical assignments are incorporated into the plan of the encampment and the order of march, as outlined in chap. 2.

It is chap. 8, however, that depicts the actual dedication of the Levites once their operative status within the cultic establishment had been established. The rites described in this chapter confirm the position of the Levites as an order subordinate to the Aaronide priesthood, who are also Levites by tribal affiliation. In this respect, the book of Numbers parts company with Deuteronomy, and in its emphasis is distinctive even within priestly literature itself. The book of Numbers highlights the internal division of the tribe of Levi into two groups: the priests, strictly defined, who constituted a limited group; and the Levites, who in effect constituted the rest of the tribe of Levi. Certain aspects of this innovation have already been discussed in the NOTES and COMMENT on chaps. 3–4.

It will be the purpose of the present discussion to address two related yet distinct questions pertaining to the Levites of biblical times: (1) Historically, was there a tribe of Levi, like the tribe of Judah or Gad, as certain biblical sources record; or did a professional class, a guild of cultic practitioners, eventually assume either the image or actual structure of a tribe? and (2) Can we trace the internal stratification of the "tribe" of Levi, so clearly detailed in the priestly accounts of Numbers, in institutional and historical terms—how did it happen, and when?

These questions require us to make certain judgments regarding the historicity and dating of various biblical sources, whose respective characterizations of the Levites and of their history differ in essential respects. On the one hand, we have relatively early Torah sources—narrative, legal, and poetic—that speak of the tribe of Levi as one of the tribes of Israel. On the other hand, virtually no biblical source outside of the Torah, whose preexilic provenance can be fairly reliably established, ever refers to the Levites as constituting one of the tribes of Israel. Which of these two sets of traditions is more accurate historically, and which is more realistic in its reflection of institutional development? Can these differing traditions be synthesized or reconciled, or must we regard them as being sufficiently distinct to require a decision about which is more historically authentic? The view adopted here is that we are, indeed, required to make such a decision.

Methodologically, it would be best to begin with the extrapentateuchal sources. From the book of Judges one would gather that, in early biblical times, a Levite was a skilled practitioner of the cultic arts, a trained professional who enjoyed considerable mobility. The narratives preserved in Judges 17–18 mention a Levite identified as a member of the clan *(mišpāḥāh)* of Judah (not of the tribe of Judah, by the way), who came from Bethlehem. This Levite had journeyed to the Ephraimite hills in search of employment. There he was retained by a certain Micah, a local leader who operated a temple and was in need of the services of a Levite. Micah appointed the Levite as *'āb* 'master' and *kôhēn* 'priest', providing him support and a modest stipend. Subsequently, this Levite was relocated in Dan, after the migrating Danites passing through Micah's town made him a better offer by appointing him priest over an entire tribe.

In Judg 19:1 and 20:4 we read that the man whose concubine had been violated in Gibeah of Benjamin was likewise a Levite from Bethlehem, living in the Ephraimite hills. When combined, both narratives point to Bethlehem as a center of levitical training and activity. It is possible, of course, that both narratives are actually referring to the same Levite! The term *lēwî* itself may be a northern locution; witness its occurrence in these early northern Israelite sources and in Deuteronomy, whose core is probably of northern Israelite origin (Ginsberg 1982). The narratives of Judges, as well as other relatively early biblical sources, say nothing about a tribe of Israel named Levi, and they clearly indicate that individuals identified as Judeans, for instance, functioned as Levites.

Second Samuel 8 (v 18) states that David's own sons were priests and that David was of the tribe of Judah. There is also the institutional dimension to be considered. Sources that document the history of Israel before the Babylonian exile, such as the books of Samuel and Kings, clearly indicate that cultic functionaries, however named, were appointed and dismissed by leaders and rulers, and served at their pleasure. These sources say nothing of tribal affiliation as the basis of the sacerdotal office. Even the Levite of Judges 17–18, whose clan affiliation is mentioned in passing, behaved as a professional, accepting employment by his own decision. In 2 Sam 15:24 we read that the royally appointed priest, Zadok, was accompanied by all of the Levites on one occasion, when he attempted to transport the Ark out of Jerusalem. There is no reference, however, to a *tribe* of Levites, and there is good reason for regarding the term *lewiyyîm* in that verse as a professional designation. We encounter, therefore, a classical problem of biblical criticism in our attempt to identify the Levites: what is the relative historical value of pentateuchal versus nonpentateuchal biblical evidence?

Let us now turn to the evidence of Torah literature. A tribe of Levi is projected in the family narratives of Gen 29:32–35, a passage usually attributed to the Yahwist, with some possible input by the Elohist. As one of Jacob's sons, Levi is the eponym of a tribe of Israel. (The genealogies of Gen 35:23–29 and 46:8–27 derive from the priestly source and probably represent relatively late traditions.)

It is in Deuteronomy, more than in any other reliably preexilic Torah source, that we find the Levites identified as a tribe, albeit one different from all others. In Deut 10:8–9 there is a clear statement to this effect: YHWH had separated the tribe of Levi *(šēbeṭ hallēwî)* for cultic service while the Israelites were still in the wilderness. This tribe was to bear the Ark of YHWH's Covenant, to serve in YHWH's presence, and to pronounce blessings in his name. As a consequence, the tribe of Levi would have no territory in the Promised Land. God would make alternative provisions for them. In several Deuteronomic passages, the Levites are designated *hakkôhanîm hallewiyyîm* 'the levitical priests', that is to say, the priests who belong to the group called Levites (Deut 17:9, 18; 24:8). That this group was defined in Deuteronomy as a tribe is further evidenced by Deut 18:1, where these levitical priests are specified as *kol šēbeṭ Lēwî* 'the entire tribe of Levi'. In other words, all Levites were priests, and all legitimate priests were Levites. In Deut 21:5, these same priests are referred to as *hakkôhanîm benê Lēwî* 'the priests, sons of Levi'.

There are, of course, serious infra-Deuteronomic problems of a source-critical nature to be considered, and as a consequence the identification of the Levites in Deuteronomy is not as consistent as has been implied up to this point. For the purposes of the present discussion, however, we can state that Deuteronomy, in all of its parts, knows of no stratification within the ranks of Levites such as is detailed in the book of Numbers. Nevertheless Deuteronomy, in some of its parts, clearly projects a tribal affiliation for the Levites, and we are left with the challenge of assessing the degree of realism in this definition. An obvious caveat is the depiction of the tribe of Levi in Deuteronomy as anomalous, with no tribal territory of its own. It is also clear, however, that in Deuteronomy Levites are cultic functionaries, the recipients of consecrated emoluments.

Turning now to the poetic sections of Torah literature, we read in Gen 49:5–7, part of Jacob's blessing, that Simeon and Levi are brothers, violent in their collaborative activities. Evoking a recollection of the Shechem narrative of Genesis 34, Jacob curses Simeon and Levi jointly:

> Cursed be their anger so fierce,
> And their wrath so relentless!
> I shall disperse them in Jacob,
> Scatter them in Israel!

The topical association with Genesis 34 raises the question of whether the narrative is the source of the poem or the poem the actual source of the narrative, or whether each was composed with a view to the other. Surely some literary relationship must be assumed for the two texts. The same problem affects our understanding of the reference to Reuben's impropriety in Gen 49:3–4, for Reuben's act is independently recorded in Gen 35:22.

For itself, the Shechem story in Genesis 34 bears clear priestly earmarks, and one wonders, therefore, how early the poetic reference to Simeon and Levi is! Unless we assume that the poem of Genesis 49 considerably antedates the narrative of Genesis 34, we are led to conclude that it, too, may be relatively late.

To be specific about Genesis 34: those who regard the Shechem narrative as very ancient must, in the first instance, account for the role of circumcision in the plot, a factor that links this narrative, not only in content but in language, to Genesis 17, a blatantly priestly text. There are further priestly associations: the clan of Jacob is offered the right of *ʾaḥuzzāh* 'acquired land' by the Shechemites (Gen 34:10). This is a feature of priestly legislation in Leviticus 25, and one that figures in other priestly narratives of the Torah as well (Levine 1983).

A possible giveaway in the poetic version is the nature of the punishment to be imposed on the tribes of Simeon and Levi, according to Gen 49:7b: they are to be dispersed throughout Israelite territory. Now it has just been noted that Deuteronomy emphasizes the anomalous situation of the tribe of Levi, a tribe without a territory of its own, with its members living in various towns and regions of the land (Deut 14:29; 18:6; Josh 13:33). This evidence suggests that the poetry of Gen 49:5–7 is etiological in character, that it was written with the purpose of explaining the origin of the Levites, and should not be considered evidence of an original tribe named Levi at all.

Others have pointed to the poetry of Deuteronomy 33 as an early source describing a tribe named Levi. There we read, in vv 8–11, that the Levites are to constitute a priestly tribe, collectively officiating in the Israelite cult. The members of the tribe of Levi are credited with having withstood a test of faith, even turning against their own relatives in order to demonstrate their fidelity to the God of Israel. According to Exod 32:26–29 this test happened when Israel sinned in the matter of the golden calf, whereas in the poem of Deuteronomy 33, the levitical act of faith is associated with the incident of Massah and Meribah. The rationale is the same, however: as a reward for loyalty, when all others went astray, the tribe of Levi was chosen for sacred service:

> They shall teach your norms to Jacob,
> And your instructions to Israel.
> They shall offer you incense to savor,
> Whole offerings on your altar.

This assignment more or less accords with what we read in Deut 10:8–9, a statement already referred to. At an earlier time, when the Israelites were in the wilderness, the God of Israel had singled out the tribe of Levi to bear the Ark, to serve in his presence, and to bless the people in his name. It also correlates with the judicial and educational roles assigned to the levitical priests in Deuteronomy 17, for instance, and with the narrative of Exodus 32 that tell of the loyalty of the Levites in rallying behind Moses.

When we combine the telltale signs of etiology evident in both Genesis 49 and Deuteronomy 33 as they speak of the tribe of Levi, we are led to doubt the very early provenance alleged for both poetic sections and their weight as historical evidence. It must be pointed out, however, that some students of biblical poetry, most notably D. N. Freedman (Cross and Freedman 1948), regard Deuteronomy 33, in particular, as representative of early biblical poetry. On literary and linguistic grounds, Freedman would logically regard its contents as expressing the realities of the early biblical period.

Were we to perceive a high degree of consistency in all biblical sources that speak of the tribal origin of the Levites, our doubts would be less compelling. As it is, we must seriously question the original tribal identity attributed to the Levites. Those who assign primacy to the poetic evidence of the Torah must postulate that the warlike, sword-bearing Levites of Genesis 49 demonstrated great loyalty to God at one or another critical juncture, and were thereupon rewarded by being declared a sacred tribe. It would then be the transformed tribe of Levi that is hailed in Deuteronomy 33.

A. Rofé sees elements of consistency in the respective depictions of the Levites in Genesis 49 and in Deuteronomy 33, the latter a poem he dates to the early ninth century B.C.E. in Transjordan (Rofé 1988: 234–249). In Rofé's view, such consistency is evident in the characterization of the tribe of Levi as a fighting force. In Genesis 49 this is a dominant theme, as we would also conclude from the narrative of the Shechem incident in Genesis 34. In Deut 33:11b, however, it is far less certain that the heroic capabilities of the tribe of Levi are being extolled. The Hebrew reads as follows:

bārēk YHWH ḥêlô; ûpôʿal yādâw tirṣeh.
meḥaṣ motnayîm qāmâw; ûmeśanneʾāw min yeqûmûn

Bless, YHWH, his wealth;
Favor his undertakings.
Smite the loins of his foes;
Let his enemies rise no more.

Understood in this way, v 11 is a blessing addressed to Levi, wishing this tribe prosperity and security from enemy attack. The text may be rendered differently, however, in a way that indeed expresses the power of the tribe of Levi:

YHWH has blessed his wealth;
You have favored his undertakings.
He smites the loins of his foes;
His foes rise up no more.

The latter rendering reads the Hebrew verbal form *meḥaṣ* as the infinitive absolute *māḥôṣ*, in the function of a finite verb, and likewise takes *bārēk* as an infinitive absolute. This method effectively changes the wished-for blessing into a fait accompli.

The former reading is more probable, however. Deut 33:11 probably does not speak of the tribe of Levi as warlike, and it cannot be cited incontrovertibly to demonstrate continuity or consistency between Genesis 49 and Deuteronomy 33.

Against persistent doubts about the historicity of the tribe of Levi as one of the tribes of Israel, there is logic in questioning whether a tribe of Levi would have been invented, if one had not existed. Would records of a tribe of Levi have been fabricated in the Jahwistic and Elohistic sources of the Torah, if no such tribe had actually existed? Would relatively early poems refer to such a tribe?

In a sense, the historicity of an ancient tribe of Levi is just one aspect of a much broader set of problems. Are the narratives of J and E, and of the combined source JE, historical? Was there actually a patriarchal age? Is the system of twelve tribes itself historical, or is it a traditional way of rationalizing a royal districting system? Depending on one's views regarding these questions and others of a historical or institutional character, one will assign greater or lesser reliability to the pentateuchal evidence.

An alternative approach, one that might yield a more realistic reconstruction of the history of the Levites, would predicate the early existence of a priestly class or guild, composed of trained groups and training centers. Such a network may ultimately have developed into a tribal structure. This model would reflect the interaction of three socioeconomic factors: family and clan, skills and training, and locale.

In ancient societies, and in some of more recent date, skills like those employed in the cult were normally transmitted within the context of the family, often from father to son or among close relatives. Such skills were generally guarded from outsiders, though it is also true that outsiders who showed talent might be adopted into the family-based group. The Shiloh narratives of 1 Samuel 1–3 reflect this process. Little Samuel is brought to the sanctuary at Shiloh, where the old priest Eli quickly recognizes his gifts. Eventually, Samuel took over Shiloh after the corruption of Eli's sons became intolerable. Though presented in moralistic terms, the takeover by an outsider of the cult of Israel centered at Shiloh may well represent a realistic case history.

Families and clans tended to live together in specific towns and areas of the country; as regards cultic personnel, near temples where their particular skills were needed. It is this pattern that best explains the rise of levitical and priestly towns (Lev 25:32–34; Joshua 21; 1 Sam 22:19; 2 Chronicles 6). The cumulative concentration of specific skills in certain families and clans might, in the course of time, produce a situation in which one clan, or several related clans, would effectively monopolize the cultic arts. When it happened most, if not all, licensed cultic practitioners would be viewed as members of the same "tribe." A proper "history" of the tribe would then be written, just as the *hieros logos* of an acknowledged cult center like Bethel, Dan, or even Jerusalem would be written and retrojected into the patriarchal age, or into the lifetime of Moses, or into both. This process was already quite advanced before the mid eighth century B.C.E., if not in Judah then surely in the northern kingdom of Israel.

This model does not, however, fully answer all of the pertinent historical questions. After all, prophetic guilds were never conceived in tribal terms, nor were the scribal families, of which we have considerable evidence. And yet, in the case of the Levites we have full-blown genealogies, etiologies, narratives, and legal enactments endorsing the tribal origins of this group! All that can be said is that, on balance, it is more realistic to suppose that the notion of the Levites as a tribe, and possibly the actual amalgamation of such a tribe, developed from family-based professional groups. It is less realistic to assume that a tribe named Levi, originally having the same status as the other tribes of Israel, was subsequently dedicated en masse to cultic service.

We may now address the second query regarding the internal division of the tribe of Levi, as mirrored in the opening chapters of Numbers. As already emphasized, Deuteronomy regards the entire tribe of Levi as priestly, and there is no indication of any stratification within that tribe. In the rest of Torah literature, even in priestly sources, there is no explicit indication of an internal division within the tribe of Levi as regards cultic functions. In Lev 25:33–34 we come closest to this possibility. There we find the exemptions from general regulations governing land tenure granted to the levitical towns, the urban dwellings of the Levites and their plots of land used for shepherding and gardening. Clearly, the author of Leviticus 25 knew of a group (not necessarily a tribe!) called Levites, and of their pattern of residence in special towns. It is not at all certain, however, that these Levites were considered separate from the priests. Conceivably, the formulations of these laws followed the Deuteronomic pattern. In fact, this passage represents a unique reference to the Levites by name in all of the book of Leviticus.

The priestly texts of Numbers constitute, therefore, a major departure within Torah literature, even within priestly literature itself. We are presented with a class of cultic servitors known as Levites who are genealogically related to the Aaronide priests, yet subservient to them and differentiated in terms of their functions.

What we read in Numbers may be regarded as the outcome of earlier institutional changes in the Israelite priesthood. It becomes necessary to review these changes so as to position the Numbers traditions historically. It is likely that the internal stratification of the Levites referred to in Numbers reflects a reorganization of the Judean priesthood that began in near-exilic times, pursuant to the edicts of Josiah the Judean king, about 622 (2 Kings 22–23). According to this view, evidence of such reorganization is reflected in Ezek 44:9–14, an interesting passage in every respect.

Ezek 44:9–14 states that the Levites are to be relegated to a subservient status in the Temple, as it was envisioned by the prophet. They are to be prohibited from officiating in the sacrificial cult. Such "demotion" is rationalized as punishment for cultic infidelity. This is a curious counterpoint to those traditions of Exodus and Deuteronomy, which explain the selection of the tribe of Levi as a reward for cultic fidelity! Henceforth, only Zakokite priests would be permitted to officiate in the Temple cult. Prior to their apostasy, however, the Levites were priests, and priests were Levites. This passage in Ezekiel firmly objects to the presence of foreigners in the Temple, and one presumes that such foreigners had previously performed those functions now to be assumed by the Levites. Most scholarly opinion concludes that Ezek 44:9–14 refer to the situation that had obtained in Judah and Jerusalem prior to the execution of Josiah's edicts. Those priests (who were Levites, as were all priests) who had been part of the *bāmāh* network outlawed by Josiah's edicts would now serve as mere workers in the Temple of Jerusalem.

For historical purposes, the textual provenance of Ezek 44:9–14 must be clarified. We should try to determine whether it is integral to the text of Ezekiel 44 or is a later interpolation. There are telling indications that Ezek 44:9–14 were interpolated in postexilic times so as to lend prophetic sanction to what had then become the division of the clergy into two ranks. There are, first of all, distinct differences in terminology and usage between vv 9–14 and the rest of the chapter. Then, too, one notes some fairly obvious dictional mechanisms that blend vv 9–14 with the texts that surround this passage.

Most telling is the fact that in Ezek 43:19 and 44:15, at some point before and immediately following the passage in question, the text of Ezekiel had been referring to *hakkôhanîm hallewiyyîm* 'the leviticial priests', using the Deuteronomic designation, but identifying these priests as Zadokites. It is only in vv 9–14 that we first encounter the independent designation *hallewiyyîm* 'the Levites', referring specifically to the now-to-be-demoted personnel. Prior to vv 9–14, the contrast that had been drawn had been between Zadokite priests and uncircumcised, impure foreigners. Only in Ezek 44:9–14 do we read that the Levites are "to serve" (the verb *šērēt*) at lesser tasks, reserving officiation exclusively for the Zadokite priests. It is curious that the same Hebrew verb, *šērēt*, is used in Ezek 44:15–16 to characterize the "service" of the Zadokite priests themselves in sacral officiation. In Ezek 44:11, part of the passage under discussion, we read that the Levites are to serve as "security guards *(pequddôt)*" and as maintenance personnel, functions conveyed by the verb *šērēt*. In effect, Ezek 44:9–14 use the verb *šērēt* much in the same way as does the priestly text of Num 8:26, whereas the surrounding texts in Ezekiel use the same verb in the Deuteronomic sense (for example, Deut 10:8–9) to connote priestly officiation specifically.

The same modulation occurs with respect to the verb *šāmar* and the noun *mišmeret.* In Ezek 44:15–16 we find the idiom *šāmerû mišmeret* 'they performed the duty of', which resumes the idiom of Ezek 44:8 and refers to the faithful duties of the priests. In v 14, however, which is part of the interpolation, *šômerê mišmeret habbayît* refers to the tasks of the Levites and means, literally, "maintainers of the Temple maintenance."

There are several indications of blending, a literary technique that goes hand in hand with the process of interpolation. A case in point is the verb *tā'āh* 'to stray', which occurs in Ezek 44:15, and whose sense seems to be restated in v 10 as part of the interpolation. In Ezek 44:15 the verb *tā'āh* refers to apostasizing Israelites. In v 10, within the interpolation, we read that those Levites who distanced themselves (the verb *rāḥaq)* from God when the other Israelites went astray (the verb *tā'āh)* were now to be demoted. In a similar vein, v 10 of the interpolation introduces the term *gillûlîm* 'fetishes', elsewhere favored by Ezekiel; but in v 13 we also find *tô'ēbôt* 'abomination', used in Ezek 44:6, in the sections preceding the interpolation.

Revealing in a different way are references to *ḥēleb wādām* 'fat and blood', an idiomatic way of describing burnt altar offerings. This idiom occurs in Ezek 44:7, before the interpolation begins, and resumes in v 15, following it, thereby punctuating the break created by Ezek 44:9–14.

I have taken up considerable space to argue for the secondary textual status of Ezek 44:9–14 because this passage is crucial for reconstructing the institutional history of the Israelite priesthood. To understand the importance of this passage requires us to return to 2 Kgs 23:8–9, where we read as follows:

> He (= Josiah) summoned all the priests *(kôhanîm)* from the towns of Judah and put the *bāmôt* out of commission, where the priests had offered burnt sacrifices, from Geba' to Beer Sheva. . . . But the priests of the *bāmôt* are not allowed to mount the altar of YHWH in Jerusalem and would only be permitted to eat *maṣṣôt* together with their brothers.

This reference alludes to the basis for the demotion of the Levites stated in Ezek 44:9–14. But we should assume considerable distance in time between 2 Kings 23 and Ezek 44:9–14. We must also recognize the difference between 2 Kings 23 and Deut 18:6–8, where we read

> Should the Levite *(hallēwî)* arrive from any of your gates, from any part of Israel, where he resides, he may enter as his feelings impel him into the cult place *(māqôm)* that YHWH shall select. He may serve in

> the name of YHWH, his God, like all his kinsmen who are stationed there in the presence of YHWH. They shall eat equal portions, without regard to personal gifts, or patrimonies.

To be precise: Ezek 44:9–14 accord with the reorganization of the priesthood provided for in Josiah's edicts. Those statements clash, however, with Deuteronomic legislation, which is at least implicitly endorsed in Ezek 43:19 and 44:15.

Whereas Deuteronomy does not identify proper priests except as Levites, Ezekiel 40–48 regularly identify them as Zadokites (Ezek 40:46; 43:19; 44:15; 48:11), in line with the narratives of 2 Samuel and 1 Kings, where we read of David's association with a priest named Zadok (2 Sam 8:17; 15:24; 1 Kgs 1:34; 2:35). Zadok's origins are never identified, as were those of the second priest associated with David, Abiathar, whose origins are told (1 Sam 23:65). It must be remembered that First Temple sources regard priests as royal appointees who could be dismissed, as was the Abiathar family for siding with Adonijah against David (1 Kgs 2:27, 35). So Zadok has no genealogy at all in First Temple sources. This is a significant difference between the historical books and Torah literature.

In summary, the Levites of whom Numbers speaks in detail, as a group distinct from priests and subservient to them, ultimately owe their existence to the edicts of Josiah, subsequently endorsed in Ezek 44:9–14. If it is agreed that Ezek 44:9–14 represent a postexilic interpolation, it is reasonable to regard the institutionalization of the subordinate Levites recorded in Numbers as decidedly postexilic. Even if original to Ezekiel 40–48, the statements in 44:9–14 are exilic at the earliest, indicating that there was no stratification within the Israelite priesthood before the Babylonian exile. Pursuant to Josiah's edicts, levitical priests from the provinces were denied the status of officiants in the Jerusalem Temple, but they could rely on the Temple for support. What is announced in Ezek 44:9–14, and institutionalized in Numbers, is an internal stratification of the Judean priesthood. When we peruse postexilic literature, in Chronicles, in Ezra and Nehemiah, and in certain late psalms, we find this "ranking" reflected at every step.

The oracle preserved in Malachi 2, a postexilic source of uncertain date, might add to our understanding of the postexilic Jewish priesthood. Malachi addresses the Jerusalemite priesthood, castigating them for their improper cultic conduct. He refers to their abrogation of "my covenant with Levi *(berîtî 'et Lēwî)*" in Mal 2:4, later referred to as *berît hallēwî* 'the covenant with the levitical group' in v 8. This covenant is one of "the life of fellowship *(haḥayîm wehaššālôm)*." The only other biblical source that employs such language in a similar context is Num 25:10–13, where Phineas, grandson of Aaron, is promised "an everlasting priestly covenant *(berît kehunnat 'ôlām)*," also characterized as *beriti šālôm* 'my covenant of fellowship'.

One could argue that Malachi does not know of the Aaronide priesthood and, more significantly for purposes of this discussion, that he does not know of any stratification within the priesthood. The priests of his time are levitical, and their ancient eponym is Levi. Quite possibly Num 25:10–13 took its cue from Malachi, rephrasing his critical words positively in an endorsement of the Aaronide priesthood. The subject of the Aaronide priesthood itself will be discussed in COMMENT 2 on Numbers 16–17.

PART VI.

NUMBERS 9: TWO MATTERS OF CULTIC SIGNIFICANCE

INTRODUCTION

Numbers 9 consists of two parts, which have little specifically to do with each other. Verses 1–14 deal with the performance of the paschal sacrifice, and vv 15–23 relate how the cloud signaled to the Israelites when to encamp and when to set out on the march. As such, Numbers 9, like a number of chapters in this book and even in Leviticus, brings together a variety of subjects that were previously unaddressed but required attention within the overall agenda of the book. The second part of the chapter (vv 15–23) prepares us for Num 10:11, where we read that the Israelites set out from Sinai in the south to Paran in the north (see the NOTES on Num 10:11).

Israelites who were impure on the fourteenth day of the first month, when the paschal sacrifice was to be performed, or who were away on a journey at the time could perform this rite on the same day a month later, in the second month. They would then perform all that was required, as if the sacrifice had been performed at its appointed time. One is inevitably reminded of the tradition of 2 Chronicles 30, which relates that Hezekiah once ordained a paschal celebration for all Israel in Jerusalem in the second month. On that occasion, we are told, there was also a problem with purity. We are likewise brought back to Numbers 5:1–4, a law requiring the Israelites to banish impure persons from the encampment. In their formulation, Num 9:1–14 bear close affinity to Exodus 12, one of the principal statements on the celebration of the paschal sacrifice.

The provision for a deferred Pesaḥ sacrifice in the second month for those too distant inevitably implies that one was obliged to perform the paschal sacrifice in a certain place. To put it another way, Num 9:1–14 presuppose cult centralization. Under the old, pre-Deuteronomic system, one had not to go very far to perform the Pesaḥ, for the sacrifice was to be offered near one's home (Exodus 12–13). It was only as a result of the Deuteronomic reform, so called, that a lengthy pilgrimage would become necessary for many Israelites (Deut 16:2–3, 5–7). Of course, one could argue that Num 9:1–14 are simply speaking of a person far from home at the original time of the Pesaḥ, but such reasoning runs into the objection that one could celebrate the Pesaḥ anywhere in the land under the old system. More likely, vv 1–14 represent a late accommodation to the Deuteronomic reform and constitute further evidence for the dependence of the priestly law on Deuteronomy.

Verses 15–23 explain, in a rather repetitive and redundant fashion, that the Israelites encamped and set out on their marches by direct divine command. This command was signaled by the cloud that accompanied the people day and night, hovering over the Tabernacle. This section of Numbers 9, which parallels Exod 40:34–37, is part of a larger group of traditions on the manifestation of God's presence during the wilderness period. It sets the stage for Num 10:1–28, where we read that the Israelites set out from Sinai, bearing with them the portable Tabernacle and its appurtenances.

TRANSLATION

9 1 YHWH spoke to Moses in the Wilderness of Sinai in the second year after their exodus from Egypt, in the first month, as follows:

2 Let the Israelite people perform the paschal sacrifice at its set time.

3 On the fourteenth day of this month, at twilight, you shall perform it, at its set time. You must perform it in accordance with all of its statutes and its rules.

4 So Moses instructed the Israelite people to perform the paschal sacrifice.

5 They performed the paschal sacrifice in the first month, on the fourteenth day of the month, at twilight, in the Wilderness of Sinai, in accordance with all that YHWH had commanded Moses. So did the Israelites perform it.

6 It happened that some persons were impure because of contact with a dead human body, and could not perform the paschal sacrifice on that day. They approached Moses and Aaron on that day.

7 These persons stated to him, "We are impure because of contact with a dead body. Why should we be deprived of presenting the offering of YHWH at its set time, together with the Israelite people?"

8 Moses said to them, "Stay here, until I hear what YHWH commands concerning you."

9 YHWH spoke to Moses as follows:

10 Speak to the Israelite people as follows: Any person who becomes impure because of contact with a dead body, or is away on a distant journey, of you or your future generations, and desires to perform the paschal sacrifice—

11 They may perform it in the second month, on the fourteenth day, at twilight. Together with unleavened bread and bitter herbs let them partake of it.

12 They may not leave any part of it until morning, nor break any bone in it. They must perform it completely in accordance with the statute of the paschal sacrifice.

13 Any person who is pure, and was not away on a journey, and yet fails to perform the paschal sacrifice—that person shall be cut off from his kinsmen, for he failed to present the offering of YHWH at its set time. That person must bear the punishment for his offense.

14 Should an alien reside among you and wish to perform the paschal sacrifice to YHWH, he must perform it in accordance with the statute of the paschal sacrifice, and according to its rule. There shall be only one statute applying to the alien, just as it applies to the native-born citizen of the land.

15 On the day that the Tabernacle was set up, the cloud covered the Taberna-

cle of the Tent of the Covenant. At evening, it appeared over the Tabernacle
as fire, until morning.
16So it was regularly: the cloud covered it, appearing as fire at night.
17As the cloud lifted off from atop the Tent, the Israelites would promptly
set out on the march. Wherever the cloud came to rest, there the Israelites
would make camp.
18The Israelites marched by order of YHWH, and by order of YHWH they
encamped. As long as the cloud rested over the Tabernacle, they remained
encamped.
19When the cloud remained over the Tabernacle for a long period of time,
the Israelites obeyed YHWH's ordinance and did not march.
20It would happen that the cloud would remain over the Tabernacle for only
a few days. In that event, they encamped by order of YHWH, just as they
marched by order of YHWH.
21It happened that the cloud would remain only from evening until morning,
and then lift off in the morning.
22Whether for two days, for a month, or for a year—when the cloud rested
over the Tabernacle for a long period of time—the Israelites would remain
encamped, and would not march. When it lifted—they marched.
23By order of YHWH they made camp, and by order of YHWH they
marched. They obeyed YHWH's ordinance, by order of YHWH, through the
authority of Moses.

NOTES TO 9:1–14: SUPPLEMENTARY PASSOVER LEGISLATION

9 1. A chronological problem is evident in the caption. The communication from God is dated in the second year after the Exodus, in the first month (or possibly on the first new moon). In Num 1:1, however, God addressed Moses on the first day of the *second* month, in the second year after the Exodus. There is a simple way of resolving this discrepancy. Most likely the caption of Num 9:1 already appeared in the text of Numbers before the opening caption of the book was added, and may take us back to Exod 40:2.

2. *Let the Israelite people perform.* The force of *weyaʿaśû* is modal. The verb *ʿāśāh* has the functional sense of worshiping or performing a religious rite, as in Num 15:3, for example. There it is employed with particular reference to performance of the paschal sacrifice, as it is below, in vv 10 and 14, and in Exod 12:48.

at its set time. Hebrew *bemôʿadô,* here and in v 3, resonates the diction of Exod 13:10, part of one of the principal statements on the paschal sacrifice. Deriving from the root *y-ʿ-d* 'to encounter, fix, designate' a time or place, or a meeting, the noun *môʿēd* became the normal term for the annual festivals that occur at the same time every year (Lev 23:2, 4, 37). The point of the statement is that this rite must be observed in its designated date to start with.

3. *twilight.* This verse recalls Lev 23:5, as well as Exod 12:6; 16:12; and 29:39, 41. The time frame indicated by the term *bên haʿarbāyîm,* literally, "between the two settings" is best defined as "twilight," a period of time between sunset and nightfall, of about one and a half hours' duration. Hebrew *ʿarbāyîm* is a dual form, conveying the sense of two "settings," sunset and nightfall. The verb *ʿārab* means "to enter, set," as in Judg 19:9: "Behold, the day has waned toward setting *(laʿarôb).*" The verb *ʿārab* is synonymous with *bôʾ* 'to enter, set', an action often said of the sun (Gen 28:11; Eccl 1:5). According to the Mishna, *Pesaḥîm* 5:1, the paschal sacrifice was offered in the Second Temple of Jerusalem at nine and a half hours into the day. In a theoretical daytime period lasting from 6:00 A.M. to 6:00 P.M., that would be at 3:30 P.M. This interpretation reflects the view in the *Mekhîltāʾ*, *Boʾ*, par. 5 (Lauterbach 1976: 39), which defines *ʿarbāyîm* as the entire period from noon to 6:00 P.M. in an ideal twelve-hour day.

All of these texts reflect, of course, the priestly law. Deut 16:6 ordains the paschal sacrifice "in the evening, when the sun sets" *(bāʿereb kebôʾ haššemeš)* or, in the preceding verse, *bāʿereb bayyôm hāriʾšôn* 'in the evening, on the first day', indicating a considerably later hour.

its statutes and its rules. Use of the terms *ḥoq, ḥuqqāh* 'statute' and *mišpāṭ* 'rule' together as a pair is typical of Deuteronomic diction (Deut 8:11; 30:16). The paschal sacrifice is designated *ḥuqqāh* in Exod 12:43 and 13:10; see below, in the NOTES on v 14.

4. *Moses instructed.* The sense of *wayyedabbēr* is closer to "he instructed" than simply "he spoke," and has been so translated.

5. The statement of compliance in this verse recalls Exod 12:50.

6. *It happened that.* Singular *wayyehî* before a plural subject would be acceptable, but here we have, most likely, an instance of narrative style: "It happened that—."

impure because of contact with a dead human body. The formula *ṭemēʾîm lenepeš ʾādām* is explained in the NOTES on Num 5:2. It recalls the language of Lev 22:4 and Num 19:13. Hebrew *nepeš* can connote a dead body.

7. *should we be deprived.* On the *niphʿal* form *niggāraʿ* also occurs in Num 27:4 and 36:4. In Deut 18:1 we read that the Israelites were forbidden to add (the verb *hôsîp)* to God's commands or to subtract (the verb *gāraʿ*) from them.

8. *Stay here.* The primary connotation of the Hebrew verb *ʿāmad* is "to stay put, to stop" (Gen 45:9; Exod 9:28; Josh 10:13; 1 Sam 20:38). The situation of awaiting a direct divine communication, so as to be able to resolve a present question of law, is also projected in Lev 24:12 and Num 15:34, where Moses

was uncertain about the penalties for particular crimes. The accused parties were detained until the word of God settled the pertinent questions of law.

concerning you. Pronominal *lākem* means "concerning you, with respect to you." One could, however, take *lākem* as indicating the accusative: "what YHWH will command *you.*"

10. The syntax in this verse is parenthetical, but the sense is clear. Idiomatic *ʾîš ʾîš* 'any person' recalls Leviticus 17 (cf. Num 4:19, 49; 5:12). The clause beginning *weʿāśāh* expresses intent, hence the translation "and desires to perform." This verse is the protasis of a prolonged conditional statement that continues into v 11.

11. The paschal sacrifice of those unable, for valid reasons, to perform it in the first month may be performed on the same day a month later. The language *ʿal maṣṣôt ûmerōrîm yôʾkelûhû* 'Let them partake of it *together with* unleavened bread and bitter herbs' recalls Exod 12:8 (cf. Deut 16:3).

12. This verse presents a third-person formulation of Exod 12:10, substituting *yašʾîrû* 'let them leave over' for *tôtîru,* with the same meaning. In Lev 22:30 the same prohibition against subsequent use of any part of a sacrifice left until the next morning is stated. There it pertains to the thanksgiving offering.

nor break any bone in it. The prohibition against breaking any of the victim's bones is first stated in Exod 12:46. It is consistent with the unusual requirement that the paschal lamb not be sectioned, but roasted whole over the fire with its head and lower legs intact. The requirement of retaining structural wholeness may be echoed in John 19:30, where we read that Jesus, as a sacrificial victim who met his death on the eve of the Passover, did not have his legs broken!

13. *shall be cut off.* One who is present and able to perform the paschal sacrifice at its proper time, but desists (the verb *ḥādal*) from doing so, is to be "cut off" from his people. On this punishment, see the NOTES on Num 19:13 (cf. Num 15:30–31).

the offering of YHWH. The designation *qorbān YHWH* is unique to this passage, but *qorban ʾelôhêkem* 'the offering of your God' in Lev 23:14 comes close to it.

That person must bear the punishment for his offense. Idiomatic *ḥeṭʾô yiśśāʾ* is explained in the NOTE on Num 18:1 (cf. Lev 20:20; 24:15). It is a variant of the more common *ʿawônô yiśśāʾ*, which has the same meaning. The term for the offense *(ḥēṭʾ)* itself expresses punishment for the offense.

14. This verse restates Exod 12:48–49, part of the laws of Pesaḥ. Here there is no requirement of circumcision for non-Israelites desiring to observe the rite, as is stipulated in the Exodus version of the law. This difference is probably due to the tendency toward abbreviation in Numbers, when previously stated priestly legislation is reformulated.

alien . . . native-born citizen. The contrast *gēr . . . ʾezrāḥ* (cf. Lev 19:33–34; Num 15:14) requires comment. The *gēr* of biblical times was usually a foreign merchant, craftsman, or mercenary. The term *gēr* connotes impermanence and derives from the verbal root *g-w-r* 'to sojourn, reside'. The Hebrew *ʾezrāḥ* is of uncertain etymology. The fuller designation is *ʾezrāḥ hāʾāreṣ* 'the native-born citizen of the land'. It is probable that *ʾezrāḥ* was originally a botanical term for a tree or plant that is well rooted in the soil. This is suggested by Ps 37:35, "well rooted like a robust native tree *(keʾezrāḥ raʿanān).*" On this basis, the *ʾezrāḥ* is one whose lineage has roots in the land, one who belongs to the people who possess the land. It is common in biblical parlance for humans, individually and collectively, to be characterized in botanical terms. The best known image is that of *zeraʿ* 'seed', in the sense of descendants. The point to be made is that the terms *ʾezrāḥ* and *gēr* never apply to the prior inhabitants of Canaan, who are most often designated ethnically as Canaanites, Amorites, Amalekites, and the like. We also encounter the collective designation *yôšēb hāʾāreṣ* 'the inhabitants of the land' (Gen 34:30; Exod 34:12, 15). W. F. Albright's earlier view (1968) that *ʾezrāḥ* meant something like "aborigine" is possible etymologically, but is not supported by biblical usage. Non-Israelite residents of the land would often be motivated to join in festival celebrations and were welcome to do so as long as they followed proper procedures. The terms *ḥuqqāh* 'statute' and *mišpāṭ* 'rule' are explained in the NOTES on Num 15:14–16.

NOTES TO 9:15–23: A CLOUD BY DAY; FIRE BY NIGHT

Verses 15–23 recall Exod 40:34–37, the first of several priestly references to the erection of the Tabernacle. They also direct our attention to the caption in Num 7:1, which ostensibly refers to the same event.

15. *cloud.* The cloud *(ʿānān)* spoken of here, which enveloped the Tabernacle during the daytime and had the appearance of fire at night, is the same cloud described in Exod 40:34 and Num 10:11; compare also Num 10:34, a probable priestly insertion into the Ark narrative, as well as Num 14:14 and Deut 1:33. The "cloud" tradition is expressed in many related ways and is an aspect of the *kābôd* theology, a way of representing the divine presence. Fire burned inside the cloud at all times, day and night, except that during the day it was not visible, whereas at night it could be seen in contrast to the enveloping darkness.

of the Tent of the Covenant. The construction *leʾōhel hāʿēdût* means, literally, "*belonging to* the Tent of the Covenant." The Tent was so called because it contained the Tablets of the Covenant *(luḥôt hāʿēdût)*; see the NOTES on Num 1:50, 53; 4:5; 7:89; 17:19.

16. *regularly*. Adverbial *tāmîd* does not mean "always, forever," but "regularly, daily," the point being that the same cloud signal occurred repeatedly (Levine 1965b).

17. As *the cloud lifted off . . . promptly*. The syntax of this verse is unusual. A time sequence is expressed as *ûlepî hēʿālôt heʿānān . . . weʾaḥarê kēn*. Idiomatic *lepî* seldom has a temporal meaning, but see Jer 29:10: *lepî melōʾt lebābel šibʿîm šānāh* 'as seventy years ended for Babylon'. In that verse, *lepî* is also followed by an infinitive construct, as is true here. Adverbial *ʾaḥarê kēn* 'subsequently' here indicates promptness. The cloud signaled not only the time for setting out on the march and for encamping, but also the place.

set out on the march. It is preferable to translate the verb *nāśāʾ* in the technical sense of "marching," because the Israelite camp is depicted as a military array, and the verb *nāśāʾ* may connote a military expedition, as in 2 Kgs 19:8 || Isa 37:8; Exod 14:10.

The cloud either "came to rest" (the verb *šākan)* or was "lifted off" (the *niphʿal* form, *yēʿāleh)*, and this contrast is repeated in the verses to follow, echoing Exod 40:34. In vv 19–22, the language is varied a bit, and we read that the cloud "remains *(yiḥyeh)*" or that it "remains for a long time *(yaʾarîk)*."

18. *marched . . . encamped*. The imperfect verbal forms *yiśʾû, yaḥanû* 'they march, they encamp' are durative in force and connote continuous action. The construction *kol yemê ʾašer* is highly unusual, but its meaning is clear. It expresses "time during which," and that is the force of the relative pronoun *ʾašer* in this construction; compare Lev 13:46.

19. *obeyed [YHWH's] ordinance*. The formula *wešamrû . . . mišmeret* simply means "they obeyed . . . the ordinance" and does not imply any "guarding" of the Tabernacle. See the Notes on Num 1:53 regarding the various connotations of the term *mišmeret* in biblical Hebrew.

20. *only a few days*. Idiomatic *yāmîm mispār* connotes paucity of time and reflects one of the polar meanings of *mispār* 'number', which ranges in its connotations from few to many. Compare its usage in Isa 10:19 and the common designation *metê mispār* 'a few persons' in Deut 4:7.

21. *It happened that*. Idiomatic *weyēš ʾašer* is circumstantial; compare the late usage in Neh 5:2–4.

would remain. The force of *yihyeh* 'it is, will be' is closer to 'it would *remain*'.

22. The progression of time is rhetorical. Compare Num 11:19–20, where the progression is from one day to two, to five, to ten, to twenty, to a month. Here idiomatic *yāmîm* means "a year." This meaning for adverbial *yāmîm* is proved by Lev 25:29, where *yāmîm* is synonymous with *ʿad tôm šenat mimkārô* 'until completion of the year of its sale'.

23. Formulaic *ʿal pî YHWH* 'by order of YHWH' is common, as is *beyad Môšeh* 'through the authority of Moses' (cf. Num 4:37, 45; 10:13). This verse

recalls Exod 17:1, which likewise records the outset of a march. The combination of God's command and Moses' authority (for that is what *beyad*, literally, "by the hand of" means) is to define the relations between the divine leader and the human leader. God issues commands and instructions, and Moses carries them out and in turn commands the Israelites. Refusal to obey Moses is tantamount to disobedience to God himself, a thought expressed in Num 14:9, 41.

PART VII.

NUMBERS 10:1–28: THE ISRAELITES ON THE MARCH

PART VII.

NUMBERS 10:1–28: THE ISRAELITES ON THE MARCH

INTRODUCTION

Numbers 10 is of two parts. Verses 1–28 belong to the priestly historiography of Numbers and are directly linked to Numbers 2, where the units comprising the Israelite fighting force were delineated and the strength of each unit recorded. Chapter 2 had also outlined the order of march, and we note that the list of chieftains given in 10:1–28 is identical to that appearing in chap. 2.

Chapter 10 begins by describing the silver trumpets to be used in mustering the forces (vv 1–10). Their utilization is explained more in religious terms than as a practical function. It should also be noted that v 10 is a unique reference, in all of the Torah, to the use of trumpets in the cult.

Beginning in v 11, the priestly historiography records that on the twentieth day of the second month of the second year after the Exodus, the Israelites set out on the march from the Wilderness of Sinai, in the southern part of the peninsula, to the Wilderness of Paran, in the north. This was, according to the reckoning of the priestly historiography, only twenty days after the date recorded in Num 1:1. There we read that on the first day of the same month, in the same year, God began to instruct Moses and the Israelites regarding all that was to be accomplished in southern Sinai—the census, the assignment of the levitical clans to their duties, the assembling of the Tabernacle and its dedication, and the dedication of the Levites.

The patterns of encampment and deployment underlying Num 10:11–18 are explained in the NOTES on chap. 2, as are the basic terms of reference—*degel, maḥaneh, ṣābāʾ*—all of which will be encountered here once again. In the present plan of march, the participation of the levitical clans is outlined. They are assigned positions in the order of march (vv 17, 21) based on their assignments as prescribed in Numbers 3–4.

TRANSLATION

10 [1]YHWH spoke to Moses as follows:

[2]Fashion two trumpets of silver; make them of a hammered piece. They shall serve you for assembling the community and for undertaking the march of the corps.

[3]When both of them are sounded, the entire community shall assemble before you, at the entrance of the Tent of Meeting.

[4]When only one is sounded, the chieftains, heads of the Israelite militias, shall assemble before you.

[5]When you sound prolonged blasts, the corps encamped on the eastern side shall set out on the march.

[6]At the second sounding of prolonged blasts, the corps encamped on the

southern side shall set out on the march. Prolonged blasts shall be sounded for their marches,

[7]but for assembling the congregation, you must sound short blasts, not prolonged blasts.

[8]The sons of Aaron, the priests, shall sound the trumpets. They shall serve you on a permanent basis, throughout your generations.

[9]When you wage war in your land, against any aggressor who attacks you, sound prolonged blasts on the trumpet, so that you will be brought to the attention of YHWH, your God, and be rescued from your enemies.

[10]And at the time of your rejoicing, on your annual festivals and your new moons, you must blast the trumpets over your burnt offerings and your sacred gifts of greeting. The [blasts] will serve as a reminder of you before your God. I am YHWH, your God!

[11]In the second year, on the twentieth day of the second month, the cloud lifted from the Tabernacle of the Covenant.

[12]The Israelites set out on their marches from the Wilderness of Sinai. The cloud settled in the Wilderness of Paran.

[13]They had commenced their march at the command of YHWH, transmitted by Moses.

[14]The *degel* consisting of the Judahite corps set out in the lead, by their divisions. In command of its (Judah's) division was Nahshon son of Amminadab.

[15]Commanding the division of the tribe of Issachar was Nathanel son of Zuar,

[16]and commanding the division of the tribe of Zebulun was Eliab son of Helon.

[17]The Tabernacle was then disassembled, and the Gershonites and Merarites, bearers of the Tabernacle, took to the march.

[18]The *degel* consisting of the Reubenite corps then set out on the march, by their divisions. In command of its (Reuben's) division was Elizur son of Shedeur.

[19]Commanding the division of the tribe of Simeon was Shelumiel son of Zurishaddai,

[20]and commanding the division of the tribe of Gad was Eliasaph son of Deuel.

[21]Then the Kohathites, bearers of the inner sanctuary, set out on the march. By the time they arrived, others would have erected the Tabernacle.

[22]The *degel* consisting of the Ephraimite corps then set out on the march, by their divisions. In command of its (Ephraim's) division was Elishama son of Ammihud.

[23]Commanding the division of the tribe of Manasseh was Gamaliel son of Pedahzur,

24 and commanding the division of the tribe of Benjamin was Abidan son of Gideoni.

25 The *degel* consisting of the Danite corps, the rear guard of all the corps, then set out on the march, by their divisions. In command of its (Dan's) division was Ahiezer son of Ammishaddai.

26 Commanding the division of the tribe of Asher was Pagiel son of Ochran,

27 and commanding the division of the tribe of Naphtali was Ahira son of Enan.

28 These were the deployments of the Israelites, by their divisions, when they set out on the march.

NOTES

10 2. The derivation of *ḥaṣôṣerāh* 'trumpet' remains elusive. Hebrew *miqšāh,* from the root *q-š-h* 'to be hard', means "hard hammered, pounded." It is a craftsman's term for metal artifacts "worked" or hammered into shape. The cherubs were fashioned in this way (Exod 25:18; 37:7, 17), as was the golden Menorah of the Tabernacle (Exod 25:31, and see the NOTES on Num 8:4; Meyers 1976: 31–34).

They shall serve you. Hebrew *haya l-* 'to be for' means "to serve as"—to be used for a certain purpose, to serve a specific function (cf. in v 8, below).

for assembling . . . for undertaking the march. The forms *lemiqrāʾ*, *lemassāʿ* are probably constructed on the model of the Aramaic infinitive, which in the simple stem has a prefixed *mem.* Thus we have *lemiqrāʾ* instead of *liqrôʾ*, for instance. This analysis was favored by Ibn Ezra. The form *lemansaʿ* becomes *lemassāʿ* by assimilation.

the community. Collectively, the Israelite people comprise the *ʿēdāh* 'community', a term prevalent in P and explained in the NOTES on Num 1:16.

3. *both.* Hebrew *bāhēn* (pausal form) 'with them' is translated "with both of them" to provide a contrast with v 4, where we read "with *one* of them."

The place of assembly, usually designated "the entrance of the Tent of Meeting," was undoubtedly a large area, as was explained in the NOTES on Num 1:1.

4. *the chieftains, heads of the Israelite militias.* The title *rāʾšê ʾalpê Yiśrāʾēl* is explained in the NOTES on Num 1:16. The title *rôʾš ʾelep* 'head of a militia' (Josh 22:21, 30) is functionally equivalent to *śar ʾelep* 'commander of a militia unit' (1 Sam 18:13), which seems to be older in biblical usage.

is sounded. The verb *tāqaʿ* means "to drive through" and is said of driving in a tent peg (Gen 31:25). When said of musical instruments, it means to blow a sound through a channel (1 Sam 13:3). In contrast to *terûʿāh,* this verb technically denotes a short blast.

5. *sound prolonged blasts.* Hebrew *terûʿāh* expresses the consequences of

the *hiphʿil hērîaʿ* 'to make a loud sound'. The prefixed *tau* often expresses the result, so that literally *terûʿāh* means "the sound that has been blasted" (1 Sam 17:20; Isa 44:3; Hos 5:8). In Jewish liturgy, where the shofar is still used, *terûʿāh* is defined as a rapid staccato of nine shofar blasts (Mishna, *Taʿanît* 2:5).

8. *on a permanent basis.* The sense of *ḥuqqat ʿôlām,* literally, "a statute forever," is less technical here, and it means simply that the use of trumpets was to be a permanent feature of the cult. It was important to the priestly school to emphasize that their descriptions were not simply historical or characteristic of a particular period.

9. *When you wage war.* The clause *wekî tābōʾû milḥāmāh,* literally, "when you enter into war," is unique in biblical Hebrew usage. Usually we find expressions such as "going to war," with the verb *yāṣāʾ*. The present expression resembles use of the verb *qārab* 'to approach', used in certain contexts to connote military onslaught. In statements about battle, prepositional *ʿal* usually means "against."

you will be brought to the attention of. The *niphʿal* passive *wenizkartem* means "you will be brought to the attention of," just as in v 10, below, the noun *zikkārôn* means "reminder." As Gray observed, gods may forget, fail to pay attention, and even slumber! This accounts for the language of supplications, in which God is implored to turn toward those who call upon him, to remember them, and to remain awake. In Ps 109:14 we read about God's attention to wrongdoing: "May the offense of his ancestors be brought to YHWH's attention *(yizzākēr ʾel YHWH).*"

10. *At the time of your rejoicing.* This phrase refers to the annual festivals, on which Israelites were commanded to rejoice, as we read of the Sukkoth festival in Deut 16:14: "You shall rejoice *(weśāmaḥtā)* on your pilgrimage festivals and be exceptionally happy!" In context, Hebrew *môʿēd,* which has many related meanings, connotes an annual festival.

new moons. These were important occasions in biblical times. The sacrificial rites ordained by the priesthood for the new moons are set forth in Num 28:11–15. The plural form "your new moons" is written defectively as *hdškm,* instead of *hdšykm.*

sacred gifts of greeting. The sacrifice known as *šelāmîm* has a long history in ancient Near Eastern religions. It was especially prominent in the Ugaritic sacrificial system. The basic provisions of the *šelāmîm* are presented in Leviticus 3 and Lev 7:11–38, and its special character is explained in the NOTES on Num 6:14. The common pair *ʿôlāh* 'burnt offering' and *šelāmîm* (Exod 32:6; Josh 8:31) customarily refers to a regimen of sacrifices, in general.

11. When the cloud lifted from the Tabernacle, the Israelites set out on the march. The term *miškan hāʿēdût* 'the Tabernacle of the Covenant' defines the Tabernacle as the place wherein "the Tablets of the Covenant" *(luḥôt hāʿēdût)* were deposited; see the NOTES on Num 1:50, where this designation

first occurs in the Book of Numbers. When a march was to begin, the cloud lifted off as a signal to move. In Num 9:15–23, part of a priestly record of the actual day on which the Tabernacle was erected, this phenomenon was described.

12. *the Wilderness of Paran.* The Israelites marched northward to the Wilderness of Paran. Some discussion of the term *midbar Pārā'n* is required because of the complex pattern of its utilization by the priestly writers, who use this designation for the northern part of the Sinai peninsula. What is, however, the most accurate geographic delimitation of the Wilderness of Paran?

In biblical geographic nomenclature, the formula "*midbār* of X-toponym" often designates the desert facing the named locality or area from one or another direction, as seems to be the case with respect to a number of desert areas in southern Judah and the Negeb. Thus we have *midbar Mā'ôn* (1 Sam 23:25), *midbar Zip* (1 Sam 26:2), *midbar Be'ēr Šeba'* (Gen 21:14), *midbar 'Ên Gedî* (1 Sam 24:1), and even *midbar Qādēš* (Ps 29:8), all in that general southern area. On the same basis, *midbar Pārā'n* would be the desert facing El Paran *('ēl ['yl] Pārā'n)*, namely, Elath *('Êlat ('ylt) / 'Êlôt ('lwt))*. This identification is made virtually explicit in Gen 14:6: *'ad 'Êl Pārā'n 'ašer 'al hammidbār* 'up to El Paran, which faces the desert', namely, *midbar Pārā'n*. It is interesting to note that David moves down to *midbar Pārā'n* after his encounters with Saul in the area of Ain Gedi (1 Sam 25:1). In a similar manner, Hagar first wanders with her son Ishmael in *midbar Be'ēr Šeba'* (Gen 21:14), and after the two of them are rescued and Ishmael grows up, he resides in *midbar Pārā'n* (Gen 21:21). Quite clearly, the Wilderness of Paran is southeast of where Kadesh is located and west-northwest of Elath.

The priestly writers greatly expanded the area of the Wilderness of Paran, it seems. In Num 13:3 and 26, verses that were both rewritten by the priestly school, an overlap occurs, with the result that Kadesh is said to be located in the Wilderness of Paran, and the Wilderness of Paran is said to be part of Sinai, so that Kadesh is not located in Canaan. According to the priestly tradition, the Israelites remained in the Wilderness of Paran, as it turned out, for about thirty-eight of the forty years of their migrations. (In the introduction to this volume, section A.5, and in the COMMENTS on chaps. 13–14, the respective itineraries of JE and P, which differ significantly from each other, are discussed.)

13. *at the command of YHWH, transmitted by Moses.* The common formula *'al pî YHWH beyad Môšeh* here serves to emphasize that the marches and their routes were specifically commanded by God. The notion that God is directly in control of everything that happens is consistent with the priestly outlook on history and government, and on life generally (cf. Exod 34:27; Lev 24:12; Num 3:39, 51; 4:37, 45; 9:23). Hebrew *'al pî*, literally, "by the mouth of," parallels the Akkadian idioms *ina pî* and *ša pî*, both of which often convey the sense of divine as well as human commands *(AHw*, 873, s.v. *pū(m)* I, 7–9).

Hebrew *beyad,* literally, "by the hand of," may connote the instrumentality of transmission; compare Gen 38:20: "Judah sent the kid goat *by the hand of (beyad)* his Adulamite companion."

14. The unit known as *degel* is defined in the NOTES to Num 2:2. The twelve tribes were divided into four *degel* units, each consisting of three tribes, with the commander of the *degel* being a chieftain of one of them. In administrative usage, the preposition *ʿal* means "in charge of, in command over" (cf. Gen 39:4; 43:16; 2 Sam 20:24; 1 Kgs 4:6; 5:28; 12:18; etc.).

17–21. The present chapter identifies the positions of the three levitical clans in the order of march, referring to their respective assignments in transporting the portable Tabernacle complex. These assignments were set forth in Numbers 3–4.

The Gershonites and Merarites set out in advance of the Kohathites so that the structural components of the Tabernacle would reach the next encampment site in time to be erected before the Kohathites arrived, bearing the interior appurtenances to be installed inside it. That is the sense of v 21b: "By the time they arrived, *others* (i.e., the Gershonites and Merarites) would have erected the Tabernacle" (cf. the similar, though less specific, statement in Num 2:17).

25. From Josh 6:9 and 13 we learn that the Israelite fighting forces included advance units, called *(he)ḥālûṣ,* and a rear guard, known as *meʾassēp,* literally, the units that "gather up" the rear. This military deployment is expressed in prophecy: "For YHWH marches in advance of you, and the God of Israel is your rear guard *(meʾassipkem)*" (Isa 52:12).

28. This final verse sums up the contents of Num 10:11–28 pertaining to the Israelite plan of march. For this reason, Hebrew *masseʿê benê Yiśrāʾēl* is translated "the deployments of the Israelites," because it would be inaccurate to understand 10:11–28 as a record of actual marches, such as we find in chap. 33, for instance.

PART VIII.

NUMBERS 10:29–12:16: ENCOUNTERS AND EXPERIENCES IN THE SINAI

INTRODUCTION

In Num 10:29–12:16 we encounter for the first time in the book of Numbers selections from the JE historiographic archive. These sources, generally considered to be earlier than the priestly texts of Numbers, preserve distinctive traditions about the wilderness period, characterized as a time in which relations between the Israelites and their God were generally harsh.

As this section of Numbers begins, we read of a meeting between Moses and his Midianite father-in-law, here named Hobab, who was apparently persuaded to accompany the Israelites on their way through Sinai (Num 10:29–32). The Israelites set out from "the mountain of YHWH," located in southern Sinai, with the Ark borne at the head of the fighting force and YHWH's cloud hovering above them (Num 10:33–34). In contrast to the priestly notice in Num 10:12, no destination is mentioned here. At this point in the narrative, a hymn to the Ark is cited from an independent source. It consists of two captioned poetic lines (Num 10:35–36).

Numbers 11 is an elaborate narrative telling of incidents on the way to Hazeroth, a site in southern Sinai. It epitomizes YHWH's wrath over Israel's rebelliousness and records a change in the governance of the Israelites, whereby Moses shared authority with a council of seventy elders *(zeqēnîm)*. Numbers 12 makes an important statement on Moses' unique status and role. It comes against the background of a challenge to Moses' authority by Aaron and Miriam. As chap. 12 ends, Miriam is punished for speaking against Moses but is ultimately healed through his intercession.

Num 12:16, at the very close of this section, is a postscript inserted by P to reconcile Num 10:12 with Num 11:35. In 10:12 (P) the Israelites are already on their way to the Wilderness of Paran, whereas in 11:35 (JE) they are just arriving at Hazeroth, and still in southern Sinai! To show awareness of the discrepancy between the sources, P says in 12:16 that "only thereafter *(we'aḥar)*," namely, after all that is recorded in 10:29–12:15, did the Israelites actually begin their march northward to the Wilderness of Paran.

TRANSLATION

10 [29]Moses addressed Hobab son of Reuel, the Midianite (the father-in-law of Moses), "We are marching to the place of which YHWH has declared: 'That very one will I grant to you!' Accompany us, and we will be generous to you, for YHWH has assured Israel of good things."

[30]He responded, "I will not come along; I prefer to return to the land of my birth."

[31]Moses went on, "Please do not part company with us; for truly, you know where we should make camp in the wilderness, and you could serve as our eyes.

32 “If you accompany us, we will share with you the good things YHWH is about to confer on us.”

33 They marched three days’ distance from the mountain of YHWH, with the Ark of YHWH’s Covenant marching ahead of them < three days’ distance > to scout out for them a place to encamp.

34 The cloud of YHWH remained above them during the day as they set forth from the encampment.

35 Whenever the Ark set out on the march, Moses proclaimed,

“Attack, YHWH!
Your enemies disperse;
Your foes flee from your presence!”

36 When the Ark came to a halt, he would declare,

“Bring back, O YHWH,
The myriads of Israel’s militias!”

11 1 The people continued to grieve bitterly, within earshot of YHWH, and YHWH overheard, and his wrath flared. The flame of YHWH blazed at them, consuming [those at] the edge of the encampment.

2 The people raised their grievance with Moses, and after Moses entreated YHWH the flame subsided.

3 That site was named Taberah, for the flame of YHWH had blazed at them.

4 The rabble in their midst had insatiable appetites. They complained again and again, as did the Israelites, in the following words:

5 “Who will feed us meat? We recall the fish we dined on in Egypt without cost; the cucumbers, melons, leeks, onions, and garlic.

6 “But now, our throats are dry; there is nothing to eat. All we can look forward to is manna.”

7 Now, manna was similar to coriander seed, and its texture was like that of bdellium.

8 The people would move about, gathering it up. They would grind it or pound it in a mortar, to be boiled in a pot or made into cakes. It tasted like creamy oil.

9 At night, when dew fell over the encampment, manna would alight on top of it.

10 Moses overheard the people as they complained, clan by clan, each person at the entrance of his tent. YHWH’s wrath had flared, and Moses regarded the situation as dangerous.

11 Moses addressed YHWH: “Why have you brought misfortune on your servant? What have I done to displease you, that you have imposed the burden of this entire people on me?

12 “Did I conceive this entire people; did I give birth to it? Yet you com-

mand me: 'Carry him in your lap!'—as a male nurse carries an infant—to the land you promised to his ancestors.

[13]"Where can I find enough meat to feed this entire people? For they complain to me, saying, 'Give us meat to eat!'

[14]"I cannot bear responsibility for this entire people by myself. It is too burdensome for me!

[15]"If you insist on treating me this way put me to death, if I displease you—but let me not witness my own misfortune."

[16]Thereupon, YHWH instructed Moses: Assemble in my presence seventy men from among the elders of Israel, whom you know to be truly the elders of the people and its senior officers. Bring them to the Tent of Meeting, and let them station themselves there, beside you.

[17]I will descend to communicate with you there. Then I will withdraw some of the spirit that rests upon you and confer it on them, so that they can share responsibility for all of the people with you, and you will not have to bear it alone.

[18]And to the people say: Make yourselves ritually fit for tomorrow, when you will eat meat. For you have been complaining within earshot of YHWH, saying, "Who will feed us meat? It was better for us in Egypt!" Indeed, YHWH will give you meat and you shall eat.

[19]You shall eat it not for one or two days, or for five or ten days, or even for twenty days;

[20]Rather, up to a whole month of days, until it comes out of your nostrils and is loathsome to you. For you have rejected YHWH who is present in your midst, and have complained to him, saying, "Why, indeed, did we leave Egypt?"

[21]But Moses spoke up: "The people in whose midst I find myself include six hundred thousand foot soldiers, and yet you say, 'I will give them enough meat to eat for a whole month of days!'

[22]"Could flocks and herds be slaughtered for them in quantities sufficient for them? Were all the fish of the sea to be caught for them, would that meet their needs?"

[23]YHWH replied to Moses: Is anything beyond the reach of YHWH's arm? You will presently observe whether what I have spoken will happen to you.

[24]Moses came out of the Tent of Meeting and conveyed YHWH's message to the people. He then assembled seventy men from among the elders of the people and stationed them around the Tent.

[25]YHWH descended in the cloud and spoke to him. He withdrew some of the spirit that had rested on him, and bestowed it on the seventy elders. As the spirit settled on them, they began to prophesy ecstatically, but did not persist.

[26]Now, two men had remained in the encampment; one was named Eldad

and the other was named Medad. The spirit had come to rest on them, for they were among those registered [as elders]. They had not gone out to the Tent, and [now] they continued to prophesy ecstatically inside the encampment.

27A youth ran over to Moses and reported to him as follows: "Eldad and Medad are prophesying inside the encampment."

28Joshua son of Nun, Moses' attendant since his youth, spoke up and said, "My lord, Moses, restrain them!"

29Moses replied to him, "Are you being zealous on my account? Would that the entire people of YHWH were prophets, if only YHWH would bestow his spirit on them."

30Moses reentered the encampment in the company of the elders of Israel.

31A wind gusted from YHWH, and swept up quail from the sea, dropping them over the encampment about the extent of one day's march in either direction around the encampment, and about two cubits over the surface of the ground.

32The people set about that entire day, the entire night and the entire day following to gather the quail—the one with the least gathered ten homers—and they spread them all around the encampment.

33While the meat was still between their teeth, even before it had been eaten, YHWH's wrath flared at the people. YHWH struck down the people in great numbers.

34That site was named Qibhroth Ha-Taavah, for those who had insatiable appetites were buried there.

35From Qibhroth Ha-Taavah, the people marched to Hazeroth, and they remained in Hazeroth.

12 1Miriam and Aaron spoke against Moses on the matter of the Cushite woman whom he had married: "He has taken a Cushite wife!"

2They went on to say, "Has YHWH spoken to Moses alone? Has he not also spoken to us?" YHWH took note of this.

3As for Moses, the man, he was exceedingly unassuming, more so than any person on the face of the earth.

4Suddenly, YHWH addressed Moses, Aaron, and Miriam: Go out all three of you to the Tent of Meeting! The three of them departed.

5Then YHWH descended in a pillar of cloud and stood at the entrance of the Tent. He called out: Aaron and Miriam! The two of them emerged.

6He said: Take heed of my words!
If there should be a prophet of yours,
[who is] of YHWH,
In a vision would I make myself known to him;
In a dream would I speak to him.
7Not so my servant, Moses!

Of all my household
He is most trusted.
8Mouth to mouth I speak to him;
In clear view, not in riddles.
He looks upon the likeness of YHWH.
How is it then, that you were not afraid to speak against my servant, against Moses?
9YHWH's wrath flared at them. Then he departed.
10The cloud moved away from the Tent, and Aaron turned to Miriam, and behold—she was covered with scales, as white as snow.
11Aaron besought Moses: "By my life, master! Pray do not impose on us punishment for the sin we have so foolishly committed.
12"May she not remain as a stillbirth, who issues from his mother's womb with half of his body eaten away!"
13Moses petitioned YHWH with these words: "*No more*, I beseech you! Heal her, I beseech you!"
14Then YHWH said to Moses: Suppose her father had spat directly in her face, would she not remain in disgrace for seven days? Let her be confined for seven days outside the encampment and only afterward be readmitted.
15So Miriam was confined outside the encampment for seven days. The people delayed their march until Miriam had been readmitted.
16Only thereafter did the people set out from Hazeroth, and they encamped in the Wilderness of Paran.

NOTES TO 10:29–32: MOSES' MIDIANITE RELATIONS

10 29. *the father-in-law of Moses.* The words *ḥôtēn Môšeh* are probably a gloss, inserted in order to identify Hobab, whose name has not been mentioned prior to this verse. There is no basis for identifying Reuel as Moses' father-in-law, by construing the syntax in that manner.

Hobab. The name *Ḥôbāb* is a passive, shortened form meaning "loved one, friend, client." We may compare the name *ʿÔbēd,* shortened from the full name *ʿÔbadyāh* 'servant of YHWH'. A cognate of Hebrew *Ḥôbāb* occurs in Sabaean South Arabic, and in Ugaritic as well *(HALAT,* 273; Whitaker 1972: 266, under *ḫbb).* In Deut 33:3 the God of Israel is characterized as "the befriender of peoples *(ḥôbēb ʿammîm).*" One named Hobab is, therefore, one befriended by a deity. This name is similar in meaning to *Reʿûʾēl* 'the friend of El', in this very verse. It is also similar to *ʾEldād* and *Mêdād* in Num 11:26–27, and to *Yedîdyāh* in 2 Sam 12:25. Like the root *ḥ-b-b,* so, too, the verbal root *y-d-d* 'to love, be in love' is expressed in personal names, and we note the Ugaritic epithet *ydd (bn) il* 'beloved of (the son of) Il (Gibson 1978: 65, on

4:vii:46; 68, on 5:i:15), and the personal name *mddb'l* 'beloved of Baal' (Whitaker 1972: 412).

the place. Reference to "the place *(hammāqôm)*" promised by God to the Israelites recalls Gen 13:14 (J): "Raise your eyes and look out from the place *(min hammāqôm)* where you are."

That very one will I grant to you! In Num 10:29 we find emphatic syntax. Hebrew *'ôtô 'ettēn lākem,* literally, "it I shall grant to you," recalls the wording in Exod 10:11: *'ôtāh 'attem mebaqqešîm* 'because that is what you are seeking'. The idiom *dibbēr ṭôb 'al* 'to speak well regarding' conveys an assurance, a promise, and also a prediction of good fortune. Note the reflex of 10:29 in Josh 23:14–15; and see 1 Kgs 22:8, 13, 18 for similar expressions.

30. *to the land of my birth.* Hebrew *'el 'arṣî we'el môladtî,* literally, "to my land and to my birthplace," is an example of hendiadys, hence "to the land of my birth." Compare E. A. Speiser's translation of Gen 12:1 in Anchor Bible 1.

31. The force of Hebrew *'al kēn* is to emphasize a fact or circumstance, not to convey purpose or result, as is its normal sense. Compare usage in Gen 2:24: "For so it is *(kî 'al kēn)* that a man leaves his father"; and in Num 14:43. The idiom *hāyāh l-*X *le'ênayîm* 'to serve for X as eyes' is unique to this biblical passage.

32. The wording of this verse suggests that the Midianites were actually being offered a share in the Promised Land. This thought is carried over from v 29. In COMMENT 1, below, this significant possibility will be discussed, and the question of the identity of the Midianites referred to in the present passage will be clarified.

NOTES TO 10:33–36: THE SONG OF THE ARK

33. *three days' distance.* In this verse, the words *derek šelôšet yāmîm* occur twice. The second occurrence is undoubtedly a dittography, a scribal error, as is shown in the translation. The Ark went at the head of the fighting force, a position basic to its function as an emblem of the God of Israel.

the mountain of YHWH. Hebrew *har YHWH,* as a designation for the mountain in the Sinai variously known as "Horeb" and "Sinai," is unique to this passage. Better known is *har hā'elôhîm* 'the mountain of God' (Exod 3:5; 4:7; and see 1 Kgs 19:20, within the Elijah tale). Elsewhere, *har YHWH* may refer to Mount Zion (Isa 2:3).

the Ark of YHWH's Covenant. The designation *'arôn berît YHWH* requires clarification. It connotes the Ark in which the "tablets of the covenant *(luḥôt habberît)*" were deposited (Deut 9:9, 11, 15). Referring to the Ark in terms of its contents is characteristic of Deuteronomy (Deut 10:8; 31:9, 25–26). In presumably earlier biblical sources, no such connection is expressed. It is likely that the Ark was originally conceived as a seat for the Deity or as an emblem of some sort. Elsewhere this designation of the Ark occurs only once, in Num 14:44, within a priestly section of the text.

scout out. The verb *tûr* 'to circumambulate, scout, survey' is frequently employed in Numbers 13–14, whose subject matter is, after all, the scouting of the land of Canaan or parts thereof. In a similar context, the same verb occurs in Deut 1:33.

a place to encamp. The Hebrew noun *menûḥāh* here connotes a place to halt, to pause. This sense is evident farther on, in v 36: *ûbenûḥoh* 'when it (= the Ark) came to a halt' (cf. usage in 1 Sam 25:9; Isa 7:19). Hebrew *menûḥāh* may also connote a permanent, secure habitation (Deut 12:9; Jer 45:3; Ruth 1:9), but this is not its sense here, where context relates to the military function of the Ark on the march.

34. *The cloud of YHWH.* Hebrew *ʿanan YHWH* occurs elsewhere only in Exod 40:28 (P), although in Num 14:14 we find reference to "your (= YHWH's) cloud *(ʿanānkā).*" More will be said about the "cloud" in remarks on 12:4–5.

There are certain problems of a source-critical nature pertaining to Num 10:33–34. It is entirely possible that these verses were interpolated by a priestly compiler who sought to make the JE account conform to priestly notions regarding the character and function of the Ark as a repository for the tablets. There are further indications that vv 33–34 were interpolated. The verb *tûr* 'to scout, survey' occurs frequently in chaps. 13–14, but only in the priestly sections of those chapters. In the JE sections we encounter a different diction: *ûreʾîtem ʾet hāʾāreṣ* 'you shall inspect the land'. The verb *tûr* occurs only once more, in Num 15:39, within a priestly code. It should also be mentioned that *ʿanan YHWH* is a priestly locution, occurring elsewhere in Torah literature only in Exod 40:38, within a priestly section. It is reasonable to suppose that the priestly compiler who interpolated vv 33–34, if he did so, was under the influence of Deut 1:30–33, where we likewise find the idiom *hahhôlek lipnêkem* 'who goes in front of you'. There it is YHWH who goes ahead of the Israelites "to scout out *(lātûr)* a place for you to encamp *(laḥanôtekem).*"

A priestly compiler probably inserted vv 33–34 between Num 10:29–32 and the Song of the Ark (vv 35–36). The original verses, now interrupted, were linked by the verb *nāsaʿ* 'to march', which occurs in vv 29, 33, and 35. In this way, the compiler modulated the import of Deut 1:30–33. Deuteronomic *hālak* 'to go' becomes *nāsaʿ* 'to march', and it is the Ark, instead of YHWH himself, that went ahead of the fighting force. Secondarily, the verb *nûaḥ* 'to halt, encamp' of v 33 links up with another form of the same verb, in the caption of v 36: *ûbenûḥoh* 'when it (= the Ark) came to a halt'.

35–36. Num 10:35–36 are set off by inverted *nuns*, which indicates an awareness on the part of the ancient Jewish scribes that these two captioned verses were either out of place here or, as is more likely, that they were cited from an independent source. This scribal convention parallels the practice of the Alexandrian scribes in their copies of Greek texts, where similar markings are evident (Lieberman 1950: 38–46; Levine 1976).

Whenever. The force of the narrative opening *wayyehî* 'so it was' is durative, not punctive; that is, the hymn was sung whenever the Ark set out on the march or came to a halt.

Attack, YHWH! The sense of Hebrew *qûmāh YHWH* is not properly conveyed by the rendering "Arise, YHWH!" *NJPS* is closer to the correct meaning when it translates "Advance, O LORD!" This is a call to the God of Israel to attack the enemy, here identified as God's own enemy. Hence I translate "Attack, YHWH!" Compare Judg 5:12: *qûm Bārāq ûšebēh šebyekā ben ʾAbînōʿam* 'Attack, Barak! Take your captives, son of Abinoam!' Somewhat less precise is usage in Pss 10:12 and 17:13.

Your enemies disperse; Your foes flee. The mood of the verbs *yāpûṣû* and *yānûsû* is indicative, not modal. We have a bold declaration of fact: when the God of Israel attacks, his enemies are compelled to disperse and flee. In early Hebrew poetry in general the prefixed, conjunctive *waw* is probably secondary. I therefore omit it here in the translation of the poetic lines, thereby resisting the tendency to interpret the hymn of the Ark as expressing a wished-for result, as if to say, "that your enemies may disperse."

We note what appears to be another version of Num 10:35–36 in Ps 68:2:

God attacks!
His enemies disperse!
His foes flee from his presence!

In the psalm, there can be doubt that the inevitable is being stated.

36. *Bring back.* In the second poetic line the precise sense of the Hebrew verb *šûbāh* (which would normally be taken to mean "Return!") has been debated since late antiquity. Gesenius, followed by G. B. Gray, maintained that in this verse we have the locative accusative, albeit implicit, as if to say, "Return, YHWH, *to* the myriads of the clans of Israel!" Ehrlich's objection to this interpretation is valid. Ehrlich maintained that there is no place-name to serve as the object of the verb, and that one is required for the locative accusative to be assumed (Ehrlich 1969: 1.255).

Ehrlich's own resolution was adopted in *NJPS*: "Return O LORD, You who are Israel's myriads." Ehrlich compared this poem to the exclamation of Elisha, recorded in 2 Kgs 2:12: "O father, father! Israel's chariots and horsemen!" There the sense is that Elijah, as the true prophet of YHWH, represented the God of Israel, the source of all power. Here too the sense would be that YHWH's hosts are the true fighting force of Israel.

Another approach, though rejected by G. B. Gray and others, may nevertheless serve us well. The verb *šûb* is almost always a verb of motion, but in certain specific constructions it may have active-transitive force: "to bring back, restore." This seems to be the case in the well-known idiom *šāb šebût* 'to restore the captivity' (Deut 30:3; Jer 29:14). The active-transitive aspect of the verb *sub* would be the appropriate sense here, as well. The role of a military commander is to lead forces into battle and to bring them back safely. This conventional role is epitomized in Num 27:17 with respect to Joshua, Moses' successor, and in 1 Sam 8:20, where the putative role of the king is characterized. In the immediate context of the present poem it is the Ark, as the manifestation of the God of Israel, that moves forward to the attack and, when the battle is over, leads the Israelite forces home safely.

The myriads of Israel's militias. In interpreting the Hebrew *ribebôt ʾalpê Yiśrāʾēl* it may be best to assume a play on meanings, whereby *ribebôt* has a numerical connotation, "myriads," but *ʾalpê Yiśrāʾēl* designates "clans," not "thousands." Admittedly, the parallelism in Deut 33:17 would suggest consistency, for there we read, "These are the myriads of Ephraim *(ribebôt ʾEprayîm)*; these are the thousands of Manasseh *(ʾalpê Menaššeh)*." Nevertheless, the meanings evident in Num 31:5 suggest another interpretation: "There were recruited from the clans of Israel *(mēʾalpê Yiśrāʾēl)* a thousand *(ʾelep)* from each tribe for military service." In the NOTES on Num 1:16 it was explained that the term *ʾelep* 'clan' is actually unrelated to *ʾelep* 'a thousand', but instead derives from *ʾelep* (Akkadian *alpu*) 'ox, bull', the lead animal of the herd and hence a way of referring to the herd itself.

The tribal militias of premonarchic Israel were recruited from the various regions of the country. How this system worked is most clearly expressed in the Song of Deborah (Judges 5). Such units were not part of a standing army, but were called up by designated leaders when needed (Judg 6:15; 1 Sam 10:19; 17:8; 18:13; Mic 5:1).

NOTES TO NUMBERS 11: INCIDENTS ON THE WAY TO HAZEROTH—REBELLION, CHARISMA, AND PROBLEMS OF GOVERNANCE

11 1. *The people.* It may not be noticed by the reader, but in this verse, for the first time in the book of Numbers, the Israelites are designated *hāʿām* 'the people'. In Num 1:1–10:28, which contain priestly material, the Israelites are designated as *ʿēdāh* 'community', as *benê Yiśrāʾēl* 'the Israelite people', and by other terms of reference, which may also occur in JE. As a rule, whenever *hāʿām* is used in the book of Numbers, we can identify the source in which this designation occurs as JE.

There are two attestations of *ʿam* 'people' in the priestly section, Num 1:1–

10:28, but in each case usage is specialized, and the term *ʿam* does not designate the Israelite people per se. In Num 5:21 *betôk ʿammēk* means "among your kin" and is part of a curse formula. In Num 9:13, *ʿam* likewise means "kin" and occurs in a formula of banishment. Farther on in Numbers, *ʿam* also occurs in priestly material, but in special contexts. In Num 27:14 and 31:2 we read that one is gathered unto his *ʿam* 'kin', a common way of referring to burial.

continued to grieve bitterly. The construction *kemitʾônenîm raʿ* is unusual, but its meaning is clear. Prefixed *kap* may have temporal force: "as the people grieved." The only other biblical attestation of the *hithpaʿel* form, *hitʾônēn,* occurs in Lam 3:39: "of what shall a living man complain *(yitʾônēn)?*" The root is either *ʾ-n-h* or *ʾ-n-n* 'to grieve, mourn', and some mingling of the two roots is possible.

2. *raised their grievance.* The idiom *ṣāʿaq ʾel* 'to cry out to' may express a formal grievance brought to the attention of a king or other person in authority. In ancient Israel, as in some other societies, private persons had the right to petition their leaders, to "cry out" to them for succor (1 Kgs 20:39; 2 Kgs 4:1; 6:28; 8:3–5).

entreated. The verb *hitpallēl* 'to pray, entreat' occurs most noticeably in Samuel and Kings. In Torah literature, the only other occurrences outside Num 11:2 are in Gen 20:7–17 and 21:7 (E). Here this verb punctuates Moses' function as an intercessor. The etymology of *hitpallēl,* and of nominal *tepillāh* 'prayer', is not entirely clear. The *piʿel* form of the same root, *p-l-l,* may mean "to judge" as in 1 Sam 2:25, where God is said to plead the cause of those who offend against others: "If one person offends against another, God will defend him *(ûpillelô ʾelôhîm)*; but if a person offends against YHWH, who will undertake his vindication *(yitpallēl lô)?*" Also note legal usage in Exod 21:22 and Deut 32:31, where we encounter the noun *pelîlîm* 'judgment', and in Job 31:11, 28: *ʿawôn pelîlî* 'a punishable offense'. On this basis *hitpallēl,* as a reflexive form of the verb, would mean "to submit oneself to judgment; to judge oneself." A person petitioning God is asking to be judged worthy, to be vindicated and, accordingly, to have his petition granted by God (Spiegel 1953).

3. The elliptical *wayyiqrāʾ* may be rendered as a passive, "it was named." Hebrew *tabʿērāh* means 'conflagration'. What we have here is a folk etymology of an unidentified locale. Perhaps a fire broke out in the encampment and was interpreted as a punishment from God. The God of Israel often used fire as a punishment for those who had offended against him. This verse contains the only biblical attestation of the combination *ʾēš YHWH* 'YHWH's fire', although in Deut 4:36 we find *ʾiššô haggedôlāh* 'his (= YHWH's) great fire'.

4. *The rabble in their midst.* The Hebrew *ʾasapsûp* is a reduplicative form of the verb *ʾ-s-p* 'to gather in', which is said of taking in foundlings as well as lost objects (Deut 22:2; Ps 27:10). The verb *ʾasap* often connotes the assem-

bling of fighting forces (1 Sam 17:11). So it remains unclear whether reference here is to auxiliary fighting forces, or to camp followers and other non-Israelite hangers-on. In the parallel account of Exod 12:38 the term used is *ʿēreb rab*, perhaps originally *ʿarabrāb*, also a reduplicative form meaning "a mixed group." In both accounts, in Numbers and in Exodus, these presumably non-Israelites are blamed for incurring God's wrath, whereas the fault of the Israelites themselves was that they followed suit.

had insatiable appetites. Hebrew *hitʾawwû taʾawāh* is a cognate accusative construction, literally, "they craved a craving." A later reference to this incident, set in the wilderness period, occurs in Ps 106:14. The *hithpaʿel* stem of the verb *ʾāwāh* 'to desire' most often, if not always, connotes an improper or excessive desire, not a bona fide one. In Deut 5:21, within the Deuteronomic version of the Decalogue, we read, "Do not covet *(lôʾ titʾawweh)* your neighbor's house," which restates *lôʾ taḥmôd* 'Do not covet' in the previous clause. The pejorative sense is common in wisdom literature (Prov 13:4; 21:26), and it also informs Amos 5:18. It is unclear whether, according to 2 Sam 23:15, David's craving for water was excessive, but it certainly led to dangerous exploits!

5. As has been pointed out by numerous commentators, the demands of the people stated here pose two apparent problems. For one thing, Rashi long ago noted that a demand for meat made little sense on the part of a people said to be rich in flocks (Exod 12:38; 17:3; 19:3; 34:5; Num 14:33; 32:1). Furthermore, the formulation of the demand is puzzling, because the people proceed to recall the fish and fresh produce they enjoyed in Egypt, but do not recall having enjoyed meat there; and yet, as the account proceeds, the demand for meat is reiterated and emphasized.

Based on what we know of the diet of the ancient Egyptians, the recollection by the people of the fish and fresh produce that had been available in Egypt is strikingly realistic. Fish was plentiful in the rivers and canals of Egypt, a fact alluded to by the author of Isa 19:8–10. Herodotus also refers to the abundance of fish in Egypt (Herodotus 1971: 11.92–93, at 1.377–379). We are told that when the rivers of Egypt turned to blood, all of the fish in the Nile died (Exod 7:21).

The detailed list of foods is entirely appropriate. (1) Cucumbers, Hebrew *qiššuʾîm (Cucumis melo var. chate Nard.)*, are native to Egypt *(EB* 7.279–280). (2) Watermelons, Hebrew *ʾabaṭiḥîm (Cucumis melo)*, are represented on ancient Egyptian wall paintings and reliefs and are still plentiful in Egypt today *(EB* 1.20–21). (3) Leeks, Hebrew *ḥāṣîr*, a collective noun *(Allium porrum L)*, were widely grown in ancient Egypt as a garden vegetable *(EB* 3.270–271). (4) Garlic, Hebrew *šûmîm (Allium sativum)*, is called in Akkadian *šūmu* (Loew 1881: 1.336–337). (5) Onions, Hebrew *beṣalîm (Allium cepa)* are mentioned only here in the Hebrew Bible, but the term is common in Late Hebrew *(EB* 2.306–307).

6. *throat.* The Hebrew word *nepeš* may designate virtually any part of the interior of the thorax, from the mouth (even from the nostrils) down to the intestines. The meaning "throat" is appropriate here, and it is also the sense in Jer 31:14 and 25, where reference is to drinking fluids. In Jonah 2:6 and Ps 62:2, water is said to reach to one's *nepěs* 'throat' (or "nostrils," perhaps), expressing the danger of drowning. The mere fact that the Hebrew language uses the same word to connote both physical and nonphysical entities is significant. It suggests the unity of body and soul, of the physical and spiritual.

manna. The Hebrew word *mān* is interpreted to mean "What?" on the basis of the explanation provided in Exod 16:15. This appears to represent a folk etymology, and the word probably has another meaning, which eludes us. During their field trips in the Sinai, modern naturalists have found insect secretions whose appearance correlates with the description of the manna in Num 11:7–9. Certain insects come to rest on a tree known as *Tamarix mannifera.* In central Sinai these trees are more specifically identified as *Trabutina mannifero Elnenberg,* and in the Sinai plains as *Najacocus supentinus Green.* The insect secretions glisten like dew and must be harvested early in the morning before ants get to them. Some excretions remain on the trees, and some fall to the ground. They may be eaten in their natural form or ground up, just as we read in Num 11:8. The sense of the present verse is dependent on the meaning of the word *bedôlaḥ* in v 7. If it refers to a type of sap, the implication of this verse is that the manna was sticky. If, however, *bedôlaḥ* designates a gemstone, bdellium, the meaning is that the secretions glistened in the sun like a brilliant stone (*EB* 5.7–10).

7. In Num 11:7–9 we have a parenthetical description of the manna that interrupts the continuing narrative. The Hebrew *zeraʿ gād* has been identified as coriander seed (*EB* 2.430). We read that the manna looked like *bedôlaḥ: weʿênô keʾên habbedôlaḥ,* literally, "Its eye was like the eye of *bedôlaḥ.*" In biblical Hebrew, *ʿayîn* 'eye' can mean "appearance, texture, color," in other words, what the eye discerns (cf. Lev 13:5; Ezek 1:4).

8. In Exod 16:14 (P) we find a description of the manna as "a flaky substance, as fine as frost on the ground." The present verse includes an unusual list of ancient implements. We know of millstones, of course, but only here do we read of *medôkāh* 'mortar', and *pārûr* 'pot' occurs elsewhere only in 1 Sam 2:14.

10. The narrative resumes here. YHWH is exceedingly angry, and Moses extremely worried. It is interesting, however, that Moses does not castigate the people for their sinfulness, but instead confronts YHWH with the problems caused by his position as leader of the Israelites. Moses' role as an intercessor is discussed in COMMENT 4, below.

11. The language used here should be compared with Gen 19:9; 43:6; and Exod 5:22, where the verb *hēraʿ* 'to hurt, do harm' is also employed. It is of

interest that Moses refers to himself as *ʿabdekā* 'your servant'. This term is characteristic of epistolary style, as known from Old Babylonian letters (*CAD* A, 2.251, s.v. *ardu,* e). It also features prominently in Hebrew letters of the biblical period, such as those from Lachish and Arad (Pardee 1982: 157–159). The self-deprecating manner of referring to oneself as a servant, especially when addressing persons in authority, is also typical of the style of the Jahwist (Gen 18:3, 5). There are many traces of epistolary style in biblical literature (Levine 1979b).

The oppressiveness of leadership, conveyed by the verb *nāśāʾ* 'to bear' and the noun *maśśāʾ* 'burden', is expressed in Exod 18:22, in the Elohist's version of the reorganization of the Israelite people; and in Deut 1:12, in the words of Moses' complaint (see below, in v 17). The idiom *māṣāʾ ḥēn beʿênê* 'to find favor in the eyes of' is typical of the Jahwist's narrative in Exod 33:12–13, 16 (see below, in v 15).

this entire people. Beginning in v 11 and carrying through v 14, Moses repeatedly refers to the Israelites as *kol hāʿām* 'the entire people', characterized as an unruly multitude who are difficult to govern effectively. This term of reference serves to link the present narrative to Exodus 18, where the context is similar: the entire people impatiently looks to Moses for leadership. With a somewhat less negative connotation, *kol hāʿām* informs other Exodus narratives as well (Exod 19:16; 20:18; 24:3, 8; 32:3; 33:8).

12. The diction of this verse is echoed in the imagery of Isa 40:11, where it is said that God will bear Israel as a shepherd carries young lambs in his lap. In Isa 49:23 we read that foreign kings will serve as Israel's nurses, and that the Israelites will be carried to their land on the backs of others, not in their laps! Here the sense of prepositional *ʿal* is 'to, toward', as is the normal meaning of Aramaic *ʿal.* Moses was being asked to bear the people all the way to the Promised Land.

13. *they complain.* The Hebrew idiom *bākāh ʿal,* literally, "to weep over," means "to complain," functionally speaking. This seems to be the sense throughout Numbers 11 (cf. also Deut 1:45; Judg 14:16–17).

15. *If I displease you.* The phraseology is deferential. Although Moses is angry, he remains respectful because he is addressing God.

witness my own misfortune. Hebrew *rāʾāh berāʾāh,* literally, "looking at the evil of," is similarly expressed in Gen 21:16; 44:34.

16. The role of the seventy elders as expressed here correlates with the definition of their role in Exod 24:1–11, where the elders participate in the enactment of the siniatic covenant. For the ongoing role of the elders in Moses' career, see Exod 3:16; 4:2; and 17:6.

officers. In Hebrew usage, *šôṭerîm* are so called primarily because they issue written documents or actually write them. This definition emerges from the Akkadian cognate, *šaṭāru* 'to write', as well as from Aramaic *šeṭār* 'written document'. A title similar to Hebrew *šôṭēr* does not, however, occur either in

Akkadian or Aramaic, as far as we know. These same officials figure in the narratives of Exodus and in the laws of Deuteronomy. In 2 Chr 26:11, *šôṭēr* is synonymous with *sôpēr* 'scribe'.

Tent of Meeting. On the meaning of *'ôhel mô'ēd* see the NOTES on Num 1:1, where this term appears for the first time in Numbers. In the Elohist tradition, represented by Exod 33:7–11, the Tent of Meeting was located outside the encampment, and that is its projected location here and in v 26, below.

17. *I will withdraw.* The fairly rare Hebrew verb *'āṣal* means "to withdraw, retain"; compare Gen 27:36: "Have you not reserved *('āṣaltā)* a blessing for me?" (Note relevant usages in 2 Kgs 2:9; Eccl 2:10.) It is of interest that this verb accounts for the preposition *'ēṣel* 'beside, near' and for *'aṣîlê yādayîm* 'armpits' (Punic *yṣlt)* in Jer 38:12; and Ezek 13:18; 41:18. In Isa 41:9 *'aṣîlê hā'āreṣ* means "the recesses of the earth." One who is the recipient of God's spirit may be called *'āṣîl* (Exod 24:11). In v 25, below, we are told that Moses had received more than enough of God's spirit so that he could spare some for the elders! (Levine 1974: 119, n. 3).

the spirit. Hebrew *hārûaḥ* refers to the spirit of prophecy and is synonymous with *rûaḥ YHWH* 'the spirit of YHWH'. In Amos 9:7 *nābî'* 'prophet' is parallel with *'îš hārûaḥ* 'a man imbued with the spirit'. According to Num 24:2, Balaam received "the spirit" of prophecy. In the determined form, *hārûaḥ* often occurs in tales about charismatic leaders (Judg 3:10; 11:29; 1 Sam 10:6; 19:20; Isa 11:2; 61:1).

18. *Make yourselves ritually fit.* The Hebrew verbal form *hitqaddēš* literally means "to consecrate oneself," as in Exod 19:10–11. In Isa 30:29, the expression *belêl hitqaddēš ḥag* is best rendered "on a night when a festival is hallowed." Such consecration often involved ritual purification, the laundering of clothing, and abstinence from sexual relations. It is doubtful, however, if such specific preparations were intended here, where the sense is more like "Prepare yourselves!"

20. *loathsome.* The rare form *zārā'*, with final *aleph,* is to be equated with *zarah* (consonantal *z-r-h),* with final *heh,* with the meaning "hateful, alien." The Hebrew verbal root *z-w-r* is cognate with Akkadian *zêru* 'to dislike, hate, avoid' *(CAD* Z, 97). In Sir 37:30 we find this word similarly written with final *aleph* as *zārā'*, whereas in Sir 39:27 it is written *zārāh,* with final *heh.* There is, however, a notation on the manuscript bearing the variant *zārā'* (Ben Sira 1973: 38, to Sir 37, line 30; and cf. 47, to Sir 39, line 27). What all of this means is that the Masoretic reading may represent a late spelling, wherein orthographic *heh* gives way to *aleph.*

you have rejected. The verb *mā'as* means more than "despise." It connotes rejection and often occurs in castigations of Israel for its hostility to God. This theme is prominent in the epilogue to the Holiness Code (Lev 26:3–46). Hebrew *mā'as* also characterizes God's ephemeral rejection of Israel, when that happens (Jer 7:29; Lam 5:22). Hebrew *mā'as* may be regarded as the antonym of *bāḥar* 'to choose, elect' (Isa 7:15–16; 41:9; Levine 1987a).

Why. Hebrew *lāmāh,* usually rendered "Why?" often has a negative connotation, as is true of Aramaic *lemāh* and Arabic *lam;* hence "we should not have."

21. *six hundred thousand.* This total count of Israelite fighting men is also mentioned in Exod 12:37 (J). The various problems raised by such an excessive total have been widely discussed, and this schematic total is usually regarded as unrealistic; see the NOTES on Num 1:46.

foot soldiers. Hebrew *raglî* is a collective term (Judg 20:2; 1 Sam 4:10; 15:4).

22. *would that meet their needs?* Idiomatic *ûmāṣā' lāhem* literally means "would that overtake them, reach them?" The sense is that of sufficiency: "would that suffice for them?" The hyperbole expressed in this verse is certainly unrealistic in the interior of the Sinai wilderness, as far as gathering fish is concerned, and should be understood as merely expressive of the people's needs. Use of the verb *'āsap* 'to gather' with respect to fishing may allude to gathering of fish on the seashore, an ancient method of fishing.

23. *Is anything beyond the reach of YHWH's arm?* Being "short" means being inadequate in many languages. The idiom *hayad YHWH tiqṣar,* literally, "is the arm of YHWH too short?" is a good example. The same idiom occurs in Isa 50:2 and 59:1.

25. More is said about the Tent of Meeting as the focus of God's presence in Num 12:5 and, of course, in Exod 33:9–11 (E), the primary statement on Tent of Meeting as an oraculum.

prophesy ecstatically. This verse contains terminology basic to an understanding of ecstatic prophecy. The verbal form *hitnabbē'* elsewhere characterizes the activity of mantic prophets. It is told of Saul that he came upon a band of prophets and was overcome by ecstasy. He could not resist its onslaught and began to prophesy ecstatically *(lehitnabbē'*; 1 Sam 10:5, 10–11; 19:20–24; and cf. 1 Kgs 22:10).

26. The names *'Eldād* and *Mêdād* have already been referred to in the NOTES on 10:29, where their meanings were explained. Eldad and Medad were two of the elders selected by Moses. For some unexplained reason, they had not followed Moses out to the Tent of Meeting, remaining inside the encampment. When the spirit of YHWH settled upon the other elders who were assembled at the Tent, it settled upon Eldad and Medad as well, even though they were quite a distance away. After the effects of the spirit had left those elders assembled at the Tent, it nevertheless remained with Eldad and Medad.

for they were among those registered [as elders]. Although the diffusion of the spirit is here perceived as erratic, its human targets were, nevertheless, precisely identified by means of their prior registration by Moses. This is what is meant by *wehēmāh bakketûbîm.* Compare Isa 4:3: "everyone who is inscribed *(kol hakkātûb)* for life in Jerusalem." Jer 22:30 is likewise instructive: "Register *(kitbû)* this man as childless." Such statements highlight the extent of writing and its authoritative function at the time that the present narrative, Isaiah 4, and Jeremiah 22 were composed.

28. *since his youth.* Joshua's status as Moses' attendant is also noted in Exod 33:11 (E). Translating Hebrew *mibbeḥûrâw* as "from his youth" posits an abstract noun, *behûrîm* 'youth', similar to *neʿûrîm* 'youth' or *zeqûnîm* 'old age'. Alternatively, we could translate "from among his select associates," assuming that this locution reflects *bāḥûr* 'chosen, select troops' (Exod 14:7; Judg 20:15–16).

restrain. It is doubtful whether the verb *kālāʾ* implies actual detention in a prison facility, as is the case in Num 15:34, where the text explicitly refers to *mišmār* 'guard house'.

29. *are you being zealous.* The verb *qinnēʾ* expresses zeal and passion. In Num 25:13 we read that Phineas, the priest, acted zealously in defending God's honor, and Elijah (1 Kgs 19:10–14) defended the honor of God, an act conveyed by the same verb. One can be overly zealous, of course!

the entire people of YHWH. The designation of the Israelites as *ʿam YHWH* 'people of YHWH', like *ʿam Kemôš* 'people of Kemosh' in Num 21:29 (cf. Jer 48:46) expresses, in the first instance, the covenant relationship between a people and its national god in terms of kinship. In several of its occurrences, *ʿam YHWH* refers specifically to the fighting forces of Israel, its militias (Judg 5:11; 2 Sam 1:12; Good 1983). Elsewhere the context pertains to governance, referring to the anointing of a king over all of the people (2 Sam 6:21; 2 Kgs 9:6). The theme of governance also informs Num 17:6, 1 Sam 2:24, and even Zeph 2:10. The people of Israel is the people of YHWH, and its fighting forces are those of YHWH. In Ps 47:10 Israel is called *ʿam ʾelôhê ʾAbrāhām* 'the people of the God of Abraham'.

30. *reentered.* Moses was at the Tent of Meeting located outside the encampment when the matter of Eldad and Medad was reported to him. The *niphʿal* of the verb *ʾāsap* 'to gather' can have the sense of reentry, as in Num 12:15, below.

31. *swept up.* Read *wayyāgēz* 'he caused to pass, he swept up', a *hiphʿil* form, from *g-w-z,* instead of Masoretic *wayyāgoz,* a *qal* form. The *qal* would mean "to pass by, pass over" and would represent a verb of motion (cf. Ps 90:10; Nah 1:12, where the *niphʿal* form occurs). What is required here, however, is an active-transitive verb; compare Arabic *jaza,* IV-form, for a sense comparable to that conveyed by the Hebrew *hiphʿil* stem (Gray—ICC, 119). God often causes winds to blow (Ps 78:26). This is a major theme in the Song of the Sea (Exodus 15). Hebrew *millipnê YHWH* 'from before YHWH' recalls 1 Kgs 19:11, in the Elijah episode, where we read of a powerful wind gusting "in front of YHWH *(lipnê YHWH).*"

quail. The Hebrew *śelâw (Coturnix coturnix)* appears as *śalwî* (collective) in Syriac and Arabic (*EB* 8.306–307). The plural form, *śalwîm,* occurring here, is predicated on just such a form. There is a later reference to the quail of the wilderness in Ps 105:40. The sea referred to is undoubtedly the Mediterranean. Quail flourished in Europe and in the Mediterranean area and migrated across Canaan, the Sinai, and Egypt into Nubia, Ethiopia, and the region of Lake Chad. Migrations occurred in spring and autumn, but not regularly every year and not always in great numbers. When passing over Egypt and the Sinai, the quail were already extremely exhausted and would drop into the foliage for shelter before migrating farther. As they always entered the foliage on the north side and exited on the south side, the Arabs would set traps for them on the south side of the foliage or place nets on the seashore. When caught, the quail were often caged and fattened, and their meat was marketed as a delicacy. Here we read that the quail were cured in the sun (Num 32:32). The verb *nāṭaš* 'to drop, leave on the ground' occurs in Exod 23:11, with reference to what grows from the earth naturally in the seventh year. Such produce was to be "left" on the ground (Gray—ICC).

32. The *ḥômer* was a large, dry measure consisting of ten ephahs (Ezek 45:11).

33. A couple of locutions in this verse require comment. Hebrew *ṭerem yikkārēt* literally means "before it was cut off," that is to say, "consumed." Hebrew *makkāh rabbāh* means "a great blow," with the verb *hikkāh* 'to strike' most often connoting a deathblow.

34. Here we have still another folk etymology for an unidentified locale, just as we had in v 3, above.

35. Hazeroth is not positively identified, there being serious doubt about the proposed identification with ʿAin Khadra (Aharoni and Avi-Yonah 1979: 40, map 48). According to Deut 1:1, Hazeroth was located near Di-Zahab (Dahab), a known site in southern Sinai.

The composition of Numbers 11 requires comment. Two discrete subjects are incorporated in the narrative: (1) the dissatisfaction of the people with respect to food, particularly their disgust with the manna and their demand for meat; and (2) the change in the governance of the people resulting from Moses' complaint about the strains of his office. As Gray has shown, one could extract the subject of governance from the chapter, leaving what remains as a coherent narrative epitomizing God's wrath and his punishment.

Nevertheless, there is a reasonable connection between food-supply problems and political leadership. One of the primary responsibilities of a leader is to provide food for his people. There are other Torah narratives in which these two concerns, stable leadership and food and water, are integrated within the same narrative: for instance, in Exod 15:22–26 and 17:1–7, the people rebelled against Moses because they had no water. It is preferable, therefore, to accept Numbers 11 as a coherent composition instead of extracting one of the two themes, which would undo the work of the authors of JE who may have fused them initially.

NOTES TO NUMBERS 12: MOSES AS A UNIQUE PROPHET

12 1. *spoke against.* Idiomatic *dibbēr b-*, which occurs again in v 8, below, connotes actual rebellion or advocacy of the same. Thus the people "speak against" God in Num 21:5–7. For the idiom itself, see Ps 50:20; Job 19:18; and Ps 78:19 for an echo of this very episode. And yet it is likely that in this chapter a play on the ambiguity of *dibbēr b-* was intended. In this verse, and in v 8, below, the sense is negative, whereas in v 2 and again in v 8, alongside the negative connotations, *dibbēr b-* means "to speak to," as God spoke to Moses.

He [Moses] has taken a Cushite wife! The verb *lāqaḥ* 'to take', when its direct object is *ʾiššāh* 'woman, wife' can mean "to take a woman as wife," as in Gen 24:3 and Deut 24:1. Moses took a Cushite wife, we are told. Cush designates the Sudan (Nubia), the land south of Egypt, though Cush is sometimes identified as Ethiopia. The woman in question was most certainly not Zipporah, who is identified as a Midianite woman. According to Exod 18:23 (E), Zipporah had been sent home earlier, but was later brought back to join Moses by Jethro, her father. Most likely, Moses had married the Cushite woman during Zipporah's absence.

The basis of the criticism by Miriam and Aaron is not explained, and there has understandably been much speculation on this subject. The inhabitants of Cush are black, according to Jer 13:23, but race could not have been the point at issue. Perhaps there was objection to the taking of a second wife, which might have been regarded as an affront to Zipporah. Gen 31:50 gives evidence of such objection, because Laban insisted in his treaty with Jacob that the latter not take additional wives beyond Rachel and Leah, his daughters. Ancient Near Eastern marriage contracts often contained provisions that a first wife's children would be protected as heirs in the event the husband in question took a second wife during their mother's lifetime.

2. *spoken to.* Here, *dibbēr b-* means either "to speak to" or "to speak through," to communicate through a human being, to transmit a message through him. The latter sense is attested elsewhere. In his farewell address to the people, David states that "the spirit of YHWH has spoken through me *(dibbēr bî)*" (2 Sam 23:2). In 2 Chr 18:27 the prophet Micaiah challenges his critics by saying, "then YHWH did not speak through me *(lōʾ dibber YHWH bî)!*" But immediate usage in Num 12:6 is simpler: "in a dream would I speak to him *(ʾadabber bô)*." This is probably the meaning here, too, for in the perception of JE as represented in Numbers, God did not speak through

Miriam and Aaron, but only to them. It is only in the priestly writings of the Torah that God regularly transmits his utterances through Aaron, alongside Moses, and instructs them both to communicate his words to the people.

3. *As for Moses.* The syntax of Hebrew *wehā'îš Môšeh* is unusual, but the meaning is clear, cf. Exod 32:23, *kî zeh Môšeh hā'îš* 'for this man, Moses'.

unassuming. As G. B. Gray correctly emphasizes, the Hebrew *ʿānâw* does not mean "meek," but rather humble before God. This is the connotation of *ʿānâw* in Zeph 2:3, where we read that the humble obey God's just laws. In Ps 22:27, the humble are those who seek the Lord.

4–5. Once again, the Tent of Meeting is assumed to be located outside the encampment, so that Moses, Aaron, and Miriam are told to "go out" to it. YHWH descends in a cloud pillar *(beʿammûd ʿānān)* when he communicates with select human beings.

6. *If there should be a prophet of yours, [who is] of YHWH.* Traditional and modern commentators have long struggled with the Hebrew wording of this verse: *'im yihyeh nebî'akem YHWH,* which we would ordinarly take to mean "if your prophet were YHWH," which is, of course, impossible. Recently, *NJPS* presented two alternative suggestions. Its preferred rendering is "When a prophet of the LORD arises among you, I make Myself known to him." A note in *NJPS* provides an alternative rendering: "If there be a prophet among you, I, the LORD, make Myself known to him."

Both suggested renderings appear to be based on the often proposed emendation *nābî' bākem* 'a prophet among you' (instead of Masoretic *nebî'akem).* Thus the Septuagint has *ean genêtai prophêtês homon kuriô* 'If there be a prophet among you to the Lord'. Compare the Latin of the Vulgate: *Si quis fuerit inter vos propheta domini* 'If there should be among you a prophet of the Lord'. Characteristically, *NJPS* appropriated the yield of the emendation without actually emending the text. Ehrlich understood the suffixed noun *nebî'akem* as an anticipatory genitive and translated "If there should be a prophet of yours, [who is] of the LORD." For the syntax, he compared Lev 6:3: "The priest shall don his vestment, [which is] of linen *(middô bad)*" (Ehrlich 1969: 1.266). This appears to be the closest we can come to an adequate rendering.

G. B. Gray suggested that the word *YHWH* was misplaced in the Masoretic text, that it had been mistakenly moved from the beginning of the verse to a point farther on in it. He also endorsed the proposed emendation, *nābî' bākem.* According to Gray, the verse may have originally read as follows:

wayyō'mer YHWH . . . 'im yihyeh nābî' bakem,
bammar'āh 'ēlâw 'etwaddāʿ

YHWH said: . . . If there be a prophet among you,
In a vision would I make myself known to him.

Whereas Gray was only guessing, the Numbers text from Qumran cave 4, published by N. Jastram (1989), actually attests *YHWH* as the explicit subject who addresses Moses, Aaron, and Miriam in the opening words of the verse. Based on the space of the gap left in the text, and on other text-critical considerations, Jastram reconstructs the Qumran reading as follows:

wy]ʾmr YHWH ʾlyhm [smʿw nʾ dbry ʾm yhyh nbʾkmh
bmrʾh ʾlyw ʾtwdʿ wbhlw]m ʾdbr bw

And *YHWH said to them:* Hear my words! If you have a prophet, in a vision I reveal myself to him, in a dream I speak to him.

As for the indirect object pronoun, *ʾlyhm* 'to them', in the Qumran text, we have the testimony of the Septuagint: *kai eippen pros autous* 'And he spoke to them'. As for the continuation of v 6, Jastram concedes that the name of YHWH may have appeared again in the Qumran text after *nbʾkmh* 'your prophet', though he doubts it because of lack of space. It would be odd, however, to find a clause that reads *ʾim yihyeh nebîʾakem* without these words being followed by an explicit predicate, or some other qualifier. We have noted only relatively few instances in biblical Hebrew in which *ʾim* is followed by a form of the verb *hāyāh,* and then by a subject: *ʾim* + *hāyāh* + subject. In every case, this sequence is followed by some component—nominal, adverbial, or prepositional—that completes the clause. Compare Gen 28:20: *ʾim yihyeh ʾelôhîm* | *ʿimmādî* 'If God will be | with me'; or Deut 30:4: *ʾim yihyeh niddaḥakā* | *biqṣēh haššāmayîm* 'If your diaspora be | at the edge of the heavens'; or Amos 3:6: *ʾim tihyeh rāʿāh* | *bāʿîr* 'If there should be an evil | in the city.' See also Num 36:4: *weʾim yihyeh hayyôbēl* | *libnê Yiśrāʾēl* 'Should the Jubilee occur | for the Israelites'. Finally, cf. 1 Kgs 17:1: *ʾim yihyeh* | *haššānîm hāʾēleh* | *ṭal ûmāṭār* 'There shall not be | in these years | dew and rain'. The point is that *ʾim yihyeh nebîʾakem* does not sound like a complete clause. In any event, the Qumran version hardly clarifies the meaning of Num 12:6, except to render the syntax more fluid in the early part of the verse and to provide an explicit subject, YHWH, who speaks to Aaron and Miriam.

Although Ehrlich's interpretation is acceptable and has been adopted in my translation, it is far from satisfying on all scores. One would normally have taken Num 12:6 as hyperbole, as if to say, "No matter how exalted your prophet may be, he would not be of the same status as Moses!" Inevitably, one suspects that the verse has been damaged in transmission and that the similarity between consonantal *yhyh* and *YHWH* may have produced the Tetragrammaton after *nebîʾakem* instead of some other divine appellation that was there originally. Add to this the clear reading *ʾlyhm* 'to them' in the Qumran text, earlier in the verse, which is consonantally similar to *ʾlhym* 'God, divine being', and it occurs to the commentator that the original statement might have read as follows: *ʾim yihyeh nebîʾakem ʾelōhîm* 'though your prophet be a divine being'—he would not have the intimate relationship with YHWH that Moses uniqely enjoys.

In the very next verse we are told that Moses was a member of God's *bayît,* his "household," which was comprised of servants. There are several clues to who these "servants" may have been. One recalls God's words to Moses in Exod 7:1: "Behold, I have made you a god *(ʾelōhîm)* to Pharaoh, and Aaron shall be your spokesman *(nebîʾekā).*" In Psalm 82 we read that the God of Israel, initially designated *ʾelōhîm,* presides over "the council of El *(ʿadat ʾēl)*" and renders judgment "in the midst of the gods *(beqereb ʾelōhîm).*" Farther on, God expresses extreme displeasure with the kind of justice dispensed by this divine council and states, "I had regarded you as divine beings *(ʾelōhîm),* all of you as sons of Elyon. But surely, you shall die as humans, as one of the princes—you shall fall dead!"

Prophets and other divine messengers had a special role, one that brought them into close contact with God. If my suggested reconstruction of Num 12:6 is regarded as at all possible textually, this verse would be saying that Moses enjoyed a degree of access to God that was even more intimate than that normally associated with God's entourage or heavenly household.

In a dream would I speak to him. Divine communication in dreams is well attested in the Hebrew Bible, a subject explored in COMMENT 4, below. It should be noted, however, that in this verse and in v 8, below, we have a phenomenological distinction that is expressed entirely by means of vocalization. Here feminine *marʾāh* designates the sort of vision normally seen by prophets, whereas masculine *marʾeh,* in v 8, means "a clear vision," something exceptional, by contrast, and reserved for Moses.

7. *my servant.* Reference to Moses as God's *ʿebed* is suggestive (cf. Josh 1:1–2). This characterization is also applied to Abraham (Gen 26:24), to Caleb (Num 14:24), and quite often to David (2 Sam 3:18). Prophets may also be called YHWH's servants (2 Kgs 9:17; 17:13; Jer 7:25; Ezek 38:17; Zech 1:6; Ps 126:5). The term *ʿebed* obviously connotes loyalty and would be reserved for those who epitomize loyalty to God.

Of all my household. The form *bêtî* elsewhere refers consistently to "my Temple" (Isa 56:7; Jer 12:7; Ezek 23:39; Zech 3:7). This is the only time in Scripture that we find YHWH's heavenly household designated by the term *bayît.* The two concepts are hardly unrelated, however. The force of *bekol bêtî neʾemān hûʾ* is superlative: "Of all my household, / He is the most trusted." Prepositional *beth* is partitive "of all."

8. *In clear view.* Read *bemarʾeh* 'in clear view', according to the Septuagint *en eidei* 'in a vision'. The translation given here resists the effort to render the differing sensory perceptions expressed in this verse consistently. The Hebrew forms *marʾeh* and *marʾāh* refer to what is seen, as is true of nominal *temûnāh* 'likeness' and the verb *hibbîṭ* 'to look upon'. By contrast, *dibbēr* connotes

speech, and *ḥiddôt* 'riddles' are heard, not seen. *NJPS* forced the text a bit by translating "plainly and not in riddles." In its sensory perceptions, biblical imagery is not always consistent, however. In Exod 20:18 we read that "all of the people were beholding *(rôʾîm)* the thunderclaps" at Sinai. We could, of course, alter the sequence of the stichs to produce greater consistency:

Mouth to mouth I speak to him, and not in riddles;
In clear view, so that he actually looks upon the likeness of YHWH.

Reference to YHWH's "likeness" recalls Deut 4:11–12, where we read that the people heard YHWH's voice but saw no "likeness *(temûnāh)*" at the Sinai theophany. In contrast, the author of Ps 17:15 does not hesitate, in another context, to state, "Now, justified, I behold your countenance; Awake, I will be sated with your likeness *(temûnāteḵā)*." This subject is explored further in COMMENT 4, below.

9. The departure of YHWH was signaled by the lifting of the cloud from atop the Tent.

10. Miriam was stricken with a disease called *ṣāraʿat*. It has long been recognized that *ṣāraʿat* is not an accurate term for Hansen's Disease, usually called leprosy; see the NOTES on Num 5:2. In ancient Israel it was believed that *ṣāraʿat* was a punishment from God, as was believed of illnesses generally. The present episode of the affliction of Miriam served as the primary basis for a body of postbiblical Jewish interpretation that regarded *ṣāraʿat* as the specific punishment for malicious talk (Babylonian Talmud, *Sôṭāh*, 15a; *Šābûʿôt*, 8a).

11. *By my life, master!* The Hebrew idiom *bî ʾadônî* 'In me, my Lord,' can mean one of two things. It can mean that one offers to assume the punishment for the other's sin by asserting that the offense lies in oneself, not in the person suffering the punishment or threatened with it. It could also be taken to mean "By my life, at the cost of my life." This meaning would predicate prepositional *beth* as *beth pretii* the *beth* of price. In effect, *bî ʾadônî* constitutes an oath formula. The speaker vows to substitute his own life for that of another person.

impose. The verb *šît (š-y-t)* 'to place' occurs in legal contexts, where it refers to the imposition of a penalty. This is the context in Exod 21:22: *kaʾašer yāšît ʿālaw* 'as he imposes on him' (cf. Exod 21:30). The Hebrew term *ḥaṭṭāʾt*, like other terms for "sin, offense, crime," may also connote the consequences of an act, the punishment incurred; and it is the sense here.

so foolishly. Though listed in the lexica under the root *y-ʾ-l*, the form *nôʾalnû* occurring in this verse is more likely derived from the root *ʾ-w-l* 'to be foolish', from which we have the noun *ʾewîl* 'fool'. Compare Isa 19:13: *nôʾalû śārê Ṣôʿan* 'the princes of Tanis were deceived', or Jer 5:4: "They were foolish *(nôʾalû)*, for they did not know the ways of YHWH, the judgment of their God." In Jer 50:36, *nôʾalû* is parallel with *ḥattû* 'they were in dread'.

12. *stillbirth.* In the immediate context, Hebrew *mēt* 'a dead person' functionally connotes "stillbirth" and has been translated accordingly.

13. *petitioned.* The verb *ṣāʿaq* 'to cry out', discussed above in the NOTES on 11:2, here expresses the language of prayer, conveying an appeal to God by one in pain; compare Ps 34:18: "They cried out *(ṣāʿaqû)*, and YHWH heard." Compare also the usages in Deut 26:7; Isa 19:20; and Ps 107:28.

No more, I beseech you! Read *ʾal nāʾ* '*Do not,* I pray!' instead of Masoretic *ʾēl nāʾ* 'O God, I pray you!' The Masoretic pointing was probably inspired by the context, because Moses was addressing God. In biblical Hebrew, *nāʾ* never directly follows a noun. The suggested reading follows logically from the previous verse: *ʾal nāʾ tihyeh* 'let her not be'.

14. Spitting is known to be a way of shaming another person. In Deut 25:9 we read that a widow without children who is rejected as a wife by her brother-in-law is to spit in his face. In Isa 50:6 the prophet declares, "I did not hide my face from insults and spittle *(wārôq)*." Spitting is associated with disgrace, here expressed by the verb *tikkālēm* 'she will be disgraced' (cf. Job 30:10).

Quarantine for a period of seven days is prescribed in Lev 13:4 and 14:3 for one who showed the symptoms of *ṣāraʿat*, a skin disease, Miriam's very affliction. This practice was undoubtedly ancient. In 2 Kgs 7:3 we read how four men afflicted with *ṣāraʿat* performed a valuable service by bringing information to the people of the city. It is clear from the narrative that they were forbidden to enter the city, and had to stand outside the gate.

Some questions have been raised about the source-critical provenance of Num 12:14–15. The specific requirement that one afflicted with the symptoms of *ṣāraʿat* is to be confined outside the encampment for seven days is known only from the priestly provisions of Leviticus 13–14, where the requisite procedure is formulated in much the same words. Some would therefore regard Num 12:14–16 as a priestly addendum. It is more likely, however, that quarantine for a seven-day period represents ancient custom, merely standardized by the priestly legislators. Furthermore, usage of the term *hāʿām* 'the people' in v 15 recommends the assignment of Num 12:14–15 to the JE source.

16. As explained in the INTRODUCTION to Num 10:29–12:16, this verse is a postscript added by P in an effort to reconcile the discrepancy between Num 10:12 (P), where we read that the Israelites had already begun their march northward to the Wilderness of Paran, and Num 11:35 (JE), where we read that they were still in the southern Sinai peninsula, having just arrived at Hazeroth. Hence I translate *weʾaḥar* 'only thereafter', as if to correct Num 11:35.

COMMENT 1: THE MIDIANITE CONNECTION

In Num 10:29–12:16 we find important statements on biblical prophecy, especially regarding the unique role of Moses. There is also the Song of the Ark, which invites discussion of the various biblical traditions on the functions of the Ark. The theme of divine providence is introduced by the narrative of the manna. Finally, the Midianite connection, epitomized in the relationship between Moses and his father-in-law, requires clarification. Before engaging these themes, some discussion about the composition of this section of Numbers, and its place within Torah literature, would be helpful.

In the general introduction to this volume, sections A.3 and A.5.c, the source-critical makeup of Numbers was discussed in considerable detail, eliminating the need to do so here. It is noteworthy, nevertheless, that this is the first appearance of JE materials in the book of Numbers. The compilers of Numbers intended that the reader who began reading chapter 1 would regard the events and activities recorded in 1:1–10:28 as chronologically prior to what is portrayed in 10:29 and thereafter. In terms of the priestly agenda it was important to date the initiation of the Israelite cult to the early wilderness period, when the Israelites were in southern Sinai, thereby linking this process to the sinaitic theophany.

JE materials were last encountered in Exodus 34, which ended with Moses' descent from Mount Sinai and his communication of God's words to the Israelites. Num 10:29–12:16 share much in common with Exodus 32–34, and even with earlier sections of Exodus attributable to the JE source. What has happened is that the priestly school positioned much of its material between Exodus 34 and Numbers 10: in fact, Exodus 35–40, all of Leviticus, and Num 1:1–10:28. With this background in mind, we can now proceed to examine in detail some of the themes found in Num 10:29–12:16.

Much has been written about Moses' affiliation by marriage either to the Midianites or to the Kenites. This problem has already been addressed in the introduction, section D.5. A consideration of the context of Numbers necessarily involves Israelite relations with neighboring peoples like the Midianites. There is, therefore, no need to repeat here all that has been already said. The most likely resolution is to assume an ethnographic substitution whereby here, and in Exodus 18, the Midianites of Moses' association were disguised Kenites. Some have suggested that the Kenites were a subgroup of Midianites, which is a possible, though not probable, way out of the problem. The traditions of Numbers 10 and Exodus 18 probably do not record an actual historical shift in Israelite-Midianite relations. The spirit of both JE and P in the book of Numbers reflects the notion that enemies remain enemies, and had always been so!

In favor of assuming substitution is the evidence of Judg 4:11 on the identity of Hobab, Moses' father-in-law, as well as the evidence of various accounts in 1 Samuel relevant to the Kenites who inhabited Judah and the Negeb (1 Sam 15:6; 27:10; 30:29). Of particular interest is the fact that 1 Sam 15:6 refers to kindnesses shown by the Kenites to the Israelites after the Exodus, an obvious reference to Exodus 18 and to Num 10:29–32. What we read in Torah literature about Jethro/Hobab would, therefore, suit what we know about the Kenites instead of the always inimical Midianites known from the narratives of Judges and Samuel. The same interpretation is suggested by the interchanges between Moses and Hobab in Num 10:29–32. In effect, Moses offered Hobab a share in the Promised Land. This offer would be a way of reflecting the actual Kenite settlements in Canaan whose inhabitants coexisted amicably with the Israelites, and were the exception to the general hostility between Israelites and Canaanites in the conquest-settlement period. It is reasonable to conclude that Hobab finally accepted Moses' offer and continued on the march in company with the Israelites. Generally, one assumes that the ending of a biblical passage produces a resolution; or, to put in another way, that a biblical account seldom leaves a situation unresolved. In this case, Hobab seems to have given up his objections, or else he would have had the last word.

The different names ascribed to Moses' father-in-law may be attributed to a difference in literary sources. Num 10:29–32 is probably taken from the Jahwist, whereas Exodus 18 derives from the Elohist (Noth 1962: 146–148). For traditional commentators like Rashi, the divergence of names was a source of fascination. Rashi suggested that Moses' father-in-law had more than one name, a decided possibility in the ancient Near East.

COMMENT 2: THE ARK TRADITIONS

Notwithstanding the source-critical analysis of Num 10:33–34 presented in the NOTES, which concluded that Num 10:33–34 were interpolated by a priestly compiler, it is precisely in v 33 that we find language referring to the battle function of the Ark, in itself an old theme in biblical literature. Furthermore, the military and protective roles of the Ark relate to the similar functions of divine emblems in other cultures of the ancient Near East.

Source-critical analysis shows how different traditions were brought to bear on one another. Related to the image, which dominates Num 10:33–36, of an emblem marching in front of the fighting force is that of one marching with or alongside it. This image is expressed as *hôlēk ʿim* rather than as *hôlēk lipnê* (cf. Deut 20:4; 31:6, 8). Both of these locutions have counterparts in Akkadian descriptions of gods and their emblems that accompanied fighting forces or proceeded in advance of them.

Thus in the annals of Adad-Nirari II, an Assyrian king, we read, *d. Ištar . . . a-lik-at pa-na-at ERIN.ḪI.A.MEŠ-ia rapšāti* 'Ishtar . . . who goes in front of my large army' *(CAD* A, 1.317). Note also the characterization *ālik maḫri* 'the one who goes in front, herald, forerunner'. It is interesting that *ālik maḫri* is said of divine emblems *(CAD* A, 1.344). There is also the designation *ālik idi* 'who/that which goes alongside'. In *Enuma Eliš* II, line 14, we read, *ilū gimiršun . . . i-da-a-ša al-ku* 'All of the gods are marching with her (Tiamat)' *(CAD* A, 1.319, under *alāku* 4c, 3′).

The explorer and student of ancient Near Eastern history A. Musil (1928: 571–574, and figs. 1–2; 623–624, line 2) found a type of enclosed litter called *al-markab,* 'chariot, carriage' in Arabic in use among the Rwala bedouin of Syria. It was made of strips of thin wood, mounted on the saddle of a camel, and adorned with ostrich feathers. This *markab* was carried into battle, with the tribesmen following behind it. The *markab* was believed to have oracular functions, signaling Allah's will for the fighting forces. Any chief who possessed the *markab* thereby enjoyed considerable authority, and it was carefully protected in battle. Another somewhat similar structure known among the Arabs is called *mahmal,* and was used in pilgrimages to Mecca. Both of these structures were conceived as replicas of the heavenly seat of the Deity, enveloped by clouds.

It requires little imagination to find indications in biblical literature of the conception of the Ark as a seat or chariot for the God of Israel as he led his people in battle. In biblical epic, the God of Israel rides astride a cherub (2 Sam 18:11 ‖ Ps 18:11). An epithet of YHWH is *yôšēb hakkerûbîm* 'the one who sits upon the cherubs' (1 Sam 4:4; 2 Sam 6:2; 2 Kgs 19:1; Ezek 10:4; Ps 80:2; 99:1). The reference in 1 Sam 4:4 actually links the cultic setting with the battle function, by relating how "the Ark of YHWH of Hosts, who sits astride the cherubs" was brought from the sanctuary at Shiloh to the battlefield at Ebenezer.

Despite evidence of deuteronomistic editing, the narratives in 1 Samuel 4–7 clearly reflect ancient attitudes about the power manifested in the Ark, in the context of battle. When the Philistines learned that the Ark had arrived on the scene of battle they exclaimed, "A divine being *('elôhîm)* has entered the encampment!" (1 Sam 4:7). They go on to express their dread of this powerful deity, represented by his emblem, and eventually they carry away the Ark so as to exercise control, as it were, over the divine power it embodied (Levine 1968a; Miller and Roberts 1977). The same function is expressed in Num 14:44, where we read that Moses and the Ark did not budge from the midst of the Israelite camp after YHWH had imposed his decree on the Israelites of the wilderness. Those who attempted to invade southern Canaan in defiance of God's edict were summarily repulsed.

Interestingly, talmudic literature also preserves a song to the Ark, which the later Sages variously associated with the Philistine episode (1 Samuel 4–7) or with the present passage, Num 10:35–36. In their homilies they interpreted the strange construction *wayyiššarnāh happārôt* in 1 Sam 6:12, which seems to mean "The cows made straight for," to mean instead, "the cows broke into song," from *sir* 'song'. The talmudic poem reads as follows:

> Be exalted, be exalted, acacia-Ark!
> Loom high in your great beauty!
> Overlaid with embroidered gold,
> Glorious in the shrine of the Temple,
> Majestic with many ornaments.
> (Babylonian Talmud, *'Abôdāh Zārāh* 22:b)

COMMENT 3: MANNA AND QUAIL AND DIVINE PROVIDENCE

As has been noted above, Numbers 11 enmeshes two themes, the burdens of leadership and problems of food supply. The latter are attended to by God, who provides for the Israelites in the wilderness with manna and quail. In Num 11:6 it is assumed that the manna had served as a staple of the diet for some time, for we read that the people are disgusted by it. Verses 7–9 are parenthetical, reminding the reader how the manna tasted and how it was harvested. All of this is preamble to a new demand by the people for meat, an appetite not satisfied by the manna. In response, YHWH provides quail to the Israelites as an addition to their diet.

When we examine Exodus 16, the only textual precedent in Torah literature on the subject of the manna, we encounter once again a highly composite text. It appears to be the work of priestly writers who were fully aware of deuteronomistic traditions. The original account, embedded in Exodus 16, might have read as follows:

> 16:4 YHWH said to Moses: I am about to rain down bread for you from the heavens. Let the people go out to harvest every day's requirement on that day, so that I may put him to the test: Will he follow my instructions or not?
>
> 16:14. The fall of dew lifted, and behold! Over the surface of the wilderness lay a fine and flaky substance, fine as the frost on the ground.
>
> 16:15. The Israelites observed [it], and remarked to each other: "What is it?" For they did not know what it was! So Moses informed them: "It is the bread that YHWH has given you to eat."
>
> 16:21. They harvested it morning after morning, each one as much as he needed for food. When the sun grew hot, it melted.

16:31. The Israelites (read: *benê Yiśrā'ēl)* named it "manna." It was like coriander seed, and white, and it tasted like wafers made with honey.

The literary links between Numbers 11 and Exodus 16 are evident in the reference to coriander seed, in the use of the verb *lāqaṭ* 'to gather, glean' (cf. Num 11:7 with Exod 16:4, 21), and in the term of reference *hāʿām* 'the people' as designating the Israelites (cf. Num 11:8 with Exod 16:4). Under priestly editorship, Exodus 16 fuses the manna with the meat, as though both were features of the wilderness period from the outset of God's providential care. In its final form, with its priestly input, Exodus 16 presupposes Numbers 11, for the earlier passages in Exodus 16, as extrapolated above, speak only of manna. In the nonpriestly passages of Exodus 16, it is YHWH who rains down manna, just as in Numbers 11 it is YHWH who causes the wind to bring the quail to the edges of the Israelite encampment.

It is insignificant that Numbers 11 does not explicitly state that YHWH provided the manna. After all, it was a known quantity, and Num 11:7–9 remind the reader (not the Israelites themselves) of its texture and substance.

COMMENT 4: MOSES AND PROPHETIC LEADERSHIP

Numbers 11 must be studied against the background of certain Exodus traditions, especially those preserved in Exodus 18 and in Exod 24:1–11 and 33:1–11. Such comparisons will help to define more precisely the theory of prophetic leadership expressed in the JE sources of Numbers.

Like Numbers 11, Exodus 18 records a change in the governance of the Israelite people. In Exodus, this change was recommended by Moses' father-in-law, Jethro. We read that every day Moses "judged" (the verb *šāpaṭ)* the people, who came to him "to inquire of God *(lidrôš 'elôhîm)*," that is to say, to make oracular inquiry. Jethro recommended that Moses' oracular role continue as part of his judicial function, but that only the most difficult cases be brought directly to him. Less involved litigations would be screened, so to speak, and handled by appointed officials without recourse to inquiry of God. The new system resembled a military or paramilitary organization, headed by chiliarchs, centurions, and heads of fifty and ten. It is worthy of note that the elders *(zeqēnîm)* have no role in this reorganization. The only reference to the elders comes in Exod 18:12, which belongs to another strand of the narrative. The various officials are to be selected by Moses on the basis of their virtues and skills, and there is nothing at all charismatic about them. Moses remains the sole person with oracular access to God.

From 1 Sam 8:12 we learn, at least by implication, that this system, or one similar to it, operated under the Israelite monarchies. There we read that it would be within the jurisdiction of the king to appoint heads of administrative units. In fact, the delegation of authority by Moses projected in Exodus 18, certainly in the elohistic sections of that chapter, seems to reflect the role and status of a king.

In Numbers 11 the charismatic principle is prominent, and although it is not limited to Moses it is controlled by him, nonetheless. Here the elders are the group from which the leaders are chosen. The seventy are to be selected from a larger group of elders. They are, in effect, the elders whom Moses considers to be the true leaders of the people (Num 11:16). He registers their names, and the spirit of YHWH invests only those whose names were registered by Moses (Num 11:26). In other words, God ratifies Moses' choice!

This process is dramatized by the incident of Eldad and Medad. Although they were some distance away from the main group of elders, they experienced prophetic ecstasy because they had been registered as Moses' selections. The narrative of Numbers 11 thus reconciles a traditional basis of authority with the charismatic principle: the best of the elders, as decided by Moses, are now declared to be God's chosen leaders as well.

We turn now to Exod 24:1–11, an account of the Covenant enacted at Sinai. As has been shown by any number of commentators, these verses preserve two versions of the Covenant: vv 1–2 and 9–11 represent one version, and vv 3–8 represent another. The elders *(zeqēnîm)* figure only in the former version, being mentioned in vv 1 and 9. The people as a whole do not make the ascent to the top of the mountain (v 2), while Moses, Aaron, and two of Aaron's sons, accompanied by the elders, ascend the mountain to meet the God of Israel. All but Moses must remain at a distance, of course. No one is harmed by proximity to the Deity.

The key words in this version are *ʾaṣîlê benê Yiśrāʾēl* 'the spirited leaders of the Israelite people' in Exod 24:11. One called *ʾasil* is one who has received the spirit of the Lord. The corresponding verb, *ʾāṣal,* signifies the withdrawal of some of the spirit invested in Moses and its conferral on the elders, in Num 11:17 and 25. Exod 24:11 thus subtly subsumes the elders under the category of charismatic leaders. Their acceptability as such is confirmed by the fact that they were not harmed when in God's presence. What was alluded to in Exod 24:11 is spelled out in Numbers 11.

There is one more strand to be woven into the fabric of the Exodus traditions having a bearing on Numbers 11. In Exod 33:7–11 there is preserved an early characterization of the Tent of Meeting as an oraculum, a concept that derives from the elohistic tradition. We read of the pillar of cloud that served as an envelope for the God of Israel, who would descend to communicate with Moses at the entrance of the Tent. This is also the setting for the conferral of the divine spirit of prophecy on the seventy chosen elders, according to the narrative of Numbers 11.

The phenomenology of charisma also invites further discussion. The verb *hitnabbēʾ* 'to experience prophetic ecstasy' describes what happens physically and emotionally when the irresistible spirit of God seizes a person. This particular form of the verb *nābāʾ* 'to pronounce, utter prophecy' is best known from the biblical stories about Saul (1 Sam 10:5–6; 18:29; 19:23–24). It is also used in connection with mantic court prophets (1 Kgs 22:10) and describes the fits of the cult prophets of Baal (1 Kgs 18:29). In Jeremiah and Ezekiel, the verb *hitnabbēʾ* is used with reference to false prophets, although in Ezek 37:10 the prophet once says it of himself.

The verb *hitnabbēʾ* expresses only one aspect of the prophetic experience, however. In Numbers 11 it is the verb *nûaḥ* 'to rest, alight' that describes the settling of the spirit on the elders (Num 11:25–26). In other words, *hitnabbēʾ* expresses an effect, something a person invested with the spirit might do, but it does not describe the original conferral of the spirit.

Is the conferral of the spirit, expressed by the verb *nûaḥ*, conceived as permanent or ephemeral? Num 11:25 informs us that the elders did not continue to experience prophetic ecstasy, but clearly the spirit withdrawn from Moses and conferred on them had altered their status permanently. The spirit that had settled on them endowed them with the continuing capability of sharing responsibility with Moses in governing the people. Their ecstasy was a passing experience, but their status, and presumably their new competence, were permanent.

It is significant that the verb *nûaḥ* 'to rest, alight upon' is never used in the heroic biblical tradition to describe the settling of the divine spirit on a human being. The verbs employed in Judges and Samuel to describe such seizure are *ṣālaḥ* 'to fall upon', *lābaš* 'to clothe, envelop', or simply *hāyāh ʿal* 'to come upon'. In Judg 13:25 it is said that the spirit of YHWH "began to pulsate in him *(heḥēl lepaʿamô)*," namely, in Samson. Sometimes the preceding verbs are used in conjunction with *hitnabbēʾ*.

There are two observable facts about usage of these verbs in the heroic tradition that are significant, in contradistinction to usage of the verb *nûaḥ*. First, seizure by the spirit of the Lord is manifested in feats of physical prowess or surprising victory. And second, in every case the effects of seizure are, by implication, ephemeral or passing, not lasting. The seizure usually precedes some particular feat or episode, and then the spirit leaves the hero. Regarding David there is one exception, recorded in 1 Sam 16:13. In that case the spirit fell upon David, we are told, "from that day forward." This is a way of saying that, having been duly anointed as king by the prophet Samuel, David would permanently retain his charismatic powers as God's elect hero. In effect, the chosen king was a charismatic hero, but one whose conferred royal status, not to speak of his anticipated dynastic position, served to institutionalize his charisma.

The dynamics differ when the verb *nûaḥ* is used outside the heroic tradition. The transfer of the spirit from Elijah to Elisha is conveyed by the verb *nûaḥ*, and it was surely perceived as permanent (2 Kgs 2:1). Similarly, the spirit of the Lord is said to rest on the prince of peace, the wise counselor (Isa 11:1–9). He will judge by exercising this power throughout his career as a king.

It is true that heroic language may be employed in connection with the verb *nûaḥ*, but when it is, the "spirit" conferred supplies other capabilities. Although Elisha calls Elijah "Israel's chariots and horsemen," the sense is that real power comes to the people from God through his prophet (2 Kgs 2:12). The prince of peace possesses *gebûrāh* 'heroism, strength', but this power is conceptualized as justice and peace, not as physical might. Justice is his soldier's belt, and he is girded with trustworthiness! In judgment he exercises skill, discernment, and knowledge of the Lord. This radical redefinition of heroic concepts comes full circle in Zech 4:6: "Not by power nor by military might, but by my spirit, says YHWH." Physical force and the spirit of the Lord have become antithetical.

The statement on the uniqueness of Mosaic prophecy in Num 12:6–8 may be seen as a reflex of the very words attributed to Moses in Num 11:29: "Would that the entire people of YHWH were prophets, if only YHWH would bestow his spirit on them." As if to counter the implication that others could attain to the status of Moses, we are informed quite promptly, in Num 12:6–8, that this is impossible. Normally, prophets see God in dreams. In fact, Deut 13:2–7 virtually equate *nabî'* 'prophet' with *ḥôlēm ḥalôm* 'a dreamer of a dream'. The same equation is fairly widespread in biblical literature and is presumed in 1 Sam 28:6, 15; and Joel 3:1 (cf. also Isa 29:7; Jer 23:25–28; 27:9; 28:18; Zech 10:2).

1 Sam 9:9 informs us that in Israel, the prophet used to be called *rô'eh* 'seer', one who beholds visions. The riddle *(ḥîdāh)* and the parable *(māšāl)*, both enigmatic utterances, also had a role in the normal functioning of the prophet (Ezek 17:2; Hab 2:6).

We are told that Moses held a unique relationship with God and did not need these forms of divine communication. Come to think of it, this view of Moses provides yet another link between Numbers 11 and Exod 33:7–11, the primary text informing us of the role of the Tent of Meeting as an oraculum. In Exod 33:11 we read that YHWH spoke with Moses "face to face *(pānîm 'el pānîm)*, just as one person speaks to another." A later writer summed up the matter as follows: "There never again arose a prophet in Israel like Moses, whom YHWH acknowledged face to face" (Deut 34:10).

Phenomenologically, Moses' uniqueness lies in the fact that God speaks to him directly, "mouth to mouth" or "face to face." There is nothing intervening between God and Moses in the transmission of God's voice. Furthermore, Moses sees God's form or likeness *(temûnāh)* in clear view. Although God is close to Moses, Moses does not actually see God's face. As Exod 33:20 states,

"You will not be able to see my face, for a human being cannot see my face and survive." The idiom "face to face" does not mean, therefore, that one sees the face of the other, but is merely a way of expressing direct communication, with nothing intervening between the two speakers. Exod 33:21 continues to explain that Moses did not see God frontally, but only as he passed by.

At the Sinai theophany, the Israelites all heard God's words but did not see any form (Deut 4:12). This information shows us how we are to understand the statement in Exod 24:10–11 to the effect that the entire group accompanying Moses saw the God of Israel. Either that statement represents a highly divergent tradition, which is unlikely, or it should be taken to mean that the company saw what lay beneath God's throne: the pure, azure sky.

Having explored aspects of phenomenology, we should now attempt to establish the *Sitz-im-Leben* of the theory of leadership expressed in Numbers 11–12. It has already been explained that the present theory differs from the heroic interpretation. In discussing Exodus 18 the point has been made that Moses is there cast as a king. Although considerable pains have been taken to bring out certain differences between Numbers 11 and Exodus 18, in phenomenological terms, it would appear that Numbers 11–12 and Exodus 18 share a common *Sitz-im-Leben.*

The link between Numbers 11 and the oracle of Isa 11:1–9, suggested by the verb *nûaḥ* 'to rest, alight upon' common to both sources, further indicates that the status of Moses in Numbers 11–12 is modeled on the royal office, not only on the prophetic role. Moses' unique prophetic role is clearly expressed in the phenomenological statements of Num 12:6–8, whereas his monarchic profile is less explicit. The key is provided by Num 12:7: "Not so my servant *(ʿabdî)*, Moses! / Of all my household / He is the most trusted."

We are led directly to courtly literature by the inclusion, in this verse, of three elements of diction: *ʿabdî* 'my servant', *neʾemān* 'trusted', and *bayît* 'household'. The same three elements elsewhere occur in a single verse, 1 Sam 22:14, where Ahimelek speaks to Saul about David: "Who of all your servants *(ʾabādekā)* is as trusted *(neʾemān)* as David, his being the king's own son-in-law, acting under your orders, and esteemed in your household *(bebêtekā)?*" In Num 12:7 Moses is characterized in virtually the same way as is David in 1 Sam 22:14!

Not only are the literary-historical affinities of these two sources significant, but so are their implications for our understanding of the the function of Torah literature. In literary-historical terms, these affinities suggest that JE, resting on its original sources, J and E, ultimately derives from the same repertoire as the accounts in 1 Samuel. Beyond this point, we begin to understand the function of Torah literature in laying the foundation for the legitimacy of the Davidic monarchy. Torah literature embodies both in the characterization of Moses' virtues and in God's stated evaluation of Moses, a model of the upright Davidic monarch.

But there is more to this comparison. A survey of the adjective *ne'emān* in biblical Hebrew shows that it has two related connotations: both "trusted, reliable, faithful" and "secure, guaranteed." We find that there is interplay between these two nuances. In 1 Sam 2:35 we are told that in place of the unfit house of Eli, God will designate "a trusted priest *(kôhēn ne'emān)*," who will in turn be granted "a secure succession *(bayît ne'emān)*." Similarly, the prophet Samuel is said to be "trusted as a prophet of YHWH *(ne'emān lenābî' le-YHWH)*."

Doubtless, the prophetic pronouncement to Eli and the statement about Samuel are modeled on characterizations of the Davidic royal house. Thus Abigail was echoing a dynastic covenant promise when she said to David, "For YHWH will surely establish for my lord a secure dynasty *(bayît ne'emān)*." (1 Sam. 25:28) The same diction is used again in recounting the anointing of Jehu, in 2 Kgs 11:38.

Discrete usage of *ʿabdî* 'my servant' (namely, God's servant) is instructive in further respects. David is *ʿabdî* par excellence, as has been shown. This status is also attributed to such leaders as Caleb, the devout conqueror who bears a Judean affiliation (Num 14:24 [J]), and to the patriarch Abraham (Gen 26:24 [J]). In Hag 2:23, Zerubbabel is called *ʿabdî*, as is the good royal steward, Eliakim, in Isa 22:20. Let us not overlook the royal servant of Deutero-Isaiah. However he may be identified, and it is likely that more than a single identity is intended in the servant passages of Isaiah 40–55, the role of the servant is projected in royal terms.

It is also true, however, that prophets are called *ʿabādaî* 'my servants'. What we have in Numbers 11–12 is the fusion of two parts of a composite, the prophetic and the royal. Moses, in the JE narratives of Numbers, is cast as the prototype of this fusion.

Numbers 11–12 project a theory of government that is worthy of our attention. The *zeqēnîm* 'elders' retained a role under the monarchy, and we are advised in 1 Kgs 12:6 that a good king heeds the counsel of the elders, whereas a bad one rejects it. The theory of government projected here accommodates the monarchy, and would appear to endorse the Davidic dynasty. Still, it expects of the monarch a prophetlike spirit of leadership, the very spirit epitomized in the oracle of Isaiah 11.

PART IX.

NUMBERS 13–14: UNSUCCESSFUL ATTEMPTS TO PENETRATE CANAAN

♦

INTRODUCTION

Chapters 13 and 14 of Numbers record that Moses and the Israelites, after having marched north to the Wilderness of Paran, dispatched a team of twelve tribal leaders to reconnoiter Canaan or, by one account, only part of Canaan. They were to report back with firsthand intelligence that would provide certain kinds of information. Their report was to include such subjects as the productivity of the land, the military capability of its inhabitants, and their settlement patterns, especially the character and extent of their urban fortifications.

In their present form, Numbers 13 and 14 represent a fusion of materials drawn from JE, from P, and perhaps even from other independent sources. At points, the fabric of the text can be unraveled easily, whereas elsewhere priestly writers have rewritten the text so that one can only guess how JE originally read.

The priestly version was unknown to the author of Deut 1:22–25, where we find a different account of the mission. It has even been suggested that the deuteronomistic version once stood at the beginning of Numbers 13 because it agrees, in most respects, with what JE has to say about the scope of the mission. One difference is that in Numbers 13, as we have it, God commands the mission directly, whereas in Deut 1:22–25 the people propose it to Moses. This shift is probably attributable to the priestly reworking of Numbers 13–14. At the very least, the deuteronomistic version can be utilized as an indication of how priestly writers adapted earlier accounts of the reconnaissance mission itself. Largely following G. B. Gray (in Gray—ICC), we may outline Numbers 13–14 as follows:

1. Num 13:1–17a (P). Priestly writers recast the undertaking of the mission to Canaan, and in so doing provided a list of the twelve *neśî'îm* 'chieftains'. These representatives of the twelve tribes departed from the Wilderness of Paran where, according to Num 13:26, a verse edited by P, Kadesh Barnea was located.

2. Num 13:17b–20, 22–24 (JE) (v 21 = P). In JE's version, the spies are instructed to traverse the Negeb and to ascend into the Judean hill country, proceeding to the area of Hebron, as is clearly indicated in Num 13:22–24 and is even anticipated in v 17b. Such a route was realistic, considering the location of the Israelite base at the time, in Kadesh. By inserting v 21, the priestly writer greatly extended the scope of the mission all the way to the northern border of Canaan. He did so, most likely, to bring the account of Numbers 13–14 into conformity with the priestly delimitation of the Promised Land, as projected in Num 34:1–15. The spies were to bring back reports and samples of produce, which they did.

3. Num 13:25–26 (P). Here, as at the beginning of Numbers 13, priestly writers rewrote the text of JE, which had recorded the return of the spies to

Kadesh. Verse 25 connects to v 17a, and like it uses the verb *tûr* 'to encircle, traverse'. In its rewritten form, v 26 locates Kadesh in the Wilderness of Paran. The spies bring back their report.

4. Num 13:27–31, 33 (JE) (v 32 = P). In JE's version, the spies report that the land is exceedingly fertile, but its inhabitants are fierce and protected within large, fortified towns. They provide a demographic sketch of the population, which also serves to outline the probable deployment of the very forces the Israelites would encounter. The spies are pessimistic about the prospects of a successful occupation of Canaan. Only Caleb is confident of victory and professes faith in God's power.

Priestly writers inserted Num 13:32 into the account to make the point that not only were the inhabitants fierce but the land itself could not sustain its inhabitants. This statement flatly contradicts v 27 and renders the report of the spies even more disillusioning. JE's version will resume in Num 14:8, with Caleb's explicit assurance of success and his profession of faith.

5. Num 14:1–7a, 10 (P) (vv 7b–9 = JE). In the priestly version, the entire *ʿēdāh* 'community' (P's term for the Israelite people) breaks into weeping. The people beleaguer Moses and Aaron, threatening to reverse course and head back to Egypt. Caleb and Joshua, son of Nun, urge the people not to despair. The enraged crowd threatens to stone its leaders and is prevented from doing so by the dramatic appearance of the *kābôd* 'the glorious presence'. Verses 7b–9 connect with Num 13:33: although the inhabitants of Canaan are gigantic they can be overcome, because YHWH is on Israel's side. The "Protector" of the Canaanites has already abandoned them.

6. Num 14:11–25 (JE?). Although the dialogue between Moses and God is surely not a priestly composition, it is uncertain whether it is attributable to JE or to an independent source. It resembles Exodus 33–34 in that it gives poignant expression to divine wrath unleashed against the rebellious Israelites. Only Caleb, here unaccompanied by Joshua, will live to enter the land, but all those who rejected God will not! The people are instructed to avoid a clash with the Canaanites and Amalekites, who inhabit the hill country, by proceeding through the wilderness to the Sea of Reeds, namely, the Red Sea.

7. Num 14:26–38 (P). The impact of Moses' dialogue with God is reinforced by priestly writers. Greater elaboration is given to the consequences of divine wrath, a theme characteristic of priestly historiography in general. The people will wander in the wilderness for forty years so that the sinful generation of the Exodus will die out. Only Caleb and Joshua are exempt from the divine decree. Together with the coming generation, these two leaders will enter the Land. A plague annihilates the spies, whose sudden death is mourned by the people.

8. Num 14:39–45 (JE). JE's version takes up where Num 14:25 left off. Resisting God's instructions, the people attempt a direct incursion through

the Judean hills, but are repulsed by Canaanites and Amalekites. The Israelites are routed at Hormah, near Arad in the Negeb.

The overall objective of Numbers 13–14 is to explain why it was that the Israelites failed to penetrate southern Canaan soon after the Exodus. In realistic terms, it is explained that the Canaanite peoples who inhabited the Judean Negeb and hill country were powerful and well fortified. This situation was interpreted theologically, so that it was Israel's lack of faith in God that had deterred the people from embarking on a direct invasion of Canaan. Priestly writers added further emphasis to both levels of interpretation: the land of Canaan was unproductive to start with, and the Israelites were sorely lacking in heroism and faith. Numbers 13–14 thus set the stage for the Transjordanian adventures.

In the introduction to this volume, section A.5.b, considerable discussion was devoted to the different itineraries of JE and P and to their divergent schedules of the wilderness period. It turns out that Numbers 13–14 are pivotal for the historiographic interpretation of the entire book of Numbers, as will be shown in the COMMENT below.

TRANSLATION OF NUMBERS 13

13 [1]The Lord spoke to Moses as follows:

[2]Dispatch important personages to scout the land of Canaan, which I am granting to the Israelite people. Send one such person to represent each of their patrilineal tribes, every one of them a chieftain.

[3]Moses dispatched them from the Wilderness of Paran, in accordance with YHWH's command. All of them were important personages; they were the heads of the Israelite people.

[4]Their names were as follows:

Representing the tribe of Reuben—Shammua son of Zaccur.

[5]Representing the tribe of Simeon—Shaphat son of Hori.

[6]Representing the tribe of Judah—Caleb son of Jephunneh.

[7]Representing the tribe of Issachar—Igal son of Joseph.

[8]Representing the tribe of Ephraim—Hosea son of Nun.

[9]Representing the tribe of Benjamin—Palti son of Raphu.

[10]Representing the tribe of Zebulun—Gaddiel son of Sodi.

[11]Representing the tribe of Joseph, that is, the tribe of Manasseh—Gaddi son of Susi.

[12]Representing the tribe of Dan—Ammiel son of Gemalli.

[13]Representing the tribe of Asher—Sethur son of Michael.

[14]Representing the tribe of Naphtali—Nahbi son of Vupsi.

[15]Representing the tribe of Gad—Geuel son of Machi.

[16]These are the names of the personages whom Moses dispatched

to scout the land. (Moses called Hosea son of Nun by the name of "Joshua.")

17 Moses dispatched them to scout the land of Canaan. He charged them, "Proceed northward through the Negeb, and make your ascent into the mountains.

18 "Observe the land: what is its condition? And the people inhabiting it: are they strong or feeble, few or numerous?

19 "And what of the land they inhabit: is it bountiful or lacking? And what of the towns where they dwell: are they built as unwalled settlements or as fortified towns?

20 "And how is the land: is it rich in produce or lean? Is it wooded or not? Make an effort to bring back some of the fruit of the land." (This was at the season of first ripe grapes.)

21 They proceeded northward, scouting the land all the way from the Wilderness of Zin to Rehob, at Lebo of Hamath.

22 They proceeded northward through the Negeb, arriving at Hebron. Ahiman, Sheshai, and Talmai, born of the Anakites, were there. (Hebron had been built seven years before Tanis, in Egypt.)

23 Arriving at Wadi Eshcol, they cut off a branch with a cluster of grapes, which they carried on a pole, [borne] by two [men], along with some pomegranates and figs.

24 That place was named Wadi Eshcol in token of the *cluster* that the Israelites had cut off while there.

25 They returned from scouting the land forty days later,

26 and went straight to Moses and the entire Israelite community, in the Wilderness of Paran, at Kadesh. They brought to them and to the entire community a report, and showed them the fruit of the land.

27 They reported to him as follows: "We entered the land to which you dispatched us. It is truly flowing with milk and sap, and here is a sample of its fruit.

28 "In contrast, the people inhabiting the land are fierce, and the cities are fortified and very large. We also noticed men born of the Anakites there.

29 "Amalekites inhabit the Negeb region, with Hittites, Jebusites, and Amorites occupying the mountains; while Canaanites are settled near the sea and along the Jordan."

30 Caleb silenced the people near Moses, exclaiming, "We should, by all means, invade and take possession of [the land], for we can certainly prevail over it."

31 But the men who had accompanied him said, "We dare not mount an attack against that people, for it is more powerful than we are!"

32 They presented the Israelite people with a discrediting report of the land they had scouted, as follows: "The land we traversed for the purpose of scout-

ing it is a land that devours its inhabitants, and all of the people whom we observed in it are of enormous proportions.

33 "There we saw Nephilim (Anakites are descended from Nephilim), and we felt like grasshoppers; and so we must have seemed to them!"

NOTES TO NUMBERS 13: THE DISPATCH OF THE SPIES AND THEIR DISCOURAGING REPORT—VARYING ACCOUNTS

13 2. *important personages.* Hebrew *ʾanāšîm* 'men, people' often implies status. This is true here, as is suggested by v 3: *kullām ʾanāšîm* 'all of them were *important personages.*' In Judg 18:2 we read of *ʾanāšîm* dispatched by the Danites to find a new tribal territory, and they, too, were leaders of the tribe. Similarly, in Judg 20:12 *ʾanāšîm* are dispatched by the Israelite tribes to demand that the Benjamites surrender those who had committed atrocities.

to scout. The verb *tur* 'to encircle, traverse' occurs again in vv 17a and 25, and is common in P. In the version of the mission preserved in Deut 1:22–25, the verb used is *ḥāpar* 'to uncover' the land, that is, to explore it. In JE's account the functional equivalent is probably *rāʾāh* 'to observe', as in v 18, below.

the land of Canaan. Hebrew *ʾereṣ Kenāʿan* as a designation for the Promised Land occurs frequently in P (Gen 23:2, 19; Genesis 36; Lev 14:34; 18:3; 25:38; Num 32:30, 32), though it is hardly limited to this source. Much has been written about the toponym *Kenāʿan,* and despite some lingering questions of etymology, it is probable that it derives from a word meaning "purple dye" or "purple cloth" (Astour 1965). The geography of this toponym will be explored in the commentary on Numbers 34, where the priestly delimitation of Canaan is presented in full.

I am granting. The verb *nātan* 'to give' expresses the granting of Canaan to the Israelite people by their God. This verb has legal and covenantal force and is often employed in P. In Gen 15:18, in a priestly version of the Abrahamic covenant, we read, "To your offspring I grant *(nôtēn)* this land" (cf. also Gen 17:8; 27:12; Num 33:53; Lev 14:34).

patrilineal tribes. Hebrew *maṭṭeh* 'staff' is the term for "tribe" in P; see the NOTES on Num 1:4. The tribal system of ancient Israel, as conceived in the priestly traditions of Numbers, is described in the NOTES on Numbers 1 and 34, and in the COMMENT on Numbers 3–4.

every one of them a chieftain. The phrase *kol nāśîʾ bāhem* means not "every chieftain among them" but rather "every one of them a chieftain," as if written *kol bāhem nāśîʾ*. As Gray has noted, tribes were not limited to one *nāśîʾ*; see the NOTES on Num 3:32.

3. *the heads of the Israelite people.* The titulary *rāʾšê benê Yiśrāʾēl* is unique

to this passage, though the term *rōʾš* usually designates the head of a clan or militia. Compare *rāʾšê ʾalpê Yiśrāʾēl* 'the *heads* of the Israelite *clans*' in Num 1:16 and 10:4. Note also *rāʾšê hammaṭṭôt* 'the heads of the tribes' in Num 32:28. In Num 25:4 (JE) we find the titulary *rāʾšê hāʿām* 'the heads of the people'.

The mission was ordered by God, and this command was transmitted by Moses. See the NOTES on Num 10:13.

4–15. In the list of *neśîʾîm* 'chieftains', prepositional *lamed* indicates representation. This usage is explained in the NOTES on Num 1:15. The list begins with Reuben, and in this respect correlates with Numbers 1 and 26, in contrast to lists beginning with Judah, in Numbers 2, 7, 10, and 34. But internally, the order of the tribes given here is distinctive. It separates Ephraim from Manasseh and Issachar from Zebulun. The tribe of Levi is consistently absent from the tribal lists of Numbers because of the cultic status conferred on the Levites.

Gray noted that many names in this list are unattested elsewhere, and certainly unattested as *neśîʾîm* of the wilderness period. Hosea son of Nun (Joshua) and Caleb are known personages, of course; but for the rest, most of the names are unusual. The name Shammua (of Reuben) occurs in 2 Sam 5:14 || 1 Chr 14:4 as one of David's sons. Zaccur *(Zakkûr)* is known as the name of a king of Hamath in epigraphic sources (Gibson 1975: 8, line 1), and elsewhere occurs in Nehemiah and Chronicles. A certain Shaphat is Elisha's father in 1 Kgs 19:16, and others with this name are mentioned in Chronicles. Hori is an Edomite eponym in Gen 36:22 || 1 Chr 1:39 and may, as an ethnonym *(haḥôrî, haḥôrîm)*, designate one of the peoples who inhabited Canaan (Gen 14:6; 36:20; Deut 2:22). Igal is a fairly old name (2 Sam 23:36) and occurs in later sources as well (1 Chr 3:22). Palti is a relatively old name (1 Sam 25:44), that of Michal's husband. Raphu, Gaddiel, and Gaddi (in contrast to Gadi), Sodi, Susi, Gemalli, Sethur, Nahbi, Vupsi, Geuel, and Machi are otherwise unattested in biblical sources. The name Ammiel is known in 2 Sam 9:4–5 and 17:27, as is Michael, the name of an angel in Dan 10:13, 21, and of several persons in Ezra and Chronicles.

The point is that this list of names differs radically from the other lists of *neśîʾîm* in Numbers. Although we cannot be certain, it may derive from a divergent priestly source.

16. Verse 16b is a gloss, intended to identify the Hosea of the list with Joshua son of Nun. Compare Deut 32:44, where the name Hosea son of Nun occurs in a priestly addendum to the Deuteronomic text. In Neh 10:24 a certain Hosea is listed as one of the "heads of the people" during the late Persian period.

17. *Proceed northward through the Negeb.* JE resumes in 17b. Hebrew *ʿalû zeh bannegeb* means "proceed directly northward." The demonstrative *zeh* may mean "here, this way," and is an adverbial indication of direction; com-

pare *bāzeh* 'in *this place*' in Num 23:1, 29; also 1 Kgs 3:8: *'ê-zeh hadderek naʿaleh* 'Where *is* the road by which we must advance?'

make your ascent. The verb *ʿālāh* does not necessarily indicate an ascent, but may refer to a northerly direction. In the ancient Near East, with the exception of Egypt, movement in a northerly direction was often expressed as "ascent" and movement in a southerly direction as "descent." This is because the Tigris and Euphrates flowed in a southerly direction, so that "up river" was "north." The point is that the spies were instructed to proceed *northward* through the Negeb and then "ascend" into the mountains (Levine 1975).

the mountains. The geographic term *hāhār* is collective: "the mountains; the mountain range." It refers to the central or interior mountain range of Canaan, as we learn from several geographic descriptions of Canaan. See v 29, below, and Num 14:45; compare also Deut 1:3; 2:37; Josh 9:1; 10:6; and especially Josh 10:40 for regionalized descriptions of Canaan.

18. *what.* The interrogative/relative *mah* 'what, which' often suggests condition or extent, and is best rendered "how" in certain contexts.

19. *is it bountiful or lacking?* The adjectives *ṭôbāh* and *rāʿāh* are translated in context as pertaining to greater or lesser fertility or productive capacity, respectively.

unwalled settlements. The plural *maḥanîm,* literally, "encampments," is unique to this passage, but we can speculate about its realistic sense. There is an increasing body of archaeological evidence pointing to the existence of sedentarized villages in various regions of Canaan, where pastoral Israelites began to settle down and engage in agriculture. I. Finkelstein (1988: 336–351) points out that in addition to the fertile areas, such as the coastal plain (Shephelah) and the northern valleys (Jezreel, for instance), which had been settled in a permanent way before the beginning of the Iron Age, there were also marginal regions in Canaan. At times sedentary communities existed in these areas, and at times not. These marginal regions included parts of the hilly regions of Upper Galilee, Ephraim, and Judea, realities revealed by recent surveys and excavations, and unknown by earlier scholars. Of particular interest to the present discussion is the fact that the semiarid regions of the Negeb highlands, the Beersheba valley, and the Judean desert were also "frontier regions." These and the Judean hills around Hebron are the very regions referred to in Numbers 13–14.

Finkelstein also explains that fortified towns existed in certain areas from the very beginning of the Israelite experience in Canaan. It is not as though there was a fixed sequence of development whereby unwalled settlements consistently preceded fortified towns, and always gave way to them. The two forms of settlements often coexisted. In this connection, an interesting term of reference is *migrāšîm,* which etymologically connotes "corrals" into which livestock is "herded," an activity conveyed by the verbal root *g-r-š* (Num 35:3;

Josh 14:4). And yet one has the impression that a *migrāš* could also serve as a garden plot on the outskirts of town (Lev 25:34).

Biblical sources also speak of *ḥaṣērîm*, a term for an unwalled settlement (Isa 42:11; Lev 25:31), which occurs together with *ṭîrôt* 'circular settlements', in which Ishmaelites were said to dwell (Gen 25:16). In Num 31:10 the term *ṭîrôt* designates the settlements of the Midianites. Most telling is the characterization of the Philistine territory in 1 Sam 6:18: "both fortified towns and unwalled villages *(mēʿîr mibṣār weʿad kôper happerāzî)*." There, as here, we find the contrast between the two patterns of settlement: walled towns and unwalled villages. The same contrast is expressed in Deut 3:5. In Judg 5:7 and 11 we are told that *perāzôn* 'open settlements' had ceased in the land because of fear of attack (cf. Esth 9:19; Hab 3:14; Ps 69:26; Ezek 25:4).

20. *This was at the season of first ripe grapes.* These words, at the conclusion of v 20, were most likely added as a gloss, identifying the time of the year when the mission was undertaken as late summer.

21. This is the verse inserted by the priestly writers to extend the scope of the reconaissance mission all the way to the northern border of Canaan, as the boundaries of the land given in Num 34:8 indicate. Rehob may be the name of either a district or a city, perhaps *Bêt Reḥôb* (Judg 18:28). In Josh 13:5 and Judg 3:3, Lebo of Hamath is depicted as being far away from the battles fought by the Israelites in Canaan. It became virtually proverbial as a faraway place in the north of the land. Both David and, later, Jeroboam passed through Lebo of Hamath on their way to the conquest of parts of ancient Syria (1 Kgs 8:65; 2 Kgs 14:25). B. Mazar (1962) identifies Lebo with *Lab'u*, mentioned in an annal of Tiglath Pileser III, and with *Libo*, mentioned in a Roman itinerary. A site by this name is probably mentioned in Egyptian execration texts. The *lamed* of *Lebôʾ* is, therefore, radical, and there is little warrant for rendering *Lebôʾ Ḥamāt* 'at the approaches of Hamath'.

22. *They proceeded northward through the Negeb.* The account of JE continues, taking up the theme of v 17b. There we read the command *ʿalû zeh bannegeb* 'Proceed [directly] northward through the Negeb', and here we read of the fulfillment of that command: *wayyaʿalû bannegeb.*

Hebron. Ancient Hebron has been identified as Tell Rumeidah, where limited excavations have been undertaken recently (see the COMMENT below). The gloss that provides a relative chronology, by stating that Hebron was built seven years before Tanis of Egypt, is most intriguing but historically incorrect. This statement merely reflects the image of Tanis held in the first millennium B.C.E., when it was thought that this town in the northern Delta had served as a capital city during the Ramesside period. The archaeologists Monet and Yoyote found at Tanis monuments and architectural fragments dating as early as the Sixth Dynasty, and many from the period of Rameses II. But it has become clear that these early artifacts were brought to Tanis as part of a program aimed at enhancing the importance of the city, which became the capital of Egypt about 1100 B.C.E. and continued in that status until 660 B.C.E.

Tanis. The name *Ṣôʿan* = Tanis has been variously identified with towns mentioned in ancient sources, including Avaris. It is known from the annals of Assurbanipal of the seventh century B.C.E. and first occurs in Egyptian sources precisely during the Twenty-first Dynasty, about 1100 B.C.E. In biblical literature, most references to *Ṣôʿan* pertain to late periods of Egyptian history (Isa 19:11, 13; 30:4; Ezek 30:14; Ps 12:43). Of interest is the fact that Rameses II is called ruler of Tanis in an Egyptian inscription dating from the time of Shishak III (Twenty-second Dynasty). In fact, Shishak III himself was called ruler of Tanis. We are dealing, therefore, with a *tradition* about the great antiquity of Tanis, not with actual historical evidence of its antiquity as a capital (S. Ahituv 1971).

The names of the Anakites associated with the Hebron area—Ahiman, Seshai, and Talmai—still elude certain identification. A. Kempinsky (1982) regards both Seshai and Talmai as Hurrian names. *Talmaî* means "great" in Hurrian. This name is attested at Bogazkoy and Ugarit in various theophoric combinations. The name Seshai was that of one of the rulers of the Hyksos dynasty (Fifteenth) in Egypt, which also ruled over southern Canaan. Furthermore, a certain Talmai son of Ammihur is named as a king of Geshur in the time of David, and he was the grandfather of Absalom (2 Sam 3:3; 13:37). On this basis, Kempinsky speculates that reference to these three Anakites ("giants") comes from an ancient epic known in the Hebron area. Hurrian names have been found in pre-Israelite inscriptions from Canaan, in fact, at Gezer. Josh 15:13–15 speaks of Anakites from the Hebron area (cf. Judg 1:10).

23. Wadi Eshcol has not been precisely identified. Hebrew *zemôrāh* designates a branch or twig, usually part of a grapevine (Ezek 15:2), which bears a grape cluster *(ʾeškôl).*

they carried on a pole, [borne] by two [men]. Adverbial *bišnayîm* 'by two [men]' is unusual; compare *ʾeḥād beʾeḥād* 'one by one' in Job 41:8. Hebrew *môṭ* 'pole, bar' usually designates a part of the yoke (Lev 26:13; Jer 28:13; Nah 1:13). It is, however, the term used to designate the carrying frame on which the Menorah was mounted when it was being transported (Num 4:10–12).

25. The account of P resumes, relating that the spies returned after forty days, a common schematic span of time, whether in days or years.

26. It is this verse that identifies the place from which the spies were dispatched as Kadesh (see the NOTES on v 3, above). In the priestly perception, Kadesh was located in the Wilderness of Paran. In the introduction to this volume, section A.5.a, Num 13:26 is analyzed, and there it is concluded that locative *Qādēšāh* 'at Kadesh' is original to the verse. In a sense, Num 13:26 is a pivotal verse for the interpretation of all of Numbers, and for that reason it was discussed in the introduction.

They brought to them . . . a report. Hebrew *wayyāšîbû ʾôtām dābār,* literally, "they brought them back word," is idiomatic for responding or reporting. In Ugaritic letters we find the parallel idiom *wrgm ṯṯb ly* 'Bring back a reply to me' *(KTU* 2.13, line 13; Cunchillos 1989: 260–261). In Josh 22:32 a delegation of tribal *nésîʾîm* also brought back a word (cf. also usage in 2 Kgs 12:9; 22:8).

27. *flowing with milk and sap.* The account of JE resumes here. The characterization *zābat ḥālāb ûdebaš* expresses an environmental perception representing the land of Canaan as abundant in flocks and herds, and rich in sap-giving trees—fig trees, for instance. Hebrew *debaš,* like its cognates in the Semitic languages, should not be taken to mean specifically bee's honey. It simply conveys the sense of sweetness. By all indications, the honey industry was not developed in biblical Israel, though the Bible occasionally speaks of the honey of bees in the carcasses of animals, in tree trunks, or in crevices (Palmoni 1954; Caquot 1977).

This characterization is, in any event, pastoral and horticultural. It refers to mountain slopes with their orchards and vines, covered by numerous flocks. Most probably this characterization was introduced by J (Exod 3:8, 17; 13:5; 33:3; Num 14:8) and was used by the Deuteronomist (Deut 6:3, 11; 27:3) as well as by priestly writers (Num 14:8; 16:13–14, Deut 31:50).

28. *In contrast.* The force of the Hebrew idiom *ʾepes kî,* literally, "naught except that," is to express contrast. Compare usage in 2 Sam 12:13–14: "YHWH has, moreover, deferred the punishment of your offense; you shall not die. In contrast *(ʾepes kî)* you have severely rejected the enemies of YHWH in this matter."

the people . . . are fierce, and the cities are fortified and very large. The report of the spies confirms the fears intimated above, in vv 18–19, in Moses' charge to the spies. There we found the term *mibṣārîm* 'fortified towns,' and here we have the adjective *beṣûrôt* 'fortified.' In v 18, the people inhabiting Canaan are characterized as "strong" *(ḥāzāq)*, whereas here it is *ʿaz* 'fierce,' an adjective which describes well-fortified boundaries in Num 21:24. The identity of the legendary Anakites was discussed in the NOTES to 13:22.

29. *Amalekites inhabit the Negeb region.* This verse is an unusual ethnographic indicator, purportedly a resume of the inhabitants of southern Canaan at the time the Israelites first attempted to penetrate the land from Kadesh. It would be very enlightening to identify the *Sitz-im-Leben* of this verse, but we can only suggest a general provenance. In the COMMENT (1), below, it is suggested that the JE traditions on Kadesh, and the events associated with this locality, may ultimately derive from the period of the United Monarchy, in the tenth century B.C.E. The same provenance is proposed in the introduction to Numbers D 2–3. On this basis, we can surmise that an author active as early as the tenth century B.C.E. sought to portray an even earlier period in this way.

Van Seters (1976) has proposed that the ethnographic terms Hittite and Amorite, as they are used in the biblical conquest traditions, are anachronistic, and reflect an orientation toward Canaan and western Asia shared by biblical and other ancient Near Eastern historiographers of the first millennium. Amorites were "westerners," among them residents of Canaan, and Hittites may have been Syrians of various types, probably including Arameans (see NOTES to Num 14:25, 45).

We can be more precise about some of the ethnonyms, however. The Amalekites are known in more than one region of Canaan, and even outside its boundaries, but their concentration in the Negeb is well attested in the premonarchic and early monarchic periods (1 Sam 15:5; 30:1, 18). The Jebusites belong in the central mountain range (Judg 19:10–11; 2 Sam 5:6; Josh 15:8, 63). In contrast, the determinate term *hakkenaʿanî* 'the Canaanites' is too generally used to allow for a precise identification.

The overall effect of v 29 is to project hostile and powerful enemies on all sides! To the west and to the east, near the sea and at the Jordan—Canaanites; in the central mountain range (Hebrew *bahar)*—Hittites, Jebusites, and Amorites; to the south, in the Negeb—Amalekites. Assuming this is a description of Judah, not of Canaan in its entirety, all directions are addressed. It has already been noted that v 21, which extends the mission of the spies to Lebo of Hamath, on the northern border of Canaan, is an addition of the priestly writer, whereas the mission, in JE's projection, reached only to the area of Hebron, in the central mountain range.

30. *Caleb silenced the people.* The rare verbal root, postulated as *hāsāh* 'to hush, silence' seems to have an acoustic character, approximating the actual sound that would be used in urging another to be silent. The present form, *wayyahas* 'he silenced' is unique in the Hebrew Bible. Elsewhere we have the form *has* 'hush!' (Judg 3:19; Amos 6:10; 8:3).

The verb *ʿālāh* 'to ascend' has been translated "invade" so as to convey the military intent of Caleb's statement. Compare Josh 10:33: "Then Horam, king of Gezer, invaded *(ʿālāh)* in order to relieve Lachish, but Joshua overwhelmed him and his army without leaving any survivors" (cf. also 1 Kgs 9:16; 14:25; 2 Kgs 17:3; 18:9). There seems to be some play on the nuances of Hebrew *ʿālāh* in this and the following verses.

It is, however, the verb *yāraš* 'to seize, take possession' that requires special clarification. Contrary to conventional opinion, the primary connotation is not "to inherit," but rather "to possess," in any of several ways. In the present verse, possession by military force is clearly indicated, and the same sense obtains in other conquest narratives (Deut 1:21; 2:24, 31). Of immediate relevance is usage of the verb *yāraš* in Num 21:24: "The Israelites defeated him, by the blade of the sword, and seized his land from the Arnon to the Jabbok, up to [the border of] the Ammonites, for the Ammonite border was strongly fortified."

Once possession is actual, subsequent generations inherit what their predecessors had probably conquered by force (Levine 1983).

In statements about physical prowess, the verb *yākôl* means "to prevail over, overpower," as in Gen. 32:25: "He (the angel) saw that he could prevail over him *(kî lōʾ yākôl lô)*, so he touched the socket of his hip" (cf. Gen 32:28; Ps 13:5).

31. *We dare not mount an attack against that people.* Once again, Hebrew *ʿālāh* connotes military action. Here, *laʿalôt ʾel hāʿām* uses prepositional *ʾel* in the sense of *ʿal* 'against.'

32. It is likely that this verse was inserted by P. It contradicts v 27, which characterizes the land of Canaan as bountiful, by condemning Canaan as a land that devours its inhabitants. Furthermore, v 32 employs the verb *tûr* 'to reconnoiter,' a favorite usage of P (Num 13:2, 17; 14:6–7, 34).

a discrediting report. Hebrew *dibbāh,* from the verb *dābab* 'to speak', represents specialized usage, always connoting evil speech. Although rare in biblical Hebrew, this verbal root has cognates in other Semitic languages, most notably in Akkadian, *dabābu* 'to speak,' and its many related forms *(CAD D,* 4–14).

Thus, Joseph brought back a bad report about his brothers' activities (Gen 37:2), whereas those suffering the calumny of evil persons, or of the community as a whole, complain of *dibbāh* (Jer 20:10; Ps 31:14; Ezek 36:3). A wise person refrains from speaking *dibbāh* (Prov 10:18; 25:10). It is difficult to pinpoint the effect of the verb *hôṣîʾ*, literally "to bring out," used here and in Num 14:36–37; Prov 10:28. Curiously, in Gen 37:21 the idiom is *hēbîʾ dibbāh* 'to bring, produce a bad report.' One is reminded of the legal formula *hôṣîʾ šēm raʿ ʿal-* 'to disseminate a bad name against' in Deut 22:14, where the sense of *hôṣîʾ* is to publicize or promulgate.

Whereas in the JE narrative, the spies are realistically concerned about force and fortifications, here in P's version, they malign the Promised Land itself. In the priestly execration, it is predicted that the Judean exiles will be consumed by the land of their enemies, which is a way of expressing extinction (Lev 26:38). Given the affinities between priestly diction and Ezekiel's rhetoric, it is relevant to cite the dramatic prophecy of Ezekiel addressed to the Land of Israel: "Because they say to you (the land personified): A devourer of people are you *(ʾôkelet ʾādām ʾatt),* and a bereaver of your nations were you! Just so, you shall no longer devour people, and your nations you shall no more bereave" (Ezek 36:13–14).

A perusal of the preceding prophecy, of Ezek 36:5–12, shows the converse of a land that devours its inhabitants, for there we read of bountiful fertility, of agricultural lands worked and sown, and of towns settled and of ruins restored; of a populous nation. In the harsh priestly view, the offense of the spies was particularly grievous.

Hebrew *'anšê middôt* means, literally, "men of large measurements, proportions." Compare *bêt middôt* 'a grand house' in Jer 22:14.

33. *There we saw Nephilim.* The JE narrative resumes here, for a brief spell, since P reenters in 14:1. See the NOTES on v 22, above, for information on the Anakites. The only other biblical mention of the *nepîlîm* comes in Gen 6:4, in a passage attributed to the Yahwist: "The Nephilim were about in the land in those days, and afterwards as well, when the young gods had intercourse with human women, who bore them children. They were the heroes of old, the men of renown."

In effect, the author, or glossator, of Num 13:33 creates a mythic affiliation between the Anakites mentioned in v 22, above, and the Nephilim of the prologue to the flood epic in Gen 6:1–4. Precisely, the Hebrew plural form *nepîlîm* represents the *qāṭîl*, active participle, predicated as singular: *nāpîl*, meaning "the faller; one who fell." One thinks of fallen gods, who had been ejected from the celestial realm, perhaps for some offense, or as a consequence of a power conflict on high.

we felt like grasshoppers. The spies felt minuscule as they gazed up at the fortified cities, and at the gigantic Anakites-Nephilim. Viewed from heaven, humans appear like grasshoppers in God's sight:

> He is seated above the vault of the earth,
> So that its inhabitants appear as grasshoppers *(weyôšebêhā kaḥḥagābîm)*.

Most likely, grasshoppers served in the proverbial idiom as the epitome of smallness, as a lilliputian image. By attributing to the Canaanites their perception of their own insignificance, the spies reveal their own feeling of inadequacy.

TRANSLATION OF NUMBERS 14

14 [1]The entire community raised [its voice] and gave forth with weeping on that night.

[2]All of the Israelite people protested to Moses and Aaron. The entire community said to them, "If only we had died in Egypt, or in this wilderness if only we had died!

[3]"Why is YHWH leading us to this land, only to fall by the sword, with our wives and small children taken as spoils? It would be preferable to return to Egypt!"

[4]They said to one another, "Let us head back and return to Egypt!"

[5]Moses and Aaron fell prostrate before the entire assembled Israelite community.

6Joshua son of Nun and Caleb son of Jephunneh, from among those who had scouted the land, tore their garments.

7They addressed the entire Israelite community as follows: "The land we traversed for the purpose of scouting it—that land is exceedingly bountiful!

8"Surely YHWH is well disposed toward us; he will enable us to enter this land, and will grant it to us—a land flowing with milk and sap.

9"As for you—do not rebel against YHWH! You must have no fear of the people of the land, for they are prey for us! Their Protector has abandoned them, and YHWH is on *our* side. Have no fear of them!"

10The entire community was threatening to stone them, when the glorious presence of YHWH appeared at the Tent of Meeting, before the entire Israelite people.

11YHWH said to Moses: How long will this people continue to reject me? How long will they refuse to place their trust in me, in all of the signs I have performed in their midst?

12I will afflict them with pestilence, and dispossess them, and then make you into a nation greater and more numerous than they.

13But Moses replied to YHWH, "The Egyptians will learn of this, for you brought this people out of their midst by your power.

14"Now, they will learn of this, and relate it to the inhabitants of this land. They, in turn, have heard how you, O YHWH, appear to them in plain view, while your cloud remains above them; how you march in advance of them, within a pillar of cloud by day, and within a pillar of fire by night.

15"If you should put this people to death, to the last person, the nations who have heard of your renown would then say,

16" 'It was because YHWH lacked the capacity to bring this people to the land he had promised them that he slaughtered them in the wilderness!'

17"Now, then, let my LORD's forbearance be great, as you, yourself, have declared, in the following words:

18" 'YHWH is long-tempered, and shows great kindness. He forgives iniquity and disloyalty, but will not grant full exoneration. Rather, he reserves the punishment due the fathers for their children; for the third and for the fourth generations!'

19"Pardon, I beseech you, the iniquity of this people, commensurate with your great kindness; just as you have pardoned this people from Egypt until now."

20YHWH responded: I grant forgiveness, in accordance with your word.

21But, as I live, and just as my glorious presence expands to fill the entire earth—

22just so, none of these men who now see my glorious presence, and [who saw] my wondrous signs that I performed in Egypt and in the wilderness, and yet challenged me [at least] ten times, refusing to heed me,

23 will ever see the land I promised to their ancestors. All who would reject me shall never see it!

24 Except for my servant, Caleb, because he was possessed of a different spirit and remained committed to me. Him will I bring to the land he has already entered, and his descendants will conquer it.

25 Now, as the Amalekites and Canaanites inhabit the valley, redirect your march into the wilderness tomorrow, on the way to the Sea of Reeds.

26 YHWH spoke to Moses and Aaron as follows:

27 How long will this evil community persist in their agitation against me? The protests of the Israelite people, which they continually inveigh against me, I have heard.

28 Say to them: As I live, says YHWH, precisely what I have heard you wish for, I will grant you!

29 Your corpses shall fall in this very wilderness, all of your numbered divisions, twenty years of age and above, who have agitated against me.

30 You will never enter the land where I swore I would settle you, except for Caleb son of Jephunneh, and Joshua son of Nun.

31 But as for your small children, who, you predicted, would be taken as spoils, these will I, indeed, allow to enter, and they will experience the land that you have disparaged.

32 But your own corpses will fall in this wilderness!

33 And your [grown] children will roam about in this wilderness for forty years, bearing the punishment for your faithlessness, until your own corpses decompose in the wilderness.

34 In proportion to the number of days you scouted the land, for each day a year, you shall bear the punishment for your iniquities; for forty years, so that you may know what the denial of me entails!

35 I, YHWH, have spoken, and this I shall surely do to this evil community who conspire against me. In this very wilderness they shall meet their end, and here they shall die!

36 (And the men whom Moses had dispatched to scout the land, and who returned to incite the entire community against him, presenting a discrediting report of the land—

37 these men who presented a discrediting report of the land actually died in a plague, in the presence of YHWH.

38 Only Joshua son of Nun and Caleb son of Jephunneh survived, of those men who went to scout the land.)

39 When Moses communicated these words to the entire Israelite people, the people mourned deeply.

40 They arose early on the morrow and climbed toward the summit of the mountain range, proclaiming, "We are ready to invade the place designated by YHWH. We have been remiss!"

41 But Moses warned, "Why are you countermanding YHWH's directive? Such a course will not succeed!

42 "Do not invade, because YHWH is not present in your midst. Or else you will be repulsed by your enemies!

43 "For the Amalekites will confront you there, and you will fall by the sword! Because you have deserted YHWH, he will no longer be at your side."

44 Nevertheless, they surged ahead, attempting to climb to the summit of the mountain range; but neither the Ark of YHWH's Covenant, nor Moses himself, budged from within the encampment.

45 The Amalekites and the Canaanites, who inhabited the mountains, swept down and pounded them to pieces all the way to Hormah.

NOTES TO NUMBERS 14: GOD'S DECREE AGAINST THE WILDERNESS GENERATION—MOSES AS INTERCESSOR

14 1–10. In their final form these verses are the work of the priestly school, though vv 1a, 2–4, and 7b–9 were taken from JE. This section amplifies the theme of Numbers 13, and further emphasizes the negativism of the Israelites on the matter of the conquest and settlement policy.

raised [its voice] and gave forth with weeping. Two familiar ways of depicting weeping are combined in v 1. There is, first of all, the notion of "raising one's voice and weeping *(nāśā' qôl . . . ûbākāh),*" as in Gen 27:28 and 29:11; and then, of "giving forth with sound *(nātan qôl),*" as in Gen 45:2 and 2 Sam 22:14. The present result is a conflation.

The separate derivation of each of the two parts of v 1 is signified by the differing terms used with reference to the Israelite people: *ʿēdāh* 'community' in the opening clause, an earmark of P, and *ʿam* 'people' in the latter part of the verse, a term characteristic of JE.

2. *protested.* Hebrew *wayyillônû,* a *niphʿal* form, connotes actual grievance (cf. below in v 36, and in Num 17:6). *Hiphʿil* forms of this verb describe the instigation of opposition on the part of others, as in v 27, below, and in Num 16:11 and 17:20.

If only we had died. In desperation the people wish they had perished in Egypt. The Hebrew *lû matnû* is unique, but the same thought is expressed through parallel words in Num 20:4–6.

3. The complaints of the people often centered around the perils and deprivations of the wilderness (Exod 14:11–12; Num 20:4). Here, however, the people speak of not wanting to face the strenuous effort of settlement, and of encountering fierce enemies in Canaan. This theme is new, and it is an extension of the fears expressed in Num 13:27–29.

taken as spoils. Hebrew *lābaz* is an adverbial form derived from the root *bāzaz* 'to despoil', and it recurs in v 31, below. In Deut 1:39 we find a similar statement. The form *lābaz* may have been coined by the Deuteronomic school: evidence its frequency in Jeremiah (Jer 2:4; 15:13).

The wish to return to Egypt when the going gets rough is introduced in Exod 13:17. There we read that the people were in despair when faced with possible war against the Philistines.

4. *Let us head back.* The Hebrew idiom *nittenāh rō᾽š* is ambiguous. The most logical sense is that of "turning about" or "heading back," as in Neh 9:17, a later echo of this verse *(NJPS)*. This sense conforms with the immediate context. But the sense could be that of "forming a column," because Hebrew *rō᾽š* has this specialized meaning (Judg 7:16; 9:34, 43). Others have suggested the notion of appointing a new "head" to replace Moses, but this reading seems less likely.

5. Falling prostrate has differing symbolic significance in varying contexts, but it invariably connotes submission. Here both Moses and Aaron fell prostrate before the Israelite community upon receiving the discouraging report of the spies. In some instances, this act bespeaks grief. In Josh 7:6 we read that Joshua and the elders, upon hearing of the Israelite defeat at Ai, tore their garments, fell to the ground, and threw dust over their heads.

the entire assembled Israelite community. The unique composite designation *qehal ʿadat benê Yiśrā᾽ēl* combines components of different origins and meanings that in time came to be used synonymously. The designation *qehal Yiśrā᾽ēl* 'the congregation of Israel' occurs in Deut 3:30, and in general the term *qahal* is favored by the Deuteronomic school. In contrast, *ʿēdāh* is a distinctively priestly term. Finally, *benê Yiśrā᾽ēl* is a term of widespread use, and one favored by priestly writers because of its genealogical orientation. See the NOTES on Num 1:2.

7. *we traversed.* Both the verb *tûr* 'to traverse, explore' and the statement of Joshua and Caleb are explained in the NOTES on Num 13:32.

exceedingly. Adverbial *me᾽ōd me᾽ōd* often expresses excessive quantity or volume (Gen 7:19; 30:43), or an intense degree of emotion (2 Kgs 10:4). On the bounty of Canaan see Deut 1:25, 35; 8:7; and cf. Exod 3:8.

8. *is well disposed.* The verb *ḥāpēṣ* expresses preference and even desire (Isa 66:3; Esth 2:14; and cf. Gen 34:19; 1 Sam 18:22; 1 Kgs 10:9).

9. The notion of rebelling (the verb *mārad)* against God is a late locution in biblical Hebrew, occurring in Joshua 22 and in Ezek 2:3; 20:38; Dan 9:5, 9; and Neh 9:26. Here it connotes activism, whereas we are more familiar with negative expressions of disobedience, such as failure to heed and turning away that are also conveyed by this verb.

the people of the land. The Hebrew term *ʿam hā᾽āreṣ* here refers to the existing landed population of Canaan. In Gen 23:7 we read that Abraham presented himself before the "Hittite" landowners of Hebron, who are identified as *ʿam hāʾāreṣ* (cf. Exod 5:5). Elsewhere *ʿam hāʾāreṣ* may have different connotations (Tadmor 1968).

for they are prey for us. Hebrew *kî laḥmēnû hēm*, literally, "for they are our bread," uses *leḥem* in the sense of "prey, spoils," to be consumed by an invader. This usage of *leḥem* is unique in biblical Hebrew, though Hebrew *maʾakāl* 'food' is once used in this way in Ps 44:14.

Their Protector. Usage of Hebrew *ṣēl* 'shade, shadow' in the present verse deserves special comment. Here *ṣēl* signifies the patronage or protection afforded by deities, as well as by kings. Isa 30:2–3 make the point that the "shade" or protection of Egypt is unreliable. Similarly, we read that the Judean exiles had hoped to remain under the "protection *(ṣēl)*" of their king in hostile lands (Lam 40:20; cf. Jer 48:45; Ezek 31:6). This connotation is well attested in Akkadian, and is said of both gods and kings *(CAD S*, 190, s.v. *ṣillu*, 4). It is even expressed in personal names, such as *Ṣi-lu-uš Dagan* 'Into-the-Protection-of-Dagan'. This is the most likely connotation of the Ugaritic cognate, *ẓlm*, in the title of an unusual Ugaritic ritual *(KTU* 1.161): *spr dbḥ ẓlm* 'the record of the sacred feast in honor of the Patrons'. This interpretation is clarified in the COMMENT, below.

The connotation of "protection, protector" derives from the realities of life in Near Eastern climes, where shade shelters humans from the life-threatening heat of the sun. Compare Ps 121:5–6: "YHWH is your guardian. YHWH is your protection *(ṣillleḵā)* at your right hand. By day the sun will not strike you, nor the moon by night." Similar language is used in Isa 25:4, in describing God's protection of the unfortunate, and in Jotham's parable, where the thorn bush invites all to seek protection *(ṣēl* 'shade') under his kingship (Judg 9:15).

The message of this verse is that the previous inhabitants of Canaan have been abandoned by their national god, who had formerly protected them, whereas Israel's God stands at the side of his people to protect them. In contrast, other biblical verses speak of the God of Israel himself as "turning away" (the verb *sûr)* from those whom he rejects (Judg 16:20; 1 Sam 28:15).

10. *was threatening.* The Hebrew verb *ʾāmar* 'to say', when linked syntactically to infinitives, may express intent. Thus Exod 2:14: "*Do you mean* to kill me *(halehorgēnî ʾattāh ʾômēr)* as you killed the Egyptian?" (Cf. also 1 Kgs 5:19; 8:12; Ezek 20:8; 2 Chr 13:8; 28:10.) The sense here is that the people *threatened* to kill Moses and Aaron.

In priestly narratives, God's glorious presence appears at critical junctures, dramatically quells rebellion, and restores order (Num 16:19; 17:7; 20:26).

11. *to reject.* Verses 11–24 are part of JE, and are remarkably similar in tone and theme to Exod 32:9–14, 30–35; 34:9. The verb *niʾēṣ*, occurring also in the *qal* stem, seems to be reserved for the human-divine encounter. One "spurns" God and his laws, just as God "spurns" people in his wrath. Hebrew *niʾēṣ* is possibly cognate to Akkadian *nâṣu* (from *naʾaṣu)* 'to scorn' *(CAD N*, 1.53,

nâṣu). As such, it would express emotion as motion, a common semantic feature of biblical Hebrew. Similar thoughts are expressed in v 22, below.

The sense of the verse is that the people failed to place their trust in God despite the wondrous acts he had performed on their behalf. This is the force of prepositional *beth: bekol hā'ôtôt 'despite* all of the signs'.

There is a lack of precise agreement between the verb *lô' ya'amînû 'they* do not have faith' and the pronominal suffix of *beqirbô* 'in *its* midst'. It seems that this discrepancy reflects the wording of the following verses, 14:12–13, where at the end of v 13 we also find *beqirbô* 'in *its* midst'. Deuteronomy is replete with similar criticisms of Israel (Deut 3:21; 4:9, 19; 7:19; 10:21). In those statements the emphasis is on the fact that the Israelites beheld God's acts with their own eyes, but the fact that it is God who performed them is also important (Deut 29:2; 34:11).

12. The thought that God would destroy Israel, replace them with another people, and make Moses the leader of that other people is expressed in Exod 32:9–10 and Deut 9:14, in much the same words. This is an ironic twist to God's promise to Abram (Gen 12:2). Abram was to become the father of a great people, whereas God, in his anger, threatens to destroy Israel and make Moses leader of another people!

13–16. These verses, which string out a series of related ideas somewhat repetitively, are difficult to interpret and present problems of style and syntax. They are best explained as follows: the Egyptians will report to the Canaanites that God had liberated the Israelites from Egypt with great acts of might. Now, if God puts the Israelites to death in the wilderness, those nations will conclude that God lacked the power to bring the people he had liberated to the Promised Land, and for that reason had allowed them to perish in the wilderness.

The difficulty lies in v 13b, which, as stated, would imply that the Egyptians had yet to hear about the Exodus! Actually, this is not the meaning of v 13b, where a sequence of tenses is operative: *wešāme'û . . . we'āmerû* 'having heard . . . they will report'. Kmowing of the Exodus, the Egyptians will report to the Canaanites how powerful the God of Israel is.

14. This verse is also problematic. As it stands, a relative clause must be assumed: "*who had heard* that you, YHWH, are present in the midst of the people." But possibly the verb *šāme'û* in v 14 should be excised. It may have been miscopied from v 13, and v 14 may have read, "and they will report *(we'āmeru)* to the inhabitants of this land that you, YHWH *(kî 'attāh YHWH)*." The sense of v 14 is that God's presence is visible, being manifest in the pillar of cloud.

in plain view. For idiomatic *'ayîn be'ayîn* 'eye to eye' see Isa 52:8; and for a similar thought, expressed differently, see Exod 33:11. The cloud tradition was introduced in Exod 13:21–22 and is referred to repeatedly (see the NOTES on Num 9:15–16 and 10:11–12, 34). During the day, God's presence appeared as a cloud, but at night the flame that was enveloped in it shone through in the dark.

15. Here we also detect a particular sequence of tenses: *wehemattah . . . we'āmerû* 'should you kill off . . . they would say'.

to the last person. Idiomatic *ke'îš 'eḥād* 'as one man' is appropriate in a reference to annihilation. In Judg 6:16 we read that with God's help, Gideon would wipe out the Midianites "as one man." The same sense is conveyed by the idiom *'ad 'eḥād* in Exod 14:28.

16. The language of v 16 is harsh. The verb *šāḥaṭ* 'to slaughter' is used to describe God's projected action against Israel. Furthermore, doubt is actually voiced about God's power, a thought shared with Deut 9:28.

17. The precise connotation of *kôaḥ* (normally "strength, power") in this verse requires comment. The sense here is "forbearance, restraint," namely, the strength to restrain the use of destructive power. Moses appeals to God, with some indirection, not to unleash his wrath against his people. This nuance is expressed in Nah 1:3: "YHWH is long tempered and of great forbearance *(ugedol kôaḥ)*." On this basis, *yigdal-nā' kôaḥ YHWH* should mean "let the *forbearance* of YHWH grow greater!" (Gray—ICC).

18. *long-tempered.* The characterizations of God expressed here recall Exod 34:6–7. The pair of divine virtues or attributes *'erek 'appayim werab ḥesed* 'long-tempered and abundant in kindness' are often cited with respect to the God of Israel (Joel 2:13; Jonah 4:2; Pss 86:15; 103:8; 145:8; Neh 9:17). The logic of Moses' argument, here and in Exod 34:6–7, is that God's reputation as a compassionate divine being, as well as a powerful one, will suffer if Israel perishes.

He forgives iniquity and disloyalty. The statement *nôśē' 'awôn wāpeša'*, literally, "forgiving of iniquity and transgression," emphasizes God's compassion (Exod 34:7; Mic 7:18; Ps 99:8), whereas *wenaqqēh lô' yenaqqeh* 'but he will surely not clear, exonerate' emphasizes his punitive tendency. In various forms, the verbal root *nāqah* is used in legal contexts. Its usage in biblical Hebrew parallels that of similar terms in Aramaic and Akkadian, all expressing the notion of "cleansing" or clearing away guilt, debt, and obligation. Thus adjectival *nāqî* means "clear, innocent" (Gen 24:41; Exod 21:28; see the NOTES on Num 5:19).

The statements occurring here are paraphrased in the Decalogue, where they are associated with the commandments pertaining to idolatry and the worship of other gods, as well as to swearing falsely in God's name (Exod 20:5–6; Deut 5:11–12).

he reserves the punishment. The idiom *pāqad 'al* connotes punishment. The basic sense of *pāqad* is "to hand over, deliver, assign," hence "to turn one's thoughts, attention to" another person or concern (Gen 21:1; Exod 4:31; 1 Sam 2:21; see the NOTES on Num 1:3). It is not entirely clear how *pāqad ʿal* came to mean "punish." Either *pāqad ʿal* means "to count against, hold accountable," or it means "to turn one's attention to"—for the purpose of punishing (Exod 32:34; Jer 21:14).

Students of biblical theology have paid considerable attention to the implied injustice of making subsequent generations pay for the sins of their ancestors. What is being expressed in the present statement is actually a two-dimensional concept. On the one hand, we are told that no one within the immediate family alive when the perpetrator committed the crime can escape divine justice, which will reach down to those of the fourth generation (Freedman 1986). On the other hand, there is currency to the notion that God does not always bring the evil in the lifetime of the perpetrator, but defers it as a concession (Muffs 1978). This question is discussed further in the COMMENT that follows.

19. This verse contains two verbs that are basic to the notion of forgiveness in biblical religion, *sālaḥ* 'to forgive' and *nāśāʾ*, literally, "to lift, carry away," hence "to remove" the offense. The verb *sālaḥ*, functionally translated "to forgive," probably means "to wash, sprinkle," as we know from its cognates in Ugaritic and Akkadian (see *CAD S*, 85–88, *salāḥu* A). In a Ugaritic ritual we find the formula *slḫ npš* 'washing of the upper part of an animal' (*KTU* 1.46, line 1). The notion of cleansing is extended to connote God's forgiveness. The verb *sālaḥ* is always said of God, who retains the exclusive prerogative of forgiveness for offenses against him, just as humans retain that prerogative for offenses against one another. These offenses cannot be ritually expiated. The verb *nāśāʾ*, when its object is a term meaning sin or transgression, projects the image of relieving or unburdening a person of offenses and of their consequent punishments. This is a very common image in biblical literature (cf. Isa 33:24; Ps 32:1).

20. God accedes to Moses' request in a uniquely dramatic statement, as if in obedience to Moses.

21. There is, however, a proviso: God will not destroy the people immediately, but he will not allow any and all who had spurned him to enter the Promised Land.

as I live. God swears by his own life, just as humans swear by God's life (see below, in v 28; and cf. Isa 49:18; Jer 22:24). God may also swear by his holiness (Amos 4:2), or by his "self" (Amos 6:8).

The perspective shifts to the third person: *weyimmālēʾ kebôd YHWH ʾet kol hāʾāreṣ* 'as the glorious presence of YHWH expands to fill the entire earth'. Compare Isa 6:3, and see the NOTES on v 10, above. This clause further enhances the efficacy of God's oath by referring, once again, to his visible presence.

22–23. The oath continues through v 23. All who had witnessed God's glorious presence and his providential acts and yet continued to doubt him repeatedly (idiomatic "ten times") will not live to see the Promised Land. There is an unmistakable emphasis on vision, conveying a cruelly ironic twist: those who *saw* God's acts and yet failed to trust him will never *see* the land!

challenged me. In v 22, the verb *nissāh* 'to try, test' bears the nuance of doubting, as if the Israelites had concluded prematurely that God was unable to bring his people to Canaan. See Exod 15:25; 17:2, 7; and Deut 6:16 for similar thoughts. One could also say that the Israelites repeatedly "tried" God's patience and forbearance.

none. In oath formulas, *'im* has assertive force, with negative implication, and is not usually conditional. Thus Gen. 14:22–23: "I swear to YHWH, EL-Elyon, creator of heaven and earth: I *will not take ('im 'eqqaḥ).*" Compare also Gen 21:23: "Therefore swear to me here by God *that you will not* deal falsely with me *('im tišqôr lî).*"

23. *All who would reject me shall never see it.* The verse concludes with a reinforcement of God's decree: "Surely, all those who spurn me *(wekol menā'asâi)* shall never see it." Conjunctive *waw* strengthens the assertion.

24. *a different spirit.* In the JE narratives, Caleb is the sole exception within the group of spies who keeps the faith (Num 13:30). Hebrew *rûaḥ* often means "a feeling, frame of mind." Compare *rûaḥ qin'āh* 'a feeling of envy' in Num 5:14 and 30. A "spirit" or attitude is said to be "with" a person (1 Sam 19:9).

remained committed to me. Hebrew *wayyemallē' 'aḥaraî* means "he followed after me," in the sense of remaining loyal when all others turned away from God (cf. Num 32:11–12; Deut 1:36). Thus Solomon did not *follow the course of* his father, David (1 Kgs 11:6). As a reward, Caleb's descendants will take possession of *(hôrîš)* the land.

25. *the Sea of Reeds.* This verse concludes the passage from JE. The people are instructed to proceed toward Canaan by a roundabout route, taking them to the area of the Red Sea. Hebrew *yam sûp* here designates the Gulf of Elath/Aqaba. The road leading to that area was known as *derek yam sûp* (Num 21:4; Deut 1:40; 2:1).

Questions remain about the precise meaning of v 25 in context, and we must backtrack in order to explain it correctly. Here we read that Canaanites and Amalekites inhabited "the valley." According to Num 13:29, the spies reported that the Negeb was inhabited by Amalekites, with Canaanites living along the coast. But aside from this inconsistency, it would make little sense to locate Amalekites and Canaanites "in the valley" *(bā'ēmeq)*, as is stated here. Which valley was intended? Verse 45, below, has the Amalekites and Canaanites living in the "hill country" *(bāhār)*, and the preceeding verses (vv 40–44) repeatedly refer to the difficulties of direct penetration into Judah through the hill country. It is possible, therefore, that the *sebîr, brh* (= *bāhār)* is correct *(BHS)*. In Gen 14:7 we read of an early battle with Amalekites in an area called *śedēh hāʿamālēqî,* best translated "the Amalekite mountains" (see the COMMENT, below).

In any event, v 25 in its totality means that the Israelites were to proceed from Kadesh/the Wilderness of Paran to the area of Elath/Aqaba, there beginning the encirclement of Edom and the ultimate penetration into Transjordan.

26–39a. The next section of Numbers 14 is the work of P, and constitutes an amplification of the divine decree stated by JE in Num 14:23–24, above. Whereas JE posed the rhetorical question in v 11, *ʿad ʾānāh* 'How long?' P asks, *ʿad mātaî* 'How long?'

persist in their agitation. Again, *hiphʿil mallînîm* connotes the instigation of others to acts of rebellion (see the NOTES on v 2, above).

28. *As I live.* Here again, God himself takes an oath formulated with assertive *ʾim* (see above, in the NOTES on vv 22–23 and below, in v 30).

what I have heard you wish for. The wording *kaʾašer dibbartem beʾoznaî*, literally, "which you spoke in my ears" suggests God's proximity to the people, even suggesting divine immanence.

29. *all of your numbered divisions.* The wording *wekol pequddêkem lekol misparkem,* literally, "and all of your arrays, with all of your numbers," appears somewhat redundant, but actually is not. The sense of *pequddîm* 'arrays, ranks' is explained in the NOTE on Num 1:21. It is a basic term of reference in the priestly traditions portraying the wilderness period. It has to do with the organization of the Israelite fighting force, and with census taking as well. At times *pequddîm* itself has a numerical connotation, but when further qualified by *mispār* 'count, number', the more basic sense of "rank, array" is preferable.

The decree was to affect all who were twenty years of age or older when they left Egypt, so that realistically a migration period of forty years, a schematic period of time, would see all of those who left Egypt gone from the scene. The significance of the minimal age of twenty years is clarified in the NOTES on Num 1:3, where the various priestly traditions on this subject are summarized. This classification system is utilized cruelly here; it serves as a context for God's horrendous decree. The verse ends with a reference to the instigation of rebellion against God.

30. Here Caleb is joined by Joshua in being exempted from the decree. Contrast v 24, above, in JE's account, where only Caleb is singled out.

I swore. Idiomatic *nāśāʾtî ʾet yādî,* literally, "I have raised my arm," means to swear (Exod 6:8; Ezek 20:6).

I would settle you. Hebrew *lešakkēn,* the *piʿel,* means "to settle, to cause one to dwell," and recalls the diction of Jer 7:3, 7, where the prophets warn the people that their continued settlement in the land is contingent on following God's ways.

31. The reference to small children who would not make it through, in the

view of the faithless, recalls v 3, above. Here the people is being taunted: you wrote off your small children, but they are the very ones who will ultimately reach the land and possess it.

32. *But your own corpses.* The Hebrew *ûpigrêkem 'attem* utilizes an independent pronoun to render direct address more emphatic (Gesenius 1960: 438, #135, no. 2).

33. *will roam about.* The grown sons of the Israelites, those over twenty years of age, who were already born at the time of the Exodus, will roam the desert aimlessly. This is a nuance of the verb *rā'āh* 'to graze; shepherd,' reflecting the shepherd's movements (Hos 12:2).

bearing the punishment for your faithlessness. The Hebrew idiom is *wenāśe'û 'et zenûtêkem.* Often words connoting sin or transgression also convey the consequences of, or punishment for, those acts (see the NOTES on Num 5:31; 15:31; and note the same connotation below, in v 34).

The verb *zānāh* means to commit a harlotrous or improper sexual act (Lev 21:14; Deut 23:19). It is one of the usual ways of conveying the infidelity of Israel as a people, and of its leaders, in metaphorical terms. The sense here is that one who disregards God's commandments is unfaithful to the Covenant (cf. Num 15:39; Judg 2:7; Ezek 20:30; Hos 9:1).

34. *for each day a year.* On idiomatic *yôm laššānāh yôm laššānāh* see Ezek 4:6.

the denial. Hebrew *tenû'āh* (the plural occurs in Job 33:10) derives from the verbal root *n-w-'* (or *n-y-'*), which in the *hiph'il* means "to negate, deny, treat as nothing" (Num 32:7; Ps 141:3). This verb also occurs in legal contexts, connoting the annulment of vows (Num 30:6, 9, 12). The sense here is that now the Israelites will experience the punishment that the denial of God will bring upon them.

35. *I shall surely do.* Again, *'im* introduces an oath, this time with positive suggestion *'im lō' zo't 'e'eséh* 'I will most certainly do this'.

who conspire against me. The idiom *hannô'adîm 'al* 'to rally against', with the *niph'al* form of the verb, figures in the account of Korah and his faction in Num 16:11 (cf. also usage in Num 27:3; 1 Kgs 8:5 ‖ 2 Chr 5:6).

36–37. These two verses are to be read continuously, without pause. They exhibit a prolonged sequence of tenses, as the translation indicates. In the priestly tradition, those who submitted a disparaging report promptly died in a plague; see the NOTES on Num 13:32.

39a. Moses, along with Aaron, had received the foregoing lecture (Num 14:26–38), and Moses now communicated it to the people assembled.

39b. Gray notes that JE resumes here. Verse 39b is to be linked either to v 24 or to v 25. Upon hearing that God was angered and had decreed that the current generation would not live to see the Land, the people mourned.

40. The fighting force began to climb the mountain range. The present

idiom, *hinnennû weʿālînû,* literally, "here we are, and we are about to ascend," is unique.

the place designated by YHWH. The same Hebrew designation, *ʾel ham-māqôm* ʾašer *ʾāmar YHWH* 'to the place that YHWH promised' occurs in Num 10:29. The people sensed that they had offended God by opposing the conquest of the land, and now sought to make amends. But it was too late!

41. *Why are you countermanding YHWH's directive?* The idiom *ʿôberîm ʾet pî YHWH* means "transgressing against the *command* of YHWH," for that is the functional connotation of *peh* 'mouth' in legal contexts. Commands were normally communicated orally.

Such a course will not succeed! The Hebrew *wehîʾ lōʾ tisḷaḥ* means "It (namely, the effort of the fighting force) will not succeed." The *qal* stem of the verb *sḷalaḥ* conveys success in Jer 12:1; Ezek 16:13; and Isa 53:10.

42. The presence of God was indispensable to victory. Without God fighting with them, the Israelites would be battered by their enemies. The *niphʿal niggap* often depicts utter defeat or retreat (2 Sam 10:15, 19; 1 Kgs 8:33; and cf. Lev 26:17). Idiomatic *welōʾ* means "lest"—lest you be battered by the enemy.

43. Referring to v 25, above, we again find two peoples, the Amalekites and Canaanites, inhabiting the hill country.

Because. The force of Hebrew *ʿal kēn* is distinctive here. Usually *ʿal kēn* connotes purpose: "therefore." But here the sense is closer to conveying result: "*because* you have turned away from following YHWH." Compare the usage of *ʿal kēn* in 2 Sam 7:22: *ʿal kēn gādaltā YHWH ʾelôhîm* 'Because you are great, YHWH, God!' (cf. also Gen 19:8, and probably Num 10:31). This part of the verse merely explains why God was not present in the midst of the people at the time in question.

44. *they surged ahead.* Hebrew *wayyaʿapîlû* is unique. We have the noun *ʿôpel,* meaning "tower" (2 Kgs 5:24; Mic 4:8), which may explain how *ʿapôlîm* became a word for hemorrhoids (1 Sam 5:6). On this basis, *wayyaʿapîlû* might be rendered, literally, "they surged up, stormed."

The Ark, the manifestation of God's presence, did not stir from the camp, nor did Moses, thus clearly indicating that the military effort did not have God's approval. On the role of the Ark in warfare, see COMMENT 2 on Num 10:29–12:16.

budged. Hebrew *mûš* is a verb of motion, meaning "to move" (Josh 1:8; Judg 6:18).

45. *pounded them to pieces.* The Amalekites and Canaanites defeated Israel and routed them all the way to Hormah, a site near Arad. It is tentatively identified as Tell Masos (Khirbet el-Meshash), a site mentioned in the Egyptian execration texts from the early second millennium B.C.E. (Aharoni and Avi-Yonah 1979: 26–27, map 23). The Hebrew *wayyaktûm,* from the verb

kātat, literally means "they beat them to pieces." The same battle is probably referred to again in Num 21:1–3. See the introduction to this volume, section A.5.c, for a discussion of the relationship of Num 21:1–3 and the present verse. In both passages we have folk etymologies of a toponym. In the present verse, the words *'ad haḥormāh* could be rendered "to utter destruction," especially because of their syntactic position: "they beat them to pieces to utter destruction." The site is called Hormah because of Israel's utter defeat. In Num 21:1–3, the same place is called Hormah, we are told, because Israel had vowed to condemn (the verb *heḥerîm*) the Canaanite cities if God granted them victory, and so they did.

COMMENT: BEGINNING THE CONQUEST OF CANAAN—WHY THE DELAY?

Numbers 13 and 14 present to the reader a panoply of themes, reflecting the highly composite character of these two chapters, which together form a literary unit. In the NOTES a source-critical analysis of Numbers 13 and 14 was presented; it remains to clarify their pivotal function within the overall historiography of Numbers, and within Torah literature as a whole.

Historiographic Considerations

The historiographic function of Numbers 13 and 14, in their final form, is to explain how it happened that the Israelites were compelled to invade Canaan from Transjordan at the end of a forty-year period. Why weren't they able to penetrate southern Canaan soon after the Exodus from Egypt?

According to Num 13:26–29, the spies reported back to Moses (and to Aaron and the heads of the community, according to P) that farther north, in the Judean hill country, there were Canaanites and Amalekites, as well as Amorites and Rephaim, living in fortified towns. At the time, the Israelites were in northern Sinai, according to P, and in Kadesh, according to JE. Notwithstanding such discrepancies in historical geography, it is clearly the message of Numbers 13–14 that the Israelites, being unable to invade Canaan from the south, were compelled to proceed eastward to the Gulf of Elath and then northward to Transjordan. Thus it is that in Num 20:14–21 we read of an Israelite delegation to the southernmost Transjordanian kingdom of Edom, dispatched from Kadesh. In Numbers 21–24 we subsequently read of Israelite victories in Transjordan. As Numbers ends, the Israelites are encamped in the Plains of Moab, preparing to cross the Jordan into Canaan.

The problems involved in reconstructing the progression of events from Numbers 13 to Numbers 21 have been discussed at great length in the introduction to this volume, sections A.4–5. Similarly, historiographic processes such as refraction and retrojection, employed by biblical authors to compose an early history of Israel before the conquest and settlement of Canaan, are also discussed in the introduction, sections D.2–4. A good part of this discussion necessarily focused on Numbers 13–14 and need not be repeated here. Suffice it to say, by way of summary, that according to JE the Israelites arrived at Kadesh early in the wilderness period (Num 13:26), whereas according to P they arrived at Kadesh only in the fortieth year (Num 20:1; 33:36–39). As a corollary, we can state that for P the wilderness of the extended wanderings was the Sinai peninsula, whereas in the view of JE it was another wilderness east of Edom and Moab.

It would be helpful, however, to review available historical and archaeological information in order to provide a more detailed analysis than was possible in the introduction. We begin with Kadesh (= Kadesh Barnea), mentioned by the JE historiographers in Num 13:26 as the site from which the spies had been dispatched; or, more precisely, the place to which they returned after completing their mission. Recent archaeological expeditions under R. Cohen in 1976 and 1982 (R. Cohen 1983) have confirmed the proposed identification of Kadesh Barnea as ʾAin Qudeirat, a site located southwest of Sedeh Boqer, along Wadi el-Ayin, at the most important crossroad in the immediate region. Y. Aharoni has suggested that the road leading from Kadesh to the Arad area, from southwest to northeast, was in fact *derek hāʾatārîm* (Num 21:1), traversed by the Israelites in their failed attempt to penetrate the southern Negeb (Aharoni and Avi-Yonah 1979: 40, map 48).

Based on the recent excavations, it emerges that Kadesh/ʿAin Qudeirat was part of a network of more than a dozen fortresses, first constructed in the mid tenth century B.C.E., most probably during the reign of Solomon. Several strata have been uncovered at ʿAin Qudeirat, and they correlate with the stratigraphy of the other sites that were part of this network. The most recent phase yielded remains of a rectangular fortress with casemate walls and eight towers. That phase is dated to the reign of Josiah in the late seventh century B.C.E. Underneath that stratum were found remains of a fortress dated less precisely to the ninth or eighth centuries, and beneath that, evidence of the tenth-century fortress. Cohen speculates that this earliest phase of the network was destroyed during the campaign of Pharaoh Shishak, ca. 925 B.C.E.

Cohen calls our attention to the geographical list preserved in Josh 15:1–4. He associates the boundary described in that list with the network of the most recent phase in the fortifications of the Negeb hill country, which included Kadesh. This latest phase was destroyed during the campaigns of Nebuchadrezzar preceding the Babylonian exile.

It is difficult, therefore, to establish the *Sitz-im-Leben* of the JE traditions of Numbers 13–14 bearing on Kadesh. What we have is the refraction into the presettlement period of a border situation that was realistic at various times during the monarchic period, most notably during the United Monarchy and during the reign of Josiah. What had served historically as a defense network, built to repel Israel's enemies on its southern border and to exercise control over the area south of Judah becomes, in the JE historiography and in the writings of the Deuteronomist, a stronghold once held by the Israelites themselves. On their way to the Promised Land after the Exodus, they had attempted to penetrate Canaan from Kadesh and to prevail over the Canaanite peoples who inhabited the southern territories of Canaan. In the introduction it was explained that an early date for the basic Kadesh tradition during the United Monarchy would correlate with what we know of the independent literary histories of J and E, on which JE is based.

Most revealing, in this regard, are the repeated references to Amalekites in Numbers 13–14. In the period of the United Monarchy, the southern border of Judah was secured by the very chain of fortifications of which Kadesh/ʿAin Qudeirat was a prominent component. The JE historiographers envisioned the very inhabitants of the Negeb whom the first kings of Israel sought to subdue and expel as those whom the Israelites would have encountered in the presettlement period, as they sought access to southern Canaan.

What is true of the Negeb also applies to Judah, especially the Hebron area, featured so prominently as the objective of the reconnaissance mission in the JE narrative. Although the archaeological record is limited in many respects, it seems reasonable to conclude that at the end of the Late Bronze Age the Judean hill country in the area of Hebron was not fortified. Some Late Bronze Age pottery has been found at such sites as Khirbet Rabud, which M. Kochavi (1973), its excavator, identifies as Debir/Qiryat Sepher (as an alternative to W. F. Albright's identification of Debir as Tell Beit-Mirsim), but the overall picture is one of a gap in fortification and large construction from the Middle Bronze Age to the Early Iron Age. The same seems to be true of Hebron/Tell-Rumeidah, where limited excavations have been recently conducted by A. Ofer (1989). Such gaps also appear at sites like Tell-Arad, which was vacant during the period between the Early Bronze Age and the late eleventh century B.C.E. (Aharoni 1976; Amiran 1980). Tell-Malkhata (Tell el-Milh), which may possibly be ancient Arad, also shows a gap from the Middle Bronze Age to the tenth or ninth century, in the Iron Age I phase (Kochavi 1970; 1977). At Tell-Masos, another suggested candidate for Arad (alternatively, for Hormah), there is likewise little evidence of fortification in the Late Bronze Age (Aharoni 1974).

With respect to the Negeb and the Judean hill country we have in Numbers 13 and 14 the same sort of historiographic refraction as we observed in the formulation of the Kadesh traditions. The realities of the period of the United Monarchy, and of various subsequent periods of biblical history, have been retrojected into the presettlement period, as conceived by biblical historiographers of several schools. The roles played by these locales and events have been modulated in the process.

The biblical historian must take into account the likelihood that Israelites, primarily Judahites and Simeonites, had actually entered the Negeb and Judah from the south separately, not as part of the major invasion from Transjordan, which are the focus of the historiography of Numbers. In other words, the Deuteronomist who gave us Deuteronomy 1–2 was bending the historical record when he intimated, in Deut 1:7–8, that the expansion into Judah and the Negeb occurred *after* the Transjordanian campaigns of Numbers 21. In fact, this expansion may have been independent of the Transjordanian adventure. If the report of an Israelite victory over Negebite Canaanites, preserved in Num 21:1–3, is, indeed, of deuteronomistic derivation, and if it is historically realistic, then we have an indication of an early penetration directly into the Negeb and southern Judah. The surprising placement of Num 21:1–3, probably the work of P, conveys the message that some Israelites did, in fact, succeed in battling the Canaanites. For the priestly writers, the interpolation of this record may have been intended to upstage the Transjordanian victories. But for the critical student of biblical historiography it serves as a clue to the existence of divergent traditions on the conquest and settlement of Canaan.

We can link the references to Caleb in Num 13:30 and 14:24, 30 to Deut 1:19–46 and to Judg 1:8–15. In a less direct way, these Torah references also relate to what is said about Caleb in Josh 14:6–14 and 15:13–14 (section D.5 of the introduction). All of these sources refer in some way to early Israelite conquests in Judah. Whatever Caleb's ethnic origin, he emerges as a Judahite leader who conquers the Hebron area. By referring to Caleb as an exception to the decree issued against the leadership of the wilderness generation, the JE historiographers of Numbers 13–14 square two agendas: they rationalize the inevitability of the Transjordanian adventure, while at the same time alluding to the record of the historical books, especially Judges, which tell of the conquest of Judah without referring to a Transjordanian campaign.

I have already mentioned the references to Hormah in Num 14:45 and 21:1. Hormah has been provisionally identified as Tell-Masos, but in any event it is located in the Negeb, in the area of Beersheba and Arad. If Mazar's identification of biblical Hormah as a town mentioned in the inscriptions of Amenemhet III of the nineteenth century B.C.E. is correct (B. Mazar 1965), we have evidence of its antiquity and possible further support for the authenticity of the report in Num 21:1–3. See the NOTE on Num 14:45.

The Dispatching of Spies: A Chronistic Typology

Reconnaissance is a familiar part of military strategy, and the reader logically expects that the Bible would record any number of instances in which this stratagem was employed (cf. 2 Sam 10:31; 15:10; 26:4; Gen 42:9).

Most relevant to the incidents recorded in the JE narratives of Numbers

13 and 14 is the brief statement in Num 21:32 that when in Transjordan, Moses sent spies ahead to scout the area of Jazer before advancing against it. A parallel to the priestly version of the mission to Canaan is the account in Joshua 2. The spies dispatched by Joshua entered Jericho, the major walled city in the Jordan valley, and secretly set about gathering intelligence on the state of the city's defenses. In its composition and emphasis, the account in Joshua 2 contrasts dramatically with what we read in Numbers 13–14. The only clear link between the diction of the two accounts is expressed by the verb *rā'āh* 'to see, observe' (Num 13:15; Josh 2:1). For the rest, we note significant differences in perspective: the Joshua account extols the awesome power of the Israelites and of their God, who fights at their side against their enemies. The Canaanites are filled with dread, as if in direct fulfillment of the poetic portrayal of Exod 15:15b–16a: "Then did all the inhabitants of Canaan melt away *(nāmôgû)*; fear and dread overcame them." This pronouncement is virtually paraphrased in Josh 2:9, where the verbal root *m-w-g* 'to melt away, dissolve' also occurs. This was the response of the inhabitants of Jericho, notwithstanding the formidable city walls that protected them. In a tale echoing the theme of the destruction of Sodom and Gomorrah, the narrative of Joshua 2 speaks of the sparing of a single family, this time headed by a woman.

In sharp contrast, the narratives of Numbers 13 and 14 project the dread experienced by the Israelites in the face of Canaanite power, the sense of being overwhelmed by the gigantic inhabitants of the land and of being deterred by the urban fortifications of the Canaanites. The situation had clearly improved from Numbers to Joshua, as if by historiographic design. The deuteronomistic recasting of early Israelite history, so prominent in the book of Joshua, has produced a more optimistic, positive portrayal of Israelite power in the settlement period.

A more subtle, but potentially more enlightening parallel to the narratives of Numbers 13 and 14 is to be found in Judges 18. With considerable insight, A. Malamat (1970) has identified significant typological parallels between the Exodus saga in Torah literature and the accounts of the Danite migration preserved in Judges. But the particular relevance of the Judges account to Numbers 13–14 has yet to be clarified.

Hard pressed by the Philistines of the southern Shephelah, the Danites sought a *naḥalāh*, a territory of their own elsewhere in Canaan. They accordingly dispatched a group of five spies, each a leading warrior, to the Ephraimite mountains. In the overall narrative, the mission of the spies serves as a rubric for an etiology of the original establishment of the northern Israelite cult center at Dan, in northern Galilee. Nevertheless, a close reading of Judges 18 reveals the essentials of the same typology that underlies Numbers 13–14.

Judges 18 begins with the charge to the spies: "Go search out the land!"

Compare Num 13:17b in the JE narrative: "Proceed directly through the Negeb. . . . Observe the land!" Compare also Josh 2:1: "Go, observe the land!" In all three sources, there is reference to *'anāšîm* 'personages', and this nuance was expressed by the priestly writers as well in Num 13:1–17a.

Whenever reconnaissance of unknown territory is undertaken, leading warriors, or tribal chieftains *(nésî'îm)*, are entrusted with the mission. They are formally charged, given their orders, so to speak, and instructed to bring back a report of their mission. Furthermore, we note that Judg 18:2 speaks of the warrior-spies dispatched by the Danites as coming "from their clan *(mim-mišpaḥtām)*," a status expressed in the priestly version of Num 13:1–17a as "one tribal chieftain *(nāśî')*, head of a patriarchal house *(bêt 'āb)*," from each of the twelve tribes.

Most interesting in the comparison of Judges 18 with the narratives of Numbers 13–14 are the reactions of the spies to what they actually observed in the target areas. As told in Judg 18:7–10, the Danite spies observe a people who are "tranquil and secure *(šôqēṭ ûbôṭēaḥ)*," living way off by themselves, unmolested and unthreatened by other nations. In the recapitulation of the story (Judg 18:27–29) we again read an idealized characterization of the most desired *naḥalāh* for the taking, an unfortified, undefended territory, whose residents have no standing army, being unaccustomed to warfare. What the spies of Numbers 13–14 are said to have encountered in Canaan is the very opposite situation! It is noteworthy that the land of Canaan itself, as described both in Judges 18 and in the JE version of Numbers 13–14, is beautiful and bountiful (compare Judg 18:9 with Num 13:27; 14:7b–8).

R. de Vaux (1978: 2.520) points to an additional theme evident in Numbers 13–14, one that epitomizes the themes of exodus and conquest. He refers to the role of Caleb, and to the defeat at Hormah recorded in Num 14:45: "What we have is a complete reversal of the themes of the Exodus and the holy war, in other words, the themes are a non-holy war and an anti-Exodus." The unwillingness of the people to undertake the invasion of Canaan represents the "anti-Exodus," because it is expressed as the desire to return to Egypt. The futile attempt to advance into the Negeb and the hill country of Judah represents the "non-holy war," a military venture that lacked divine sanction. Moses and the Ark did not budge from within the Israelite encampment (Num 14:44). The people are warned not to attempt an attack, that God was not "with" the people in this undertaking.

The JE narrative resonates a mythological theme associated with the giants and Nephilim of yore, even mentioning the names of three notables of that awesome group (see the NOTES on Num 13:22). The Rephaim, elsewhere associated with the giants, are not mentioned explicitly, and yet it is obvious that we should relate the brief references in Numbers 13 and 14 to more expansive passages on the same theme preserved in Deut 2:11–12a and 22–23.

Those passages were probably inserted by the Deuteronomist, who excerpted them from an independent chronicle. The style and syntax of these particular verses differ from the surrounding deuteronomistic narrative itself.

The pre-Israelite residents variously called Nephilim, Rephaim, Anakites, and designated by other more elusive names such as *ʿAwwîm* and *ʾÊmîm* (the dreadful ones?), inhabited diverse regions of Canaan and Transjordan, ranging all the way from Bashan (Golan) in northern Transjordan, through Hebron in the Judean hill country and down to Seir and the southern coastal plain. What is most significant about these traditions is the consistent identification of those almost mythic creatures as non-Israelites, as having descended from other groups, some identifiable and others not, but decidedly not from Israelite ancestors.

This perception differs essentially from what we find at Ugarit, for instance, where traditions about Rephaim are prominent. At Ugarit, the Rephaim are explicitly identified as the ancestors of the Ugaritic dynasty. In a royal text *(KTU* 1.161) we read how the ancestors of the ascendant Ugaritic king, Ammurapi (who, as it turned out, was the last king of Ugarit), were summoned to his coronation. The record lists several known dynastic predecessors of Ammurapi, but also refers to ancient personages designated as *rapiūma* (Hebrew *repāʾîm),* much in the same way that Mesopotamian king-lists refer to antediluvian kings, or as Genesis 1–6 refer to heroes of the generations from creation to the flood (Levine and de Tarragon 1984).

In the Ugaritic perception, the ancestral kings and heroes who were summoned to the coronation were important ancestors, whose endorsement of the new king was vital and indispensable. In contrast, the Rephaim of the Hebrew Bible and the Nephilim of antediluvian times bear no genealogical or ethnographic relationship to the Israelites. In Numbers 13–14, these giants are part of the Canaanite environment and were perceived as a danger to the Israelites.

The references to giants in Numbers 13 and 14 recall the Ugaritic royal liturgy in yet a more specific way. In Num 14:9 we find a statement that has eluded certain interpretation until quite recently. Verse 9 occurs in a passage that is part of the JE historiography (Num 14:7b–9). There the people are admonished as follows: "do not rebel against YHWH! You must have no fear of the people of the land, for they are prey for us! Their Protector *(ṣilllām)* has abandoned them, and YHWH is on *our* side. Have no fear of them!" Usage of Hebrew *ṣēl* 'shadow' as a divine epithet is explained in the Notes on Num 14:9. What is important for our understanding of the theme expressed is that the Ugaritic royal liturgy is entitled *spr dbḥ ẓlm* 'the record of the sacred celebration [in honor] of the *Patrons*'. The Rephaim and earlier dynastic kings are referred to as *ẓlm* 'protectors, patrons', just as in Num 14:9 the henotheistic deity projected for the Canaanites is referred to as "their Protector *(ṣillām)*."

By referring to the protector deity of the Canaanites as *ṣēl,* the author of Num 14:9 resonates the epic tradition of the West Semitic peoples preserved in one of its phases at Ugarit. A polytheistic culture has many *ẓlm,* the beatified kings and heroes of the distant past. The biblical writer was thinking in henotheistic terms. And yet that same biblical author is reminding us that the Rephaim and other heroes bore no relation to Israelite ancestors, but were rather part of the ethnographic makeup of Canaan when the Israelites commenced the process of conquest and settlement.

There is also a theology underlying the reference to the protector deity, the *ṣēl* of the Canaanites and their quasi-mythic heroes: each nation has its divine protector(s). The wars between the Israelites and other peoples, undertaken as part of the conquest of Canaan, were, in a different dimension, battles between their respective divine protectors.

Just as YHWH threatens to abandon Israel, and on occasion actually does so, so do the gods of other nations abandon their peoples. What we have, therefore, is a mirror image of Israelite epic projected onto the Canaanites. Their divine protector has abandoned them for the same reasons that YHWH abandons Israel; or he threatens to do so, in extreme anger. The Canaanites must have angered their protector by their sinfulness, and thereby fell out of favor with him. This conception is implied in Gen 15:16, in an account of the Abrahamic covenant, where it is stated that four generations would have to pass before Abraham's descendants would possess the land of Canaan, "because the sin of the Amorites would not be complete until that time." Only at that future time would the protector of the Amorites abandon them, thereby leaving Canaan open to the invading Israelites.

The same theology informs the Moabite inscription wherein the Moabite king Mesha of the ninth century B.C.E. explained the occupation of his country by the northern Israelites as a consequence of the wrath of Kemosh, the Moabite deity, that had been directed against his own people (Gibson 1971: 1.74, Mesha, lines 5–6).

The Attributes of God and the Intercession of Moses (Num 14:11–25)

Y. Muffs (1978) has clarified the subject of the prophetic role as it is expressed in biblical literature, showing how complex and subtle this role was understood to be. There has been a tendency to interpret the Israelite prophets as primarily the bearers of God's word to Israel and to other nations. This emphasis ignores, to a considerable extent, the effectiveness of the prophet as an intercessor on behalf of a distressed and threatened people.

Muffs explains that "the hand of YHWH" *(yad YHWH),*" the symbol of God's dominance over the prophet, must be understood in tandem with prophetic prayer and supplication, the expressions of the individuality of the prophet and of his conscience, one might say. In Muffs's view biblical literature conceives of the God of Israel as a deity who, if truth be said, favors individuals for the prophetic assignment who are not "yes men." He chooses persons who dare to challenge him. Note that Abraham is called a prophet in Gen 20:7, even though he was not sent to bear a message to a people. In part, Abraham's relation to God seems to have been that of an advocate, negotiating with God over Sodom and Gomorrah, for instance.

In Num 13 and 14 we observe a significant development in Moses' role as an intercessor on behalf of his people, Israel. This role was first portrayed in Exodus 32 and 34, as well as briefly in Numbers 11–12. In literary terms, it seems reasonable to regard Numbers 13–14 as having been based to a considerable extent on Exodus 32 and 34. We have in Num 14:11–25 the reuse of themes first conveyed in the context of the Sinai theophany, and reapplied, as it were, to the situation at Kadesh.

Israel's sin of worshiping the golden calf, committed at the very time that Moses was atop Sinai receiving God's covenantal gift to his people, generated the need for intercession when God threatened to annihilate Israel. The same role comes to the fore after Israel balks at the challenge of the conquest of Canaan, when Israelite forces were positioned to penetrate Canaan from the south.

The nexus of Exodus 32 and 34, on the one hand, and Numbers 13–14, on the other, reveals the fullness of God's plan for Israel. At Mount Sinai the God of Israel informed his people of its proper way of life *in its land.* The centrality of the land is expressed in Moses' appeal to God not to renege on his promise of granting the land to his people (Exod 32:13–14). The orientation toward the Promised Land is again conveyed in Exod 34:10–26, pursuant to God's forgiveness in response to Moses' entreaty. There Israel is admonished concerning proper worship once it defeats the Canaanites and settles Canaan with God's assistance.

The same dynamics informs Num 14:11–25, albeit with some differences. Moses taunts God about what the Egyptians will conclude from the premature extinction of Israel in the wilderness, thus resonating the theme of the promise of the land. Keeping more to the role of Moses himself, we note that both in Exod 32:10 and 32, and in Num 14:12, God is said to have offered Moses the leadership of another people, only to have Moses flatly refuse such an opportunity. As a prophetic leader, Moses is fiercely loyal to Israel, and his major effort is aimed at persuading God to forgive his sinful people and to bring his plan for them to fruition. In both Exodus and Numbers, the liturgical invocation of God's attributes of compassion serves to announce divine forgiveness.

The version of the attributes is abbreviated in Num 14:18, as compared with the version found in Exod 34:6–7, and it is also introduced in a different way. In Exodus, God's compassion allows for a second transmission of the covenantal tablets, whereas in Numbers it signals God's forbearance, his *kôaḥ* (Num 14:17). God will not cancel his program with respect to the land, only delay it, thereby preventing the current leadership and probably the entire people from entering the land.

Muffs calls attention to the deferral of punishment that is basic to the statement of divine attributes and is voiced in the Decalogue in association with the prohibition of pagan worship (Exod 20:5–6; Deut 5:9–10). This emphasis makes it quite clear, by the way, that Exodus 34 is the source of Num 14:11–25, where the context shifts from the issue of pagan worship to that of the lack of faith in God's promise and his power to accomplish the conquest of Canaan.

Exod 32:34 also implies that deferral of punishment and its visitation on the second, third, or fourth generation was at times perceived as a merciful act. God's kindness lasts a thousand generations, whereas deferral of punishment has a statute of limitations, we might say. If God can be persuaded to extend his grace beyond the fourth generation, Israel will not be punished for ancient sins! This conception is in tension with another biblical viewpoint, which regards delayed punishment as unjust, as punishment of the innocent by substitution.

It would be ironic if unjust cruelty were to be cited as evidence of God's covenant love *(ḥesed)*. We cannot, therefore, interpret the delaying of punishment stated in the pronouncement of the attributes as an injustice, and must regard deferral as essentially an act of divine kindness. It allowed the conquest of Canaan to proceed, albeit with some delay. This interpretation is suggested by Exod 32:34: "But for now, go lead the people to the place that I have specified to you. Behold, my divine messenger shall go ahead of you. But, on the day of my punitive visitation, I shall hold them accountable for their sin." We note that similar notions inform Amos 3:14 and Jer 27:2 and 32:5, where exile is the punishment of reference.

In summary, Num 14:11–25 reuses the themes of Exodus 32 and 34 in composing the Kadesh historiography, as these themes bear on the enterprise of conquest and settlement, so as to explain how it was that the fulfillment of God's promise took so long.

PART X.

NUMBERS 15: UNFINISHED CULTIC BUSINESS

♦

INTRODUCTION

At a certain stage in the development of the Israelite cult, the primary offerings of public worship, as well as of certain private sacrifices, were embellished by the addition of accompanying offerings on a regular basis. By this process the two major sacrifices, the *ʿôlāh* 'burnt offering' and the *zebaḥ* 'sacred feast', so often offered together, were regularly accompanied, in many rites, by a grain offering *(minḥāh)* and a libation *(nesek)*, consisting of wine. In themselves, grain offerings and libations of wine were ancient sacrifices, each with a life of its own in Israelite worship. What changed was their regular involvement as accompaniments to animal sacrifices. The four-part sacrificial ritual—*ʿôlāh, minḥāh, zebaḥ, nesek*—became fairly standard, and its specification is the burden of Num 15:1–16. Frequently a *ḥaṭṭāʾt* 'sin offering' was required, both in private and public rites, thereby generating a sequence of five sacrifices.

The frame of reference of Num 15:1–16 is ambiguous. On the one hand, its provisions seem to be addressed to the individual Israelite who would offer the usual sacrifices, informing him that when he does, he must include the grain offering and libation. On the other hand, there is reference to festival offerings, which would presumably be part of the public cult. In fact, such a system of composite rites, including grain offerings and libations, is prescribed for the public cult in Numbers 28–29.

The function of Num 15:1–16 is to detail the ingredients of the grain offerings and libations that were to be offered together with the major sacrifices. In this respect, Num 15:1–16 complements Leviticus 1–3 and Lev 6:1–11 and 7:11–34. One notes that the provisions of Num 15:1–6 were progressively incorporated into various composite rites. We see evidence of this development in Ezek 45:17, part of the regimen projected for a restored temple.

Following upon this code of ritual law, Num 15:17–21 ordain a "levy" (Hebrew *terûmāh)* taken from dough made from grains. Normally, the substances for cultic offerings were set aside or dedicated in the first instance before being converted into food. The present provision is an exception, because it applies to the dough, not to the grain used to make dough, or even to the flour. Perhaps this law represents a change in procedure, a possibility suggested by the wording of Num 15:20, where the present requirement of offering dough is compared to the more common requirement of offering grain. The normal pattern is evident in the respective requirements to set aside the firstfruits (Deut 26:1–11) and to collect tithes (Deut 14:22–29).

Three additional subjects are addressed in Numbers 15. (1) Num 15:22–31 restate the sacrifices required for the expiation of inadvertent offenses, a subject first addressed in Leviticus 4–5 and in Lev 6:17–17:10. (2) Num 15:32–36 report an instance of Sabbath violation and the punishment of the offender by divine command. Such reports occasionally appear in priestly literature, and serve to impress upon the reader the severity of religious prohibitions. (3) Num 15:37–41 state the duty of every Israelite to affix a blue cord to the corner of his garment, so as to be reminded at all times during the day of God's commandments.

Like several other sections of Numbers, chapter 15 represents, in large part, an addition or appendix to other cultic codes, especially those of Leviticus. Numbers thus emerges as a repository of late ritual law.

TRANSLATION

15 [1]The LORD spoke to Moses as follows:

[2]Speak to the Israelite people, and say to them: When you arrive at the land of your settlement, which I am granting to you,

[3]and perform a sacrifice by fire to YHWH, consisting of a burnt offering or a sacred feast, for the purpose of setting aside a votive, or as a voluntary offering, or on the occasion of your festivals—producing a pleasing aroma for YHWH, from the herd or from the flocks—

[4]the one making his offering to YHWH shall present a grain offering consisting of a one-tenth measure of semolina flour, mixed with one-fourth of a *hin* of oil;

[5]also wine for the libation, in the amount of one-fourth of a *hin*. [These] you shall perform in addition to the burnt offering, or for the sacred feast, for each head of sheep.

[6]Or in the case of a ram, you shall perform a grain offering consisting of two one-tenth measures of semolina flour, mixed with one-third of a *hin* of oil;

[7]also wine for the libation in the amount of one-third of a *hin*. These you shall present, [producing] a pleasing aroma for YHWH.

[8]In the event you perform a burnt offering or a sacred feast, consisting of a head of large cattle, for the purpose of setting aside a votive, or as a sacred gift of greeting to YHWH,

[9]you must present, together with the head of large cattle, a grain offering, consisting of three one-tenth measures of semolina flour, mixed with one-half of a *hin* of oil;

[10]also wine for the libation, in the amount of one-half of a *hin*, to produce a pleasing aroma for YHWH.

[11]The same shall be performed for each ox and for each ram, or other head of small cattle, sheep, or goats.

[12]For as many as you perform, so shall you do for each one, corresponding to their number.

[13]Every native-born citizen of the land shall perform these [rites] in this

way, when presenting an offering by fire, to produce a pleasant aroma for YHWH.

14When an alien who resides among you, or anyone else who may be among you at any time in the future, wishes to perform a sacrifice by fire, producing a pleasing aroma for YHWH, he shall perform [it] just as you perform [it].

15For the congregation [as a whole] there is only one statute, for you as well as for the resident alien; an everlasting statute throughout your generations. It shall [always] be the same for the alien as it is for you, in the presence of YHWH.

16There shall be only one prescription and rule applying both to you and to the alien who lives among you.

17YHWH spoke to Moses as follows:

18Speak to the Israelite people, and say to them: When you enter the land to which I am bringing you,

19and partake of the food of the land, you shall collect a donation for YHWH.

20The first product of your baking utensils, the round loaves, you shall collect as a donation, collecting it just as you do the donation from the threshing floor.

21You must prepare a donation to YHWH from the first product of your baking utensils, throughout your generations.

22In the event you inadvertently fail to perform all of these commandments, which YHWH communicated to Moses,

23including all that YHWH commanded you through Moses from the day that YHWH first issued commandments, and forward, throughout your generations:

24If an offense was inadvertently committed without the awareness of the community, the entire community must offer the sacrifice of one bull from the herd as a burnt offering, producing a pleasing aroma for YHWH, with its accompanying grain offering and libation, according to the rule; also one he-goat as a sin offering.

25The priest shall perform rites of expiation for the entire Israelite community, and they shall be pardoned. For it was, after all, an inadvertent offense, and they have duly presented their offering, a sacrifice by fire to YHWH, as well as their sin offering to YHWH consequent to their inadvertent offense.

26Pardon shall therefore be granted to the entire community of the Israelite people, as well as the alien residing among them, for the offense was committed by the entire people inadvertently.

27If an individual commits an offense inadvertently, that person must offer a yearling she-goat as a sin offering.

28The priest shall perform rites of expiation for that person who commits an inadvertent offense (because that person offended only inadvertently), in the presence of YHWH, securing expiation for him so that he may be pardoned.

29 As regards both the permanent resident of the land from among the Israelites and the alien residing among them, there shall be one prescription for all of you, for one who acts inadvertently.

30 But the person who acts defiantly, either permanent resident of the land or alien, is maligning YHWH. That person must be cut off from among his people.

31 For he has shown disrespect for the word of YHWH and has transgressed his commandment. That person must surely be cut off and bear the punishment for his iniquity.

32 While the Israelites were in the wilderness, they found a man gathering wood on the Sabbath.

33 Those who discovered him gathering wood brought him before Moses and Aaron, and before the entire community.

34 They placed him under guard, for it had not yet been specified what was to be done with him.

35 YHWH said to Moses: That man must be put to death! The entire community must stone him to death outside the encampment.

36 So the entire community took him outside the encampment and stoned him to death, just as YHWH had commanded Moses.

37 YHWH addressed Moses as follows:

38 Speak to the Israelite people and say to them that when they fashion fringes for themselves on the corners of their garments throughout their generations, they must join a cord of blue cloth to the fringe, at each corner.

39 It (= the cord) shall serve you as a fringe, and when you see it, you will be reminded of all of YHWH's commandments and perform them. Then you will not be drawn after your heart and your eyes, which you follow so faithlessly!

40 You must remember to perform all of my commandments and thereby be consecrated to your God.

41 I am YHWH, your God, who brought you out of the land of Egypt, thereby becoming your God. I am YHWH, your God.

NOTES TO 15:1–16: ACCOMPANYING GRAIN OFFERINGS

15 1–2. *the land of your settlement.* The combination *ʾereṣ môšebōtêkem* is unique, though we frequently encounter the term *môšābôt* 'settlements'. Whereas the plural form of this noun may signify numerical plurality, here it expresses a qualitative plural, focusing on the *act* of settlement. Compare the sense of plural *megûrîm* 'sojourning' in Gen 28:4: "to possess the land *of your sojourning ('ereṣ megûrêkā)*" (cf. also Gen 17:8; 37:1; Exod 6:4).

The formula "When you arrive at the land . . . which I am granting to you," and variations of the same, are well known (cf. Exod 12:25; Lev 14:34). This formula expresses the future orientation of priestly historiography, whose literary setting is in the period prior to the Israelite settlement of Canaan. Usage of the verb *nātan* 'to give, grant' signifies the basis of Israel's claim to the land: God had granted it to the Israelite people under the terms of the covenant relationship. The formulation is casuistic and predictive, which represents one of the functions of the particle *kî* 'when, as' (cf. Exod 21:2, 33; Lev 1:2).

3. *perform.* One "performs" (the verb *ʿāśāh)* a sacrifice; compare Exod 12:48: *weʿāśāh pesaḥ l-YHWH* 'and he would *perform* a paschal sacrifice to YHWH', or *weʿāśāh 'et ʿôlātô* 'and he *performed* his burnt offering' (Lev 16:24). This meaning recurs farther on in chap. 15, in vv 5–6, 8, and 11–14, and it corresponds to that of Akkadian *epēšu* 'to do, make', when said of cult and worship. On this basis, the repeated statements in 2 Kgs 17:29–32 to the effect that the foreigners *ʿāśû* 'did' their various gods, means that they performed sacrifices or worshiped them (Levine 1968b).

burnt offering. The term *'iššeh* most probably derives from *'ēš* 'fire' and means "a burnt offering, an offering by fire." It may refer to parts of various sacrifices that were burned on the altar or to complete sacrifices, where applicable. J. Hoftijzer (1967) attempted to relate the Hebrew *'iššeh* to a Ugaritic term, *iṯt*, which he translates "gift of devotion." Because the meaning of the Ugaritic term itself is uncertain, it is preferable to stay with the customary derivation from *'ēš* 'fire' (Levine 1974: 6, n. 6). See further below, in the NOTES on Num 15:25; and cf. Lev 1:9; Num 18:17; 28:6.

Still another indication that *'iššeh* derives from *'ēš* 'fire' comes from Num 18:9, where we read, "This is what you are to receive from the most sacred offerings *(miqqôdeš haqqodāšîm)*, from the offerings by fire *(min hā'ēš)*." We have, therefore, alternate ways of referring to sacrifices of which substantial portions were burned on the altar.

The pair *ʿôlāh* + *zebaḥ* occurs frequently, because we often find these two sacrifices, each of which represents a distinct mode of worship, offered together (Exod 18:12; Lev 17:8; and below, in v 8). The two terms are explained in the NOTES on Num 6:17, where they first occur in the book of Numbers.

to set aside a votive. The idiom *lepallē' neder* requires comment. The verb *p-l-'* is a variant of *p-l-h*, as usage indicates. In Exod 33:16 *wenipletnû* means "that we may be distinguished, differentiated," just as *hiphʿil wehiplāh* in Exod 9:4 means "He (God) will discriminate, differentiate"—between Israelites and Egyptians. On this basis, *yaplî'* *neder* 'to set aside a votive' in Lev 27:2 parallels *lepallē' neder* of the present verse, and of Lev 22:21. (Levine 1989b: 151, on Lev 22:21; 193, on Lev 27:2). See the NOTES on Num 6:1.

The term *neder* connotes both the initial pronouncement of the votive pledge and its payment, in the form of a sacrifice or some valuable object. Compare Gen 28:20 and Num 21:2, where vows are pronounced, with Lev 22:23 and Ps 65:2, where we read of the payment of votives.

a voluntary offering. The sacrificial offering called *nedābāh,* which is often accompanied by *tôdāh* 'thanksgiving offering' (Amos 4:5; Num 29:29; Deut 23:24; etc.), conveys the sense of an offering brought voluntarily, out of generosity. The basic procedures for a sacred feast offered as *nedābāh* are prescribed in Lev 7:16–17, where it is also paired with *neder* 'votive'. In postexilic biblical literature *hannedābāh* 'the voluntary offering' served as a generic term for designating several classes of cultic donations (Ezra 1:4; 3:5; 8:28).

your festivals. As a term for "festival," Hebrew *mô'ēd* is explained in the NOTES on Num 9:2. It signifies a recurring, annual occasion.

a pleasing aroma. The Hebrew idiom *rēaḥ nihôaḥ* occurs frequently in Leviticus and Numbers. The geminate form *nihôaḥ* probably derives from the verb *nûaḥ* 'to rest, be at ease', hence "experience comfort, pleasure." Rabbinic interpretation links *niḥôaḥ* to the noun *naḥat* 'comfort, pleasure', conveying the thought that sacrifices properly offered bring pleasure to God *(Midrash Hagadol* 1932: 36, line 10). The regular requirement that offerings be of a pleasant aroma implies, of course, that aromatic substances were regularly utilized in biblical sacrifices, as was true of ancient Near Eastern sacrificial cults generally. The biblical Tabernacle was censed regularly (Exod 30:24–28). In Num 19:6 we read that cedar wood and hyssop were to be cast into the fire when the red heifer was burned to ashes. There was also a daily incense offering (Exod 30:7–10, 32–33), and Leviticus 2 prescribed aromatic substances for the grain offering, as a rule.

from the herd or from the flocks. The formula *min habbāqār ûmin haṣṣô'n* follows traditional generic classifications. Note the classification of sacrificial animals in Leviticus 1.

Num 15:3 is loosely formulated, which may be the result of parenthetical editing, as the translation indicates. This verse means that whenever sacrifices of the kinds listed are offered they are to be accompanied by what is prescribed in Num 15:4–7, namely, a grain offering and a libation. Num 15:3 may be seen as the protasis, and vv 4–7 as the apodosis of a prolonged statement.

4. *the one making his offering.* The Hebrew formulation *wehiqrîb hammaqrîb 'et qorbanô* 'the offerer shall offer his offering' is unique. The closest to it is in Num 7:12: *hammaqrîb 'et qorbānô* 'the one who offers his offering'. The term *qorbān,* which is generic for all types of cultic offerings, including sanctuary vessels and appurtenances, is explained in the NOTES on Num 7:17.

grain offering. The term *minḥāh* itself says nothing about the substances used in its preparation. Its primary meaning is "gift, tribute" (Gen 32:14; 1 Kgs 10:25; 2 Kgs 17:4). Like many other terms for cultic offerings, *minḥāh* was appropriated by priestly writers from the administrative vocabulary precisely because it conveyed the subservient relationship of the worshiper to God so exactly. In the first stage of its appropriation, *minḥāh* might have designated any type of sacrifice. In Gen 4:3–5 the differing sacrifices of Cain and Abel, one consisting of grain and the other of animals, are both termed *minḥāh* (cf. also 1 Sam 2:17; Ps 141:2).

It is not entirely clear just how the term *minḥāh* came to designate grain offerings in particular. Perhaps the manner of presenting grain offerings holds the answer. Hebrew *minḥāh* derives from the verb *nāḥāh* 'to lead, conduct, bring', and literally means, "what is placed before one, presented, brought." In earliest times, grain offerings were probably not burned on an altar at all; they were set before the Deity to be viewed by him, and in this manner accepted by the Deity. This was true of the bread of display, as prescribed in Lev 24:5–9, and of the offerings of firstfruits, ordained in Deut 26:1–11. According to Lev 7:12–15, the thanksgiving offering *(tôdāh)* was to include two loaves, which were placed before God, but of which no part ascended the altar. In the course of time, as burnt altar offerings came to predominate in the Israelite cult, presentation offerings were adapted to that mode of sacrifice. The term *minḥāh*, which antedated this development, was nonetheless retained.

If this is how *minḥāh* came to designate the grain offering, then we can easily understand its connection with the late afternoon, or early evening, for that is when grain offerings were customarily presented (2 Kgs 16:15; Ps 141:2; Ezra 9:4; Dan 9:21).

semolina flour. Hebrew *sôlet* specifically designates semolina, as is explained in the NOTES on Num 6:15.

The measurements of dry and liquid commodities prescribed here are well attested: (1) *ʿiśśārôn* 'one-tenth' = .1 *ʾēpāh*, which is a term for both a dry and a liquid measure of approximately 22 liters. It is also called *ʿaśîrît hāʾēpāh* 'one-tenth ephah' in Num 5:15, as well as in Exod 16:36; and Lev 5:11 and 6:13. One-tenth of an ephah was therefore approximately 2.2 liters. (2) *Hîn* was a liquid measure of approximately 3.6 liters. Libations of .25 *hîn*, and the use of the same amount of oil for mixing with flour in the preparation of the *minḥāh*, were routine in priestly prescriptions. The most complete table of weights and measures used in the Israelite cult appears in Ezek 45:11–12 (Scott 1959).

Olive oil was mixed with or poured over (the verb *bālal)* the semolina flour. Various recipes for preparing grain offerings are found in Leviticus 2. The Akkadian cognate, *balālu*, in the simple stem is also used to describe the process of kneading dough, whereas in Akkadian the intensive form, *bullulu*, more properly means "to mix, smear." In Hebrew usage the meaning is less precise. When the verb *bālal* is used with oil, the sense is "to pour over, smear" (Ps 92:11), as is likewise indicated by ritual prescriptions that speak of "pouring" or "placing" oil over dough (Lev 2:1, 6, 15; 5:11).

5. *wine for the libation.* No specific code for the preparation of libations exists in the Torah, such as we have for grain offerings. And yet libations are often prescribed, and they represent an ancient form of worship. Note the reference to libation jugs in Num 4:7; cf. also Num 6:17 and 28:10.

in addition to. Here, the preposition *ʿal* means "in addition to" or possibly "together with," as is often its connotation in codes of sacrifice. Thus Num 28:10: "It is the burnt offering of each Sabbath in turn, in addition to (*ʿal*) the regular burnt offering and its libation." The preposition *ʿal* makes the point that the provisions of Num 15:4–5 complement the main sacrifices.

4–11. The scaled requirements of Num 15:4–11 may be tabulated as follows:

class of animal	*grain offering (+ oil)*	*libation (wine)*
sheep or goat	.1 ephah + .25 *hin*	.25 *hin*
ram	.2 ephah + .33 *hin*	.33 *hin*
large cattle	.3 ephah + .5 *hin*	.5 *hin*

8. The casuistic wording of Num 15:8 does not precisely parallel that of v 3. In that verse, which opens the section on small cattle, one sets aside a votive as a voluntary offering, whereas in v 8, which opens the section on large cattle, one sets aside a votive as sacred gifts of greeting (Hebrew *šelāmîm*). The discrepancy is hardly consequential, in ritual terms, and seems merely to echo the original emphasis on the *šelāmîm* sacrifice in Lev 7:11–18. We are warranted in assuming that large cattle were also utilized for the *nedābāh*.

11. *The same shall be performed.* Again, *yēʿāśeh* 'it shall be performed' conveys the precise sense of the verb *ʿāśāh* in cultic contexts. See above, in the NOTES on v 3.

for each ox. Laššôr hāʾeḥād is idiomatic; compare *laʿeḥād* 'for each one' in v 12, below. The present law includes goats in its provisions, whereas v 5 only mentioned sheep. This discrepancy, too, is hardly significant in cultic terms. Whereas Hebrew *kebés* 'lamb, head of small cattle' never includes goats, *śeh* 'head of small cattle' is more general (Levine 1963).

12. The effect of this verse is mathematical: the number of accompanying grain offerings and libations must equal the total number of the major offerings to which they were joined, namely, the burnt offerings or sacred feasts, for whatever purpose they were presented.

13. *native-born citizen.* The Hebrew term *ʾezrāḥ* is often paired with *gēr* 'alien', as it is here and in vv 14–16 that follow. Functionally, the *ʾezrāḥ* is contrasted with non-Israelites, who have come from other lands. The rendering "native-born citizen" may be anachronistic, but it is apt, nonetheless, because it conveys the sense of belonging to the group of reference—in the biblical ethos, the Israelites. See the NOTES on Num 9:14.

14. Many priestly laws include special provisions for foreigners (cf. Exod 12:48; Lev 19:33; Num 9:14). Biblical law tended increasingly to make legal practice uniform for all residents, both Israelites and others, especially when the quality of collective existence might be affected. There were two sides to the coin. There was, first of all, the principle of equity. Foreigners should be protected from abuse prompted by xenophobia (Exod 22:20; 23:9; Lev 19:33–34; Deut 10:19). But for his part, the *gēr* was expected to respect the laws of the country, especially those of the dominant religion, as we see here. This was particularly relevant in biblical Israel, where the new monotheism was different in kind from other contemporary religions.

or anyone else who may be among you. The formulation *ʾô ʾašer betôkekem* employs an unusual syntax, suggestive of Aramaic.

Stylistically, the cliché *kaʾašer taʿáśû kēn yāʿăśeh* 'As you perform [it], so shall he perform [it]' recalls Lev 24:19: *kaʾašer ʿāśāh kēn yēʿāśeh lô* 'As he has done, so may be done to him!'

15. The style here is laconic. Compare Gen 44:18: *kî kāmôkā keparʿôh* 'for you are the same as Pharaoh!' or *kāmônî kāmôkā, keʿammî keʿammekā,* literally, "like me, like you; like my fighting force, like your fighting force" (Deut 1:17; 1 Kgs 22:4; 2 Kgs 3:7). Such phrasing probably reflects the spoken, conversational language of biblical times (Levine 1978: 155–160).

in the presence of YHWH. The phrase *lipnê YHWH* often has a spatial connotation, referring to an area in which sacrifices were offered. Less technically, this phrase may refer in a relational sense to all sacrifices offered to the God of Israel, which seems to be the meaning here.

16. The overall formulation in vv 15–16 is redundant, utilizing three related legal terms—*ḥuqqāh* 'statute', *tôrāh* 'instruction', and *mišpāṭ* 'rule, legal norm' (cf. Num 9:3–4, 14). The Hebrew term *tôrāh* signifies what has been taught or shown, hence "instruction." One is obliged to obey a *tôrāh* (or the Torah) because it has been taught by God or transmitted by authoritative human teachers such as priests (Deut 17:11). One is expected to obey the *ḥuqqāh* (or masculine *ḥôq)*, in the first instance, because it had been inscribed (the verb *ḥāqaq)*. The basis for obedience to *mišpāṭ* emerges from judicial procedures, and relates to what is determined to be just.

NOTES TO 15:17–21: DESACRALIZING THE DOUGH

17. Verse 17–21 ordain that a donation be taken from the dough before baking, from the "first" of the dough, so to speak. The amount of the offering is not specified, though talmudic tradition fixed suggested quantities for this offering, which remained customary in postbiblical Judaism. See Mishna, *Ḥallāh*, 2:6.

18. The futuristic orientation of the opening statement in this section of Numbers 15 is common: "When you enter the land. . . ." The precise formulation used here, *bebō'akem* (a declined infinitive construct), is rare in such statements. Normally, we find *kî tābō'û* 'When you enter', expressed by an imperfect form (as in v 2, above). Deuteronomic diction yields *'ad bō'akem* 'until you came' to the land (Deut 1:31; 9:7; 11:5).

19. *the food of the land.* The term *leḥem hā'āreṣ*, literally, "bread of the land," is unique. In Ps 104:14 we find *leḥôṣî' leḥem min hā'āreṣ* 'to bring forth bread from the earth', which endures as the theme of the blessing recited before partaking of bread to this day. It seems that *leḥem hā'āreṣ* is synonymous with *'abûr hā'āreṣ* 'the harvest of the land' in Josh 5:11–12, where we actually find the same syntax: *be'oklām mē'abûr hā'āreṣ* 'when they ate of the harvest of the land'. The point is that the donation is to be set aside before one partakes of prepared food, more precisely, before baking the bread. The Hebrew term *terûmāh* is explained in the NOTES on Num 5:9.

20. *The first product.* Hebrew *rē'šît* connotes both the "first" in sequence and the "first" in quality. The same semantic range is known in many languages. Use of this characterization here recalls the rites of the first-fruits (Exod 23:19; 34:26; Deut 18:4; 26:10). Here it is the "first" of the dough.

bread-baking utensils. The Hebrew word *'arisāh* has not been definitively explained. Some take it as cognate to *'arsān*, a barley food, *arsanu* in Akkadian (Gray—ICC, 177; *CAD* A 2.3.6). It is also possible that *'arisāh* designates a baking vessel. Just as the word *miš'eret*, a vessel for dough or grain, probably derives from *śe'ôr* 'leavened dough', so *'arisāh* may derive from *'arsān* 'barley'. Hebrew *'arisāh* occurs in Ezek 44:30 and Neh 10:38, in versions of the present law. Some have proposed that *'arisāh* may be related to *'ereś* 'crib, bed', reflecting the forms of baking vessels. Although the derivation remains uncertain, it is evident that *'arisāh* designates a kind of vessel, not a foodstuff. The offering is to be extracted from the vessels before baking.

Hebrew *ḥallāh* designates "round loaves" (so Ibn Ezra). The basic sense seems to be "roundness" (the verb *ḥ-w-l*) rather than "piercing" (the verb *ḥ-l-l*). This word is mentioned only in cultic contexts (Exod 29:2; Lev 2:4; 2 Sam 6:19). In Lev 2:4 *ḥallāh* contrasts with thin wafers or crackers mentioned in that chapter, as one of the forms taken by the grain offering (Levine 1965b). See the NOTES on Num 6:15, 19.

donation from the threshing floor. The present offering of dough parallels offerings collected at the threshing floor (*gôren*). Deut 15:14 requires Israelites to give to the poor a part of what they process at the threshing floor and vat. Most cultic assessments of grain, fruits, and oil were collected at that stage, when natural products first become usable as food, a point noted in the introduction to this chapter. The present law diverges from this pattern, but carefully states that the offering from the dough counts for the same, to the credit of the offerer. In Num 18:27 we read that the one percent owed by the Levites to the priests (the tithe of their tithe) is regarded as "grain from the threshing floor and ripe fruit from the vat." This is a way of saying that this newly prescribed donation has the same force as the others, and counts to the credit of the offerer in the same way.

NOTES TO 15:22–31: A SUPPLEMENTARY CODE OF SACRIFICES

Verses 22–31 continue to introduce innovations, following the pattern evident in vv 1–16, in requiring grain offerings and libations as accompaniments to the expiatory sacrifices. When either the community as a whole or individual Israelites inadvertently transgressed against God's commandments, a regimen of composite sacrifices became obligatory. At points, the formulation of vv 22–31 is difficult and legally imprecise, employing an unusual syntax and rare vocabulary. These verses are modeled on the formulation of Leviticus 4–5, the primary priestly codes governing the inadvertent offenses of the Israelite community and of its individual members.

22. *you inadvertently fail.* The verbs *šāgāh* and *šāgag* are virtually synonymous despite differences in usage. The geminate form yielded the noun *šegāgāh* 'inadvertence'. The primary connotation of *šāgāh* is "to stray, meander," hence "to err" in a general way (1 Sam 26:21; Prov 19:27). The geminate form *šāgag* and the noun *šegāgāh* pertain more particularly to ritual and legal offenses (Lev 4:2, 22, and farther on in these verses).

Acts so classified were understood by the Jewish sages to encompass two related situations. The first was inadvertence with respect to the facts of law involved in the offense. The offender either did not know that what he had done was in violation of the law, or was unaware of the penalties prescribed for the offense. Ignorance of the law was often a mitigating factor, especially in matters of ritual. The second was inadvertence with respect to the nature of the act itself. A person may have eaten forbidden food, such as *ḥēleb,* a term for the fat covering certain internal organs of animals, thinking it was ordinary fat, *šûmān,* which was permitted (Mishna, *Hôdāyôt,* 2:1–2; *Kerîtût,* 4:1f.).

This verse appears to be speaking of "sins of omission," of the failure to perform God's commandments, a notion conveyed by the negative formulation *welōʾ taʿaśû* 'In the event you fail to perform'. In contrast, the legislation of Leviticus 4–5 deals quite clearly with "sins of commission," with acts of disobedience. Normally, this distinction is consequential in Torah legislation, and for this reason one wonders just how technical the formulation is here. More likely, it is rather loose, and vv 22–31 were composed simply to extend the requirement of grain offerings and libations to apply to the expiatory sacrifices. Note that in v 24 the language of commission, conveyed by the verb *ʿāśāh* 'to do', resumes.

commandments. The term *miṣwāh* has an interesting history. It was favored by the Deuteronomist (Deut 4:2, 40; 5:31) and represents one of the ways of characterizing divine authority. In fact, it is the most authoritarian of the several terms employed to rationalize the basis of obedience to God. One obeys a *miṣwāh* or a collective body of *miṣwôt* because they were ordered by God. Priestly law often speaks of specific rituals as God's *miṣwāh*.

Another indication of imprecision is the fact that whereas v 22 speaks of commandments conveyed by God to Moses, v 23 speaks of those transmitted via Moses, *beyad Môšeh* 'by means of Moses'. This formula is common in the book of Numbers (cf. Num 4:33).

23. *from the day that.* Idiomatic *lemin hayyôm* is known in Deuteronomy (4:32; 9:7), while the fuller formula, *min hayyôm hahûʾ wāhālʾāh* 'from that day onward' appears in 1 Sam 18:9 and Ezek 39:22.

24. *without the awareness.* Reference to concealment "from the eyes" of the community *(mēʿênê hāʿēdāh)* again recalls Lev 4:13 and 22. The normal syntax is *ʿāśāh bišegāgāh* 'to do inadvertently', with the adverbial force conveyed by prepositional *beth.* Here we have *lišegāgāh,* with prefixed *lamed.* Below, in vv 26–28, we again find *bišegāgāh*. Curiously, the verb *ʿāśāh* here has two different connotations in the same verse. Thus, *neʿeśtāh lišegāgāh* literally means "was committed inadvertently," whereas *weʿāśû kol hāʿēdāh* 'the entire community shall perform' conveys the particular sense of ritual performance noted above in the NOTES on v 3.

According to Lev 4:13–21, a sin offering *(ḥaṭṭāʾt)* consisting of a bull was required in order to expiate an inadvertent transgression on the part of the entire community. Here a bull is also required as a sacrifice, but it is termed *ʿôlāh* 'burnt offering', not *ḥaṭṭāʾt* 'sin offering'. In addition, a kid goat *(śāʿîr)* is to be offered together with the bull as a sin offering! This modified structure generally accords with the procedures of festival worship in the public cult, as prescribed in Numbers 28–29. It is also the pattern in Numbers 7, a record of the offerings brought at the dedication of the Tabernacle. A certain degree of blending is to be assumed, whereby combinations characteristic of the public cult were superimposed on the expiatory process, when it concerned communal atonement and, in that sense, represented public worship.

with its accompanying grain offering and libation, according to the rule. The formula *ûminḥātô weniskô kammišpāṭ* refers to the provisions of vv 4–5, above. That is to say, a sacrifice of a bull requires an accompanying grain offering *(minḥāh)* of one-third *ʾēpāh* of semolina mixed with one-half *hîn* of oil, and a libation of one-half *hîn* of wine. Adverbial *kammišpāṭ* 'according to regulation' occurs repeatedly in Numbers 29 (v 18 et passim) and in Lev 5:10 and 9:16. It is a mechanism for abbreviating the formulation of the law. Compare Exod 21:9, *kemišpaṭ habbānôt* 'according to the regulation [governing] daughters' or Deut 21:17, *mišpāṭ habbekôrāh* 'the regulation of primogeniture'. In all cases, one assumes that the reader was expected to know the reference, which did not have to be repeated, probably because the essential codes of law were available. What we have, therefore, is an editorial statement.

The term for sin offering, normally written *ḥaṭṭāʾt,* is here spelled defectively: *ḥṭṭ,* without *aleph.*

25. *rites of expiation.* The all-important verb *kippēr* 'to expiate' is explained in the NOTES on Num 6:11 (see also v 28, below). The construction *kippēr ʿal* has relational force here: the priest performed rites of expiation "with respect to" or "in relation to" the community, not physically "over" them. Compare the formulation here with Lev 4:20 and 26.

they shall be pardoned. The verb *sālaḥ* 'to forgive' is explained in the NOTES on Num 14:19.

they have duly presented. The force of prefixed *waw* in *wāhēm* is circumstantial: "they, having brought their sacrifice," may now be forgiven.

the entire Israelite community. The Hebrew *ʿadat benê Yiśrāʾēl* is quite common in priestly sources, first occurring in Exod 16:1 (cf. Josh 22:12). It reflects the blending of two discrete formulas for designating the Israelites: *benê Yiśrāʾēl* 'members of the Israelite people, Israelites' and *ʿēdāh* 'community', a term of reference distinctive to priestly sources. Note *ʿadat Yiśrāʾēl* 'the Israelite community' in Exod 12:3.

consequent to their inadvertent offense. Hebrew *ʿal šigegātām* means "on account of their inadvertent act." Similar usage of prepositional *ʿal* is common in other legal texts (Lev 4:3; 5:18).

26. *the alien.* Reference to the *gēr* recalls vv 14–16, above, where this term is explained. There is a further reference in v 29, below.

27. *she-goat.* Verses 27–29 present the rules for an individual Israelite who is required to bring expiatory offerings. They parallel Lev 4:27–5:14, with the significant addition of grain offerings and libations. Here the required sacrifice consists of a yearling she-goat *(ʿēz),* whereas in Lev 4:28 we read of *śeʿîrat ʿizzîm* 'a female goat'. The difference is merely terminological. The animal is brought as a sin offering, which is consistent with the law of Leviticus, where, however, the offender has the option of offering a ewe. Why a female animal was specifically required is not clear.

28. *that person who commits an inadvertent offense.* The construction *hannepeš haššôgeget,* literally, "the person who offends inadvertently," is a relative reflex of casuistic or conditional formulation, another way of implying contingency without using a particle such as "if." Compare Ezek 18:4 and 20, *hannepeš haḥôṭēʾt* 'the person who sins'.

because that person offended. Masoretic *beḥeṭʾāh* is a conflate form, in place of *beḥoṭʾāh* a declined infinitive construct, literally, "by its offending, through its offending."

The lack of agreement in gender between *nepeš*, a feminine noun, and *lekappēr ʿālâw wenislaḥ lô* 'to perform rites of expiation on *his* behalf so that *he* may be forgiven' is hardly significant, because *nepeš* effectively connotes what *ʾādām* 'person, human' does in similar formulations of priestly law.

29. See the NOTES on v 16, above. Again, the syntax is somewhat unbalanced. Prepositional *lamed* of v 28 *(wenislaḥ lô)* probably conditioned *welaggēr* 'and for the alien' in this verse.

30. *defiantly.* The Hebrew idiom *beyad rāmāh* literally means "high-handedly." It conveys the sense of brazen or blatant behavior. Compare Exod 14:8 (paralleled in Num 33:3), where we read that the Israelites departed from Egypt *beyad rāmāh,* in open defiance of the Egyptians. In a legal context, *beyad rāmāh* connotes premeditation and contrasts with *bišegāgāh* 'inadvertently', in other words, without prior intent.

must be cut off. The penalty of being "cut off" from one's kinsmen *(ʿam)* is discussed in the NOTES on Num 19:13.

31. The parallelism of *bāzāh* 'to despise' and *hēpēr* 'to breach' may be found in Ezek 10:59 and 17:18–19.

must surely be cut off. Use of the infinitive absolute, followed by the finite verb, *hikkārēt tikkārēt,* is unique to this passage. Usually we find a finite form of the *niphʿal* stem: *wenikretāh* 'it shall be cut off'.

the punishment for his iniquity. Here the sense of the Hebrew *ʿawôn* 'transgression' is "punishment for transgression." This meaning is demonstrated in Num 18:1, where it is stated that the Aaronide priests will bear the punishment (the idiom *nāśāʾ ʿawôn)* of the Sanctuary. In effect, they bear responsibility for any impurity that might defile the Sanctuary. The semantic transaction whereby both an act and its effects, or consequences, are conveyed by the same word is well attested in biblical Hebrew. Thus Hebrew *pôʿal,* feminine *peʿullâh* means "deed, act" (Ps 44:2; Jer 31:16[15]), but in Isa 40:10 we read, "See, his reward *(śekārô)* is with him, his recompense *(ûpeʿullātô)* before him." Compare also Isa 62:11, Ruth 2:12, and priestly law—Lev 19:13—where *peʿullâh* designates the wages of a hired laborer. Similarly, Hebrew *ʿāmāl* means "toil, pain, effort" (Job 5:7; Ps 25:18), but also the consequence of effort, namely, wealth (Eccl 2:24; Ps 105:44).

NOTES TO 15:32–36: A TELLING INCIDENT OF SABBATH VIOLATION

Verses 32–36 relate an incident of Sabbath violation. In tone, this report resembles what is told in Lev 24:10–14, where a case of blasphemy is reported. In both texts instructions from God are awaited, and in both instances the accused is detained, pending disposition of the case.

32. *gathering.* The Hebrew *meqôšēš,* probably a denominative of *qaš*

'straw', means "to assemble, gather" into a bunch or bale. In Exod 5:7 and 12 it is said of gathering straw for making bricks, and in 1 Kgs 17:10–12 of gathering sticks to make a fire. It can also be said of assembling people (Zeph 2:1). One assumes that, in this instance, wood was being gathered in order to make a fire for cooking, which is expressly forbidden on the Sabbath, according to Exod 35:3, also a priestly law.

34. *They placed him under guard.* Hebrew *mišmār* may designate a detention facility, literally, a "guard house." This term occurs several times in the cycle of Joseph stories (Gen 40:4; 41:10; 42:17), where we read that a *mišmār* held persons who had committed some offense against the pharaoh. Lev 24:12 reports that a blasphemer was similarly detained, and in Num 11:22 there is the implication that a detention facility was in use, because Joshua suggested that Moses "arrest" (the verb *kālāʾ*) the elders who were discovered prophesying in the camp.

In biblical law, as in the ancient Near East generally, incarceration was not part of the penal system, as such, but was used primarily for detention. Detention was necessary, in this case, "because it had not been specified *(kî lōʾ pôraš)*" how the offender was to be punished. Rashi, quoting the Sifre, states that the Israelites must have known that Sabbath violation entailed the death penalty from Exod 31:14–15, but they were uncertain what particular form of execution was called for. In his comment on Lev 24:12 Rashi states that it was not known, by contrast, what penalty was in store for the blasphemer, because the law prohibiting blasphemy in Exod 22:27 had not specified this point. This is, of course, a traditional answer to the problem of sequence in Torah legislation.

it had not yet been specified. The verb *pôraš* (in the *hophʿal* stem) reflects the sense of the *piʿel, pērēš* 'to decide, specify'. Aramaic attests two phonetic manifestations of this Semitic root, *pērēš* (written with a *samekh)* 'to cut, divide' and *pēraš* (written with a *shin)* 'to specify, decide'. Akkadian has *parāsu* 'to cut, divide' *(AHw,* 830–832). The primary sense is "to cut," just as in English, based in this instance on Latin, "decide" literally means "to cut." Verbs with this meaning often appropriate legal connotations, and the same is true within many language groups. It is of interest that Targum Onkelos (Sperber 1944) renders *wayyiqqôb* 'he blasphemed (literally, pierced) . . . the (= God's) name' in Lev 24:11 by Aramaic *ûpārēš* 'he specified (literally, "cut")' God's name.

35. *must stone him.* Infinitive absolute *rāgôm* is used in place of the finite verb. This verb always involves the use of stones. The fact that stones are consistently mentioned whenever this verb is used indicates that its original meaning may have been "to cast" but that its usage was frozen, or specialized, so that it could only be said of stoning. The same penalty befell the blasphemer of Leviticus 24.

Executions normally took place outside the camp, at least in part to avoid defiling the area of settlement by introducing an impure corpse. It was also because the taking of human life, though pursuant to just laws, was a horrible act. Deut 17:5 ordains that one convicted of a capital offense was to be taken outside the city gate for execution. Note that even Naboth, who was falsely condemned to death, was executed outside the city (1 Kgs 21:13; and cf. Num 31:19).

36. *as YHWH had commanded Moses.* The compliance formula *ka'ašer ṣiwwāh YHWH 'et Môšeh* is common in Leviticus and Numbers. See the NOTES on Num 1:19.

NOTES TO 15:37–41: THE CORD OF BLUE

Verses 37–41 ordain that all Israelites (most probably, all adult Israelite males) were to affix blue cords as fringes on the "corners" of their garments so as to be reminded of God's commandments. This custom continues in Jewish practice to this day.

38. Hebrew *ṣiṣît* appears to represent the feminine of *ṣîṣ*, an ornamental floral design used in fashioning the frontlet worn by the high priest (Exod 28:36; 39:30; Lev 8:9). The basic sense is botanical, for *ṣîṣ* is synonymous with *peraḥ* 'blossom' (Num 17:23; and cf. Isa 28:1; 40:5–8; Pss 72:16; 103:15). In 1 Kgs 6:18 we read of *ṣiṣṣîm* 'calyxes', decorations on the walls of the Solomonic temples. The fact that *ṣiṣṣîm* is written with a small *i* vowel, followed by augmentation, rather than with a long *i* vowel, as is *ṣiṣît*, is probably not significant. Akkadian *ṣiṣṣātu*, plural *ṣiṣṣētu*, means "ornament" (*CAD S* 214, *ṣiṣṣātu*), and it is cognate to the Hebrew forms. The Hebrew forms are not related to Akkadian *ṣiṣītu*, a part of the loom (*CAD S*, 214, *ṣiṣītu*).

The same requirement of symbolizing the commandments is stated in Deut 22:12: "You shall make tassels (*gedîlîm*) on the four corners of the garments with which you clothe yourself." The two terms, *ṣiṣît* and *gādîl*, are virtually synonymous, for in 1 Kgs 7:17 we read of *gedîlîm* adorning the capitals of columns in Solomon's temple, just as we read in 1 Kgs 6:18 of *ṣiṣṣîm* as wall decorations. One can also speak of the *ṣiṣît* 'braids, curls' of one's hair (Ezek 8:3).

a cord. Hebrew *pātîl*, from a verb meaning "to wind, twist," means "fillet, cord," such as was used in tying a cylinder seal to one's belt or pocket (Gen 38:18, 25; and cf. Exod 28:28).

blue cloth. Hebrew *tekēlet* is a dye or pigment, often listed together with *'argāmān* (see the NOTE on Num 4:13). It is of greenish-blue color and is taken from snails known as *Murex trunculis* and *Murex brandaris* (also *Purpura haemastonea*). These snails are found along the Mediterranean coast (and along the Atlantic and Pacific coasts, as a matter of fact). Akkadian attests *takiltu*, related to the Akkadian adjective *taklu* 'consistent, fast'. This etymology reflects the fact that the dye in question maintains a highly consistent or permanent hue. The Palestinian Talmud *(Berākôt* 1:5) describes this color as that of the sea, and at Ugarit it was called *uqnû*, the word for lapis lazuli. A great deal of information is available from Roman authors concerning the manufacture of this dye, and there is archaeological evidence at Ugarit, where the dye was extracted extensively in the Late Bronze Age (M. Eilat 1982; Burshtin 1988; Milgrom 1989: 410–414, 516). *Tekēlet* was exceedingly costly because it required enormous quantities of snails to produce even a gram of pure pigment. For this reason, *tekēlet* was reserved for royalty and for cultic vestments.

The primary difficulty in understanding this verse and the next is syntactic. How are we to render the Hebrew clause *wenātenû ʿal ṣiṣît hakkānāp petîl tekēlet* 'they shall affix *to* the corner fringe a cord of blue?' Logically, this clause means that a cord of blue was to be added to or included among the ordinary tassels. Its striking color would make it stand out from the other fringes, thereby reminding its wearer of God's commandments.

Verse 38 is composed of sequential clauses, each introduced by *waw*, where the first *waw* has temporal or circumstantial force. Therefore I have translated v 38 to read "and say to them that *when they fashion* fringes for themselves on the corners of their garments . . . *they must join* a cord of blue cloth to the fringe, at each corner."

39. *It shall serve you.* Elliptical *wehāyāh 'that* shall serve' has no explicit antecedent. What is it that should serve as *ṣiṣît?* Elliptical *wehāyāh* should be understood as referring to the complete parcel that was prescribed. Attempts to identify *petîl tekēlet* 'the cord of blue' as the direct antecedent of *ṣiṣît* run into difficulty because the blue cord was only part of the fringe. There need not be agreement in gender between v 39 and v 38, because *wehāyāh* and *ʾōtô* 'it' (both masculine) do not refer directly to the *ṣiṣît*, which is feminine, but to "that," namely, to what was commanded.

you will not be drawn after. The connotation of the verb *tûr* is a bit different here. Usually it means "to move about," literally, "tour, explore," whereas here it means to follow passively, to be led about, with the result that one strays from the path. This meaning is conditioned by prepositional *ʾaḥarê* 'after'. One who is led about by his desires, or by the temptations of what he sees, will most assuredly disregard God's commandments.

which you follow so faithlessly! The verb *zānāh* means to commit harlotry or an improper sexual act (Lev 21:14; Deut 23:19). It is one of the usual ways of conveying the infidelity of Israel as a people, and of its leaders, in metaphorical terms (Deut 31:16; Hos 2:7). The sense here is that one who disregards God's commandments will be unfaithful to the covenant.

40. To be holy in relation to God is a thought basic to the priestly outlook, best stated in Lev 19:2: "You shall be holy, for I, YHWH your God, am holy" (Levine 1989b: 256–257).

41. This statement recalls the opening of the Decalogue (Exod 20:2; Deut 5:6), where, however, the form of address is singular rather than plural. YHWH became the God of the Israelite people when he redeemed them from Egyptian bondage. Liberation was, simultaneously, the event that made Israel a nation.

PART XI.

NUMBERS 16–17: THE KORAH INCIDENT

♦

INTRODUCTION

Chapters 16 and 17 of Numbers relate an involved tale of insurrection when Moses was leader of the Israelites. Only through divine intervention was the insurrection put down and Moses' leadership (in the priestly view, also Aaron's) sustained. According to the schedule of JE, the incident would have taken place in Kadesh, whereas P would place it in the Wilderness of Paran; but nowhere in Numbers 16–17 is it stated where the insurrection occurred.

It has long been recognized that these two chapters, which together form a literary unit, were composed from more than one source, and that more than one set of issues informs them. At least two literary strata can be identified: the historiography of JE and various priestly materials. The source-critical makeup of these two chapters may be outlined as follows:

JE—Num 16:1–2 (rewritten by P), 12–15, 25–34 (with several priestly insertions)

P—Num 16:3–11, 16–24, 35, and chap. 17.

Originally Num 16:1–2, the opening verses of the narrative, probably contained no reference to Korah and spoke only of a rebellion against Moses led by a group of Reubenites, and one that did not involve the Levites. What we find in Numbers 16 is, however, a pattern of linkage whereby priestly compilers or editors enmeshed JE and P, using well-placed interpolations in the process. The structural situation resembles that of Numbers 13–14 in many respects.

In JE's version the issue is the leadership and authority of Moses. This single theme informs all of the JE verses, Num 16:12–15 and 25–34. Moses claims that God had commissioned him to lead the Israelites and that in opposing him the insurgents were virtually rejecting God. He insists on the fairness of his leadership. The grievances stated by the Israelites pertain to the perils of the wilderness and to the delays in arriving at the Promised Land. The relevant passages read like any of several other challenges to Moses' authority recounted in Exodus, Numbers, and Deuteronomy. With poignant irony, it is Egypt that is characterized as a land of milk and honey.

Moses warns all Israelites to disengage from the insurgents, Dathan and Abiram, lest they share in the punishment awaiting them. Moses calls upon God for a sign to demonstrate his own selection as legitimate leader. In response to Moses' entreaty, the earth swallows up the entire dissident faction, their families and possessions, in a sudden, unnatural way.

The various priestly materials incorporated in Numbers 16 and 17 transform the challenge to Moses' authority, which had been instigated by several Reubenites, into a protest by another levitical family against the exclusive right of Aaron's family to the Israelite priesthood. It is difficult to agree with

G. B. Gray that two discrete conflicts inform the priestly materials themselves: (a) Moses, Aaron, and the Levites versus the rest of the Israelites; and (b) The family of Aaron versus the rest of the tribe of Levi, on the issue of which levitical family should control the priesthood. It is more likely that the issue for all of the priestly writers of Numbers 16 and 17 is the same: Which "person" (Hebrew *'is*, in Num 16:5–7; 17:20) is the divinely designated high priest? Although the two ordeals projected in the priestly sections of Numbers 16–17, that of the incense offerings and that of the sprouting rods, are presented independently, it appears that the real issue to be decided by both of them is the Aaronide priesthood. Korah, a Levite and Moses' fellow Kohathite, was introduced by the priestly writers so as to convert the context of the insurrection. Effectively, this shift made of the incident an internecine struggle between the family of Aaron, the Amramite, and the family of Korah, the Izharite.

The lines of textual demarcation between JE and P in Numbers 16–17 are quite distinct, despite their linkage. JE never mentions Aaron, for instance, nor does it contain any references to the Levites as such. The only overlap pertains to the names of Korah, Dathan, and Abiram (cf. Num 16:1, 24, 27, 32). As will be shown, the names of Dathan and Abiram were inserted into priestly passages, and that of Korah into JE, as part of the enmeshing process, what some have called "braiding."

The unfolding of the priestly materials reveals the central issue of the priestly school. Thus, Num 16:8–11 amplify and clarify Num 16:3–7 by focusing on the internecine struggle for power within the tribe of Levi, even within the specific clan of Levites to which Korah, Moses, and Aaron all belonged, the clan of Kohath (Num 3:14). In a somewhat propagandistic manner, Moses attempts to persuade the dissident Levites that they, too, are God's intimates and that they enjoy a degree of sanctity. The persuasion hardly succeeds, however, and the ordeal of the incense offerings proceeds as planned. This ordeal is anticipated in Num 16:5–7 and is carried forward in Num 16:16–24. Its horrendous conclusion is stated in Num 16:35, and its cultic implications are projected in Num 17:1–5. Korah and his faction are repudiated by God, and this repudiation expresses itself in the rejection of their incense offerings, contrasted to the dramatic acceptance of Aaron's offerings. More than that, the dissidents are destroyed by God's fire as punishment for their rebellion. The ordeal of the sprouting rods (Num 17:16–25) appears to derive from a different priestly tradition and serves further to confirm Aaron's selection.

Common to all of these accounts is the theme of divine wrath, so basic to the ideology of P, but certainly not limited to priestly writings. In Num 16:20–22 God threatens to annihilate the entire Israelite community. The same theme is reflected in the account of the plague in Num 17:6–15 and in the regulations subsequent to the ordeal of the sprouting rods (Num 17:26–28).

The problem of identifying historical settings appropriate to the various literary strata that are represented in Numbers 16–17 will be addressed in the COMMENTS on these chapters.

TRANSLATION

16 1Korah son of Izhar, son of Kohath, son of Levi, took counsel, along with Dathan and Abiram, and On son of Peleth, all Reubenites.

2They confronted Moses, accompanied by 250 personages from among the Israelites; chieftains of the community, those called in the assembly, men of renown.

3They rallied en masse against Moses and Aaron, and charged them, "You seek too much! The community in its entirety is sanctified, for YHWH is present in their midst. Why, then, do you exalt yourselves over YHWH's congregation?"

4When Moses heard this, he fell prostrate.

5He addressed Korah and his entire faction as follows: "In the morning YHWH will make known who is consecrated to him, and will declare [him] his intimate. He will declare as his intimate the one whom he chooses.

6"Do the following: Provide yourselves with firepans, Korah and his entire faction.

7"Place hot coals in them, and put incense over them when you stand in the presence of YHWH tomorrow. The person whom YHWH chooses—he is the sacred one! It is you who seek too much, you Levites!"

8Then Moses said to Korah, "Pay attention, you Levites!

9"Is it of so little importance to you that the God of Israel has distinguished you from the community of Israel by declaring you his intimates? He has assigned you to the maintenance of the Tabernacle of YHWH, to stand in attendance before the community to serve them.

10"He has declared you and all your Levite kinsmen his intimates. Do you seek priestly status as well?

11"In truth, it is against YHWH that you and your entire faction are conspiring! As for Aaron—what has *he* done that you incite grievances against him?"

12Moses sent word to summon Dathan and Abiram, sons of Eliab, but they replied, "We refuse to appear!

13"Haven't you done enough harm by leading us out of a land flowing with milk and sap, only to bring about our death in the wilderness, that you also persist in lording over us?

14"You have not even brought us to a land flowing with milk and sap, or granted us fields and vineyards as our estate. Do you intend to gouge out the eyes of those men? We refuse to appear!"

15Moses became exceedingly angered and addressed YHWH: "Do not ac-

cept their offering! I have never misappropriated the mule of a single one of
them, nor have I ever harmed one of them!"
16 Then Moses said to Korah, "You and your entire faction be present before
YHWH; you and they, along with Aaron, tomorrow!
17 "Let each person bring along his firepan and place incense over [the
coals] and offer it in the presence of YHWH; each person with his own
firepan, 250 firepans, in addition to you and Aaron, each with his firepan."
18 So each person took his firepan, they put coals in them, and they placed
incense over them, and stood at the entrance to the Tent of Meeting, alongside Moses and Aaron.
19 Korah then rallied his entire faction against them, at the entrance to the
Tent of Meeting. The presence of YHWH appeared in view of the entire
community.
20 YHWH spoke to Moses as follows:
21 Break away from this evil faction that I may annihilate them instantly!
22 They fell prostrate, exclaiming, "Lord, God of the spirits of all flesh!
When only one person has offended, will you become enraged at the entire
community?"
23 YHWH addressed Moses, saying:
24 Speak to the community as follows: "Withdraw from the area around the
residence of Korah, Dathan, and Abiram!"
25 Moses then went over to Dathan and Abiram, and the elders of Israel
followed him.
26 He addressed the assemblage as follows:
"Move away from the tents of these wicked men and have no contact with
anyone aligned with them, lest you, too, be terminated because of all their
offenses!"
27 So they withdrew from the area around the residence of Korah, Dathan,
and Abiram, as Dathan and Abiram were standing outside the entrances of
their tents, along with their wives, their grown children, and their infants.
28 Then Moses spoke: "By this shall you know that it is YHWH who has
sent me to carry out these actions; that they are not of my own devising.
29 "If these persons die in the manner usual for all human beings, if the fate
of all mankind befalls them, then it is not YHWH who has sent me.
30 "But if YHWH creates a [special] creation and the earth opens its mouth
and swallows them up, as well as all aligned with them; so that they descend
live into Sheol—then you must acknowledge that these persons have rejected
YHWH."
31 Just as he finished speaking these words, the earth beneath them split
open.
32 The earth opened its mouth and swallowed them up, and their families,
and all personnel who belonged to Korah, and their possessions.

[33]They, and all associated with them, descended live into Sheol. The earth closed over them, so that they vanished from the midst of the congregation.

[34]All Israelites who were in their proximity fled at the sound of their [cries], for they said, "The earth may swallow us, too!"

[35]A fire issued forth from YHWH and consumed the 250 men, the offerers of the incense.

17 [1]YHWH spoke to Moses as follows:

[2]Order Eleazar son of Aaron the priest to remove the firepans from the remains of the fire and to scatter the incense away, for they have [both] become holy—

[3]the firepans of those persons whose sinfulness cost them their lives. Let them be hammered into sheets as plating for the altar. Once having been offered in the presence of YHWH they had become holy. Let them serve as a sign to the Israelite people.

[4]So Eleazar the priest took the copper firepans offered by those who perished in flame, and they were hammered into plating for the altar;

[5]< as YHWH had commanded him through Moses. > This was a reminder to the Israelite people to ensure that no outsider, one not of the seed of Aaron, would ever approach, bearing incense, into the presence of YHWH, or behave in the manner of Korah and his faction.

[6]On the morrow, the entire community of Israelites protested to Moses and Aaron, saying, "You have brought death upon the people of YHWH!"

[7]As the community rallied en masse against Moses and Aaron, they turned toward the Tent of Meeting, and behold! The cloud had enveloped it! The glorious presence of YHWH had appeared.

[8]Then Moses approached the Tent of Meeting.

[9]YHWH spoke to Moses as follows:

[10]Withdraw from the midst of the community and I will annihilate them instantly! They fell prostrate.

[11]Thereupon Moses instructed Aaron, "Take one firepan and put hot coals from the altar in it, and add incense. Quickly carry it over to the community and perform a rite of expiation over them. For the fuming rage has issued from the presence of YHWH; the plague has begun!"

[12]Aaron took what Moses had instructed. He ran into the midst of the congregation, and behold! The plague had begun among the people. He prepared the incense and performed a rite of expiation over the people.

[13]He stood between the dead and the living, and the plague was contained.

[14]The number of those who died in the plague was 14,700, not counting those who perished in the Korah incident.

[15]Aaron returned to Moses at the entrance of the Tent of Meeting. The plague had been contained.

[16]YHWH spoke to Moses as follows:

17Speak to the Israelite people. Collect from them one rod apiece from each patriarchal house, from all of the chieftains, for their patriarchal houses; twelve staffs. Write the name of each person on his rod.

18And the name of Aaron you shall write on the rod of Levi, for there is also to be one rod for the head of their patriarchal house.

19Place them inside the Tent of Meeting, in front of the Ark of the Covenant, where I customarily meet with you.

20The man whom I select—his rod shall sprout, and I will then be relieved of the grievances of the Israelites that they incite against you!

21Moses spoke to the Israelite people, and all of their chieftains delivered to him one rod for each chieftain, for their patriarchal houses, twelve rods. The rod of Aaron is [to be placed] among their rods.

22Moses placed the rods in the presence of YHWH, inside the Tent of the Covenant.

23It happened on the morrow that when Moses arrived at the Tent of the Covenant—lo and behold! The rod of Aaron, of the house of Levi, had sprouted. It gave forth sprouts, produced blossoms, and bore almonds.

24Moses brought out all of the rods from the presence of YHWH before the entire Israelite people. Each person identified and retrieved his own rod.

25YHWH then spoke to Moses: Replace Aaron's rod in front of the Ark of the Covenant for safe keeping, as a [warning] sign to rebellious persons; so that their protestations against me may cease, and they will not die.

26Moses did as YHWH commanded him; so he did.

27The Israelite people then addressed themselves to Moses as follows: "Surely, we are about to perish; we are all lost; we are all lost!

28"Every person who ever approaches the Tabernacle of YHWH will die! Will we ever cease perishing?"

NOTES TO NUMBERS 16: BRAIDED ACCOUNTS OF INTERNECINE STRIFE IN THE WILDERNESS

16 1. The syntax of v 1 is problematic, because the verb *wayyiqqaḥ* 'he took' has no direct object, as we would expect.

When or *what* did Korah and his cohorts "take"? Some suggest that the simple removal of a *waw*, presently prefixed to the name *Dātān*, would make those named—Dathan, Abiram, and On—the direct objects of the verb, not its coordinate subjects. In other words, Korah "took" them; he recruited them for his faction. It has also been proposed that we read *wayyāqom* 'he arose' instead of *wayyiqqaḥ*, as is suggested by v 2. Perhaps we should read *wayyāqāṣ* 'he was alarmed' (cf. Num 22:3) or *wayyāqôt* 'he became antagonistic' (cf. Ps 95:10). All of these suggestions are plausible, but hardly demonstrable.

Akkadian attests an extended meaning for the cognate *leqû* 'to take', namely, "to learn, understand," reflecting the nuance of "grasping" facts or knowledge. In rare instances, this connotation in Akkadian is conveyed by Akkadian *leqû* without an object (*CAD L*, 137, *leqû*, 4′). A similar semantic range is known for the Akkadian verb *aḫāzu* 'to seize, hold' and related forms, such as nominal *iḫzu* 'idea, wisdom' (*CAD I/J*, 47, *iḫzu* A).

The sense of v 1 may be that the persons named "grasped" what was happening and consequently confronted Moses with their grievances. The Jewish exegetical tradition, summarized by Rashi, also offers several suggestions of interest. Midrash *Tanḥûmā'* states, "He betook himself to one side, to be separated from the community, so as to bring a grievance regarding the priesthood." Rashi notes that this interpretation underlies the rendering of Targum Onkelos (Sperber 1944): *we'itpelēg* 'he cut himself off, entered into a dispute'. Another interpretation: *wayyiqqaḥ* 'he *drew* the leaders of the courts among them with words'. This interpretation is intimated by the language of Hos 14:3: *qeḥû ʿimmākem debārîm* 'take counsel among yourselves with words'. The last interpretation has been adopted in my translation, but it merely expresses a nuance. When all is said, the opening verse of Numbers 16 defies certain interpretation.

Dathan and Abiram are known from Deut 11:65, which echoes the present narrative (cf. also Num 36:9; Ps 106:17). The name *'Abîrām* means "the high god is my father" (cf. 1 Kgs 16:34). The meaning of Hebrew *Dātān* remains elusive. Perhaps it is related to Akkadian *Ditānu*, an ancient Syro-Mesopotamian eponym, also attested in Ugaritic (Levine and de Tarragon 1984: 654–655). It may also be related to the biblical personal name *Dôtān*.

The name *Qôraḥ* occurs in 1 Chr 1:43 and is probably related to the personal name *Qareah* in Jer 25:23, listed as an Edomite eponym (Gen 36:5, 14; 1 Chr 1:35). Its connotation is uncertain, but the obvious possibility is "baldness." *'Ôn* and *Pelet* are elsewhere unattested. *'Ôn* may be related to such personal names as *'Ônām*, listed as a Hurrian (Gen 36:23), or even *'Ônān*, Judah's son (Gen 38:8). The sense would be "strength, wealth" (Mazar 1950). *Pelet* suggests the Aegean mercenaries of David, the *Kerētî* and *Pelētî* (2 Sam 15:18), and the reference to *negeb happelētî* 'the Negeb of the Pelethites' (1 Sam 30:14) suggests an area of residence for this ethnic group. Korah's full genealogy is supplied so as to set the stage for the internecine conflict among the Levites. He was the first cousin of Moses and Aaron.

2. *personages*. On this sense for Hebrew *'anāšîm* see the Notes on Num 13:3.

The two titles "chieftains of the community (*neśî'ê hā-ʿēdāh*)" and "those called in the assembly (*qerî'ê môʿēd*)" function synonymously here, but derive from different literary traditions. Priestly writings often mention "chieftains of the community" (Exod 16:22; Num 31:13; 32:2; Josh 9:18). The term *ʿēdāh*, a characteristic priestly term, is explained in the Notes on Num 1:2. This titulary was most probably introduced by the priestly compiler, who was also responsible for introducing the name and lineage of Korah in v 1, as explained in the INTRODUCTION to Numbers 16–17.

By contrast, *qerîʾê môʿēd* is a unique titulary, though we do find *qerîʾê hāʿēdāh* 'those called in the community' (Num 1:16; and Num 26:9, in a reference to this incident). Because it is appositional with *ʾanšê šēm* 'men of renown' (cf. Gen 6:4), the sense is fairly clear: these are personages called by *name* in the assembly of the people. In Ezek 23:23 *qerûʾîm*, the normal form of the passive participle, appears together with other known titles for "governor" and "commander." The present verse may represent the only explicit reference to the existence of a body known as *môʿēd* in ancient Israel. Isa 14:13 mentions the mountain where the divine *môʿēd* assembles, and this is correctly perceived as a projection of the human polity (Cross 1953). We also read of the divine council, known as *pḫr mʿd* 'the assembled council' in Ugaritic literature (Gibson 1978: 40; Baal and Anath, 2, col. i, line 14), and as *mwʿd* in the Balaam inscription from Deir ʿAlla in Transjordan (Hoftijzer and van der Kooij 1976; Levine 1981: in Deir ʿAlla, combination I, line 19). It is probable that *qiryat môʿadēnû* 'the city of our assembly' in Isa 33:20 refers to Jerusalem as the seat of the national âssembly, though a less technical interpretation of that verse is also possible.

3. *rallied.* Here the first priestly section begins (vv 3–11). Idiomatic *wayyiqqāhalu ʿal* means "to demonstrate against, to beleaguer." Note similar usages in Num 17:7 and 20:2; and cf. Exod 32:1.

You seek too much! The Hebrew idiom *rab lākem* "It is more than enough for you," recurring in v 7, below, contrasts with *ha-meʿaṭ mikkem* 'is it of little importance to you?' in v 9, below. This idiom expresses severe criticism (cf. Deut 1:6; 2:3; 3:19, 26; Ezek 44:6; 45:9).

exalt yourselves. The *hithpaʿel* form *titnaśśeʾû* conveys arrogance or presumption. Compare 1 Kgs 1:5: "Now, Adonijah, son of Haggith, *presumed to think (mitnaśśēʾ lēʾmôr)*: I will be king!" An instructive analogue is to be found in Ezek 17:14: "so that it (= Judah) might be a humble kingdom, and not exalt itself *(lebiltî hitnaśśēʾ)*" (cf. Dan 11:14).

4. The significance of prostration is discussed in the NOTES on Num 14:5. In v 22, below, we read that Moses and Aaron again fell prostrate and appealed to God for assistance. Here it is reasonable to interpret Moses' act as one of surrender or submission to God's will after his leadership had been repudiated by some of the Israelites.

5. *In the morning.* The Hebrew *bōqer* has adverbial force. Compare Exod 16:7: "and *in the morning (ûbôqer)* you shall see" (cf. also Hos 7:6; Ps 5:4).

who is consecrated to him. The syntax of v 5 is subtle. Hebrew *ʾet ʾašer lô weʾet haqqādôš*, literally, "who belongs to him and who is sacred," is best taken as hendiadys.

his intimate. The sense of *hiphʿil hiqrîb* requires comment. The priests are "close" to God, in a spatial sense, because they officiate in sacred precincts. Functionally, *qārôb* expresses a relational "closeness"; compare Lev 10:3: "I will be sanctified by *my intimates (biqerôbâi 'eqqādēš).*" That verse likewise refers to the status of the Aaronide priests.

Ultimately, what we have is courtly language applied to sacral status. In Gen 45:10, Joseph assures his father, Jacob, that he will be his son's intimate *(qārôb),* and under his protection. In Esth 1:14, the highest advisers of the Persian king are collectively called *haqqārôb 'ēlâw* 'those closest to him'. In the present context, *hiqrîb* means to declare or designate an intimate. See below, in vv 9–10.

6. The style of this verse is laconic. One almost suspects that the words *Qorah wekol ʿadātô* 'Korah and his entire faction' were inserted from v 5, above. The text would read smoothly without them.

9. *the maintenance of the Tabernacle of YHWH.* The construction *ʿabôdat miškan YHWH* does not refer to worship, and it is synonymous with *ʿabôdat 'ôhel môʿēd* 'the maintenance of the Tent of Meeting' in Num 3:1 and 8:4, 23, and 35, where reference is also to the duties of the Levites. The Levites were explicitly excluded from officiating in the cult. See the Notes on Num 8:26, and cf. usages in Exod 30:16 and 36:3.

Is it of so little importance to you that. The idiom *ha-meʿaṭ mikkem kî* rhetorically implies a negative response, as does the similar idiom *ha-meʿaṭ kî* in v 13, below (see above, in v 3; and cf. Gen 30:15; Josh 22:17; Isa 7:13; Ezek 34:18; Job 15:11).

to stand in attendance. Idiomatic *ʿāmad lipnê,* literally, "to stand before," means "to wait upon, to attend" (cf. Judg 20:28; 1 Kgs 1:2). The Levites served the community by attending to the functions necessary for the operation of the cult.

11. The syntax of this verse is ambiguous. One could translate, "Therefore you and your entire faction are the ones who are rallying against YHWH." But, in context, the point is that the actions of Korah's faction constituted rebellion against YHWH, not just against Aaron! Idiomatic *hannôʿadîm ʿal* means "to assemble against," hence, "to conspire." Conceivably there is a play on sound and meaning between *ʿadātekā* 'your faction' and *hannôʿadîm* 'that are conspiring', even though etymologically the two words derive from different verbal roots *(ʿēdāh* from *ʿ-w-d,* and *nôʿād* from *w/y-ʿ-d).*

incite. The *qere tālînû* (cf. Num 14:36) means "to instigate," that is, to arouse others to press their grievances, in this case against Aaron.

What has he done. Rhetorical *mahû'* may mean "what is it with him; what is wrong with him?" Compare *mî 'attāh* in Isa 51:12: "what is wrong with you?" The sense is similar to *mah l-* 'what is wrong with so-and-so?' Compare also the Ugaritic idiom *mat Krt k ybky* 'what is it with Keret, that he weeps?' (Gibson 1978: 83; Keret, col. i, lines 38–39).

12. The JE narrative resumes here, as the story reverts to the challenge to

Moses' authority. The verb *šalaḥ* means "to send word, send a message" and does not require a direct object to convey this sense. In fact, the combination *šālaḥ liqrō'* 'send . . . to summon' occurs in Num 22:5 and 37; and 1 Sam 22:11, though *šālaḥ . . . weqārā'* 'he sent and called' is more common.

13. On "a land flowing with milk and sap" see the NOTES on Num 13:27. The idiom *ha-meʿaṭ kî* 'haven't you done enough [harm]?' echoes similar idioms occurring in vv 9 and 10, above. *Hithpaʿel tiśtārēr* is unique to this verse, and is correctly analyzed as a denominative of *śār* 'prince, officer'. Compare Exod 21:14 for similar grievances, also addressed to Moses.

The sequence *kî* + verb . . . *gam* + the same verb, as we have it here *(kî tiśtārēr ʾālênû gam histarer* 'that you continue to lord over us', is rare.

14. *not even.* The combination *ʾap lōʾ* is unique to this verse. More common is *ʾap kî* 'even if'. The thought expressed here is reminiscent of Exod 3:8, presented here with irony. The pair *śādeh* + *kerem* 'field + vineyard/orchard' is proverbial (Exod 22:4; Num 20:17; 21:22) and pretty well covers the two main types of productive land: sown fields of grain and fruit-bearing trees and vines.

the eyes of those men. Reference to the eyes of "those men" is euphemistic for "our eyes." Compare 1 Sam 29:4, where "the heads of 'those men' *(haʾ anāšîm hāhēm)*" means "our heads." When some awful harm or evil is spoken of, it is customary to deflect its effects onto a third person or persons. Gouging out the eyes was a known punishment imposed on runaway slaves, prisoners, and rebellious vassals (see Judg 16:21; 2 Kgs 25:4–7; Jer 39:4–7; 52:7–11). The verb *niqqēr* almost always pertains to eyes, but may also be said of cutting stone. It is related to the law of retaliation—"an eye for an eye" (Exod 21:24; Lev 24:20; Deut 19:21).

15. A common theme in treaty curses and in the execrations included in royal inscriptions is the plea to a god, or to gods, not to accept the offerings of any who violate the terms of the treaty or show disrespect to the king. This subject is discussed in the COMMENTS that follow. "Turning toward" is idiomatic for acceptance, or the granting of favor. Thus God turned toward (the verb *šāʿāh)* Abel's offering, but did not turn toward Cain's (Gen 4:4). This idiom is expressed in Mal 2:13: "so that he refuses to *regard* the oblation *(penôt ʾel hamminḥāh)* any more, or to accept what you offer" (cf. 1 Kgs 8:28 ‖ 2 Chr 6:19). Akkadian idiom attests *pani suḫḫuru* 'to turn the face toward', with the same connotation *(CAD S,* 49–50, under *saḫāru* 11).

Moses' insistence that he has not misappropriated even a work animal nor harmed a single person is reminiscent of Samuel's apologia: "Whose ox have I taken, and whose ass have I taken? Whom have I defrauded or whom have I robbed?" (1 Sam 12:3f.). The verb *nāśāʾ* means both "to lift up" and "to carry away."

19. *rallied . . . against. Hiphʿil wayyaqhēl ʿal* means "to demonstrate against" and is analogous to *tallînu ʿal* in v 11, above.

21. God would not annihilate evildoers while Moses and Aaron were in proximity to them. Num 16:26, below (JE), and a further statement in Num 17:10 (P) both attribute the same concern to God. Also compare Ezra 6:21; 10:8, 11, 16; and Neh 9:2 and 10:29 for usage of the verb *hibbādēl* 'to remove oneself, secede'. This verb is used to convey a major theme in the characterization of the postexilic community: social and religious separatism. In 1 Chr 23:13 we read that Aaron was "separated" in the process of being consecrated.

that I may annihilate them. The verb *killāh* 'to destroy, annihilate' is often said of God's punitive actions. Compare Num 25:31; and Exod 32:12; 33:5 (E); Deut 28:21; Josh 24:20; Jer 5:3; and Ezek 22:31.

22. Moses and Aaron fell on their faces. The meaning of this act is explained in the NOTES on Num 14:5, where at another critical moment they did the same.

Lord, God of the spirits of all flesh. The epithet *ʾel ʾelôhê hāruḥôt lekol bāśār* requires comment. In Num 27:16, in the context of Joshua's appointment to succeed Moses, YHWH occurs instead of *ʾel: YHWH ʾelôhê hāruḥôt* 'YHWH, God of the spirits'. In a similar way, one notes that in Gen 33:20 we have *ʾēl ʾelôhê Yiśrāʾēl*, literally, "El, the God of Israel," whereas in Judg 5:3 we read *ʾazammēr lYHWH ʾelôhê Yiśrāʾēl* 'I sing to YHWH, the God of Israel'. These phenomena relate to the synthesis of El and YHWH, a major aspect of the early development of biblical monotheism (Eissfeldt 1956).

all flesh. Hebrew *kol bāśār* can refer to all living creatures, including animals (Gen 7:15; Ps 104:29), or simply to humans (as is probably the sense in Job 12:10; 34:14).

The argumentation here has been correctly interpreted by G. B. Gray as unusual, and relatively latecoming in biblical thought. Abraham appeals to God's justice as judge of the world not to destroy the righteous along with the sinful wicked (Gen 18:23–25). The diction of Ezek 18:4 is closer to that of the present verse: "the very person who commits an offense *(hannepeš haḥôṭēʾt)* shall die!" In Lev 10:6 the priests are instructed to act in a way that will spare "the entire community *(kol hāʿēdāh)*" from God's rage. The theme of *qeṣep* 'wrath' (literally "foam" of the waves—Hos 10:7) will be discussed in the COMMENTS that follow.

24. *Withdraw.* The verb *hēʿālû* parallels usage of *hibbādelû* in v 20, above, and *sûrû* 'turn away' in v 26, below. In biblical usage, *ʿālāh* 'to ascend' and verbs with the same meaning can mean "to retreat, withdraw" especially in military contexts. Thus 2 Sam 20:2: "all of the men of Israel *left (wayyaʿal)* David and followed Sheba, son of Bikri"; or 2 Sam 23:9: "the Israelite soldiers *retreated (wayyaʿalû Yiśrāʾēl).*"

The names of Dathan and Abiram were probably interpolated in v 24 by the priestly compiler, as a way of linking P to JE, which resumes in v 25, where there is no mention of Korah!

residence. The use of *miškān* in the singular to designate a family dwelling is unattested outside the present chapter. In v 26, below, it reappears in a priestly interpolation within JE. This usage has attracted considerable comment. Some have gone so far as to suggest that Korah and his faction had set up a rival tabernacle, but this reading is not indicated in any way. There is nothing unacceptable about usage of the singular *miškān* for a private dwelling, because the plural is used in this way (Num 24:5). The term used in JE is *ʾōhel* 'tent' (v 26).

25. JE resumes here, and again Dathan and Abiram are the actors. This is the first reference to the elders of Israel in Numbers 16. The elders *(zeqēnîm)* were first mentioned in Num 11:16, where this Israelite institution is discussed.

26. *He addressed the assemblage as follows.* The introductory words were formulated by a priestly writer (Gray—ICC). The admonition against touching anything belonging to the dissidents is conventional. It is a way of saying "Keep away!" (cf. Gen 3:3; Exod 19:12; Isa 52:11; Lam 4:15).

you, too, be terminated. Use of the verb *sāpāh* evokes the saga of Sodom and Gomorrah. Lot is warned to leave Sodom with the members of his family "lest you be terminated *(tissāpēh)* because of the sin *(ʿawôn)* of the city" (Gen 19:15, 17). Similarly, in Gen 18:23 Abraham questions God about whether he would "terminate" the righteous along with the wicked. We have, therefore, the theme of the divine destruction of wicked communities.

27. The words *miškan Qôraḥ* 'the dwelling of Korah' were probably inserted by a priestly writer. In the second part of the verse, it is only Dathan and Abiram who stand outside their tents.

28. *by this shall you know.* Idiomatic *bezōʾt tēdʿûn* often introduces the presentation of proof or the granting of a sign (Gen 42:33; Exod 7:16–17).

has sent me. The verb *šālaḥ* 'to send' is basic to the biblical concept of prophecy. The basic claim of the Israelite prophet is that God sent him to deliver his message and to perform acts on his behalf. Samuel was sent to anoint Saul as king (1 Sam 15:1), as was Moses himself sent to the Israelites (Ps 105:26). In fact, the verb *šālaḥ* is central to the diction of the Moses stories (Exod 3:13–15; 7:16), indicating that he was the first prophet, the first to be sent in the historiography of the Torah. Jeremiah insists that only he was sent by YHWH, not the false prophets who were persecuting him (Jer 25:17; 26:12, 15; and especially 28:9).

that they are not of my own devising. Idiomatic *kî loʾ millibbî* is reminiscent of what Balaam said about his powerlessness to act on his own devices (Num 24:13).

29. *if the fate of all mankind befalls them.* Elsewhere Hebrew *pequddāh* designates a state or situation in which God is turning his attention to the punishment of evildoers; compare Isa 10:3: "What will you do on the day of punishment *(leyôm pequddāh)*, when the calamity comes from afar?" (cf. Hos 9:7; Mic 7:4; and frequently in Jeremiah). The punishment that God imposes

on all mortals is, of course, natural death. This reality is alluded to in the statement of Zelophehad's daughters that their father had not perished as one of Korah's faction, but because of his own transgression (Num 27:3). Idiomatic *kol hāʾādām* means "everyone, all humans" (Ps 116:11; 1 Kgs 5:11; 8:38).

30. *a special creation.* The form *berîʾāh* is a hapax, serving as a cognate accusative. Similar syntax and morphology are to be found in Jonah 3:2: *weqārāʾ ʿālêhā ʾet haqqerîʾāh hazzōʾt,* literally, "he pronounced over it this pronouncement."

opens its mouth. The verb *pāṣāh* 'to open' is specialized, always taking as its object *peh* 'mouth'. On the theme of being swallowed up by the earth see the COMMENTS that follow.

35. The version of P resumes here. What P states is in direct contradiction to the account of JE (Num 16:25–34). Instead of perishing by being swallowed up by the earth, the dissidents perish by fire. Fire regularly "issues forth" (the verb *yāṣā*); compare Lev 9:24; 10:2; and in ancient poetry, Num 21:28.

NOTES TO NUMBERS 17: THE AARONIDE PREROGATIVE

17 Num 17:1–5 follow directly upon Num 16:35. The copper firepans utilized by the insurgents had become holy in the process of being offered to God. Their further use by worshipers was, therefore, forbidden. Eleazar son of Aaron is instructed to retrieve them and to use the copper in refurbishing the altar of burnt offerings.

2. Eleazar's assignment, according to Num 4:16, was to attend to the interior appurtenances of the Tabernacle, and what he is instructed to do here falls within that assignment. In Num 19:3–8 we read that Eleazar took charge of the purification rites involving the red heifer. In Num 20:28–29 we are told that Eleazar was invested as high priest just before the death of his father Aaron. Still later, it is Phineas son of Eleazar who assumes leadership in a crisis (Num 25:7–15). A line of succession through Eleazar is thereby indicated.

Order . . . to remove. The verb *weyārēm* is translated "let him remove" because verbs meaning "to lift" can carry the idiomatic sense "to remove, carry away." See the NOTES on Num 16:24.

incense. Hebrew *ʾēš* here designates the incense itself. In other instances, *ʾēš* may refer to hot coals (see v 11, below, and cf. Num 16:7). In Lev 10:1, *ʾēš zārāh* 'alien fire' also refers, in substance, to the incense improperly offered by Aaron's two sons. Hebrew *qeṭôret* 'incense' is explained in the NOTES on Num

7:14. The verb *zērāh* 'to scatter' is normally said of winnowing, sowing seed, or scattering dust (Exod 32:20; Isa 41:16; Ezek 5:2; Ruth 3:2).

they have become holy. In varying contexts the verb *qādaš* means (a) "to become holy," initially; (b) "to remain holy"; and (c) "to be holy," existentially. The first sense suits the immediate context. The import of *qādaš* is restrictive, by implication, imposing prohibitions on the use of the copper firepans. At this point, the text has not yet explained on what basis the firepans became holy. This explanation comes in v 3.

3. *cost them their lives.* Hebrew *benapsōtām* incorporates *beth pretii.* Similar usage occurs in 1 Kgs 2:23: "so may God do to me, and even more, if speaking of this matter does not cost Adonijah his life *(kî benapšô dibbēr 'Adôniyāhû).*" Also note usages in 2 Sam 14:7; 23:17; and Jonah 1:14. *Beth pretii* is most obvious in such statements as *nepeš benepeš* 'a life for a life' in Deut 19:21, which restates *nepeš taḥat nepeš* in Exod 21:23.

Let them be hammered into sheets. Hebrew *riqqu'ê paḥîm* means, literally "hammerings of sheets" of metal. In the *pi'el* stem, the verb *r-q-'* means "to hammer, to work metal," as in Exod 39:3: *wayyeraqqe'û* 'they hammered' sheets of gold. Compare also Isa 40:19: *weṣôrēp bazzāhāb yeraqqe'ennû* 'a smith overlays it with gold', where reference is to a statue of wood; and Jer 10:9: *kesep meruqqā'* 'hammered silver sheets'.

plating. Hebrew *ṣippuî* is a *pi'el*-based noun, from the verb *ṣippāh* 'to cover, overlay'. Compare Isa 30:22: "the overlay *(ṣippûi)* of your silver statues." See also Exod 36:38; 38:17–19; and 1 Kgs 6:35, all of which pertain to the fashioning of cult objects and edifices. In the ancient Near East, statues of gods were often fashioned of wood and overlaid with silver or gold. This was true of the Tabernacle altars, which were made of wood and were overlaid with gold and copper.

having been offered . . . they had become holy. The precise sense of verbal *hiqrîbûm* 'they offered them' (namely, the firepans) holds the key to a proper understanding of the phenomenology expressed in Num 17:1–5. Some scholars, among them G. B. Gray and more recently M. Haran (1960), have explained the phenomenology in spatial terms: once the firepans had been brought inside the sacred space of the Tabernacle complex they had "contracted" holiness, which is, in this view, a contagious condition.

This interpretation of the disposition of the firepans is actually part of a larger point of view on the character of holiness itself. In Exod 29:27 and several similar statements we read, *kol hannôgē'a bammizbēaḥ yiqdāš,* which Haran takes to mean "anyone who touches the altar *is thereby rendered holy.*" In other words, the holiness of the altar "rubs off" on all who touch it. This interpretation is problematic, however. In Lev 6:11 the statement *kol 'ašer yigga' bāhem yiqdāš* must be understood to mean "anyone who touches them (namely, the expiatory sacrifices) must be *in a holy state.*" In other words, only priests who are properly consecrated and purified may have physical contact with sacrificial materials. This interpretation is borne out by Lev 6:20: *kol 'ăšer yiggaʿ bibeśārāh yiqdāš* 'anyone who touches its flesh (namely, the flesh of the sin offering) *must be in a holy state*'.

Now the preceding two statements cannot refer to contagious holiness because, in fact, one would not be sanctified through contact with sacrificial substances. Hag 2:11–13 explicitly states as much; there a hypothetical inquiry into cultic law is addressed to the postexilic priests of Jerusalem:

> "If a man is carrying sacrificial flesh in a fold of his garment and with that fold touches bread, stew, wine, oil, or any other food, will the latter *become holy (ha-yiqdāš)?*"
>
> The priests responded by saying, "No!"
>
> Haggai then said, "If one impure through contact with a dead person should touch any one of these [substances], would it thereby be defiled?"
>
> The priests replied by saying, "It will be defiled!"

Foodstuffs do not become sanctified through contact with other already sanctified foodstuffs, nor do persons become holy through contact with holy objects.

The explanation of the phenomenology of sanctification in the present instance lies elsewhere, primarily in the force of the verb *hiqrîb* in this verse. Its sense is functional: "to offer, assign," as it is in Num 15:4, where we read of one who donates a sacrifice. The point is that once a sacrifice is assigned to be a particular offering, and once the act of offering is completed, the objects or substances so assigned become God's property. The offering is a gift, and it does not matter whether the recipient, once the gift is delivered to him, decides to reject it, as is the case here. At a certain moment, the firepans had become the property of the Deity. That God subsequently rejected them as offerings did not undo that conveyance or transfer of ownership. The reason for restricting subsequent utilization of the copper firepans was that they had been assigned to God and could not be used by worshipers for other purposes.

Let them serve as. The idiom *hāyāh l-* means "to serve as"; see the NOTE on Num 10:1. The new plating would serve as a visible sign and a warning. All would know where the copper plating came from (see below, in v 25, for a more forceful statement to this effect.)

5. *This was a reminder.* Hebrew *zikkārôn* connotes a visible reminder, such as a written document or an inscription appearing on a statue or artifact. See the NOTES on Num 5:15 and 10:10 for more on usage of the term *zikkārôn.*

outsider. Hebrew *zār* literally means "a hated person," a meaning shared by the Akkadian cognate *zêru* 'to hate'. That foreigners should be referred to in this way attests to the prevalence of xenophobia. The same animus accounts for Hebrew *nokrî* 'stranger' (cf. Akkadian *nakāru* 'to hate'). Depending on immediate context, *zār* has differing meanings. Here the sense is made explicit: the *zār* is one not of the seed of Aaron (cf. Exod 29:33; Lev 22:10–12 [Milgrom 1970: 5–8]).

the seed of Aaron. The convention of referring to hereditary successors as *zeraʿ* 'seed' probably originated in the royal context and was appropriated as a classification for hereditary priests. Compare 1 Kgs 11:14; 2 Kgs 25:25; Jer 41:1; Ezek 17:13; and elsewhere. *Zeraʿ ʾAharôn* is paralleled by *zeraʿ Ṣādôq* 'the seed of Zadok' in Ezek 43:19.

The arrangement of v 5 requires some comment. *NJPS* juxtaposes the clause *kaʾăšer dibbēr YHWH beyad Môšeh lô* 'as YHWH had commanded him through Moses' to the beginning of v 5, regarding it as a logical continuation of v 4. I have translated accordingly. The logical antecedent of *lô* 'to him' must be Eleazar.

6–15. The next section of Numbers 17 describes a mass demonstration against Moses and Aaron, and God's wrathful response to it in the form of a plague. Aaron used incense in an apotropaic manner so as to contain the plague and protect the living from its onslaught. God's wrath has already been recorded in Num 16:20–22 and is again referred to in Num 17:9.

protested. Niphʿal wayyillōnû means "to complain, bring a grievance." Contrast the factitive force of the *hiphʿil* in v 20, below, and in Num 16:11.

the people of YHWH. On *ʿam YHWH* see the NOTES on Num 11:29.

You have brought death. The force of *hēmattem* is causative; compare similar meanings in Gen 18:25; Exod 16:3; and 2 Sam 20:19.

7. *rallied en masse against. Niphʿal behiqqāhēl ʿal-* connotes a demonstration *against* Moses and Aaron. Contrast *wayyaqhēl ʿal,* the *hiphʿil* factitive, "to instigate protests against," in Num 16:3.

glorious presence. In Num 16:19 we also read that God's *kābôd* appeared at a critical moment. For the phenomenology of the "cloud," see the NOTES on Num 12:4.

10. *Withdraw.* Hebrew *hērōmû (niphʿal)* means, literally, "lift yourselves." In the same way, *hēʿālû* 'raise yourselves' in Num 16:24 effectively means "to withdraw." On the meaning of falling on one's face, see the NOTES on Num 14:5.

11. The procedure for preparing the incense in the firepan is the same here as it was in preparation for the ordeal of the incense offerings in Num 16:6.

perform a rite of expiation over them. The precise force of *wekappēr ʿalêhem* is important for a proper understanding of the phenomenology underlying the apotropaic uses of incense. The sense is functional: the verb *kippēr* does not mean "to cleanse," but rather to perform a rite whose *result* is a kind of purification. Furthermore, this formula expresses the spatial factor in expiatory rites, performed in close proximity to persons or objects. Here Aaron was positioned between those already stricken by the plague (the "dead" of v 13) and those still unaffected (the "living"). He waved the incense over the living, and it protected them from the advancing plague. What Aaron did on this occasion represents an adaptation of procedures involved in expiation rites, and conveyed by the verb *kippēr*. These rites normally required the utilization of sacrificial blood, placed on the horns of the altar of burnt offerings and occasionally on other interior appurtenances of the Tabernacle (Levine 1974: 63–77).

the fuming rage. Hebrew *haqqeṣep* is explained in the NOTES on Num 16:22, where the verb *qāṣap* occurs. This is the only instance in which this noun is determinate, indicating that to the author it represented a known phenomenon.

plague. Hebrew *negep* occurs in Exod 12:13 with reference to the smiting of the firstborn in Egypt. Ironically, the Levites were supposed to protect the Israelite community against *negep* by attending properly to the tasks of the Tabernacle. The proper maintenance of the Tabernacle was requisite to averting God's wrath (Num 8:19). When, however, a group of Levites rebelled against the leadership of Moses and Aaron and thereby aroused God's wrath, the result was *negep!*

13. *was contained*. The verb *ʿāṣar* means "to hold back, contain," with reference to the holding back of rain from heaven (1 Kgs 8:35). See Ps 106:30 for a literary echo of the present verse, and 2 Sam 24:25 for similar usage.

15. *had been contained*. Hebrew *neʿeṣārāh* is pluperfect. The plague had been contained before Aaron returned to the Tent of Meeting.

16–26. The next verses project a second ordeal aimed at confirming Aaron's selection by God as the legitimate priest. Although this ordeal is orchestrated between the Levites and the other eleven tribes, its true purpose was to determine which *ʾîš* 'person' (in v 20) had been designated for the priesthood.

17. *one rod apiece*. The doubling of Hebrew *maṭṭeh maṭṭeh* means "one rod each"; see below, in v 21, where the syntax is different but the sense is the same. Compare also *ʾîš ʾeḥād ʾîš eḥād* 'one person apiece' in Num 13:2.

Usage of the socioeconomic term *bêt ʾāb* 'patriarchal house' here, and throughout the ordeal, is less than precise. In the NOTES on Num 1:2 it was explained that *bêt ʾāb* represented a unit within the larger *maṭṭeh* 'tribe'. Here it is effectively synonymous with *maṭṭeh*, it being assumed that there were, in all, twelve *neśîʾîm* 'chieftains', who were heads of patriarchal houses. In the NOTES on Num 13:2 it was explained that there was more than one *nāśîʾ* in each tribe, and more than one *bêt ʾāb* as well.

18. *on the rod of Levi*. Hebrew *ʿal maṭṭeh Lēwî* is unusual usage, for *maṭṭeh* in the priestly source of the Torah almost always has the extended meaning "tribe." There is an ambiguity here, and it is amplified in v 21, below. Are we to understand that the rod of Levi was one of the twelve rods, each of which

represented a tribe? The dominant tradition of the priestly source in Numbers, set forth in Numbers 3–4, is that the Levites were not counted as one of the twelve tribes. The point already made here in v 18, and reinforced in v 21, below, is that there was also a rod representing Levi, in addition to the twelve rods of the tribes (see below, in the NOTES on v 21). A special rod representing the tribe of Levi would have been necessary for the ordeal to yield its expected verdict.

19. It seems that here there is a play on the similarity in sound between *'ēdût* 'the [Ark of the] Covenant' and *'iwwāʿēd* 'I meet with', even though there is, in fact, no etymological connection between the two words (see the NOTES on Num 16:31). In a similar statement in Exod 16:34 an etymological connection exists, because it is at *'ôhel môʿēd* 'the Tent of Meeting' that God says "I meet with you *('iwwāʿēd leka)*" (cf. also Exod 29:42; 30:6, 36).

20. Poles and rods are involved in other magical occurrences, such as the mating of Jacob's flocks (Gen 30:37–41), but nowhere in biblical literature do we have the sprouting of a rod detached from the soil, serving as a sign. Further information on this phenomenology will be provided in the COMMENTS that follow.

I will then be relieved. Hebrew *wahašîkkôtî* is a unique locution, from *š-k-k* 'to recede' when said of water (Gen 8:1), and "to be assuaged" when said of anger (Esth 2:1; 7:10). God will relieve himself of the grievances incited against Moses and Aaron. Compare Num 16:11, where the grievances are said to be leveled against God himself. Opposition to Aaron is, in effect, opposition to God!

21. *The rod of Aaron is [to be placed] among their rods.* The concluding words of v 21, *ûmaṭṭēh 'Aharôn betôk maṭṭôtām,* constitute an explanatory statement informing the reader that, in addition to the twelve rods representing the tribes of Israel, there was also a rod representing the Levites placed together with the others. It would be incorrect to translate "and the rod of Aaron was counted among them," for the tribe of Levi was not one of the twelve tribes (see above, in the NOTES on v 18).

22. *the Tent of the Covenant.* Hebrew *'ôhel hāʿēdût* designates the tent where the Ark of the Covenant was deposited. In Num 1:53 we find the term *miškan hāʿēdût,* which bears the same meaning.

23. *the house of Levi.* The designation *bêt Lēwî* is relatively rare; compare Ps 135:20, where *bêt hallēwî* contrasts with *bêt 'Aharôn* 'the house of Aaron'. In Zech 12:13 *bêt Lēwî* is classified as a *mišpāḥāh* 'clan'. The writer of the present passage probably intended to resonate the diction of Exod 2:11, where the lineage of Moses is first recorded: "a certain man of the house of Levi *(mibbêt Lēwî)* went and married a Levite woman." In priestly tradition, Aaron is Moses' brother (Exod 4:13).

The process of sprouting, blossoming, and bearing almonds is beautifully expressed here. *Hiphʿil wayyôṣēʾ* means "to bring forth" vegetation (Gen

1:12). For similar imagery, compare Isa 18:5; 40:6–8; Ps 103:15; and Job 14:7–11. This passage is singled out for discussion in the introduction to this volume, section B.

25. *for safe keeping*. Here Hebrew *lemišmeret* could be interpreted to mean "for observation" (cf. Exod 12:6; 16:23, 34). The term for "sign", Hebrew *ʾôt*, often connotes a warning sign.

rebellious persons. Usage in Ezek 12:9 and 44:6 suggests that *benê merî*, as it occurs here, is a derogatory reference to *benê Yiśrāʾēl* 'the Israelite people'. In Ezekiel we frequently encounter *bêt hammerî* 'the rebellious house/family' (Ezek 2:5; 6:8); compare also *ʿam merî* 'a rebellious people' in Isa 30:9. In Deut 31:27 Israel's rebelliousness is sharply criticized.

may cease. The form *ûtekal* is the jussive of the *qal* stem of the root *k-l-h*: "let it cease!"

26. This is the common compliance clause, which expresses the priestly ideology. In the days of Moses, the Israelites were quick to carry out God's commands, especially those relevant to ritual worship (Levine 1965).

27. Adverbial *hēn* 'surely' is followed by a verb in the perfect; compare Deut 5:21 and 31:14 for similar syntax. The verb *gāwaʿ* may refer to natural death or to death as a result of some catastrophe, such as the flood, as we read in Gen 6:17. In Num 20:3 the same verb refers to this very incident.

28. *Will we ever cease perishing?* Hebrew *tamnû ligwôʿa*, literally, "we have reached the end of perishing," is reminiscent of Deut 2:16, where we find *tamnû . . . lāmût* 'they reached the end of dying'.

COMMENT 1: ECHOES OF AN INSURRECTION—THE JE NARRATIVE

Pursuant to the source analysis of Numbers 16–17 presented in the NOTES, it is appropriate to explore the themes expressed distinctively in both the priestly and nonpriestly sections of these chapters.

In their received form, Numbers 16 and 17 confirm the priestly traditions of Numbers that regard the Levites as a distinct class of cultic servitors, separate from the Aaronide priesthood. In the COMMENTS to Numbers 3–4 and 8 it was explained that the reorganization of the Israelite priesthood, highlighted in the book of Numbers, represents the ultimate outcome, in postexilic times, of a process initiated in the late seventh century B.C.E., subsequent to the edicts of Josiah, king of Judah, in 622.

Numbers presents its view of the Levites in several related ways. In chaps. 3–4 the levitical clans are assigned their specific tasks, necessitated for the most part by the portable character of the Tabernacle, which had to be dismantled and reassembled at intervals. The plan of the Israelite encampment, as set forth in chap. 2, had special locations for the Levites, who were, we were told in chap. 1, to be mustered and counted separately from the rest of the Israelite tribes. Finally, chap. 8 records the dedication of the Levites as a class (actually, a tribe) of servitors, subordinate to the Aaronide priesthood, who were the only ones permitted to officiate in the Israelite cult.

Once these broad organizational patterns are recognized, it is possible to focus on the narrower internecine conflict projected by the priestly writers of Numbers 16–17. Their immediate purpose was to lock in the exclusive sanction of the Amramite family, the family of Moses and Aaron, within the larger Kohathite clan of Levites, as the sole legitimate priests.

It would be best to discuss the themes expressed in the JE narratives of Numbers 16 first and then examine precisely how the priestly writers transformed the context of the conflict so markedly. From a literary point of view, what we have in Numbers 16–17 resembles the situation in Numbers 13–14, the account of the reconnaissance of Canaan. In both instances, priestly writers modulated earlier JE narratives in ways that enabled them to present their distinctively priestly agenda. In fact, Numbers 16–17 may serve as a paradigm of the source-critical method.

As outlined in the INTRODUCTION to these chapters, the JE stratum may be found in the following verses: 16:1–2 (adapted by P), 12–15, and 25–34 (containing several priestly interpolations). Num 16:1–2, which were rewritten by priestly authors, introduce the main characters of the episode. It was a priestly writer, most likely, who interpolated the name and levitical lineage of Korah in v 1, making him the leader of the insurgents. The same interpolation is to be assumed in Num 16:27 and 32, farther on in the JE narrative. These insertions of Korah's name served to link the JE and P versions to each other internally. In v 2, the formula *neśîʾê hāʿēdāh* 'chieftains of the community' was also added by a priestly writer, for these terms of reference are distinctively priestly locutions.

In analyzing the core of JE content in vv 1–2, it becomes clear that all of the persons named by JE—Dathan, Abiram, and On (whose name never occurs elsewhere)—are identified as Reubenites. This affiliation is assumed by the author of Deut 11:6, who listed all of these persons in genealogical sequence as "sons of Eliab, sons of Reuben." The same affiliation is also indicated by Num 26:8–9, part of a priestly genealogy that, as a matter of fact, purposely digresses so as to refer to the present incident.

There have been ample speculations about what was at issue in the dispute, as it was originally perceived in the JE narrative. Were the Reubenites disaffected over the loss of their status as the firstborn, the first of the tribes? This interpretation attributes too much reality to a tradition of eponyms. More likely, the issue in Numbers 16–17 was related to the Transjordanian dispute and to Moses' insistence that all of the tribes take part in the conquest of Canaan, west of the Jordan. The Reubenites were historically one of the Transjordanian tribes. Perhaps Num 16:14, in particular, presages the narrative of chap. 32. In that verse the Reubenites complain that they have not yet received *naḥalat śādeh wākārem* 'fields and vineyards as estates', indicating their dissatisfaction at the delay in settling their own territories. If it is accurate to translate *lōʾ naʿaleh* as "we will not go forth on the march!" in Num 16:12 and 14, then the repetition of that assertion may allude to the refusal of the Reubenites to fight west of the Jordan, alongside the main group of Israelite tribes. On this basis, the subsequent claims pressed by the Transjordanian tribes—Reuben, Gad, and the Machirite clan affiliated with Manasseh—were anticipated by earlier challenges to Moses' leadership, also on matters of settlement policy.

The narrative in Numbers 32 is admittedly etiological in that it explains how it was that some Israelite tribes settled in Transjordan. It is also likely, however, that it preserves a realistic recollection of problems affecting the conquest, settlement, and distribution of land, both in Canaan and in Transjordan. Behind the severely judgmental tone criticizing all who questioned the policy of settling in Canaan, we may perceive in the JE narratives of Numbers 16–17 allusions to real disputes among the Israelite tribes on this very policy. This agenda has been submerged in the final redaction of the text, as priestly writers sought to transform the earlier JE narratives into an endorsement of the exclusive Aaronide priesthood.

Actually, the statements in Num 16:12–15 sound very much like other challenges to Moses' authority. A key locution is the verb *heʿelāh* 'to lead out, bring forth', introduced here by rhetorical *hameʿaṭ kî*: 'haven't you done enough by bringing us forth?' In Exod 17:13 a similar challenge is introduced by *lāmāh heʿelîtānû* 'why have you brought us forth?' from the land of Egypt. In Num 21:5 (reflected, perhaps in Num 20:5), a similar rhetoric is evident.

The narrative here resonates these Torah sources in additional ways: the danger of death and extinction in the wilderness further links Num 16:13 to Exod 16:3. In a somewhat larger perspective, Exod 17:3 relates to Numbers 32 in alluding to a pastoral economy, whereas in Num 16:13–14 and 20:5 the potential of agricultural productivity is suggested. Most poignant in Numbers 16 is the characterization of Egypt, not Canaan, as a land flowing with milk and sap, which in its expression of anger and frustration recalls Exod 16:3.

Within the JE narratives, Num 16:15 is perhaps the most suggestive verse because, in its two parts, it leads us to comparative sources of considerable interest. The apologia of Moses in Num 16:15b recalls, of course, Samuel's parting words in 1 Sam 13:3, even to the point that both passages refer specifically to the misappropriation of a mule! We know now that there were conventional formulas or statements of innocence—disclaimers, if you will—that may have been required of those in positions of accountability. Thus in an Amarna letter (Knudtzon 1964: 1.849; EA 280:24–29) we read the words of a vassal to his suzerain: "Furthermore: Let the king, my lord, inquire if I have misappropriated a single person, or if a single ox, or if a single mule *(ú šum-ma l imēra)* from him. And so is his right!" This statement serves to affirm the vassal's loyalty and probity, as he urgently seeks the assistance of his suzerain. He had undertaken hostile action against an enemy of his king, only to arouse a counter-action by the ally of the king's enemy that caused him to lose his own town to the enemy. To press home the point that he is worthy of aid, he states in hyperbolic fashion his innocence of all wrongdoing. In the case of Moses, and in Samuel's parting words, we find leaders protesting their honor before the people whom they lead; Samuel, as he was about to retire and make way for the monarchy, and Moses, in the face of a threatened rebellion.

One further recalls the negative confessions known from ancient Egyptian literature. A classic example from the Book of the Dead was entitled by its translator, John A. Wilson, "The Protestation of Guiltlessness" (Wilson 1969). We may also cite the biblical negative confession of one seeking entry into the Temple, expressed so beautifully in Psalm 15.

The first part of Num 16:15 contains a brief entreaty to God in which Moses, severely angered by the rebellion, asks God not to accept sacrificial offerings from Dathan and Abiram and their faction. This petition recalls ancient Near Eastern treaties and royal inscriptions that contain conventional curses and threats. Would-be treaty violators and detractors of royal ancestors are threatened, among other things, with the rejection of their sacrificial offerings and, further, with the revocation or denial of their very right to offer sacrifices and to appear before the gods in their temples.

We encounter similar statements even in Scripture. Condemning the abominations practiced in the Second Temple of Jerusalem, the postexilic prophet Malachi (2:13) invokes God's punishment upon the offenders: "And this further shall you do: Cover the altar of YHWH with weeping and moaning, for there will be no further turning toward offerings *(mēʾēn ʿôd penôt ʾel hamminḥāh)*, nor their favorable acceptance from your hand *(welāqaḥat rāṣôn miyyedkem)*." One recalls the hope expressed in the temple prayer attributed to Solomon, in 1 Kgs 8:28: "May you turn toward *(ûpānîtā)* the prayer of your servant. . . ." Using a different verb, Gen 4:4b–5a express the alternatives of acceptance and rejection of sacrifice as follows: *wayiššaʿ YHWH ʾel hebel weʾel minḥātô, weʾel Qayîn weʾel minḥātô lōʾ šāʿāh* 'YHWH turned toward Abel and toward his sacrifice, but toward Cain and toward his sacrifice he did not turn'.

In the recently discovered royal inscription from Tell-Fekherye in Syria, dated to the ninth century B.C.E. (an inscription preserved in both Assyrian and Aramaic versions), we find the same themes expressed negatively as a curse. Adad-itʾi, the governor of Gozan, the area in which Tell-Fekherye was located, admonishes as follows any who would erase his name from the furnishings of the Adad temple: "Whosoever removes my name from the furnishings of the temple of Hadad, my Lord, may Hadad, my Lord, not receive either his food offerings or his libations from his hand." In Aramaic, which is closer to Hebrew than Assyrian, this statement reads in part, *lḥmh wmwh 'l ylqḥ mn ydh* 'his bread and his water let him not take from his hand.' The text invokes both the male divinity Hadad and his female consort, in the repetition of the threat (Abou-Assaf 1982: 65).

In the foregoing citations, both biblical and extrabiblical, the theme of "receiving from one's hand" expresses acceptance of gifts. In the Hebrew Bible we note additional instances of this idiom in Gen 33:10, with reference to Jacob's gifts to his brother Esau, and in 1 Sam 25:35, where we read that David accepted Abigail's gifts. Of particular interest are the words of Manoah's wife in Judg 13:23: "had YHWH indeed sought to cause our death, he would hardly have received from our hand *(lō' lāqaḥ miyyādēnû)* burnt offerings and offerings of grain, nor would he have announced all of these things to us at this time."

Turning again to comparative evidence, we are led to the Yaudian Aramaic inscription of Panamuwa I, found in Zinjirli and dated to the first half of the eighth century B.C.E. We first encounter a positive, self-adulatory statement by the king: "And during the days of my succession (?) [offerings] I proffered to the gods (or "to my gods"), and they always received them from my hands *(wmt yqḥw mn ydy)*. And whatever I asked from the gods they always granted me" (Aramaic text in Gibson 1975: 2.66, no. 13, lines 12–13). Contrast this statement with what Panamuwa wishes on any of his royal successors who would fail to honor him: "and he offers sacrifice to this same Hadad, but does not pronounce the name of Panamuwa . . . [may Hadad not receive] his sacrifice nor view it with favor; and whatever he asks, may he (= Hadad) not grant to him" (Aramaic text in Gibson 1975: 2.67–68, no. 13, lines 21–23).

Num 16:15 is part of the JE narrative (vv 12–15). At an early stage in the formation of chap. 16, v 15 was not followed by vv 16–24. The JE narrative only resumes in v 25, which records an act of divine punishment. The insurgents and their households were swallowed up alive. The point is that Num 16:15a should first be understood as a general petition, conveying a curse that was promptly answered by God, who destroyed Moses' enemies. We may view the priestly section that was later added, namely, vv 16–24, as commentary on Num 16:15a: Moses asked God to reject the *minḥāh* of his enemies, using *minḥāh* as a collective term for "offerings" and referring to those who were his enemies in the JE version of the insurrection. In response, the priestly writers lend specificity to Moses' more general petition by recording, in vv 16–24, that God instructed Moses to have Korah and his group present an incense offering, which he then rejected in Num 16:35 by destroying the rebellious faction in a consuming fire.

The value of source analysis thus extends beyond the mere reconstruction of a particular document by tracing its formation. Source analysis shows us how the priestly writers, in the present instance, interpreted a more general statement in specific terms. This method also led us to a broad consideration of themes that might have passed us by had we failed to attribute to each source its own distinctive agenda.

When the JE narrative resumes in Num 16:25–34 we read of the elimination of the insurgent faction by divine wrath, realized as an earthquake. We encounter a melange of themes associated with cataclysm and with signs from God, most of which have been noted in the NOTES. It might be worth mentioning the function of idiomatic *bezō̂ʾt* + *y-d-ʿ* 'by this + know' used in v 28. Compare Gen 42:33: *bezō̂ʾt ʾēdaʿ* 'by this [sign] I shall know', words spoken by God to Pharaoh, via Moses. Similar diction informs Gen 42:15; Josh 3:10; Mal 3:10; and Ps 41:12.

Being swallowed up by the earth is a known depiction of catastrophe in epic poetry (Exod 15:12), and it recurs in echoes of the present incident, of course (Deut 11:6; Ps 106:17). A similar scene is evoked in Exod 14:3, when Pharaoh surmises that the Israelites will perish because "the desert has closed over them *(sāgar ʿalêhem hammidbār)*." We also read of being swallowed up by mighty waters (Ps 69:16). The same symmetry of land and sea is evident in descriptions of the splitting of land and sea (Judg 15:19; Isa 48:21; Ps 141:7). The descent into Sheol is expressed in Ps 55:16: "He imposes death upon them; they descend live into Sheol, for evil doings were present in their habitations."

COMMENT 2: THE STRUGGLE OVER THE PRIESTHOOD—THE PRIESTLY AGENDA

G. B. Gray saw evidence of a two-pronged challenge within the priestly sections of Numbers 16–17. He interpreted Num 16:3, in particular, as reflecting a dispute between all of the Levites and the rest of the Israelite people: *kî kol hāʿēdāh qedôšîm* 'for the entire community are holy'. He saw evidence of the same tension in Num 17:16–26, the test of legitimacy in which Aaron's rod sprouted almonds.

It is more likely that the priestly argumentation relates to one issue alone, but that it develops in several stages, moving from more general or loose statements to the more specific agenda of the priestly writers, namely, the exclusive election of the Aaronide priesthood. This progression is developed in Num 16:5–7 and following: Korah, leader of the rebellion in the priestly versions, was in fact Aaron's (and Moses') first cousin, the son of Uncle Yizhar. We are told as much in Num 16:1, as it was adapted by the priestly writer. Most probably Korah was insistent that the entire Kohathite clan be included in the priesthood, instead of relegating most of its families to the subordinate status of Levites, just like the other clans of Gershon and Merari.

The development of the priestly argument may be understood as telescopic: it begins by questioning what special right the Levites had, as a tribe, to a more sacred status (v 3), and then proceeds to zoom in on individuals ("that person" in v 7), thereby narrowing the context of the dispute. This narrow context continues to inform vv 8–11, so that when the priestly version resumes in v 16 the issue is clearly drawn between Korah and his faction, on the one hand, and Aaron, on the other.

In v 3 we find the notion expressed that the entire Israelite community shared in sanctity; that they were all, in a sense, "sacred *(qedôšîm)*" by virtue of the divine presence in their midst. This view contrasts with the singular form, *qādôš* 'sacred' in v 5, which is applied to the single individual specifically chosen for the priesthood. The priestly writer is transparently playing on the nuances of adjectival *qādôš*.

The divine presence was manifested in the Tabernacle, located at the center of the Israelite encampment. The preposition *betôk* 'in the midst of' emerges as a revealing figure of speech, used frequently in statements affirming God's presence, together with the verb *šākan* 'to dwell, reside'. An example is to be found in the instructions for constructing the Tabernacle in Exod 25:8: *weʿāśû lî miqdāš wešākantî betôkām* 'let them build me a sanctuary that I may reside in their midst' (cf. Exod 29:45–46; Lev 15:31; 16:16; Num 5:3; 35:34; Josh 22:31; 1 Kgs 6:13). The notion of divine immanence is expressed most eloquently in Ezek 37:28: "The nations shall know that I, YHWH, sanctify Israel by the presence of my sanctuary in their midst forever *(biyhôt miqdāšî betôkām le ʿôlām)*" (cf. also Ezek 43:9).

The priestly writers played on the ambiguities of yet another verb, *hiphʿil hiqrîb*. In Num 16:5, *hiqrîb* means "to bring near, include" in an inner circle of intimates whose members operated within the sacred precincts. This is also the sense in Num 16:8–9, where those whom God has brought near are the Levites. So the verb *hiqrîb* may signify varying degrees of intimacy with God. But the priestly writers further employ the verb *hiqrîb* in its cultic sense of "presenting an offering," in this instance the incense offerings of Aaron and Korah and his 250 cohorts (Num 16:17).

In the discussion of the assignments of the three major levitical clans in the COMMENT on Numbers 3–4, I noted the preeminence of the clan of Kohath over the other two levitical clans. It is significant that of the Kohathites, the Korahites in particular appear to have enjoyed considerable status in the practice of the cultic arts. On a jar base dated to the latter half of the eighth century B.C.E., found at Arad, a Negeb site (stratum VII at the site), we find a personnel list that includes *bny qrḥ* (= Hebrew *benê qôraḥ)* 'members of the Korahite guild' (Aharoni 1981: 80–84, no. 49, line 2). This translation of the term *bny* (literally, "sons of") is not meant to negate actual family affiliations at Arad by craftsmen and cultic servitors, but only to emphasize the convention of employing familial nomenclature for institutional or professional categories, as well. In other words, *bny qrḥ* at Arad were most likely cultic functionaries, for many of the names of personnel occurring in the horde of ostraca found at the site are those of the staff of the temple that stood at Arad. The formula *bn x* 'son of So-and-So' is a common way of listing members of such groups (Levine 1963).

Archaeological evidence seems, therefore, to support the theory that, prior to the institutionalization of a tribe of Levites, there were families of skilled practitioners in the cultic arts residing in special areas, usually in proximity to cult centers, who more or less monopolized these arts and transmitted them to their sons and relatives. This subject is discussed at some length in the COMMENT on Numbers 8.

What we have in the priestly reworking of Numbers 16–17 is, then, the record of a grievance brought by the most probable rival of the Amramite family of Aaron and Moses within the Kohathite clan, namely, the Korahites. Would that we possessed historical evidence from later periods of biblical experience bearing on this dispute. Are there other echoes of tension within the Kohathite clan itself? Perhaps Joshua 21, a late source of priestly provenance, echoes just such a situation. The subject of Joshua 21 is the relinquishing of forty-eight towns to the Levites by the Israelite tribes in fulfillment of the dictate of Num 35:7. The Levites were to receive these towns from the Israelite tribes in lieu of the arable land that the other tribes had received, and of which none had been allotted to the Levites.

As related in Joshua 21, the clan of Kohath won the first lottery and was allocated a total of twenty-three towns in Canaan. Of the twenty-three, thirteen went to the Aaronide family of priests, leaving only ten towns for the remaining Kohathites. So whereas belonging to the same clan as the Aaronide priests undoubtedly brought certain privileges, the nonpriestly families of the Kohathite clan—that is to say, three out of the four Kohathite families altogether—received fewer towns than did the Merarites or Gershonites.

Although we are unable to pinpoint a particular historical circumstance as background for the internecine dispute within the clan of Kohath, there would be a certain logic to expecting such disputes in the postexilic community. It must be remembered that the actual history of the Aaronide priesthood still eludes us. As a result, it is most difficult to link a traditional account, such as is preserved in Numbers 16–17, to historical situations. Perhaps Numbers 16–17, in their priestly version, mask a rivalry within the postexilic priesthood. In any event, these chapters establish within Torah literature a unique sanction for the Aaronide priesthood, expressed as the triumph of Aaron over his first cousin, Korah. It may be significant that in the priestly genealogy recorded in 1 Chr 5:29–41 Zadok, the high priest, is affiliated with the Amramite family. In 1 Chr 6:35–38 Zadok is registered as a descendant of Aaron.

In the preceding discussion of the JE narratives in Numbers 16–17 the interaction of JE and P in Num 16:12–35 was clarified. Moses' implied curse in Num 16:15, in the JE narrative, served as a cue for the orchestration of the incense offerings as a test of legitimacy. The priestly narrative actualizes the threat conveyed in Moses' entreaty.

The priestly narrative also involves God's glorious presence, the *kābôd.* When all were assembled in the courtyard of the Tent of Meeting, the glorious presence *(kābôd)* of God appeared before the entire people. Here the *kābôd* appears as a primitive force when God acts to annihilate the insurgent faction and its leader, which prompts Moses and Aaron to intercede and to ask God's mercy (Num 16:20–21). The same dynamic obtains in Num 17:7, when the appearance of the *kābôd* likewise precedes punitive action by God. These scenes recall an earlier crisis of divine wrath, recounted in Num 14:10. On that occasion the derogatory report of the delegation sent to reconnoiter the land of Canaan aroused God's anger.

In the present narrative God agrees to restrict punishment to the insurgent group, and Num 16:35 records their death by a divine fire. There is a parallelism between this narrative and the briefer one in Leviticus 10, which tells of the death of two of Aaron's sons after they had presented an improper incense offering. The theme of improper sacrifice is elsewhere specifically related to incense. In 2 Chr 26:16–21 we read that in his arrogance Uzziah, king of Judah, made an offering on the incense altar within the Temple of Jerusalem, an act properly reserved for priests. He was punished with the skin disease known as *ṣāraʿat*. In chaps. 16–17, more precisely in Num 17:5, we find it explicitly stated that offering incense is the exclusive prerogative of the Aaronide priests.

Numbers 17 is comprised of three sections, two of which surely belong to the priestly source. Most of the specific content of Numbers 17 has been treated in the NOTES. The apotropaic function of incense is exploited by Aaron in stemming a divine plague (Num 17:6–15). Earlier in the chapter, the copper firepans used by the insurgents in presenting their incense offerings are consigned for use in the Sanctuary as an overlay for the altar of burnt offerings (Num 17:1–5). What remains to be elaborated is the separate tale about Aaron's rod (Num 17:15–26), which may derive from a different priestly archive.

Folklorists have noted that the rapid, miraculous sprouting of a dry stick or rod is a motif evident in myth and legend. Herodotus (1971: book iv, 265–266, pars. 67–68) relates that the hero, Heracles, once deposited his club beside a pillar in Traezen, and that the pillar then put forth blossoms. The parallel is not exact, but the result was similar (Gaster 1969: 301, 397).

The literary relationship of the tale in Num 17:16–28 and the rest of Numbers 16–17 is not immediately evident. This tale uses social terms of reference in a way similar to their application in Numbers 1–4, but less precisely. The term *bêt ʾāb* 'patriarchal house' is functionally synonymous, in this tale, with *maṭṭeh* 'tribe'. This usage represents an extension of the social organization projected in Numbers 1–4, namely, that every *naśîʾ* 'chieftain' was, at the same time, the head of a patriarchal house. There is, of course, a play on the term *maṭṭeh*, which means both "staff, rod" and "tribe." But further, there is the clear implication in Num 17:21 that a choice would be made by the Deity from among the thirteen staffs, each with the name of a chieftain written on it. There were twelve rods, plus Aaron's rod, which was placed among them. When Aaron's rod sprouted almonds, it was an indication that the "house of Levi" had been chosen. Retention of Aaron's rod in the Sanctuary was a warning to all who would challenge the chosen status of the tribe of Levi.

The problem with this analysis is that the selection of the tribe of Levi is strictly old business by the time we get to the book of Numbers! In addition, there is a certain ambiguity in Num 17:20, which speaks of the election of a particular person, not of the selection of a tribe, which, in turn, recalls Num 16:6–7. Could it be that this tale was intended to establish Aaron's undisputed leadership of the tribe of Levi?

Perhaps we are wrong to expect consistency in this tale, or to expect that its presuppositions would correlate with those of Num 16:1–17:15, the texts that precede it. In 17:28 we find an allusion to the prohibitions of access associated with earlier rationalizations of levitical functions. Having Levites maintain the Tabernacle complex assured that no "alien *(zār)*"—in this case, no non-Levite—would draw near to the sacred precincts and meet death (cf. Num 1:51; 3:10, 38; 18:7). In Num 17:27–28 this very fear is expressed.

The agenda of Num 17:16–28 is perhaps not the same as that of 16:1–17:15. In the former, the singular role of the tribe of Levi, whose overall chieftain is Aaron (Num 3:32), is different. It is to approach the sacred precincts in order to attend to the operation of the Tabernacle, thereby preventing the threat of a plague, a threat already voiced in Num 8:19, in the record of the dedication of the Levites.

PART XII.

NUMBERS 18: THE DUTIES AND PERQUISITES OF THE PRIESTS AND LEVITES, A SUMMARY STATEMENT

♦

INTRODUCTION

Chapter 18 is composed of a series of laws governing the duties of the Aaronide priesthood and those of the Levites associated with them. In exchange for their services on behalf of their fellow Israelites, priests and Levites were entitled to certain emoluments, which combined to serve as a support system for the clergy. For the most part, the specific provisions of Numbers 18 are anticipated in prior legislation. Numbers 18 presents these requirements in a summary fashion, and regards them as known facts of law. The one exception is an innovative provision, stated in Num 18:25–32, that obligates the Levites to withhold one-tenth of all they receive from the Israelite people as tithes ("a tenth of the tithe"). This quantity was to be remitted by the Levites to the priests.

Two concerns dominate the varied legislation of Numbers 18. The first is the purity of the Sanctuary and of its interior space and contents, and the corresponding purity of the priesthood. Preserving such comprehensive purity required that access to the Sanctuary be restricted to properly consecrated personnel and, further, that the consecrated personnel themselves attend to their own purification. The edifices, furniture, and sacred vessels also had to be protected from defilement. These tasks were among the responsibilities of the priesthood. The other issue at stake is support or compensation for the priests and Levites and for their families. In theory, priestly law, pursuant to Deuteronomic legislation, justifies the entitlements of the clergy in lieu of the territories that were not granted to them, as they were to the other tribes of Israel. The tribe of Levi, to which the Aaronide priesthood also belonged, was not granted a territory in the Promised Land, but was instead guaranteed certain forms of regular income from the revenues of the Sanctuary.

Cultic taxes and sacrificial offerings designated "for YHWH *(l-YHWH)*," or "consecrated for YHWH *(qôdeš l-YHWH)*" were usually earmarked for the priests, in reality. More precisely, those parts of the sacrificial offerings which were not consumed on the altar were usually assigned to the priests. Thus we encounter the formula *qôdeš . . . l-YHWH lakkôhēn* 'consecrated . . . for YHWH, for the priest' (Lev 23:20). In a similar manner, tithes were allocated to the Levites.

The varied contents of Numbers 18 may be outlined as follows:

1. 1–7: The respective duties of the priests and Levites are enumerated. Priests bore primary responsibility for preserving the purity of the Sanctuary and its contents, most notably the altar. The priesthood was also obliged to monitor the purity of its own members. Priests would defile the Sanctuary if, for any of several reasons, they penetrated its space when in an impure state. The Levites, who assisted the priests, had access only to the outer areas of the Sanctuary complex. The overall effect of this legis-

lation was to prevent unconsecrated Israelites, as well as all non-Israelites, of course, from entering sacred space and from having contact with any sacred object or consecrated material. This section of Numbers 18 relates most specifically to Leviticus 8–10 (cf. Exod 29:1–37), where the consecration of the Aaronide priesthood is recorded. Also relevant are Num 8:5–26, containing a parallel description of the dedication of the Levites. The system of levitical assignments that is reflected here was first set forth in Numbers 3–4.

2. 8–20: The priestly emoluments are delineated. Individually and collectively, the Israelite people were obligated to convey to the priests the following types of revenue:

   a. All portions of the "most sacred offerings *(qôdeš haqqodāšîm)*" not consigned to the altar fire. This category included most of the grain offerings, along with the sin and guilt offerings. The basic legislation is stated in Lev 6:1–7:10. The edible portions of the most sacred offerings were to be consumed by pure priests, within the sacred precincts of the Sanctuary (Num 18:8–10).

   b. Specified portions from "the sacred gifts of greeting *(šelāmîm)*" went to the priests. These portions are here referred to as *terûmāh* 'levied donation' and *tenûpāh* 'presentation offering'. The basic legislation appears in Lev 7:11–38 (Num 18:11).

   c. All offerings of firstfruits and of the first yields of grain, wine, and oil went to the priests. This provision recalls various laws appearing in Exod 23:16–19; Deut 18:4; 26:1–11; and Lev 2:14; and 23:17–18 (Num 18:12–13).

   d. Anything proscribed under the provisions of the *ḥērem* 'ban' went to the priests. This law recalls Lev 27:21 and 28–29, which speak of fields that had become temple property under the law of *ḥērem*. In a more general way, the present law relates to the entire subject of the *ḥērem*, as expressed in Deut 7:28 and 13:18, and in the narratives of Joshua 6–7.

   e. All firstborn males, of man and beast, went to the priests. Firstborn human males were to be redeemed, and their value, plus a surcharge, remitted to the priests. Firstlings of impure species of animals, unfit for use as sacrifices, were also to be redeemed, and their value, plus a surcharge, remitted to the priests. These laws recall Exod 13:2, 11–13; 22:28; 34:19–20; Deut 12:17; 14:23; 15:19–23; and Lev 27:1–13, all of which are statements pertaining to the widespread practice of devoting the firstborn to God (Num 18:15–18). Verses 19–20 summarize the theory underlying the provisions of Numbers 18. The grants to the priests and Levites were intended to compensate for their exclusion from the land grants awarded to the tribes of Israel as a whole (cf. Num 18:18, above).

3. 21–24: The Levites were to collect from the Israelites one-tenth of the annual produce of the fields, vineyards, and orchards. The primary laws governing tithes are found in Deut 12:17–19 and 14:22–29, as well as in Lev 27:30–32, which, however, differ among themselves in their specific provisions.
4. 25–32: This section presents a novel law, requiring the Levites themselves to contribute to the priests one-tenth of all they collected as tithes. This gift counted as their way of supporting the Sanctuary, in lieu of what Israelites would contribute in other forms. The Levites had little wealth of their own. They were, however, only auxiliary personnel, and for this reason were not exempt from supporting the cultic establishment. This requirement epitomized their subserviance to the Aaronide priests.

It is of interest to note that in Ezek 44:29–30 we find a brief statement that incorporates much of the legislation summarized in Numbers 18.

TRANSLATION

18 [1]YHWH said to Aaron: You, your sons and your patriarchal house with you shall incur [punishment] for defilement of the Sanctuary, just as you and your sons with you shall incur [punishment] for the defilement of your [own] priestly group.

[2]Dedicate as well your kinsmen with you, the tribe of Levi, your paternal tribe, that they may be associated with you and assist you and your sons with you in front of the Tent of the Covenant.

[3]They shall be charged with caring for you, and with maintaining the overall Tent structure, but they may not have access to the vessels of the Shrine, or to the altar, lest both they and you meet with death!

[4]They shall be associated with you in maintaining the Tent of Meeting, in all tasks pertaining to the Tent structure. No alien shall encroach upon you,

[5]but you, yourselves, must undertake the maintenance of the Shrine and the altar, so that wrath may never again assail the Israelite people.

[6]I hereby select your kinsmen, the Levites, from among the Israelite people to be given in service to you. [They are] dedicated to YHWH, to perform the tasks that pertain to the Tent of Meeting.

[7]But you, and your sons with you, shall carefully fulfill the charge of your priesthood in all that pertains to the altar, and to what is located inside the *pārôket* screen. I will make of your priesthood a service of dedication, and any alien who intrudes shall be put to death.

[8]YHWH spoke to Aaron: I hereby grant to you control over my levied

donations, including all of the sacred offerings of the Israelite people. To you and to your sons I grant them as a share, as a permanent entitlement.

9 This is what you are to receive from the most sacred offerings, from the offerings by fire: all of their offerings, including all of their grain offerings and sin offerings, and guilt offerings that they must deliver to me as most sacred offerings—all this shall belong to you and your sons.

10 You must eat this in the most sacred precincts. Every male shall partake of it; it shall be consecrated as yours.

11 This, too, shall be yours: the levied donations that comprise their gifts, as well as all of the presentation offerings of the Israelite people, to you have I granted them and to your sons and your daughters with you, as a permanent statutory allocation. Every pure person in your household may partake of it.

12 All of the richest, new oil and all of the richest contents of wine and grain, their prime yield, which they [regularly] devote to YHWH—to you have I granted them.

13 The first yield of all that grows in their land, which they [regularly] convey to YHWH, shall belong to you. Every pure person in your household may partake of it.

14 Whatever has been proscribed on the part of Israelites shall be yours.

15 The first issue of the womb of every living creature, which they [regularly] dedicate to YHWH, of human and beast, shall be yours. But you must provide for the redemption of the first issue of humans, and redeem as well the firstlings of impure animals.

16 You shall collect their redemption payments, on behalf of all over one month of age, in the equivalent of five shekels of silver, according to the shekel of the Sanctuary, which contains twenty grains.

17 You may not, however, permit the redemption of the firstlings of oxen, or the firstlings of lambs, or the firstlings of goats. These are preconsecrated; their blood you must dash on the altar, and their fatty portions you must burn as an offering by fire, producing a pleasant aroma for YHWH.

18 Their flesh shall be yours, like the breast of the presentation offering; like the right thigh—they shall belong to you.

19 All of the sacred levied donations that the Israelite people raise for YHWH have I granted to you and to your sons and your daughters with you, as a permanent statutory allocation. It is like the permanent rule [requiring use] of salt in the presence of YHWH, for you and your descendants with you.

20 YHWH said to Aaron: You will not be granted an estate in their land, nor any territory among them. I represent your territory and the estate you are granted among the Israelite people.

21 To the Levites I have awarded every tithe in Israel, in lieu of a land grant; as exchange for the tasks they will be performing by attending to the Tent of Meeting.

[22]This is so that Israelite persons will no longer encroach upon the Tent of Meeting, thereby incurring the penalty of dying.

[23]It is the Levites who shall perform the tasks pertaining to the Tent of Meeting, and they shall bear any punishment for their neglect. It (= the tithe) is a permanent statutory allocation throughout your generations. But they (= the Levites) will not receive a land grant among the Israelite people.

[24]For I have given to the Levites, in lieu of a granted estate, the tithes of the Israelite people, which they collect for YHWH as levied donations. Consequently, I have informed them that they will not receive a land grant among the Israelite people.

[25]YHWH spoke to Moses as follows:

[26]You shall address the Levites and say to them, "When you collect from the Israelite people the tithe that I have given to you in lieu of your land grant, you shall withhold from it as the levied donation for YHWH a tenth of the tithe.

[27]"Your levied donation will count for you the same as grain from the threshing floor and ripe fruit from the vat.

[28]"In this way you shall withhold the levied donations for YHWH from all of your tithes, which you collect from the Israelite people. Out of that you shall remit the levied donation for YHWH to Aaron, the priest.

[29]"From all gifts conveyed to you, you shall withhold the entire levied donation for YHWH; from all of its richest contents—the consecrated portion of it."

[30]You shall say to them, "When you have withheld [an amount] from its richest contents, it shall count for the Levites the same as the yield from the threshing floor and the yield from the vat.

[31]"You may then partake of it (= the tithe) anywhere, you and your household. For it is compensation to you, in exchange for performance of your tasks relevant to the Tent of Meeting.

[32]"By withholding its richest contents from it, you will avoid bearing punishment over it, and will not cause the defilement of the sacred offerings of the Israelite people and thereby meet with death."

NOTES

18 1. Hebrew *ʿawôn* and similar terms such as *ḥēṭʾ*, which mean "sin, offense," often connote not the act itself but the consequences of the act. Thus *yiśśeʾû ʾet ʿawôn hammiqdāš* precisely translated means, "they shall bear the *consequences of* the defilement of the Sanctuary." But there is an added dimension of meaning, as though *ʿawôn* were doing "double duty." The offense or sin being referred to here is either initial defilement or the failure to restore the purity of the Sanctuary after it had been defiled. So I translate

"you shall incur *punishment* for the *defilement* of the Sanctuary." Compare Num 9:13: "that person shall bear the punishment for his offense *(ḥeṭ'ô yiśśā')*." Note similar usages in Exod 28:43; Lev 5:1; 19:8; and farther on in Num 18:22 and 32.

Two defilements are indicated here: the defilement of the Sanctuary and "the defilement of your priestly group *('awôn kehunnatkem)*." Hebrew *kehunnāh* may refer, in the abstract, to the priestly office or "the priesthood" (Num 25:13; Exod 40:15; Josh 18:7). Here it seems likely that reference is to the fellowship of priests, as is the sense in 1 Sam 2:36, where a disenfranchised priest pleads, "please assign me to one of the priestly groups *('el 'aḥat hakkehunnôt)* so that I may have a morsel of bread to eat." For this usage compare Ezra 2:62; Neh 7:64; 13:29; and in Late Hebrew, Mishna, *Yômā'*, 1:5, 7, *Sanhedrîn* 9:6.

you and your sons with you. Numbers 18 uses declined forms of the preposition *'et* quite regularly, as in the present verse: *'attāh ûbānêkā 'ittak*; see below in Num 18:7, 9, 19.

2. *kinsmen.* Hebrew *'aḥ* 'brother' here has the sense of "kinsman" in general, referring to members of the same household, clan, or tribe. It may even designate a fellow Israelite in contradistinction to non-Israelites. See below in Num 18:6; and compare Deut 1:16; 15:11; 18:18; and in priestly legislation, Lev 25:14.

the tribe of Levi. The designation *maṭṭeh Lēwî* first occurs in Num 1:49, where it is explained. It recurs in Num 17:18. In Numbers 7, which records the donations of all tribal chieftains, Hebrew *maṭṭeh* is the consistent term for "tribe." Although *maṭṭeh* is a distinctively priestly term of reference, with *šēbeṭ* 'staff, tribe' being a term of more general use, the two terms are virtually interchangeable in Numbers. Both express the semantic transaction by which a word meaning "staff" designates the unit arrayed around, or organized under, such a symbol of jurisdiction.

your paternal tribe. The designation *šēbeṭ 'ābîkā* is unique to this verse. Most likely it represents a variation on the better-known term *bêt 'āb* 'patriarchal house' employed above in v 1. The intent may have been to emphasize the contrast between v 1 and v 2. Verse 1 speaks of the restrictive "house" of Aaron, whereas v 2 deals with the broad tribal base of the Levites as a group.

Dedicate. Hebrew *hiqrîb* means "bring near, dedicate." Compare its sense in Num 8:9–10, where we read of the actual dedication of the Levites. Note also the provisions of Num 3:6–10 concerning the status of the Levites (cf. Exod 28:1; 29:4; 40:12; Lev 7:35).

It is worth mentioning that the verb *qiddēš* 'to consecrate', used in reference to the ordination of the priests in Leviticus 8, is never employed to describe the dedication of the Levites, only verbs such as *hiqrîb* 'to bring near' and *nātan* 'to dedicate, hand over'. This distinction reflects the difference in status between priests and Levites.

they may be associated. Use of the verb *weyillāwû* (literally, "they shall encircle, accompany"), is probably a wordplay on the name *Lēwî,* deriving it from the verb *lāwāh* 'to encircle, accompany'. Presumably Levites received their name from their function, as those who marched around the Sanctuary or carried cultic furnishing "around." The same derivation is assumed in the *Namengebung* of the child *Lēwî* in Gen 29:34, and some modern scholars have actually adopted this transparent etymology.

Use of the *niph'al* of the verb *lāwāh,* such as we have here and in v 4, below, is relatively late in biblical Hebrew. In Isa 14:1 and 56:6, both late passages, this verb characterized the activity of non-Israelites who joined the people of Israel, both in exile and later on in the homeland. Similar contexts are evident in Jer 50:5; Zech 2:15; and Esth 9:21. In Ps 83:9 the verb *lāwāh* characterizes a military alliance.

Another verb intimately associated with the Levites is *šēret* 'to serve', which almost always refers, in context, to cultic service. In Num 8:26 it is used to characterize the service to be rendered by the Levites, and the same is true in Deut 18:7. This verb is prominent in the stories about young Samuel, serving at the shrine of Shiloh (1 Sam 2:18; 3:1), and in Ezek 44:11–12 and 16 it again classifies the specific function of the Levites in contradistinction to that of the Zadokite priests. Here, too, the verb *šēret* contrasts with *qārab* 'to approach' the altar, which characterizes the exclusive role of the priests. See below, in v 3.

the Tent of the Covenant. The relatively rare designation *'ôhel hā'ēdût* also occurs in Num 9:15 and 17:22–23. It is synonymous with *miškan hā'ēdût* in Num 1:53.

3. *They shall be charged.* Hebrew *mišmeret* attests several principal connotations, sometimes confused by scholars who expect a consistent meaning. In the Notes on Num 1:53 these nuances are explained. The sense most appropriate here is that of performing a charge or duty, of whatever nature is required. The Levites were to do what the priests instructed them to do, along with maintaining the Tent.

vessels of the shrine. Hebrew *kelê haqqôdeš* is ambiguous, because *qôdeš* can mean "holiness," expressed adjectivally as "sacred," or "a holy place, Shrine." Here "vessels of the Shrine" is better, for it indicates where the relevant vessels were positioned. In Num 18:7, below, these vessels are further identified as those situated inside the *pārôket* screen. Levites were forbidden to have contact with vessels so placed.

lest . . . they . . . meet with death. The negative formulation *welō' yāmûtû* has a preventive connotation: "lest they die!"

4. *alien.* The various nuances of Hebrew *zār* are governed by context. Here *zār* refers to an Israelite who is neither a consecrated priest nor a devoted Levite. Elsewhere, *zār* may define one's position as an outsider with respect to the family (Deut 25:5). The basic sense of *zār* is "hateful," from a verbal root

z-w-r, cognate to Akkadian *zeru* 'to hate'. The term *zār* expresses the phenomenon of xenophobia.

5. *undertake the maintenance.* Here the formula *šāmar mišmeret* means, literally, "to maintain the maintenance," as explained above, in the NOTE on v 3.

wrath. The reference to *qeṣep* 'froth, wrath' takes us back to the preceding chapter, 17, where we read that divine wrath was unleashed against the Israelites during the Korah insurrection (see the NOTES on Num 17:5, 10–15). At the conclusion of Numbers 17 (vv 27–28), we read that the people were anxiety-ridden over the problem of approaching the Sanctuary, fearing they would be stricken once again by God's wrath. Numbers 18 addresses this problem at the outset; it states quite emphatically that divine wrath can be averted if the priests and Levites fulfill their respective charges properly. If only those permitted to do so "approach" the Sanctuary and Shrine, the people will be safe. This is the force of Num 18:1: only the Aaronide priests may penetrate the inner precincts of the Sanctuary.

6. *to be given in service to you. [They are] dedicated to YHWH.* The phrasing of the Masorah is somewhat misleading. Hebrew *mattānāh* is not the object of *netûnîm*, and the clause is not to be rendered "devoted to you as a grant." Rather, we have appositional statements: *lākem mattānāh—netûnîm l-YHWH* 'to be given in service to you—they are dedicated to YHWH'.

This proposed phrasing accords better with the next verse, where we find the composite term *ʿabôdat mattānāh* 'a service of dedication'. It also corresponds to what is said of the Levites in the record of their dedication (Num 8:16) and earlier, in the work assignments of the levitical clans (Num. 3:9). The point is that the Levites are devoted not to the priests, but ultimately to YHWH. They work for the priests, but are bound to God (Speiser 1963b).

Just as forms of the verb *šāmar* 'to guard, keep' were subject to subtle nuances, so the verb *ʿābad* 'to serve' has differing applications. Here, the formula *laʿabôd ʾet ʿabôdat ʾôhel môʿēd* means "*to perform the tasks* pertaining to the Tent of Meeting." Clearly it does not refer to officiating in the cult! The same is true of usage in v 7, which follows. Compare Exod 30:16 for the same formula, and Num 4:23 and 27 for the same work assignment (cf. also Num 16:9).

7. The priests are to perform their special "charges *(mišmeret)*." Once again, see the NOTES on Num 1:53 for the several connotations of the Hebrew term *mišmeret.*

inside the pārôket screen. In the phrase *ûlemibbêt lappārôket* we have a cluster of prefixed elements: *w* + *l* + *m(n)*, and in the following word we have an additional prefixed preposition, *lamed.* The doubling of prepositional elements was characteristic of early Phoenician syntax. In the Phoenician inscription of Kilamuwa from Zinjirli (Gibson 1982: 34, line 12) we read, *lmnʿry* 'ever since my youth', and in the Karatepe inscription (Gibson 1982: 46, line

4), *lmmṣ' šmš* 'from the rising of the sun'. Ugaritic attests the same phenomenon in such forms as *wlbbt* 'and well inside the temple' *(Ugaritica* V, no. 11, line 11; Rainey 1973), and *lbrmṣt* 'inside the corral' *(KTU* 1.41, 18–19). We encounter such proliferation in late biblical texts; compare 1 Chr 15:13 *lemibbārî'šônāh* 'from the very beginning', and rabbinic Hebrew (Levine 1985a: 151, n. 24).

Elsewhere, the term *pārôket* occurs only once in the book of Numbers, at Num 4:5, in the construction *pārôket hammāsāk* 'the screened *pārôket*', and there the term itself is explained.

As described in Exod 25:1–27:21, the interior of the Tent of Meeting was divided into two areas separated by the *pārôket* screen. The area behind the screen, the innermost part of the Tent, was known as "the Holy of Holies." This name actually occurs in Num 18:10, below, where its significance is explained. In this section of the Tent stood the Ark, covered by its sculpted lid, the *kappôret.* In front of the screen, in the area first encountered when entering the Tent, stood the Menorah, the golden incense altar, and the presentation table. The outer entrance of the Tent was covered by a drape or curtain. The entire Tent structure stood within a bounded courtyard, open to the sky, with the altar of burnt offerings positioned in line with the entrance to the Tent.

As in Num 18:9 and 11, below, prepositional *lamed* here connotes relevance. Thus *lekol debar hammiqdāš* means "in all that *pertains to* the altar."

8. The sense of this verse is that all income deriving from the levied donations of the Israelites, to be specified farther on, and from sacred offerings as well belongs to the priests as their entitlement.

control. Here the sense of *mišmeret* is "control, jurisdiction"; see the NOTES on Num 1:53, where this connotation is mentioned. A similar sense is probably expressed in 1 Chr 12:30: *šômerê mišmeret bêt Šā'ûl* 'protecting the *interests* of the House of Saul' (so *NJPS).* Perhaps we could translate "the *executors* of the House of Saul."

levied donations. The Hebrew term *terûmāh* first occurs in Num 5:9, where it is explained. It recurs in this chapter in various combinations (see below, in vv 12, 24, 26–32). It may refer to a variety of levies and donations, including those contributed voluntarily. Thus, in Exod 25:1 the voluntary gifts of the Israelites to the Sanctuary project were termed *terûmāh.*

as a share. Hebrew *lemošḥāh* requires specific comment because it has often been confused with the verb *māšaḥ* 'to anoint'. We have homonyms in biblical Hebrew: (1) *māšaḥ* I 'to anoint', a denominative of *mešaḥ* 'oil', a word common in Aramaic; and (2) *māšaḥ* II 'to measure'. This verb is reflected in Ezek 28:14: "I created you as a cherub with *long-extended,* protecting [wings] *(mimšaḥ hassôkēk).*" It is in Aramaic, however, that we find nominal forms of this verb. In the Elephantine legal papyri of the fifth century B.C.E. we find the term *mišḥetā'* 'measurement'. Akkadian attests the cognates *mišiḥtu* (Late

Babylonian *mĕsḥatu)* 'measure'. So in Num 18:8, *lemošḥāh* means "as a share, for a share."

The situation in biblical Hebrew is, however, a bit more complex, when we consider Lev 7:35: "This shall constitute the share of *(mišḥat)* Aaron, and *the share of (ûmišḥat)* his sons." The form *lemošḥāh* in the present verse is a variant of *mišḥāh,* vocalized as a cohortative infinitive, probably because it was misunderstood as deriving from *māšaḥ* I 'to anoint'. There is, however, no mention in this passage of anointing. In Lev 7:35 there is, indeed, reason for confusion, because in the subsequent verse we have a reference to the anointing of the priests: *beyôm mošḥô ʾōtām* 'on the day of his anointing them'. Accordingly, the Septuagint renders *mišḥat ʾAharôn : hei chrîsis* 'unction', but in Num 18:8 it renders *lemošḥāh* as *eis geras* 'for a share'. This translation is in context and indicates an awareness of *māšaḥ* II 'to measure'. It is likely, however, that in Lev 7:35 we have the same word as we have here, further demonstrating the link between this chapter and Leviticus 6–7 (Levine 1982a).

9. *from the offerings by fire.* The words *min hāʾēš,* literally, "from the fire," have occasioned comment. M. Haran (1962) sees in them evidence of a development that occurred in the mode of Israelite sacrifice. In the course of time, parts of certain sacrifices came to be kept from the altar fire in offerings that had previously required the total burning of the victim on the altar, in the manner of the *ʿôlāh.* Haran actually bases his analysis on Num 18:9, arguing that the parts allotted to the priests were "rescued" from the altar fire, *min hāʾēš.*

More likely, however, *min hāʾēš* has a different meaning: "from the fire [offering]" (cf. the rendering in *NJPS*). As such, *ʾēš* has the same function as *ʾiššeh* 'offering by fire', below, in v 17. See the NOTES on Num 15:2.

The second part of v 9 delineates the types of offerings that come under the provisions of Numbers 18. We find repeated forms of the particle *kol* 'all, every', emphasizing the inclusiveness of the law, its broad scope. A whole array of grants was awarded to the priests. For similar administrative listings see Lev 11:46 and 22:18.

offerings. The term *qorbān* is generic, designating all sorts of offerings and votives, and not necessarily sacrifices per se. In Numbers 7 it is used to refer to the sacred vessels that were donated by the tribal chiefs at the dedication of the Tabernacle. Literally, *qorbān* means "that which is brought near, presented." Artifacts bearing the inscription *qorbān* have been discovered in archaeological excavations, dating from the period of the Second Temple of Jerusalem. The objects themselves were forms of *qorbān* (Fitzmyer 1959; Mazar 1969).

The three types of "most sacred offerings" mentioned here require special comment. (There is no reference to the *ʿôlāh* 'burnt offering', which is of this class of sacrifices, for the obvious reason that it was offered as a holocaust. Except for hides, nothing of value would remain from such sacrifices.)

grain offerings. There were several types of *minḥāh,* which had a role in both private and public ritual. Except for the daily grain offering brought by the high priest (Lev 6:12–16), which was a holocaust, grain offerings were baked or fried, and only a small part of the dough was placed on the altar. The term *minḥāh* is explained in the NOTES on Num 4:16, and its basic features are legislated in Leviticus 2. We find this type of sacrifice being used for different ritual purposes, and the NOTES on Num 5:18, 25; 6:17; 7:13; 8:8; and 15:4 provide information on such utilization of the *minḥāh.*

sin offerings. The meaning and functions of the two principal types of *ḥaṭṭā't* are discussed in the NOTES on Num 8:8. Clearly, reference here is to the type of *ḥaṭṭā't* of which parts were eaten by the priests.

guilt offerings. This type of sacrifice had no role in the public cult. It was actually a penalty, and it was only paid in the *form* of a sacrifice. The *'āšām* was required, along with restitution, for certain offenses involving the misappropriation of sacred property, an offense known as *ma'al* (Lev 5:14–26).

that they must deliver to me as most sacred offerings. Use of the verb *hēšîb* "to restore, return" in v 9 is of interest. In certain contexts *hēšîb* means "to remit, repay," as in Num 5:7–8, where it likewise expresses payment of the penalty called *'āšām.* The verb *hēšîb* derives from the administrative vocabulary.

In the clause *'ašer yāšîbû lî qôdeš qodāšîm* we have an instance of adverbial force being expressed without the usual prepositional *lamed,* whose use would have produced *leqôdeš qodāšîm.*

10. *the most sacred precincts.* Here, in contrast to the preceding verse, *qôdeš haqqodāšîm* has spatial meaning, demarcating an interior area of the Tabernacle (see above, in the NOTES on v 7). Only male priests in a state of purity were permitted to partake of these offerings, not the female members of their families (see Lev 6:11, 22). The families of priests were permitted, however, to eat foodstuffs coming from less sacred donations, as provided in v 11, directly below.

11. This verse lists additional grants to the priesthood, which is the force of the Hebrew *wezeh lekā* 'This, too, shall be yours'.

the levied donations that comprise their gifts. The composite term *terûmat mattānām* is somewhat ambiguous. Either it means "the levied donation of their giving," in which case *mattānām* (from an original form, *mantānām)* represents an infinitive; or it is to be rendered "their gift of the levied donation," in which case *mattānām* represents a noun, *mattān,* a masculine counterpart of the more common feminine *mattānāh* 'gift'. In Gen 34:12 we have the parallelism of *môhar* 'connubial gift' and *mattān* 'gift', suggesting that here, as well, *mattānām* is simply a declined noun.

The Hebrew term *tenûpāh* and the essential rite it designates are explained in the NOTES on Num 8:11. Reference here is to the law of Lev 7:28–34, where it is stipulated that certain sections of the *šelāmîm* offerings were given to the priests.

In Lev 7:28–34, however, the relevant sections are called *hazeh hattenûpāh* 'the breast of the presentation offering' and *šôq hatterûmāh* 'the thigh of the levied donation' (Lev 7:34). Compare also similar usage in Lev 8:27, 29; and Num 6:20. The essential character of the *šelāmîm* offering is explained in the NOTES on Num 6:14.

Daughters of priests and the other females in their households could partake of the preceding offerings because, in contrast to those which were "most sacred," these were of "lesser sanctity," in the language of the Mishna, *qodāšîm qallîm* (Mishna, *Qiddûšîn,* 2:8).

12–13. These two verses enumerate various kinds of firstfruits and first yields of grain. The governing principle was that before one could enjoy the produce of the land, an offering to God, the source of the bounty, was required. Only once this was done were humans free to benefit from the yield of the earth. Hebrew *ḥēleb* means "fat," both of animals (Gen 4:4; Isa 1:11) and of grains, such as wheat (Deut 32:14; Ps 81:17). It is less usual to find *ḥēleb* characterizing wine and oil (but see Gen 45:18).

The original order in which the three forms of yield were listed was *dāgān, tîrôš, weyisḥār* 'grain, wine, and oil', as in Hos 2:10 and 24; and Deut 7:13. The order here is inverted, which probably indicates the adaptation of the formula by priestly writers.

The first yields of field, vineyard, and olive grove must be devoted to God. The two terms for first yield, *rēʾšît* and *bikkûrîm,* interact in vv 12–13. (The two terms occur in construct in Exod 23:19; 34:26.) Hebrew *rēʾšît* is explained in the NOTES on Num 15:20–21. The Hebrew term *bikkûrîm* occurred once before in Num 13:20, in a passing reference. Its matrix is in the animal kingdom. A firstling is called *bekôr* (see below, in vv 15–17). *Piʿel bikkēr* 'to declare as firstborn, to produce a firstling' (Deut 21:16; Lev 27:26) is denominative of *bekôr,* and in turn gave us the noun *bikkûrîm* 'firstfruits' (Exod 23:16; Lev 2:14). Here we have an example of the semantic transaction whereby "first" means "foremost, best." Actually, the best oil comes from the first pressing of the olives.

Verses 12b–13a restate the principle underlying most of the provisions of Numbers 18: in practical terms, whatever the Israelites devote to YHWH goes to the priests. The gifts are first presented to God and then allocated to the priests. All members of priestly households may partake of these donations, as long as they are ritually pure at the time.

14. *Whatever has been proscribed.* The *ḥērem* operated in ancient Israel as a major practice (Stern 1991). Essentially, the verb *ḥāram,* which has cognates in other Semitic languages, means "to separate, set aside." Compare the

Akkadian name of a certain grade of sequestered priestess, *ḫarimtu*, and the attendant status *ḫarimūtu* (*CAD Ḫ*, 101–102). This vocabulary expresses the semantics of the sacred, whereby holiness is perceived as "otherness," as something apart from the profane or ordinary.

In biblical Hebrew, usage of the verb *ḥāram* and related forms is consistently negative, bearing the sense "to condemn, proscribe." Num 18:14 is referring to laws governing the appropriation of condemned property by the Temple establishment. Thus one condemned to death for sacrificing to other gods lost possession of his property (Exod 22:19; Lev 27:21, 29). In Ezra 10:5–8 we read of a decree adjuring all the Jews to assemble in Jerusalem on a particular date. Those failing to appear would have their property condemned! Spoils seized in the wars of conquest were *ḥērem* and became Temple property (Deut 13:18; Joshua 6–7; 1 Sam 15:8–9).

15. *of every living creature.* The formulation *lekol behēmāh* is further specified as *bā'ādām ûbabbehēmāh* 'of human and beast'. This method of explication, by which a general category is stated and then defined more specifically, is common in legal and ritual texts. The primary law was stated in Exod 34:19–20, against the background of the earlier provisions of Exod 13:1 and 11–16 regarding the laws of redemption.

of every living creature. The nuances of Hebrew *bāśār* are well known. In Gen 6:12 *kol bāśār* 'all flesh' most probably included reference to the animal kingdom, in the context of the flood narrative. "All flesh" had been corrupted.

redeem. The verb *pādāh*, used here, also occurs in the Exodus passages. This passage does not, however, specify what is to be done with impure firstlings left unredeemed. The purpose of the law is to afford the Sanctuary the equivalent value in silver of firstlings unfit for sacrifice. The wording of this verse and the next, recalls Lev 27:11 and 27, where the specifications of the system of votive redemptions are spelled out. The Sanctuary, through its administering priesthood, established valuations based on age and gender and imposed a surcharge of 20 percent on redemptions. Firstborn sons of Israelites must always be redeemed. God had first claim on them.

first issue of the womb. Hebrew *peṭer reḥem* appeared for the first time in Num 3:11, where it is explained. In Num 8:16 it occurs again in the feminine construction, *piṭrat reḥem*, with reference to the devotion of the Levites, who substituted for the firstborn sons of the Israelites.

16. This verse expands on the previous one and states that humans became eligible for redemption upon reaching the age of one month. At that point a child was considered viable and likely to survive.

their redemption payments. The passive participial form *pedûyâw* means "its redemption payments," as is explained in the NOTES on Num 3:46. The plural expresses abstraction, in the same way that *neʿûrîm* means "youth, youthfulness" and *zeqûnîm* means "old age."

the equivalent. The meaning of *ʿerkekā* is clear; but the specific form used here, with the pronominal suffix, requires explanation. This bound form occurs in Lev 5:15 and 25; and 27:1–8, in the actual sources of the present legislation. The second-person masculine form, *ʿerkekā*, literally, "your equivalent," became a bound form, so that we can refer to *hā-ʿerkekā* 'the "your equivalent"' (Lev 27:23). In Lev 27:1 we find the formulation *beʿerkekā nepāšôt* 'in the "your equivalent" of lives', which corresponds to 2 Kgs 12:5: *ʾîš kesep napšôt ʿerkô* 'the silver of each person's life equivalent' (Levine 1989b: 30–31, 203, n. 24).

Pursuant to the provisions of Leviticus 27, the present law assigns the redemption payments of firstborn Israelites to the priests. The price was set at five shekels by the sanctuary weight for a child of one month's age. Each shekel weighed twenty grains of silver. For further information on weights and measures, see the NOTES on Num 3:47–48.

17. *These are preconsecrated.* Firstlings of animals fit for sacrifice, such as large cattle, or sheep and goats, could not be redeemed because they were sacred by the fact of their birth. God had prior claim on them. This is the force of *qôdeš hēm.* Such firstlings could only be used in sacrifices unless they originally had, or subsequently developed, blemishes of the kinds that rendered animals unsuitable for sacrifice (cf. Lev 22:19–22). This matter was the subject of extensive legislation by the Jewish Sages in postbiblical times, who established criteria for releasing firstlings who developed blemishes or had exhibited them initially. Tractate *Bekôrôt* of the Babylonian Talmud deals with the relevant procedures.

Hebrew *šôr, keśeb, ʿēz* 'ox, lamb, goat' is a common combination (Lev 7:23; 17:3; 22:27). Idiomatically, it is a merism, referring to all classes of domestic livestock.

In the usual procedures for sacrificing *šelāmîm* offerings, blood from the sacrificial victim is dashed on the altar, and the fatty portions of the animal are burned in the altar fire (Leviticus 3; Lev 7:11–34). The term *ʾiššeh* 'offering by fire' was explained in the NOTES on Num 15:3.

18. The flesh of firstlings offered as sacrifices, more precisely, those portions of meat not placed on the altar accrue to the priests. The point is that there is a difference between the disposition of the *šelāmîm* according to Lev 7:11–34 and the present legislation. The unburned flesh of firstlings is not divided between priests and donors, as is that of *šelāmîm* offerings, but is entirely assigned to the priests.

Although the law here is clearly modeled on the law of the *šelāmîm* offering, as its formulation indicates, it applies the provisions of that law to another category. The law states that all of the unburned flesh of firstlings is of a status comparable with the specific sections of the *šelāmîm*, the breast and thigh, which go to the priests. See the NOTES on v 11, above, for the sense of the term *tenûpāh* 'presentation offering'.

19–20. The next two verses recapitulate the provisions of vv 8–18.

the permanent rule [requiring use] of salt. The formulation *berît melaḥ ʿôlām* deserves comment because it has been the subject of considerable discussion. Some scholars have assumed that salt had a particular role in covenant enactment, and that *berît melaḥ* meant "a covenant made binding by salt," or the like. They have referred to treaty curses found in ancient Near Eastern documents, which refer to salt. These statements admonish anyone who might violate the treaty that his arable land or towns would be sown with salt as punishment. Some have referred to the symbolic use of salt in the conventions of hospitality as indicating its legal effects (Fensham 1962).

It is more likely, however, that the law of Lev 2:13 and its reflex in the present verse have nothing to do with covenant enactment or with treaty curses. The term *berît,* in these statements, simply means "binding obligation, rule, commitment." It is said of the Sabbath that it is *berît ʿôlām* 'a binding observance for all time' (Exod 31:10). The bread of display is termed *berît ʿôlām* in Lev 24:8, whereas in the next verse, Lev 24:9, it is designated *ḥôq ʿôlām* 'a statutory obligation for all time', thus suggesting that the two terms, *berît* and *ḥôq,* are synonymous. The point is that it is the actual requirement to use salt that constitutes the *berît.* What the present verse states is that the entitlements assigned to the priests in vv 8–19 have the same binding force as the rule requiring the salting of sacrifices stated in Lev 2:13. There it is stated emphatically that the salting of sacrifices must never cease!

20. This verse expresses the underlying theory of the priestly support system, ordained in Deut 18:1–2. Deuteronomy addresses the levitical priests rather than the Aaronide clan because Deuteronomy classifies all priests as Levites and does not project the distinction between priests and Levites so basic to the book of Numbers. The principle is the same, however: the priesthood would receive no grant of land or territory in Canaan, unlike the tribes of Israel as a whole. The priests would be granted cultic entitlements in place of territory. The key terms are *ḥēleq* 'area, territory', and *naḥalāh* 'possession, estate'. These two terms often occur together synonymously (Gen 31:14; Deut 10:9; 12:12).

Whereas *ḥēleq* is merely a term of measurement, *naḥalāh* reflects a complex legal system. In biblical Hebrew, the verb *nāḥal* means "to possess, appropriate," and its connotations always reflect the orientation of the recipient. A *naḥalāh,* however acquired, represents what is received. From the Mari dialect of Akkadian we learn that the cognate, *naḫālu,* means "to hand over (property), to convey" (*CAD* N, 1.126, *naḫālu* B). The related noun *niḫlatu* means "property handed over, transferred" (*CAD* N, 2.219, *niḫlatu*). The Ugaritic attestations of the cognate *nḥlt* are especially instructive. Baal speaks of "the mountain of my estate (*ǵr nḥlty*)" (Gibson 1978: 49, 3c, lines 26–28). The home of Kothar-wa-Hasis in Memphis is referred to as *ḥkpt arṣ nḥlth* 'Memphis, the land of his estate' (Gibson 1978: 55, F 16), and the term *arṣ nḥlth* 'the land of his estate' recurs in a description of the habitat of the god Mot (Gibson 1978: 66, 4.viii.13–14). In biblical Hebrew, the cognate of this noun, *naḥalāh,* may have generated a denominative verb, *nāḥal* 'to receive, possess a *naḥalāh*'. So we end up with two sides of the coin: receipt and conveyance.

Initially the verb *nāḥal,* and the term *naḥalāh,* had nothing necessarily to do with inheritance, but because land was the mainstay of family estates, it is understandable that these terms would appropriate the sense of "inheritance." In reality, the *naḥalāh* was initially obtained by a family or clan either by conquest or by purchase or grant. Only subsequently was it transmitted through family lines. Here we are told that God himself will provide the estate of the Aaronide priesthood, to be granted them in the form of entitlements from Temple income.

21–24. These verses prescribe the principal entitlements of the Levites, as distinct from those of the priesthood. The Levites are to receive one-tenth of the annual yield of the fields, orchards, and vineyards, to be remitted to them by all Israelites.

every tithe. The term *maʿaśēr* means "a tenth part." The earliest biblical source to refer to tithes is undoubtedly 1 Sam 8:15–17, where we read that kings normally taxed their subjects one-tenth of their grain crops and fruits and of the increment of their flocks. As such, the tithe was a form of royal taxation. It first emerges as a form of temple taxation in Deuteronomy (Deut 12:6, 17–18; 14:22–29; 26:12–15), and Lev 27:30–33 restate the duty to consecrate the tithes from the yield of the land and the herds and flocks. Against this background, it would appear that the tithe was a form of temple taxation. However it was specifically earmarked in Torah legislation, its cultic provisions undoubtedly reflect a system of royal taxation. In fact, the history of the tithe in biblical Israel, as sketchy as it is, demonstrates nonetheless that the temple establishment and the priesthood were rooted in royal administration.

Now, whereas Deuteronomy also assigns tithes to "the Levite *(lallēwî),*" the term *lēwî* refers to all priests in the Deuteronomic system and does not stand in contradistinction to priests, as it does in Numbers; see the NOTE on v 20, above. The stratification of the tribe of Levi into the two groups, priests and Levites, first occurs explicitly within Torah literature in Numbers. It may be implied in Lev 25:32–33, a law dealing with the so-called "levitical" towns, but this is far from certain. In any event, it is undoubtedly Numbers that unambiguously assigns the tithes to the Levites, as emoluments distinct from those assigned to the priests.

As for Lev 27:30–33, the law requiring Israelites to consecrate a tenth part of the annual yield of the land and of the increment of the herds and flocks, it is not formulated in terms of priestly or levitical income. Although the formula *qôdeš l-YHWH* used in those priestly statements functionally connotes temple income, it does not specifically identify the Levites as recipients of tithes. The legislation summarized in Numbers 18 represents, therefore, the end of a long process.

The formulation *kol maʿaśēr* 'every tithe' is vague. Does *kol maʿaśēr* refer to the two principal kinds of tithes, from agricultural produce and from the increment of herds and flocks, as stipulated in Lev 27:30–33? Gray is doubtful, and correctly so.

Logically, "the tithe from the tithe," which the Levites themselves were to remit to the priests (as prescribed below, in Num 18:27, 30), consisted only of agricultural produce and did not include animals. Furthermore, if we conclude, as the text specifies, that the Levites were to pay the priests one-tenth of all they received from the Israelites, it is logical to conclude that they did not receive from the Israelites tithes from the herds and flocks. This is Gray's reasoning, and he also notes that Neh 10:36–38; and 13:5 and 12, which are very late postexilic sources, mention only tithes from produce of the land as the obligation of the community.

And yet tithing of animals was a relatively old practice in biblical Israel. It is mentioned as a royal prerogative in 1 Sam 8:17 and is referred to by both Jeremiah (Jer 33:13) and Ezekiel (Ezek 20:37). Interestingly, both Abraham (Gen 14:20) and Jacob (Gen 28:22), at various times, pledged tithes "of all *(mikkol)*" they possessed, and both were noted for possessing extensive herds and flocks! Most likely, tithing of animals was a known practice when Numbers 18 was written, but such tithes are not, nevertheless, covered by its legislation. It must be conceded that we know relatively little about the realities of temple funding in biblical Israel, and this situation requires the commentator to be tentative in the interpretation of specific priestly statutes.

The pertinent tithes were assigned to the Levites "in exchange" (Hebrew *ḥēlep)* for their "service *(ʿabôdāh)*" in the Sanctuary. The preposition *ḥēlep* occurs only here and in v 31, below. In the Aramaic Targum and the Peshitta, *ḥālap* normally translates Hebrew *taḥat* 'in place of' (cf. the formulations in Num 8:16, 18).

tasks. The term *ʿabôdāh* has been explained in the Notes on Num 10:9, and in the comments on v 9, above. It is central to the functions of the Levites, as these functions are outlined in Numbers 3–4. Hebrew *ʿabôdāh* is a thoroughly ambiguous term, connoting both cultic officiation (Num 8:7) and maintenance functions, as is its meaning here.

22. The careful attention of the Levites to their assigned tasks will prevent ordinary Israelites from encroaching on the area of the Sanctuary, from which they are barred. This is a veiled reference to the episodes related in Numbers 16–17, especially Num 17:28.

incurring the penalty. The idiom *lāśēʾt ḥēṭʾ* 'to bear the punishment for an offense' is a variation on the more common idiom *nāśāʾ ʿawôn* in Num 18:1, above. This variation recurs below, in v 32.

24. *which they collect for* YHWH *as levied donations.* The clause *ʾašer*

yarîmû l-YHWH terûmāh belies the etymology of the term *terûmāh* itself. The *terûmāh* consists of what is "raised."

Consequently. Idiomatic *ʿal kēn* has its normal sense here, expressing the rationale of one's actions.

25–32. The remaining verses of Numbers 18 introduce a novel provision, actually a variation on the law of the tithe. The Levites were not to be relieved of all obligation to support the cult and priesthood. The status of the Levites, as defined in the book of Numbers, made them auxiliary personnel—dedicated to God, but subservient to the Aaronide priesthood.

26. This verse states an operative principle: the Levites are required to "withhold" one-tenth of the tithes they collect from the Israelites. This is what is meant by the verb *wahharîmôtem* 'you shall withhold', exactly as we, today, speak of withholding taxes. In this way, the tithes were desacralized. God's claim to them had been satisfied. Speaking more realistically, the priesthood would enjoy added income.

in lieu of your land grant. In v 26, the basis for these entitlements is laconically restated: *benahaḷātkem* 'in place of your land grant'. Prepositional *beth* in this construction is *beth pretii* 'the *beth* of price', a function explained in the NOTES on Num 17:3.

27. *will count for you. Niphʿal neḥšāb* here functions as part of the accounting vocabulary, as is generally true of other forms of the verb *ḥāšab* 'to figure, calculate'. Compare 1 Kgs 10:21: "silver does not count for anything *(lōʾ neḥšāb . . . limeʾûmāh).*" Here the sense is that the materiel that the Levites withheld and then remitted to the priests would be credited to them as if they were desacralizing their own produce—grain and ripe fruit. The notion that the contribution of the Levites to the priests would "count" for them is repeated in v 30 below. In actuality, the Levites had virtually no arable land, with the possible exception of small plots for gardening.

ripe fruit. Hebrew *melēʾāh* is a rare term. In Exod 22:28 it occurs in a law requiring payment of the first ripe fruits from the vat, and in Deut 22:9 its usage pertains to the prohibition against sowing seed in proximity to vines. One who does so loses his ripe fruit.

28. *In this way.* Here the force of adverbial *kēn* is "so." It expresses the anticipated result of the Levites' action in donating a tithe from what they had collected.

29. *from all of its richest contents.* In the second part of the verse, Hebrew *ḥelbô mimmennû* '[an amount] from its richest contents' illustrates that Hebrew *ḥēleb* 'fat' can refer to the choicest grain, as is explained in the NOTES on vv 12–13, above.

the consecrated portion of it. The parallel statement, *ʾet miqdešô mimmennû,* is an old crux of interpretation, both because of the Masoretic pointing *(miqdešô* instead of *miqdāšô)* and because the usual meaning, "sanctuary," does not fit here. The Septuagint reads *to hagiasmenon ap autou* 'the sacred part of it,' suggesting a Hebrew pointing *mequddāšô*. Curiously, in 2 Chr 31:6, a passage dealing with tithes, we find the construction *qodāšîm hammequd-dāšîm,* literally, "sacred donations that have been consecrated" (see below, in the NOTES on v 32). As it stands, the Masoretic pointing is anomalous and probably represents a tendentious vocalization, intended to differentiate this word from *miqdāš* 'sanctuary', which would make little sense here.

31. *of it.* The object pronoun *'ôtô* has many antecedents in the preceding verses. Ultimately, it reverts to *mimmennû* 'from it' in v 26, namely, from the tithes collected by the Levites.

Once having desacralized the tithes the Levites were free to partake of them anywhere because, unlike sacrificial materiel, tithes did not have to be eaten in sacred precincts.

32. The sense of this verse is that the Levites could avoid punishment for defiling the sacred donations of the Israelites by properly contributing one-tenth of the tithes they collect to the priests.

the sacred offerings of the Israelite people. It is admittedly unusual to refer to tithes as *qodšê benê Yiśrā'ēl,* a designation normally reserved for sacrificial offerings. And yet in 2 Chr 31:6, a passage already mentioned, we find *ma'aśar qodāšîm hammequddāšîm,* literally, "tithes of sacred donations that have been consecrated."

We should assume a degree of license in technical usage here, in contrast to Gray, who interpreted this provision differently. He understood this verse as admonishing the Levites against partaking of priestly entitlements, which would be an act of defilement. More likely, the sense is that by paying their dues, the Levites would be acting properly.

PART XIII.

NUMBERS 19: THE IMPURE DEAD

INTRODUCTION

The subject of Numbers 19 is the impurity resulting from contact with or proximity to a human corpse, a grave, or bones from a corpse. The formulation of the law suggests that it intended no distinction between Israelites and non-Israelites as regards the impurity of the dead; all human corpses and bones were impure. This type of impurity was regarded by the priests of biblical Israel as the most severe of all. It was the urgent need to eliminate such impurity from the Israelite areas of settlement that gave rise to the complex regulations and rituals of Numbers 19.

If left unattended, the impurity of the dead would ultimately defile the Sanctuary, located within the encampment *(maḥaneh)*, even if no direct physical contact with or proximity to the Sanctuary might be involved. The mere likelihood that a contaminated individual might enter the sacred space of the Sanctuary was sufficient to pose a real threat to its purity, even if the event did not actually occur, because the impurity of the dead generated additional impurity. The danger to the Sanctuary is explicitly stated in Num 19:13 and repeated in Num 19:20, so that both sections of the chapter, as it turns out, convey this principle. Proper purification after contamination by the dead became a vital concern.

Numbers 19 is clearly divided into two discrete sections, which differ in their terms of reference and perspective. Whereas Num 19:13 refers to a Tabernacle *(miškān)*, v 20 of the second section, in a variation of the same statement, uses the term *miqdāš* 'sanctuary'.

Furthermore, each section deals with a separate dimension of the purification process. Num 19:1–13 are devoted primarily to the preparation of a mixture of ashes and living water, to be used in purifying persons and objects that had been contaminated by the dead. This mixture required the total destruction of a red cow in the course of a rite of riddance. The ashes of the bovine victim, which was slaughtered and destroyed outside the encampment, were gathered up and stored in a pure place. Mixed with living water, the ashes would be sprinkled over those persons and objects requiring purification. All persons involved in administering these procedures, the priests and those who burned the cow and gathered its ashes, were themselves required to undergo purification, albeit of a lesser severity, through ablutions and the laundering of their clothing.

The former section of Numbers 19 concludes with an admonition: anyone who had contact with the dead and subsequently failed to purify himself would be ostracized from the Israelite community. The point is stressed that purification was to be accomplished in two stages, on the third and seventh days of the period of impurity. Num 19:13 charges any person who fails in this duty with defiling the Sanctuary itself, because "water of lustration *(mê niddāh)*," the mixture of ashes and living water prescribed in this section, had not been sprinkled on him. A relation to the Sanctuary is also expressed by the requirement that blood from the cow be sprinkled in the direction of the Sanctuary (v 4).

The second section of Numbers 19 (vv 14–22) sets forth the specific conditions of contact and proximity that had the effect of contaminating persons, places, and objects with the impurity of the dead. Essentially, anyone standing within the same roofed structure as the dead (the "tent" of v 14) became impure merely by sharing that space. Furthermore, any substances left in open vessels within that enclosure contracted the impurity of the dead. Only vessels closed and sealed were protected. In open air, it was tactile contact with a corpse, or with bones from a corpse, or with a grave that rendered a person impure.

Whenever this contact occurred, the prescribed mixture was to be utilized. A pure person was to sprinkle living water, in which the ashes of the red cow had been mixed, on the tent, vessels, or humans requiring purification. This ritual was to be repeated on the third and seventh days of the period of impurity, and only then, after ablutions and the laundering of clothing, would the contaminated person be restored to a pure state. Verse 20 restates the impact that the impurity of the dead would have on the Sanctuary itself.

In the COMMENT on this chapter the overall significance and phenomenology of priestly legislation pertaining to the dead will be discussed. Here it would be helpful merely to note several features of Numbers 19 that have a direct bearing on its interpretation.

Within the first section (Num 19:1–13) we note a further internal division: vv 1–10 constitute a unit entirely devoted to the preparation of the means of purification; while vv 11–13 anticipate the second section of Numbers 19 by discussing how the mixture would be utilized, and emphatically state the admonition against failure to undertake the required purification. Possibly vv 11–13 were later inserted after v 10 in an effort to join the two sections of the chapter. The sequence of the two parts of Numbers 19 would seem to be determined by a principle evident in many priestly prescriptions: before the actual law with its contingencies is stated, the means for fulfilling it are prescribed.

In the second section of Numbers 19 (vv 14–22) no specific role is projected for priests. It is required only that "a pure man *('îš ṭāhôr)*" perform the rite of lustration. The implications of this shift will be discussed in the COMMENT, below. Quite possibly, the lustration rite prescribed in the latter section of this chapter had a popular rather than a priestly origin.

TRANSLATION

19 1 YHWH addressed Moses and Aaron as follows:

2 This is the statute of the prescribed instruction that YHWH has ordained, as follows: Order the Israelite people to provide to you a red cow, physically perfect and without blemish, one that has never borne a yoke.

3 Deliver it to Eleazar, the priest, and let it be taken outside the encampment and slaughtered in his presence.

4 Eleazar, the priest, shall take some of its blood on his finger and sprinkle [it] seven times in the direction of the Tent of Meeting.

5 The cow shall then be burned in his presence; its hide, meat, and blood shall be burned, together with its dung.

6 The priest shall take cedar wood, hyssop, and crimson cloth, and cast them into the fire where the cow is being burned.

7 The priest must then launder his clothing and bathe his body in water, after which he may reenter the encampment. He remains impure until evening.

8 The person who burned [the cow] must likewise launder his clothing in water, and bathe his body in water. He remains impure until evening.

9 A pure person shall gather up the ashes of the cow and deposit them in a pure place. This shall be conserved by the community of the Israelite people as water of lustration; it is a sin-offering.

10 The person who gathers up the ashes of the cow shall launder his clothing. He remains impure until evening. This shall be a permanent statute for the Israelite people, as well as for the alien who resides among them.

11 Whoever had contact with the corpse of any human being shall be deemed impure for seven days.

12 He must purify himself with [the ashes] on the third day and on the seventh day, and then shall become pure. Should he fail to purify himself on the third day and on the seventh day, he shall not be deemed pure.

13 One who had contact with a corpse belonging to any human being who had died, but failed to purify himself, has defiled the Tabernacle of YHWH. That person shall be cut off from Israel, because water of lustration was not dashed on him. He remains impure; his impurity endures within him.

14 This is the prescribed instruction: in the event that a person dies inside a tent, everyone who enters that tent and everyone found inside that tent becomes impure for seven days.

15 Every open vessel that does not have a lid fastened around it becomes impure.

16 Anyone having contact, in the open field, with a slain human body, or a corpse, or a human bone, or a grave, becomes impure for seven days.

17 Some of the "dust" of the burned sin-offering shall be used for the impure person, and living water shall be poured over it, into a vessel.

18 A pure person shall then take hyssop and dip it into the water, and sprinkle it on the tent, and on the persons who were there, and on the one who had contact with the bone, or the slain body, or the corpse, or the grave.

19 The pure person shall perform the sprinkling over the impure person on the third day, and on the seventh day, finally removing the impurity on the seventh day. He must then launder his clothing and bathe in water, and at eventide he is restored to purity.

20 But any person who becomes impure, but fails to purify himself—that person shall be cut off from the midst of the congregation, for it is the Sanctuary of YHWH that he has defiled. Water of lustration was not dashed on him: he remains impure.

21 This shall be a permanent statute for you. The person who sprinkled the lustration water must launder his clothing: and anyone who had contact with the water of lustration remains impure until evening.

22 Anything that the impure person touches is rendered impure, and a person who [in turn] touches [such objects] remains impure until evening.

NOTES TO 19:1–13: METHODS OF PURIFICATION

19 2. *the statute of the prescribed instruction.* The combination *ḥuqqat hattôrāh* is redundant. It is unique to this verse, though each of its two components, *tôrāh* and *ḥuqqāh,* occurs frequently in priestly texts.

The term *ḥuqqāh* is explained in the NOTES on Num 9:12, and the term *tôrāh* in the NOTES on Num 15:16. In Leviticus 6–7, for instance, the term *tôrāh* occurs repeatedly as a way of designating manuals of instruction for the priests. Thus in Lev 6:2 we read, *zō̂'t tôrat hāʿôlāh* 'this is the prescribed instruction for the burnt offering'.

Order [the Israelite people] to provide to you. Idiomatic *weyiqqeḥû 'ēlêkā* has the sense of "let them *provide* to you." Actually it is a rare formulation, but its meaning is established by the more common construction *lāqaḥ + l-* in v 17, below: *welāqeḥû laṭṭāmē'* 'let them provide for the impure person' (cf. similar usages in Lev 14:4; Ezek 5:1).

red. It seems inescapable that the ruddy color of the cow symbolized blood. More will be said of this in the COMMENT, below. Here we note that the adjective *'ādôm* itself may be related to *dām* 'blood', expressed with prothetic *'aleph.* This relation is suggested by the Akkadian forms *adamu* 'blood' (*CAD* A, 1.95) and *adamatu* 'black, blood' (*CAD* A, 1.94). The same phenomenolgy would, of course, account for the utilization of scarlet cloth in rites of purification, as we shall observe below, in the NOTES on v 18.

cow. Hebrew *pārāh* tells us little about the precise age of the requisite animal, because *par* 'bull' and *pārāh* 'cow' are used rather loosely in biblical Hebrew. English "heifer" designates a cow that has not borne a calf, and it is nowhere near certain that such an animal was intended by the present law. One assumes that a degree of physical maturity is implied by the term *pārāh*, though we lack detailed information on animal husbandry in biblical Israel. Clearly, a *pārāh* is older than an *ʿeglāh* 'calf' (female), and, according to Mic 6:6, a yearling is called *ʿēgel.*

physically perfect and without blemish. The red cow had to be, literally, "complete, having no blemish in her *(temîmāh ʾašer ʾên bāk mûm).*" Those blemishes which rendered an animal unfit for sacrifice are enumerated in Lev 22:20–25. Most of them are congenital.

The requirement that a cow be used that had never borne the yoke recalls a similar provision in Deut 21:3. The calf put to death over a perennial stream to expiate an unidentified murder was to be one that had never "drawn" the yoke (the Hebrew verb *māšak).* Further, we note that the expiatory gifts dispatched by the Philistines to propitiate the God of Israel were put in a wagon drawn by cows that had never borne the yoke (1 Sam 6:7). It is clear from context that those cows were intended as sacrifices (1 Sam 5:14). The notion underlying such requirements is that animals used in purificatory rites, like those in more usual types of sacrifices, should represent the best available, and should never have been employed for any profane purpose (Gray—ICC).

3. *Deliver it.* Here the sense of Hebrew *nātan* is "to deliver." The subject of the statement shifts in the course of the verse. The verbs *nātan* 'to deliver' and *hôṣîʾ* 'to take out' have as their subject Eleazar, the priest, while the subject of the verb *wešāḥaṭ* 'he shall slaughter' is elliptical. The subject is unspecified, and this verb could just as well be translated as a passive: "it shall be slaughtered." This manner of expressing actions recurs in vv 5 and 17, below.

The entire riddance ritual was performed outside the encampment, with no recourse to a sacrificial altar. This rite was not sacrificial, in the usual sense, but it bore a similarity to certain major expiatory sacrifices in which the element of riddance was operative. Rites of riddance were normally enacted outside the camp, for the obvious reason that the objective was to eliminate impurity through its distancing and destruction. Furthermore, as will be discussed in the COMMENT, riddance implies the transfer of sinfulness and impurity to the victim, in this case, to the red cow. Whenever such transferral occurs, we are dealing with a contaminated object, and it would make little sense to retain such contamination inside the encampment.

Examples of sacrificial rites in which riddance figured prominently are the sin-offerings brought in order to expiate major offenses on the part of the entire Israelite community or its chief priest, as set forth in Lev 4:1–21. The same enactment of riddance was part of the Yom Kippur purification ordained in Leviticus 16 and the purification of Aaron and his sons at the time of their investiture, rites described in Leviticus 8–10. Especially significant are the similarities between the present legislation and the rites prescribed for the purification of one suffering from the symptoms of *ṣāraʿat*, a skin disease, according to Leviticus 14. In the NOTES on Num 2:3, the significance of the term *maḥaneh* 'encampment' was discussed.

It is of interest to note that Eleazar, Aaron's son and designated successor (Num 20:25–29) was to administer these riddance procedures. He had already begun to assume certain duties in the aftermath of the Korah episode, as is recorded in Num 17:1–5.

4. Blood from the slaughtered red cow was to be sprinkled by Eleazar "in the direction of" the Tent of Meeting. The Hebrew construction *ʾel nôkaḥ* 'facing, in the direction of' is actually unique to this verse, though we often find other expressions with *nôkaḥ* 'facing, immediately present' (Gen 25:21; Exod 26:35). The Sifre comments, "he (= the priest) must consciously look at the entrance of the Temple while sprinkling the blood." This comment, reflecting later Jewish practices, emphasizes the importance of the orientation or orchestration of this ritual. The impurity of the dead impacted the Sanctuary, and its elimination was to be visually and geographically linked to it, even though great distance from the Sanctuary was required because of the impurity realized in the rite itself.

Sprinkling blood taken from a sacrificial victim, and doing so seven times, are normal acts of purification (cf. Lev 4:6, 17; 14:7; 16:14–15; Num 8:7).

5. The entire cow, even including its blood, was to be burned as the priest watched. Nowhere else in Torah ritual do we find the explicit requirement of burning the blood of a ritual victim.

shall be burned. The verb *weśārap* 'he shall burn' has an elliptical subject (see above, in the NOTES on Num 19:3). The force of prepositional *ʿal* is "together with." The cow was to be burned together with its dung (Hebrew *pereš*), the undigested contents of the stomach normally not burned on the altar from considerations of delicacy (cf. Lev 4:11; 8:17; 10:27). This sensitivity is echoed in Malachi's condemnation of improper sacrifice: "I will strew dung on your faces, the very dung of your festal sacrifices!" (Mal 2:3).

6. The three specified ingredients—cedar wood, hyssop, and scarlet cloth—all figure as well in the rites of purification undertaken for one thought to have *ṣāraʿat*, according to Lev 14:4–6. According to the present verse, these ingredients were to be cast into the fire, but below, in v 17, hyssop is again used when sprinkling the water of lustration over contaminated persons and objects.

Obviously we are dealing with ingredients that had a broad role in purification and riddance. Hyssop (Hebrew *ʾēzôb*) is mentioned in this connection by the Psalmist, who probably had rites such as the present ones in mind: "Purge me with hyssop till I am pure!" (Ps 51:9). In fact, the verb *ḥiṭṭēʾ* used

in Ps 51:9, which means "to remove impurity," is employed in this chapter in vv 12–23 and 20, in the derived, *hithpa'el* form, *yiṭhaṭṭā'* 'he purifies himself'.

crimson. Hebrew *šenî tôla'at*, literally, "the scarlet of the worm" (cf. *tôla'at šānî* in Num 4:8), precisely refers to the insects from whose eggs crimson dye was extracted. These insects live in the fronds of palm trees. Hebrew *šānî* thus describes the color, not the cloth, which was traditionally identified as wool.

Cedar wood was prized for its aromatic qualities. In the COMMENT, below, an attempt will be made to rationalize the particular appropriateness of these substances to the objectives of riddance and purification, based on comparative evidence.

7. Laundering of garments and ablutions were regular features of purification. Before the Sinai theophany, the Israelites were commanded to launder their clothing as part of their preparations for that momentous event (Exod 19:10). According to Num 8:7, the Levites were ordered to launder their garments in preparation for the rites celebrating their dedication to Tabernacle service.

The point is that the priests, like the others involved in administering the riddance rites, had themselves become impure in the process, and could reenter the encampment only pursuant to their own purification.

8. The same rule governing the presiding priest applied to the person who had burned the cow.

9. A pure man *('îš ṭāhôr)* was then to gather up the ashes of the burned cow and store them outside the encampment, in a pure place. Were an impure person to do this, the effect of the whole rite would be undone.

This shall be. The direct antecedent of *wehāyetāh*, literally, "It shall be," is imprecise. Grammatically, it should be the cow (feminine) and not the ashes, but such license is normal in biblical Hebrew syntax.

the community of the Israelite people. The composite term *'adat benê Yiś-rā'ēl* is common in priestly writings (cf. Exod 10:1; Lev 16:5; 19:2; Num 1:2; 17:26). Several similar classifications were discussed in the NOTES on Num 1:2.

conserved. Here *lemišmeret* means "for safekeeping, conserving." The Hebrew term *mišmeret*, which has a wide range of connotations, was discussed in the NOTES on Num 1:53.

water of lustration. A problematic term is *me niddāh*, which recurs below, in vv 13 and 20, and in Num 31:23 (see further in the NOTES on v 13, below). For the most part, commentators have tended to interpret Hebrew *niddāh*, which elsewhere signifies "menstruation" (Lev 12:2; 18:19; Ezek 18:6; 36:17) and pertains to the prohibition of sexual relations with a woman during her period, at times metaphorically.

The form *niddāh* is a *niph'al*-based construction, based on the verbal root *n-d-h*, probably cognate with Akkadian *nadû* 'to hurl, cast off'. The question is whether the "casting off" refers to the menstruating woman, who is to be removed in some way, or to the flow of her blood, which leaves her body.

Although it is true, as Gray emphasizes, that Hebrew *niddāh* virtually always pertains to impurity, even metaphorically so, it is more likely that it originally referred merely to physiological processes, or simply, as in the present case, to the sprinkling or splashing of water. Most likely, Hebrew *n-d-h* is a variant of *n-z-h* 'to spatter', which is said of blood (Lev 6:20; 2 Kgs 9:33). Rashi probably held this view, by the way, before Akkadian cognates were known.

On this basis, *mê niddāh* means "water of lustration; water for sprinkling," and the characterization *niddāh* literally means, as applied to a menstruating woman, "one who is spilling" blood. Such a woman was declared to be impure during her period, but it is not the word *niddāh* that, by itself, connotes that impurity!

Gray cites as a parallel of *mê niddāh* the term *mê ḥaṭṭā't* 'water of purification' in Num 8:7 and suggests that both mean the same thing. This suggestion is tempting, but is no more than functional. In both instances, in the present rite of riddance and in the purification of the Levites, water is instrumental, but the term *mê niddāh* itself does not convey the same meaning as *mê ḥaṭṭā't*. See the NOTES on Num 8:7.

it is a sin offering. The concluding words of this verse, *ḥaṭṭā't hî'*, require comment precisely because of the ambiguity attendant upon the term *ḥaṭṭā't* itself. Normally *ḥaṭṭā't* designates a sin-offering, more literally, one aimed at removing or eliminating the impurity occasioned by a sin. Some consider that meaning inappropriate here, because this riddance rite is not a sin-offering in the usual sense of the term. Nevertheless, "it is a sin-offering" may be the closest we can come to a precise rendering of *ḥaṭṭā't ḥî'*. The antecedent of pronominal *hî'* 'it' is the same as that of *wehāyetāh* 'it shall be', earlier in the verse; namely, the red cow that had been reduced to ashes.

NJPS translates "It is for cleansing," and Gray, "It is a means of removing sin." Here it is indeed tempting to compare *mê ḥaṭṭā't* 'water of purification', just mentioned. It occurs in Num 8:7, where the term *ḥaṭṭā't* also seems to have a more general meaning. On this basis, the form *ḥaṭṭā't* would be infinitival—"cleansing, purifying"—and perhaps should be vocalized *ḥaṭṭō't*. And yet it should be remembered that the term *ḥaṭṭā't* itself literally means "an offering for the removal of sin" (see the NOTES on Num 8:12). The Sages of the Sifre, surely aware of the problem in this verse, emphasize that the regulations affecting the sin-offering applied as well to the water of lustration. So I see no reason not to translate *ḥaṭṭā't* here as "sin offering." Note that the ashes are also referred to as a *ḥaṭṭā't* in Num 19:17, below.

10. The man who gathered the ashes of the red cow was rendered impure by that very act, and he required the usual purification before being readmitted to the encampment.

the alien who resides among them. What is of greatest interest in this verse is the reference to resident aliens. The verse emphasizes that the foregoing, namely, the preparation of the water of lustration from the ashes of the burned cow, is to be a permanent statute not only for Israelites, but for the *gēr*, the alien resident within the Israelite settlement. The status of the *gēr* was explained in the NOTES on Num 9:14 (cf. Num 15:15). This term designates non-Israelites who came from foreign lands, or whose families had done so at an earlier time.

Two questions are raised by the inclusion of the alien in the requirement of purification: (1) Was the corpse of a non-Israelite also a source of impurity? (2) Would a non-Israelite be contaminated by contact with a corpse, in the same way as would an Israelite? The wording of v 11 would seem clearly to assume as much, for it speaks of corpses and bones "belonging to any human being *(lekol nepeš ʾādām)*," and v 14, below, also uses the term *ʾādām* generically. Although later Jewish law restricted the provisions of this chapter to Israelite dead, the original intent of the law was to deal with all death occurring within the bounds of the Israelite settlement.

11–13. The next three verses constitute a subunit, in which the provisions of vv 14–22 are anticipated in a summary fashion. These verses may have been inserted editorially so as to link the two sections of the chapter.

11. *Whoever had contact with the corpse.* The Hebrew *hannôgēaʿ bemēt* has relative force: "whoever touches, anyone who touches, a dead body." This syntax, wherein the definite article has relative force, is typical of late biblical and of postbiblical Hebrew. Relative formulations are, however, quite common in the exposition of biblical law. Most often, an indeterminate participle is used, as in Exod 21:12: "Anyone who strikes another person *(makkeh ʾîš)*" (cf. also Num 35:12).

In certain contexts, Hebrew *nepeš* may designate a dead person (cf. Lev 22:4, and see the NOTES on Num 6:6). It does not necessarily do so here, because the sense of *lekol nepeš ʾādām* 'belonging to any human being' suggests that the reference may be to living persons, and because the text adds *ʾašer yāmût* 'who dies'.

The seven-day duration of impurity is common in priestly law, especially for the more severe forms of impurity. Compare the provisions of Leviticus 13–15 on illnesses and their effects.

12. *He must purify himself.* The *hithpaʿel* form *yiṯḥaṭṭāʾ* links this law with the provisions of Num 31:19–24, and in general with the overall provisions of Numbers 31 relevant to the disposition of the spoils of war. In Num 31:19 and 23 we also find this unusual *hithpaʿel* form, which elsewhere occurs only in Num 8:21 (and metaphorically in Job 41:17). In Num 8:21 we read that the Levites *underwent purification* as part of their dedication, and this process is conveyed by the *hithpaʿel*, *wayyiṯḥaṭṭeʾû* 'they purified themselves'.

The laws of Numbers 31 require Israelite warriors who had killed human beings in battle to remain outside the encampment for seven days and to undergo purification in two stages, just as is provided in Num 19:16. Furthermore, metal objects, and those made of other materials, had to be purified.

This process involved use of *mê niddāh* 'water of lustration'. Inevitably, the provisions of Numbers 31 represent a direct application of the laws of the present chapter. Num 19:12 states the requirements of the law both positively and negatively.

13. This verse expresses the same admonition as we find farther on, in v 20. The impurity of the dead was so powerful that it affected the Sanctuary (see the INTRODUCTION to this chapter).

shall be cut off. The penalty of being "cut off" (the verb *nikrat)* from the Israelite community is common in priestly writings. This penalty originally meant banishment from one's clan or territory, but in the course of time it was perceived somewhat differently. It came to connotate premature death, loss of status or office, and finally "death at the hands of heaven *(mîtāh biydê šāmayîm),*" as it is characterized in the Mishna *(Kerîtût* 1:2; Levine 1989b: 241–242).

The penalty of *kārēt,* as it is known, is ordained for such offenses as violation of the Sabbath and holy days (Exod 12:15–19; 31:12; Lev 23:29), the eating of blood and fat from sacrifices (Lev 3:17; 19:8), and the failure to circumcise one's son at the age of eight days (Gen 17:14; Lev 12:3). It is also the penalty for certain sexual offenses (Lev 18:19; 20:17–18).

The sense of the Hebrew *ʿôd ṭumʾātô bô* is "his impurity endures within him." This is often the force of Hebrew *ʿôd,* as in Gen 8:22: "as long as the earth endures *(ʿôd kol yemê hāʾāreṣ).*"

dashed. The sprinkling of the special mixture of living water and ashes was absolutely indispensable for purification. The verb *zāraq* often describes cultic acts involving blood as well as water (cf. Lev 1:5). The prophet Ezekiel was probably referring to rites such as those presented in this chapter when he predicted God's purification of Israel: "I will sprinkle *(wezāraqtî)* pure water upon you, so that you may become pure!" (Ezek 36:35).

NOTES TO 19:14–22: DEFINING CORPSE CONTAMINATION

The remaining verses of Numbers 19 comprise the second part of the chapter. Once the preparation of the instrument of purification has been prescribed it is now appropriate to state the conditions requiring such purification.

14. *inside a tent.* The law here refers to the tent that one lives in: *bāʾôhel* 'in the tent'. This wording merely reflects the overall orientation of the priestly writings of the Torah and of Numbers specifically. The laws and rituals ordained here were addressed by Moses to the Israelites before their occupation of Canaan. The scene is the migratory experience of Sinai and Transjordan, when the Israelites dwelled in tents. Later Jewish interpreters, whose

legislation is preserved in such talmudic tractates as *ʾAhîlôt* (literally, "enclosures, tenting") translated the dicta of the Torah to fit the structural requirements of buildings and homes.

This is the prescribed instruction. For the formula *ẑoʾt hattôrāh* see the NOTES to v 2, above. This construction occurs elsewhere (Lev 7:37; 14:54), but nowhere else as a complete caption. In Deut 4:44 it occurs in a postscript, referring to what had been stated earlier.

The law is that a person found under the same roof with the dead, so to speak, or who entered that space, was rendered impure merely by reason of propinquity. No direct physical contact with the corpse was necessary, because it was thought that its impurity was trapped within the covered, enclosed structure, and had pervaded its atmosphere.

15. The contents of any open vessel located inside the enclosure when death occurred, or during the subsequent period of impurity, are rendered impure, and ultimately so is the vessel itself. The operative principle is that the impurity present within the structure invades all of its interior air, or space, and only sealed vessels are protected. The open vessel becomes impure because its unprotected contents had been contaminated, a conclusion proved by the fact that sealed vessels resist the impurity of the atmosphere.

a lid. The terminology of this verse is elusive, and has been recognized as such since late antiquity. Hebrew *ṣāmîd* is a term for bracelet (Num 31:50; and cf. Gen 24:22), but this meaning seems unsuited to the present context. Lexicographers posit a second meaning, "lid," such as was used to seal ceramic vessels in antiquity. The verbal root *ṣ-m-d* means "to join, connect, bind," and both terms merely represent different realizations of the same verbal root.

fastened around it. The form *pātîl* follows the model of the Aramaic passive participle, and means "wound around, sealed around." The Sifre therefore defines *ṣāmîd* as *dôpēq* 'cover, stopper' and *pātîl* as *ʿôdēp* 'overlapping' or the like. Lids were sealed onto ceramic vessels with plaster or some similar adhesive substance, as is explained in the Mishna *(Kēlîm,* chap. 10). This explanation is preferable to interpreting *pātîl* as "fillet," which is the meaning of this noun in certain contexts (Exod 38:37).

16. *Anyone having contact, in the open field.* In contrast to what or who shares the same "tent" space with the dead, one "in the field *(ʿal penê haśśādeh),*" that is to say, in open air, must have direct physical contact in order for contamination to result. That is the sense of *wekol ʾašer yiggaʿ*, literally, "anyone touching" in this verse. The several contaminating objects are listed: one slain, one who died a natural death, a human bone, or a grave.

The impurity of the dead is permanent. Even an old grave or an ancient human bone contaminates. The resultant impurity affecting humans lasted for seven days—assuming, of course, that proper purification was undertaken.

If not, the resultant impurity endured, as is clearly stated in v 13, above, in anticipation of the present law.

17. This verse refers to the ashes of the burned cow as a *ḥaṭṭā't* 'sin offering' (see the NOTES on v 9, above). Although the riddance procedures prescribed in Numbers 19 did not constitute a sin offering in the usual sense of an altar sacrifice, they resembled such sacrifices in many respects, certainly in their common objectives.

"dust." What is puzzling here is the use of Hebrew *'āpār* 'dust' instead of *'ēper* 'ashes', the term found in v 9, above. One immediately recalls the cliché *'āpār wā'eper* 'dust and ashes' in Gen 18:27, echoed in Job 42:86. We must infer that Hebrew *'āpār* here describes the dusty physical character of the cow's ashes.

living water. Living water was to be poured over the ashes, into a container. *Mayîm ḥayyîm* means, in effect, fresh water from a source, not from a cistern or the like (cf. Gen 26:19; Jer 17:13). Utilization of living water is also ordained in the purification of one suffering from the symptoms of *ṣāra'at* in Lev 14:5 and 50.

18–19. The prepared mixture was to be sprinkled (the verb *hizzāh)* upon whatever object or structure, or whichever person, was being purified. A hyssop branch was to be used for this purpose (see the NOTES on v 6, above). In the purification of disease, ordained in Lev 14:6 and 49, hyssop was also used for sprinkling. A pure person was to perform this task. The purification was to be performed in two stages, on the third and seventh days of the period of impurity, and the laundering of clothes as well as ablutions were also required.

20. This verse reiterates the admonition in v 13, above, except that it uses a significantly different term of reference. The community is the *qāhāl* 'congregation', not the *'ēdāh* 'community', and the term for the Sanctuary is *miqdāš* 'Sanctuary', not *miškān*, a more particularly priestly term.

21. This verse states the permanence of the foregoing requirements, adding the duty of the person who accomplished the sprinkling to undergo proper purification.

22. The impurity of the dead was communicable, so whatever had been touched by one so contaminated became, in time, impure itself. One who, in due course, touched such objects was also rendered impure, albeit to a lesser degree than one having direct contact with the dead.

COMMENT: THE CULT OF THE DEAD IN BIBLICAL ISRAEL

Chapter 19 of Numbers is the primary statement in Torah literature regarding the impurity generated through contact with a corpse, with human bones, or with graves presumed to contain bones. This type of impurity is the most severe ever legislated in the Torah. Even a person under the same roof (in the words of Num 19:14, within the same "tent") as a corpse is defiled thereby, because the entire interior space of the dwelling had been polluted by the corpse. What is more significant, however, is the fact that the mere presence of the impurity of the dead is sufficiently potent to threaten the purity of the Sanctuary situated within the Israelite encampment. This notion is repeated in Num 19:13 and 20: one who failed to undergo the required purifications subsequent to pollution by a corpse "has defiled the Tabernacle/sanctuary of YHWH *(ʾet miškan/miqdaš YHWH ṭimmēʾ)*." This would be so even if the impure person had not actually entered the area of the Sanctuary.

The relatedness of the impurity of the dead to the status or condition of the sanctuary is also signaled in the procedures for preparing the ashes of the incinerated cow: the priest, standing outside the encampment, must sprinkle some of the blood taken from the slaughtered cow in the direction of the Sanctuary, located inside the encampment.

G. B. Gray saw nothing distinctively Israelite in the provisions of Numbers 19, insisting that in most ancient societies, as well as in more recent ones, a corpse is regarded as impure in some sense and, as such, an object to be disposed of carefully. This claim is assuredly true, yet the permanent effects of the impurity of the dead stated in the provisions of Numbers 19 are decidedly unusual. At no future time do corpses or graves undergo a change of status; their impurity is permanent. An impure person and certain kinds of impure vessels may be purified, but not the bones of human dead or a grave containing them. Similarly, there is no dimension of sanctity that ever accrues to them.

T. Frymer-Kensky (1983) emphasizes the importance of defining boundaries, in this case between the world of the living and the world of the dead. It is the withdrawal of one defiled by a corpse from the encampment and his readmittance only after extensive purifications that express the polarity of the two universes, the worlds of the living and the dead. Such withdrawal is a reaction common to any number of threats posed against the purity of sanctuary and community, as we find in the treatment of diseased persons, for example, as prescribed in Leviticus 13–14.

And yet there is a difference as regards the priestly legislation of the Torah: the procedures attendant upon the dead are consistently disassociated from the Sanctuary and, for the most part, distanced from the encampment as well. In all other priestly rites of riddance there is, along with procedures taking place outside the encampment, a certain aspect of the rite that must be enacted "in the presence of YHWH *(lipnê YHWH)*," that is to say, in the area of the Sanctuary. Ultimately, those involved would have to present themselves before God. The same was true of the major sacrifices prescribed in Lev 4:1–21 in expiation of offenses committed by the Israelite community at large or by its chief priest, the functional leader of the community. It was likewise true of the expiations scheduled for the Day of Atonement in the provisions of Leviticus 16. Even the purification of diseased persons, prescribed in Leviticus 13–14, which is closest in its specifications to Numbers 19, ultimately required sacrificial offerings in the Sanctuary in order to render the purification efficacious (Lev 14:11). Riddance rites were normally combined with altar sacrifices in priestly legislation.

Numbers 19 provides a unique instance in priestly legislation of riddance rites entirely separate from the Sanctuary and its sacrificial altar. Consider the following of its features: the slaughter of the red cow took place outside the encampment. The cow was totally incinerated in a single procedure. The ashes yielded by the incinerated cow were to be stored in a pure place outside the encampment, not within the Sanctuary, as was customary for consecrated substances. The pattern of purifications on the third and seventh days is likewise unique, and is mentioned again only in Num 31:19–23, in connection with purification after battle, a rite clearly modeled on the legislation of Numbers 19.

Now, priests participated in the rites of Numbers 19, of course. It would have run counter to the legitimate interests of the Israelite priesthood to have any except priests officiate in the purification rites. It is significant, however, that nonpriests assisted in the preparation of the purificatory substances. There is, first of all, the man who slaughtered the cow, as well as the one who incinerated it to ashes; and it is stipulated that "a pure man *(ʾîš ṭāhôr)*" must gather up the ashes and store them.

The officiating priest became impure in the process of preparing the ashes, which, when mixed with fresh water, would serve as the purificatory substance. In fact, the preparation of these ashes is the only instance in priestly legislation wherein it is explicitly stated that a priest was defiled *(ṭāmēʾ)* as a direct result of performing a ritual. In the rites of the Day of Atonement, the high priest was required to bathe himself at one point before undertaking the burnt offerings, undoubtedly because he had become impure in the course of officiating at the prior expiatory sacrifices and in the dispatching of the scapegoat (Lev 16:23–24). This reason is not stated, however, and in most cases the performance of purificatory rites and involvement with impurity did not directly render a priest impure.

The stipulations for selecting the red cow are readily comprehensible. Prior utilization of the animal would have disqualified it. The same is indicated in the rites prescribed in Deuteronomy 21 for requiting the blood of the slain, where a female calf *(ʿeglāh)* was utilized rather than a cow. Further comparison of the two rituals is even more instructive: both rites were performed outside the encampment. In Deuteronomy the realities required it: the person had been slain in the open field, outside the jurisdictional limits of any town. In Numbers 19, however, the location of the riddance rites outside the encampment was due to priestly notions of impurity. In the Deuteronomic rite, blood is the functional substance, and the implications of the procedures are ultimately juridical, with the elders in charge. In the rites of Numbers 19, the ashes of the incinerated cow represent the operative substance, and the implications are cultic, with the priests in charge.

Blood symbolizes life, whereas ashes represent death, the ultimate biodegradable condition of a mortal being, human or animal. The abject quality of ashes is epitomized in several biblical statements that emphasize human mortality, significantly attributed to Abraham and to Job (Gen 18:27; Job 30:19; 42:6). Deuteronomy 21 fails to inform us how the calf is to be disposed of subsequent to the utilization of its blood. In that context, riddance was not the central concern. In Numbers 19, riddance is the main concern.

In Ezek 28:11–19 we find a dramatic oracle predicting the downfall of the Phoenician city-state of Tyre. This oracle, which expresses the theme of the Garden of Eden, resonates cultic language:

> Because of your abundant sinfulness *(ʿawônekā)*, and through your commercial wrongdoing, you have desecrated your sanctuaries *(ḥillaltā miqdāšekā)*. I have, therefore, brought out fire from your midst; it has consumed you. I have reduced you to ashes *(leʾēper)*, in view of all who behold you. All your partners among the nations are devastated at the sight of you; you have become a shock, a permanent nonentity *(weʾênkā ʿad ʿôlām)*. (Ezek 28:18–19)

This passage not only refers to the desecration of sanctuaries and to sinfulness, the more obvious cultic nuances, but also depicts fire issuing forth from the midst of the city, much as divine fire emits from God's presence (Lev 9:24; 10:2; Jer 4:4; 21:12; Ezek 5:4; 19:14). Most instructive for the present discussion is the reduction of the city to ashes by that same fire. God would rid the world of an evil regime by reducing the king and kingdom of Tyre to ashes (cf. Mal 3:21). This explains why sitting amidst ashes and casting ashes on one's head were forms of abject mourning (2 Sam 13:19; Isa 58:5; Jer 6:26; Ezek 27:30; Jonah 3:6; Esth 4:1–3; Dan 9:3).

The operative magical principle in the rites of Numbers 19 is sympathetic: death rids the community of death! Ashes represent annihilation and are, therefore, effective when applied to persons and objects defiled through contact with the dead. The mixture of ashes and living water had a primarily practical basis: in liquid form, this mixture could be applied to persons and objects. The operative cultic principle is substitution.

The symbolism of "red" is uncertain. Some have associated it with blood. To the extent that blood itself was functional in the processes prescribed in Numbers 19, it operated at an early stage prior to the actual rites of riddance. The sprinkling of blood taken from the slaughtered red cow in the direction of the Sanctuary (Num 19:4) was prophylactic, or perhaps apotropaic. Its intent was to shield the Sanctuary from contamination.

The hidden agenda of Numbers 19 is the cult of the dead. Directly relevant to its provisions are the laws of Lev 21:1–15 forbidding that Israelite priests come into contact with the dead in the funerary process. Numbers 19 establishes the severe impurity of the corpse, contact with which defiles all Israelites, not only priests, of course. But whereas no initial prohibition was placed on Israelites generally, who were permitted to be present at burials, priests were allowed to attend only to the burials of consanguineous relatives. Rabbinic law endorsed the same dispensation for the wife of a priest. The high priest enjoyed no exemptions whatsoever, and was forbidden even to attend to the burial of his own parents!

The incompatibility of consecration, on the one hand, and the impurity of the dead, on the other, is further reflected in the law of Num 6:1–12 that prohibits the Nazirite from any contact with the dead, even in the case of his own parents, because he, too, was a consecrated person during the period covered by his naziritic vow. In effect, the Nazirite shared the stringencies imposed on the high priest.

It seems inescapable that the priestly regulations of Leviticus 21 were aimed at eliminating a funerary role for the consecrated Israelite priesthood and at distancing funerary rites from the Sanctuary and its cult. We encounter a policy that, if fully implemented, would prevent any cultic celebration of death and would make of burial, and all that went with it, a nonpriestly activity, a duty resting with the family of the deceased. As a corollary, it is proper to see in the legislation of Numbers 19 an attempt to prevent the establishment of cults of the dead in biblical Israel, and to uproot them where they existed.

We must, however, clearly define what was meant by a cult of the dead in the ancient Near Eastern context. Not all funerary practices qualify as such, for some are prophylactic and apotropaic measures addressed primarily to the living as part of the mourning process. Cults of the dead, properly speaking, involve propitiation of the dead through sacrifice and other forms of ritual activity, as well as by magic. By their very nature, cults of the dead exhibit two complementary objectives: first, they are aimed at affording the dead what they seek, namely, an agreeable afterlife. Second, in so doing, cults of the dead seek to ensure that the powerful dead will not forget the living and will act benevolently rather than malevolently toward them, especially toward their own descendants. Ultimately, a society or community that celebrates a cult of dead ancestors considers the dead part of the community and the family. Their approval is required for the major decisions of the community, and their presence is desired at major events in communal life. The priestly program expressed in Leviticus 21 and Numbers 19, and in other biblical sources to be examined presently, rejects all of these attitudes. The dead have no power, and they are no longer members of the ongoing community. Their exploits during their lifetimes are a source of inspiration and guidance to their descendants, but the community itself looks forward to the future and consigns ancestors to the realm of memory.

Most of what we have learned about ancient Near Eastern cults of the dead pertains to departed royalty and dead heroes, two categories that often overlap. In part, this selectivity is due to the nature of the evidence uncovered by archaeologists, which existed initially and was later preserved by the ancients precisely because it had to do with their kings and heroes. Then, too, it is quite possible that cults of the dead may have been concentrated in leadership circles and largely limited to elites. In recent studies W. W. Hallo (1991a; 1991b) has gathered extensive evidence from all of the major civilizations of the ancient Near East on worship of dead ancestors, and from some of the smaller societies as well. His main focus is on Mesopotamian societies, but by way of a method he calls "contextual," Hallo discusses the biblical world as well. He is particularly interested in the relation of such cults to concepts of monarchy.

We are fortunate in having a recently discovered liturgy from the royal cult of the dead at Ugarit. This text, registered as *KTU* 1.161, preserves the complete text of the liturgy recited at the ascension of Ammurapi III, who was, as circumstances had it, the last king of Ugarit (Levine and de Tarragon 1984). The liturgy is entitled *spr dbḫ ẓlm* 'the written record of the sacred celebration [in honor] of the "Patrons" '. The Patrons were the protectors and guarantors of the Ugaritic royal dynasty. Included in this group were both the former kings of Ugarit and those to whom we may refer as the predynastic dead, known as *rpim,* the biblical Rephaim. The liturgy opens with the summoning of the mythic Rephaim and the historic kings (at least some of them), a series of actions repeatedly expressed by the verb *qra* 'to call'. The officiant at the ceremony, which most probably took place in the royal palace of Ugarit, near the tombs of the kings, summoned *rpim qdmym* 'the very ancient Rephaim', who were *rpi arṣ* 'the Rapha-beings of the netherworld'. They comprised "the Council of the Ditanites *(qbṣ ddn),*" which was headquartered in the northeastern sector of ancient Syria, an area to which the Ugaritians traced their origins.

The liturgy continues with words of lamentation over the immediately departed king, Niqmadu III. His throne, footstool, and royal table all shed tears! The sun goddess, Shapshu, is enlisted to locate the royal dead in the netherworld during her nocturnal circuits of the earth. She announces that the departed kings are deep down below, near the very ancient Rephaim. Niqmadu has also arrived there. Those assembled are to identify psychologically with the dead.

When all were present—the living king and his court, along with the departed kings and the Rephaim—seven sacrifices were offered. This scene recalls the Syro-Mesopotamian *kispum* 'funerary offering' and Egyptian feasts held in the company of the dead *(CAD K,* 425–427, *kispu).* The shared feast signified the endorsement of the new king by his royal ancestors. Such endorsement was deemed requisite to the legitimacy of the royal succession at Ugarit.

The liturgy concludes with words of blessing pronounced over the new king and his queen, as well as the city of Ugarit itself:

Hail *(šlm)!*
Hail Ammurapi,
and hail to his household!
Hail Tharyelli,
and hail to her household!
Hail Ugarit,
and hail to her gates!

In light of the recent discovery of extensive archives at Ebla in Syria, dated to the latter part of the third millennium B.C.E., it becomes possible to trace the development of royal cults of the dead back further in time than early first-millennium Mari, where considerable evidence on this subject has emerged. G. Pettinato (1979) has published a collection of texts pertaining to the cult of the royal family at Ebla during the reign of Ibbi-Sipis. These texts list offerings donated and presented to the major deities of Ebla on the part of the king and his family and members of his court.

On the first day of the eleventh month, the month of the Ishtar festival, we read a list of offerings including animals presented as si-dù si.dù en.en 'the laments of the kings' (Pettinato 1979: 127–128). The term si-dù is listed in the Eblaic bilingual lexical texts, also edited by Pettinato, where it is translated *di-mu-mu* 'lament, weeping' (Pettinato 1982: 320, no. 1116). The same rite is again performed, perhaps at the middle of the month, when the very same person donated offerings in honor of the place—in the palace garden, most likely—where the si-dù laments took place. Pettinato regards the si-dù laments as part of the royal cult of the dead.

Biblical authors surely knew of the themes reflected in royal cult of the dead in the ancient Near East, especially at Ugarit. This fact is revealed most dramatically in the oracle of Isaiah 14 predicting the demise of the king of Babylon (historically, the king of Assyria). In the prophetic oracle we are told that the king of Babylon will be denied a proper afterlife alongside the Rephaim of the netherworld, who will reject him from membership in their esteemed fraternity. We also find passing references to the Rephaim of Sheol in Proverbs (2:18; 9:18; 21:16), in Psalms (88:11), and in Job (20:5). Isa 26:14 and 19, part of a late passage, speak of the dead as being among the Rephaim.

There is a significant difference, however: the Rephaim of whom the Bible speaks are never identified as the ancestors of the kings of Judah and Israel, or of the Israelites as a nation. In biblical traditions, the Rephaim are viewed as a component of the pre-Israelite demography of Canaan, noted for their unusual stature and enormous prowess, a few of whom still survived into the Israelite period (see the COMMENT Numbers 13–14).

In Gen 6:1–4 we read another kind of objection to the apotheosis of heroes:

> When humans began to multiply on the earth and daughters were born to them, young gods *(ḇenê hāʾelôhîm)* saw how beautiful human women were, and took wives from among those who pleased them. YHWH said: "My spirit shall not retain its vitality in humans *(lōʾ yādôn rûḥî bāʾādām)* forever, because they are merely flesh. The limit of their days shall amount to one hundred twenty years."
>
> The Nephilim were present on earth in those days (and later, too), so that young gods had intercourse with human women, who bore them children. They (= the children) became the primeval heroes, the men of renown.

It would take us far afield to discuss all of the implications of this statement. While acknowledging the existence of mythic heroes, this passage from Genesis defines the boundary between the divine and the human. The heroes are not immortal, even those born of unions between gods and human women. Their divine heredity, so to speak, had not made them immortal or divine in any sense. One may conclude that upon their death such heroes would not be worshiped or have divinity attributed to them. In any event, they existed only in primeval times and are carefully separated from Israelite origins, as were the Rephaim.

Do we have evidence of royal or other cults of the dead in biblical Israel? The evidence is not unequivocal, but it is sufficient to allow for the conclusion that a royal cult of the dead was operative in biblical Israel, but that objection to it arose in the near-exilic and exilic periods.

In Jer 34:5 we find a statement by the prophet addressed to Zedekiah, the tragic king of Judah, assuring him that he would not die in battle: "You shall die peacefully, and they shall burn [offerings] for you, like the burnt offerings of your ancestors *(miśrepôt ʾabôtêkā)*, the former kings who preceded you. They shall mourn you: 'Ah, Lord!' *(hôi ʾādôn)*" (cf. Jer 22:18). The same burnt offerings are mentioned in 2 Chr 16:14, in connection with the burial of Asa, an earlier king of Judah: "They buried him in his gravesite, which he had hewn for himself in the City of David. They laid him to rest in his bed, which he had filled with spices of all kinds expertly blended, and they burned for him a great burnt offering *(śerēpāh gedôlāh)*" (cf. also 2 Chr 21:19).

Amos (6:10) refers to an uncle whose duty it was to attend to the funerary burnt offering attendant upon the burial of his clan relative. We are not informed what materials were to be burned, and some have suggested that only the burning of incense was involved. More likely, reference was to other forms of burnt offerings as well. In Ugaritic terminology *šrp*, a cognate of biblical Hebrew **miśrāpāh*, means "burnt offering," and Ugaritic rituals make it certain that this sacrifice usually consisted of animals (Levine and de Tarragon 1991; and see *KTU* 1.41 || 1.87). At Ebla, sheep were sacrificed as *sà-ra-pá-tum* 'burnt offering(s)' (Pettinato 1979: 42). In any event, it is difficult to avoid the conclusion that these burnt offerings were forms of worshiping the dead.

The kings of Judah were customarily buried in the City of David (2 Chr 21:20; 24:25; 35:24). The first overt protest against this burial practice is voiced in Ezek 43:7–9:

> O mortal man! This is the place of my throne and the place for the soles of my feet, where I dwell in the midst of the Israelite people forever. The House of Israel and their kings must never again defile my holy name by their faithlessness and by the corpses of their kings at their death (read: *bemôtām*).
>
> They position their threshold next to my threshold and their doorpost next to my doorpost, with only the wall between me and them. . . . Now, therefore, let them distance their faithlessness and the corpses of their kings from me, so that I may reside among them forever.

An explanatory note in *NJPS* explains that the southern wall of the First Temple was also the northern wall of the royal enclosure, with the two locales connecting through the Gate of the Guard (2 Kgs 11:19). Kings buried in the palace would, therefore, be within the same architectural complex as the temple; within the same "tent," to use the archaizing language of Num 19:14. In fact, whenever a king died in the palace, the temple would be automatically defiled. In Ezek 45:15 we read further that the restored temple, as the prophet envisioned it, would have a different plan. Considerable space would separate the sacred precincts from the royal palace, in order to avoid the pollution of the temple by the dead.

Even prior to the time of Ezekiel (or the other author of Ezekiel 43), we find indications of a toughening attitude regarding cults of the dead as part of the reforms of Josiah, king of Judah, decreed in 622 B.C.E. It is surely not coincidental that Josiah targeted the necropolis on the mountainside of Bethel for destruction (2 Kgs 23:16), as part of his overall effort to uproot pagan worship and to eliminate the cults of the *bāmôt*, principally in the area of Jerusalem. Nor is it insignificant that the method of destroying cult places, *maṣṣēbôt* 'cultic stelae', and altars involved burning such objects to ashes, literally, "to dust *(leʿāpār)*." More precisely, we should be interested in one of the methods used for invalidating altars or other cultic appurtenances for further use. It was to burn human bones upon them, or to fill them with bones (2 Kgs 23:14, 16, 20).

The verb used to convey the desecration of altars and Asherah columns is *ṭimmēʾ* 'to pollute, defile'. Implicit in these horrendous accounts is the notion that bones of the dead are irreversibly impure and would defile a cultic place or altar permanently. In fact, if bones were left in place, they would render the ground on which the altar or *bāmāh* stood impure, just as they rendered a grave impure. The author of 2 Kings 22–23 was operating with the concept that the bones of the dead were the most impure objects around, and that their impurity never ceased. He also assumed that reduction to ashes was the most effective method of riddance.

The sources in 2 Kings document a reversal of customary practice by establishing a new category of impurity associated with the dead, the same type of impurity as is legislated in Numbers 19! It would appear that the severe impurity of the dead legislated in Numbers 19 had not been the norm in preexilic times. There had been objection to certain aspects of cults of the dead, as we shall see, though some form of a royal cult of the dead had been authorized, if my reading of Jeremiah 34 is correct. But the author of Ezekiel 43, whether or not he was the prophet himself, is announcing a new policy. It came to legislative fruition in Numbers 19 and Leviticus 21, in the restrictions there imposed on the priesthood. The new direction may have been dictated during the reign of Josiah.

In preexilic Israel, certain aspects of the cults of the dead were outlawed as part of more comprehensive objections to pagan forms of magic and mourning, such as necromancy (Lev 19:26–28; Deut 18:11). Deut 26:13–15 preserve the text of a declaration to be pronounced by Israelites every third year, after the appropriate tithes had been remitted. An Israelite would make his appearance at the Temple and would declare,

> I have removed the consecrated material *(haqqôdeš)* from the house and have, moreover, disbursed it to the Levite, the alien, the orphan, and the widow, in accordance with all your commandments which you have commanded me. I have not transgressed against your commandments, nor have I been negligent. I have not eaten any of it while I was in mourning, nor have I disposed of any of it while I was impure, nor have I offered any of it to the dead. I have heeded the voice of YHWH, my God, and have performed all that you have commanded me.

The blatant funerary references in this declaration demonstrate that it was aimed at outlawing participation by Israelites in cults of the dead. An Israelite was required to disavow any such practice, precisely at the time that he was remitting his cultic dues. It would have been especially sacrilegious to set aside any produce as *maʿaśēr* that had come from a lot of which other parts had been used as offerings to the dead. What is more, tithes would have been polluted if they had been handled by an impure person who had been in contact with the dead. It is this prohibition that most clearly establishes the intent of the law: mourning and tithing are mutually exclusive.

It is not certain that all funerary rites described in the Hebrew Bible qualify as worship of the dead. Proper burial and lamentation need not imply a cult of the dead. Thus the often-cited passage in Jer 16:5–8 may have been misunderstood, and its provisions may be directed toward comforting the living, not worshiping the dead. The prophet is instructed not to mourn or grieve over his people, because there is no possibility of consolation. He is not to enter *bêt marzeāḥ*, a place in which mourning took place, because he would not be comforted by doing so. Many will die in the land, but will not be properly buried. Mourners will not gash themselves or pull out their hair, or prepare food and drink to console the bereaved. There is no indication that any of these activities is improper under normal circumstances. They would be superfluous because they would be ineffectual. The emphasis seems to be on consoling the living rather than on propitiating the dead.

And yet the needs addressed by cults of the dead are primal in their force. Israelites inevitably engaged in rites that would qualify as worship of the dead, notwithstanding deep-rooted objections from priestly and prophetic quarters. In its purest forms, biblical monotheism was incompatible with cults of the dead. To empower the dead with lasting influence over the living would serve to undercut the power of the God of Israel, as perceived by his worshipers. The worshiped dead also became divine, at some point, because the ongoing process of worship tends inevitably to attribute divinity to the objects of worship.

Antagonism to communication with the dead is expressed in the harsh oracle preserved in Isa 8:16–22. Isaiah is bereft of communication from YHWH, awaiting word from a God who had hidden his face from his people in anger:

> If people say to you: "Inquire of the ghosts and familiar spirits, who chirp and moan. May not a people inquire of its divine beings *(ʾelôhîm)*, on behalf of the living to the dead, for instruction and authority?"
>
> Surely, one who counsels thus shall see no dawn! He shall go about, wretched and hungry; and when he is hungry, he will rage and rebel against his king and his divinities. Whether he turns his face upward, or gazes downward into the netherworld, behold! Distress and darkness, with [the dawn] fled; stress and gloom, with [the dawn] cast away!

The import of this desperate prophetic statement is that communication with the spirits of the dead is futile and produces no enlightenment whatsoever. The language of this oracle recalls the incident of Saul's communication with the departed Samuel, through the services of a medium (1 Sam 28:13). There it is stated that Saul saw "divine beings *('elôhîm)* rising from the netherworld *(ʿôlîm min hāʾāreṣ).*"

In summary, certain notions of the impurity of the dead and serious objections to cults of the dead go far back in the Israelite mentality. Nevertheless, the specific category of impurity legislated in Numbers 19, and the restrictions on priestly activity prescribed in Leviticus 21, seem to reflect a religious movement that is heralded in Ezekiel 43 and generated by the policies of Josiah, and that was to gain in strength during the postexilic period of the Second Temple. Thus in Isa 57:9 and 65:3–7 we find cryptic references to worship of the dead, to which there is intense objection, and in Hag 2:12–14 we have an explicit protest against the pollution caused by contact with the dead. Similarly, in Num 9:9–14 we find a provision allowing those impure subsequent to contact with the dead to defer the celebration of the paschal sacrifice.

PART XIV.

NUMBERS 20: THE END OF THE WILDERNESS PERIOD —MIRIAM AND AARON PASS AWAY

INTRODUCTION

Numbers 20, as presented by the priestly school, brings to an end the era of the wilderness generation, the Israelites of the Exodus. Gray is undoubtedly correct in concluding that the unspecified date of the Israelite arrival at Kadesh recorded in Num 20:1 was, in fact, the first month of the fortieth year, the year in which Aaron died (cf. Num 20:22–29; 27:12–14; Deut 32:48–52).

In the introduction to this volume, section A.4, a lengthy discussion was devoted to assessing the historiographic implications of Numbers 20 as regards the priestly schedule, which differs substantially from that of the historiographers of the JE source. According to JE, the Israelites had arrived at Kadesh within a year or so after the Exodus and were already in Kadesh when they dispatched the spies to reconnoiter southern Canaan (Num 13:26; 32:8).

For reasons not entirely clear to us, the priestly writers sought to retain the Israelites in Sinai until the last of the forty years of the wilderness period. They had gone to considerable effort in construing the existing sources to attain this result. So it is that the caption in Num 20:1, and Numbers 20 as a whole, highlight the different wildernesses of the JE and P sources, respectively: according to P, the wilderness of reference was northern Sinai, the Wilderness of Paran; while according to JE, thirty-eight of the forty years were spent on a route that led the Israelites east of Edom to Nahal Zered, in Transjordan, which joins the King's Highway on the southern border of Moab. In textual terms, P creates a time warp, shifting the date of the mission to Edom to the fortieth year. In JE's schedule, this mission was undertaken soon after the spies returned to Kadesh with their discouraging report, and the Israelites were told to proceed toward the Reed Sea (Num 14:11–25, 44–45; see the NOTES on Num 20:1).

Numbers 20 is composed of three principal sections. Verses 1–13, primarily attributable to P in their present form, recount an incident of popular rebellion against Moses and Aaron prompted by a lack of water and by overall dissatisfaction with conditions of life in the wilderness. In response, Moses provided water for the people and their livestock by hitting the rock with his staff, undoubtedly thinking that he had thereby demonstrated God's providence.

As the text continues, in v 12, we are startled to learn that Moses' action bespoke a serious lack of trust in God, and for this reason, Moses and Aaron would not live to bring the Israelites into the Promised Land. This decree is restated in v 24, after the priestly record resumes (Num 20:22–29), in the passage recording Aaron's death. The reader has the sense that he is missing something. After all, Moses had been instructed by God to take his staff with him when he stood before the rock, though a literal reading of the text reveals, to be sure, that Moses was told to speak to the rock, not to strike it (Num

20:8). Is it because of this imprecision that Moses was denied entry into Canaan?

Quite possibly the priestly writers were echoing the theme of the Deuteronomist (Deut 3:23–29), who dramatizes the tragedy of Moses' death before Israel entered Canaan. They stopped short, however, of recording Moses' death, as they did the deaths of Aaron and Miriam. On this basis, v 12 may have been interpolated, so as to link two subjects originally unrelated to each other: the supplying of water by a providential God, and the decree against Moses and Aaron.

There are possible traces of JE material in Num 20:1–13, but they have been reworked by priestly writers. Some of vv 1 and 3–5, the words of the complaint that the people addressed to Moses, probably come from JE. Nevertheless, the reference to dying *lipnê YHWH* 'in the presence of YHWH' (v 3) recalls Num 16:16, a priestly passage.

Actually, Num 20:1–13 (with the possible exception of v 12) represent a parallel priestly version of Exod 17:1b–7, part of the JE narrative. According to Exod 17:1b–7 the incident of reference occurred at a site named Massah and Meribah, so that the themes of testing and contention are present, but that site was located close to Mount Horeb, in the south of the Sinai peninsula near Rephidim, not in the Wilderness of Zin.

Nevertheless, the two reports have in common hitting a rock to bring forth water, the use of Moses' staff with which he had struck the Nile and performed wonders in Egypt, and shared diction. Both Exod 17:2 and Num 20:3 say that the people contended *(wayyāreb)* with Moses, and in both Exod 17:3 and Num 20:5 the Israelites complain that Moses (and Aaron) brought them up (the verb *heʿelāh)* from Egypt. Both versions include a grievance about the loss of livestock (cf. Exod 17:3 with Num 20:4).

The differences between the two accounts are equally significant. In the JE version of Exod 17:1b–7, the sin of the people is testing God (the verb *nissāh*). With the elders lending legitimacy to Moses, he produces water from a rock, and the people are satisfied. In the priestly version of Num 20:1–13, the legitimacy of Moses (and Aaron) is established by the appearance of the *kābôd,* and God is sanctified after the contention is over (Num 20:6, 13). There is also a relation to the Tent of Meeting. In fact, the staff had been placed in the sacred area (Num 20:9). The people's complaints are voiced more bitterly, and the entire episode is characterized by a forensic quality. Moses is told to speak to the rock, an aspect missing from Exod 17:1b–7.

So it is that we have two accounts of the same kind of crisis, one at the beginning of the wilderness period, and one at its end; one as the Israelites enter Sinai and one as they are about to leave it. Furthermore, Exod 17:1b–7 precede a war with Amalek (Exod 17:8–16), and Num 20:1–13 and 24 precede a battle with the Negeb Canaanites (Num 21:1–3). In both instances, God's power, appealed to in different ways, turned the battle in Israel's favor.

Num 20:14–21 are part of the JE historiography in Numbers. They record a mission to the king of Edom from Kadesh (here described as a town on the Edomite border), requesting permission for the Israelites to traverse the land of Edom. This permission was denied, and what is more, the Edomites confronted Israel with a large force, making it necessary for them to turn away and, as we know, to proceed on a route from Elath, east of Edom. In the introduction to this volume, section D.4, the differing attitudes of the JE historiographers and of the Deuteronomist (Deut 2:1–8) about Edom/Seir were discussed. According to the Deuteronomist, the Israelites did, indeed, pass through Edom/Seir, exactly as they pledged to do in Num 20:14–21 when they were refused.

The priestly record resumes in Num 20:22–29, which recount the death of Aaron at Hor Hahar, an unidentified site near Kadesh. The incident at the Waters of Meribah is blamed for Aaron's premature demise. Before his death, Aaron transferred the high priesthood to his son, Eleazar, in a ceremony over which Moses presided, and the people mourned Aaron.

TRANSLATION

20 [1]The Israelite people, the entire community, arrived at the Wilderness of Zin in the first month, and the people were residing at Kadesh. Miriam died there, and was buried there.

[2]There was no water for the community, and they assembled en masse against Moses and against Aaron.

[3]The people quarreled with Moses, expressing themselves as follows: "Had we only expired when our kinsmen expired in the presence of YHWH!

[4]"Why did you bring the congregation of YHWH to this wilderness to die here, we and our livestock?

[5]"And why did you take us up from Egypt to bring us to this awful place; not a place of seed, or fig trees, or vines, or pomegranates, and with no water to drink?"

[6]Moses and Aaron withdrew from the advance of the congregation to the entrance of the Tent of Meeting, and they fell on their faces. The glorious presence of YHWH appeared to them.

[7]YHWH addressed Moses as follows:

[8]Take the staff and assemble the community, you and Aaron, your brother. Both of you speak to the rock in sight of them, and it will produce its water. You shall extract water for them from the rock, and provide water for the community and their livestock.

[9]Moses took the staff from the presence of YHWH as he had commanded him.

[10]Moses and Aaron assembled the congregation in front of the rock. He

said to them: "Take heed, then, O rebellious ones! Shall we from this rock actually extract water for you?"

11 Thereupon Moses raised his arm and hit the rock with his staff twice. Abundant water gushed forth, and the community and its livestock drank.

12 But YHWH said to Moses and to Aaron: Because you did not place your trust in me, which would have affirmed my sanctity in the sight of the Israelite people—for that reason you shall not bring this congregation to the land that I have granted to them.

13 Those are the Waters of Meribah, where the Israelite people quarreled with YHWH, and through which his sanctity was affirmed.

14 Moses dispatched messengers from Kadesh to the king of Edom. Thus says your brother, Israel: "You are surely aware of all of the distress that has overtaken us.

15 "Our ancestors descended to Egypt, and we resided in Egypt for many years, but the Egyptians dealt harshly with us and with our ancestors.

16 "We cried out to YHWH, who heard our voice. He sent an angel who brought us out of Egypt, and now we are in Kadesh, a town bordering on your territory.

17 "May we traverse your land? We will not pass through fields or vineyards, nor will we drink well water. We will travel on the King's Highway, without turning to the right or to the left, until we have traversed your territory."

18 But Edom said to him, "You shall not pass through me, lest I come out to meet you with the sword!"

19 The Israelite people said to him, "We will make our way up the highway, and should we drink of your waters, I or my livestock, I will remit their cost. Only make no issue of it; let me traverse on foot."

20 But he said, "You shall not pass through!" Then Edom came out to confront him with a large fighting force and with a powerful arm.

21 Edom refused to allow the Israelites to pass through his territory, and Israel turned away from him.

22 They marched from Kadesh, and the Israelite people, the entire community, arrived at Hor Hahar.

23 YHWH said to Moses and to Aaron at Hor Hahar, on the Edomite border, as follows:

24 Let Aaron be taken away to his kin, for he shall not enter the land that I have granted to the Israelite people, because [the two of] you disobeyed my command at the Waters of Meribah.

25 Take Aaron and Eleazar, his son, and bring them up to Hor Hahar.

26 Divest Aaron of his garments, and clothe Eleazar, his son, with them, and let Aaron be taken away, and let him die there.

27 Moses did as YHWH had commanded him. They ascended Hor Hahar in sight of the entire community.

28 Moses divested Aaron of his garments and clothed his son, Eleazar, with

them. Then Aaron died there, atop Hor Hahar. Moses and Eleazar came down from the mountain.

29The entire community saw that Aaron had expired, and they mourned Aaron for thirty days, the entire household of Israel.

NOTES TO 20:1–13: INCIDENTS AT KADESH

20 1. According to the priestly schedule, the Israelites first arrived at Kadesh in v 1, and in v 22 departed from Kadesh, but only to a nearby site, Hor Hahar, where Aaron died. They did not start their encirclement of Edom until Num 21:4a.

and the people were residing at Kadesh. There is subtlety in v 1, which is a pivotal statement in the priestly historiography of Numbers. The words *wayyēšeb hāʿām beqādēš* probably derive from JE, as is suggested by use of the term *hāʿām* 'the people' to designate the Israelites. Originally, these words may have had circumstantial force and may have come at the beginning of Num 20:14: "While the people were residing at Kadesh, Moses dispatched messengers from Kadesh to the king of Edom." By positioning these words in v 1, however, the priestly writers associated them with the Israelite arrival at Kadesh, not with a prior circumstance. As a result, Num 20:1, as we have it, explicitly records the Israelite arrival in the Wilderness of Zin, but is less explicit regarding when, precisely, they had begun their residence at Kadesh.

the Wilderness of Zin. The Hebrew *midbar Ṣin* is a well-known toponym in P (Num 27:14; 33:36; Deut 32:51). It is one way of indicating the southernmost extent of Canaan (Num 13:21; 34:3–4; Josh 15:1–3). It defines an area north-northeast of the brook of Egypt, considerably south of Arad, west of a line running from the Dead Sea to Elath, and northeast of Elath (Aharoni and Avi-Yonah 1979: 40, map 48; 41, map 50). In the NOTES on Num 13:26 it was explained that the schedule of the wilderness period projected by P required that the spies report back to the Wilderness of Paran, in Sinai. Kadesh is correctly to be located in the Wilderness of Zin, in southern Canaan, not in Sinai; but the geography of the various sources seems to move or slide in more than one direction (see the COMMENT on Numbers 13–14).

Gray was of the opinion that according to JE's schedule the Israelites spent the better part of thirty-eight years in Kadesh. He understood the verb *yāšab* in Num 20:1 as indicating a prolonged habitation, citing usage of *yāšab* in Num 21:25 and 31, where the sense is that the Israelites "settled" in the Amorite cities of Transjordan. Gray's reference to Judg 11:17, where the same clause occurs in Jephthah's recounting of the wilderness experience, is hardly supportive of his view, however. In fact, Judg 11:17–18 should be rendered as follows: "Israel dispatched messengers to the king of Edom, saying, 'Let me pass through your land.' But the king of Edom did not comply. He also sent word to the king of Moab, but he would not agree. *This was while Israel was residing in Kadesh.* So he walked through the wilderness and encircled the land of Edom and the land of Moab. . . ." If anything, Judg 11:17–18, where the reference to the Israelite residence at Kadesh is juxtaposed and placed subsequent to the mission to Edom (and Moab), support the view that the Israelites did not remain very long at Kadesh. Soon after being refused passage through Edom, they began to go around it.

Furthermore, the verb *yāšab* often connotes only brief residence (Num 25:1; Exod 2:15; Gen 29:14 [one month]; Judg 19:4 [three days]; 1 Sam 23:14). It is more reasonable, therefore, to conclude that the Israelites remained only a relatively short while in Kadesh, according to the view of JE, a view shared by the Deuteronomist (Deut 2:14).

It was most probably P's view that both Miriam and Aaron died in the fortieth year. In Numbers 20, P intimates the end of the wilderness generation by recording the passing of two members of Moses' family.

2. *they assembled en masse against.* The idiom *wayyiqqāhalû ʿal* also informs Num 16:3 and 17:7 (P), where rebellion is likewise described. In Exod 32:1 the same diction is expressed in a passage attributed to JE: *wayyiqqahēl hāʿām ʿal ʾAharôn* 'the people assembled en masse against Aaron' (cf. also Ezek 38:7).

3. *quarreled.* Hebrew *wayyāreb,* from the verbal root *r-y-b,* may connote violent conflict, as in Ps 35:1, where it is parallel with *lāḥam* 'to do battle'. Violence is also intimated in Gen 26:20–22, where we read of a fight over a well (cf. Exod 17:2; Judg 8:1). Often a forensic encounter or a quarrel over some issue is indicated, as may be true here, although what begins as an argument may develop into a physical encounter. For the same scene and the same idiom see Exod 17:2, a comparison that suggests that Num 20:3a may derive from JE.

expired. The reference to the death of kinsmen recalls use of the verb *gāwaʿ* 'to expire, die' in the diction of Num 17:27, where the congregation expresses fear of dying in the aftermath of the Korah incident. The Hebrew verb *gāwaʿ* seems to indicate a state immediately prior to death (Gen 25:8, 17; 35:29). There is also the nuance of disappearance (Job 10:18; 14:10).

4. *livestock.* Note the different words for livestock in this chapter. P uses *beʿir* for cattle here, but in Num 20:19 (JE) the term for livestock is *miqneh,* as in Exod 17:3, also from JE.

the congregation of YHWH. Reference to *qehal* YHWH recalls Num 16:3, further linking the rebellion of Numbers 20 to the Korah incident of Numbers 16–17. In itself, *qehal* YHWH appears to be a deuteronomistic designation (Deut 23:2–3, 4; Mic 2:5) adopted by P and its successors (1 Chr 28:8).

this wilderness. The Hebrew *hammidbār hazzeh* can refer to more than one region, depending on who is using this term of reference. In Deut 2:7 *ʾet hammidbār haggādôl hazzeh* 'this vast wilderness' refers to the Edomite/Seirite desert, whereas in Exod 16:3 and Num 14:2 and 32 (P), reference is to Sinai. In the present verse, the most immediate reference is the Wilderness of Zin; but in the larger context of P, it is likewise Sinai.

5. *this awful place.* The negative characterization of the wilderness echoes in a pathetic manner Deut 8:7–8, where Canaan is described as "a beautiful land; a land of water-filled wadis, with springs and artesian waters flowing in hills and valleys; a land of wheat and barley and vines and fig trees and pomegranates; a land of olive oil and nectar." Instead of *'eres tobah* 'a beautiful land', the Israelites found themselves in *hammāqôm hāraʿ hazzeh*—"this awful place; not a place of seed, or fig trees, or vines, or pomegranates, and with no water to drink."

6. Falling on one's face before God was a sign of submission to his will; see the NOTES on Num 14:5 and 10. The appearance of the *kābôd* 'glorious presence' at a moment of crisis is a recurrent phenomenon in the priestly literature of the Torah and is associated with a crisis of leadership or faith, the very occasions on which Moses and Aaron usually fell on their faces (Exod 16:10; Num 16:19, 22; 17:7, 10). In fact, Num 20:6 and 14:10 resemble each other considerably. A typology is formed: the leaders fall on their faces in an appeal to God's rescue, and the divine *kābôd* appears in response.

7–13. These verses provide a resolution of the crisis of vv 1–6.

8. *staff.* The staff *(hammaṭṭeh)* that Moses is instructed to take is undoubtedly the one he used in Egypt to perform the signs (Exod 17:5, 9; and see Exod 4:2–4, 17; 7:10–20; 8:1, 12; 14:16–18; 17:5, 9).

in sight of them. It was important for the community to see God's act of providence with their own eyes, hence Moses and Aaron were to speak to the rock *leʿênêhem* 'in sight of them' (cf. Exod 17:6).

9. *as he had commanded him.* In priestly narratives, Moses acts in response to specific divine commands. The formula *ka'ašer ṣiwwāh (YHWH)* 'as YHWH commanded' is an earmark of priestly style.

10. *assembled the congregation.* The cognate clause *wayyaqhîlû . . . 'et haqqāhāl,* literally, "they congregated the congregation," is stilted.

in front of the rock. Idiomatic *'el penê hasselaʿ* means "facing the rock." Gray (Gray—ICC 144, in a note to Num 13:26) cites a naturalist and explorer named Clay Trumbull who describes a huge cliff formation at Ayn Qudeis, with a deep well cutting down through it. Now although Kadesh Barnea is no longer identified with 'Ain Qudeis (which nevertheless expresses the name *Qādēš*) but with 'Ain Qudeirat, the two sites are actually not far from each other. Often tales about miracles are stimulated by unusual natural phenomena.

The Septuagint suggests the reading *šemaʿûnî* (plural imperative): "Hear me!" instead of *šimeʿû -nā'* 'Take heed, then!' In the present verse we have a unique occurrence of the plural participle *hammôrîm* 'O rebellious ones'. The verb *mārāh* itself is common and expresses conscious disobedience of God's will or willful infraction of the law.

Moses' words are best understood as a taunt: "Do you disbelieving rebels think we can really bring forth water for you from this rock?" Moses himself was given to irony in questioning God's power. Thus we read similar rhetorical questions introduced by interrogative *heh* in Num 11:22, as Moses appears to doubt God's capacity to provide for the Israelites: "Could flocks and herds be slaughtered for them in quantities sufficient for them? Were all the fish of the sea to be caught for them, would that meet their needs?"

The notion of speaking to the rock, instead of striking it, points to the interaction of two motifs: using a staff to strike a rock is functionally logical. Although a normal staff would not split a rock, the miraculous one that Moses used would. However, speaking to the rock implies that Moses' command, his word, is powerful, that the rock obeys him. It is a case of "Open, Sesame!" Now v 8 is confusing, because why would the staff be needed if Moses was only to command the rock verbally? Possibly the author who interpolated v 12 also introduced the notion of speaking to the rock in the present verse, in order to provide a basis for divine disapproval.

11. Moses raises his staff so as to be able to strike hard; cf. Exod 14:16.

12. The criticism leveled against Moses and Aaron is unclear. The sense seems to be that if Moses had spoken certain words, which were not specified in v 8, God would have been sanctified in the sight of the Israelites. Presumably Moses doubted that merely commanding the rock would produce water, so he hit the rock to make certain. Seeing this action, the people did not get the same message as they would have received had he commanded the rock.

There may be some significance to the fact that Moses struck the rock twice. We note that Elisha had to strike the water twice in his attempt to replicate Elijah's miracle, undoubtedly because nothing happened the first time (2 Kgs 2:13–15). Conceivably, Moses showed impatience or a lack of faith, or perhaps it was normal in magical activity to repeat specific actions.

All of this reasoning is, however, hypothetical. What is clear is the agenda: Moses and Aaron would not live to bring the Israelites into the land YHWH had granted them. As suggested earlier, this decree resonates Deut 3:23–29.

13. In a sense, this verse contradicts the preceding, further suggesting that v 12 was interpolated. Verse 12 states that Moses and Aaron had failed to sanctify God in the sight of the people, whereas v 13 records that subsequent to the conflict, God was sanctified *(wayyiqqādēš)* by virtue of his demonstrated power, here employed to produce water. Gray suggests that repeated use of the verb *qādaš* 'to be holy' is a play on the toponym *Qādēš. Hiphʿil hiqdîs* 'to proclaim holy' requires a leader to show the people God's acts or to recount them to the people (Isa 29:23).

The Waters of Meribah. Mê merîbāh is a two-dimensional name, referring to an incident of contention and at the same time to a presumed toponym, *Merîbāh.* An examination of the variations of this toponym in biblical literature yields the following information: first, there is a place named *mê merîbāh* 'Waters of Meribah' (Num 20:24; Deut 33:8; Pss 81:8; 106:32); second, there is a place named *mê merîbat Qādēš* 'Waters of Meribath Kadesh' (Num 27:14; Deut 32:51; Ezek 47:19; 48:28); and, third, there is also a place named *Massāh Ûmerîbāh* (Exod 17:7).

NOTES TO 20:14–21: THE MISSION TO EDOM

Verses 14–21 are taken from the JE historiography, primarily from E. Moses refers to *'aḥîka Yiśrā'ēl* 'your kinsman, Israel', which recalls the law of Deut 23:8: "do not despise an Edomite, for he is your kinsman *(kî 'aḥîkā hû')*." Compare also Amos 1:11; Obad 10:12; and Mal 1:2.

Gray comments that whole peoples and other large groups can be referred to in the singular, as here. Thus in Exod 14:25b, the Egyptians speak as one person: "Egypt said: I must flee from before Israel, for YHWH is doing battle for them against Egypt." Compare also Num 21:1–3, 22; Josh 9:7; 17:14; Judg 1:2–3; 19:44; and Lam 1:15–22.

14. *distress.* Use of the rare word *telā'āh* (literally, the effects of exhaustion, weariness) recalls Exod 18:8, also part of a speech by Moses, in which he similarly characterizes the pressures of migration (cf. Neh 9:32). Speeches are often introduced by *kôh 'āmar* 'Thus he has spoken' (Levine 1979b).

15–16. The historical review presented in vv 15–16 may be compared to other similar summaries. Closest in diction are the statements in Deut 26:5–8, part of a declaration to be made when firstfruits were presented in the Sanctuary. Common to the two sources are references to the descent into Egypt, to crying out to God (the verb *ṣā'aq)*, to God's hearing the outcry (the verb *šāma'*), and to the mistreatment of the Israelites by the Egyptians: *wayyārē'û lānû ('ôtānû) hammiṣrîm* 'the Egyptians dealt harshly with us'.

16. What is distinctive here is the reference to an angel sent by God to liberate the Israelites from Egypt. Exod 14:19 relates that the angel of God *(mal'ak hā'elôhîm)*, who had been proceeding in advance of the Israelites as they began to leave Egypt, changed position and fell back to protect them from behind as the Egyptians pursued them. Elsewhere, in Exod 23:20 and 33:2, we read that God will send an angel to protect Israel on their journey to the Promised Land and to facilitate their victory over the Canaanites. Num 20:16 brings us back to the Exodus, as if to say that all the way from Egypt to the settlement of Canaan, Israel had the benefit of angelic protection. Contrast this concept with Hos 12:14: "It was by means of a prophet that YHWH brought Israel up out of Egypt, and by means of a prophet that he was protected."

a town bordering on your territory. In the introduction to this volume, section D.5, it was explained that the stated location of Kadesh as *ʿîr qeṣēh gebûlekā* 'a town bordering on your territory', namely, on the territory of Edom, is a telling contextual indicator. It suggests that the author of Num 20:14–21 wrote at a time in which Edomite territory extended west of Elath–Ezion Geber and ran along the southern border of Judah. Based on the diction of v 18, below, which recalls the language of Amos 1:11, and upon historical considerations pertaining to the westward expansion of Edom, it was suggested that Num 20:14–21 reflects the realities of the mid to late eighth century B.C.E., though a later date is also possible. In the late thirteenth and early twelfth centuries B.C.E., the traditional period of the wilderness wanderings, one could not have referred realistically to Kadesh as being adjacent to Edomite territory, because the Edomites had not expanded west of Elath (Bartlett 1989: 90–93).

17. *fields or vineyards.* The pair *śādeh wākerem* is proverbial (Exod 22:4; Num 16:14), and it is repeated in Num 21:22, in a similar request for passage through Amorite territory.

the King's Highway. Reference to *derek hammelek* requires comment. This designation recurs in Num 21:22 (and only there), in the similar request for passage through Transjordan, farther north in Amorite country. Clearly, Num 20:14–21 and 21:21–23 are modeled on the same typology.

According to Bartlett (1989: 38, 92, 128–130) a designation such as the King's Highway might suit the Assyrian period, which began after the campaigns of Tiglath-Pileser III in Transjordan, perhaps as early as 735 B.C.E. It was then that Qosmalak was appointed the vassal king of Edom. It is probable, however, that this major roadway was known as *derek hammelek*, or by cognate names, before that time, because the roadway itself was very ancient. It led from Damascus to the delta of Egypt via Elath. In the north, it intersected with the Via Maris at Damascus. At various times Madeba, Dibon, Heshbon, Rabbath Ammon, as well as Shawe-Kiryathaim, Ramoth Gilead, and Ashtaroth-Karnaim served as stations on the King's Highway.

The King's Highway was important in the perfume trade coming from southern Arabia, through Teima. In Transjordan, this route runs north and south just east of the major wadis—the Yarmuk, the Jabbok/Zerqa, the Arnon, and the Zered—in the desert. At Damascus one could turn northeast and continue to Tadmor/Palmyra, and then to the Euphrates, or one could continue northward to Qatna, Hamath, and Aleppo. At Damascus, those coming from a northerly direction could switch to the Via Maris and continue down to Gaza and Egypt. Aharoni suggests that the northern part of the King's Highway was probably known as *derek habbāšān* 'the Bashan Road', traversed by the Israelites as they proceeded northward to do battle with Og, king of the Bashan (Num 21:33; Deut 3:1; Aharoni 1979: 16, map 9; Aharoni 1979: 54–58).

R. de Vaux (1978: 22) calls attention to the importance of Genesis 14 in tracing the history of the King's Highway. In fact, that early source may hold the key to the name *derek hammelek.* In effect, it relates that the four kings of the north came down the route of the King's Highway to the region of the Dead Sea and farther south, to El Paran/Elath. Gen 14:5–8 mention Ashtaroth-Karnaim, Ham, and, most notably, Shawe-Kiryathaim, all towns along that route. Especially important for present considerations is Gen 14:17: "The king of Sodom came out to greet him (= Abram) after he had returned from defeating Chedor-laomer and the kings allied with him, at the valley of Shawe[-Kiryathaim]; that is, the royal valley *(ʿēmeq hammelek).*" We thus have a symmetry of sorts in the nomenclature, *ʿēmeq hammelek* and *derek hammelek,* in the zone east of the Dead Sea, at its northern extent. Exactly how ancient the two discrete sections of Genesis 14 are cannot be determined, but it is an early biblical source, perhaps the earliest text in the Torah. For some reason, both the road itself and a valley situated along its route were dubbed "royal," the valley so called in an early record of a battle between two coalitions of kings (see the NOTES on Num 14:25, 45).

18. In refusing, the king of Edom speaks in the language of Amos 1:11, where Edom is condemned: "because he pursued his kinsman with the sword *(ʿal rodpo baḥereb ʾahiw).*" Here the king of Edom threatens *pen baḥereb ʾēṣēʾ liqrāʾtekā* 'lest I come out to meet you with the sword!" The dictional link with Amos 1:11 further recommends assigning Num 20:14–21 to the eighth century B.C.E.

19. Hebrew *mesillāh* indicates a flattened, or at least graded, road from which rocks had been removed (Isa 62:10). The verb *naʿaleh,* literally, "we shall ascend," indicates a northerly direction in some ancient Near Eastern geographical descriptions (Levine 1975).

Reference to paying for food and water and proceeding on foot recall Deut 2:27–28, part of a similar request to Sihon, the Amorite king, for passage through his territory. Compare also Judg 11:17.

Only make no issue of it. Idiomatic *raq ʾên dābār* is unique to this verse. Part of the idiom, *ʾên dābār* 'it doesn't matter', is common in modern Hebrew parlance. Here the sense appears to be that Moses is urging the Edomite king not to block the route of the Israelites because of fear that his fields would be damaged or his resources depleted.

on foot. Perhaps *beraglaî* does not mean "by foot," but rather "with my foot soldiers," expressing an otherwise unattested plural of the collective *raglî* 'foot soldiers, infantry' (Num 11:21).

20. One recalls Gen 32:6, where Esau "comes out to confront *(hôlēk liqrāʾt-)*" Jacob, the same language used in the present verse. Hebrew *ʿam* 'people' here connotes a military force.

21. *to allow.* The sense of the verb *nātan* is "to permit," and the meaning and syntax of the present verse resemble Num 21:23, once again linking Num

20:14–21 with the parallel request for passage addressed to Sihon, the Amorite.

NOTES TO 20:22–29: THE FIRST PRIESTLY SUCCESSION

The final verses (P) record the passing of Aaron and the succession to the high priesthood of his son, Eleazar. This account has the effect of keeping the Israelites in the Kadesh area a little longer. The result is that Aaron dies before the Israelites enter the Promised Land, for in the priestly geography Kadesh is still in the Wilderness of Paran (Num 13:26). To put the matter another way: the Wilderness of Zin (Num 20:1) and the Wilderness of Paran overlap just enough to obscure the southern border of Canaan, allowing the Israelites to be in Kadesh, but not actually in Canaan! This is the probable reason for creating Hor Hahar, an unidentified locale and a toponym that undoubtedly means "the mountaintop" (Num 20:28; and cf. Num 33:38–40; Deut 32:50). The result is that Aaron dies near the Edomite territory, and not technically in Canaan, thereby fulfilling the priestly version of the decree that the entire Exodus generation will perish in Sinai (Num 14:32). Moses was not included in this decree (introduction, section A.6.a); nor were Caleb and Joshua, in the combined traditions of JE and P.

24. The part of v 24 that explains why Aaron died in the area of Kadesh correlates with v 12 in offering the same reason for his premature death: he and Moses had disobeyed God's order at the Waters of Meribah. Note that both Moses and Aaron had been commanded to speak to the rock, so that even though Aaron did not actually strike the rock, only Moses, the outcome implicated him as well.

be taken away to his kin. The idiom *ne'esap 'el 'ammâw* exhibits more than one dimension of meaning, because of the ambiguity attendant on the verb *ne'esap*. It can mean to be brought back, to be taken in (Num 11:30; 12:14–15; Judg 19:15, 18), or to be gathered up and taken away, which is probably what is conveyed by the present idiom. On the simplest level, the sense is that one is not left unburied, but rather brought to a grave (Jer 8:2; 9:21; 25:33). An obvious inference is that bones would be gathered up for secondary burial, but this sense was not always intended, to be sure. One may also perceive the sense of bringing a dead person to a family grave where he would join his "kin," which is the sense of *'am* here (cf. Lev 21:1, 4). On another plane, the sense is that one rests with his ancestors in Sheol (Judg 2:10; 1 Kgs 1:21; 14:31).

26. Investiture was instrumental in transferring the office of the high priest, just as it had been in the initial consecration of Aaron and his sons (Exod 29:1–37; Leviticus 8). The verse reads "and Aaron shall be taken away

and die there," which seems to reverse the order of events. There may be a subtle allusion to a faraway grave to which Aaron was led.

27. Moses complies, *ka'ašer ṣiwwāh YHWH* 'as YHWH commanded', the typical priestly formula. It was important for the people to witness the ascent on the mountain, and then to realize that Aaron did not return. One inevitably associates this scene with the Akkadian idiom connoting death, *šadāšu īmid,* literally, "he entered into his mountain" (*CAD E,* 140, *emēdu,* d, 3').

29. The thirty-day period of mourning was also observed when Moses died (Deut 34:8). The priestly school established a symmetry between the death of Moses and the death of Aaron. When Aaron was about to die, he was succeeded by his son, Eleazar; when Moses was about to die, he was succeeded by his disciple, Joshua.

Moses saw his people through the Transjordanian campaigns of the fortieth year and, at the very least, lived to see a new generation of Israelite heroes. In the JE historiography, the new generation enters on the scene after the Israelites arrive at Nahal Zered (Num 21:12) and prepare for their inevitable encounter with the Amorites of Transjordan.

Map I
The Sinai Phase of the Wilderness Period:
Identifiable Stations on the Priestly Route
Time Frame: Years 1–39 following the Exodus

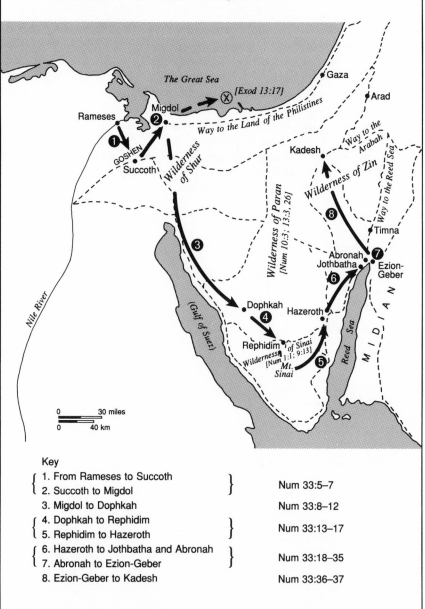

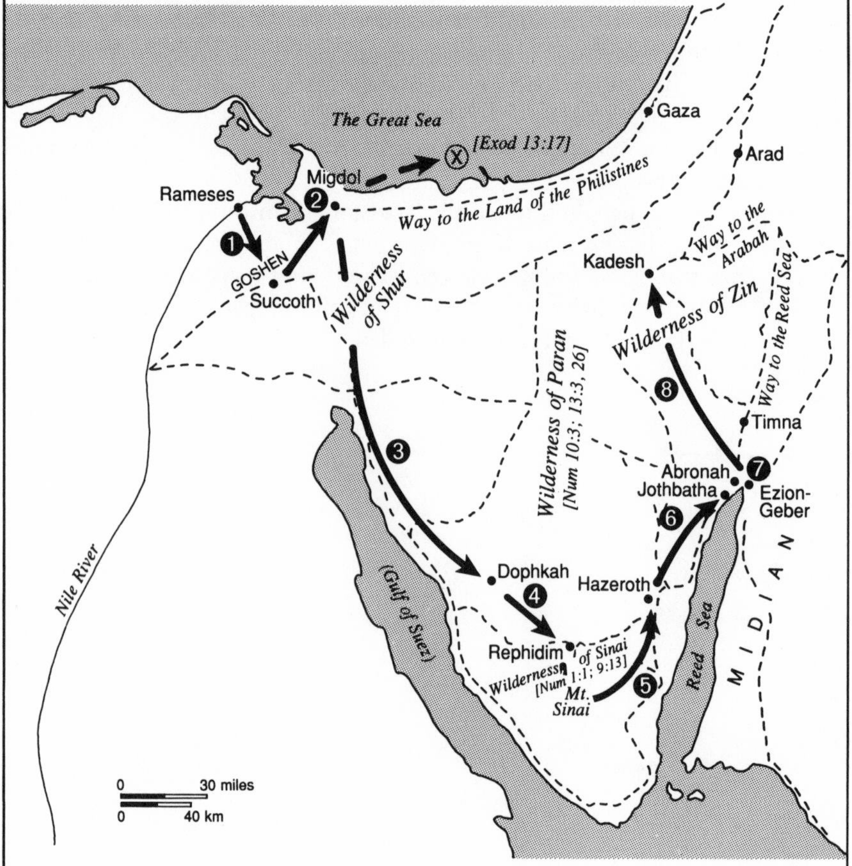

Key

1. From Rameses to Succoth 2. Succoth to Migdol	Num 33:5–7
3. Migdol to Dophkah	Num 33:8–12
4. Dophkah to Rephidim 5. Rephidim to Hazeroth	Num 33:13–17
6. Hazeroth to Jothbatha and Abronah 7. Abronah to Ezion-Geber	Num 33:18–35
8. Ezion-Geber to Kadesh	Num 33:36–37

Map II
The Sinai Phase of the Wilderness Period:
Identifiable Stations on the JE Route
Time Frame: Years 1–2 following the Exodus

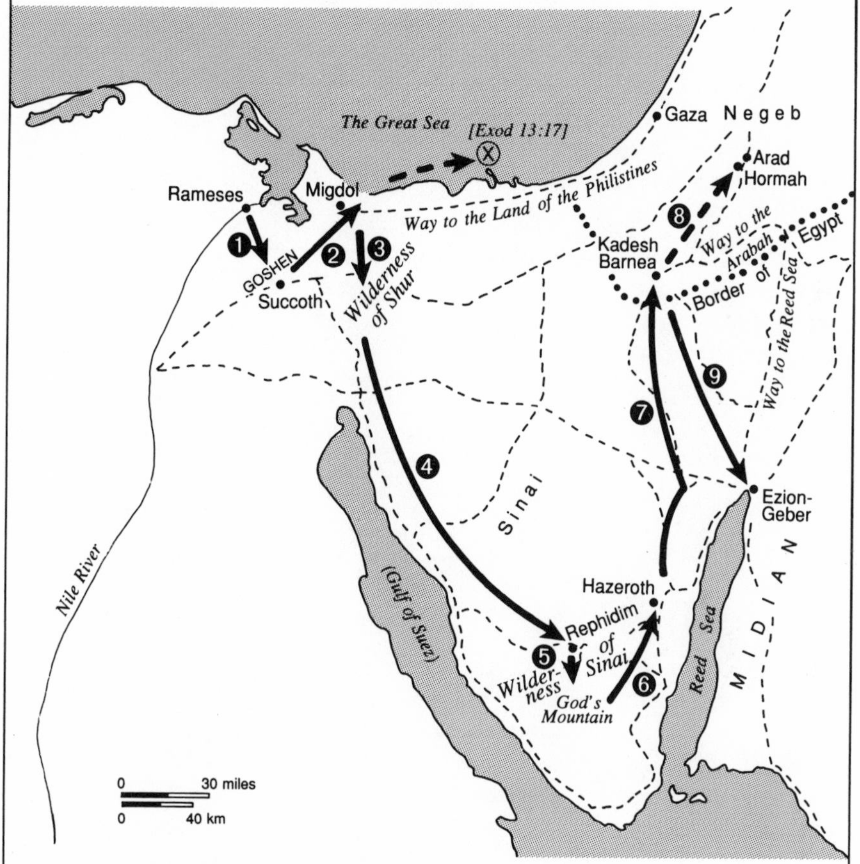

Key

1. From Rameses to Succoth	Exod 13:37
2. Succoth to a point between Migdol and the sea	Exod 14:1
3. From that point into the Wilderness of Shur	Exod 15:22
4. From the Wilderness of Shur to Rephidim	Exod 17:1b, 8
5. Rephidim to God's Mountain	Num 10:33
6. God's Mountain to Hazeroth	Num 11:35
7. Hazeroth to Kadesh	Num 13:26; 32:8
8. Foray into the Negeb	Num 14:44–45; 21:1–3
9. Kadesh to the Reed Sea	Num 14:25; 20:21

Subject Index

♦

SUBJECT INDEX

SUBJECT INDEX

Modern Authors Index

♦

MODERN AUTHORS INDEX

Sources Index

SCRIPTURE

SOURCES INDEX

SOURCES INDEX

SOURCES INDEX

SOURCES INDEX

SOURCES INDEX

SOURCES INDEX

RABBINIC / MEDIEVAL JEWISH SOURCES AND AUTHORS

MISHNAH

TOSEPHTAʾ

JERUSALEM TALMUD

BABYLONIAN TALMUD

MEKHILTAʾ

SIFRE

MEDIEVAL AUTHORS

ANCIENT SOURCES

UGARITIC

ARAMAIC/REGIONAL CANAANITE

PHOENICIAN

AKKADIAN

MOABITE

HEBREW

DEAD SEA SCROLLS

CLASSICAL